Kiss of the Yoginī

Kiss of the Yoginī

"TANTRIC SEX" IN ITS SOUTH ASIAN CONTEXTS

David Gordon White

THE UNIVERSITY OF CHICAGO PRESS
CHICAGO AND LONDON

The University of Chicago Press, Chicago 60637
The University of Chicago Press, Ltd., London

Paperback edition 2006
Printed in the United States of America

Kamil Zvelebil's translation of the late medieval Tamil poem the *Kāmapānacāstiram* ("Treatise on the Arrow of Lust") on pp. 74–75 was previously published in *The Siddha Quest for Immortality: Sexual, Alchemical and Medical Secrets of the Tamil Siddhas*. Oxford: Mandrake of Oxford (1996).

11 10 09 08 07 06 2 3 4 5

ISBN 0-226-89483-5 (cloth)
ISBN 0-226-89484-3 (paperback)

Library of Congress Cataloging-in-Publication Data

White, David Gordon.
Kiss of the yoginī: "Tantric Sex" in its South Asian contexts / David Gordon White.
p. cm.
Includes bibliographical references and index.
ISBN 0-226-89483-5 (cloth : alk. paper)
1. Tantrism—South Asia. 2. Sex—Religious aspects—Tantrism.
I. Title.
BL1283.842 .W45 2003
294.5′514′0954—dc21 2002029031

mama mātṛpitṛbhyāṃ yayor dravyair vinā idaṃ pustakaṃ nāsambhaviṣyat

Contents

List of Illustrations ix
Preface xi
Note on Transliteration xvii
Abbreviations of Titles of Sanskrit Works xix

1. Tantra in Its South Asian Contexts 1
2. The Origins of the Yoginī: Bird, Animal and Tree Goddesses and Demonesses in South Asia 27
3. The Blood of the Yoginī: Vital and Sexual Fluids in South Asian Thought and Practice 67
4. The Mouth of the Yoginī: Sexual Transactions in Tantric Ritual 94
5. The Power of the Yoginī: Tantric Actors in South Asia 123
6. The Consort of the Yoginī: South Asian Siddha Cults and Traditions 160
7. The Flight of the Yoginī: Fueling the Flight of Tantric Witches 188
8. The Sublimation of the Yoginī: The Subordination of the Feminine in High Hindu Tantra 219
9. Tantra for the New Millennium 258

Notes 273
Bibliography 335
Index 357

Illustrations

1.a.	Goddess Caṇḍikā, riding a corpse	9
2.a.	Childbirth scene	42
2.b.	Bird-headed Grahī	43
2.c.	Goddess shrine beneath *khejaṛa* tree	56
4.a.	*Kāmakalā* yantra according to the *Śilpa Prakāśa*	95
4.b.	*Kāmakalā* yantra superimposed upon erotic sculpture	98
4.c.	Initiate collecting sexual fluids	107
4.d.	*Yonipūjā*, "Veneration of the Vulva"	110
4.e.	Female sexual display	111
4.f.	Kālī and Tārā venerating Śiva as a *liṅgam*	119
5.a.	Rajasthani *kuladevī*s and popular goddesses	128
5.b.	Navadurgā masks	130
5.c.	Khoḍīyār, *kuladevī* of the medieval Cūḍāsamā dynasty	131
5.d.	Detail from image of Bhāvnā Yoginī	138
5.e.	Orgy scene	145
6.a.	Rajput prince kneeling before Nāth Siddha	170
6.b.	Thāṇī Yoginī	172
6.c.	Siddhaloka	176
6.d.	Seated yogin	178
7.a.	Cobra-headed Yoginī	190
7.b.	Vetāla-possessed corpse looking up at Yoginī for whom it is a vehicle	205
7.c.	Animal- or bird-headed Yoginī	206
7.d.	Yoginī beating a drum	208

7.e. Dancing Śiva shrine 214

7.f. Yoginī standing above representations of human head and jackals 216

8.a. *Kāmakalā* yantra according to the *Yoginīhṛdaya Tantra* 238

9.a. Bound male victim being led away by two female figures 260

9.b. Painted stones representing Yoginīs outside Līlāḍ temple 268

Preface

As far as I can recall, my searches for an authentic Tantric practitioner began in 1974 in Benares, where I was a study-abroad student in my senior year from the University of Wisconsin. One fine day in the postmonsoon season, I walked down to Kedar Ghat in search of a holy man who could initiate me into the mysteries of Tantra. Standing near the top of the stairs leading down to the churning brown waters of the Ganges, I spied a late-middle-aged man with a longish graying beard and a loincloth, seated in what appeared to be a meditative pose. I approached him and, summoning up my best Hindi, asked him if he was a renouncer (*sannyāsin*), and if he was, what could he tell me about Tantra? His reply was in English: he was a businessman from Bengal who, having had all his belongings stolen from him on a train a month before, had alighted at Benares to take a break from his work. He had family in the neighborhood and enjoyed spending his afternoons on Kedar Ghat. As for Tantra, he didn't practice it, and in any case, all that was worth knowing on the topic could be found in the books of Arthur Avalon.[1] This was the first time I had heard the pseudonym of the English court judge who, based in Bengal, had become the father of Tantric studies and, by extension, of the emergence of "Tantric" practice in Europe and the United States. This was also my first introduction to the funhouse mirror world of modern-day Tantra,[2] in which Indian practitioners and gurus take their ideas from Western scholars and sell them to Western disciples thirsting for initiation into the mysteries of the East. Nearly thirty years have passed since that encounter. Today Assi Ghat, just a short way upriver from Kedar Ghat, will, on any given day in the same postmonsoon season, sport a number of North Americans and Europeans dressed up as Tantric specialists. California, France, and Italy, in particular, are crawling with such people, many of whom advertise New Age "retreats" or "workshops" in "Tantric sex" and many other types of hybrid practice on the Internet.

Medieval Indian literature had an overarching term for entrepreneurs of this type, who targeted a certain leisured segment of the population in their marketing of a product nowadays known as "Tantric sex": they were "impostors."[3] Now, there was and remains an authentic body of precept and practice known as "Kaula" or "Tantra," which has been, among other things, a sexualization of ritual (as opposed to a ritualization of sex, one of many fundamental errors on the part of the present-day "Tantric sex" entrepreneurs). In about the eleventh century, a scholasticizing trend in Kashmirian Hindu circles, led by the great systematic theologian Abhinavagupta, sought to aestheticize the sexual rituals of the Kaula. These theoreticians, whose intended audience was likely composed of conformist householder practitioners, sublimated the end and raison d'être of Kaula sexual practice—the production of powerful, transformative sexual fluids—into simple by-products of a higher goal: the cultivation of a divine state of consciousness homologous to the bliss experienced in sexual orgasm.[4] At nearly no point in the original Kaula sources on sexualized ritual, however, is mention made of pleasure, let alone bliss or ecstasy.[5] Nonetheless, it was this experience of a blissful expansion of consciousness that became the watchword of later scholasticist revisions of Tantra. Now it was precisely these second-order, derivative developments that early-twentieth-century Tantric scholar-practitioners, both Asian and Western, emphasized in their attempts to rehabilitate Tantra. Here, I am referring specifically to the "reformed" Tantra of Bengal and the influence it exerted on Sir John Woodroffe, a.k.a. Arthur Avalon, the father of Western Tantric scholarship.

These scholar-practitioners were, for their part, responding to an earlier Western distorted image of Tantra, namely the sensationalist productions of Christian missionaries and colonial administrators, who portrayed Tantra as little more than a congeries of sexual perversions and abominations. These two interpretive strategies of praising and blaming Tantra are foundational to the image of "Tantric sex" that a number of Indian and Western spiritual entrepreneurs have been offering to a mainly American and European clientele for the past several decades. Presenting the entire history of Tantra as a unified, monolithic "cult of ecstasy" and assuming that all that has smacked of eroticism in Indian culture is by definition Tantric, New Age Tantra eclectically blends together Indian erotics (*kāmaśāstra*, *ratiśāstra*), erotic art, techniques of massage, Āyurveda, and yoga into a single invented tradition. Furthermore, its emphasis on ecstasy and mind expansion draws on what was already a second-order reflection on the original meaning and power of Kaula ritual, a cosmeticized interpretation offered to a stratum of eleventh-century Kashmiri society for whose members the oral consumption of sexual fluids as power substances, practices that lay at the heart of Kaula ritual, would have been too shocking and perverse to contemplate.[6] Abhinavagupta's "packaging" of Tantra as a path to ecstatic, exalted god-consciousness was pitched at a leisured Kashmiri populace whose "bobo" profile was arguably homologous to the demographics of the twentieth- and twenty-first-century New Age seekers who treat "Tantric sex" as a consumer product. The reader is invited to consult the fine work of Hugh Urban on the demographics and history of this modern-day phenomenon.[7]

New Age Tantra is to medieval Tantra what finger painting is to fine art, a remarkably unimaginative "series of yogic exercises applied to the sexual act . . . a *coitus reservatus par excellence* . . . a sad attempt to mechanize the mysteries of sexual love."[8] Yet its derivative, dilettante, diminished rendering of a sophisticated, coherent, foreign, and relatively ancient tradition is not unique to the history of religions. For example, the "Egyptian Mysteries" that were all the rage in the Hellenistic and Roman world were neither Egyptian nor *mysteria* in the original sense of the term; and they flourished at a distance of over a thousand years from the original centers of the cults of Isis and Osiris. In this respect, New Age Tantra is as "Tantric" as the Egyptian Mysteries were "Egyptian" or "mysteries." Already in medieval times, the Indian Ocean was a "dream horizon" for the West, the oceanic boundary of a geographical void that came to be peopled by the marvels and monsters craved and feared by the European mind.[9] And whereas India has changed radically over the centuries, Western attitudes toward it have not. "India," as the epitome of the "Mysterious East," continues to constitute an empty category that Europeans (and now North Americans) have seen fit to fill with their own fantasies, pulsions, and phobias, such that this India of the imagination has remained little more than a dumping ground of sorts for Western psychological cathexes.[10] The invented tradition of New Age Tantra is but the latest avatar of this antiquated mind-set, which has been exploited to great advantage by such self-appointed gurus as Rajneesh (also known as Osho), Margo Anand, Charles Muir, and others. At the same time, it must be acknowledged that Indian religious polity—or the near total absence thereof—has contributed to this laissez-faire situation. India has no centralized church, no legislating theocracy, and no authorized canon (although this has not been for lack of trying by the sectarian leaders of the present-day Viśva Hindu Pariṣad and its narrow definition of *hindutva*, "Hindu-ness"). There is not and never has been a hegemonic religious institution in India to protect itself and counter what may be qualified as heretical appropriations of Indian religious precept and practice, and so the entrepreneurs of ecstasy are able to ply their trade with impunity.

This colonization and commodification of another people's religious belief system, and the appropriation and distortion of its very use of the term "Tantra," is not only deceptive; it also runs roughshod over the sensibilities of authentic modern-day Asian practitioners of Tantra, the silent Tantric majority. Imagine an analogous scenario in which an Indian entrepreneur began running "Christian sex" workshops in South Asia, claiming that they drew on the secret practices of Jesus and Mary Magdalene as transmitted through the Albigensians, or some other such invented nonsense. Or New Age basketball clinics without baskets. Of course, the "Tantric sex" websites are full of testimonials by satisfied customers that it makes them feel good, and that it has improved their lives in every way, well beyond the level of their libidos. No doubt this is true in many cases, and no doubt many "Tantric sex" entrepreneurs are well-meaning people who have offered their clients a new and liberating way of experiencing and enjoying their sexuality.[11] Here I am not taking issue with the sex in "Tantric sex," but rather the use of the term "Tantric," which is entirely misplaced. When the Disney Corporation makes an animated film about Pocahontas, it does not make any claim to historical accuracy; it is simply selling a product for its "feel-good" entertainment value. This is what the "Tantric sex" business is doing here in the West, with the important difference that it *does* in fact make the implicit and bogus claim—by its abusive appropriation of the adjective "Tantric"—that it is reproducing a body of practice with an Indian historical pedigree.

In this, New Age "Tantric sex" further breaks with another set of traditions, those of the many Asian countries into which Indian Tantra was imported from the very beginning. For any lineage-based Tantric body of practice (*sādhanā*) to be legitimate in Chinese (Ch'an), Japanese (Zen, Tendai, etc.), or Tibetan Tantric traditions, both past and present, its translated root text must be traceable back to an Indian original written in Sanskrit. The banalities and platitudes spouted by today's Western Tantric gurus have no such pedigree.[12] Furthermore, the transmission of these teachings must be traceable through an unbroken lineage of gurus and disciples, going back to Indian founders. Today's Western Tantric gurus belong to no such lineages of transmitted teachings. New Age "Tantric sex" is a Western fabrication, whose greatest promise, if one is to take its Internet advertising at face value, is longer sexual staying power for men and more sustained and frequent orgasms for women. None of this has ever been the subject matter of any authentic Tantric teaching. All is Western make-believe but for one detail: the pricey weekends and workshops the "Tantric sex" merchants are selling cannot be had with play money.

Although I will but rarely address or describe this New Age phenomenon, I intend, by reconstructing the medieval South Asian Kaula and Tantric traditions that involved sexual practices, to deconstruct the "product" that these modern-day entrepreneurs of ecstasy are selling to a benighted Western public.

This book would not have been possible without the scholarly, material, and moral support of a great many colleagues, friends, and present and former graduate students: Rick Asher, Marcy Braverman, Gudrun Bühnemann, Kalyan Chakravarty, Ashok Das, Dan Ehnbom, Mark Elmore, Mike Gill, Ann Gold, Bhoju Ram Gujar, Paul Hackett, Sattar and Dominique-Sila Khan, Naval Krishna, Jeffrey Lidke, L. L. Lodhi, Elisa McCormick, Paul Muller-Ortega, André Padoux, Michael Rabe, Arion Roşu, Jeffrey Ruff, Bhagavatilal Sharma, Nutan Sharma, R. K. Sharma, Lee Siegel, Kerry Skora, Micaela Soar, Tony Stewart, and Dominik Wujastyk. I must single out for special thanks Professor Sthanesvar Timilsina of Mahendra University, Kathmandu, for his many hours of guidance in decrypting and translating Tantric manuscripts; Professor Mukunda Raj Aryal of Tribhuvan University, Kathmandu, for guiding me (often on the back of his motorcycle) to dozens of Tantric temples and sites in the Kathmandu Valley; and most especially Dr. Mark Dyczkowski, the remarkable sage of Narad Ghat in Benares, who remains a deep well of knowledge for scholars thirsting to comprehend the complex traditions of South Asian Tantra. My heartfelt thanks as well to David Brent, the editor who has steered me through what is now my third book at the University of Chicago Press with his light and expert hand. Finally, I kiss the lotus feet of Catherine, my precious Yoginī, for her unwavering support and patience in listening to me talk about sexual fluids at all hours of the day and night for the past seven years.

Research for this book was supported by a Fulbright Senior Research Fellowship, which permitted me to carry out fieldwork in India and Nepal during the first half of 1999. In South Asia I was fortunate to enjoy the cooperation and support of the directors of the Archaeological Survey of India, the Archaeological Survey of Madhya Pradesh, the American Institute of Indian Studies, the Man Singh Library, the Nepal National Archives, and the Nepal Research Centre.

A number of passages found in this book are revisions of articles or chapters that I have previously published in various academic journals and edited volumes. I am grateful to the editors of these publications for their permission to reproduce those passages here.

Portions of chapter 4, parts 1, 2, and 4; and chapter 8, parts 4–6, have appeared in "Transformations in the Art of Love: Kāmakalā Practices in

Hindu Tantric and Kaula Traditions," *History of Religions* 38:2 (November 1998), pp. 172–98. Portions of chapter 5, parts 1 and 6; and chapter 9, part 1, have appeared in "Tantra in Practice: Mapping a Tradition," in *Tantra in Practice*, ed. David Gordon White (Princeton: Princeton University Press, 2000), pp. 3–38. Portions of chapter 5, parts 8 and 9, have appeared in "Tantric Sex and Tantric Sects: The Flow of Secret Tantric Gnosis," in *Rending the Veil: Concealment and Secrecy in the History of Religions*, ed. Elliott Wolfson (New York: Seven Bridges Press, 1999), pp. 249–70. Portions of chapter 6, parts 4 and 6, have appeared, in French, in "Le Monde dans le corps du Siddha: Microcosmologie dans les traditions médiévales indiennes," in *Images du corps dans le monde hindou*, ed. Véronique Bouillier and Gilles Tarabout (Paris: Editions du CNRS, 2002). Portions of chapter 7, parts 3–7, have appeared in "Aviators of Medieval India," in *Notes on a Mandala: Essays in Honor of Wendy Doniger*, ed. David Haberman and Laurie Patton (New York: Seven Bridges Press, 2002). Portions of chapter 8, parts 1–3, have appeared in "Yoga in Early Hindu Tantra," in *Yoga Traditions of India*, ed. Ian Whicher (London: Curzon Press, 2002). Portions of chapter 8, part 8, have appeared, in French, in "Possession, rêves, et visions dans le tantrisme indien," in *Rêves et visions révélatrices*, ed. Maya Burger (Studia Religiosa Helvetica 6/7) (Bern: Peter Lang, 2002).

Note on Transliteration

Unless otherwise noted, all transliterations from the Sanskrit follow standard lexicographical usage, except for toponyms still in use, which are transliterated without diacritics (thus Srisailam and not Śrīśailam). Words from medieval and modern north and south Indian languages are transliterated according to standard lexicographical usage for those languages (the Tamil Murukaṉ, for example). Names of authors from the colonial and postcolonial periods are transliterated without diacritics (thus Gopinath Kaviraj and not Gopīnāth Kavirāj).

Abbreviations of Titles of Sanskrit Works

AH	*Aṣṭāṅga Hṛdaya* of Vāgbhaṭṭa
AV	*Atharva Veda*
BhP	*Bhāgavata Purāṇa*
BY	*Brahmayāmala*
HT	*Hevajra Tantra*
HYP	*Haṭhayogapradīpikā* of Svātmarāman
JY	*Jayadrathayāmala*
KĀN	*Kaulāvalinirṇaya* of Jñānānanda Paramahaṃsa
KCT	*Kulacūḍāmaṇi Tantra*
KJñN	*Kaulajñānanirṇaya* of Matsyendranātha
KKV	*Kāmakalāvilāsa* of Puṇyānandanātha
KM	*Kubjikāmata*
KSS	*Kathāsaritsāgara* of Somadeva
KT	*Kulārṇava Tantra*
MBh	*Mahābhārata*
MBhT	*Manthānabhairava Tantra*
NT	*Netra Tantra*
PC	*Prabodhacandrodaya* of Kṛṣṇamiśra
RA	*Rasārṇava*
RV	*Ṛg Veda*
SP	*Śilpa Prakāśa* of Rāmacandra Kulācāra
SS	*Suśruta Saṃhitā*
SŚP	*Somaśambhupaddhati*
TĀ	*Tantrāloka* of Abhinavagupta
YH	*Yoginīhṛdaya Tantra*
YS	*Yoga Sūtras* of Patañjali

Chapter 1

TANTRA IN ITS SOUTH ASIAN CONTEXTS

Je ne suis pas seul dans ma peau—
Ma famille est immense.
—Henri Michaux

Curiously, the most balanced overview of Tantra in South Asia written to date is the work of a Sinologist. This is Michel Strickmann's posthumous *Mantras et mandarins: Le Bouddhisme tantrique en Chine,* which, in giving an account of the origins of Tantra in East Asia, brings together textual, art historical, and ethnographic data to sketch out the broad lines of South Asian Tantra.[1] The present volume will continue Strickmann's project, within a strictly South Asian focus, bringing together text-based Tantric theory and exegesis (that has been the subject of work by scholars like Woodroffe, Silburn, Padoux, Gnoli, Goudriaan, Gupta, Sanderson, Dyczkowski, Muller-Ortega, Brooks, and others), Tantric imagery (the stuff of the pop art books by Rawson, Mookerjee, and others, but also of serious scholarship by Dehejia, Desai, Donaldson, Mallmann, and Slusser), and Tantric practice (the subject of a growing number of studies in ethnopsychology by Kakar, Obeyesekere, Caldwell, Nabokov, etc.). While each of these approaches has its merits, and while many of the studies published by various scholars in these fields have been nothing short of brilliant, the nearly total lack of attention to complementary disciplines (of art history and ethnography for the textualists, for example) has generated three very different and truncated—if not skewed—types of scholarly analysis of one and the same phenomenon. The life of Tantric practitioners has never been limited to textual exegesis alone; nor has it been solely concerned with the fabrication of worship images or the ritual propitiation of the Tantric pantheon. Yet such is the impression one receives when one reads one or another of the types of scholarly literature on the subject.

Here, by paralleling these three types of data, as well as attending to accounts of Tantric practice and practitioners found in the medieval secular literature, I intend to reconstruct a history as well, perhaps, as a religious anthropology, a sociology, and a political economy of (mainly Hindu) Tantra, from the medieval period down to the present day. In so doing, I will also lend serious attention to human agency in the history of Tantra in South Asia. Most of the South Asian temples upon which Tantric practices are depicted in sculpture were constructed by kings—kings whose involvement in Tantric ritual life is irrefutable. When the king is a Tantric practitioner and his religious advisers are Tantric "power brokers," how does this impact the religious and political life of his kingdom? What is the relationship between "popular" practice and "elite" exegesis in the Tantric context? What has been the relationship between "pragmatic" and "transcendental" religious practice in South Asia?[2] These are questions whose answers may be found in texts and in stone, in medieval precept as well as modern-day practice. This book will grapple with these questions, and in so doing resituate South Asian Tantra, in its precolonial forms at least, at the center of the religious, social, and political life of India and Nepal. For a wide swath of central India in the precolonial period, Tantra would have been the "mainstream," and in many ways it continues to impact the mainstream, even if emic misappreciations of Tantra tend to relegate it to a marginal position. In present-day Nepal, Bhutan, and Tibet, Tantra remains the mainstream form of religious practice.

1. Revisioning the "Mainstream" of Indian Religion

Viewed through the lens of present-day reformed Hindu sensibilities as spread through the printed word and other mass media, "classical Hinduism" evolved directly out of the speculative hymns of the *Ṛg Veda* and the Upaniṣads and down through the teachings of the *Bhagavad Gītā* into the predominantly Vaiṣṇava forms of devotionalism that predominate in north India today. Most Indian and Western scholars of the past century have consciously or unconsciously adopted this reformist agenda, devoting their interpretive efforts to Hindu religious texts in the Sanskrit medium or to living vernacular traditions that partake of *bhakti* religiosity and neo-Vedantic philosophy. In so doing, they have succeeded in mapping, often in great detail, a thin sliver of the history of South Asian religions, which they have generally mistaken for a comprehensive history of the same.[3]

However, this selective chronology bears no resemblance to what may be termed the truly "perennial" Indian religion, which has generally remained constant since at least the time of the *Atharva Veda*, as evidenced in over three thousand years of sacred and secular literature as well as medieval iconography and modern ethnography. For what reformist Hindus and the scholars who have followed their revisionist history of South Asian religion have in fact done has been to project—backward onto over two millennia of religious history, and outward onto the entire population of South Asia—the ideals, concerns, and categories of a relatively small cadre of Hindu religious specialists, literati, and their mainly urban clientele. While it is the case that those same elites—the brahmin intelligentsia, a certain Indian aristocracy, and the merchant classes—have been the historical bearers of much of Indian religious *civilization*, their texts and temples have had limited impact on the religious *culture* of the vast majority of South Asians. "Classical" *bhakti* in some way corresponds to the religious productions of post-Gupta period elites—what royal chaplains and their royal clients displayed as public religion—as well as the religion of what Harald Tambs-Lyche has termed "urban society" in South Asia.[4]

The distorting effect of the hegemonic voices of these elites on the ways that twentieth- and now twenty-first-century India has imagined its past has been the subject of no small number of scholarly works, if not movements, over the past twenty-five years. The critical (or postcolonialist, or subalternist) approach to Indian historiography has been quite successful in deconstructing colonial categories.[5] Where it has markedly failed—*postmodernisme oblige?*—has been in generating other nonelite, noncolonial (i.e., subaltern) categories through which to interpret the history of Indian culture. Yet such a category exists and is possessed of a cultural history that may be—and in many cases has been—retrieved through literary, art historical, and ethnographic research. That category, that cultural phenomenon, is Tantra, the occulted face of India's religious history. In many ways the antitype of *bhakti*—the religion of Indian civilization that has come to be embraced by nineteenth- to twenty-first-century reformed Hinduism as normative for all of Indian religious history—Tantra has been the predominant religious paradigm, for over a millennium, of the great majority of the inhabitants of the Indian subcontinent. It has been the background against which Indian religious civilization has evolved.

A preponderance of evidence supports this conclusion. In ancient times as in the present, village India has had its own local or regional deities that it has worshiped in its own ways and in its own contexts. These deities, which are multiple rather than singular, often form a part of the geographical as well as human landscapes of their various localities: trees, forests, mountains, bodies of water; but also the malevolent and heroic dead, male and female ancestors, and ghosts, ghouls, and rascally imps of every sort. As will be shown in detail in the next chapter, these multiple (and often feminine) deities are, before all else, angry and hungry, and very often angry because hungry. Their cultus consists of feeding them in order that they be pacified.

As far back as the time of Pāṇini, Brahmanic sources have qualified these as *laukika devatās* (popular deities), while Jain and Buddhist authors have termed them *vyantara devatās* (intermediate deities, as opposed to enlightened *jinas* and *tīrthaṃkaras*), and *devas* (unenlightened deities, as opposed to enlightened Buddhas and bodhisattvas), respectively. Yet when one looks at the devotional cults of the gods of so-called classical Hinduism, the gods of the Hindu elites, one finds remarkable connections—historical, iconographic, ritual, and regional—between these high gods and the deities of the preterite masses. Whereas the gods Viṣṇu, Śiva (Maheśvara, Śaṅkara, Mahākāla), and Skanda (Kārttikeya) likely have their South Asian origins in local or regional Yakṣa cults,[6] and Kṛṣṇa-Gopāla and Gaṇeśa were likely first worshiped in the form of mountains,[7] the great Goddess is a theological abstraction of the multiple tree, forest, and water goddesses of popular Indian religion, as well as of the complex image of the multiple Mothers of earlier traditions. Nearly every one of the *avatāras* of Viṣṇu has its own regional and historical antecedents, which have little or nothing to do with the great god Viṣṇu per se, with whom they are later identified in Sanskritic traditions. The earliest Kṛṣṇa traditions portray him and his brother Balarāma as tributary to the great Goddess Ekānaṃśā: this "Vṛṣṇī triad," rather than the much-vaunted *trimūrti* of Brahmā, Viṣṇu, and Śiva, was the original Hindu "trinity."[8] Prior to the eleventh century, there were no temples to Rāma, who theretofore had been revered more as an exemplary human king than as a god.[9]

Devotional vernacular poetry and literature, the strongest evidence we have for the flourishing of *bhakti* as a regional phenomenon, emerged slowly, and in an uneven and discontinuous way. The earliest *bhakti* poems, the sixth-century works of the Vaiṣṇava Āḻvārs and Śaiva Nāyaṉmārs in the Tamil medium—and whose content and tenor would be barely recognizable to a present-day devotee of one of the great Hindu gods—date from the sixth century C.E. *Bhakti* poems in the Kannada medium appear in the same century; in Marathi in the eleventh century; Gujarati in the twelfth century; Kashmiri, Bengali, Assamese, and Maithili in the fourteenth century; and Oriya in the fifteenth century. It is not until the sixteenth century that the *bhakti* poetry considered to be definitive for the cults of Kṛṣṇa and Rāma, in the Braj and Avadhi dialects, first appears.[10]

So much for the great gods of *bhakti*. What then of Tantra? As William Pinch has demonstrated, brahmin pandits themselves categorized the religion of the Indian masses well into the nineteenth century as "Tantra," in the sense of rustic mumbo-jumbo. (Most orthodox Hindus continue to qualify *tantra-mantra* in this way: we will return to this point in the final chapter of this book.) Throughout north India, the nineteenth- to twentieth-century social uplift of the same masses took place through the mechanism of religious "conversion" to an especially Ramaite form of Vaisnavism based on the *Rām Carit Mānas* of Tulsidās.[11] This is the basis for what is termed *sanātana dharma*, an "old-time religion" that never existed prior to the nineteenth century,[12] as evidenced in the ethnographic surveys undertaken by Bengali pandits on the behalf of the British civil servant Francis Buchanan in the early 1800s. In a typical district of Bihar, these pandits reported that one-fourth of the population's religion was "unworthy of the note of any sage"—that is, they consisted of cults of (predominantly female) village deities whose worship was often conducted by the socially and culturally marginalized, in other words, Tantric cults. Of those "worthy of note"—that is, the remaining 75 percent of the population, one-fourth were Śākta (devotees of the Goddess as Śakti); one-eighth Śaiva; one-eighth Vaiṣṇava; three-sixteenths "adher[ing] to the sect of Nānak"; and one-sixteenth Kabīrpanthīs or followers of the doctrine of Śivanārāyaṇ.[13] In other words, less than one hundred years prior to the "Rāma-fication" of this part of the "Hindu heartland," less than 10 percent of the total population, and one-eighth of the middle- and upper-middle-class religiosity reflected in Buchanan's survey, considered itself to be Vaiṣṇava, while over 40 percent were either Tantric or Śākta. Buchanan further observed that most of the pandits in the Bihar and Patna Districts worshiped Śakti as their chosen deity and were "Tantriks." As he moved northwest toward Ayodhya, he recorded increasing numbers of brahmins serving as Vaiṣṇava gurus.[14] The same has been the case farther to the north, where, in spite of the implantation of Krishnaism as the court religion in recent centuries, "*bhakti* seems to have always been marginal in the [Kathmandu] valley of Nepal . . . it could never rival Tantra, which dominated the religious scene."[15]

In south India the "new orthodoxy"—what Fred Clothey has termed "neo-*bhakti*"—has tended to be either Śaiva or related to the Saivized cult of Murukaṉ;[16] but it, too, is a very recent overlay of far more ancient Tantric traditions involving spirit possession by the dead, demons, and female deities. On the one hand, as scholars like Gananath Obeyesekere, Sarah Caldwell, Jackie Assayag,[17] and others have demonstrated in their ethnographies, the goddess cults that have predominated in traditional South Indian societies have only recently become masculinized, "Saivized."[18] On the other hand, as Douglas Brooks has shown, even the most orthodox (and orthoprax) Śaivas of South India, the Smārta brahmins, continue their Śākta Tantric devotion to the Goddess, covertly.[19] (Here, it is also important to note that "Śākta" is a relatively late technical term applied to those cults, scriptures, or persons associated with the worship of the Goddess as Śakti: prior to the eleventh century, the operative term for the same was simply "Kula" or "Kaula": the term "clan" being applied implicitly and exclusively to female lineages.[20] I will, however, continue to use the term "Śākta" in its broadly accepted sense.)

Well into the nineteenth century, the mainstream Vaiṣṇava and Śaiva religious orders themselves termed their own practice "Tantric": in the words of Sanjukta Gupta and Richard Gombrich, "[The Vedic] stratum of ritual has never become wholly obsolete, but throughout Hinduism it has long been overlaid by the ritual of the monotheistic sects, ritual which is accurately known as *tāntrika*."[21] Sir John Woodroffe makes much the same observation:

> "Medieval Hinduism" . . . was, as its successor, modern orthodoxy, is, largely Tāntric. The Tantra was then, as it is now, the great Mantra and Sādhanā Śāstra (Scripture), and the main, where not the sole, source of some of the most fundamental concepts still prevalent as regards worship, images, initiation, yoga, the supremacy of the guru, and so forth.[22]

Fifty years before Woodroffe, in about 1865, a leader of the Rāmānandī monastery of Galta—the Vaiṣṇava center most intimately linked to the Kachvaha dynasty of Jaipur from its foundation down to its dramatic ouster in the middle of the nineteenth century—described his own "Vaiṣṇava Dharma" in the following terms:

> The Vaiṣṇava Dharma with the mantras of Nārāyaṇa, Rāma and Kṛṣṇa, the adoration (*upāsanā*) of the chosen deity (*iṣṭa-devatā*), the vertical mark (*ūrdhva-puṇḍra*), the white clay *tilaka*, the basil and lotus seed necklace . . . the nine forms of *bhakti*, and the Tantric rites (*anuṣṭhāna*): all of these things have always existed. . . .[23]

The ritual of the nineteenth-century Vaiṣṇava orders included *anuṣṭhāna*, ("practice"), Tantric rites whose aim was to harness supernatural powers for the attainment of material gains, on the behalf of a clientele that was, in the case of the Rāmānandīs of Jaipur, none other than the royal family itself.[24] Echoing Kullūka Bhaṭṭa, the fifteenth-century commentator on the *Manu Smṛti*, other north Indian Vaiṣṇava sectarian ideologues of nineteenth-century north India from the Nimbārkī and Vallabhī orders also described their practices as twofold: Vedic and Tantric.[25] The Tantric tradition to which these Vaiṣṇava leaders were referring was that of the Pāñcarātra, whose "Man-Lion Initiation" (*narasiṃha-dīkṣā*) was administered to kings by Vaiṣṇava sectarians throughout medieval India.[26]

Far earlier, a 788 C.E. inscription from the Alwar region of eastern Rajasthan records a king's "monthly gift of wine made for the worship of Viṣṇu (probably in the Tantric fashion)." We will return to the place of Tantra in rituals of royalty in chapter 5; suffice it to say here that the self-understanding of the Vaiṣṇava orthodoxy was very much Tantric well into the nineteenth century, a self-understanding that would be quickly forgotten or censored. So it is that in 1927 a Rāmānandī polemic, published in Allahabad and entitled *Devībali Pākhaṇḍ*, "The Heresy of Sacrifice to the Goddess," utterly condemns Tantra—which it identifies with extreme forms of Durgā worship—and whose main proponents, it alleges, were Maithili brahmins.[27]

Most adherents of India's postreformation Hindu "mainstream" have been possessed of the same sort of selective amnesia concerning both their own past and the multiplicity of practices that currently surround them, and that they themselves engage in on particular occasions.[28] In this regard, one could drive an overloaded Tata truck through their blind spot—but blind spots are not contagious, and scholars ought not to let themselves be led by the blind when generating a history of Hindu religious practice.

2. A "Tantric Sex" Scenario

It is beyond the scope of this work to present an exhaustive history and anthropology of South Asian Tantra. Rather, its focus will be on that element of Tantra that, as I will argue, has given it its specificity over and against other South Asian religious traditions. That distinctive element is a form of sexualized ritual practice that first makes its appearance in circa seventh-century Hindu and Buddhist medieval sources, and has continued to the present time in a significant number of "popular" South Asian traditions. My analysis of this body of practice will be based to a certain extent on a *literal* reading of a small grouping of Sanskrit terms—*kula* ("family, "clan"), *dravyam* ("fluid"), *mukham* ("mouth"), *vīra* ("Virile Hero"), *siddha* ("Perfected Being"), and *khecara* ("flight")—complemented by iconographic and ethnographic evidence from the medieval as well as the modern periods. The term *dravyam* and its Kaula uses will be the focus of chapter 3; *mukham* that of chapter 4; *vīra* and *siddha* that of chapter 6; and *khecara* that of chapter 7.

Such a literal, rather than a symbolic or metaphysical, reading of these terms and their attendant practices in Hindu Tantra requires some justification. Not all religious language is literal in its intentionality. The Christian Eucharist, for example, if taken literally, would reduce that sacrament to a sort of cannibalistic practice of eating the flesh and drinking the blood of a religious founder and savior. In what ways does the spirit of Hindu Tantra so differ from Christianity as to justify a literal reading of certain of its core terms? There are a number of grounds upon which such a reading becomes justifiable and, I would argue, necessary. First, such a reading forms a part of the history of Hindu religious ideas, going back to the time of the Brāhmaṇas. As Sylvain Lévi argued nearly a hundred years ago, the circa tenth- to eighth-century B.C.E. Brāhmaṇas, whose liturgies and mythology lent ritual a "procreative" power, "led inexorably to an expansion of the real or symbolic reproductive powers of the sexual act. The Brāhmaṇas opened the way to the pious obscenities of the Tantras."[29] This tendency, toward a literalization of symbolic statements or practices, is one that David Shulman has also identified as a hallmark of many extreme forms of south Indian devotionalism.[30] Most importantly, as I hope the balance of this book will make clear, much of the Tantric terminology makes sense only if it is read literally; indeed, I would argue that the ritual edifice of early Tantra only stands, that early Tantra only functions as a coherent system, if these terms are put into literal practice.

As Alexis Sanderson has convincingly argued, a reformation of sorts occurred in the South Asian proto-Tantric milieus in about the tenth century. This reformation especially involved a shift away from early forms of practice, which had involved cremation-ground-based asceticism featuring the use of blood sacrifice and alcohol as means to feeding and satisfying a host of terrible Kula ("Clan") deities.[31] In the ninth or tenth century, a paradigm shift of sorts occurred, with a change in emphasis away from the feeding of these ravening deities and toward a type of erotico-mystical practice involving a female horde collectively known as the Yoginīs, led by the terrible male Śiva-Bhairava, together with his consort, the Goddess (Aghoreśvarī, Umā, Caṇḍī, Śakti, etc.).[32] The Kaula rites were grounded in the cults of the Yoginīs, medieval heiresses to the Mātṛ[kā]s (Mothers), Yakṣiṇīs (female Dryads), and Grahaṇīs (female Seizers) of earlier traditions who, like them, were often represented as supernatural or preternatural hybrids between the human, animal, bird, and plant worlds (fig. 1.a). These petulant female divinities, located at a shifting threshold between the divine and the demonic, were by turns terrible and benign with regard to humans, who traditionally worshiped them with blood offerings and animal sacrifice. Once gratified by said oblations, the Yoginīs would reveal themselves as ravishing young women and gratify their human devotees in return with supernatural powers, most particularly the power of flight.

Induced possession by these Yoginīs was the prime means to the ends of the Kaula, the "clan-generated" practices, also termed the "clan practice" (*kulācāra*), "clan religion" (*kuladharma*), or the "clan-generated gnosis"

Figure 1.a. Goddess Caṇḍikā, riding a corpse in the midst of a cremation-ground scene. Bheraghat Yoginī temple, ca. 1000 C.E., Jabalpur District, Madhya Pradesh. Courtesy of the American Institute of Indian Studies.

(*kaulajñāna*).[33] Kaula practitioners were primarily concerned with this-worldly powers (*siddhis*) and bodily immortality (*jīvanmukti*), with the enjoyment (*bhukti*) of said powers and immortality taking precedence over any ideal of consciousness raising or disembodied liberation from cyclic rebirth (*mukti*), embraced by more conventional Tantric practitioners. These powers were gained by transacting with Yoginīs, who, in the Kaula context, were also identified with the female ritual consorts of the male practitioner. That is, the Yoginīs of the Kaula and Tantric traditions were at once regarded as flesh-and-blood women with whom male practitioners interacted, and the devouring semidivine beings who were the object of their worship cults. In the secular literature, these Yoginīs were often portrayed as sorceresses or witches, ambiguous, powerful, and dangerous figures that only a heroic male would dare to approach, let alone attempt to conquer. It is for this reason that the fully initiated male practitioners of the Kaula termed themselves Champions or Virile Heroes (Vīras); alternatively, they referred to themselves as Perfected Beings (Siddhas), by way of identifying themselves with another order of semidivine beings, the male counterparts to the Yoginīs of Epic and medieval Indian mythology. That mythology, to which the Yoginīs and Siddhas of the Kaula were the heirs, will be the subject of chapters 2 and 7 in particular.

Unlike the Kula before it, which openly transgressed in the public space of a town and its cremation grounds—and unlike the Tāntrikas, most often householder practitioners of relatively conventional, nonsexual Tantric liturgies, whose goal was liberation rather than supernatural enjoyments—members of the Kaula tended to carry out their sexual rites in relatively remote areas and at times known only to its initiates. However, when the king and his court were Kaula initiates, this may not have been a particularly well-guarded secret. On certain nights of the lunar month[34] and solar year, Kaula practitioners would assemble on cremation grounds, or at clan "mounds" or "seats" (*pīṭhas*),[35] "clan-mountains" (*kula-parvatas*), or "fields" (*kṣetras*). These gatherings, called "minglings" (*melakas*, *melanas*, *melāpas*), involved the union of female and male initiates, of Yoginīs whose presence and interaction with their heroic (Vīra) or perfected (Siddha) male counterparts were the sine qua non of Kaula practice.

At these gatherings the Yoginīs would descend from the sky to meet their male consorts awaiting them on the ground. These Yoginīs' flight was fueled by the human and animal flesh that was their diet; however, the Siddhas or Vīras, by virtue of their own practice, were able to offer the Yoginīs a more subtle and powerful energy source. This was their semen (*vīrya*), the distilled essence of their own bodily constituents. The Yoginīs, gratified by such offerings, would offer their form of grace to the Siddhas or Vīras. Instead of devouring them, they would offer them a counterprestation of their own sexual discharge, something these male partners would have been as needful of as the Yoginīs were of male semen.

This male requirement stemmed from an altogether different set of needs than those of the Yoginīs, however. According to the Kaula worldview, the godhead—the source of all being and power in the world—externalized himself (or herself, in the case of the purely feminine hierarchy of the Kālī-Krama of Kashmir) in the form of a series of female hypostases, a cluster of (often eight) great Goddesses, who in turn proliferated into the multiple circles of feminine energies (often sixty-four) that were their Yoginī entourage. These semidivine Yoginīs and the human women who embodied them therefore carried in their bodies the germ plasm of the godhead, called the "clan fluid" (*kuladravyam*), "clan nectar" (*kulāmṛta*), "vulval essence" (*yonitattva*), the "command" (*ājñā*), the "real thing" (*sadbhāva*), or simply the "fluid" (*dravyam*),[36] or the "clan" (*kula*). While this fluid essence of the godhead flowed naturally through these female beings, it was absent in males.[37] Therefore, the sole means by which a male could access the flow of the supreme godhead at the elevated center of the mandala, the clan "flow chart," was through the Yoginīs, who formed or inhabited its outer circles.

Only through initiation by and continued interaction with the Yoginīs could these male practitioners access this fluid essence and boundless energy of the godhead. It was therefore necessary that male practitioners be "inseminated," or more properly speaking "insanguinated," with the sexual or menstrual discharge of the Yoginīs—rendering the "mouth" of the Yoginī their sole conduit to membership in the clan and all its perquisites. Here, the "mouth" of the Yoginī was her vulva, and "drinking female discharge" (*rajapāna*), the prime means to fulfilling these male needs. Therefore, the erotico-mystical practice, the "Tantric sex" practiced by the Kaula practitioners, mainly involved *drinking* the "power substances" that were sexual fluids, either through "mutual oral congress" or through a form of genital sex called *vajrolī mudrā* ("urethral suction"), by which the male partner was able, following ejaculation, to draw up into himself the sexual discharge of his female partner. The "happy ending" of this body of practice is described time and again in the Tantras as well as the adventure and fantasy literature of the medieval period (most particularly in the circa 1070 C.E. *Kathāsaritsāgara* [KSS], the "Ocean of Rivers of Story" of Somadeva): both Yoginī and Vīra fly up into the sky, to sport there together for eons of time.[38] The *Rudrayāmala Tantra* states the matter most eloquently:

> By virtue of the Vīra mental disposition, one becomes a regent of the directions, having the form of Rudra. This universe is subservient to (*adhīnam*) the Vīra; [yet] the Vīra is dependent on (*adhīnam*) the clan

> [fluid] (*kula*). Therefore, by choosing the clan [fluid], a [previously] unconscious being (*jaḍaḥ*) becomes the master of every supernatural power.[39]

The Kaula path, with its claims to direct access to power in and over the world, was attractive to no small number of kings and princes in the medieval period, and it was South Asian royalty and aristocracy that formed the principal clientele of Kaula specialists. The latter were of two sorts: wild, itinerant, charismatic thaumaturges, on the one hand, and, on the other, royal chaplains (*rāja-purohitas*), literate brahmins sometimes attached to monasteries, who tended to be more sedentary and conventional in their practice and lifestyle.[40] Toward the end of the first millennium, the royal patrons of the Kaula began to commission the construction of permanent structures for the Kaula rites. This was the case in central India in particular, where a significant number of Yoginī temples were constructed between the eighth and eleventh centuries C.E. Yoginī temples were unique in that they were circular and roofless constructions: they were hypaethral, open to the heavens, and as such served as landing fields and launching pads for Yoginīs. At the center of these temples, there often stood an ithyphallic image of Śiva or Bhairava, who represented the male godhead at the center and source of the Yoginī clans;[41] as for the Yoginīs themselves, they were sculpturally represented on the inner wall of these temples' circular enclosures, facing Bhairava. It was here that royal cult rituals of the Yoginīs would have been enacted, with blood sacrifices and sexual transactions between male and female clan members taking place around the person of the king himself, the "god" of his kingdom.

When the king was himself a Vīra—and this was the case in this period for certain dynasts of the Somavaṃśi, Kalacuri, Chandella, and other royal houses—Yoginī temples became the focal point of the kingdom's religious life, which would have been, by definition, Kaula. An example of such is the early-eleventh-century Yoginī temple at Bheraghat (Bhairavaghāṭ), located across the Narmada River from the site of the old Kalacuri capital of Tripurī, which would have constituted the greatest religious building project of that entire dynasty.[42] As with the Kalacuris, Kaula or Tantric practice was—and in some cases has remained—the royal cultus, in addition to being the religion of the popular masses. Such was the case, in particular, across a wide swath of central India between the ninth and thirteenth centuries (as well as the "Greater India" of the Southeast Asian kingdoms of present-day Indonesia, Cambodia, and Burma), and such remains the case in present-day Nepal and Bhutan, Himalayan kingdoms whose state ceremonial has been Tantric for centuries. There was a direct relationship between Kaula practice and temporal power, and it is no coincidence that in an eleventh-century "Mirror of Kings" from western India, "The Circle of Yoginīs" is the title of a chapter on military strategies.[43]

3. Tantra and Kaula

Like any phenomenon that a scholar would choose to interpret, Tantra will be best defined in terms of that which gives it its specificity, of that which differentiates it from other phenomena. As such, I find it useful to speak of both a "soft core" and a "hard core" of Tantric practice. The former more or less corresponds to accounts that most present-day practitioners who consider themselves to be Tantric give of their practice; that is, their emic perspective. The latter consists of those practices found mainly in early medieval Tantric texts, liturgies, and imagery, and nowhere else in the range of (South) Asian religious traditions. This latter, exclusivist, account of Tantric practice will not correspond to any single emic perspective, nor will it correspond to the sum of all emic perspectives.[44] Because I am a historian of South Asian religions and not a Tantric practitioner, it is this "hard-core" etic perspective that I unabashedly take here in my interpretive efforts. It is for this reason that this study will privilege "Tantric sex" over all other aspects of Tantric or Kaula practice, because sexualized ritual practice is the sole truly distinctive feature of South Asian Tantric traditions. All of the other elements of Tantric practice—the ritual use of mandalas, mantras, and *mudrās*; worship of terrible or benign divinities; fire offerings; induced possession; sorcery; and so on—may be found elsewhere, in traditions whose emic self-definitions are not necessarily Tantric. In addition, all of the elements of Tantric exegesis, that is, Tantric "mysticism," are second-order reflections not unique to Tantra, and that in fact have, over time, brought Tantra back into the fold of more conventional forms of South Asian precept and practice.[45]

At this point an essential definitional distinction must be made. Since its origins in the sixth or seventh century, Tantra has essentially consisted of a body of techniques for the control of multiple, often female, beings, both for one's own benefit and as tools to use against others. These may be reduced to three principal types: (1) mantras, acoustic formulas that, when enunciated properly under the proper conditions, control said beings; (2) techniques of possession, in which the same beings act through one's own body; and (3) the gratification of these beings through sacrificial offerings, with or without the transformative medium of fire. In this last case, the supreme offering is none other than the bodily constituents of the practitioner himself. Here, coercion is replaced by an exchange of prestations, in a heroic mode. Human practitioners make the supreme sacrifice of their own person, moving the Tantric deity to reciprocate with untold powers and supernatural enjoyments. It is these three types of practice that have constituted the Tantric "mainstream" in the history of South Asian religions, to which we will return in the final chapter of this book.

So, while my prime focus will be on hard-core "Tantric sex," such does not constitute and has not ever, as far as can be determined, constituted the mainstream of Kaula or Tantric practice in South Asia. It is rather the more soft-core practices listed above, in which feeding is brought to the fore, that form the Tantric mainstream, at the same time as it has been the hard-core rituals practiced by a limited inner circle—in which pleasing supernatural beings through sexual emissions is paramount—that have given Tantra its specificity. A single Sanskrit term, *bhoga*, covers the notions of "feeding on," "food," and "sexual enjoyment," with the first of these being its primary meaning. Whereas the Tantric mainstream as I have described it reads and practices *bhoga* in its primary sense of satisfying multiple and petulant divinities by feeding them, the elite practitioners whose sexualized rituals are what have given the Tantric and Kaula traditions their specificity read the same term in its secondary senses, of giving pleasure through sexual enjoyment ambiguously understood as enjoyment through the consumption of sexual emissions as food. In both cases, the female Yoginī "seizes" or "possesses" her male counterpart. However, whereas in the former case, she simply preys upon her human victim (*paśu*), in the latter, the male partner takes an active role, inducing a sort of "mutual possession" (*samāveśa*) in a sexual mode. It is for this reason as well that Kaula virtuosi practiced in sites most frequently haunted by these semidemonic beings: mountains, caves, forests, at the foot of isolated trees, deserted buildings, crossroads, remote temples of the Mothers, and cremation grounds.[46]

A second important terminological point must also be made here, on the basis of historical data, both in the content of the early Tantric literature, liturgies, and iconography and in their reworking by later Tantric exegetes. What I am calling the "Tantric mainstream" here refers to the popular practices, found throughout South Asia, to which I referred in the first section of this chapter. This is to be distinguished from the "high Hindu" Tantric mysticism of the later Tantric exegetes, which was generated, as I will show, in an effort to win a certain support base, of generally high-caste householders in Kashmir and, later, in Tamil Nadu, from the tenth century onward. Whereas the sexual content of Kaula practice had the production of a sacramentally transformative ritual substance (*dravyam*) as its principal goal, later Tantric sexual practice came to be grounded in a theory of transformative aesthetics, in which the experience of orgasm effected a breakthrough from "contracted" self-consciousness to an expansive "god-consciousness," in which the entire universe came to be experienced as

"Self."[47] The exegetical syntheses of these thinkers, arguably the greatest metaphysical writings of the entire medieval period in South Asia, have become the basis for the "soft-core" practice of the great majority of high-caste Hindu Tantric practitioners of the Indian subcontinent. But these practices do not constitute the Tantric mainstream so much as a Tantric orthopraxy whose practices shade into those of orthoprax brahmanic ritual. So it is that the majority of Tamil Tantric practitioners are Smārta brahmins, whose Śrīvidyā or Śaivasiddhānta rituals are expanded variations on brahmanic rites.[48] This type of practice, comprised of highly elaborate, semanticized rites, has prevailed among elite Indian practitioners, whose numbers, in comparison to those of what I am calling the Tantric mainstream, are relatively insignificant. I will return to brahmanical appropriations of Kaula and Tantric practice in chapter 8.

South Asian Tantra can neither be reduced to an elite corpus of texts nor to a body of mystical practices amputated from "real-world" concerns, and even less to the late-twentieth- and early-twenty-first-century fad that the French novelist Michel Houellebecq recently characterized as "a combination of bumping and grinding, fuzzy spirituality, and extreme egotism."[49] What, then, is Tantra? What were its South Asian origins? What are its modalities? Who are its principal actors? Over fifteen years ago, André Padoux, citing Madeleine Biardeau, offered an overarching definition of Tantric doctrine that has since held the field:

> [Tantra is] . . . an attempt to place *kāma*, desire, in every sense of the word, in the service of liberation . . . not to sacrifice this world for liberation's sake, but to reinstate it, in varying ways, within the perspective of salvation. This use of *kāma* and of all aspects of this world to gain both worldly and supernatural enjoyments (*bhukti*) and powers (*siddhis*), and to obtain liberation in this life (*jīvanmukti*), implies a particular attitude on the part of the Tantric adept toward the cosmos, whereby he feels integrated within an all-embracing system of micro-macrocosmic correlations.[50]

This definition, which concentrates on the goals of Tantric practice, is best applied to scholasticist Tantric traditions, or better still to the textual corpus known as Tantraśāstra, in the sense of "Theoretical Treatises on Tantra," ritual exegesis. This corpus, which appears later than the original Tantric texts themselves—the Tantras properly speaking—of which it constitutes the commentary, generally consists of "signed" works written in excellent Sanskrit by members of the brahmin intelligentsia. The title of the most renowned of all such works, the eleventh-century *Tantrāloka* (TĀ) of Abhinavagupta, makes this abundantly clear: *Tantrāloka* means "Elucidation of the Tantras."[51]

The two ritual components of Abhinavagupta's system are *tantra prakriyā*, the exoteric, normative liturgy of the entire community, centered on the god Bhairava or Śiva; and *kula prakriyā*, the esoteric, secret rites of the inner circle, the "clan" of initiates, centered on the Goddess and her proliferation into multiple goddesses.[52] The former form the "soft core" of Tantric practice, rituals observed by, but not exclusive to, Tantric practitioners. Generally speaking, the latter constitute the "hard core" of such practice, that which makes it distinctive, as opposed to other forms of practice or systems of thought. In his exegesis of the *kula prakriyā*, Abhinavagupta sublimates, cosmeticizes, and semanticizes many of its practices into a type of meditative asceticism whose aim it was to realize a transcendent subjectivity. In the process, he transforms ritual from a form of "doing" to a form of "knowing."[53] Exegetical or scholasticist Tantric works, then, constitute a secondary development, a hermeneutical transformation of an earlier body of practice into a mystical metaphysics, which often systematically distorts the meaning of the original practice itself. Prime examples of this are Kṣemarāja's eleventh-century Trika commentary on the *Netra Tantra*,[54] and Abhinavagupta's forced reading of the dualist principles of the *Mālinīvijayottara Tantra* into a nondualist Trika mold in his TĀ.[55]

In fact, it has been this corpus of Kashmiri exegesis—datable to the tenth century and after—rather than the Tantras themselves, that has been the focus of nearly all serious Western scholarship since the pioneering work of Woodroffe, Silburn, Padoux, and others. Tantraśāstra, whose expressed end is to provide a theoretical, doctrinal basis for Tantric practice, is a systematic reflection on Tantra. As such, I can think of no better translation for the term "Tantraśāstra" than "Tantrism."[56] There is a certain irony here, since the term "Tantrism" is the very Orientalist bogey that Western scholars have, of late, been attempting to exorcise from their discourse,[57] even as the focus of their scholarship has remained, precisely, more squarely based on Tantraśāstra than on Tantra.

If, then, the Western scholarship that has purportedly focused on "Tantra" has in fact been a study of "Tantrism," what is this thing called "Tantra" that has been left relatively unexplored? The textual pedigree of the term "Tantra" goes back to the pre-fifth-century B.C.E. *śrauta sūtras*, a corpus of ritual instructions for Vedic specialists. So, for example, the opening verses of the *Āśvalayana Śrauta Sūtra* employ the term "tantra" to mean "ritual framework,"[58] or "interweaving of rites"; and such is precisely the subject matter of the Tantras. Tantra is ritual practice, and the Tantras are unembellished compendia of ritual practice, with a minimum of the explanatory material and erudite exegesis found in later works of Tantraśāstra.[59] One may also resort to a tautological definition: Tantra is the subject matter of works that call themselves "Tantras." This definition is valuable to a point and applies to both Hindu and Buddhist texts; however, not all texts calling themselves "Tantras" are ritual texts. So, for example, perhaps the best known of all "Tantras" is the Pañcatantra ("Five Treatises"), a collection of animal stories and fables. Elsewhere, works on grammar, astronomy, as well as certain alchemical works consisting of procedural, but not necessarily ritual, instructions have also called themselves Tantras. In addition, a number of works devoted to the ritual practices that typify Tantra call themselves by other names: these include Matas (the *Kubjikāmata* [KM], *Kākacaṇḍeśvarīmata* [KCM], and *Siddhayogeśvarīmata*), the Yāmalas (*Brahmayāmala* [BY], *Jayadrathayāmala* [JY], etc.), the Nirṇayas (*Kaulajñānanirṇaya* [KJñN] and *Kaulāvalinirṇaya* [KĀN]), as well as such works as the *Tantrasadbhāva* and *Kriyākālaguṇottara*. Finally, a number of works that closely resemble the Tantras in their ritual focus call themselves Āgamas or Saṃhitās. These are works belonging to the coeval Śaivasiddhānta and (Vaiṣṇava) Pāñcarātra schools, respectively.[60]

The "hard-core" Tantric or, more properly speaking, Kaula practices are, I would maintain, what give Tantra its specificity and distinguish its rituals from rituals that are not Tantric. Generally speaking, these are ritual acts addressed to a multiplicity of goddesses, which often involve human sexuality and sexual interactions between male practitioners and their female counterparts. It is in this context that the two most salient elements of Tantra, *eros* and *thanatos*, emerge. The decapitated and dismembered bodies that litter the myriad tableaux of Tantric expression exemplify the practitioner who heroically gives up that which is most precious to him, and which is restored to him by the Tantric deity. There is, however, a more effective way to sacrifice one's life's essence, which does not involve losing one's head. This is the offering of one's sexual emissions, which are at once the stuff of life itself (according to Indian medicine) and the staff of life and preferred food of several classes of Tantric deities, generally female. There is a Sanskrit term that denotes both of these types of offerings, a term that one encounters as frequently as the other blanket terms for (male) Tantric practitioners in the medieval period. This is the term *vīra*, which, commonly translated as "hero" or "champion" in the martial sense of the word, has for its primary meaning "one who is virile, possessed of virility."[61] It is the practices of these Virile Heroes—heroic in their interactions with the powerful beings they attempt to control, as well as in the war of the sexes in which their partners are assimilated to the terrifying female deities, the Yoginīs, to whom their sexual fluids (*vīrya*) are offered, or with whom they are exchanged—that exemplify the "Tantric sex" that is the subject of this book.[62]

Another term that comes to be applied to the elite male Tantric initiate in the early sources is *kulaputra*, "son of the clan" (*kula*), or *kaulavit*, "one possessed of the clan-generated gnosis."[63] Kula and Kaula are at once metaphysical categories, categories of texts and their liturgies, and kinship terms. I begin with a discussion of the former, more technical uses of the terms. In much of the later Tantric exegetical literature, the term *kula* becomes "semanticized" into a broad range of significations,[64] most felicitously encapsulated by Paul Muller-Ortega in the term "embodied cosmos."[65] Important among these is a Hindu classification of texts and their corresponding liturgies and cults. Here, I am referring to the self-proclaimed "Kula Tantras," which distinguished themselves from all other types of Tantra by referring to themselves as "Kaula," and others as "Tāntrika" collectively. Some time in the eleventh century, these Kaula traditions were systematized into *āmnāyas* ("transmissions"), comprising the cults of the goddesses[66] of the (1) Trika, named Parā, Aparā, and Parāparā (the *pūrvāmnāya*, the "prior" or "eastern transmission"); (2) Kālī (the *uttarāmnāya*, the "higher" or "northern transmission," also known as the Krama, "sequence"); and (3) Kubjikā (the *paścimāmnāya*, the "final" or "western transmission"). Later the cult of (4) Tripurāsundarī would be added as a fourth Kaula tradition, the *dakṣiṇāmnāya* ("southern transmission");[67] still later the *Kulārṇava Tantra* would claim to represent a fifth tradition, the *ūrdhvāmnāya* ("upper transmission").[68]

A number of Kaula sources state that these five traditions flow from the five mouths of Śiva, evoking either the five-headed Sadāśiva of the Śaivasiddhānta[69] or the *pañcamukha liṅga*, the five-faced phallic image of Śiva.[70] Many of the same sources also posit a sixth mouth, called the "nether mouth" or "mouth of the Yoginī"—a reference to the yoni, the vulva-shaped chasing in which the *liṅga* is inserted—as the source of a sixth stream of teachings and clan lineages;[71] and Kaula systems of the Kathmandu Valley and elsewhere have been classified as the *ṣaḍāmnāya* ("six transmissions") since the thirteenth or fourteenth century.[72] Above all else, these comprise "systematic genealogies" or "flow charts," in which the flow in question is one of teachings, traditions, and liturgies—but ultimately of sublimated sexual fluids, emanating first from the supreme godhead and radiating outward, via goddesses and Yoginīs, through the transmission of the clan fluid, into the various suborders of the clans.[73]

This brings us to the nontechnical meanings of the term *kula*, which are of paramount importance to this study. The primary sense of the term *kula* is simply "family," "line," "lineage," "(noble) race," or "clan." The term also is applied to birds, quadrupeds, and insects: a herd of buffalo, a troop of monkeys, a flock of birds, and a swarm of bees are all signified by *kula:* as we will see, this polyvalence is of signal importance for the cults of the Yoginīs, the female consorts of the male Vīras and Siddhas.[74] In his *Parātriśika*

Vivaraṇa, Abhinavagupta derives the term *kula* from the root *kul*, which means "coming together as a group."[75] In this nontechnical usage, *kula* is at once a kinship term and a term applied to voluntary associations of beings. This allows for ambiguity and redundancy, which is altogether appropriate. In many cases the Tantric clan is at once composed of the initiated members of an inner circle, related to one another through the Goddess or Mother who is the progenetrix of the clan, as well as to the biologically related members of human families who form that inner circle. It is this sense of the term *kula*—as a "segmentary lineage system," both biological and sociological—that has obsessed political historians of the Indian Rajputs for decades.[76] This sociological reality of biological families participating in nonbiologically determined clan practices reinforces the solidarity of the Tantric clan group. Biological fathers, mothers, sisters, and brothers initiate their kin into the Goddess's family, the Tantric clan. Such is strikingly the case of the Charans of western India, the bards to the same Rajputs, who term themselves "Sons of the Goddess," and whose women call themselves "Sisters of the Goddess," with whom they identify.[77] At the level of royal cults, entire lineages of princes and kings may be initiated by parallel lineages of royal Tantric gurus.[78] Clearly, the use of *kula* as a kinship term predates and flows into its application to the segmentary lineage systems of religious societies: such was also the case in Jain religious and sectarian society, in which *kula* was an operative term as well.[79]

In the KJñN and many later works, Śiva is referred to as *akula*, "clanless," in opposition to the Goddess, who is said to be *kula*, "clanned": the Kaula ("Clan Generated" [lineage]) arises from their union.[80] While many commentators interpret this classification to mean that Śiva is ontologically prior to the Goddess—a reading that only applies to Śākta-Śaiva metaphysics—this usage also privileges the Goddess as the authentic source of the life of the clan, her family, in opposition to the solitary male, Śiva.[81] In this context, two epithets of the Goddess, found in the KJñN, take on great significance: she is *kulagocarā*, "she who is the channel of access to the clan,"[82] and *kulāgamā*, "she whose issue of blood gives rise to the clan."[83] The Goddess, through the channel of her vulva and its emissions, is the mother of the entire flow chart of the clan, indeed of the entire embodied cosmos.

Of course, in early works on Tantric sorcery, the sole importance of knowing a devouring Yoginī's clan was as a means to controlling her. In the words of the *Netra Tantra*, "In every case in which someone is 'sealed [in]' or 'nailed [down]' [by a Yoginī or a demon] from a given clan (*kula*) [or] who is a portion of a given power, he can only be released from his ills by an offering to the [leader of] that family."[84] So, for example, a person tormented by the Yoginīs and their ilk is to worship their leader, Bhairava.[85] The Kaula began as an endeavor to tame the wild Yoginīs and assume the place of Bhairava at the heart of their ravening hordes.

The relationship between the Tantric clans, on the one hand, and human women and the family units of their fathers and husbands, on the other, is also illuminating here. Describing the latter in a twentieth-century Orissan context, Frédérique Apfel-Marglin explains that

> the wives—who also belong to the clan—come from different lines (*kulas*) and are incorporated into the husband's line by the marriage ritual, and at the same time are severed from their father's line. . . . The fertility of women in the shape of sons preserves the *kula*. . . . The continuity of the line therefore is achieved through the seed [of the male], and the maintenance of the line depends on the feeding by the woman, both in terms of food and in terms of feeding the embryo with the woman's blood. . . .[86]

Even though a human woman preserves the *kula* by giving life to her sons (and daughters) through her nurturing bodily fluids, she is nonetheless not the source of the continuity of the clan line, which is ensured through male semen. Indeed, a human woman is seen to have no *kula* of her own: rather, upon marriage, her bodily substance changes from that of her father to that of her husband.[87] This is, in fact, but a restatement of the old commonplace that the woman is the field in which the man plants his seed—or more precisely, an embryonic form of himself, contained in his seed.[88] This "spermatogenetic" model of animal (and human) reproduction[89]—which was superseded in the medical literature by a combinatory model near the beginning of the common era—served as the basis for Hindu inheritance law, according to which the corporate wealth of the family was always transmitted patrilineally.

There have been, however, important exceptions to this religious construction of biological or genetic categories. First, as will be shown in chapter 3,[90] the Tantric authors were aware of the role of "female seed" in human reproduction and of the fact that both male and female sexual fluids were necessary to conception.[91] Second, as Catherine Weinberger-Thomas and Harald Tambs-Lyche have noted for the Rajput and Charan communities of western India, women play a prominent role in defining their husbands' clan identities, with human women sometimes retaining their own clan identities after marriage.[92] More importantly, royal Rajput marriages have often involved the adoption by the groom of his bride's *kuldevī* (the vernacular form of the Sanskrit *kula-devī*), her "clan" or "lineage goddess." Such have both cemented alliances between royal families and symbolically wed the king to the goddess of the land itself. As Tambs-Lyche explains:

> The queen's role . . . shows the fundamental importance of marriage alliance in Rajput polity. . . . The idea of Rajputhood, as it emerges, involves a complementarity of male and female, of brotherhood and alliance. . . . In this kinship nexus, the place of the *kuldevī* or clan goddess is central; linking her to the king are her brothers the bards [the Charans, mentioned above], from whose caste the goddess is herself recruited. . . . [I]n a context where no state deity . . . is found . . . caste and lineage . . . become sacred, and over this sacred entity the *kuldevī*, herself a Charanī [a Charan woman], presides. . . . [T]he Goddess, representing the integrity of the royal lineage as well as the fruits of alliance in the form of fertility, becomes the perfect symbol of what the king is supposed to achieve, and by implication the obvious source of the power to succeed.[93]

As we will see, these Rajput *kuldevīs* bear a strong resemblance to the Tantric Yoginīs in their appearance, vehicles, and roles. And while in the Rajput case, Charan women are identified with their clan goddess, it is important here to bear in mind that the great Goddess or multiple goddesses of the Tantric clans were neither human nor married. Independent sources of life and energy, they defined clan continuity, in a reversal of the fate of human daughters and wives. Here, their status and role appear to reproduce that of the "woman who wears flowers" (*pūvāṭaikkāri*) in modern-day Tamil rituals: a family's tutelary deity—in whose supernatural person the entire host of family ancestors coalesce—is invested and enshrined in the family compound as a bride, a "woman who wears flowers," to ensure the very generational continuity that the human bride shatters when she marries a son of the family.[94]

Whereas the Tantric *kula* flowed naturally through the wombs of these goddesses and their human counterparts or incarnations, the Yoginīs, the most that a male could hope for was to become a *kulaputra*, a son of the (female) clan, through initiation. Indeed, while the Goddess is sometimes referred to as *śukradevī* ("goddess semen") or *bindupuṣpā* ("she whose menses is semen") in these traditions, her male counterpart Śiva-Bhairava is never given such an androgynous qualifier.[95] Alexis Sanderson summarizes the Tantric understanding of female predominance in the Kula in the following terms:

> The rites of the Yoginī cults and the fruits they bestowed were called *kaulika* or *kaula* in the texts which prescribed them, these terms being

> adjectives derived from the noun *kula* in its reference to the families or lineages of the Yoginīs or Mothers. Thus a Kaulika rite was one connected with the worship of these *kulas*, and a *kaulika* power (*kaulikī siddhiḥ*) was one that was attained through that worship, above all assimilation into these families (*kulasāmānyatā*). Kaulism developed from within these Yoginī cults. It preserved the original meaning of the term *kula* and its derivatives but it introduced a new level of esotericism based on a homonym. For *kula* was also taken to mean the body and, by further extension, the totality (of phenomena), the "body" of power (*śakti*). This last meaning neatly encompassed the original, for this cosmic "body" was said to consist of the powers of the eight families of the Mothers. One was believed to enter the totality (*kula*) through that segment of its power with which one had a special affinity, determined as before by the casting of a flower during possession (*āveśa*).[96]

The importance of a substantive link, in the form of the *kuladravyam*, cannot be underestimated here, since it was this, the germ plasm of the divine, literally flowing through the clan, that made it a unified family. For all intents and purposes, the Kaula disappeared, in the twelfth and thirteenth centuries, with a catastrophic break in most of the guru-disciple lineages, a break most likely occasioned by the progressive Muslim conquest of north India. Thereafter, it is only appropriate to speak of Tantric or Kaula "revivals."[97]

4. Introducing the Kaula Universe

A number of sources attribute the reformation of the Kula, which brought about the emergence of the Kaula, to Macchanda (or Matsyendranātha), a Siddha who incorporated the teachings and practices of a group called the Yoginī Kaula into his *Kaulajñānanirṇaya* (KJñN), for which reason he is exalted, in later works, as the founder of the Kaula. Because it is arguably a foundational text of the Kaula corpus, and because it offers the most complete and straightforward descriptions of the Kaula—mythical origins, specific doctrines and practices, and principal actors, the male Siddhas or Vīras and the female Yoginīs—a presentation of selected passages of the KJñN will be essential to this study. As is well known, an edition of this text was published in 1934 by Prabodh Chandra Bagchi on the basis of the sole extant manuscript of the work, held in the Nepal National Archives, which Bagchi dated to the mid-eleventh century.[98] Matsyendra's foundational role in the Yoginīkaulamata, the "Doctrine of the Clan-born Sons of the Yoginīs," has been acknowledged in Kubjikā sources,[99] while Abhinavagupta lauds Matsyendra as the revealer of the Kaula.[100] On the basis of these outside references, I prefer to date the KJñN to the ninth or tenth century. As such, it is coeval with, if not earlier than, such core Kaula texts as the *Jayadrathayāmala*, *Brahmayāmala-Picumata*, *Tantrasadbhāva*, *Mālinīvijayottara Tantra*, *Siddhayogeśvarīmata*, *Netra Tantra*, *Svacchandabhairava Tantra*, and the *Kubjikāmata*.[101] It is far earlier than the core texts of the "Tantric revival" of the thirteenth and fourteenth centuries, the "later" *Rudrayāmala Tantra*,[102] *Kulacūḍāmaṇi Tantra*, *Kulārṇava Tantra*, *Śāradātilaka*, et cetera. Still later than these are two other works to which I will nonetheless refer in these pages: the sixteenth- to seventeenth-century *Yoni Tantra*,[103] and the *Kaulāvalinirṇaya* (KĀN) of Jñānānanda Paramahaṃsa,[104] which are representative of a still later Tantric revival which was likely based in eastern India and that may have been one of the wellsprings of the "Tantric Renaissance" that took place in the Kathmandu Valley under the Malla kings.[105]

Reading the KJñN, one is struck by the coherence and comprehensiveness of the Kaula system as a body of practice encompassing the human, divine, and semidivine realms of being. In chapter 16 of this work, the Śākta-Śaiva concept of Kaula as a cosmic "clan" or "family," whose lines extend from the great god Śiva-Bhairava himself down into every human initiate, is made clear in one of the rare cosmogonic (or ethnogenic) myths of the entire Hindu Tantric corpus. This cosmogony, presented in the form of a genealogy, is divided into two parts and interspersed with another myth, that of the loss and recovery of the Kaula scriptures in the Kali Yuga. This latter myth will be discussed in detail in chapter 4; here we focus on the Kaula cosmogony, which begins with the divine narrator of the work identifying himself with the *paramaṃ tattvam*, the "highest essence" of the universe:[106]

> I am the Highest Essence; I am the Bhairava [of the Kaula]; I am Sadāśiva, the Supreme, Śrīkaṇṭha, and Rudra.[107] I am that fisherman. . . . I am the Lord of the Virile Heroes. . . . I annihilate the entire universe: [therefore] I am the Annihilator (*saṃhāra*), O Clan Mistress! Following that, I am the Emitter (*sraṣṭāra*) in the creative emission of mobile and immobile beings. . . . I constantly protect the ordered universe; therefore I am the Orderer (*vidhātṛ*).[108]

Following this, Bhairava presents a list of six other names by which he is known, each based on what appears to be a fanciful etymology: he is also called Viśvapāda, Vicitra, Śvetapāda, Bhṛṅgapāda, Bhaṭṭāraka-Bhaṭṭapāda, and Rūrūpāda.[109] He then begins an account of how the Kaula gnosis was brought down to earth:

> Thou, O Great Goddess, art Umā and I, dear, am thy husband. I am [the goddess] Śrī's lord (*nātha*); therefore I am [called] Śrīnātha. . . . When the [clan] gnosis was brought down at Kāmarūpa[110] by thou and I, the essence of [our son], the six-mouthed [Skanda], descended into thee. The [clan] gnosis [was placed] in the clan scripture by him. . . . I inhabit Moon Island in my nonmanifest (*avyaktam*) form. . . .[111]

It is here that an account of the theft and recovery of the Kaula scriptures intervenes, after which the narrator Bhairava's description of the clan genealogy continues, beginning with a clear reference to the Samkhyan categories of *avyaktam* and *mahātman:*[112] "The great self (*mahātman*) was formed, in the beginning, by the nonmanifest (*avyaktam*). By it, the channel of access (*gocaram*) to the nonmanifest was brought into being through the clans."[113] At two points in the following seven verses, the clans and deities who transmitted the Kaula gnosis to them are enumerated:[114] the Goddess told it to the clans of Skanda and Gaṇeśa; Nandin told it to the clan of Mahākāla; and Jayā told it to the clan of Vijayā and others.[115] Also mentioned in these enumerations are the Harasiddhi deities, a possible reference to the goddess Harasiddhi, whose worship is widely attested in medieval Nepalese sources.[116] Finally, the text gives special precedence to "the Yoginī named Kālikā, whose exalted position is equal to my [Bhairava's] own."[117] Here, the reference to Kālikā may be to her central place in the important Kashmir-based Kaula tradition called the Kālī-Krama ("Sequence of Kālīs"), in which she stands alone at the heart of the clan mandala. Interspersed between these two more or less parallel lists of clans and their respective transmitters of the Kaula gnosis is an explanation of the relationship between god and his creatures:

> That [the nonmanifest godhead] is clanless (*akula*) where I dwell [on Moon Island]. Then, at the end of a cosmic eon and the end of a cosmic age [everything] dwells inside my body. Just as there is in an individual seed (*jīva*) the origins of a tree possessed of flowers, roots, fruit, leaves, and branches, so it is as well with the other beings that are generated within my body. . . . [But] steeped in nescience (*ajñānam*), [creatures fall into] the condition of the brutish individual soul (*paśu*).[118]

Here, the term *paśu*—"domesticated animal," "animal victim of a sacrifice"—is employed in the same sense as that found in the Āgamas of the Śaivāsiddhānta: the individual soul or self (*paśu*) is virtually identical to the supreme male godhead (*pati*), but remains separated from the latter due to its bondage to matter (*pāśa*). In Tantric parlance, the uninitiated are called *paśus* ("ignorant brutes") in opposition to the Vīras, whose knowledge is in no small part carnal. The former share the lot of all sacrificial victims—they are mere "food for the Yoginīs"—whereas the latter, the elite, become the "darlings of the Yoginīs," who share sexual fluids and pleasures with these otherwise predatory female beings. It is noteworthy in this context that virtually none of the sculptures found in the medieval Yoginī temples portray sexual intercourse between Yoginīs and male practitioners, whereas horrific depictions of the consumption of animal and human flesh by human "witches" and ghouls are legion.[119] In the KJñN the way to break the bond of brutish attachment to matter is gnosis (*jñāna*)—the opposite of nescience—in this case the Kaula gnosis that was disseminated, in the beginning, through the various divine clans, and that now, having been recovered, is being revealed by Bhairava in this text, the "Bringing Forth of the Kaula Gnosis."

> From the Mahākaula [arose] the Siddha Kaula; from the Siddha Kaula the Fish-Belly. It was uttered by me upon each of the divisions of the four ages (*yugas*). In the first [age] the bringing forth (*nirṇiti*) [was made] to the Kaula; in the second to the [Kaula] known as Mahat; in the third, to the [Kaula] named Siddhāmṛta [and] in the Kali [age] to the Fish-Belly.[120]

Here, we are in the presence of a mythohistorical account of the emergence of the very Kaula tradition that is being presented in the KJñN. The final two members of the series are of particular significance, since they appear to be the two strands of Kaula practice that Matsyendra is credited with having fused together to found the "mainstream" Kaula tradition lauded by Abhinavagupta and others as authoritative. The Siddha Kaula, Matsyendra's own "male" tradition of worship of a male supreme godhead, became fused with the Yoginī Kaula, here referred to cryptically as the "Fish-Belly," for two reasons. The first of these is mythological: in this same chapter we read that Bhairava, having transformed himself into a fisherman, retrieved the Kaula scriptures from the belly of a fish. The second is sexual, and evocative of the practices associated with the Yoginī Kaula. As Lilian Silburn has explained, the belly of the fish, because it expands and contracts automatically, is connected in Kaula theory with sexual experience, since the sexual organs expand and contract in a similar way.[121]

A passage from the twenty-first chapter of the KJñN[122] gives a variant and expanded list of the various subclans of the Kaula, some of which appear to be stages or phases in a creation process: these are the Sṛṣṭikaula ("Clan of Emission, Creation"), Mahākaula, Timiri[-kaula] ("Clan of Darkness"), Siddhāmṛta[-kaula], Mātakaula ("Clan of Mothers"), Śaktibhedakaula ("Clan of the Divisions of Goddesses"), Urmikaula ("Clan of the Serpent")—which constitute "the coming together of the Jñānakaula in the four yugas"—as well as the Siddheśvara[-kaula] ("Clan of [Śiva,] the

Lord of the Perfected Beings"), the Vajrasambhavakaula ("Clan Generated from Lightning"), and the Meghajā-kaula ("Rainwater Clan"), "which issued, long ago and far away, into this Kaula."

In spite of the many breaks in its narrative as well as its repetitions and inconsistencies, chapter 16 of the KJñN presents a mytho-logic of the Kaula, both as a clan or family and as a form of gnosis, consisting of the knowledge of the true nature—but also the fluid "sap" (*sadbhāva*) of that same family tree. Through the clan gnosis that was transmitted via these divine intermediaries to "the Yoginī named Kālikā," individuals, seemingly cut off by ignorance from their divine origins, may find a way to return to their divine source.

Chapter 2

THE ORIGINS OF THE YOGINĪ: *Bird, Animal, and Tree Goddesses and Demonesses in South Asia*

1. Vedic Origins: The Kiss of the Yoginī

The Yoginīs whose cults were central to Kaula practice had the following features: (1) they were a group of powerful, sometimes martial, female divinities with whom human female "witches" were identified in ritual practice;[1] (2) their power was intimately connected to the flow of blood, both their own menstrual and sexual emissions, and the blood of their animal (and human?) victims; (3) they were essential to Tantric initiation in which they initiated male practitioners through fluid transactions via their "mouths"; (4) they were possessed of the power of flight; (5) they took the form of humans, animals, or birds, and often inhabited trees; (6) they were often arrayed in circles; (7) their temples were generally located in isolated areas, on hilltops or prominences and were usually round and often hypaethral; and (8) they were never portrayed as practicing yoga for the simple reason that yoga as we know it had not yet been invented.[2] In this chapter we examine the origins of these defining features of the Yoginīs and their cults.

While the earliest mention of Yoginīs in Indian literature is to be found in a circa sixth-century C.E. chapter of the Hindu *Agni Purāṇa* (AP)[3] and the circa seventh-century C.E. Buddhist *Caryāgīti*, their origins may be traced back to Vedic, if not Indo-European, sources. The content of a number of Buddhist *caryā* songs is highly sexual, and one finds an indication in at least one that the Yoginī's role as the consort of the male practitioner had already been established at this early date:

Pressing the triangle [of the yoni], give, O Yoginī, an embrace; in the rubbing of Lotus [vulva] and Vajra [penis], bring on the evening;

O Yoginī, without you I cannot live for a moment; having kissed your mouth [vulva], I drink the juice of the Lotus.[4]

The general scholarly consensus has been that the Yoginī cults so foundational to early Tantra emerged out of an autochthonous non-Vedic Indian source. This analysis is of a piece with a more general view of Tantra, that it rose up out of the soil of India to graft itself onto more elite orders of precept and practice. This argument takes two forms. The first maintains that goddess traditions and Tantra are forms of indigenous or tribal religion that welled up to the surface of the religious practices of urban and rural elites in the late Gupta and early medieval periods.[5] The second finds strong iconographic evidence for cults of multiple goddesses, Śiva Paśupati, and a number of other fixtures of later Hinduism in the clay seals of the Indus Valley civilizations (ca. 2500–1750 B.C.E.). Here, the argument is that these cults persisted in spite of the Indo-Aryan incursions but were occulted from the scriptural and sculptural records for over two thousand years by triumphant Aryanism. This second argument only stands if one assumes that Vedic religion was itself a purely Indo-Aryan affair that remained totally untouched by the ambient culture of the subcontinent. However, as Asko Parpola, Frits Staal, and, more recently, Bernard Sergent have emphatically demonstrated, the religion of the Vedas was already a composite of the Indo-Aryan and Harappan cultures and civilizations. In the words of Sergent:

> At present, it is clear that the Indo-Aryans, upon arriving in India, drew heavily upon the Harappan heritage, incorporating some of its ritual customs (the construction of fire altars, indoor rituals, the use of the stellar mantle [in the *rājasūya*[6]], ritual bathing, the fixing of festival days [of the Goddess[7]] on the equinoxes . . .) into their own religion. The Indus Valley civilization displays features linked to Varuṇa but not to Mitra, to a "Śiva," but not to Viṣṇu, and overall very few deities in comparison with the abundant Vedic pantheon. It is not the direct source of Vedic and Indian religion, but rather a quite important component of it.[8]

As for the origins of multiple goddesses or of a single great Goddess, many scholars have seen evidence for their cults in Indus Valley seals that portray a female figure with a lotus stem emerging from her vulva;[9] the sexual union of a buffalo and a woman (prefiguring the south Indian cults of the great Goddess as spouse of the Buffalo Demon);[10] and of a grouping of seven female figures, on the so-called Mohenjo-daro "fig deity seal," whose connection with the Kṛttikās of later Indian mythology has been demonstrated by Parpola.[11] Beyond this, as Parpola has also shown, the Sumerian word for "constellation" is expressed through a pictogram comprising three stars. In the post-Vedic tradition, Apabharaṇī, the last of the twenty-eight asterisms or lunar mansions (*nakṣatras*)—a configuration also borrowed from Harappan civilization—is called a yoni. Much earlier the *Ṛg Veda* (RV) calls a fire altar composed of three stones the "belly of Agni." Śvetāmbara Jain traditions consider the Apabharaṇī asterism to have the form of a vulva (*bhaga*), while Digambara Jain traditions describe the same asterism as having the form of "a fireplace consisting of three stones."[12] In Tantric imagery, triangles composed of three points generally represent the yoni; and in goddess traditions of northwest India, Vaiṣṇo Devī, one of the Seven Sisters who is considered to be an aspect of the great Goddess, is worshiped in the form of three stone outcroppings called "lumps" (*piṇḍīs*) that represent the three members of the Śākta trinity: Mahālakṣmī, Mahāsarasvatī, and Mahākālī.[13]

The point I wish to make here is that it is quite artificial to inject a distinction between "Vedic" or " Indo-Aryan" tradition, on the one hand, and "non-Vedic" or "Indus Valley" civilization, on the other. The religion and culture of the Indus Valley civilization is already present in the Vedas, together with the more predominant Indo-Aryan material, and is no more "indigenous" to the Indian subcontinent and no more "alien" to the Veda than the latter. At a remove of nearly four thousand years and hundreds of miles (from the valley of the Indus to the Gangetic Doab, the heartland of the Indian subcontinent), such distinctions break down.

The former assertion—that Indian goddess traditions and Tantra are forms of tribal cults that, occulted for centuries by Indo-Aryan hegemony, erupted into mainstream Indian religion in the Gupta period—will be tested and, I believe, disproven in the balance of this chapter. It suffices to scratch the surface of the salient features of the Yoginī cults to find a vast reservoir of Vedic and classical Hindu precursors, in (1) the cults of Vedic goddesses, the Apsarasas (Nymphs), the Grahīs or Grahaṇīs (female Seizers), the Yakṣiṇīs (female Dryads[14]) and Ḍākinīs (Flyers or Noisemakers) of Hindu, Buddhist, and Jain mythology; (2) the various groupings of unnumbered Mother goddesses and other multiple feminine entities; and (3) in general attitudes toward women and femininity. Here, textual and iconographic data are further supported by ethnographic material from modern-day India, in ways that indicate that these semidivine (or, if one prefers, semidemonic) female deities have been a permanent fixture of Indian religions for well over three thousand years.

It is generally accepted that human women played a necessary, if not an extensive role in Vedic ritual. A recent study by Fred Smith is particularly enlightening in its careful attention to the types of ritual activities and the sorts of Vedic deities with which women interacted. One of these was the offering, made in the context of the full- and new-moon sacrifices, to the wives of the gods, an offering that was combined with those made to the lunar goddesses Rākā, Sinīvālī, and Kuhū (also goddesses of childbirth), who represented the full-moon day, the fourteenth day of the waning moon, and the new-moon day, respectively.[15] The principal activity of the sacrificer's wife in this ritual was to pour water down her right thigh (or between her thighs) after exposing her thigh or lower abdomen, while the *neṣṭṛ* priest recited: "You are Prajāpati, the male, the bestower of semen; place semen in me!" The wife herself then recited a verse in which she urged the wives of the gods to follow the path of the Gandharvas, possibly identifying the former with the Nymphs, that is, the wives of the Gandharvas.[16]

The same female ritual participants, divine and human, are brought together in another Vedic context: this is the fashioning of the fire pot (*ukhā*) in which the new fire is to be kindled for the ritual "piling of fire" (*agnicayana*). Here, the fire pot that will serve as Agni's womb is appropriately fashioned by the sacrificer's wife, who is identified with Sinīvālī. While the firing of the pot falls to the ritual priest, who is compared to the sons of Aditi, the mantras that are intoned at this time all invoke female deities: Aditi, the wives of the gods, the divine women, the Protectresses, Females with Uncut Wings (*achinnapātrāḥ*), and other female figures.[17]

The bared thigh is brought to the fore in at least three other rituals from the Vedic period,[18] all of which involve demonstrations of unbridled female sexuality, if not witchcraft. The first is a "husband-finding" (*pativedana*) rite, which occurs at the end of the Sākamedha, the third of the four-monthly (*caturmāsyam*) seasonal rituals. Here, the ritual participants take a detour, leaving the ritual ground proper and proceeding northward to a crossroad, where an apotropaic offering is made to the dread god Rudra Tryambaka, "Rudra of the Three Little Mothers." The participants make offerings to both Rudra and Ambikā ("Little Mother"), who is identified as his sister.[19] The offering cakes, which are placed on a molehill,[20] are one more in number than the members of the sacrificer's family, with the extra cake being identified with an as-yet-unborn descendant. With this the sacrificer's unborn descendants are released from the power of Rudra. Next, a group of people circle the fire, moving three times from right to left, slapping their left thighs, and then reversing their direction and slapping their right thighs.

A similar rite takes place on the Mahāvrata day of the Gavāmayana ritual, as well as during the preliminary ceremonies of the Aśvamedha. In the former, a group of eight female slaves (*dāsīs*) carrying water jars circle the *mārjālīya* (the heap of earth to the right of the altar upon which sacrificial vessels are cleaned) singing, making ritual exclamations, slapping their thighs, and stamping their feet, while a prostitute and a chaste student engage in ritual intercourse nearby.

In the Aśvamedha rite, following the killing of the horse, the king's wives approach the horse, and whilst the senior queen (*mahiṣī*) prepares for her ritual copulation with that animal, the other queens (sometimes accompanied by hundreds of female slaves) perform a series of ritual circuits, in which they slap their thighs as they circle the horse three times to the right, three times to the left, and three times to the right again. The mantra that accompanies the entrance of the three queens in this rite evokes the name Rudra Tryambaka: "O Ambā, Ambālī, Ambikā. No one is leading me. The horsikins is sleeping."[21] These three names also resonate with those of the three princesses of the Kāśis, kidnapped by Bhīṣma for marriage to his younger half-brothers, in the first book of the *Mahābhārata* (MBh). Ambā, the eldest of these, becomes a powerful avenging figure, first undertaking terrible austerities, then becoming partially transformed into a crooked (*kuṭila*), dried-up river teeming with crocodiles, and finally becoming a male warrior in a later rebirth through a genitalia exchange with the male Dryad Sthūṇākarṇa ("Stump-Ears").[22]

In all three of these rites, the prominent role of sexually powerful women moves Stephanie Jamison to affirm:

> The models furnished by the circumambulations at the Mahāvrata day and the Aśvamedha make the maiden's participation [in the husband-finding rite] all the more remarkable for [the fact that] . . . those performances increased almost to frenzy the air of abandon created by the illicit and dangerous sexual unions at those two rituals. That a presumably chaste and guarded daughter of the Sacrificer is encouraged, indeed required, to swirl around the fire slapping her thighs and begging for a husband, as if attending on ritual copulation, suggests that sexual display rather than maidenly modesty contributed to the marital negotiations.[23]

In Vedic mythology it is a woman named Apālā who performs the prototypical "husband-finding" rite, using the equipment and mantras of the Soma sacrifice to attract to her the god Indra and ultimately win a husband.[24] In the myth the maiden Apālā "comes down to the water," finds the soma, and "presses it in her mouth" (i.e., chews it), and then offers it to Indra to drink. She has sexual intercourse with Indra, after which he makes her beautiful and causes hair to grow in her pubic region. This is the same Indra who fights witches, as well as an Amazonlike woman with one breast and a "rusty vagina," in two Rigvedic passages.[25] The Brāhmaṇa commentary on the Apālā myth states that she transfers the soma to Indra—mouth to mouth—through a kiss. Alf Hiltebeitel sees in this hymn an alloform of Indo-European myths of the goddess of sovereignty, known as Śrī in India, who is, like her Irish counterpart Flaith, associated with "liquids of sovereignty," water and soma (replaced by beer in Ireland).[26]

Here, then, the "kiss" of the Yoginī, and the fluids drunk from her vulva in the Old Bengali *caryā* song with which we opened this section are shown to have their antecedents in Vedic if not Indo-European traditions, in myths and rituals that bring the powerful and dangerous sexuality of women to the fore.

2. Apsarasas

Ambā, who in the *Mahābhārata* (MBh) is partially transformed into a "crooked (*kuṭila*), dried-up river," shares her fate in modern-day Maharashtra with river goddesses known as or intimately associated with the Sātī Āsarā, the "Seven Nymphs." Quite often, Maharashtran glorification texts (*māhātmyas*) describe these river goddesses as "liquifactions" of heavenly Nymphs, cursed by this or that ascetic for having attempted to seduce him. The Sātī Āsarā, who resemble ghosts (*bhūtas*) or ghouls (*piśācas*) more closely than they do deities, can either be itinerant or localized—at certain wells, ravines, rocky shorelines, deep river pools, and so on.[27] They are unmarried and have associations with black magic, generally through their brother or guardian, Mhasobā (sometimes identified with Mahiśāsura, the Buffalo Demon), who is their "eighth."[28]

The identification in South Asia of rivers with goddesses, or of goddesses with rivers, is so ancient and common as to be overlooked in terms of its intrinsic meaning. From the very beginning, first in Vedic traditions of Sarasvatī (the Sarasvati River) and later in the Epic and Puranic Gaṅgā (the Ganges River), goddesses are identified with flows of nurturing, vivifying fluids. More than this, every goddess, every river, is in some way a replica, a "hologram," of the great riverine goddess, Gaṅgā, whose flow from heaven is present in every localized goddess of flowing water—including the crooked, dried-up Ambā and the various waterholes and wells identified with the Āsarā. Just as local traditions throughout India identify this or that temple tank or stream with the "mother" stream, Mā Gaṅgā,[29] or claim that an underground passage connects said water source with the Ganges, so, too, every local or minor goddess is recognized to be a manifestation of the great Goddess. In all cases, every individual case of a river/goddess replicates "holo-grammatically," the Mother/Goddess as the fluid source of all life. By extension, because all women are potential mothers and, to borrow Stanley Kurtz's insightful aphorism, because "all the Mothers are one,"[30] every woman also replicates the great Goddess as mother.

This also means that a woman's sexual and menstrual fluids are as potent and dangerous as those of the Goddess, and are in fact the *same* as those of the Goddess, whose fluids flow through every woman, indeed every female creature that can be construed as a "mother." However, it is important to note what the term "mother" has implied in the history of South Asian religions, and here again, the Yoginīs and their many historical and literary forerunners play a part.

The pedigree of the Nymphs goes back to the Vedas. The Vedas and Epics refer to the Nymphs as inhabiting trees, a feature that links them as well to the Yakṣiṇīs, the female Dryads or tree spirits of ancient Indian tradition.[31] In a Rigvedic reference to ritual practice involving women, we find an association of a longhaired ascetic (*keśin*) with a female figure named Kunaṃnamā, "Unbowed,"[32] who has prepared a poison (*viṣa*) for him, which he drinks from a cup, together with Rudra. This longhaired ascetic, clad in dirty red rags, is also possessed of the power of flight and is said to follow the course of the female Nymphs, the male Gandharvas, and the beasts of the forest.[33]

In the Vedic literature, the Nymphs, whose name associates them with the waters, are the spouses of the atmospheric Gandharvas, whose realm they share when they are not wandering the earth.[34] While it is the alluring seductiveness of Nymphs that is stressed in classical Hindu mythology, Vedic portrayals of them are rather more ambiguous. In the celebrated myth of Purūravas and Urvaśī, found in the *Śatapatha Brāhmaṇa*,[35] the heroine and her fellow Nymphs have taken the form of waterbirds when Purūravas approaches them. In their Rigvedic dialogue (10.95.1, 9), Purūravas calls his nymphen wife a "dangerous woman" and alludes to the avian form taken by her race. The same song cycle of the RV describes a being named Śakuna ("Bird") as a bearer of evil, while the *Atharva Veda* (AV) refers to "Black Śakunī" as the female bearer of evil omens or bad luck. In a long hymn against sorcerers of various kinds, the RV mentions "she who ranges about at night like an owl, hiding her body in a hateful disguise," as well as a rogue's gallery of dog sorcerers, owl sorcerers, owlet sorcerers, cuckoo sorcerers, eagle sorcerers, and vulture sorcerers.[36] There is an ambiguity here that we will encounter again with the Yoginīs: it is difficult to determine whether the sorcerers and sorceresses here are super- or subhuman beings, or simply humans in the guise of birds or animals of various sorts. Of course, in later traditions *śakuna* becomes the general term for omen or portent; and, as we have seen, the eighth- to fifth-century B.C.E. *Mānava Śrauta Sūtra* invokes the Females with Uncut Wings in an altogether auspicious context, that of the firing of the pot out of which fire, the god Agni, will be reborn.[37]

The *Atharva Veda* has more to say about the Nymphs, most especially in the second chapter of its second book, which is referred to, in *Kauśika Sūtra* 8.24, as the *mātṛ-nāmāni*, the verses on the "Names of the Mothers," and which consists of a hymn in five verses to a figure called "the Gandharva" and his wives. In the final verse, the poet calls the Nymphs "noisy, dusky, dice-loving, and mind-confusing." As Jagdish Narain Tiwari notes, there is no clue in this hymn itself as to why it should have been classified the "Names of the Mothers" by the *Kauśika Sūtra*.[38] It is noteworthy, however, that these *mātṛ-nāmāni* verses are used, according to Sāyaṇa's commentary on *Kauśika Sūtra* 26.29, "against seizure by the Gandharvas, Nymphs, demons, etc.," who, he asserts, citing *Taittirīya Saṃhitā* 3.4.8.4, are the cause of madness. Sāyaṇa also quotes the *mātṛ-nāmāni* hymns from a work called the *Śānti Kalpa*, with the indication that these are to accompany an offering made in the course of the sacrifice to the Seizers (*graha-yajña*).[39] While Whitney takes *graha* to mean the planets here, an alternate reading is possible, and preferable, especially when one notes that in later works the ritual pacification (*śānti*) of another type of Seizer (*graha*) is central to the treatment of mental disorders.

Furthermore, there are other Atharvavedic hymns that are also referred to as *mātṛ-nāmāni*. AV 6.111 calls upon the Nymphs and other deities to cure a man of insanity, while AV 8.6 is a hymn intended to guard a pregnant woman against a (generally male) group of demons. Yet another Atharvavedic hymn calls upon a Nymph, who "dances" with the thrown dice, for luck in gambling, asking her to "seize" (*grah*) for him the winnings in the "clutch" (*glaha*) of dice he holds in his hand.[40] The term *glaha* in fact alternates euphonically with *graha*, whose semantic field is much broader, referring to any sort of grasping, seizing, or clutching.[41] It is undoubtedly in this context that an early, unusual, and—as it turns out—Indo-European cure for epilepsy draws together the dual sense of the term *graha*. A boy who is suffering from an epileptic seizure (*śva-graha*, "seizure by the dog") is brought into a gambling hall through a hole in the roof and laid upon its round gaming board (actually a depression in the ground), which has already been strewn with a large number of dice. The term for gaming board (*dyūta-maṇḍala*) and the identification of the dice with the gods moving about in the heavens make this an implicitly astrological rite: the dice are asterisms and the gaming board the vault of heaven.[42] The boy is then sprinkled with salt and curds, while mantras are pronounced in which the Dog-Seizer causing the attack is requested to release him.[43] Through the rite, the boy is released from the bondage of the seizures caused by the demonic Seizers, which are perhaps further identified with the stars or planets (*grahas*) symbolized by the dice.

Now, from at least the time of the Vedas onward, this same term, *graha*, has been employed in Indian medical sources to designate the demonic agents of mental illness, childhood diseases, and complications in childbirth.[44] This tradition is not restricted to Hindu India. The *Kālacakra Tantra,* an eleventh-century C.E. Buddhist Tantric work, prescribes that a woman afflicted by Seizers in childbirth, or a child afflicted with some childhood disease, be placed on a circular mandala and sprinkled or bathed in the five nectars: milk, sour milk, clarified butter, honey, and molasses.[45] It is in this light that the use of the *mātṛ-nāmāni* of AV 2.2 "against seizure (*grāhi*) by the Gandharvas, Nymphs, demons, etc.," and the use of the same, in the *Śānti Kalpa,* in the context of a *grahayajña,* a "sacrifice to the Seizers," take us back to the archaic context of a healing rite, performed on a circular gaming board and involving oblations to and praise of noisy, dusky, dice-loving Nymphs. The Nymphs were among the forerunners of the female Seizers of later medico-demonological traditions, which we will discuss at length in the next section.

Thirty-six Nymphs are listed by name in the MBh—names that accentuate their feminine wiles;[46] and in fact, the Epic's first mention of incarnations of feminine deities concerns the sixteen thousand Nymphs who become the queens of Kṛṣṇa's harem.[47] It is also Nymphs who, according to the Epics, come by the thousands to usher heroes slain on the field of battle up to heaven, exclaiming, "Be my husband."[48] These martial Indian Valkyries would appear again, a thousand years later, on the sculpted walls of the "Tantric" temples of Khajuraho.[49]

3. Female Seizers

More than any other group of multiple female divinities, it is the female Seizers (*grahīs*)—also referred to as Mothers—who are the direct forerunners of the Yoginīs of the later Kaula and Tantric traditions. The earliest and most important textual window onto these deities is found in the account of the birth of the boy-god Skanda, in book 3 of the MBh (hereafter referred to as MBh III). In this narrative, which runs for a dozen chapters, several groups of "Mothers" (*mātṛs* or *mātṛkās*) are introduced, quite unsystematically, as the enemies, protectresses, minions, or siblings of the boy-god, whose own birth story is no less tangled than their own, and whose own divine nature is equally ambiguous, ranging from the sublime to the demonic. Out of these converging and diverging narrative strands, a canonical number of nine Seizers is generated. In addition, there is in this long passage a great wealth of data on Kushan-era goddess cults in India, data that is supported by textual, sculptural, and ethnographic evidence spanning nearly two millennia.[50]

In this section I will present the tortured story line of Skanda's birth as given in MBh III, pausing frequently to present external sources to prove that many of the names found in this account actually corresponded—and in some cases continue to correspond—to important goddess cults. For purposes of organization, I will present *groupings* of female deities under Roman numeral headings; and *individual* goddesses/demonesses for whom literary and iconographic evidence indicates an important cult tradition under Arabic letter headings.

I. Mothers of the World

After having listed several of the great river systems of South Asia, the *Mahābhārata* states that all rivers are mighty (*mahābalāḥ*) "Mothers of the Universe" (*viśvasya mātaraḥ*).[51] A comparable term (*mātṛtamā viśvasya*) is already found in the RV in reference to the waters from which the god Agni is engendered.[52] The same term is also applied to the female Seizers, who are additionally called "Maidens" (*kumārīs*) in MBh III. This group is also closely linked to the Mothers of the Kushan era, on whom we will focus in what follows. In Vedic mythology (RV 1.141.2), Agni is said to have seven mothers, or seven spouses, who are the Kṛttikās, that is, the Pleiades. Katherine Anne Harper argues that the Epic association of these multiple goddesses with Skanda (and thereby with Śiva) is necessitated by the fact that Agni, whose Vedic mythology later becomes linked to that of Śiva, was considered to have been the husband of the Kṛttikās in the *Śatapatha Brāhmaṇa* (2.2.1). In the Epic and Puranic mythology then, the Kṛttikās are "transferred" into the Śaivite pantheon through their "son" Skanda, who is the son of both Agni and Rudra-Śiva.[53]

A word on the canonical grouping known as the Seven Mothers (*saptamātṛkā*) is in order here. This is, in fact, a late configuration: it is not until the fifth century C.E. that such a named group of goddesses emerges in India. This series, whose members are identified with the energies of the principal male deities of the Hindu pantheon and associated with Śiva or Gaṇeśa rather than with Skanda, has an iconography that is quite entirely different from that of the Kushan-age Mothers.[54] We will therefore have little more to say about this grouping of seven, who become supporting players of later mainstream Śākta-Śaiva traditions, and who were "fabricated" for all intents and purposes by Vaiṣṇava and Śaiva sectarians of the post-Epic period in the face of the burgeoning popularity of the cults of the (unnumbered) Mothers.[55]

In the MBh III account, Agni is seduced six times in succession by the goddess Svāhā, who has taken the form of six of the Seven Ṛṣis' wives. After each bout of sex, she takes his seed in her hand and, assuming the form of a female kite (*garuḍī*), drops it into a golden basin on the reed-covered summit of White Mountain. The spilled seed heats up to engender Skanda.[56] The boy-god's power is so great that Indra fears he will conquer the universe. On the advice of the other gods, he sends the "Mothers of the World" (*lokasya mātaraḥ*) to attack him.[57] When they see he is invincible, however, they say to him, "You are our son. The world is upheld by us. Acknowledge us [as your mothers]! Agitated by our affection for you, all of us are flowing with milk."[58] Maternal instinct transforms these bloodthirsty, potentially infanticidal harpies into wet nurses for the child god and calms their fury. This mytheme, which is also found in numerous myths of Śiva and the fierce goddess Kālī,[59] is likely grounded in perennial Indian (if not Indo-European) notions of the relationship between conception, lactation, and menstruation, which we will revisit in the next chapter.[60]

The Mothers thereafter watch over Skanda like their own child, with one of the Mothers, Lohitāyanī, the "daughter of the Ocean of Blood who feeds on blood," standing guard over him with a pike in her hand,[61] and his father Agni taking the form of the goat-headed Naigameya to play with the boy. Of course, the goat is Agni's sacred animal, and a circa 700 C.E. sculpture of Agni depicts one of his two attendants as goat-headed.[62] This nativity scene of Skanda, a Mother, and a goat-headed figure appears to have been quite popular iconographically. In fact, all three figures were, as Parpola has argued, deities of childbirth, from the time of the Indus Valley civilization.[63] A Kushan-era panel housed in the State Museum of Lucknow (panel no. D-250) shows a standing Skanda flanked by a cylindrical jar bearing a goat's head on its rim to his right, and by a single lion- (or goat- or bird-) faced Mother to his left. This goddess's right hand is raised in the "fear not" pose, and her left hand holds a baby, lying horizontally, between her knees: this would be a representation of her role as the infant Skanda's nurse. To her left stand four other female figures.[64] Another Lucknow Museum sculpture (no. 0250) and a Kushan-age panel held in the Mathura Museum (no. 00.U9) have also been identified as Skanda nativity scenes.[65] A sixth-century panel from Jogesvari in western Rajasthan depicts Skanda together with a series of goat-headed figures to his right and, to his immediate left, a figure with birdlike legs, feet, and beak; a similar tableau is found in Cave 21 at Ellora.[66] A ninth- to tenth-century panel (no. H. 33) from the State Museum of Lucknow collection depicts six goat-headed goddesses, each holding a child on her lap. In this later context, however, the image has become explicitly Śaiva: these mothers appear in the company of Śiva, who is seated over the demon of epilepsy (*apasmāra*).[67] A bust of a female Dryad recently acquired by the Mathura Museum and dating back to the second century B.C.E. has a goat's face and ears shaped like bells. In Jain tradition, this goddess was the female counterpart of Naigameṣa or Hariṇegamesī, who, like his Hindu counterpart, presided over procreation and childbirth.[68] This complex appears to continue down to the present day in the Maharashtran cult of Khaṇḍobā, who some scholars consider to be a modern form of Skanda. In his modern-day mythology, Khaṇḍobā grants a boon to the demon devotee Malla by cutting off his head and replacing it with that of a goat. That head is visible in Khaṇḍobā temples, beneath the threshold to the shrine.[69]

The earliest textual mentions of nine Seizers (*grahas*) are in fact found in the eighth- to fifth-century B.C.E. *śrauta sūtras*, works on stately or public ritual. Here, the term *graha* is employed for a group of ritual goblets or ladle bowls, fashioned from the wood of a number of trees, or for the libations poured from them. Mainly named after the deities to whom the various soma libations are offered, the Maitrāvaruṇa or Ajakāva *graha*, the fourth of this group of nine, is remarkable for its description in a number of sources: it is marked with "the nipples found on the throat of the goat."[70] Here again, the juxtaposition of a group of nine "Seizers," of which one is in some way identified with a recipient bearing a caprine marking on its carved lip, seems to find a later resonance in this passage from the mythology of the birth of Skanda and in the sculpture mentioned a moment ago of a cylindrical jar bearing a goat's head on its rim.

II. The Daughters/Mothers, Part 1

We now return to the MBh III account. In a final effort to defeat him, Indra pierces Skanda's right side with his thunderbolt. Out of Skanda's wound, a youth bearing a spear and divine earrings emerges: this is Viśākha.[71] Indra then seeks refuge with Skanda, and the battle is at its end. The text then continues:

> Hear now of the terrible attendants of Skanda, who are of supernatural appearance, the dreadful Youths (*kumārakāḥ*), who, born from the thunderbolt's impact on Skanda, cruelly snatch away infants, both newborn and still in the womb. From the thunderbolt's impact on him were also born mighty Daughters (*kanyāḥ . . . mahābalāḥ*).[72]

After this, the text becomes very difficult to follow. The Youths take Viśākha to be their father,[73] and he, like Agni himself, becomes goat-faced in this role. He stands guard over them in battle, surrounded by the host of Daughters and "all of his own sons," while Skanda is said to be the joy of the onlooking Mothers. Now, the *Daughters*, "born of the Fire called Tapas," appear before Skanda, and he says to them, "What am I to do?"[74] At which point the *Mothers* reply: "By thy grace, let us be the highest

Mothers of all the World (*sarva-lokasya . . . mātaraḥ*), and objects of its worship. Do us this favor." "So be it," Skanda replies. "You shall be of the following sorts: malignant (*aśivā*) and benign (*śivā*)." Thereupon the host of Mothers (*mātṛgaṇa*), having taken Skanda to be their son,[75] go their way.

III. The Mothers of Infants

At this point in the MBh III account, the names of these "Mothers of Infants" (*śiśumātaraḥ*) are given: Kākī ("She-Crow"), Halimā, Rudrā, Bṛhalī ("She Who Makes Strong"), Āryā, Palālā, and Mitrā ("Lady Friend").[76] Skandas Mothers Each of these Mothers has a powerful, terrifying son—yet, as a group, these sons of seven mothers are called the Group of Eight Heroes (*vīrāṣṭaka*). Taken together with Skanda's *goat-faced head,*[77] the sixth of his heads, they are called the Group of Nine. This sixth head, called Bhadraśakha, is "that from which he emitted the goddess Śakti"—and it is noteworthy that these verses constitute the sole mention of Śakti as a goddess in the entire Epic.[78] This host of Mothers, whose names appear nowhere else in Indian sources, nonetheless forms a part of the Indian religious landscape. Halīmaka ("Yellowness") is a form of jaundice described in the Ayurvedic classic, the *Suśruta Saṃhitā* (SS), while Palāla ("Sorghum Stalk") is the name of a male demon inimical to children in the *Atharva Veda*.[79] Rudrā and Mitrā are feminine forms of the male gods Rudra and Mitra. Kākī shares her birdlike nature with Vedic Nymphs and a great number of other female deities, also enumerated in the MBh. A passage from this Epic's first book states that Kaśyapa and Tāmrā ("Copper Woman") are the parents of five bird-daughters: Kākī, Śyenī ("Falconess"), Bhāsī ("Vulturess"), Dhṛtarāṣṭrī,[80] and Śukī ("She-Parrot"). "Kākī gave birth to the owls, Śyenī to the kites, Bhāsī to the vultures and birds of prey. . . . Dhṛtarāṣṭrī . . . bore all the geese and ducks . . . and Śukī . . . gave birth to the parrots."[81] An important feature of the Kushan-age Mothers is their avian nature. It is this that underlies the power of flight of the later Yoginīs, who inherit much of their character as well as their iconography from the Mothers. ✗

A. Āryā

Of all the members of this list, it is Āryā who has the most broadly attested cult in the Kushan period. Later in this passage, she is called "the mother of Kumāra (Skanda)" and singled out as the recipient of a special sacrifice.[82] She is referred to in the contemporaneous Jain *Aṅgavijja* as "the great Āryā (*Ajja-mahā*),"[83] as well as in the fifth- to third-century B.C.E. *Mānava Gṛhya Sūtra*, which mentions a festival to Āryā (*ajjamaha*), the "mother of

Skanda."[84] In his sixth-century C.E. *Kādambarī*, Bāṇabhaṭṭa describes an image of Āryā that was placed upon the rice scattered near the head of Queen Candrāpīḍa's bed, in her lying-in chamber.[85] A fifth- to sixth-century C.E. Gupta inscription from the Patna District in Bihar mentions "the Excellent Āryā" (Bhadrāryā) together with Skanda and the Mothers.[86] Perhaps the earliest hymn of praise to the great Goddess in all of Sanskrit literature is the twenty-nine-verse "Hymn to Āryā," inserted into the late-third-century C.E. *Harivaṃśa*'s account of the exchange of Kṛṣṇa's embryo with that of his "sister," who is an incarnation of the goddess Ekānaṃśā. It identifies Āryā with quite nearly the entire panoply of early non-Vedic goddesses, including Kātyāyanī, Durgā, Kauśikī, Jyeṣṭhā, Śakunī, Pūtanā, and Revatī, and, in some recensions, a Yoginī whose hunger moves her to devour all living things.[87] Elsewhere, Arjuna, in the so-called "Durgā Stotra"—an interpolated passage found in certain manuscript traditions of the Bhīṣma Parva of the MBh—calls that goddess by a host of names including Āryā, Kumārī, Kālī, Bhadrakālī, Kātyāyanī, Kauśikī, and Skandamātā.[88]

We are far from the end of MBh III's presentation of multiple goddesses, however. Skanda is now anointed general of the gods by Indra, and the text explains that Skanda is at once the son of Agni, Rudra (Śiva), Svāhā, and the six women (i.e., the Kṛttikās, the wives of the *ṛṣis*).[89] The gods then choose a queen for Skanda: this is Devasenā, who the text identifies with yet another long list of goddesses: Ṣaṣṭhī ("Sixth"), Lakṣmī ("Prosperity"), Āśā ("Hope"), Sukhapradā ("Bestower of Happiness"), Sadvṛtti ("Good Conduct"), Aparājitā ("Unvanquished"), Śrī ("Sovereignty"), Sinīvālī, and Kuhū.[90] Most of these names appear to be simple deifications of abstract qualities, although Lakṣmī and Śrī were already goddesses with significant cults by this time. Of the three names that are not mere abstractions, two (Sinīvālī and Kuhū) are lunar Vedic goddess of childbirth and fertility,[91] while Ṣaṣṭhī is a goddess, closely associated with Skanda since Kushan times, who continues to enjoy a pan-Indian cult as a goddess of childbirth.

B. Ṣaṣṭhī

Scholars tend to refer to cults of goddesses like Ṣaṣṭhī as "folk" traditions, because they lack the prestige of the Seven Mothers or the great Goddess of Gupta-age, medieval, or modern-day Saktism.[92] This is a mistake. First, *all* Hindus, whether they be benighted villagers or dazzling urbanites, worship Ṣaṣṭhī on the sixth day after childbirth. Second, textual and iconographic evidence indicates that this has been the case since at least the Kushan age. Third, worship of Indian goddesses of this sort, more than that of any other Indian group of deities, has spread well beyond the borders of

India, into Southeast, Central, and East Asia.[93] Fourth, these may in fact be Indian versions of far more ancient Indo-European traditions of disease-causing deities, as a passage from Hippocrates would appear to indicate.[94]

The *Kādambarī* mentions images of Skanda and Ṣaṣṭhī painted on the wall of Queen Candrāpīḍa's lying-in chamber, and such was the most common mode of representation of the female Seizers.[95] An undated red ocher cave painting in the Bhimbhetka complex near Sanchi in Madhya Pradesh appears to depict just such a scene: a women in childbirth is shown next to a multi-armed goddess (fig. 2.a). In fact, Ṣaṣṭhī had two principal names in this period: the "Ṣaṣṭhī of Women in Childbirth" (*sūtikā-ṣaṣṭhī*) and the "Winged Ṣaṣṭhī" (*pakṣa-ṣaṣṭhī*)—for Ṣaṣṭhī, too, is a bird goddess.[96] A significant number of coins, sculptures, and inscriptions from the Kushan and Yaudheya periods picture the six-headed Ṣaṣṭhī, often on the reverse of coins upon which Skanda is figured on the obverse; and she is figured in Kushan-age "Vṛṣṇi triads" from the Mathura region, flanked by Skanda and Viśākha in a way that replicates the Balarāma-Ekānaṃśā-Kṛṣṇa trinity.[97] In addition, Kushan images of the six-headed Ṣaṣṭhī may have inspired the iconography of the *caturvyūha* ("four sheaths") forms of the emerging high gods Viṣṇu and Śiva of the same period.[98]

If nearly every Hindu in India has been worshiping Ṣaṣṭhī since Kushan times, hers is no more a "folk" cult than those of the great Goddesses Durgā or Lakṣmī: in fact, the *Mānava Gṛhya Sūtra,* which describes a ritual to her called the Ṣaṣṭhī-Kalpa, identifies her with Śrī, the great Goddess of royal sovereignty.[99] The same holds for all the other Kushan-era Mothers under discussion here: they were widely worshiped in the Kushan and early Gupta eras, whence the abundance of sculptural and scriptural evidence of their cults. Furthermore, many of them continue to be worshiped in India, especially in the contexts of childhood diseases and natural disasters. That they never belonged to the highest strata of the Indian pantheons may or may not be true; however, for the diseases and conditions with which they have been identified, they were and sometimes remain objects of universal worship.

Ṣaṣṭhī's "six-ness" manifests itself in a number of ways: she is the spouse (or sister) of the six-headed Skanda;[100] she is the sixth in a series of deities including Skanda and his "four brothers";[101] like Skanda, she has six heads; and also like Skanda, she is worshiped on the sixth day of the lunar month[102] and the sixth day after childbirth.[103] She continues to be worshiped down to the present day, at childbirth as well as in puberty and marriage rites, in north India.[104] In Bengal, where her cult is particularly prominent, Ṣaṣṭhī is worshiped as a bird-headed goddess and is portrayed together with anywhere from one to eight infants. There she is also closely associated with Manasā, the Serpent Goddess, a most archaic pairing that

Figure 2.a. Childbirth scene, first millennium C.E.?, Bhimbhetka Caves, Sanchi District, Madhya Pradesh. Photograph by David Gordon White.

Figure 2.b. Bird-headed Grahī, folio 13 of "Appeasement of the Grahas" manuscript, Nepal, 1480 C.E. Wellcome Library, London, Oriental Collections, MS Indic 1936. By permission of the Wellcome Library, London.

is elsewhere represented in an illuminated Nepalese Sanskrit manuscript inspired by the medical classic the *Suśruta Saṃhitā* (SS), in which all of the nine Seizers, of which several are bird-headed, have the bodies of serpents (fig. 2.b).[105] There may also be a connection here with the later depiction of female energy in the yogic body, now as a serpent (*kuṇḍalinī*) and now as a bird (*haṃsa*). We will return to this imagery in chapter 8.

At the same time, Ṣaṣṭhī is closely identified with her cat (sometimes she bears its face, rather than that of a bird),[106] a trait that closely links her to another important Kushan- if not Maurya-age goddess, Harītī, the "Kidnapper" of infants, who is particularly important in Buddhist mythology, and of whom massive second-century C.E. images of a Greco-Bactrian stamp, portraying her surrounded by babies, have been found in the region of Patna, the most important stronghold of the early Buddhist community. We will return to Harītī in our discussion of female Dryads, later in this chapter.

IV. The Mothers, Part 2

At this point in the MBh III account, the six wives of the Seven Ṛṣis who had been impersonated by Svāhā in her seduction of Agni, and who had been repudiated by their husbands, are dispatched skyward by Skanda with the words: "Indeed, you are my mothers and I am your son"; they continue to shine there as the visible stars of the Pleiades, the Kṛttikās.[107] Hereupon, Vinatā—known elsewhere in the Epic as the mother of the divine bird Garuḍa[108]—appears seemingly out of nowhere to remind Skanda that she is his natural mother and to declare that she wishes to remain together with him forever. Skanda assures her that she is indeed the "matriarch of his household," by promising that she will always dwell with him, honored by her daughter-in-law, that is, Devasenā. Now the entire host of Mothers (*sarva mātṛgaṇa*)—the same group that had adopted Skanda as their son, and whom he had established as the auspicious and inauspicious "Mothers of the World"[109]—addresses him:

> We are praised by the poets as Mothers of all the World. We wish to be a mother to thee, and that thou honorest us! . . . Those who were formerly appointed[110] as Mothers of the World—may that office be ours, and no longer theirs! Let us be worshipful to the world, may they not be worshipful. . . . Our children were stolen by them, for thy sake. Give them to us![111]

It is important to note that Skanda gives the same response to the Mothers of the World as he had to the Kṛttikās a few verses earlier: "Indeed, you are my mothers and I am your son."[112] Who the former Mothers of the World would have been is something of a mystery, especially given the fact that a late-sixth-century C.E. inscription from the Deogarh Fort (Jhansi District, Uttar Pradesh) speaks of the "circle of the Mothers and of the Mothers of the World."[113] Are these the Mothers of the World originally sent to kill Skanda? The Mothers/Daughters who adopt Skanda as their son? The Mothers of Infants and their offspring, called the Eight Heroes? Or some other group? What is crucial here is that the present group is claiming that their own children had been stolen away, by the former group, for Skanda's sake—and they are now demanding reparations.[114] The narrative continues, with Skanda replying:

> "Children that have been given away are not to be pursued by you. What other children shall I give you?—those which you desire in your hearts." To which the Mothers reply: "The children of those mothers are what we desire to eat. Give them to us, together with their [those mothers'] husbands—those who have turned away from thee." Skanda answers: "I give you the children, but you have said an evil thing. When you are well honored, if you please, protect the children."[115] The Mothers say: "We will protect the children (may it please thee Skanda!) as thou desirest. A long life together with thee is what we long for. . . ."

In a note to this passage, J. A. van Buitenen opines that in the eyes of these (patently demonic) Mothers, the "former Mothers of the World" could be none other than the real biological mothers of human children.[116] I am inclined to agree with this interpretation, which psychologizes the demonic Mothers as a group of powerful female figures who are, in fact, childless and therefore jealous of biological mothers, whose children they rationalize as having originally been their own. Gail Hinich Sutherland gives the following succinct analysis: "Women, it is believed, are defined and compelled by overwhelming reproductive needs that, when denied or truncated, result in their actual transformation into a demonic form."[117] This reading is supported by the "Revatī Kalpa" of the circa seventh-century C.E. *Kāśyapa Saṃhitā* (KS), which lists over fifty *jātahāriṇīs*—"child-snatchers" who enter into pregnant women to steal their progeny—according to caste and subcaste. These wrathful females possess women (of their own caste?), who then communicate them to others of their caste through various forms of contagion.[118] This meshes with another plausible interpretation, put forward by Albrecht Weber, that the Mothers are the female counterparts of the Fathers (*pitṛs*), to whom offerings are made in the context of postmortem *śrāddha* rites: these would therefore be the wrathful shades of Mothers who had died childless or in childbirth.[119] In this context, it is noteworthy that Vinatā asserts her motherhood to Skanda with the words: "You are my son to offer the funerary oblation."

Several modern-day popular traditions support these readings. Throughout north India, women whose natural fulfillment of their domestic potential has been cut off—either through death in childbirth, within the period of postpartum pollution, or prior to marriage—are transformed into haunting demonesses called *curel, curail, alivantin,* or *jakhin* (a vernacular form of *yakṣī,* "female Dryad"), that take their own children from their stepmothers, or who simply kill babies.[120] In Bengal and Kerala, Joginīs and Yakṣīs are identified as demonic spirits of women who died in childbirth.[121] In Tamil Nadu unmarried virgins are compared to the Seven Mothers, who are termed "fertile virgins" (*kaṉṉimār*) and if they die before marriage, are thought to merge with them.[122]

V. The Skanda-Seizers

Now the tone of the MBh III account changes yet again, as a new group of powerful demonic figures is introduced. Skanda says to the Mothers:

> "Torment the young children of humans in your various forms until they reach the age of sixteen. I shall give you a 'Rudraic' (*raudra*) imper-

ishable soul. With it, you shall receive worship and dwell in complete happiness."

Thereupon a mighty man, shining like gold, issued from Skanda's body to eat the children of mortals. It then fell to the ground hungry and unconscious. By Skanda's leave it became a Seizer possessed of a Rudraic (*raudra*) form. Brahmins call that Seizer "Skanda's Epilepsy" (*skandāpasmāra*).[123]

Now, Vinatā is said to be a very violent female Bird Seizer (*śakunigraha*). Pūtanā ("Stinky") is called a Protectress: know her to be Pūtanā the [female] Seizer. . . . There is a female Ghoul (*piśācī*) with a fearsome form called Śītapūtanā ("Cool Stinky"). Horrible to behold, she robs human fetuses. People call Aditi [by the name of] Revatī: her [corresponding male] Seizer is Raivata ("Born of Revatī"). He too is a great and terrible Seizer who torments young and infant children. Diti, who is the mother of the Daityas, is called Mukhamaṇḍikā. Nothing pleases her more than infant flesh in great helpings. . . . These Youths (*kumāras*) and Maidens (*kumārīs*) who are said to have been born from Skanda are all fetus-eaters [and] the greatest of Seizers. [The male Seizers] are renowned as the husbands of the Maidens. Violent in their acts, and uncanny in their ways, they seize children.

Surabhī is called the Mother of Cows by those who know. Together with the bird perching on her, she eats infants [left lying] on the ground. The one who is named Saramā is the divine Mother of Dogs. She is constantly snatching away human fetuses. She who is the Mother of Plants has her lair in the *karañja*[124] tree. Therefore, persons wishing to have sons bow to her in the *karañja*. Now these and the others [i.e., the nine named above plus their male or female counterparts] are verily the eighteen Seizers. They love their meat and drink. They always remain for ten nights in the lying-in chamber.

When Kadrū, taking on a subtle form, enters a pregnant woman, she eats the embryo inside, and the mother gives birth to a snake. She who is the mother of Gandharvas seizes the fetus and goes off. That woman is then viewed on earth as one whose fetus has melted away. The progenetrix of Nymphs takes the embryo and sits down: the wise thereupon declare the embryo to be "seated" [in the position of a breech birth]. The virgin daughter of the Ocean of Blood is rememorated as Skanda's nurse.[125] She is worshiped as Lohitāyanī in the *kadamba*[126] tree. Just as Rudra dwells in men, so Āryā dwells in wanton women. Āryā, the mother of Kumāra (Skanda), is offered sacrifices separately for the fulfillment of desires.

Herewith the Great Seizers of youths have been enumerated by me. Until [boys reach the age of] sixteen, these [Seizers] are malignant;

> thereafter, they are benign. Those previously mentioned as the "host of Mothers" (*mātṛgaṇa*) as well as those who are male Seizers—all of these are to be forever known to embodied beings by the name of Skanda-Seizers. Their pacification rites include bathing, incense, collyrium, food oblations of various types, and especially "Skanda's offering." When these are worshiped in this way, they all confer happiness, long life, and virility. . . .[127]

This last detail, of the alternation between benevolence and malevolence on the part of the Seizers (*grahas*) is, as will be demonstrated, a leitmotiv of Yoginī traditions. It is their alternation between behaviors of "seizure" (*nigraha*) and "release" (*anugraha*) that define the ways in which Yoginīs are approached by male Virile Heroes seeking union (*melaka*, *melāpaka*) with these volatile (in every sense of the word) female beings. We will return to the issue of *nigraha* and *anugraha* in chapter 7. Also in the later Tantric traditions, the divine creation of such malevolent beings constitutes nothing less than a theodicy. The *Netra Tantra*, for example, goes to great lengths to explain that the great god Śiva originally created the ravening Seizers, Mothers, and so on, to destroy the demon enemies of the gods, but that when he rendered them invincible and they began to torment the entire universe, including the gods, he also created the mantras with which beings could protect themselves from the same.[128]

In the MBh III account, whereas it is the "host of Mothers" who are female Seizers of children, it is Seizers of different sorts that afflict males between the ages of sixteen and seventy: these are the Divine Seizers (*deva-grahas*), Father Seizers (*pitṛ-grahas*), Siddha Seizers, Protector Seizers (*rākṣasa-grahas*),[129] Gandharva Seizers, Dryad Seizers (*yakṣa-grahas*), and Ghoul Seizers (*piśāca-grahas*). The passage concludes by stating that Seizers do not touch human devotees of the god named Mahādeva, that is, Śiva, an indication of that god's links to these beings well before the time of the *Netra Tantra*.[130] Skanda's link to Śiva is further emphasized in the following chapter of this narrative, in which it is stated that Agni had been penetrated by Rudra, and Svāhā by Umā, to produce the boy-god. The male gods' dual paternity is curiously bipolar, given that the Vedic Rudra was often an afflicter of the same women and children of whom Agni was the Vedic protector.[131] The text goes on to say that the seed from which the boy-god would arise had fallen onto a mountain, giving birth to two beings named Miñjika and Miñjikā, while the rest had drained into a river of blood, into the rays of the sun, onto the earth, and into trees. This is of course reminiscent of the Vedic distribution of the stain of Indra's crime of brahmanicide into earth, women, and trees.[132] Furthermore, as this chapter declares, Skanda's terrible flesh-eating entourage is none other than

Śiva's host (*gaṇas*), and it singles out one group, the man-eating Vṛddhikās "sired on trees," as worthy of worship by persons desirous of having children.[133] The narrative then shifts to other of the boy-god Skanda's feats, including the slaying of the Buffalo Demon, a feat later attributed to Durgā, in the "Glorification of the Goddess" of the *Mārkaṇḍeya Purāṇa*.[134]

This long passage from MBh III, the richest early textual source on agents of miscarriage and childhood diseases, divides the Skanda-Seizers into male Youths, female Maidens, and female Mothers. The first group it introduces is comprised of two Youths—(1) Skandāpasmāra and (2) Raivata (who is nonetheless linked to the goddess Revatī)—and four Maidens: (3) Vinatā, (4) Pūtanā, (5) Śītapūtanā, and (6) Mukhamaṇḍikā. With the exception of Skandāpasmāra, who is clearly identified with Skanda, all of these are identified with different classes of beings: Pūtanā is a Protectress (*rākṣasī*); Śītapūtanā is a Ghoul (*piśācī*); Mukhamaṇḍikā is a Demoness (*daityā*); and Vinatā a bird: Raivata, the Seizer son of Revatī—who is identified as Aditi, mother of the gods—represents the Ādityas. We are reminded here of the lists, already found in a variety of Kushan- and Gupta-age textual sources, of the host of semidivine or semidemonic beings of the Indian universe. Sharing the stage with the high gods of classical mythology are the various classes of deities or demigods known as Perfected Beings (Siddhas), Coursers (Cāraṇas), Gandharvas, Wizards (Vidyādharas), Secretives (Guhyakas), Who-People (Kinnaras), Nymphs, Serpents, Mothers, Protectors, Ghouls, Ghosts, Beings, Victors (Vināyakas), Sorcerers (Yātudhānas), Vampires (Vetālas), Seizers, and so on. All have their place in the teeming superhuman world, their roles being noted in shrines, texts, and inscriptions.[135]

Following its enumeration of these six deity and demon "types," the MBh III account lists the names of three Mothers: (7) the Mother of Cows (and the bird on her shoulder—perhaps identifiable with Vinatā, the female Bird Seizer listed above); (8) the Mother of Dogs; and (9) the Mother of Plants. These nine, together with their consorts, constitute the eighteen Seizers, male and female, who, remaining in the lying-in chamber for ten nights, seize newborn infants.

Next follows a separate grouping of three additional Mothers—(11) Kadrū, the Mother of Snakes;[136] (12) the Mother of Gandharvas; and (13) the Mother of Nymphs, all of whom seize fetuses still in utero, causing monstrous births or the loss of the child. In addition, these three figures are named and set apart from the others: (14) Lohitāyanī, the nurse of the infant Skanda; (15) Āryā, the "mother" of Skanda; and (16) Rudra (who is to be identified with Śiva Mahādeva, named at the end of this passage). Lastly, the text lists a series of male Seizers, many of which appear to be the male counterparts of a number of the Maidens and Mothers named above.

The Divine Seizers would correspond to (2) Revatī, who is identified with Aditi, Mother of the Ādityas; the Protector Seizers to (3) Pūtanā; the Ghoul Seizers to (5) Śītapūtanā; and the Gandharva Seizers to (12) the Mother of the Gandharvas.

In the final analysis, the list presented here is quite systematic. On the one hand, it presents the Skanda-Seizers as representatives of all the major classes of beings, from gods to ghouls, and including mammals, birds, reptiles, and plants. On the other, it divides them into four types: (1) those that attack the unborn, who are eighteen in number, although only nine —two male and seven female—are listed (this configuration of seven females and two males is precisely that found in the later "standard" representations of the Seven Mothers: a set of seven goddesses are flanked by two male figures, comprised of some combination of Skanda, Gaṇeśa, Vīrabhadra, or another form of Śiva); (2) those that attack children up to the age of sixteen (three listed); (3) Āryā and Lohitāyanī, the "mother" and nurse of Skanda; and (4) male Seizers that attack males between the ages of sixteen and seventy. Additionally, most of the Seizers of the first type are listed in the medical literature (which is only slightly later than the Epic material found in the MBh III account), together with the symptomology of and treatment for the childhood diseases they embody.[137] While the symptoms of each of the nine Skanda-Seizers' seizures is the object of its own specific healing treatment in the SS and other medical works, the following general treatment is prescribed: in a purified spot upon which mustard seeds have been strewn, and around which mustard-oil lamps have been placed and oblations of various aromatics (such as cardamom) have been offered, the child is smeared with rancid butter, with the words: "To Agni and the Kṛttikās, *svāhā! svāhā!* Adoration to Skanda, to the god who leads the Seizers, adoration! I bow my head to you: accept my oblation! May my child no longer suffer, may [his health] no longer waver—hurry up!"[138] Parallels to the treatments of epilepsy on the Vedic gaming board are obvious.[139]

A first-century C.E. column from Uttar Pradesh, likely dedicated to Skanda-Kumāra, offers a rare iconographic representation of what appears to be a group of these Seizers.[140]

C. Revatī

Revatī ("Lady Opulence"),[141] who is mentioned together with her male counterpart Raivata in this list, is a goddess who enjoyed a broad-based cult for several centuries following the Kushan age. She is identified in the Vedic literature as an asterism (*nakṣatra*), which may have been the starting point of her career as a demoness of disease: deities of Indian astrological cults, such as Jyeṣṭhā, are often of a malevolent nature.[142] Epic,

Puranic, and sculptural data identify Revatī as the wife of Kṛṣṇa's brother Balarāma. These sources make her the daughter of the mountain named Raivata, which I have identified elsewhere as the modern-day Girnar.[143] In one place the MBh calls Skanda the "son of Revatī."[144] Revatī is one of the many goddesses (together with Pūtanā and Śakunī) that the *Harivaṃśa* identifies with Āryā.[145] The SS lists five names or qualities by which Revatī is known: Lambā ("Tall"),[146] Karālā ("Gape-Mouthed"), Vinatā (the Bird Seizer), Bahuputrikā ("Having Many Children"),[147] and Śuṣkanāmā ("She Who Is Called Parched").

Following the *Tāṇḍya Brāhmaṇa* (13.9.17), the KS uses the name Revatī in the plural (and interchangeably with *jātahāriṇī*), as a synonym for the Mothers or female Seizers—that is, as a generic term encompassing no fewer than twenty individual names (including Pūtanā and Mukhamaṇḍikā)[148]—and devotes an entire section to her, called the "Revatī Kalpa."[149] This section of the KS opens by explaining that Prajāpati created Revatī for the destruction of a demoness named Dīrghajihvī ("Long-Tongue"), whose Brahmanic mythology links her in a number of ways to the mythic she-dog Saramā, about whom more below. This myth ends by stating that Revatī-Jātahāriṇī possesses pregnant women and kills their fetuses or newborns because that is where Dīrghajihvī and her fellow demonesses fled into their bellies when she took the form of a bird (*śakunī*) to hunt them down.[150] As a bird, the KS continues, Revatī is "feral, with her folded wings, diamond-hard beak, talons, teeth, and fangs . . . her great wings are many-splendored." In her avian form, she is specifically referred to as a female Seizer and sister of Kārttikeya, that is, Skanda.[151] This encyclopedic source in fact enumerates three types of Revatīs or Jātahāriṇīs: the divine, the human, and the Revatīs of the lower animals and plants (of which the avian is the primary subset); as we will see in chapter 7, the KJñN will classify the Yoginīs into the same three groups. In the case of birds, cows, snakes, fish, and plants, these Revatīs avenge themselves on women who have participated in their "killing" by possessing them and destroying their offspring, unless their crimes are expiated.[152]

A Kushan-age sculpture of a four-armed female divinity with snake armlets, housed in the Mathura Museum (GMM. 17. 1357), shows her holding two children in her respective hands as if intending to kill them by dashing their heads together. Near her feet another boy (an epileptic?) is shown lying facedown. Still another boy (also exhibiting seizure symptoms?) is shown standing stiffly and very erect with both hands hanging down. A squatting male Dryad completes the tableau. Noteworthy is the setting of this ensemble: the goddess's "seat" is not the usual bench or four-legged slab altar, but rather the top of a small hill, the rocks and stones of which can be clearly seen. N. P. Joshi surmises that this may be an image of

Jātahāriṇī: given Revatī's identification with Mount Raivata, it is possible that it is she who is represented here. Of course, in a later period *all* Yoginī temples would be built on prominences or atop mountain peaks.[153]

D. Pūtanā

"Stinky" is very likely so named because she embodies the pustulant sores whose eruptions are symptoms of chicken pox.[154] Her near-namesake, Śītapūtanā ("Cool Stinky"), evokes the later smallpox goddess Śītalā, the "Cool One," who is so called in order that, precisely, she cool herself down and desist from afflicting her victims with burning smallpox sores.[155] The two are explicitly connected in Śītalā's modern cult, inasmuch as this goddess's weapon or disease-causing emanation is named Pūtanā.[156] While the sixteenth-century *Bhāvaprakāśa* may be Śītalā's earliest textual mention in connection with smallpox (*masūrika*), a goddess named Śītalā is already named several centuries earlier in the Kāśī Khaṇḍa of the *Skanda Purāṇa*. A tenth-century image of a goddess mounted on an ass, and bearing other elements of Śītalā's iconography, is held in the Allahabad Museum (no. 554): this may, however, be an image of the goddess Jyeṣṭhā, who also has an ass for her mount.[157]

Pūtanā also receives a great deal of attention in the medical texts. An undated manuscript of the *Bālatantra* states that its purported author, Daśagrīva ("Ten Throats," i.e., Rāvaṇa), had sixteen sisters, all of whom were known by the common name of Pūtanā. By virtue of a boon from Śiva, they were permitted to eat the flesh of newborns. The same work opens by classifying childhood diseases according to four agents of possession: sterile female birds, female birds, male birds, and sterile male birds.[158] In the fourth- to fifth-century C.E. appendix (Uttara Sthāna) to the SS,[159] Pūtanā is described as "black in color, with a gaping mouth and projecting teeth and disheveled hair, clad in filthy garments, very smelly, and dwelling in empty, broken-down buildings."[160] In addition to anointing and fumigating the child with elaborate medicinal preparations, the SS prescribes an offering, to be made to Pūtanā in an abandoned building, consisting of crow dung, fish, a rice dish, ground sesame, and alcohol. The child is to be bathed in water remaining after the performance of religious ablutions (of an image of Pūtanā?) and have mantras uttered over him urging Pūtanā to protect him.

Of course, the most elaborate mythology of Pūtanā links her to the infant Kṛṣṇa, a fact of which the MBh itself is aware.[161] It is, however, in the sixth- to tenth-century C.E. *Bhāgavata Purāṇa* (BhP) that we find this myth in its full-blown form. Pūtanā comes to Kṛṣṇa's village, flying through the sky, using her *māyā* to assume the form of a woman. She gives her poisoned breast for the infant god to suck, which he does forthwith, sucking the life out of her without himself being harmed. After she has fallen dead to the ground, once again in her original demonic form, Kṛṣṇa's parents wave a cow-tail brush over him, bathe him in bovine urine, and using cow dung, write the names of Viṣṇu over his twelve limbs to protect him. The cowherding women then utter mantras over each of his limbs, as they invoke the various demonic minions of childhood diseases against which their formulas are meant to protect him. Among those mentioned are the Ḍākinīs, Ghouls, Dryads, Protectors, Vināyakas, Revatī, Jyeṣṭhā, Pūtanā, and the other Mothers, and the male Epilepsy Demons (*apasmāras*).[162]

The BhP account ends on a *bhakti* note: although she was a Protectress, Pūtanā, who offered her breast to Lord Kṛṣṇa, is elevated to heaven. The technique she employs in her attempted infanticide of Kṛṣṇa is, however, illuminating, inasmuch as it corresponds to what the canons of Āyurveda present as the raison d'être for their prescribed treatments against childhood diseases. Termed Kaumarabhṛtya ("Child-Rearing") or Kaumaratantra ("Rituals Related to Childhood"), this, the fifth of the eight branches of Āyurveda, is stated by the SS (1.1.4) to "have for its goal the healing of problems of gestation and changes in the milk of nursing mothers, and the pacification of diseases that arise from the empoisoned milk of the Seizers." Closely related to Kaumarabhṛtya is Indian demonology, Bhūtavidyā ("Esoteric Knowledge of [Diseases Caused by] Beings"), which is defined in the previous verse as "having for its goal, for those whose minds are possessed by . . . Seizers, to appease [these] Seizers with propitiatory rites, the offering of oblations, etc."[163] Human beings who leave openings, called "shadow cracks" (*chāyāchidrāṇi*) for Seizers to penetrate become possessed by these beings, these demons, who make them ill, drive them mad, and destroy them. Cracks in the human immune system may be opened by a number of means or dispositions: pollution, sinful behavior, straying into demonic habitats (cremation grounds, desolate forests, crossroads, and so on), or simply one's gender or stage in life.[164] Pregnant women are especially vulnerable, because attractive to demons: "Some people say pregnant women smell sweet, like a melon, and that is why they attract evil spirits."[165] The prime means for combating these seizures of these Seizers is to seize or bind (*bandh*) them back, usually through the use of mantras; or to drive them away through medical preparations, or to satisfy them through a sacrifice, usually a blood offering.

Pūtanā is portrayed as a bird, in sculpture as well as myth, in the Epic period, with Kushan-age images of Pūtanā in the form of a bird being found in Mathura, Deogarh, and Mandor.[166] In the earliest textual version of the Kṛṣṇa legend, found in the late-third-century C.E. *Harivaṃśa*, Pūtanā, called the "nurse of Kaṃsa," comes to the child "in the shape of a bird (*śakuni*)."[167] She is but one of a host of birdlike female divinities found in this "appendix" to the MBh. These include the owl-faced goddess Nidrā-Vindhyavāsinī,[168] who, fond of animal sacrifices and worshiped with urns of liquor and flesh, inhabits a wood that resounds with the cries of wild cocks and crows.[169] Elsewhere, a number of *Harivaṃśa* manuscripts provide two of the longest early lists of Mothers in Hindu literature. The first of these, a list of eighteen Divine Daughters (*devakanyās*), describes these as resembling Vindhyavāsinī, "enjoying lymph and marrow, enamored of liquor and flesh, having the faces of cats and leopards, faces resembling those of elephants and lions, as well as faces identical to those of herons, crows, vultures, and cranes."[170] The second, a list of female Seizers, names Mukhamaṇḍī, Viḍālī ("Kitty"), Pūtanā, Gandhapūtanā ("Aromatic Stinky"), Śītavātā ("Cooling Breeze"), Uṣṇavetālī ("Hot Vampiress"), and Revatī, and ends with the plea "may the Mothers protect my son, like mothers, perpetually."[171]

Pūtanā is named twice in the AP, once as a female Seizer (where she is called Pūtanā Śakunī, "Stinky Female Bird"), and once as a Yoginī;[172] she is listed (along with Viḍālī) as a Yoginī in the *Śrīmatottara Tantra*.[173] Pūtanā is the sole Mother or Maiden of the MBh III account to be named in the same work's list of 201 Mātṛkās; she is also termed a Maiden and a Protectress Seizer in this source, and she is listed twice in the *Harivaṃśa*.[174] The *Saddharmapuṇḍarika Sūtra* ("Teaching of the Lotus of the True Law"), an important Buddhist work perhaps as early as the MBh III account, provides a list of multiple demons that includes the Protectors, Protectresses, Dryads, Epilepsy Demons, and Pūtanās.[175] The 1131 C.E. *Mānasollāsa*, an encyclopedia attributed to Someśvara III, a Cāḷukya monarch whose kingdom encompassed much of the Deccan plateau, offers a similar list in its classification of goddesses: these include the Revatīs, the Śuṣkarevatīs, the Yoginīs, Yoga-Mothers, Ḍākinīs, Pūtanās, Śākinīs, and Mukhamaṇḍitās.[176] About a century later, the *Śrīmatottara Tantra*'s list of beings to whom blood offerings are to be made comprises the Yakṣas, Rākṣasas, Bhūtas, Vetālas, Kṣetrapālakas, Ḍākinīs, Rāmās, Pūtanās, Kaṭapūtanās, and the youthful Yoginīs who are inhabitants of various countries.[177] The *Hārītā Saṃhitā* and *Brahmāṇḍa Purāṇa* mention the Pūtanās as a group of Mothers or Seizers, whose individual names include Kālī and Ḍākinī.[178]

E. Saramā, the Mother of Dogs

There is no evidence for a Kushan- or Gupta-era cult of Saramā, the Mother of Dogs; hers is, however, a most archaic mythology, extending back to the RV, if not to Indo-Iranian sources.[179] She also has a place in Epic mythology. In the MBh frame account of Janamejaya's snake sacrifice, she curses that king for mistreating her pups, the Sārameyau.[180] She is also present in the *Rāmāyaṇa:* Vibhīṣana's wife, Saramā, the most sympathetic of the Protectresses of Rāvaṇa's fortified capital of Laṅka, offers comfort to the imprisoned Sītā.[181] Saramā's presence in this list of Skanda-Seizers is apposite for two reasons. First, she is the mythological Mother of dogs, a major domestic animal; and her role, in the *Jaiminīya Brāhmaṇa,* as eater of the "outer membrane of the waters"[182] prepares the way for her role, in MBh III, as a snatcher of human fetuses. Second, there is in the medical literature a close link between the childhood disease of epilepsy (embodied as Skandāpasmāra) and epileptic seizures, which are called "dog-seizures" (*śva-graha*), no doubt because foaming at the mouth is a trait shared in common by epileptics and dogs suffering from distemper. It is only, however, male Seizers who are identified with epileptiform seizures in the medical literature; this is presumably because it is especially young males who are subject to them.[183] Perhaps for this reason, the *Aṣṭāṅgahṛdaya* lists the (male) Śvagraha ("Dog-Seizer") in place of Saramā in its list of Seizers. A figure by the name of Kumāra—if the term is not simply being used generically as "boy"—is associated if not identified with a dog in a number of Vedic and medical sources, which associate him with pathological conditions suffered by women and boys.[184]

F. Surabhī, the Mother of Cows

Like Saramā, Surabhī seems not to have had a worship cult at any period in India's religious history. However, she, too, is possessed of a rich mythology, which more often than not presents her (or her alloforms) as a dangerous, feral creature. The sage Vasiṣṭha's wish-fulfilling milch cow (*kāmadhenu*) is named Surabhī in MBh 1.93.8–33; however, elsewhere in the same book of the Epic, this cow is named Nandinī. Nandinī, whom Vasiṣṭha's rival Viśvāmitra is attempting to steal, becomes enraged and excretes armies of outcastes from her every orifice: anus, mouth, and urethra.[185] David Shulman notes that the Goddess is symbolized in many of her local shrine myths—in which she is depicted as a "murderous mother" who "gives birth to her consort after slaying him"—as a "black and white cow, the violent Kāmadhenu who gives milk to the deity and yet draws forth his blood."[186] Shulman also notes that in Tamil Nadu, the shrines of a murderous goddess figure named Mūḷi ("Defective") are guarded by a black cow, and that barren black cows are offered to Nirṛti, the divinization of evil fate. Since the time of the Vedas, Nirṛti has been viewed as a dread goddess of disease, with hymns to Rudra (himself a Vedic god of disease) requesting that he hold her at bay.[187] Mūḷi is further identified as an outcaste equivalent of the equally dire goddess Jyeṣṭhā, who is accompanied, in her south Indian iconography, by a bull-faced son.[188] The feral cow has been a symbol of danger since the time of the Vedas[189] and continues to be so down to the present day, as my cowpuncher friends inform me.

G. Kadrū and Vinatā

Kadrū ("Tawny") is named as the Mother of Serpents and Vinatā ("Curved"), the Mother of Birds in a number of MBh myths; however, there is no evidence for their worship per se. There is, on the contrary, ample evidence for the worship of serpents (*nāgas*) and birds (*śakunis*), both in literary and iconographic sources. An important Epic myth that makes Kadrū and Vinatā rival sisters, and that dates from perhaps the sixth century B.C.E., is one of the oldest stories in the entire Epic.[190] In fact, this story is older still, being found as it is in the *Taittirīya Saṃhitā*—with the important difference that in this version Kadrū and Vinatā are *both* birds.[191] This is in fact one of the most widely told stories in ancient mythology, with parallels found in Norse, Greco-Roman, Iranian, and Babylonian sources.[192] An equally pervasive mytheme, that of a flock of ravening bird goddesses, is found across a wide array of Indo-European traditions, including the Scandinavian Valkyries, the Irish Deichtíre and her fifty companions, the Greek Erinnyes and Maenads, and European witches in general.[193]

VI. Tree Goddesses

The types of divinities presented in the MBh III account are, generally speaking, horrific, and it bears noting that the entire class of texts known as the Forest Books (*Āraṇyakas*)—texts that do not lose the forest for the trees—define themselves according to two criteria: for a work to be called an *Āraṇyaka*, it must be esoteric (*rahasya*), and it must make mention of the horrible, *ghora*, divinities.[194] As we have already observed, the MBh III narrative introduces a class of horrific female tree deities, called the Vṛddhikās ("Crones") or Vṛkṣakās ("Females of the Tree"), about which it states: "Women who are known by the name of Vṛddhikās are eaters of human flesh. Those desiring children should worship these goddesses, who are born in trees."[195] A number of coeval Buddhist *Jātakas* describe analogous instances of blood offerings made to tree spirits for the birth of children.[196]

As we will see in chapter 4, many Tantric goddesses are identified with flowering trees, with the six-sided *saṃvarta* mandala, the mystic diagram of the goddess Kubjikā, being modeled after a traditional Indian tree shrine with its series of surrounding walls.[197] Tree shrines of this sort, which continue to be essential to goddess worship throughout South Asia, likely number in the millions, given the fact that they are found in every South Asian village and town, as well as along the roadsides linking them (fig. 2.c). In many parts of north India, these tree shrines are identified with the goddess Śītalā, whose function and cult continue those of the earlier Pūtanā.

Figure 2.c. Goddess shrine beneath *khejaṛa* tree, Pali District, Rajasthan. Photograph by David Gordon White.

In the Gangetic plain, it is nearly always the margosa (*Azadirachta indica;* Sanskrit *nimba*; Hindi *nīm*; Tamil *vēmpu*) tree that serves as the shrine of this goddess, for a number of reasons. First, just as her devotees pray to Śītalā to be "cooling"—for this is the meaning of her name—the margosa is also the tree reputed to offer the coolest shade during the killing heat of the hot season, the period of the year most identified with smallpox and its burning pustules. The trunk and branches of the margosa itself appear to exhibit symptoms of "possession" by Śītalā, inasmuch as their trunks are often deformed by large bolls or burrs.[198] At the same time, margosa leaves have traditionally been used as poultices to cool the burning of such cutaneous eruptions, as well as to promote the flow of breast milk.[199] Precisely the same associations—of the margosa tree, the believed medicinal properties of its leaves, smallpox, and the goddess—are found in south India, with the exception that the goddess is named Māriyammān, "Mother Death."[200] In much of Rajasthan, it is more often the *khejaṛa* (*Proposis spicagera*), a thorny multipurpose desert tree, that is identified with the Goddess. As such, this tree is traditionally worshiped by Rajasthani kings; yet, at the same time, it is identified with, or considered to be the haunt of, the male god Bhairava as well as a variety of ghosts and demons, most particularly female demons called *bhūtnīs*.[201] Caṇḍeśvarī ("Our Lady of Fury"), an important Nepali goddess whose temple is located in Banepa at the eastern edge of the Kathmandu Valley, is said to have arisen from the trunk of a *raktacandana* (red sandalwood) tree. Her sacred grove is in fact dominated by this species, and barren women bathe in a pool there in order to conceive. In the upper Kulu Valley of Himachal Pradesh, the *yoginīs* are said to inhabit nut trees, the bases of which are often surrounded by a platform of stones or by wooden shrines. A tenth-century Pratīhāra stone inscription from Partabgarh in Rajasthan commemorates a shrine to Vaṭayakṣiṇidevī, the "Yakṣinī Goddess of the Banyan Tree."[202]

These tree goddesses are identified with trees in a number of ways. In certain cases, the goddess effectively *is* the tree; in others, she inhabits, haunts, the tree with which she is identified, but is capable of leaving it to possess another "host"—an animal, human adult (most often a pregnant woman), or child. These modes of being in a tree are illustrated in mythology and iconography alike. Buddhist iconography found both at the ancient Bharhut site and eighteenth-century paintings of Ceylon portray tree spirits in a minimalist fashion, as a face, two hands, or a half-body emerging from the branches or half seen amongst the leaves of a tree.[203] A story from the KSS provides a narrative parallel to this iconographic representation. A sorceress named Siddhikārī impersonates a tree goddess in order to draw into her clutches a merchant's unwitting servant. Seeing him coming from afar, she climbs into a tree and, rustling its branches, calls out: "You have always been dear to me. Climb up here; here is wealth; take your pleasure with me." When the servant climbs up to her, she embraces him, kisses his mouth, and with her teeth bites off his tongue. He falls out of the tree spitting blood. Then the sound of "lalala" is heard coming from the tree, and the merchant and servant, thinking she is a *bhūtnī*, run away.[204]

A second KSS story, involving a Wizard Maiden (Vidyādharī) named Anurāgaparā and a stone pillar, illustrates the second mode of being in a tree. An impoverished gambler named Niścayadatta, having no wife or lover, is reduced to smearing sandal paste on his back by applying it to a stone pillar and then rubbing his back against the pillar. One day an artist and a sculptor come and draw a picture and carve the image of the goddess Gaurī into that pillar. Alighting there on the same day, Anurāgaparā sees the goddess's carved image, and thinking the goddess is close at hand, enters into the pillar. The next time Niścayadatta returns to anoint himself, Anurāgaparā stretches her hand out from inside the pillar and affectionately rubs his back. He feels her presence, hears her bangles tinkling, and quickly grabs her hand, forcing her to reveal herself to him. She emerges from the pillar and reveals her love for him. She leaves him, but shortly thereafter Niścayadatta, recalling the hand that burst out of the pillar "like a shoot sprouting out of a tree," is smitten by love for her.[205] We will return to Tantric associations and identifications of trees and plants with Yoginīs and goddesses in chapter 4.

4. Skanda-Seizers: General Remarks

The preceding discussion of the Skanda-Seizers, from both inside and outside the MBh III account, permits us to make a number of general remarks concerning the multiple Mothers of the Kushan age in their relationship to the Yoginīs, who would emerge, in the seventh century, as an independent category of female deity or demoness. First, it is evident that nearly all of the female Skanda-Seizers, as well as most of the other multiple feminine deities of the Kushan age and beyond, are portrayed as either feral domestic animals (cow or dog) or as birds. Most fall in the latter category: these include Kākī, Ṣaṣṭhī, Vinatā, Revatī, and Pūtanā, as well as the many nameless bird-headed Mothers depicted in Kushan-age sculpture.[206] There is a certain logic to such portrayals. On the one hand, it is disclosive of a notion of contagion: birds, which fly from one place to another, from the wild forest to the domestic space of the household, can easily be imagined as disease carriers. This seems to have been understood by the redactors of the *Kauśika Sūtra*, according to whom demons were to be dispelled into the ground or carried away by birds to places where they could no longer harm the human community. In addition, avian infestation was a plague compared to war in a number of medieval encyclopedias.[207]

How such bird demonesses flew is also important, especially with relation to the later Yoginīs who inherited so much of the winged Mothers' legacy. In a discussion of the *rākṣasamātaraḥ*, the Mother Protectresses (which are subdivided into eight groups, one of which is comprised of the Pūtanās), the *Brahmāṇḍa Purāṇa* states that "those beings among them whose energy is drawn upward (*utkṛṣṭa*) are known as 'airborne.'"[208] In other words, their food fuels their flight. Dogs as well as feral cows also tread the line between the wild and the domestic spheres, with the ever-present potential for causing damage to the latter. More immediate still is the image of the great birds and dogs — or their animal cousins, jackals and wolves — as carrion feeders, which tear apart dying or dead bodies with formidable and fearsome rapacity, or wolf down the charred remains of animals caught in brushfires.[209]

As I have shown, certain of the Skanda-Seizers are clearly embodiments of disease symptoms: Skandāpasmāra, Pūtanā, Śītapūtanā, and Mukhamaṇḍikā are to be counted in this number. In a general way, the fiery nature of these goddesses or Seizers is of a piece with their disease pathology:

the cutaneous eruptions so often associated with such deadly diseases as smallpox—as well as the more benign but also potentially fatal childhood conditions of chicken pox, measles, et cetera—are the somatization of their presence. The victim's body is on fire from within, his skin set aboil with these goddesses' fury, with the pustules and pox that erupt being so many marks (or eyes, or fiery vaginas) of these goddesses.[210]

Earlier in this chapter, I indicated who the Skanda-Seizers' cultic forerunners would likely have been: names and descriptions of several of their number actually correspond to deities whose cults are attested in other contemporaneous sources. As I will demonstrate in the balance of this book, these Skanda-Seizers are, furthermore, the prototypes of the Yoginīs of Kaula and Tantric traditions. In fact, a straight line of textual transmission can be drawn from the MBh III account, through the medical demonological literature of the SS, KS, *Aṣṭāṅgasaṃgraha*, and other sources, and into such early works of Tantric sorcery as the *Kriyākālaguṇottara* and *Netra Tantra*. The eleventh-century Trika Kaula theoretician Kṣemarāja wrote a commentary on this last work, making it the basis for the continuation of these traditions into the Yoginī cults of high Hindu Tantra. There is virtually no Kaula work that does not devote long passages to the Yoginīs, passages that describe their appearance, behavior, and worship in ways that directly link them to the earlier female Seizers, female Dryads, and other divinities of the Vedic and Epic periods. With increasing frequency, it is Yoginīs, rather than female Seizers, female Dryads, or Mothers, who are singled out for propitiation against the childhood diseases and miscarriages of which they are the cause, whence the Yoginī names Garbhabhakṣī ("Fetus-Eater") and Śiśughnī ("Baby-Slayer"); and a fourteenth-century record from Gujarat, which held the Yoginīs to have been the cause of an epidemic that ravaged that country.[211]

It is important to note here that these goddesses are only tangentially related to the Seven Mothers of "domesticated" Śākta traditions.[212] This is in fact the great divide between the Kaula, on the one hand, and later Śākta devotionalism and high Hindu Tantra, on the other. Whereas the former's cults of multiple Yoginīs are based on the Kushan-age cults of multiple disease-bearing Mother goddesses, the latter's foundational *Devī Māhātmya* (Glorification of the Goddess) and its set of Seven Mothers is a quite arbitrary standardization of the feminine energies of the great male gods of emergent classical Hinduism. The gulf between these two traditions only widens over the centuries; however, since the time that Hindu Śākta Tantra became hegemonic, in the eleventh and twelfth centuries, the multiple Mothers and Yoginīs of the Kaula have been relegated to the outer fringes of the mandalas of the great Goddess's entourage. In both cases—the Kushan- and Gupta-age attempts at classifying the multiple

Mother goddesses and the Śākta classification of the Seven Mothers—what can be said is that canonical numbers (especially the numbers seven, eight, nine, and sixty-four) were more important than the plethora of names haphazardly offered to fit those slots, names that were only occasionally grounded in actual cults. Cāmuṇḍā was the sole Mother of this group of seven to have had an independent cult prior to this Gupta-age classification, and as the sole Mother to *not* have a male spouse, she represents, precisely, the authentic Kushan-age cults of the multiple Mothers that we have been discussing.

There remains the question of what caused the Skanda-Seizers to disappear, as a group, from the Indian religious landscape. Recall here that the Sanskrit term I have been translating as Seizer is *graha*, and that, according to the MBh and the SS, the Seizers are nine in number.[213] In fact, the SS refers to these as the Nine Seizers (*navagraha*). The term *navagraha* is much better known from another realm of Indian culture: astronomy and astrology. However, the worship of the nine heavenly bodies—sun, moon, Mercury, Venus, Mars, Jupiter, Saturn, Rāhu, and Ketu—as planetary deities only emerges in the middle of the first millennium of the common era, in the wake of the importation of Greek astronomical knowledge to India.[214] The earliest textual source to list the planets in the temporal order of their regency over days of the week is a circa 300–325 C.E. astrological work by Mīnarāja;[215] there is no iconography of the planetary *grahas* prior to circa 500 C.E. images from Madhya Pradesh; and they do not become a pan-Indian phenomenon until the beginning of the second millennium.[216] A late-sixth-century insertion in the *Matsya Purāṇa* (93.1–161 and 94.1–9) on the planetary *grahas* and their worship is the first textual source to provide an anthropomorphic description of them as a group, under the heading of *navagrahas*.[217]

Now, it is the case that the influence of the planets as principles of childhood disease can be as baneful as that of the Skanda-Seizers, and the heavenly bodies continue to be worshiped, down to the present day, in an apotropaic mode. This association of the nine planetary *grahas* with birth and the maintenance of life is found in several medieval eastern Indian sculptures that depict the birth scene known as "Reclining Mother and Child," images in which the planetary deities are frequently figured above the recumbent pair.[218] It is this similarity of function, combined with identity of name and number, I believe, that led to the gradual disappearance of the grouping of the nine Skanda-Seizers from Indian sculpture and literature. This identity is noted by N. M. Penzer in his voluminous notes to the *Kathāsaritsāgara* (KSS) when he states that "as the Mothers are supposed to be the planets which influence the unborn child, they are also worshipped to bring about an easy delivery."[219] In present-day Nepal, there is a similar identification between the Nine Durgās (*navadurgā*), who are also called Mothers, and the *navagrahas* as the nine planets. As Mary Slusser explains:

> Not only do the Mātṛkās guard the compass points but they are also regarded as regents of the sky. As the Navadurgā they are equated with the Navagraha, the male personifications of the so-called Nine Planets. . . . They [the planets] can "possess" individuals—hence their collective name, "Seizers." . . . Given the similarity of name and the correspondence of number and malevolent disposition, it is little wonder that the Navagraha and Navadurgā came to be identified as one manifestation.[220]

However, whereas Slusser sees a conflation of two ancient and coeval groups, I see these striking parallels in number and function as so many indications that the latter group is but a relatively recent overlay onto the former.

Further evidence for the sequential replacement of the female Nine Seizers by the male nine planets may be found in the *Bṛhat Saṃhitā* of Varāhamihira and *Viṣṇudharmottara Purāṇa,* both circa sixth-century texts that immediately juxtapose their discussions of pacificatory rites to the Mothers with cognate rites to Rudra, the planets (*grahas*), and asterisms (*nakṣatras*).[221] This is further reflected in pairings of Saptamātṛka and Navagraha panels, which begin to appear on northern and southern doorway lintels to central Indian temples in the early ninth century and continue in one form or another for hundreds of years.[222] Coeval with these iconographic developments, the eighth- to ninth-century *Netra Tantra* (2.13–15) names the *grahas* twice in its enumeration of baneful beings: according to Hélène Brunner, the repetition is intended, with the first mention referring to the demonic Seizers and the second to the nine planets.[223] At Khajuraho the parallels occur, but the chronology is reversed: images of the nine planets found in the principal niches of the podium encircling the 954 C.E. Lakṣmaṇa temple are replaced on the later (ca. 1031 C.E.) Kandariyā Mahādeva temple with images of the Seven Mothers, Vīrabhadra, and Gaṇeśa.[224] The nine planetary *grahas* continue to be a common fixture of Śaiva temples throughout India, continuing a primordial link between Śiva or his son Skanda with the multiple Mothers or Seizers in Kushan- and Gupta-period traditions.

This cluster of identifications also brings us back to what I believe to have been the earliest use of the term *graha:* the divinatory, exorcistic gambling ritual of the Vedic period. Here, the boy afflicted with "dog-seizure" was stretched out over a gaming board strewn with dice, which represented the stars or planets moving across the vault of heaven.[225] Nearly all of the uses of the term *graha* seem to be present here; all that is missing is a feminine figure of the Skanda-Seizer variety. Yet this missing link appears also to be provided by a commonplace of the Indian medical tradition on the Skanda-Seizers, first found in the circa eighth-century C.E. *Kumāratantra* of Rāvaṇa: this is the identification of the female Skanda-Seizer afflicting an infant child on the basis of the day, month, and year in the life of the child. Thus, for example, all childhood afflictions falling on the third day, the third month (beyond the age of twelve days), or the third year (beyond the age of twelve months) of a child's life are attributed to Pūtanā, regardless of the child's symptoms.[226] Another such system is found in the three hundredth chapter of the AP, appended to that work after the eleventh century.[227] Three parallel systems are found in a circa twelfth-century Hindu work entitled the *Tithiḍākinīkalpa*, of which the sole extant manuscript is found in Jammu, in northwestern India. Here, while the female disease demon is identified as a Ḍākinī rather than a Yoginī, the basic system is the same: the fifteen dates of the lunar fortnight are identified with fifteen diseases, with a particular *ḍākinī* to be worshiped in each case.[228] As we will discuss in later chapters, the terms *ḍākinī* and *yoginī* are nearly synonymous in Tantric traditions, with Buddhist sources favoring the former and Hindu the latter. Here it should be noted that *mkha' 'gro ma*, the Tibetan translation of the term *ḍākinī* is also the colloquial term for "bird" in that language, but with a feminine ending.[229]

A nearly identical system, currently in use in Kerala,[230] is found in the circa seventh-century KS and the coeval fifty-second chapter of the AP.[231] This last source further emphasizes the connection between the Yoginī temples and the sun: arrayed around the twelve-armed (representing the solar months) Bhairava,[232] the gnomon at the center, the circle of the Yoginīs represent the "female Seizers" (*grahaṇīs*) governed by the solar orb. In fact, this configuration of a circle of goddesses arrayed around a form of Śiva is one that goes back to at least the period of the Ellora cave temples.[233] Furthermore, as we will see, this was a goal of the Kaula practitioner, who, imitating Śiva-Bhairava, sought to become the "Lord of the Circle" (*cakravartin*) of circles of Yoginīs as well as of the entire embodied universe.[234]

In this particular context, the round hypaethral Yoginī temples may be viewed as massive sundials, with the shadow of the central Bhairava gnomon pointing to a different one of the sixty-four Yoginīs every five to six days of the solar year.[235] A similar configuration appears on a tenth-century sculpture, found at Khiching in Orissa, which depicts the *navagrahas* arrayed around a polycephalic deity located at the center of a solar "axle," with twelve spokes radiating out beyond the "Circle of the Nine Seizers."

This appears to reproduce the relationship of Skanda—as well as of Bhairava, who succeeded him in this iconographic complex—to the female Seizers and Yoginīs as well as to the *navagrahas* as planets and the solar year.[236] Similar sculptural configurations are found on miniature tenth- to eleventh-century C.E. Sūrya shrines at Khajuraho, called *ravi pīṭhas*, "Sun Mounds."[237] Finally, a type of astrological numerology, called *Yoginīdaśa*, remains popular in modern-day South Asia and is featured on a number of India-based Internet websites.[238] Here, the term *daśa* refers to the particular positioning of stars and planets at the time of a child's birth,[239] with eight Yoginīs being linked to the nine planets (the eighth Yoginī, Saṅkaṭā, linked with two of the nine, Rāhu and Ketu, the ascending and descending nodes of the moon in lunar eclipses). Because of her extended presence in a person's astrological house (eight years instead of four), Saṅkaṭā is the most powerful of the eight Yoginīs of this tradition, and as such continues to receive worship in Kathmandu, at her temple located on New Road.[240]

5. Yakṣiṇīs

In her Buddhist legend, the demoness called Harītī ("Kidnapper") is converted by the Buddha and elevated into a protectress of children.[241] In the Pali literature as well as on the sculpted railings of Bharhut, she is accompanied by other female figures named Jarā,[242] Jyeṣṭhā, Culakokā, and Mahākokā.[243] In different sources she is identified as the consort of the goat-headed Naigameṣa (also considered to be a Dryad),[244] or, much later, of the Tantric deity Ucchiṣṭa Gaṇeśa.[245] Harītī may be further identified with Jātahāriṇī ("Child-Snatcher"), of whom long descriptions are given in the KS and *Mārkaṇḍeya Purāṇa*. She is called "one who feeds on flesh" (*piśitāśanā*) and is an agent of miscarriage who feeds on newborn children, whence warnings to guard against her in the lying-in chamber.[246] In the sixth-century *Harṣacarita* (4.6–7), she is mentioned in the context of Harṣa's birth: in his post-ninth-century commentary on this work, Śaṅkara explains that a figure with a cat's face and surrounded by a crowd of children was set up in the lying-in chamber.[247] Harītī is represented very frequently in Buddhist sculpture as the consort of Kubera, the king of the Dryads, and the two are represented together on a sculpture from Mathura with eighteen children at their feet.[248]

In all of these respects, Harītī is a garden-variety demoness of childhood diseases. Indeed, certain early Buddhist sources identify her as a smallpox goddess;[249] and Harītī is worshiped today as Śītalā, in her temple at the Svayambhunāth stūpa site in Kathmandu. However, a detail from the Chinese version of her Buddhist legend is of salient interest here: Harītī began her career as a Yakṣiṇī, a female Dryad, named Abhirati: it is only as a result of her depredations that the townspeople of Rājagṛha call her "Kidnapper."[250] More than this, Buddhist mythology tells us that Harītī's wrathful behavior stems from wrongs committed against her in a previous life: forced to dance at a festival while pregnant, she had miscarried and lost her child.[251]

Harītī is not the sole female Dryad to have gone bad. In the *Rāmāyaṇa*, one of the earliest exploits of young Prince Rāma is to slay Tāḍakā/Tāṭakā/Tāraka, a beautiful female Dryad who, due to a curse, has been transformed into a man-eating Protectress with a hideous face.[252] Fully as much as the Mothers and female Seizers, the female Dryads are forerunners of the Yoginīs of Tantric tradition. They are also closely connected with the Protectresses, as evidenced in the two myths mentioned above, as well as an Epic etymology, which states that when Prajāpati created beings to protect the waters, some of them said "rakṣāmaḥ" ("let us protect") and others said "yakṣāmaḥ" ("let us gobble")—and so the two were called Rākṣasas and Yakṣas, respectively.[253] Slightly later both the Buddhist *Jātakas* and the Hindu *Matsya Purāṇa* document the fact that Dryads received blood offerings.[254]

Dryads, while generally auspicious, are at times portrayed in literary and popular traditions as giant cannibals. In the case of female Dryads, it is most often their seductiveness that is highlighted: even Tāḍakā began as a beauty. Conversely, Kuvaṇṇā, the Yakkhiṇī (the Pali form of Yakṣiṇī) queen of the island of Ceylon, first appears as a bitch and then as an alluring maiden to the conquering Prince Vijaya, in the *Mahāvaṃsa*.[255] Comparisons with the Indian Śrī, the Greek Circe, and the Irish Flaith are perhaps in order here.[256] The *Mahāvaṃsa* portrays other Yakkhiṇīs as zoomorphic or zoocephalic beings: Cetiyā, for example, has the face of a mare.[257] It should be noted here that in present-day Sri Lanka, nearly all disease demons are called Yakas (the Singhalese form of Yakṣa).[258] The Buddhist *Jātakas*, a rich source of data on Yakkhiṇīs, casts these female Dryads in ways that both evoke the coeval Epic data on the female Seizers and anticipate the nature of the Tantric Yoginīs. In a story from the *Valāhassa Jātaka*, female Dryads entice shipwrecked men into their city, bind them with magic chains, and force them to marry them, before eating some of their number.[259] The *Telapatta Jātaka* relates that female Dryads entice men passing through a forest and "seduce them with the charm of their wanton beauty. But, having excited their lust, they have intercourse with them and then they kill them and eat them while the blood flows."[260] This theme is one that recurs in both the KSS and in present-day descriptions of the nature and activities of Yakṣīs in Kerala,[261] where "Yakṣīs are ghosts," women who have died by accident, beating, suicide, or miscarriage, and who prey on men to avenge themselves for male abuse from previous lives. Perching herself atop a *karimpana* (a type of palm) tree, the Yakṣī kills men and drinks their blood. Women never have such problems with Yakṣīs.[262]

The female Dryad who most closely resembles the Seizers of Hindu tradition is a queen-turned-Yakkhiṇī, whose story is told in the *Jayaddisa Jātaka*.

> A rival queen cursed her senior queen with the words "Some day I shall be able to eat your children alive," whereupon she was turned into a female Dryad. Then, she seized her chance and grabbing the child in full view of the queen she crunched and devoured it as if it were a piece of raw flesh, and then ran off. In this fashion she killed another of the queen's newborns, but in her attempt to devour a third, the queen's guards diverted her, and not having time to devour the child, she hid him in a sewer. The infant, thinking she was his mother, took her breast in his mouth and she conceived a love for this son, and went to the cemetery where she placed him in a rock cave and looked after him.[263]

Here, we find an analogue to the MBh III account, in which the infant god Skanda's appearance awakens the maternal instincts of the Mothers who had been sent to kill (and presumably eat) him. Similarly, the location of the dwellings of the Dryads parallels that of many of the earlier Mothers, as well as of the later Yoginīs: outside the city, in a tree or grove, or on a mountaintop. A slab altar at the foot of a tree was an essential part of the Dryad shrine (*caitya*), and clearly was the parallel or forerunner to the bench, seat, or mound (*pīṭha*) of the Mothers and Yoginīs of Hindu tradition.[264] A number of other elements link the male and female Dryads to Skanda and his cult. A Jain work, the *Abhidhāncintāmaṇi*, lists Kumāra-Ṣaṇmukha as one of the Dryads devoted to the *tīrthaṃkaras*.[265] One of Skanda's names is Guhya. As such, he is said to be lord of the Guhya[ka]s (the "Secretive Ones"), a distinction shared by Kubera, king of the Dryads. These have the special task of supporting Kubera's flying palace: they are possessed of the power of flight and are described as birdlike steeds, or simply as birds.[266] Skanda is also related in the MBh to the Gaṇas, Śiva's host, a role later assumed by Gaṇeśa (Lord of the Host). This big-bellied deity, who takes Skanda's place in the later iconography of the Seven Mothers, is identified with the Dryad named Vināyaka: in the Epic literature, the multiple *vināyakas*, like the Gaṇas, are imps who possess humans and create obstacles for them.[267] According to the AP, shrines of the Dryads, Kubera, and Guha (Skanda) are to be situated in northern parts of towns; in present-day Kerala, blood sacrifices are offered on the northern side of temples to ancestral spirits, and it is here that their bloody feasting takes place.[268] Shrines of the Mothers are also often located on the northern side of temple complexes;[269] over the northern door of the sanctum of the famous Vadakkanathan Śiva in the center of Trichur town is an image of a completely naked woman, her legs parted in childbirth. Above this are bas-relief images of roosters, her sacrificial victims, shown in profile.[270]

As was the case with the Mothers and female Seizers, the collective name of these groups of female divinities becomes transformed in the medieval period from Yakṣiṇī to Yoginī, with their function remaining the same. For example, the *Bhūtaḍāmara Tantras* (BT), of which there exist both Buddhist and Hindu versions (the Buddhist version being the earlier of the two), recommend a type of mantra-based practice called *yoginīsādhanā*. Both sources contain multiple lists of eight goddesses, together with their mantras. In one case, parallel lists from the Hindu and Buddhist BT call the objects of the *yoginīsādhanā* Yakṣiṇīs rather than Yoginīs.[271] This transfer of the role played by the Hindu, Buddhist, and Jain female Dryads onto the Yoginīs has been noted by Gail Hinich Sutherland as one of the "earliest examples of the enshrinement and employment of demigods as instruments of power" typical of the later Śākta and Tantric traditions.[272] The magical (and sometimes sexual) subjugation of these figures is central to the Kaula and Tantric quest for occult powers, and the medieval literature is full of instructions for and accounts of aspiring *tāntrikas* seeking to win the wild hearts or bend the savage wills of Yakṣiṇīs or Yoginīs in order to succeed in their practice.[273] Indeed, as Hermann Goetz has noted, the alluring, naked broad-hipped nymphs that one finds in sexual union with their male partners on erotic medieval temple sculptures "are nothing but the ancient *yakṣas* and *yakṣīs* . . . popular local fertility deities."[274]

Yet, as Wendy Doniger O'Flaherty has noted with regard to Śītalā, it is a dangerous game that one plays when one seeks to become the darling rather than the food of these powerful female beings:

> The worshiper invokes [her] even though she will infect him with smallpox if she comes to him. . . . Even when she is gracious, to receive her grace is a terrifying and painful form of religious passion. But one has little choice: if that is the way that god is, what can one do? If she is denied, she is certain to be destructive; if she is worshiped, she may or may not be destructive, and the worshiper may become immortal.[275]

Chapter 3

THE BLOOD OF THE YOGINĪ: *Vital and Sexual Fluids in South Asian Thought and Practice*

1. What Makes Sexual Fluids "Power Substances"?

My original impetus for writing this book was my dissatisfaction with the treatment I had given of sexual fluids as "power substances" in *The Alchemical Body*. There is no question that mercury and sulfur are the mineral correlates of male and female sexual fluids, the *dravyams* that are so praised in a number of alchemical works, but this masks the deeper question of what it is about sexual fluids that causes them to be viewed as such. The following appear to be the most plausible reasons, which, combined, account for this ideological complex: (1) Indian traditions have always viewed sexual fluids, and most particularly uterine or menstrual blood, as polluting, powerful, and therefore dangerous substances.[1] (2) Ancient cults of "Earth Mother" goddesses, found throughout India, portray her fertility as requiring counterprestations of vital fluids in the form of male seed, animal sacrifice, or some ritual substitute. (3) Tantra originated among a subaltern stratum of the Indian population that, lacking the means to procure the *dravyams* of orthodox worship rites, made use of readily available human sexual fluids in its practice.[2] (4) Women reputed as "witches," sometimes called Yoginīs, consumed vital fluids in their "covens," including both the blood of child and adult victims, and the sexual fluids of their male partners.[3] (5) Emergent medical understandings of the role played by sexual fluids, both male and female, in conception, gave rise to the concept of these as power substances and to the notion that a transfer of the same to the initiand was a requisite moment in Tantric initiations.[4]

(6) Elite Tantric practitioners self-consciously subverted orthodox purity codes by manipulating sexual fluids as a means to effecting a powerful expansion of consciousness from the limited consciousness of the conformist brahmin practitioner to the all-encompassing "god-consciousness" of the Tantric superman.[5] In Kaula traditions, all of these elements are combined into an elaborate system of human, animal, vegetable, and mineral homologies, often expressed in an encoded form.

2. Bloody Dangerous Women

An etiological myth of menstruation, found in the Vedic literature, describes the transfer of one-third of the "stain" the god Indra has incurred for his crime of brahmanicide (*brahmahatyā*), committed in the killing of Vṛtra, onto women.[6] Just as the two other recipients of this transfer—trees and the earth—exude sap and are marked by fissures, respectively, so too a woman exudes menstrual blood from the fissure that is her vulva.

India has long portrayed the vulva, or "nether mouth," of postmenarchal women as both bleeding and bloodthirsty, and thereby doubly devouring. On the one hand, a woman must compensate her monthly loss of blood by drinking blood or blood substitutes; on the other, menstrual or uterine blood is intrinsically "hot" and "fiery," burning up and consuming the "cool" male semen that comes into contact with it.[7] Already in the *Ṛg Veda*, a woman's uterine blood is a source of anxiety. Two difficult and much-discussed passages enjoin the husband—who wishes to avoid the immediate destruction of his person from the lethal power of the virginal blood shed on his wedding night—to give the bloodstained cloth of defloration to a brahmin priest conversant in the magic of Sūryā, the daughter of the Sun and the spouse of the Moon.[8] The same ideas are taken up in the *Atharva Veda*, whose obsessive concern with the defiling power of virginal blood requires that a second complete marriage ritual be held, in the husband's home, following the consummation of the actual marriage. Here, a "scapegoat" brahmin priest absorbs and purifies the bride's virginal blood of its magical dangers through this second ceremony, in which he refers to the original wedding ceremony, which had taken place in the house of the bride, as "witchcraft" (*kṛtyā*).[9]

In modern South Asia, the wedding ritual is all that protects most bridegrooms against the awesome powers of their virgin brides. This ceremony is, however, supplemented in many parts of India by an intervention on the part of the bride's mother or some other close female relative, who ensures that the hymen is broken prior to marriage.[10] Alternately, the role of absorbing the magical dangers of virginal blood, in puberty and marriage rites, will be filled by a female specialist, such as a midwife or the wife of a barber.[11] Yet, in at least one case, the role of the male brahmin priest appears to have remained operative, at least until recent times. The "tying of the *tāli*," a mock marriage practiced among the high-caste Nāyar communities of Kerala, was, until recent date, a ritual defloration of a virgin by a surrogate "husband," often a brahmin priest, enacted to defuse the power of menstrual blood shed following menarche.[12] Interestingly, the present-day rationale for this rite is that it protects a traditional Hindu girl from dying a widow, regardless of her future sexual life.[13] Another such mock marriage, practiced among the Newars of the Kathmandu Valley, follows a similar pattern: the *ihi* ceremony, in which as many as thirty virgin girls are married in a single two-day ceremony to a *bel* fruit, constitutes a religious sanction for widow remarriage.[14]

Another Newar ritual also appears to echo Vedic concerns.[15] During her first menstrual period, a maiden releases poisons from her womb such that were they to be exposed to the sun, would render that heavenly body impure. In this particular context, the danger of this and every successive menstrual flow is neutralized through the use of a *barha khya*, a cotton effigy of a part-deity, part-spirit that is believed to possess the girl and is hung on the wall of the seclusion room. The *khya*, commonly represented as a dwarfed and pudgy figure who is black in color with curly hair and red pouting lips, would appear to be a surrogate vulva.[16]

Karin Kapadia, noting that female puberty rites, while absent from the north, are widespread in the south, points to the fact that these rituals take the form of a symbolic marriage.[17] Here, menstruation is viewed as a second birth for females, since it is with menarche that the mysterious power of creating children is "born" in women; in fact, a woman is not considered gendered until she menstruates.[18] It is, however, among the non-brahmanic communities of Tamil Nadu (Pallars, Chettiars, Christian Paraiyars, and Muthrajahs) that female blood is accorded its greatest symbolic importance. These groups view female blood as a living stream through which kinship and family connectedness (*sambandham*), as well as the menarchal girl's kinship with the stars and the destiny-giving planets, are transmitted. It is for this reason that menstrual horoscopes are cast, with calculations based on the moment at which the girl's bleeding first began (however difficult such is to determine).[19] In present-day Kerala, rituals surrounding the menses of the goddess Chengannur Bhagavatī explicitly reenact the traditional puberty ceremony of high-caste Keralan girls, in which an examination of a girl's first menstrual bloodstains on her petticoat serve to divine her future.[20]

The connection between menstruation and fertility is made explicit in textual sources from at least the time of the *Bṛhadāraṇyaka Upaniṣad*, which urges a man to lie with his wife on the morning following her menstrual bath.[21] Kauṭilya echoes this concept in his *Arthaśāstra*, stating that a husband who neglects to lie with his wife following her menses is to be fined the sum of ninety-six *paṇas*.[22] In its Paṇḍu-Kuntī dialogues, the MBh opines that adultery is not a sin if committed with a woman who would otherwise not make her menstruation fruitful.[23]

Menstruation—a woman's "seasonal fault," *ṛtu doṣa*—can only be palliated by a stream of cooling, nourishing, fecundating male vital fluids. In many regions of India, local goddesses are identified with Mother Earth, an identification that is made clear through the many myths of local goddesses whose presence first becomes known when a farmer strikes a stone with his scythe or plow, causing blood to ooze out.[24] Such goddesses are said to menstruate during the heat of the summer, at which time the red earth has become the most dried and cracked. According to an ancient south Indian belief system, only the sacrifice of male blood-seed, through war and vegetal offerings (such as coconut, jackfruit, squash) to the hot and thirsty feminine body of the earth, allows for the perpetuation of life. This is of a piece with hot season rituals observed throughout India.[25] The essential component of many of these rites is the feeding or offering of ritual equivalents of vital or sexual fluids to these goddesses as a means to restoring their energy, which is primarily sexual, and which expresses itself in the emission, the counterprestation of *their* sexual fluids, the source of their fertility.

The Keralan theater form known as *muṭiyettu* is the enactment of this ritual, in which the blood-seed of the demon Dārika is spilled on dry lifeless paddy fields after the harvest, to ensure future fertility in the next rainy season. The hot red earth in this dry season is the visible womb of the earth goddess in her season of menstruation, and offerings of *guruti* (a mixture of yellow turmeric, mineral lime, and water) represent her menstrual flow. When the Keralan goddess Kodungallur Bhagavatī has her annual festival in the midst of the hot season, she is considered to be in her fierce mood, that of a menstruating virgin. At this time her shrine is ritually polluted with blood sacrifice, filth, obscenity, and possession.[26] Conversely, during the fertile rainy season of the month of Kanni (September–October), the south Indian earth goddess is an erotic wife, wet, cool, fertile, and impregnated by continual infusions of semen in the form of the "cool" milk and bananas offered to the serpents identified with her cult.[27]

As with the primal "Earth Mothers" of India, so with the Tantric nature, forest, tree, and flower goddesses who are their later evolutes: their perennial favorite meal is a revivifying offering of sexual fluids. These are the subjects of a ritual that, described in the tenth-century *Kubjikāmata* (KM), is termed the "bolt-practice[s], beginning with that of the knife." Having entered into a forbidding forest, one uses one's blood to trace a fearsome diagram (*maṇḍala*), at whose six corners one situates a series of terrifying goddesses. One worships these with mantras, and then places them in the midst of one's own body. They are then worshiped with pieces of one's own flesh, as well as an offering of blood, by which they are compelled to reciprocate. Then, having pierced his eight body parts (hands, breast, forehead, eyes, throat, and middle of the back), and having mixed (this blood and flesh) together with urine, feces, and some liquor, the practitioner places the mixture in the offering bowl. Having thus offered his own bodily constituents, he then worships these goddesses with food offerings, incense, and so on.[28] Each of seven Yoginīs is called upon and exhorted to eat one of the practitioner's bodily constituents: semen, bone, marrow, fat, flesh, blood, and skin. The practitioner who has so sacrificed his body then exhorts these goddesses: "Take now that which is given by me. . . . Afflicted am I, drained of blood (*virakta*) am I, broken in pieces am I. . . . O ye goddesses, quickly take this, my own body, that has been given by me. . . ." The passage then concludes:

> When he whose body has been so drained of blood [performs this rite] daily, then the resplendent Yoginīs come on the seventh day. At the end of the seventh night [of such offerings], they [afford] the supernatural power of supreme knowledge to him who is accomplished in his practice. Contrary [to what one would expect] they in no way destroy [him]; [rather] they instantaneously bind together [again all of the parts he has offered to them]. But if one carries out this [rite] *in reverse order* [it affords] the destruction (*nigraha*) of wicked ones [and the Yoginīs] do not consume any of the fluids arisen from his [the practitioner's] body parts.[29]

Yet this same source describes the hexagonal configuration of these Yoginīs to be that of a "thunderbolt-lotus" (*vajrapadma*), a thinly veiled reference to the penis (*vajra*) engaged in the vulva (*padma*).[30] The gradual shift—from being fed upon by feminine powers or beings to sharing in their pleasure through sexual intercourse and more sublimated forms of interaction—was one that took place over a period of centuries, with important regional or sectarian variations in practice.

As noted in the previous chapter, the Yoginīs and their forerunners usually helped themselves to such offerings without being asked, stealing away embryos or newborn infants from their mothers, or draining adults males of their vital fluids. The twelfth- to thirteenth-century *Śrīmatottara Tantra*'s enumeration of beings to whom "semen food" (*vīryabhojam*) and blood offerings (*bahirbali*) are to be made names a number of demonic beings—Yakṣas, Rākṣasas, Bhūtas, Vetālas, Kṣetrapālakas, Ḍākinīs, Rāmās, Pūtanās,

Kaṭapūtanās—to which it adds a list of ambiguous Yoginīs: "the "Mound-born, Field-born, Clan-born . . . and the youthful Yoginīs who are inhabitants of various countries, all come together into this circle."[31] A fifth-century pre-Tantric Buddhist text, in its description of strategies to be employed by monks to battle obstacles to meditation, speaks of a Yakṣiṇī named Bhūtī, the "demoness of dreams," who causes nocturnal emissions.[32] The *Netra Tantra* (19.188b–90b) describes these beings' activities in the following terms:

> When a woman has been marked by the Beings, then the embryo cannot be conceived. . . . Because the body of every living creature is made of semen and blood, the protection of both is to be effected by utterers of mantras. The Seizers who are fond of sexual pleasure have various sexual comportments. They drink semen and blood.

The extraction techniques of these female entities are described in detail in the eleventh-century C.E. *Rasārṇava* (RA), a classic Hindu alchemical text. In the context of a discussion of the necessity of using protective mantras in the consumption of perfected mercury, the RA states:

> The goddesses—both Airborne and Land-based—partaking (*bhajayitvā*) of him while he is asleep indeed steal away his semen and life's blood. It is via the seminal duct itself that they eat the mercury [that the mantra-less practitioner has] consumed. . . . In a human form, they eat [him] while he is asleep. They eat [men's] bones and flesh while they are sleeping, O Fair Lady of the Gods! At the end of [his] sleep, [he] is perplexed. . . . They steal the very diamond-ash [mercury he has consumed] and at the end of his sleep, they make him ejaculate (*kṣobhayanti*).[33]

This, the Tantric explanation for wet dreams, remains a prevalent Indian male fantasy, as has been widely documented in Hindu and Buddhist sources alike. Ravenous goddesses descend upon the sleeper, "partaking" of his vital fluids through his penis, with the ambiguity of the verbal *bhaj* leaving open the question of whether they are extracting the same with their upper or nether mouths. The answer may be "both," as a passage from the *Telapatta Jātaka* describes, with reference to Yakṣiṇīs. When men pass through their forest, the Yakṣiṇīs "seduce them with the charm of their wanton beauty. But, having excited their lust, they have intercourse with them and then they kill them and eat them while the blood flows."[34]

In modern-day Kerala, fierce tree goddesses of this sort are termed Yakṣīs, who are often considered to be young women who died in or before childbirth, often as the result of spousal abuse. Keralan folklore depicts the Yakṣīs as bloodthirsty, night-stalking vampiresses, with an explicit connection made between them and living virgin girls, who are viewed by Keralan men as so many succubae. Dead virgins of the Nāyar *jāti* can themselves become forms of Bhagavatī, to whom a shrine must be erected—and it is through her identity with these powerful and dangerous virgins that this Keralan goddess herself comes to be viewed as a vampiress whose primary means of sexual satisfaction is the oral ingestion of a man's vital fluid of life, his *bījam*, or blood-seed: all of her cult rituals point to this.[35] As in the *Rasārṇava* passage, these succubae are the cause of nocturnal emissions. The words of one of Sarah Caldwell's Keralan informants—"they drain us and drink it"—is a leitmotiv found in Indian literature and folklore since the Vedic period.[36] Tamil notions of women increasing their own *śakti* by draining men of their sexual fluid (*intiriam*)—sometimes fatally—through intercourse, follow the same pattern.[37] So, too, do Baiga beliefs concerning the disease goddess Cuṛelin Mātā, who goes to young men in their sleep and robs them of their seed, making them impotent.[38] Quite often the effects of the relatively innocuous phenomenon of nocturnal emissions (*svapnā doṣ*, the "dream fault") will become magnified in Indian male fantasies, with a Jala-joginī (Water-Yoginī), in a case reported by Sudhir Kakar, eating a young man alive.[39]

3. Tantric Appropriations

Originally, "Tantric sex" was nothing more or less than a means to producing the fluids that Tantric goddesses such as these fed upon, without losing oneself entirely in the process. Here, we begin by presenting descriptions of such as found in three Tantric sources from three different traditions, regions, and periods. In the circa eighth-century Buddhist *Hevajra Tantra* (HT), the Great Adamantine (or Great-Penised) One (*mahāvajrin*) states:

> Listen, O Goddess, to the service of worship. In a garden, in an uninhabited country, or within the inner chamber of one's own dwelling, one possessed of yogic knowledge should always worship the naked "Great Seal" consort. Kissing and embracing her, and touching her vulva, he should effect the drinking of the fertilizing drops of the "male nose" and of the honey down below (*adharamadhu*).[40] . . . He attains abundant *siddhi* and becomes the equal of all the Buddhas. White camphor [i.e., semen] is drunk there, and especially wine. One should undertake the eating of tonics for the production of semen.[41]

In Hindu contexts, the Tantric Virile Hero generated and partook of his own and his consort's vital fluids in a "eucharistic" ritual, whose ultimate consumer was the Goddess herself, who, pleased, would afford the supernatural enjoyments and powers the practitioner sought. A late Kaula compilation, the circa sixteenth-century[42] *Kaulāvalinirṇaya* (KĀN), describes the high Tantric Goddess's taste for vital fluids in the clearest possible terms:

> The Goddess is fond of the vulva and penis, fond of the nectar of vulva and penis. Therefore, one should fully worship the Goddess with the nectar of vulva and penis. A man—who worships the Goddess by the drinking of the virile fluid and by taking pleasure in the wife of another man, as well as with the nectar of the vulva and penis—knows no sorrow and becomes possessed of perfected mantras. But he who worships Caṇḍikā without the clan-generated fluids (*kulodbhavairdravyair vinā*) [will see] the good deeds of thousands of lifetimes destroyed.[43]

The male practitioner makes offerings of his seed to the Goddess as fluid oblation. Of greater importance to himself, however, is the female discharge of his female counterparts, without which it is impossible for him to become a fully realized Siddha or Virile Hero. In this regard, Kamil Zvelebil's translation of a late medieval Tamil poem, the *Kāmapānacāstiram* ("Treatise on the Arrow of Lust")[44] deserves to be quoted in full:

First Stage:

> Like a cow which licks tenderly its calf
> spread out your tongue broad
> and lick her yoni
> lapping up the juices oozing out
> like a thirsty dog which laps cool water.

Second Stage:

> Like a worshipper who circumambulates the shrine
> pass your tongue over her yoni
> round around from left to right,
> moving in ever narrowing circles
> till you reach the very centre.
> Her yoni will open up
> like a dark and gaping chasm.
> Open then the vulva's lips
> with firm pressure of your tongue
> and insert its stiff tip inside
> like a spear's powerful thrust,
> digging, poking deep and far.

Third Stage:

> With your nose pressing against the *yonimani* [clitoris]
> your tongue enters her innermost shrine
> thrusting and digging and piking deep.
> searching for hidden treasures inside.
> Inhale deeply, breathing in the mellow odours
> of the juices of her yoni.

Fourth Stage:

> Taking the protruding, throbbing jewel of her yoni
> gently, gently between your teeth and tongue,
> suck it like a suckling feeding at the breast;
> it will rise and glisten, stand up from its sheath.
> It will swell like a large ruby.
> The fragrant copious discharge
> appearing like sweet foam
> between the lips of the vulva
> is a rejuvenating drink when mixed with your milk-white,
> lustrous, thick and fragrant sperm.

As far as the specifically Tamil context of this poem is concerned, Zvelebil notes that in some "extremist" Tamil Tantric groups, it is recommended that sexual union take place precisely with a menstruating woman, so that the merging union is effected of *velli*, "silver," that is, male seed, and *pon*, "gold," that is, menstrual blood. The same traditions, which maintain unanimously that there is a female flow (*tiravam*, "liquid, juice") corresponding to that of male semen (*vintu*), recommend the fresh mixture of male semen and this female discharge as beneficial for potency and general health when swallowed immediately after coitus. Special pills are prepared from male semen and female discharge (or menstrual blood) to heal certain types of mental illness.[45] Zvelebil's work is on the Sittars, the Tamil branch or offshoot of the Siddha traditions of north India; and while I have argued elsewhere that the northern and southern groups have a common historical background, I would maintain that the Tamil tradition is in many ways a later, somewhat eccentric tradition. This having been said, it nonetheless remains that Siddhas or Vīras are in fact portrayed in dozens of Tantric texts and sculptural images as engaging in such practices as have been poetically sung above.

A celebrated example of such is a tongue-in-cheek account, found in the twelfth- to thirteenth-century *Rudrayāmala*, of the orthodox brahmin sage Vasiṣṭha's forays into "Greater China" (*mahācīna*), to which the

Buddha tells him to go in order to learn the "Chinese practice" (*cīnācāra*) of worshiping the goddess Tārā.[46] There, Vasiṣṭha stumbles upon a Tantric orgy, in which "all the eminent naked Siddhas were actively engaged in the drinking of blood (*raktapānodyatāḥ*). "They were drinking again and again [and] taking carnal pleasure in beautiful women,[47] all of them red-eyed, stuffed, and drunk on meat and liquor."[48] There are no grounds for reading the "blood" of this passage as that of a sacrificial victim: it is menstrual or uterine blood that the naked, fornicating Siddhas are drinking. Furthermore, in this and nearly every other early and authentic Kaula source, sexual intercourse is never portrayed as an end in itself, nor as a means to attaining the bliss of god-consciousness. Rather, it is simply a means to generating the clan nectar (*kulāmṛta*), the various mixtures of sexual fluids whose "eucharistic" offering and consumption lay at the heart of Kaula practice. In the words of the KĀN, "Having collected that semen [shed in sexual intercourse], one should place it in the special fluid-offering [vessel]. The best of practitioners should quench the Goddess's thirst with that nectar. [When] the Goddess draws near, one will obtain all that one desires."[49]

Already in the ninth- to tenth-century KJñN, such drinking was essential to Kaula practice and the attainment of the Kaula gnosis, and thereby prohibited to non-initiates:

> [Concerning] brutish non-initiates (*paśus*) who are bereft of gnosis, ill behaved, and without clan authorization: sexual union is not to be enjoyed by them, nor should they consume the fluid (*dravyam*).[50] The wise [initiate] should consume the oblation [of sexual fluids]; one should not allow it to be given to pledges.[51] [The mantra] *hro hraḥ* [effects the power of] extraction of the blood of the Yoginīs.[52] The clan essence (*kaulikam sāram*), generated through intercourse with the Yoginīs, is not to be given away.[53] Poison, menstrual blood (*dhārāmṛtam*), semen, blood, and marrow: this mixture of the "Five Purifiers" [is to be employed in] the daily ritual (*nityam*). . . .[54] [Here is] the means by which one may constantly consume the extraction: one should propitiate the assembly of Yoginīs with all sorts of edible and pleasurable items. Thereafter, one should practice the drinking of [their] menstrual blood (*dhārapāna*) if one wishes to have a long life.[55] One should constantly drink blood and semen, i.e., the oblation so dear to the Siddhas and Yoginīs, in that [vulva] in which an embryo ripens. Flesh is the favorite [food] of the Śākinīs. Hear [now] the favorite [foods] of the Goddesses: *buka* flower, "Śiva-Water," blood, semen, and alcohol.[56]

Numerous references to such practices are found in chapter 18 of the same source, which devotes itself to the worship of the Siddhas and Yoginīs located within the body, to the performance of the prescribed rites of the "Clan Island," and to the consecration of clan practitioners, for the attainment of supernatural powers.[57] The first of these, which involves the use of mantras and the "orthodox" ritual supports of cow dung and powdered grains, affords the practitioner the permission or the power of "mingling, i.e., sexual union, with the Yoginīs" (*yoginīmelakam*), and affords both enjoyments and liberation.[58] Following this, Bhairava, the divine revealer of this text, turns to the consecration (*abhiṣeka*) of the fully initiated clan practitioner. The ritual begins with the consumption by the master and his consort of menstrual blood (*vāmāmṛtam*) alone or in combination with semen (*kuṇḍagolaka*), alcohol, and a number of other substances, including the *buka* flower and the extract of the *kṛṣṇa* flower, and concludes with the placing of "that which is to be raised into the head"—that is, the conjoined sexual emissions of the master and his consort—into the mouth of the initiate: "Thereafter, he becomes a yogin."[59]

These practices have not altogether disappeared from the Indian subcontinent. Among the Bāuls of Bengal, the male practitioner will drink a drop of his consort's menstrual blood once on each of her three days of menses. The blood becomes progressively clearer and more fluid and so is compared to the three *guṇas*: here it is understood that the woman exudes the *guṇas* in her role as Prakṛti, "Mother Nature." The secretion on the fourth day that is subtle and clear, the Bāuls say, represents the *kuṇḍalinī*, the "half part" that is beyond the *guṇas*. After drinking this, the practitioner may have intercourse with the consort and gather the energy of the *kuṇḍalinī*.[60] We will discuss the origins and yogic practices relating to the *kuṇḍalinī* at length in chapter 8. As June McDaniel notes, Bāul ritual practice is based on a quadernity, called the "four moons" (*cāricāndra*), which,

> . . . in the context of ritual practice, become *biṣṭha* (excrement, or in Bāul language *māṭi*), *mūtra* (urine or *rasa*), *rajas* (blood, called *rūpa* or *strīvīrya*); and *śukra* (semen, also called *rasa*). . . . These substances are used for the ritual piercing of the four moons. . . . [I]t is implied that these four substances are mixed together and drunk. . . . Blood (*rajas*) is the main moon of the four: it is gathered on the third day of menstruation. . . .[61]

Similar practices, found among present-day Nizarpanthis, "Hinduized" Ismai'ilis of western India, are referred to as *kuṇḍā panth*, the "way of the basin." According to Dominique-Sila Khan's informants:

> It is *mithun* [the product of ritual copulation] . . . which supplies the main offering to the deity (here supposed to be the Tantric Goddess revered by the Nāth Jogis, Hiṅglāj Mātā). After the ritual copulation each woman must collect in the palm of her hand the semen virile of her partner, which she deposits into a round flat earthen vessel called *kuṇḍā*. At

> the end of the ceremony all the sperm is mixed with *chūrma* (a traditional food offering made of millet, *ghī* and sugar) and partaken as *prasād* by all the members of the sect. It is named *pāyal*.[62]

The term *kuṇḍā* is the vernacular form of the Sanskrit term *kuṇḍa*, which, in addition to its standard meaning of "basin" or "vessel," has a specialized sense in Tantric parlance. In its description of "that which is arisen from the basin" (*kuṇḍottham*), the KĀN states that "even with one thousand pots of liquor and one hundred-weight of meat, the Goddess is not pleased [if these are offered] without the 'emissions of the basin and the ball'" (*kuṇḍagolaka*).[63] Most of the forty verses that follow this preamble comprise an extended description of foreplay, of "drinking the liquor churned out by the tongue of the Śakti" (*śaktijihvāviloḍitam*), the "churning of the vulva" (*yoneḥ pramanthanam*), the "gathering of the fluid known as 'arising from the basin'" (*kuṇḍodbhava*), and the "arising of the ball" (*golodbhava*), that is, female and male sexual emissions. These combined fluids (*kuṇḍagolakodbhava*) are then purified and offered to the gods.[64] *Kuṇḍagolaka* is a term found in nearly every Tantra to denote the sexual fluids employed sacramentally in the various rites. In TĀ 29.141–42, Abhinavagupta simply states that "Śakti is the basin (*kuṇḍa*), Śiva the phallus (*liṅga*), [and] their union (*melaka*) the supreme ground."[65] While this and the KĀN imply that *kuṇḍagolaka* is a combination of male and female emissions, other sources restrict the use of the term to specific types of female discharge. So, for example, the *Samayacāra Tantra* calls the menstrual blood of a married woman "arisen from the basin" (*kuṇḍodbhava*), and that of a widow "generated from the ball" (*golodbhava*).[66] The *Mātṛkabheda Tantra* lists six types of menstrual blood, according to the marital situation and age of the source: *kuṇḍagolaka* is included in this list.[67] According to the *Śyāmarahasya*, *kuṇḍa* refers to male and female sexual fluids together, and *gola* is the menstrual fluid of a widow. Louise Finn, the translator of the *Kulacūḍāmaṇi Tantra*, gives the following nomenclature of types of female discharge, as reported to her by Sri Batohi Jha, a contemporary Śākta pandit from Mithila: *kuṇḍa* is the first menstruation of a maiden born out of wedlock and *gola* her first menstruation after her father's death. Other types of menstrual blood include "adamantine flower" (*vajrapuṣpa*), the first menstruation after defloration; "self-arisen" (*svayambhū*), any woman's first menstruation; the "flower of generation" (*bhavapuṣpa*), a woman's regular monthly period; "white clay" (*gopīcandana*), a mixture of semen and menstrual blood; and the "crest jewel of the clan" (*kulacūḍāmaṇi*), menstrual blood freely offered for the purpose of Tantric practice.[68] The *Muṇḍamālā Tantra* praises the blood of a virgin as the optimal offering to the Goddess in the following terms: "The flower or blood (*kusuma*) generated from the twining tendrils (*latā*) [of a maiden], who has not had sexual intercourse with a male, is known as the 'self-arisen flower' (*svayambhūkusuma*) or 'red sandalwood' (*raktacandana*), which is to be fed to the great Goddess."[69] A number of Buddhist Tantras also employ the term "self-generated sandalwood" for uterine blood;[70] while the alchemical RA botanizes the term *kuṇḍagolaka* into a combination of the herbal essences of the *cāṇḍālī* and *rākṣasī* plants.[71] We will return to a discussion of the Tantric consort as a "flower-maiden" in the next chapter.

4. Fluid Gnosis

Because all life, all fluids, flow from the womb of the Goddess, the original source of the female discharge consumed by Kaula initiates is, of necessity, the Goddess herself, a role that is supported by an epithet encountered several times (in the vocative) in the KJñN: this is the epithet *kulāgamā*. Here, unlike *āgama*, "scripture," the feminine term *āgamā* has a physiological sense attested in the *Manu Smṛti* (8.252) and *Suśruta Saṃhitā* (SS), in which it means "issue" of blood or "course" of a fluid. Referring to the Goddess, *kulāgamā* should thus be read as "She Whose Issue of Blood Gives Rise to the Clan."[72] Here, the ambiguity between the masculine term *kulāgama*, "Clan Scripture," and the feminine *kulāgamā* is likely intended, since female discharge did in fact contain a "fluid gnosis," in much the same way that the female discharge of the Wisdom Maiden of Buddhist Highest Yoga Tantra initiations injected the initiate with the fluid wisdom (*prajñā*) of the goddess Wisdom (Prajñā) herself, the source of the Perfection of Wisdom (*prajñā-paramitā*) teachings. This distinction, between "masculine" textuality (*kulāgama*) and "feminine" orality (*kulāgamā*) is one that is treated mythologically in the sixteenth chapter of the KJñN, to which we will return in chapter 4.

Mark Dyczkowski has argued that the technical term *ājñā* ("command") bears a similar double sense of medium and message in Kubjikā traditions:

> The drop of the vital seed which is generated thereby [by the churning of phallus and vulva in the womb of energies] is the empowering Command (*ājñā*), which is both the source of the universe and the means to attain the supreme state.[73] . . . The . . . *ājñā* is her seminal fluid that is released through the conjunctio with her male partner. The god encourages her to unite with him by reminding her that the . . . *ājñā* she has to give is a product of their reciprocal relationship.[74]

A number of post-twelfth-century Kubjikā sources support this reading, including the massive twelfth- to thirteenth-century *Manthānabhairava*

Tantra (MBhT): "[The Goddess] is the bliss of the Command (*ājñā*), pure with blissful sexual intercourse.[75] . . . [The Command is the goddess named] Perpetually Wet (Nityaklinnā) who, aroused by her own passion (*svaraktā*), is free. . . ."[76] It is this divine command, god-consciousness in the form of a drop of sexual fluid, that flows through the wombs of the female Kaula consorts in initiation. This bloodline, this flow chart, the fluid source of the Goddess's family, clan, and house, constitutes her external manifest form.[77] An elaborate discussion of fluid gnosis, found in the seventeenth chapter of the KĀN, homologizes sexual intercourse with a series of offerings and liturgies:

> Without a doubt, female discharge is consciousness (*saṃvit*) in manifest form. [The goddess] Parameśānī is "Prakṛti," and the drop [of male seed, *bindu*] is called "Puruṣa." Without a doubt, "yoga" is the conjunction of Śiva and Śakti. . . . Speaking is "praising," and embracing is musk, and kissing is camphor. The wounds, etc. [raised] by the nails and teeth are worshiping with flower garlands, etc. Loveplay and so on are incense and oil lamps, kneading the breasts is the praising of Śiva. Know [the product of] sexual intercourse [to be] the water-offering, and the shedding of semen [the concluding rite of] releasing [the image of a deity into holy water]. Having purified [the body] with the clan fluid (*kuladravyam*), one becomes comprised of Śiva and Śakti.[78]

The same dynamic is presented in the *Kāmākhyā Tantra* (8.23a–24b), a relatively late work from eastern India, when it states that "the seer of the Kula path is favored by the Goddess. Initiation [transmitted] from the lotus mouth of the guru takes the form of the clan [fluid] (*kulātmikā*), O Goddess! Devotion [that lies] in the clan fluids is considered to be liberating. The wise man, knowing this alone, through effort, partakes of the clan knowledge." One finds the same dynamic, this time on a mineral register, in the *Kākacaṇḍeśvarīmata* (KCM), the "Doctrine of the Fierce Crow Goddess," a twelfth-century alchemical Tantra, in which *dravyam* has the sense of mercury and sulfur:

> Without the fluid substance (*dravyam*), there can be no *siddhi*, and no enjoyment or pleasure. Without the fluid substance, men become disembodied ghosts (*pretas*) when they die. They who employ inferior substances in life roam about blindly in the world of the dead.[79]

This emphasis on a concrete substance as substrate for the transmission of liberating gnosis is also one that is borrowed from the old Śaiva orthodoxy. In both orthodox Śaivasiddhānta and heterodox "Kāpālika" epistemology and soteriology, the root of ignorance is impurity (*malam*), which is a material substance (*dravyam*).[80] According to Śaivasiddhānta doctrine, this "atomic impurity" (*āṇavamalam*), this substance, can only be removed through the ritual act of initiation (*dīkṣā*), in which Śiva, through his grace, effects its removal, using *śakti* as his tool.[81] The Kāpālika view is summarized in the twenty-third chapter of Ānandagiri's fourteenth- to fifteenth-century *Śaṅkaradigvijaya*, in which a figure named Bodholbaṇa Nityānanda praises fearless Kāpālika sages who are "always dependent on the knowledge (*bodha*) produced from fluid (*dravyam*), whose hearts are gratified by the embrace of Kāpālika *śaktis*, [and] who are addicted to drinking the excellent nectar arising from sexual union."[82] Only in such nondualist circles as the Trika Kaula would cosmic ignorance become desubstantialized, and ritual "doing"—that is, drinking—replaced by simply "knowing."[83] Yet it should be noted that in the same Trika Kaula, the highest form of the feminine, the transcendent and consortless Goddess from which the three Trika goddesses and their Bhairava consorts emanated, was known as Mātṛsadbhāva, the "Real (Fluid) Being of the Mothers."[84]

5. *Rājayoga, Mudrā,* and *Maithuna*

When subject to scrutiny on the basis of the Tantric sources, the general consensus regarding the meanings of the technical terms *rājayoga*, *mudrā*, and *maithuna* is shown to be misplaced. The much-vaunted tradition of *rāja-yoga* itself, a term that is generally translated by commentators to signify the most elevated, "royal" practice of yoga, is read in at least one tradition to denote the consumption of male and female sexual emissions. So, the twelfth-century *Amanaskayoga* of Gorakṣanātha states that "some [practitioners], overstepping the limit [of conventional propriety], resorb semen from young girls' yonis. Without *rājayoga*, free of mental construction, there can be no perfection of the body for them."[85] The *Yogaśikhopaniṣad* (1.136, 138), a later work, states that red-colored *rajas*, which is the true form of the Goddess's essence (*devītattvasvarūpa*), resides in the great mound (*mahāpīṭha*) of the vulva; while in the place of the moon, within the upper circle of the moon, it is the *bindu* ("drop") or *retas* ("sperm") that is the true form of Śiva's essence. So it is that the two essences are constantly mingled (*milita*) in the path of *brahman* "between the two Merus." The passage concludes: "From [the fact that there is] union (*yoga*) of uterine blood and semen, this is known as *rājayoga*."[86] Both of these sources read *rāja* here as a strengthened form of *rajas*, that is, "deriving from female discharge," rather than from the standard reading of "royal." Both of these works predate the fifteenth-century *Haṭhayogapradīpikā* and its commentaries; and we may therefore conclude that their readings of the compound *rājayoga* are earlier than the more widely accepted reading of the term as the "royal" path of yogic practice.

When *rāja-yoga* is read in this way, the use of the term *mudrā*—generally read as the "parched grain, kidney beans, or any cereal believed to possess aphrodisiac properties"[87]—also becomes subject to revision. Of course, the primary sense of *mudrā* is "seal," whence the term *vajrolī mudrā*, "seal of the place of the male organ" for the technique of urethral suction by means of which the Tantric yogin, having ejaculated into his partner, draws his semen together with her sexual emission back into his penis. Without the vacuum created by such a seal—and it must be recalled here that the haṭha yoga of the Nāth Siddhas was, before all else, a hydraulic body of practice—urethral suction would not be possible.[88] The Bāuls, whose drinking of menstrual fluid was documented above,[89] also undertook this practice, which is termed "Catching the Uncatchable" in their songs. Here, the Bāul practitioner's elusive game is the "Natural Human Being" (*sahaj mānuṣ*), who is naturally present in female practitioners alone. On the third day of a woman's period, the Natural Human Being, who feels an irresistible attraction to the *śakti* in menstrual blood, descends from the woman's cranial vault to her *triveṇī* (the place in her lower abdomen where the three subtle channels, the *nāḍīs*, meet). Through coitus, the Natural Human Being is separated out of the menstrual blood, attracted into the male practitioner's penis, and brought back to *his* cranial vault.[90]

Toward the conclusion of its longest chapter, the KJñN, evoking "this *mudrā* that is called 'Unnamed'" (14.92a)—a likely reference to Kubjikā,[91] the hunchbacked goddess whose form prefigures that of the coiled *kuṇḍalinī*—together with a yogic technique involving five internal seals (*pañcamudrā*) (14.92b), states that

> one should, by means of the Śakti practice, pierce [upward] as far as the "End of the Five Times Twelve" [i.e., a point sixty finger-breadths above the fontanelle or, perhaps, the navel]. Those who have been brought under the power of the circles (*cakras*)—of Devīs, Dūtīs, Yoginīs, and Mātṛs—become absorbed in the *khecarī-cakra* [the fifth and highest *cakra* in the Kubjikā system]. This causes the arousal (*kṣobhayet*) of the supreme nectar [in them?]. Without nectar, O Goddess, how can there be immortality? Listen: nectar is the true clan-born essence (*kaulasadbhāva*), which is born from the triangle of love (*kāmakalātmaka*) [i.e., the pubic triangle].[92]

Here, the five inner seals would correspond to the five circles (*cakras*) of goddesses who become aroused, and who emit the clan nectar from their vulvas. This reading is supported by another passage from the same chapter, which relates the best *kaulasadbhāva* to the "Gandharvī, Kinnarī, Yakṣī or female dweller of the underworld, or again the Asurī, or Vidyādharī [who is] aroused" (*kṣubhyate*).[93] So, too, the *Mahiṣamardinī Stotra* and the *Kaulacūḍāmaṇi* indicate that the Kaula practice of *rajapāna*, the drinking of female discharge, becomes sublimated into the yogic technique of *khecarī mudrā*, in which the practitioner internally consumes the nectar produced through his yogic practice.[94] Once this reading of *mudrā* is accepted, a number of other usages become comprehensible. David Lorenzen has drawn attention to the ambiguous use that the philosopher Rāmānuja makes of the term, with reference to the "Kapālas," that is, the Kāpālikas.

> As the Kapālas declare: "He who knows the essence of the six insignia (*mudrikā-ṣaṭka*), who is proficient in the highest *mudrā* (*paramudrā-viśarada*), and who meditates on the Self as seated in the vulva (*bhagāsana-stha*), attains *nirvāṇa*."[95]

As Lorenzen argues, the "highest *mudrā*" ought not to be construed here as one of the six insignias (*mudrikās*) that were the distinctive regalia of the Kāpālikas. Its juxtaposition in this passage to the vulva and to *nirvāṇa* makes it clear that we are here in the presence of a Hindu homologue of the Tantric Buddhist use of the term "Seal," *mudrā* (or "Great Seal," *mahāmudrā*; or "Action Seal," *karmamudrā*), for the practitioner's female consort.[96] It is this consort's vulva that constitutes the seal here, as in the oft-repeated Tantric Buddhist aphorism that the Buddha once dwelt "in the vulvas of the Adamantine Maidens."[97] Other Buddhist Tantric sources, such as the *Sekoddeśaṭīkā* (ST), *Kālacakra Tantra*, *Hevajra Tantra*, and *Caṇḍamahāroṣaṇa Tantra*, further confirm this identity of the consort as the seal, and her vulva as the locus of initiation.[98] A passage in the TĀ speaks of a supreme *mudrā* that it quite clearly identifies with the subtle physiology of the yoni;[99] in his commentary on another passage from the same text, Jayaratha identifies the illustrious *khecarī mudrā* as a six-angled diagram comprising two interlocking triangles: one triangle is the male Siddha and the other the female Yoginī.[100] This use of the term also appears in the circa eleventh-century *Toḍala Tantra*, whose use of the term *mudrā* also clearly denotes the female consort.[101]

However, the same *Toḍala Tantra* verse includes *maithuna* as the fifth of its "set of five M-words" (*pañcamakāra*), which raises the question of what this term should mean, if not "sexual intercourse," which is its most widely accepted translation. In all of the aforementioned sources, *mudrā* clearly signifies the vulva of the consort, and is as such a code word for the more conventional terms *bhaga* and "yoni." Now, earlier Kaula works list only three M-words: *madya* (liquor), *māṃsa* (meat), and *maithuna*: the *pañcamakāra*, although better known, is in fact a secondary expansion on an original set of three. Here, there would be no redundancy, since the term *mudrā*, together with "fish" (*matsya*)—also a later addition—is omitted altogether.[102] It is also useful to note that the term *pañcatattva* is frequently used as a synonym for the *pañcamakāra* in both Hindu and Buddhist Tantra. *Tattva* may be read in many ways. In its most abstract sense, it means "essence" or "category," while in more concrete terms, it simply means "substance." Many Tantras characterize the substances denoted by the first four M-words as aphrodisiac preparatory stages or substances for the culminating *maithuna*, which is also a substance to be ritually consumed. The KĀN is most explicit in its identification of the five M-words with five substances (*pañcatattvas*) or fluids (*dravyams*) to be consumed by the practitioner.[103]

In addition, the formation of term *maithuna* presents problems of its own. *Maithuna*, which is generally translated as "sexual intercourse" or "couple engaged in sexual intercourse," is a strengthened form of *mithuna*, a term whose primary sense is "pair, couple." However the neuter form, *mithunam*, attested as early as the *Taittirīya Saṃhitā*, itself takes on the abstract sense of "pairing," "copulation."[104] This being the case, the strengthened form *maithuna* (also a neuter, when the strong sense of sexual intercourse is intended) becomes an abstraction of an abstraction: "that which pertains to, is derived from sexual intercourse." In fact, a number of sources appear to read the term *maithuna* in just this way. The KĀN speaks of an offering of the five *tattvas*, which are to be covered with a red cloth, in such a way as to leave no room for doubt that all are substances. Later, the same source compares *maithuna* to the water offering made to the ancestors (*tarpaṇa*): "Know *maithuna* [to be] the water-offering, and the shedding of semen [the concluding rite of] releasing [the image of a deity into holy water]."[105] More forcefully, the same source states, at the end of a long panegyric to the fifth *tattva*, that "one should vigorously drink the unrefined fluid of intercourse (*maithunam dravyam*)."[106] So, too, the *Āgama Prakāśa*, a nineteenth-century diatribe against Kaula practice, declares in its discussion of the five M-words that the fifth "is considered as *amṛta* and is produced from [the] Śakti; and hence it is that cohabitation with the woman is termed *yajña* (sacrifice) or the *dūtīyāga* (sacrifice to the Female Messenger)."[107]

A similar reading of *maithuna* as the fluid product of sexual intercourse may be elicited from a passage of the TĀ. After explaining that the true celibate student (*brahmacārin*) is one who experiences the bliss of the absolute *brahman* within the body in the form of the three M's (which the commentator Jayaratha glosses as "liquor, flesh and *maithuna*"),[108] the text continues: "Those who offer into the circle to the exclusion of eating the euphoric three M's are brutes (*paśus*), excluded from bliss [and thereby] excluded from that [absolute *brahman* itself]." In his commentary, Jayaratha glosses *trimāhārās* as "not eating the three M's."[109] Here, *maithuna* can only be read as "sexual emission": otherwise, it could not be eaten, consumed, together with and in the same way as alcohol and meat. In his autobiography, the twentieth-century practitioner scholar Agehananda Bharati subscribes to this broad reading of *brahmacārin* and, in his inimitable way, launches a broadside against Hindu reductions of the same to something resembling modern-day Victorian sensibilities:

> The god Kṛṣṇa had sixteen thousand wives, all of whom he enjoyed simultaneously, believe it or not, yet he was a *brahmacārī*. However, before long the meaning of the term changed and it came to refer, as it does today, merely to sexual continence, primitive celibacy. For my own part I have always held to the original meaning of the term, in which mere sexual continence is the least important characteristic. In fact in many esoteric disciplines which are taught to lead to spiritual emancipation, it is probably a hindrance—not from the psychological angle of threatening complexes and disorders (I couldn't care less about them), but on the path of deepest intuition. Thanks to the perseverance of Hindu philistine medievalism, to Christianity, to Gandhism, and to the puritanism of an inceptive industrial India, the infinitely delicate and profound balance between celibacy and erotocentric ritualism has been lost in a welter of narrow-minded, collectivizing religious observances which are Hindu only in name. . . .[110]

Frédérique Apfel-Marglin's description of the rites practiced by Tantric specialists at the famous Jagannātha temple of Puri, on the coast of Orissa, based on two undated Oriyan manuscripts, offers a similar reading of the fifth *makāra:* liquor, flesh, fish, and parched grain are transformed, through the utterance of a mantra, into nectar (*amṛta*), and are in turn combined with the *kulāmṛta*, female discharge, and a drop of the menstrual blood of a girl in her first menses. All of the five M's are then combined in a conch shell, from which they are drunk by the officiant in the course of the ritual.[111] This also squares with present-day Kaula and Tantric precept and practice, in which the production of the fluid *dravyam* is the desideratum and culmination of the practice of the five M's, and the sine qua non of Kaula initiation (*dīkṣā*).[112]

6. The Pleasures of Betel

First-time visitors to India usually do a double take the first time they see men chewing *pān* in public.[113] *Pān*, India's favorite chew, exudes a juice that has the same brilliant red color as blood in low-budget Bollywood movies. Filling the mouth of the chewer, it is periodically ejected from the same in a copious stream of red expectorate. I have met people who thought *pān* chewers were hemorrhaging from the mouth the first time they observed them.[114] Of late, chewing *pān* in public has become an all-male affair; while women will chew *pān* at home or among friends, public chewing by women is considered rustic or improper behavior, for reasons that will be made clear.[115]

In many parts of India, the offering of *pān* forms an integral part of a number of life-cycle and other rituals, as well as contractual agreements.[116] These include the marriage ritual, in which *pān* is an intimate prelude to its consummation.[117] Feeding one's beloved is an intimate act, and the effect of the chew is mildly inebriating if not arousing;[118] but there is a great deal more behind the act than this. In the intimacy of their bedchamber, a man will feed his wife *pān*, and she, him, as a part of foreplay.

We read of this in no less an orthodox source than the *Bhāgavata Purāṇa*, in its description of the dalliance of Kṛṣṇa, the alluring blue-skinned god, and the cowherding girls (*gopīs*) of Vṛndāvana, the Thick Forest. The *gopīs* are not Kṛṣṇa's lawful wives, and it is precisely the unlawful nature of his love affairs in the BhP that is interpreted by the Gauḍiya and Sahajiyā Vaiṣṇava theologians to epitomize the nature of the unbounded, unmitigated love between the male godhead and his devotees, who are, in this system, female by definition. God is the sole "real man" in this world; even men are as women before god, adoring him like a lover who awaits his sporadic visits with impatient and feverish passion. This explains the transvestitism of Caitanya, the charismatic founder of the Gauḍiya Vaiṣṇava sect: he was Rādhā to his divine lover Kṛṣṇa.

This is not all. When Kṛṣṇa incarnates himself in this world in order to fully enjoy the play of his own creativity, he does so together with his entire *dhaman*, a fully formed replica of his entire heavenly realm, complete with every aspect of himself and every form of his own divine energy. These energies come down to earth, precisely, as his *gopīs*, the cowgirls with whom he makes love, "in order to enjoy his own sweetness," and in this sense, Rādhā, his favorite, is none other than the first hypostasis of Kṛṣṇa himself. Kṛṣṇa, the male godhead, manifests himself through female energy (*śakti*) in the form of Rādhā, who proliferates into circles of lesser energies, the multiple *hlādinī* ("gladdening") *śakti*s.[119]

In its description of Kṛṣṇa's loveplay with these, his *śakti*s, the BhP tells us that "a slender maiden received with joined hands his chewed betel."[120] That is, she shared Kṛṣṇa's chew, in other words, put into her mouth, the meaning of which is clear: "bloodying" a woman's mouth with red betel is the precursor to bloodying her vulva, her "nether mouth" in Tantric parlance, with the blood of defloration. Kṛṣṇa, the androgyne in a number of

Gauḍiya Vaiṣṇava traditions, whose mouth is already red with the blood of intercourse, transfers the nectar of his sweet lips to his female hypostases in the form of chewed betel leaf. Here, we are reminded as well of the "Kiss of the Yoginī" with which we opened the second chapter of this book,[121] in which the female partner transmits her sexual fluids, real or sublimated, through her lower "mouth." We should also recall the Vedic husband-finding ritual of the maiden Apālā, who transmits the soma she has chewed, through a kiss, to the god Indra, following which they engage in sexual intercourse.[122] It is worth noting here that soma juice is described as having a reddish color; this is mixed with white milk to form the fluid offered and drunk in Vedic soma sacrifices. With these two examples, we have both Vedic and Puranic models for a type of mouth-to-mouth exchange of reddish vegetable fluids as preludes to the emission of human sexual fluids.

How does this transference between two types of fluids occur in Tantric theory and practice? Much of *pān*'s sexual symbolism has to do with the nature of its combination of ingredients. Although there are a wide variety of additional "fillings" to what is sold as *pān* in India today, it has historically been composed of four substances: (1) the shiny, bright green heart-shaped leaf of the betel tree (*tāmbūla* in Sanskrit), which is coated with (2) white caustic lime paste made from crushed shells (*cūrṇa*) and (3) blood-red catechu paste extracted from the wood of an Indian variety of mimosa (*khadīra*) and wrapped around (4) a piece of nut from the areca-nut palm (*supārī*). According to a Benares temple priest, these four ingredients represent the form and substance of the *liṅgam-yoni*, the iconographic representation of the sexual organs of Śiva and the Goddess in union. The betel leaf is the yoni; the areca nut placed atop it, the *liṅgam*; and the white and red pastes, divine semen (*vīrya*) and female discharge (*rajas*).[123]

To be sure, this esoteric symbolism is unknown to the vast majority of *pān*-chewing Indians (including non-Hindus). Nonetheless, when viewed in the light of the wide variety of ritual contexts in which it is found, it becomes apparent that the form, substance, ritual dynamics, and erotic connotations of *pān* chewing were overcoded in a number of ways in the various medieval Tantric traditions. A medieval play, the eleventh-century *Prabodhacandrodaya* of Kṛṣṇamiśra, includes a veiled allegorization of Kāpālika practice, in which an exchange of betel, from mouth to mouth, occurs.[124] The *Caryāgīti*, the same anthology of early Buddhist Tantric songs that includes the "Kiss of the Yoginī," unambiguously uses the term *tāmbūla* to denote menstrual blood:

Eating the betel-leaf of Thought and the camphor of Great Bliss,
She gives delight as she clings to his neck,
increasing his joy in Great Bliss,

and night becomes dawn.
With your Guru's word as your bow
Hit the target with the arrow of your mind.
Apply just one shaft and pierce, O pierce, supreme *nirvāṇa*.[125]

Here, white camphor (*karpūra*) is to male semen what red betel leaf is to female discharge: a homologue. We in fact find an alternation in the Tantric sources between the metonymic evocation of a sexual or vital fluid through its vegetable or mineral homologue and its literal ritual use. The KJñN states: "This is the Śakti [whom] the great-souled ones [call] 'last-born' [i.e., an outcaste] and 'garlanded by sky' [i.e., naked]. Her mouth is filled and smeared with *tāmbūla*, and her hair hanging loose."[126] This description of the Tantric consort portrays her like a wife—or, better yet, a paramour, like Kṛṣṇa's *gopīs*—in the privacy of the bedchamber: she is naked with hair hanging free, her mouth running over with *pān*.

The *Ratirahasya* (14.17), a medieval treatise on erotics, gives the following instructions for attracting the woman of one's desire: "'Oṃ Cāmuṇḍā! *Hulu hulu! Culu culu!* Bring the woman [named X] under my power! Hail!' If a man pronounces this seven times with an offering of betel-leaf, he attracts her to himself."[127] The *Kulacūḍāmaṇi Tantra*, a circa eleventh-century work, connects betel chewing either with the attraction of a female consort, the state of possession (betrayed by her rolling eyes), or with the consumption of sexual fluids in a number of its descriptions of practice.[128]

> The guru, who is wise and unagitated, [and] whose mouth is filled with a chew of betel leaf, should draw [the Śakti Cakra] on the forehead [of the practitioner's consort,] a virtuous clan-born (*kulajā*) woman whose eyes are flickering in the fluid of the highest bliss (*parānandarasāghūrṇalocanā*). . . .
>
> When he has finished the repetition of the mantra called *kulākula*, the *kula* [maiden] whose mouth is full of betel leaf . . . and whose eyes are rolling . . . is brought [to him]. . . .
>
> Then in the middle of the pavilion he should offer . . . food to be chewed, sucked, licked, and drunk [by eight women who incarnate eight goddesses]. . . . And when they have rinsed their mouths [after eating], he should offer them betel leaf and something aromatic to sweeten their breath.
>
> . . . Naked, with betel leaf in his mouth, his hair [hanging] free, his senses under control, with eyes rolling from the effect of wine and in union with another woman, the [male] jewel of the clan should worship with aromatics and flower[s] the naked women. . . .[129]

This passage concludes with a description of the Goddess, whose mouth is filled with oblations, much like the consort in the KJñN passage whose mouth and face are filled and smeared with *pān*. Similar imagery may also be present, in an occulted fashion, in the iconography of Śrī Nāthjī, the deity whose Nathdwara temple in southern Rajasthan is identified by his Vallabhī-Puṣṭimargī devotees as a form of Viṣṇu. In the foreground of nearly every painted tableau of this deity, one observes, in the lower left, a scrotum-shaped vessel, and in the lower right, a number of prepared chews of *pāns* or else a *pān* box. The relationship between this pair of images and male and female sexual fluids is supported by two types of evidence. On the one hand, as Charlotte Vaudeville has demonstrated, the original cult of the image worshiped today as the "Vaiṣṇava" Śrī Nāthjī combined the "Tantric Śaiva" cults of Jagannātha, Narasiṃha, and Ekapāda Bhairava.[130] On the other hand, the eleventh-century *Dhanyaśloka* of Madhurāja, an "eyewitness" description of Abhinavagupta, his guru's guru, seems to bring together the same two elements in an overtly Tantric context:

> Abhinava is attended by all his numerous students, with student Kṣemarāja, at their head. . . . To his side stand Female Messengers (Dūtīs), partners in Tantric rites, who hold in one hand a jug of wine (*śivarasa*) and a box full of betel-rolls, and in the other hand a lotus and a citron. . . .[131]

Similarly, Jayaratha, in his commentary on TĀ 29.68–69, describes the Dūtī as one who is "eager for a good [chew of] betel."[132] The KĀN blends betel chewing with the offering and consumption of sexual fluids. Under the heading of "Offerings to the Female Messenger (Dūtī)," this text enjoins the practitioner to worship the vulva of his consort as well as his own penis (called his "Śiva-self") with aromatics, flowers, unbroken rice grains, incense, oil lamps, and various kinds of food. Following this, he worships the goddesses Avadhūteśvarī-Kubjā-Kāmākhyā, Vajreśvarī, Dikkāravāsinī, Mahācaṇḍeśvarī, and Tārā on the triangle of the pubis.[133] Then,

> having been entreated [by her], and having eaten a fine chew of betel leaf, and having inserted his penis with the elephant-trunk *mudrā*, he should, devoid of agitation, perform the repeated utterances (*japa*) 1,008 times and then 108 times. . . . At the end of the *japa*, having then offered that *japa* to the Goddess [i.e., his consort], he should worship with the pleasures of love she who is agitated, and should remain [in that state] for a long time. The "moon" [will be] melting and flowing (*galaccandradravam*): having taken [his semen] from that [moon], he should take it [and] make a water offering of it (*tarpayet*) to Śivā [i.e., his consort].

> Praising and circumambulating [her] constitute the completion of the practice.[134]

All of these data point to the incorporation of *pān* chewing into Kaula ritual as an "overcoding" of parallel or concurrent transactions involving the male consumption of female discharge.

7. Conceiving Conception

Perhaps the most transgressive blending and consumption of female emissions by male practitioners is that described in a passage from the *Manthānabhairava Tantra*. In the fourth chapter of its "Yoga Khaṇḍa,"[135] this text discusses the "Milk of the Yoginī" (*yoginī-kṣīra*) in terms that betray a comprehensive and "subversive" understanding of the relationship between menstruation, lactation, and, to a lesser degree, conception. A knowledge of these relationships is intimated in a slightly later work, the thirteenth-century *Mātṛkābheda Tantra*, which states that when a woman conceives, uterine or menstrual blood is transformed into breast milk.[136] The *Manthānabhairava Tantra* takes matters much further, with the Goddess stating on the subject of menstrual blood that

> the source of [this] "milk" is the stoppage of [breast] milk. One should mix [this] "milk" in [breast] milk. This is a secret without equal, not to be divulged. It affords the highest supernatural powers. Because it has arisen from a Yoginī's breast, one should always use [this] milk. With this milk, she [the Yoginī] whose soul is pure is always nourishing (*puṣṭikara*) [and] auspicious. The flower [i.e., menstrual discharge] is the appearance of the milk of the vulva (*catuṣpīṭha*).[137] One should practice with it. . . . Milk is to be mixed with [female] discharge (*kṣaram*). One should always drink her milk [with] the fluid that has its origin in milk, O God. One should always practice [with] her milk.[138]

Also mentioned in this passage is a "Clan of the Cowrie Maidens" (*kākinī-kula*), that is, of those consorts renowned in alchemical texts for the regularity of their menses, which always fell during the dark half of the lunar month, the optimal period for nocturnal Tantric rites: their menstrual blood was used to catalyze sulfur, its mineral homologue, in the activation of mercury, the mineral equivalent of semen.[139] The MBhT passage also stipulates that this menstrual "milk" is "emitted via the lunar progression," and that the "solar progression" should be shunned.[140] This linking—of milk, menses, and moon—is one that occurs in other Tantric contexts. The connection between the lunar month and a woman's monthly cycle is an obvious one that is as explicit in the West as it is in India, as evidenced in the etymology of the word *mensis* in Latin. The identification between milk and menses in this ritual description is what makes the practice so powerful.

The relationship between milk and moon, as well, is one that also has its place in Tantric symbol systems. So, for example, a work entitled the *Nāthaṣoḍaśāmnāyakrama*, having listed a set of six "Mother Dūtīs"—each of whose names contains the term "yoni" (Mahāyoni, Śaṅkhayoni, Padmayoni, etc.), together with their "Siddha Nātha" consorts—makes the statement: "The moon, granter of all boons, was born from the rising Ocean of Milk. One should always imagine it as full-rayed, and flowing with nectar."[141] One of Agehananda Bharati's *tāntrika* informants, evoking the same nectar that arose from the churning of the Ocean of Milk, identified it with *kulāmṛta*, that is, female discharge or menstrual blood. The same identification (or juxtaposition) is made, on a mineral register, in the eleventh-century RA: the Goddess's menstrual blood, transformed into sulfur, rose to the surface of the Ocean of Milk, together with nectar.[142] Finally, the sixteenfold nature of the moon itself, reflected in the title of the *Nāthaṣoḍaśāmnāyakrama* ("The Sequence of the Sixteen Nāth Transmissions"), is intimately related to the menstrual cycle. In the words of the *Yājñavalkya Smṛti* (79), "sixteen nights are the season of a woman . . . from the appearance of menses, sixteen nights is for a woman the season. . . ."[143] The KĀN and other Tantric works in fact describe the worship of two sets of sixteen *kalās*, the sixteen goddesses of the *kāmakalā*, followed by the sixteen digits of the moon (*somakalā*).[144]

A number of other observations are in order. As the aphoristic opening line of the *Manthānabhairava Tantra* passage makes clear, Kaula practitioners were aware that when lactation ceases, menstrual flow begins, and vice versa. Female discharge is the "milk of the vulva," and a Yoginī's menstrual blood, which has its origins in her breast, is nourishing (*puṣṭikara*). As for the mixing of the two "milks," it would be physiologically impossible for both to be the emissions of the same woman. At the same time, Yoginīs are always described in texts and portrayed in sculptures as lithe seductresses with perfect bodies unmarked by the trammels of pregnancy and childbirth.[145] In other words, because Yoginīs—like the divine Mothers of the myth of the birth of Skanda in MBh III, who are also childless—are never portrayed as biological mothers, one wonders when and under what conditions a Yoginī would ever lactate. No Yoginī images ever show them suckling children. Indeed, some scholars have viewed the injunction, found in a number of Tantras, to engaging in sexual intercourse with menstruating women as a "rhythm method" type of birth control. Clearly, the mixing of a Yoginī's two "milks" is as powerful a form of Tantric transgressivity as one could hope to find, and it is probably on this level that one should read this passage: as a piece of the Tantric "prescriptive imagination." It also demonstrates that Hindu Tantra had found a way to overcome the apparent antithesis between so-called goddesses "of the breast" and goddesses "of the tooth."[146]

Behind this description of an impossible ritual practice, however, we may glimpse a widespread vision of female fertility and of the dynamics of conception, a vision that was not unique to India. A short excursus into comparative theories of lactation shall prove illuminating here. As in India, the premodern West postulated a channel between a woman's breasts and her womb: one finds this in the drawings of Leonardo da Vinci.[147] Here, it was further assumed that the essential component of female semen was nothing other than milk, which was funneled internally from the breasts to the genital organs for so long as there was no infant to be nursed. A woman was thought to support and "give flesh" (*puṣṭikara*, in Sanskrit) to the embryo with "uterine milk" before birth, and with "breast milk" postpartum. As such, a woman's sexual fluid was conceived as being naturally white, and only became reddened when mixed with menstrual blood. However, as Aristotle's *Generation of Animals* clearly explains, menstruation was itself nothing other than a necessary discharge of unused female semen.[148]

Certain parallels to this ancient and medieval complex may be elicited from present-day Indian data. Apfel-Marglin's study of modern-day Orissa clearly indicates that similar notions of the nurturing qualities of female "semen" remain operative.

> A child is produced by the mixing of the man's seed (*bīrjya* [*vīrya*, in Sanskrit]) and the woman's secretion (*rāja*). The word *rāja* in this context refers to the colourless (*sādhā*) vaginal secretion which is said to be ejaculated by the woman during intercourse, in much the same way as a man's semen is ejaculated. However, the word can also mean menstrual blood. . . . Women are said to have more blood than men. The greater abundance of blood in women is evidenced in their menstruating. . . . The continuity of the line therefore is achieved through the seed, (*bīrjya*), and the maintenance of the line depends on the feeding by the woman, both in terms of food and in terms of feeding the embryo with the woman's blood. . . .[149]

Here again, we see that a woman's sexual emission, beyond being simply homologized with blood or milk, is identified as the source of both, according to her sociobiological role: when she is not a mother, its excess is discharged as menstrual blood; when she is pregnant, it becomes the "uterine milk" that feeds the embryo in her womb; when she is a mother, it becomes the milk that feeds her child.[150] Now, the KĀN (17.159a) states in no uncertain terms that a woman's blood is the fount of life itself: "a woman's blood is the supreme fluid (*paramaṃ dravyam*): by means of it a body is generated." The great Tantric Goddess is, however, a special sort of woman, possessed of a unique sort of sexual fluid, whence the names, found in Kubjikā sources, of "Goddess Semen" (*śukradevī*) or "She Whose Menses Is Semen" (*bindupuṣpā*).[151] Here, it is not the Goddess herself who is androgynous (as in the case of Śiva Ardhanarīśvara); rather, it is her sexual fluids that are so. The KĀN offers an expanded discussion of this notion, explaining that both male and female sexual fluids are the source of the Goddess's creativity:

> The penis and the vulva, the nectar of the penis and vulva, comprise the Goddess's true self. Dwelling in semen (*śukra*), she has the form of semen; dwelling in menstrual blood, she has the form of menstrual blood. Dwelling in the drop [of combined sexual emissions], she has the form of the drop, she whose own form is comprised of menstrual blood and the drop.[152]

The *Kularatnoddyota* mythologizes the same: the Goddess, dwelling alone in a cave, becomes weary of asceticism and begins to lick her own yoni, which emits the semen (and not blood) that gives life to the entire universe. It is because she bent over to lick herself that she became the "Crooked One" (*kubjikā*).[153]

These sources offer an important insight into the bio-logic of the "pure Saktism" found in a number of Kaula traditions. Even as these traditions celebrated the Goddess as the sole source of the *kula*, in the sense of the clan of male and female practitioners as well as that of the entire embodied cosmos, it nonetheless recognizes the biological truth—known in India since at least the time of the *Caraka Saṃhitā*—that an embryo is conceived through the intermingling of male and female sexual fluids, which, combined, form the "drop," the zygote that gives rise to a new being.[154] In other words, even as these traditions enshrined the female Kālī, Kubjikā, or Tripurāsundarī alone as the yoni, the triangular "heart" or "source" of their mandalic universe, and even as they dispensed of the presence, or at least the hegemony, of the male god at the center, they could not do away with male sexual fluid in their reckonings of how that universe was sexually embodied. Both male and female fluids were necessary to embryogenesis, to the wondrous power to create life, even if their respective functions were different. However, extant, even classical, medical notions made it possible for Kaula theoreticians to speak of the androgynous sexuality and creativity of these goddesses who were so many childless Mothers of the Universe.

Chapter 4

THE MOUTH OF THE YOGINĪ: *Sexual Transactions in Tantric Ritual*

1. The *Kāmakalā* Yantra in the *Śilpa Prakāśa*

The *Śilpa Prakāśa* (ŚP), a ninth- to twelfth-century work on temple architecture, is signed by a certain Rāmacandra Kulācāra, whose name, together with the title of his work, tells us much about his sectarian orientations. Rāmacandra was a native of Orissa, and to all appearances, his work was nothing less than an architect's or builder's manual for the sorts of temple constructions that we most readily identify with the medieval Orissi style: the older temples of Bhubanesvar and its environs, temples renowned for their beauty but also for the proliferation of erotic sculptures on their walls.[1]

In Rāmacandra's text, the most comprehensive extant work on Tantric temple architecture, we find a number of departures from "classical" *śilpa śāstra* traditions. Most important for our concerns are the construction, consecration, and depositing of various yantras in the foundations and underneath various sections of temples as well as below or behind their sculpted images. Especially distinctive are the installation of two particular yantras. The first of these, termed the "*yoginī* yantra," is to be installed beneath the inner sanctum, called the "womb house" (*garbhagṛha*) (ŚP 1.90–96);[2] the second, called the "*kāmakalā* yantra," is the most pivotal decoration of the entire temple pavilion's (*vimāna*) outer walls, from which are generated, in accordance with Kaula rites, all of that structure's erotic sculptures (*kāmakalā-bandha:* ŚP 2.508).[3] This is of a piece with the author's overarching method, which requires that all images of divinities that

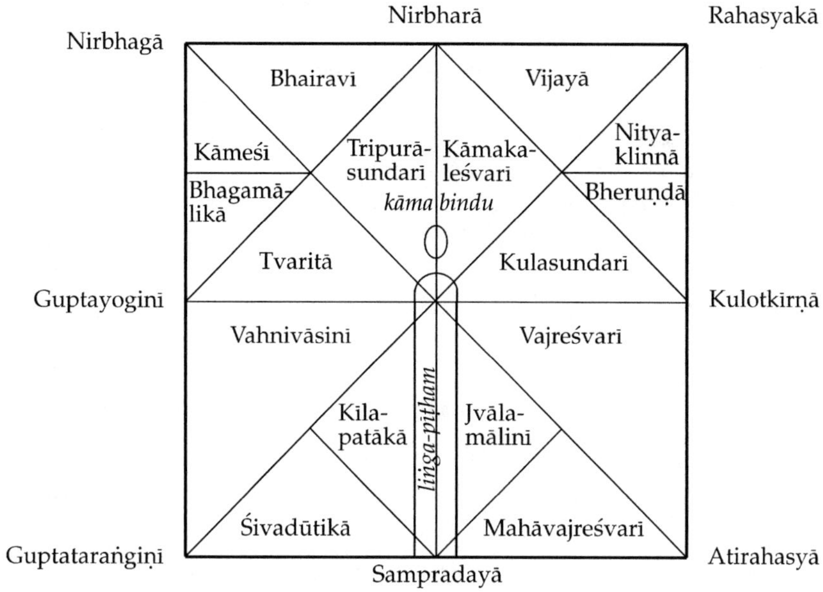

Figure 4.a. *Kāmakalā* yantra according to the *Śilpa Prakāśa*. Adobe Photoshop image.

adorn the temple be composed on yantras (here the term means "blueprint" or "model") and visualized by their sculptors through meditation on them.[4] The *yoginī* yantra, comprised for the most part of intersecting upturned and downturned triangles, bears a certain structural resemblance to the famous *kāmakalā* diagram of Śrīvidyā tradition, which will be discussed in chapter 8. While both *kāmakalā* diagrams ostensibly constitute Kaula or Śākta depictions of the Goddess's proliferation from the one into the many, the male Śiva is nonetheless present in both. So it is that, although all of the energies depicted on the ŚP *kāmakalā* yantra are feminine ("there are sixteen Mātṛkās resting on the Yoginī-*bindus*, on every *bindu* there are four Yoginīs in regular order"), these nonetheless surround an abstract representation of the male Śiva as the "liṅga-pīṭham."[5]

The ŚP *kāmakalā* yantra (fig. 4.a) consists of a standing (i.e., erect) *liṅgam* in its chasing (*liṅga-pīṭham*) with sixteen triangles grouped in geometric fashion around it, nearly all of them contiguous with the *liṅgam*. Above the *liṅgam* is a small egg-shaped drop, called the "drop of love" (*kāmabindu*). The *liṅgam* is Śiva, the triangles that converge on it are explicitly identified as vulvas (*bhagas*), and it is "only by joining the lines to the *bindu* that the *kalās* [i.e., the triangles, which represent feminine energy] are formed." These "energy-triangles," called the *kalā-śaktis*, bear the names of sixteen different goddesses, while "in the place of the egg at the center is the supreme Śakti called 'Our Great Lady of the Arts of Love'" (*mahā-kāmakaleśvarī*).[6] These interlocking triangles combine to form a square, on the perimeter of which are located eight protective Yoginīs, called the Yoginīs of the outer entourage (*bāhyāvaraṇa*).[7] This yantra, which was to be *concealed* by a love scene carved over it, was a required fixture on temples dedicated to Śiva or Rudra. Radiating outward (at least conceptually) from this yantra were the erotic sculptures of the *kāma-bandha*, which, in the case of the early-tenth-century Vārāhī temple in Caurasi, Orissa, depicted the eight-stage process of the powerful Kaula rite known as *aṣṭa-kāmakalā-prayoga*, the "practice of the eight types of *kāmakalā*," about which more shortly.[8]

The earliest depiction of this configuration is alluded to in Bhavabhūti's eighth-century C.E. play, *Mālatī-Mādhava*, whose fifth act opens with a Kāpālika consort, a Yoginī, flying onstage with the words:

> Victorious is the lord of Śakti surrounded by the Śaktis, whose self is situated in the midst of the wheel of sixteen channels (*nāḍīcakra*), [and] who, when his form is realized as dwelling in the heart, affords *siddhis* to persons possessed of this arcane knowledge, [and who is] sought after by practitioners whose minds are unwavering.[9]

Here as well, the image is one of sixteen *śakti*s converging on the male deity at the heart of a *maṇḍala* composed of channels or lines of energy. The term *nāḍī* may also be translated here as "vein," in which case we appear to be in the presence of a configuration similar to that found in the Buddhist Cakrasaṃvara Maṇḍala. Here, the names of the eight female door guardians of this mandala share their names with those of the eight principal veins that radiate outward from the vaginal nerve center, according to an Indian understanding of female anatomy reflected in the Tantric texts. The use of deity names for these veins conflates the vulva with the mandala in this symbolic realm.[10] As will be shown in chapter 8, it is the names of the sixteen *kalā-śakti*s who converge on the center of this Kaula version of the *kāmakalā* yantra that serve as the most obvious bridge between this and the later Śrīvidyā version of the same, given that these sixteen names—some of which are quite evocative (Bhagamālinī, Nityaklinnā)—are identical to those of the sixteen Nityā goddesses of the latter tradition.[11]

The ŚP's discussion of the *kāmakalā* yantra occurs in the context of Rāmacandra's long general description of the construction of the *vimāna-mālinī* temple type.[12] The joining (*jāṅgha*) wall[13] that supports the roof of such a temple is subdivided into a number of horizontal sections, of which one is the *kāma-bandha*, the place for the insertion of love scenes.[14] The ŚP offers the following rationale for such sculpted scenes:

> Desire (*kāma*) is the root of the universe. From desire all beings are born. . . . Without Śiva and Śakti creation would be nothing but imagination. Without the action of kāma there would be no birth or death. Śiva himself is visibly manifested as a great phallus (*mahāliṅgam*), and Śakti in the form of a vulva (*bhaga*). By their union the whole universe comes into being. . . . A place without love-images (*kāmakalā*) is known as a "place to be shunned." In the opinion of the Kaulācāras it is always a base, forsaken place, resembling a dark abyss, which is shunned like the den of Death. Without offering worship to the kāmakalā-yantra, Śakti worship and the [Kaula] practice (*sādhanā*) become as useless as the bath of an elephant. The shrine on which that yantra stands is a "Temple of Virile Heroes" (*vīra-mandira*). . . .[15]

Then follows the description of the *kāmakalā* yantra, which has already been outlined above, followed by these theoretical observations:

> These are the sixteen Śaktis, all being the very essence of Desire (*kāmakalātmikā*) placed inside the square field.[16] . . . In the "jewel-area" (*maṇideśa*) below [the central Śakti, Mahākāmakaleśvarī] is Śiva Kāmakaleśvara . . . always in union with Kāmakaleśvarī, established in the *ājñā cakra*, always delighting in drinking female discharge (*rajapāna*). He whose sign is the ascetic's garb, the yogin Kāmakaleśvara, the Śaṅkara of dark colour, is the Lord of the Kāmakalā Mahāyantra. . . . This yantra is utterly secret, it should not be shown to everyone. For this reason a love-scene (*mithuna-mūrti*) is to be carved on the lines of the yantra. . . . In the opinion of Kaulācāras it should be made on the lovely *jāṅgha*, on the upper part of the wall. The *kāmabandha* is placed there to give delight to people.[17]

Devangana Desai has suggested that the famous erotic *ménage à quatre* sculpted into the joining wall of the circa 1030 C.E. Kandariyā Mahādeva temple at Khajuraho is just such a love scene, as well as a case of "architectural punning" (fig. 4.b).[18] We will return to the Kaula symbolism of this temple in the next chapter.

The early-tenth-century Śākta temple of Vārāhī at Caurasi, Orissa, has been identified by Alice Boner as the paragon of the temple style described in the ŚP,[19] and it is on its walls that we find what I would argue is a depiction of the original *practice* of the *kāmakalā* [yantra]. First of all, the placement of these erotic images is telling: beginning with the circa 800 C.E. Vaitāl Deul temple at Bhubanesvar, they replace the entourage deities (*āvaraṇa-devatās*) standard on Śaiva temples.[20] There is evidence as well for parallel developments on Vaiṣṇava temples, in the placement of the

Figure 4.b. Kāmakalā yantra superimposed upon erotic sculpture from joining wall of Lakṣmaṇa temple, Khajuraho, ca. 950 C.E. Composition by Michael Rabe. Courtesy of Michael Rabe and Princeton University Press.

image of Mohinī on the circa 770 C.E. Vaikuṇṭha Perumal temple at Kancipuram (Tamil Nadu), and that of the *devadāsī* on the Jagannāth Puri temple (Orissa).[21] More important is the content of the Vārāhī sculptures, which J. N. Banerjea tentatively identified, on the basis of an unpublished manuscript of the *Kaulacūḍāmaṇi* ("Crest-Jewel of the Kaula"), as illustrations of the "practice of the eight types of *kāmakalā*." In the first three of these scenes, beginning on the southern facade of the Vārāhī temple,

> the Vīra "Kaula Sādhaka" and the Kumārī "his Śakti or Uttarā Sādhikā" are depicted standing side by side in suggestive poses and represent

> 1) *vaśīkaraṇa*, "bringing the Kumārī under control"; 2) *sammoha*, "enchanting her"; and 3) *ākarṣaṇa* and *uccāṭana*, "attracting and preparing her for ritual sex." . . . In the next two scenes are 4) *yoni-abhiṣeka* and 5) *puraścaraṇa*, "the preliminary stage of the act." . . . [On the Vārāhī temple] scene 6), which Banerjea interprets as *rajapāna*, actually depicts fellatio. The last two scenes possibly represent the final stages, 7) *prastava* and 8) *nivṛtti* with the Vīra and the Kumārī returning to the normal state after the sexual act.[22]

Similar sequences are found on the Kiñceśvarī and Gaṇeśvara temples from the same period and region of Orissa.[23] It is the sixth stage of the rite, *rajapāna*, the drinking of female discharge, that I wish to concentrate on here. While it is "substituted" on the Vārāhī temple with a depiction of fellatio, the fact remains that for a period of about two hundred years, between the tenth and twelfth centuries C.E., *rajapāna*, the drinking of female discharge, was a commonplace of Kaula (or Kaula-inspired[24]) temple sculpture in Orissa, where the greatest wealth of such medieval sculpture remains intact. No less than twenty sculptural representations of this practice, found on over a dozen temples from every corner of Orissa,[25] have survived from this period, the earliest likely being from the tenth-century Kiñcakeśvarī temple at Khiching.[26] Its representation was gradually phased out in favor of scenes of fellatio, a phenomenon that Thomas Donaldson attributes to the eleventh-century institutionalization of the *devadāsī* system and the general "hedonization" of erotic temple sculpture.[27] What was it, then, about *rajapāna*, the climax and seemingly the raison d'être of the Kaula *kāmakalā* practice, that made it meaningful to its practitioners? In what way did practice relate to precept, and precept to transcending the human condition, the goal that seems to constitute the motor of every religious system?

2. Sexually Transmitted Messages

It is this Kaula practice of *rajapāna* that renders the term *kāmakalā* meaningful in an obvious and direct way, in contradistinction—as will be shown in chapter 8—to its semanticized and bowdlerized uses in the later Trika and Śrīvidyā systems. The term *kāmakalā* ("Arts of Love" or "Love's Lunar Portion"), intimately associated with goddesses named Our Lady of Love, She Who Is Garlanded by the Vulva (Bhagamālinī), and She Who Is Always Wet (Nityaklinnā)—and described in terminology that consistently borders on the orgasmic—only makes sense in the sexual context provided by the Kaula practices portrayed on Orissan and other medieval

Indian temples. Drinking female discharge is not, however, highly arousing—and it certainly has nothing to do with the "bliss" and "fun" offered by the modern-day Tantric sex trade. What, then, can or could have been meaningful about the male consumption of female discharge?

Matsyendra's use of the term *kāmakalā* in his KJñN is an important one, inasmuch as it may be the earliest use of the term in Kaula traditions. He mentions the term but twice, relating it to a system of five *cakras* fully developed in later Kubjikā traditions, and identifying it with the nectar of immortality, that is, the clan essence (*kaulasadbhāva*).[28] The connection between yogic practice, the cranial vault, the production of nectar that is the root of immortality, and the sexual agitation of circles of goddesses brings us back to a cryptic portion of the passage, already mentioned, from the ŚP (2.534): ". . . In the jewel-area . . . is Śiva Kāmakaleśvara . . . always in union with Kāmakaleśvarī, established in the *ājñā cakra*, always delighting in drinking female discharge." The *ājñā cakra*, the sixth of the yogic centers, is located precisely in the cranial region, behind the eyebrows, which is where the nectar of immortality is produced internally through yogic practice. This nectar, termed *rajas*, "female discharge," in the *Śilpa Prakāśa*, is said to be synonymous with *kaulasadbhāva* in the KJñN; and in this and other sources, the term *kaulasadbhāva* is identified with the clan fluid or clan nectar that flows through the wombs of the Yoginīs, Goddesses, and other female beings with which the clan identifies itself. The arising of these female deities, and their arousal in the cranial vault through the nectar they drink there, is of a piece with early accounts of the yogic process, in which it is circles of goddesses, rather than lotuses or wheels, that form the energy centers of the subtle body: this is in fact the original sense of the term "*cakra*" in subtle body mapping.[29]

In these early systems, these goddesses, gratified by the bodily fluids offered to them internally by the practitioner, rose along his spinal column to converge in his cranial vault. As will be discussed in chapter 8, this dynamic flows into the practice of *khecarī mudrā*, through which the practitioner internally drinks the nectar raised and refined through his hathayogic practice, thereby rendering himself immortal. These being early Kaula sources, however, the sexual valence is still explicit: it is the sexual fluids of female deities that are being generated and absorbed in the *ājñā cakra*.[30]

This reading is further supported by the use of the term "jewel area" (*maṇideśa*) in this passage. Just as in the case of the Tantric Buddhist expression "the jewel in the heart of the lotus," here, as well, the jewel area refers first and foremost to the clitoris,[31] the egg-shaped drop or point of love (*kāma-bindu*) located just above the *liṅga-pīṭham*, and that place at which Śiva drinks feminine discharge.[32] Now, the technical sense of the term *liṅga-pīṭham* is the "seat" or "chasing" of the *śiva-liṅgam* as such is found in Śiva temples, and that chasing is nothing other than the Goddess's vulva, her yoni in which the *liṅgam* is engaged. Therefore, what the text is saying here is that Śiva is drinking feminine discharge from the sexual orifice of the Goddess. He is moreover said to be in union with the Goddess in the *ājñā cakra*, which is located directly behind the place of the third eye. But the third eye is itself an emblem of the female vulva on the forehead of the male Śiva.[33] Furthermore, as noted in the previous chapter, the term *ājñā* itself has the technical meaning of "fluid gnosis" in the Kubjikā traditions.[34]

Elsewhere, the KJñN states that "the secret channel of access to the *siddhis* consists of the Five Streams."[35] This term, the Five Streams or Five Currents (*pañcasrotas*), is in fact the earliest term that one encounters in the Śaivāgamas for the lines of transmission of that tradition's teachings.[36] In these sources the five streams or currents are said to flow from the five mouths of the god Śiva.[37] Later, Kaula traditions would posit a sixth mouth, called the "nether mouth" or "mouth of the Yoginī," the source of its teachings and clan lineages, from which a sixth current streamed.[38] This is called the *picuvaktra* ("cotton mouth"), whence the name by which the *Brahmayāmala* calls itself in its colophons: *Picumata*, the "Doctrine of the [Nether] Cotton Mouth."[39] We have already postulated that the mouth—and particularly the nether mouth—of the Tantric Yoginī was not her oral cavity, but rather her vulva. The use of a term connoting fluid transfer (*srotas*) also supports a hypothesis that in the early Tantric context, oral transmission was an affair of sexually transmitted fluid messages. This reading is further supported by the iconography of Śiva. Quite often, the *liṅgam* will be represented with a face of Śiva superimposed upon the phallic image, in which case it is called an *ekamukha liṅgam*, a one-mouthed or one-faced image. Not infrequently, five faces of Śiva will be superimposed, with four facing in the four cardinal directions and the fifth facing upward. This is a *pañcamukhi liṅgam*, a five-faced or five-mouthed image. The Śiva *liṅga* is often set in a *pīṭha* having the form of a stylized vulva:[40] this would be the nether mouth of the Yoginī, the source of the sixth stream. What flows forth is at once the germ plasm of the old Kaula lineages and the esoteric teachings of these clans: these are the sources of the Tantric flow charts, which simultaneously constitute a flow of information, of sexually transmitted messages.

It is, moreover, this flow of fluid gnosis that constitutes the "edible grace" (*prasāda*) of Śiva and the Goddess in Śiva temples: fluid offerings poured over the *liṅgam* run into the sculpted labia of the yoni, along which they are channeled through an opening in the northern wall of the temple shrine. There, these conjoined sexual fluids of the divine pair may be collected by devotees. A mythological precedent for this practice of drinking the waters in which the Goddess's yoni has been bathed (*yonisalila*) is found in the *Kālikā Purāṇa*, in which it is the gods who do so, at the goddess Kāmākhyā's command.[41]

A comic rendering of the ambiguity of the term "mouth" is found in the *Nalavilāsanāṭakam* of Rāmacandrasūri,[42] a medieval north Indian play. In act 2, Lambastanī ("Tube Boobs")—a Kāpālika consort and abortionist who is described as "fooling with her mouth" and "kneading her groin area with her hand, and screwing up her mouth"—is being verbally abused by a king and his jester. At one point, the king states that "her mouth isn't worth looking at," and then asks, "Will we gain any benefit from having had a vision of you?" She answers that he will, and loosens the waistband of her skirt, exposing herself to him.

3. Oral Transmission in the KJñN

The oral transmission of fluid messages is described in a mythic mode in the sixteenth chapter of the KJñN, which opens with the Goddess asking Bhairava to enumerate the sites at which he stands during the "three times," past, present, and future. After evoking Srisailam, Mahendra, and Kāmākhyā (the "Place Called Love") as the sites at which mingling or union (*melāpakam*) with the Yoginīs and the obtainment of supernatural powers from them occurs,[43] Bhairava concentrates on two toponyms. These are Kāmarūpa (Love's Body), where he and the Goddess are present together, and Candradvīpa, Moon Island, where he dwells alone in a nonmanifest form.[44] To which the Goddess replies with a query:

> "For what purpose did I go to Moon Island, O Lord, and for what reason was the gnosis[45] of [our son] the primal Six-Mouthed [Kārttikeya] swallowed up?"[46] [Bhairava replies]: "I and thou . . . are the bringers-down of all of the teachings.[47] When I went to Moon Island together with thee, Kārttikeya came along, in the form of a boy."[48]

Bhairava then explains to the Goddess that at Moon Island their child, the boy-god Kārttikeya, flew into a rage and, taking the form of a mouse, stole the clan scripture (*śāstra*). Bhairava located the stolen scriptures in the belly of a fish, which he hauled out of the ocean, splitting open its stomach, to recover that "tablet of gnosis" (*jñānapaṭṭa*), which he hid in a secret place.[49] The entire scenario is then repeated: the clan scripture is again stolen by the mouse Kārttikeya, again thrown into the sea, and again swallowed by a great fish. This time, however, the fish's strength proves to be equal to that of the god himself, and so Bhairava "abandons his brahminhood" to become a low-caste fisherman. It is with this that Matsyendra's name is explained. Bhairava becomes a "Lord of Fishes," Matsyendra, to recover the Kula scripture with a "net of feminine energy" (*śaktijālam*).[50] It is this role that is memorialized by Abhinavagupta in an opening verse of his monumental TĀ (1.7): "May Macchandanātha be propitious to me, he who tore apart the rosy net of knots and holes, made of so many bits and pieces, unfolding and spreading everywhere."[51]

The text then goes on to detail the original descent of the Kaula gnosis in ages prior to this, the present Kali Yuga, data presented in chapter 1. Following this, it lists the names of the sectarian groups through which this gnosis was transmitted, down to the "Fish-Belly" in the present age.[52] With this piscine reference, we are given to understand that the Fish-Belly is the repository of the Kaula teachings in the present Kali Yuga, teachings in the form of a tablet, a text. It is in the light of this that the verses that follow are of signal interest. Here, Bhairava states:

> I will now discuss to thee, in their entirety, those [teachings] that were lost [in transmission], O Goddess! [The teaching known] by the name of [the Bringing Forth of the Kaula] Gnosis came through this Clan of the Yoginīs. In the [course of its] bringing forth, the Yoginī, together with the Goddess, was immediately aroused. But, [the male] Vināyaka [and] the four Kula Siddhas [the four semidivine male founders of the clan in the four ages], who had been asking questions, became possessed, with all their hair standing on end, and flowers [used in clan initiation rites] in their hands. Awakened, they fell to the ground, stiff as rods, speaking in tongues.[53]

What is being described here is the prototype of a consecration rite through which humans are initiated into the divine family or clan of the Goddess and divine Mothers or Yoginīs themselves. Here, the male adept entered into a trance in which the possessing power of the deity caused his hand to cast a flower into a mandala enthroning these goddesses. The segment into which the flower fell revealed that Yoginī with whom he had an affinity. This established a link between him and the human Yoginīs, for they belonged to the same families as the divine Mothers themselves.[54]

In the mythic past of this KJñN narrative, the first initiates to receive the Kaula gnosis were members of the Yoginī clans as well as the four founders of the Siddha clans. It is from these that all the Kaula practitioners are descended and linked through the ritual transmission of the clan gnosis (*kaula-jñāna*). Six chapters later, this narrative seems to pick up where it left off: "Hearing Bhairava's speech, all of those [Siddhas] who had . . . transcended the Kula state of mind, had goose bumps and hair standing on end . . . delighted in mind, they all fell stiff to the ground."[55] The Goddess then compares the universe to a great spreading tree of ignorance, which has "today been felled by you, O Lord,"[56] and continues, stating that this teaching was "extracted upward" (*samuddhṛtam*) and is now found in every one of the Yoginīs' lodges in Kāmākhyā. "That which was in the condition of the Fish-Belly— the great [textual] teaching (*mahāśāstra*) that was brought down at Moon Island, O Mistress—is *sung* in Kāmākhyā."[57]

Several data relevant to the early history of the Kaula may be elicited from this early source. First, there is the person of Kārttikeya. This deity, considered to be a son of Śiva and the Goddess, was, in a number of early Kaula sources, a figure to whom Śiva transmitted several teachings,[58] or at least an important intermediary in the transmission of that teaching.[59] However, as one moves forward through the history of the early Kaula sects and schools, one witnesses a gradual phasing out of male deities like Kārttikeya in this role, in favor of the Goddess. This trend is brought to its logical conclusion in developments within the Kashmir-based Kālī-Krama (or Krama Kaula), in which Śiva disappears entirely and Kālī stands at the heart of a circle of twelve Kālīs and sixty-four Yoginīs.[60] Here, we should recall that in the same sixteenth chapter of the KJñN, Śiva describes the transmission of the Kaula gnosis to "Kālikā, known as the Yoginī . . . [who] is my equal."[61]

The esoteric meanings of the terms "Moon Island," the "Place Called Love," and "Fish-Belly" need also to be elucidated. The first two are endpoints of the subtle body of yogic practice. Moon Island is the cranial vault, the abode of the solitary Śiva, at which human sexual fluids become fully sublimated into the nectar of immortality, and at which mundane human consciousness is fully sublimated to god-consciousness. Both Love's Body (Kāmarūpa) and the Place Called Love (Kāmākhyā) signify the vulva, the abode of the Goddess, a center of transformative sexual energy, also identified as the locus of the subtle "mouth of the Yoginī."[62] In slightly later Kubjikā traditions, the cosmic vulva of the Goddess, called the "fourfold mound" (*catuṣpīṭha*), becomes situated *above* Moon Island, at the *dvādaśānta*, the "End of the Twelve," a point twelve finger-breadths above the fontanel. In these traditions the Goddess's sexual energy *descends* into the yogic body at Moon Island.[63] Although it is located outside the physical body, it is nonetheless within the subtle body.

Fish-Belly is a term that connotes the alternating movements of cosmic expansion and contraction in yogic practice, the transformation of consciousness, and the physiology of sexual orgasm.[64] Here, it may be that the image of a fish's swim bladder, which expands and contracts like a bellows, aided the Kaula theoreticians in conceptualizing the Yoginīs' upward extraction of the Kaula gnosis: they did so by upward suction through their nether mouths. The same dynamic would also have been responsible for their power of flight: we will return to this question in chapter 7.[65]

By virtue of their femininity and female organ, the Yoginīs were natural conduits for the transmission of something that was missing or lost from the earlier male-specific Kula gnosis, which previously had to be transmitted textually. This natural, sustained quality of a woman's flow is alluded to in the *Kāma Sūtra* of Vatsyāyana[66] as well as a number of Tantric and hathayogic sources.[67] According to the TĀ, women are "soaked in an excess of Clan Fluid" with the "Śakti [being] one whose central space is wide open." In his commentary on this latter verse, Jayaratha quotes an unknown source that states that a woman obtains in a single day the supernatural enjoyment a male practitioner procures after a full year of uninterrupted observance.[68] The twelfth- to thirteenth-century *Akulavīratanta* of Mīnasahajānanda echoes Jayaratha: "That which is difficult to obtain for the gods and Siddhas is easy of access (*sugocaram*) to the Yoginīs." Elsewhere, Bāul traditions view the woman to be "perfected of herself" (*svayaṇ siddhā*), naturally perfected without having to do the practice (*sādhanā*).[69] So it is that in this KJñN passage, the female Yoginī and the Goddess are immediately "aroused" by the great teaching, which is sung in every one of their lodges in the Place Called Love. In contrast, Moon Island is identified with the cranial vault, the solitary abode of the male Śiva-Bhairava, a repository of refined semen, of "seminal teachings" in the form of texts. The Kaula, of which Matsyendra was the founder, is a new synthesis of the old all-male Kula or Siddha Kaula and the all-female Yoginī Kaula in which male textuality is transmuted into or complemented by female orality.[70]

On a practical level, as anyone who has worked in manuscript archives in India knows, mice are notorious for eating through manuscripts. Texts do not have the same staying power as do orally transmitted teachings. Yet we also know that oral transmission has been, since the time of the Vedas, a male affair, transmitted from male guru or father to male disciple. The orality of the Yoginīs is of another order: they "sing" the Kaula gnosis in the Place Called Love. Nonetheless, the KJñN is a text, a text that cites its sources. In its twenty-first chapter, no less than nine "clan scriptures" are named, and it is noteworthy that two titles—the *Kulasāgara* ("Clan Ocean") and the *Kulogha* ("Clan Stream")—denote the fluid emphasis of the Kaula traditions, an emphasis reflected in other Kaula and Tantric titles, such as the *Kulārṇava Tantra* ("Tantra of the Clan Flood") and the *Mantramahodadhi* ("Great Ocean of Mantras").[71]

A number of male/female oppositions emerge out of this mythic narrative:

Male	*Female*
Bhairava and Kārttikeya	Bhairava and the Goddess
male Siddhas	female Yoginīs
questioning/possession	immediate arousal
cranial vault (Moon Island)	vulva (Kāmarūpa/Kāmākhyā)
inferior, lost teaching	superior, essence of lost teaching
swallowed at Moon Island	sung at the Place Called Love
textuality	orality

4. Sexually Transmitted Messages in Kaula and Tantric Initiation and Rites

At the conclusion of this myth, then, it is once again the nether mouth of the Yoginī, her vulva, that transmits the Kaula gnosis in an initiation ritual. It is this contribution on the part of the Yoginī Kaula that marks the watershed between the earlier Kula and later Kaula in the history of medieval Hinduism, with the gnosis that is the subject of the *Kaula-jñāna-nirṇaya*, the "Bringing Forth of the Kaula Gnosis," being brought forth through the nether mouth of the Yoginī. Late Tantric and Tantraśāstra traditions stress the transmission of the Tantric gnosis by word of mouth, "from ear to ear" in the Sanskrit parlance, "according to the succession of deities, Siddhas, and humans."[72] In the KJñN and other early Kaula sources, however, it is not only from "ear to ear," but also from "mouth to mouth" (*vaktrādvaktram*)[73] that this gnosis is transmitted. When the transmission is mouth to mouth, the ambiguity of the term "mouth" once again arises. A number of iconographic representations of *rajapāna* from the four corners of the Indian subcontinent support a reading of "mouth" as vulva. In Tantric worship of the vulva (*yonipūjā*),[74] the "primal sacrifice" (*ādiyāga*)[75]— one of the six types of "clan sacrifice" (*kulayāga*)[76]— and Tantric initiation, we find repeated descriptions of the transmission of sexual fluids from the mouths (both upper and nether) of a Yoginī into the mouth of a male practitioner. In sculptural representations of the worship of the vulva, which are frequent in the medieval period in India and Nepal, we see male practitioners crouching beneath the vulva of a female figure, in order to catch her sexual or menstrual discharge in their mouths (fig. 4.c).[77] In addition, the most powerful yantras are those drawn with the "ink" of this female discharge.[78] Two rituals described in the eighteenth

Figure 4.c. Initiate collecting sexual fluids of Tantric master and Dūtī consort. Painted wooden sculpture on roof-support strut of Paśupati-Yakṣeśvara temple, Bhaktapur, Nepal, 1460 C.E. Photograph courtesy of Sthanesvar Timilsina.

chapter of the KJñN highlight mouth-to-mouth practices. The first of these is a description of the Kaula consecration ritual (*abhiṣeka*):

> One should fill [a vessel] with blood together with an equal amount of semen, as well as with the *kuṇḍagolaka* secretion. This is combined with honey and clarified butter. [Menstrual] blood, a woman's nectar (*vāmāmṛtam*),[79] [and] semen are mixed with alcohol by the brahmin practitioner. It is [also] mixed with [the essence of] the *buka* flower and the [fermented] extract of the *kṛṣṇa* flower. That great-souled one who is accompanied by his female consort[80] [thereby realizes] a state of intoxicated bliss. . . . Having worshiped that [mixture], which is placed in a conch shell or in a pot, in proper sequence, O Goddess, the Master (*ācārya*) of one who is resolute in his devotion [i.e., the initiate who is being consecrated] . . . [should proceed as follows]: cannabis, and all of the other consciousness-altering plants . . . should be wrapped in red cloth together with the five precious gemstones. [These are accompanied by a food offering of] molasses, milk, yogurt, liquor, and sugarcane juice. He should distribute[81] [these], in sequence, into that which gives sweetness and that which eats babies [i.e., the mouth of the female consort in this rite, the Yoginī], into one mouth [that of the initiate] after the other [that of the Yoginī]. . . . Together with a prostitute or a maiden, or likewise with his own hands, the preceptor should place "that which is to be raised into the head" [i.e., sexual fluid] [into the mouth of the initiate]. Thereafter, he [the initiate] becomes a yogin.[82]

Immediately following the consecration ritual, the KJñN describes "another offering" (*punas tu yajanam*) in the following terms:

> One should effect that auspicious sequential worship with [the offerings made] in conjunction with the sixty-four-fold sequence. The high-minded Master, adorned with multicolored regalia, [worships] with celestial aromatics and flowers. Once he has brought together all the requisite materials [for the worship] of the Yoginīs, Siddhas, and Vīras, he becomes the darling of the Mothers. He should fully sate [them] with liquor, flesh, all types of food,[83] clarified butter, sugar candy, ground sugar, etc. . . . Offering one measure [of this mixture] to the guru, one [effects] the worship of the guru, separately. Then, having performed the worship of the Vīras, one should gratify [them] with that [offering],[84] again and again. The wise initiate should consume the offering: one should not allow it to be given to pledges.[85] He who wishes to partake of *siddhis*, especially, [should distribute the offering] from mouth to mouth, as [one would do] to one's equals. In the case of a common vessel shared

> by all, [one should distribute the offering] singly, from a conch shell into the mouth.[86]

These elliptical descriptions from the KJñN may be enhanced by juxtaposing them to a series of consecrations found in early Tantric Buddhist sources. In the *Caṇḍamahāroṣaṇa Tantra*, the "Secret Consecration" (*guhyābhiṣeka*), the second in a set of three consecration rituals, is described in the following terms:

> . . . The teacher . . . should worship himself with intoxicants, meats, etc., and having satisfied Wisdom (Prajñā, his female consort), being in her embrace, he should place the resulting white and red on a leaf, shaped into a funnel, etc. Then, having summoned the student, he should take that substance with his ring finger and thumb, and write the letters "Hūṃ phaṭ!" on the student's tongue. . . .[87]

Similar descriptions are found in the early *Hevajra Tantra* (1.10.5–7, 2.3.13–14) as well as a significant number of later Buddhist sources on the Secret Consecration in Highest Yoga Tantra (*anuttarayoga*) traditions. Taken together, these constitute clear proof that, as in the Hindu case, Buddhist "Tantric sex" originally involved the shedding and consumption of sexual fluids in initiation and other ritual contexts.[88] In New Age Tantra, it is a male's ability to bring his female partner to sustained, abundant orgasm, without himself shedding his seed, that is stressed, with reference to an erroneous paradigm that Buddhist "Tantric sex" always remained unconsummated, that is, that it ended in coitus interruptus and an ecstatic mystical experience for both partners.[89] While such does become the rule in later conformist Buddhist Tantric sources, it was not the original practice,[90] and, once again, the New Age paradigms are shown to be without historical foundation.

Like the consecration rituals, the *yonipūjā*, "Veneration of the Vulva,"[91] a ritual described in a multitude of Tantric texts and frequently represented in Tantric art (fig. 4.d), has for its final end the consumption of the *yonitattva*, the female discharge of the Tantric consort.[92] This is of a piece with mainstream Hindu worship rituals, in which the deity, having been gratified with various sorts of offerings, returns the offering in the form of his or her *prasāda*, their "edible grace." In this role the Yoginī serves as a conduit, through initiation and ritual, for the transmission of the clan essence that uninitiated males intrinsically lack: there is a literal fluid flow from the "mouth" of the supreme deity, either Śiva or the Goddess (who even in her role as transmitter of mantras in "high" Hindu Tantra is termed *bhinnayoni*, "she whose vulva is open"), to a Śakti, a lower female emanate of herself,

Figure 4.d. Yonipūjā, "Veneration of the Vulva," detail from the image of the "Kāmadā" Yoginī, Bheraghat Yoginī temple, ca. 1000 C.E., Jabalpur District, Madhya Pradesh. Photograph by David Gordon White.

to a guru and his Yoginī or Dūtī ("Female Messenger") consort, and thence to a male Siddha initiate. This is stated explicitly in Jayaratha's commentary to TĀ 1.16. Quoting an unidentified source that states that "gnosis is to be cast into a woman's mouth and then taken out of her mouth," he goes on to say that in the *kula prakriyā*, the secret clan rites, the disciple receives the gnosis from the lineage (*āmnāya*), via the mouth of the Dūtī, and by means of the unified emission (*samaskandatayā*) of the guru and the Dūtī. He repeats the same aphorism concerning gnosis in the mouth of a woman in his commentary on TĀ 29.122, giving further explanation in his rich commentary to Abhinavagupta's account of the *ādiyāga*. Abhinavagupta's discussion of oral transmission recalls the KJñN's mythic treatment of the bringing down of the Kaula gnosis:

> It is said in the treatises that the Śakti is one whose central space is wide open (fig. 4.e). The guru should cause the "Clan Object" (*kulārtham*) to pass to her alone; and she should cause it pass into males through her orifice, according to the aforementioned sequence. The venerable Kalaṭanātha has declared a woman to be soaked in an excess of Clan Fluid

Figure 4.e. Female sexual display, Basantpuri temple, Kathmandu, seventeenth century. Photograph by David Gordon White.

> (*sadbhāva*). . . . This, her principal cakra, has been called the "mouth of the Yoginī"[93] by the Lord, because it is there that this transmission (*sampradāya*) [takes place], and from there that gnosis is obtained. That "gnosis" which was "discoursed" cannot be committed to writing, and is said, quite appropriately, to be passed from mouth to mouth. The mouth is the principal cakra. How could consciousness itself be committed to writing? . . . Those [men] who wish to obtain supernatural enjoyments should therefore eat the combined sexual emission,[94] and worship with it alone. . . . Furthermore, that emission goes from the principal mouth [of the Yoginī], out of which it was "discoursed" to the mouth [of the male practitioner] and back again.[95]

This long passage, together with Jayaratha's *viveka* that follows, is a most precious source of data on the "mouth-to-mouth" transmissions that lay at the heart of Kaula practice.[96]

> It is said: "The best of elixirs is an excellent fluid deposited within one's own body. . . ." [It] is known as "kula." . . . It is said: "By simply eating it, a man becomes immortal and praised as 'Śiva.' . . . Elsewhere, the man who continuously eats [this fluid] in its mixed form becomes . . . the darling of the Yoginīs. . . ." It is said in all the teachings that non-aging and immortality are afforded through the primary mouth, that is, the mouth of the Yoginī [and that] it is passed back and forth, from mouth to mouth. Here, this means: from the mouth of the Yoginī into one's own mouth, then into the mouth of the Śakti,[97] then into one's own mouth. Thereupon, the guru should cast it into the offertory bowl, etc. It is said: "Taking with one's mouth the 'ball' (*golaka*) of that which will have oozed out [i.e., male semen] and the 'basin' (*kuṇḍa*) [i.e., female discharge] located there at the level of the loins; [taking] that great fluid (*mahādravyam*) at the level of the loins, [one should transmit it] to the mouth [of one's consort]. Causing it to pass back to one's own mouth, one should fill the [offertory] vessel with that. . . . Having mixed together the great fluid (*mahārasa*) by passing it from mouth to mouth, one should feed the circle . . . of the [female?] deities and [male] Virile Heroes with it." It is said: "Having aroused the Dūtī, he whose [own] desire has [also] been quickened should eat the accumulation of fluid (*dravyanicayam*) that has come forth [from them], back and forth [with her]."[98]

What is being described here is the dynamic of the lower end of the flow chart of the Kaula gnosis, in the form of the clan fluid emitted by the guru and his consort in sexual intercourse, and consumed by the initiate. It is this that makes the latter a member of the clan, of the family of Śiva, the

Goddess, and the Yoginīs, Dūtīs, and Siddha teachers through whom that clan fluid flows. This clan genealogy, this flow chart, has been mapped in the form of the Siddha Cakra,[99] which is described by Abhinavagupta in the verses immediately following his presentation of the *ādiyāga*.[100] At the center of this mandala are the supreme deity Bhairava and Kuleśvarī ("Our Lady of the Clan"), surrounded by the eight Mothers and other lower emanates of the central pair. Working downward and outward from this center—from the eternal into the historical present, as it were— one eventually comes, in the eastern quadrant, to the four mythical Siddha founders of the clan tradition together with their Dūtīs, and, lastly, the offspring of these couples and their Dūtīs. In the present Kali age, these are Macchanda and his consort Kuṅkuṇāmbā, the "Mother of Koṅkaṇa," an apparent reference to the coastal strip of modern-day Maharashtra, Goa, and Karnataka.[101] Of their sons, the twelve "princes" (*rājaputras*), six are noncelibate (*adhoretas*), and therefore specially revered as qualified (*sādhikāra*) to transmit the Kaula cult. They are revered as the founders of the six initiatory Kaula lineages (*ovallis*). At the time of consecration, an initiand enters into one of these lineages and receives a name whose second part indicates this clan affiliation.[102] These lineages, Jayaratha tells us in his commentary, constitute the "flow of gnosis" (*jñāna-pravāha*);[103] and "those who are conversant in the secret signs and meeting places of the various lineages, if they should be desirous of obtaining supernatural enjoyments, may range among the mounds (*pīṭhas*). After a short time, they will receive that which is to be obtained from the mouth of the Yoginī."[104]

With this, we find ourselves at the interface between the divine hierarchy and human practice, through which male Kaula practitioners gain access to the powers enjoyed by the denizens of that same hierarchy. In fact, the semidivine Kaula "princes" and their consorts continue to participate in the Kaula rites. How they do so is explained by the *Kālīkula Tantra* (quoted by Abhinavagupta in the TĀ): these disembodied beings spontaneously sport with one another in the bodies of human Kaula practitioners, male and female.[105] That is, the human partners in these sexual rituals are in fact inhabited, possessed by the semidivine Siddhas and Yoginīs themselves. This follows the logic of the demonological traditions we reviewed in chapter 2, in which all manner of male and female Seizers inhabited the bodies of persons open to penetration by them, and the *Caraka Saṃhitā* in fact evokes the case of possession by Siddhas in its *bhūtavidyā* section.[106] This appears to imply that the Kaula practitioners were without free will in such matters, that they would have been the unwitting vessels for these superhuman beings. Yet the verses that follow in this TĀ passage clearly indicate that the Siddhas and Yoginīs had to be actively sought out, and constitute a road map of sorts to lead the aspiring male practitioner to the right place, the right time, and the right consort.[107] As if to emphasize her transmissive role in these interactions, the Kaula consort is termed, precisely, the Dūtī, the "Female Messenger,"[108] a role emphasized by Jayaratha, who also terms *ādiyāga* the "Female Messenger Practice."[109]

Now, Jeffrey Masson and M. V. Patwardhan have argued that Abhinavagupta's use of the term *dūtī* is one that he derived from love poetry and incorporated into his philosophy of aesthetics: in Indian love poetry and drama, every heroine has her Dūtī, her "go-between," and the goal of his aestheticized account of Kaula practice was the same as that of drama: to reach a state of perfect equanimity and blissful repose.[110] But this does not justify or explain the use of the term in Kaula parlance. On the one hand, the term *dūtī* is one that was employed in Kaula sources well before Abhinavagupta's aestheticizing synthesis. On the other hand, the Kaula Dūtī, if she is a female messenger, a go-between, is a mute one. Given the fact that the Kaula sources at no time describe the Female Messenger as speaking, the question that arises is: What is the Female Messenger transmitting?[111]

When Marshall McLuhan stated that "the medium is the message," he was referring to television and other technologies. When the Kaula practitioners made essentially the same statement through their use of the term *dūtī*, their medium-*cum*-message was, instead, sexual fluid. In worship, initiation, and ritual practices involving the transmission of the clan essence from the Absolute to male practitioners through the conduit of the upper and nether mouths of the Goddess and the Yoginīs or Dūtīs, it was this fluid essence, which manifested in the form of sexual fluids, that made these practitioners part of a clan or family (*kula*). Here, the fluid medium itself was the message that, once internalized, transformed the very being of the male practitioner, injecting him with the fluid stuff of the divine, transmitted through the Yoginīs, in whom it naturally flowed.[112]

In the early Kaula transmission of tradition, the female consort, by virtue of the natural presence of the clan nectar in her menstrual or sexual emissions, was vital to aspiring male practitioners who wished to be "inseminated" or "insanguinated" with fluid gnosis, and thereby become enlightened members of the clan family (*kula*). Absorption of the clan fluid was effected through the drinking of such emissions as described, or through the practice of *vajrolī mudrā*, urethral suction. In both cases the male partner gained what he was lacking—the fluid gnosis naturally present in the Dūtī or Yoginī—while the female partner gained raw materials necessary for her refinement of the high energy fuel that powered her flight, a subject to which we will return in chapter 7.

5. The "Flowery" Mouth of the Yoginī

The identification of the body of a woman (or a goddess) with a flower or tree, her anatomy with plant and flower anatomy, human reproduction with plant reproduction, and female sexual emissions with plant or flower essences are developed at every level in these traditions. On the broadest level, the KSS, whenever it refers to Vindhyavāsinī, the "Goddess Who Dwells in the Vindhya Mountains," describes her in terms of her abode, which is an extension of herself: a vast forest teeming with plant and animal life, a place of savage energy, at once alluring and terrifying, nurturing and deadly to the men who would attempt to penetrate it; as we have already noted, a similar earlier description is found in the *Harivaṃśa*.[113] The pre-tenth-century *Netra Tantra* (12.11–12) states that at the time of universal dissolution, the Mothers hold the world inside of themselves, in the form of seeds that they will then plant again, in order that it might reappear.[114] In a discussion of ritual substitutes "for the twice-born and persons of discriminating minds," the KĀN prescribes the combination of pollens from two flowers, of which the anatomy of one, the *aparā*, resembles the female yoni. The *kuṇḍagolaka* offering is replaced here by sprinkling the pollen from the mouth of the *hayāri* (*Nerium odorum*) flower, identified with Sadāśiva, onto the mouth of the *aparā* flower.[115] The name of this "female" flower evokes the Vedic husband-finding ritual of the maiden Apālā, who transmits the soma she has chewed, through a kiss, to the god Indra, following which they engage in sexual intercourse.[116] In Vedic descriptions of the soma ritual, the juice of this plant, reddish in color, is mixed with white milk to form the fluid offered and drunk in the sacrifice.

The lotus is the flower most intimately identified with feminine beauty and femininity *tout court*. In Indian treatises on erotics (*kāmaśāstra*), the ideal lover is termed "Lotus Woman" (*padminī*). And whereas beautiful women and men may be described as lotus-faced, lotus-eyed, or lotus-mouthed, only a woman may be called "lotus-vulva-ed." Everywhere in the Tantric literature, the term *padma* is employed in the sense of "vulva," as in the case of the Lotus Maiden of Buddhist Tantra. A very well-known image bringing both feminine "lotus mouths" together is a circa eighth-century sculpture from Saṅgameśvara (Andhra Pradesh) of a *nagnakabandhā*, that is, a naked headless female figure, in prone position (perhaps that of childbirth), and with prominently displayed genitalia, but whose head has been replaced by a lotus flower. In its original worship context, the image was laid horizontally, and libations poured over the body were carried away by a channel and a spout.[117] Here again, it is the "mouth" of the female consort that becomes the transfer mechanism for the germ plasm of the divine. And, once again, we can imagine that the fluids that flowed over her lotus face and open yoni were later consumed as this figure's *prasāda*, her "edible grace."

In her commentary on the TĀ's exposition of the *kulayāga*, Lilian Silburn evokes a Kashmiri marriage custom in which a piece of food is passed from the mouth of the groom into that of the bride, in a practice analogous to those involving betel, discussed in the last chapter.[118] In the third act of the eleventh-century *Prabodhacandrodaya* (PC) of Kṛṣṇamiśra, an exchange of betel, from mouth to mouth, is preceded by another type of oral transmission. The passage is a rich one inasmuch as it compares the essence of another plant, the *bakula* (*Mimusops elengi*) flower, with both alcohol and the fluids that flow from the "mouth" of a Kāpālinī, a female Kāpālika. While the metaphor is a stock one in Indian literature—the *bakula*, whose extremely fragrant tiny white flowers appear at night during the months of the hot season, is said to put forth blossoms when sprinkled with nectar from the mouth of beautiful women[119]—it appears to take on an additional layer of meaning here. The scene in question opens with a Buddhist mendicant asking the question "How shall I drink the alcohol left over by the Kāpālika?" The Kāpālika then turns to his consort, allegorically named "Faith, Daughter of Rajas," in this play, and says in an aside, "Faith . . . they think that this alcohol which has come in contact with my mouth is impure. Therefore you purify it with the liquor of your mouth and then take it to them; for even the holy people say that 'the mouth of a woman is always pure.'" The Kāpālinī then brings the liquor pot and gives over the remains of it. The mendicant then says a mouthful:

> Great is the favor (takes the vessel and drinks from it). Ah, the beauty of alcohol! How many times have we drunk alcohol with prostitutes, alcohol that is made sweet with the fragrance of the fully opened *bakula* blossoms and that is left over after coming in contact with the mouth of beautiful-faced women. We think that the gods crave for nectar (only) because they do not get the alcohol that has been made fragrant with the nectar of the mouth of the Kāpālinī.

A Jain renouncer then enters the conversation: "O mendicant! Do not drink the whole thing. Keep some alcohol which is left over from the mouth of the Kāpālinī. (After drinking) Ah! the sweetness of the alcohol; what taste, what smell, what fragrance! By falling into the teachings of the Arhata, I have been deceived for a long time from drinking this kind of alcohol." The mendicant, laughing, says, "This poor man is very much out of his senses, through the liquor which he is not used to drinking. Therefore, let his drunkenness be removed." To which the Kāpālika replies, "Let it be so," as he gives the chewed betel leaf from his mouth to the Jain. The Jain, instantly detoxed, asks whether "women and men possess the power of attracting as much as this liquor of yours?"[120] The ambiguity of the terms denoting betel, *bakula*, and alcohol are heightened by that of the term "mouth" in this passage. Is this simply a pot of liquor that has touched the lips of a Kāpālika woman or prostitute that is being evoked? Why, then, does the Jain refer to it as "this kind of alcohol" (*īdiseṇa sulālaseṇa*)? Once again, it is the female consort's vulva, her "nether mouth," that is the referent here, with the alcohol, *bakula*, and betel as multiple evocations of her menstrual or sexual emission.

This reading is supported by a passage from the KĀN that states: "The one going to [having intercourse with] a woman should drink the nectar of her tongue in the mouth. The clan liquor (*kulamadyam*) once collected is perfected with the mantra of Varuṇa. . . . Purified with [this], the king of mantras, he should at every moment drink the beverage churned out by the *śakti*'s tongue."[121] The term "tongue" would appear to correspond, here as well, to a portion of the female anatomy, of a woman's nether mouth, with the beverage being churned out by it her female discharge. These sorts of analogies between human and plant anatomy and, in the former case, between a woman's upper and nether mouths are frequent in the mythology of wild, sexually powerful goddesses. In the Keralan mythology, temple art, and religious performance depicting Bhadrakālī's slaying of the "Blood-Seed" demon Dārika, the goddess's *female* vehicle and minion, named Vetālam, is portrayed as a hideous haggard old woman whose pendulous tongue hangs down precisely to the level of her vulva. It is this tongue that feeds on and is coated and dripping with the blood of the Goddess's demonic rival.[122] These same bloodthirsty goddesses of Kerala demand the "blood-seed," the fruit- or flower-based liquor[123] of the toddy palm, which is intimately associated with the upper and nether mouths of powerful female beings. As Caldwell explains:

> The action of toddy-tapping has obvious parallels to human sexuality. Toddy drains the essential fluid from the tree through its flower bud, which is metaphorically associated with the female genitals in . . . [Keralan] puberty rite[s]. . . . The phallic appearance of the bud and obvious symbolic parallel of the tapping action to the production of semen from the penis, by heating and stimulating the exterior surface in order to draw the clear milky fluid from the rounded tip, is hard to miss. . . . Toddy is in a sense the *bījam*, the essential blood-seed of the coconut tree itself. It is not surprising that certain fierce goddesses and demonic spirits in village shrines demand the offering of toddy, as well as blood sacrifice and meat, to satiate their thirst.[124]

The mythology and symbolism of the goddess Kālī is particularly rich in images of the female tongue as a double for her sexual organ.[125] So, for example, an Oriyan myth relates that when the furious Kālī impaled herself on the penis of the sleeping Śiva, her tongue came out of her mouth as he penetrated her.[126] Here, again, I would maintain that it is not only the blood of demons or the red juices of *pān* or other plants that coats the tongue, cheeks, and chin of this dread goddess in her iconography: rather, or additionally, it is her own female discharge, provoked by the "oblation" offered her, that is being shown, flowing out of and around her "upper mouth." This imagery is particularly arresting in late-twentieth-century poster art of Kālī and Tārā (fig.4.f).

A similar mixing or matching of flower essences, sexual fluids, and liquor is enjoined in the Kaula consecration ritual described in KJñN 18.7–9, translated above.[127] In it, the compound *bukapuṣpa* may simply be read "flower of the *Agati grandiflora* plant" or as a code term for menstrual blood. This latter interpretation is supported by KJñN 11.33: "Flesh is the favorite [food] of the Śākinīs. Hear [now] the favorite of the Goddesses: *bukapuṣpa*, *śivāmbu* ('Śiva-Water'), blood, semen, and alcohol."[128] The same ambiguity is found here in the compound *kṛṣṇāsava*, which is mixed together with the essence of the *buka* flower, blood, semen, and alcohol. Derived from the verbal root *ā-su* ("press out"), *āsava* is the distillate or extract, the nectar or juice of a flower; however, in the *Śāntiśataka* of Bhartṛhari, the term refers to the "nectar or juice of the lips of a woman."[129] *Kṛṣṇāsava* would therefore either mean the extract of a black flower or the nectar of the lips of a dark-skinned woman.

A long passage of the KĀN presupposes the symbolic interplay of flower and vulva in its description of a series of types of Śaktis, which, while reminiscent of classifications of women by animal types as found in *kāmaśāstra* literature, is perhaps unique in its assignment of flower names to its maidens.[130]

> I will now speak of fluids (*dravyams*), [as classified] by types of Śaktis. She who is slim and long-haired is [called] "Perfumed Flower": the practitioner should, with pure mind, worship [her as] the Goddess, with saffron flowers and aromatics. With her "flowers," a man may, with great effort, obtain all that he desires. She who is tall, long-eyed, dark, and shameless is [called] "Perfumed Bilva Leaf." While engaged in sexual intercourse, etc., one should energetically worship the supreme Goddess with her "flowers." A maiden who is fair-limbed, having plump buttocks and pudgy hands, and who is mad with passion is called "Intoxicating Fragrance" (*madagandhā*). She [should be worshiped] with *khārjura* (*Phoenix sylvestris*) and *palāśa* (*Butea frondosa*) flowers.

Figure 4.f. Kālī and Tārā venerating Śiva as a *liṅgam*. Polychrome from Bengal, ca. 1995.

After a total of ten "flower types" have been described in this way, the passage concludes:

> Then, by taking the fluid of [all of] these women, one should fully purify that [i.e., each woman's fluid] with these very objects [flowers etc.], sequentially. Having worshiped with each of those "flowers," one shall gain all the supernatural powers. If [however] one were to worship the Goddess, without knowing this sequence [i.e., which woman's fluid corresponds to which "flower" type], all his offerings would become absolutely fruitless, like [an offering] without clarified butter.[131]

These classifications of Śakti types presuppose an identification between flowers, vulvas, and the exudations (recall that *rajas*, in addition to meaning "female discharge," also means "pollen" in Sanskrit) emitted from these two sorts of "mouths." Flowers are identified with the female organ in a significant number of Tantric works, both Hindu and Buddhist. The Hindu *Mantramahodadhi* of Mahīdhara, a 1588 C.E. work, describes a rite in which the practitioner worships the goddess while sitting on a corpse with flowers sprinkled with the practitioner's own semen.[132] More recently, David Knipe, when he participated in a Tantric *pañcamakāra* ritual in an underground crypt in Benares in the 1970s, was made to meditate on a mandala composed of red and white flowers while the leader of the group performed sexual intercourse in an adjacent cell.[133] Buddhist Tantric identifications of this sort have been treated at length by Miranda Shaw.[134] The *Cakrasaṃvara Tantra* instructs that "a skillful one worships the Yoginī's stainless lotus of light," while in the *Caṇḍamahāroṣaṇa Tantra,* the goddess Vajrayoginī instructs the male practitioner to

> Look at my three-petaled lotus,
> Its center adorned with a stamen.
> It is a Buddha paradise, adorned with a red Buddha,
> A cosmic mother who bestows
> Bliss and tranquility on the passionate.
> Abandon all conceptual thought and
> Unite with my reclining form;
> Place my feet on your shoulders and
> Look me up and down.
> Make the fully awakened scepter
> Enter the opening in the center of the lotus.
> Move a hundred, thousand, hundred thousand times
> In my three-petaled lotus
> Of swollen flesh.
> Placing one's scepter there, offer pleasure to her mind.

Wind, inner wind—my lotus is the unexcelled!
Aroused by the tip of the diamond scepter,
It is red like a *bandhūka* flower.[135]

The Hindu Kubjikā tradition is particularly rich in botanical identifications, in which that goddess's origins as a female Dryad, a Yakṣiṇī who has assumed the form of a tree or who dwells inside a tree are made explicit. In a long section of the *Manthānabhairava Tantra* entitled the "Great Description of Authority Over the Seats (of the Goddess)," Kubjikā's power is shown to flow through the transmission of her teachings, whose conduits are represented as living plants: trees, creepers, roots, and vines.[136] A number of later Kubjikā sources depict her as a tree with orange- or red-colored blossoms—either a tamarind (*ciñca*), a *kiṃśuka*, or a *kadamba*. This is not a recent development: recall here that the female Seizer Lohitāyanī is said, in the MBh, to reside in the *kadamba* tree.[137] Furthermore, the tree of these Kubjikā traditions is said to grow from the vulva of the Goddess's "command" (*ājñā*), specifically identified with the *kadamba*'s flower, which is perfectly spherical in shape, and whose color changes from white to red as it matures, reproducing, in a botanical mode, the *bindu* of the Goddess's sexual discharge.[138] The *kadamba* flower is also evoked in a passage from the *Siddhayogeśvarīmata*, in which the goddess Parā is to be visualized in the midst of a *kadamba* grove and wearing a necklace strung with gems having the "appearance of the globular *kadamba* (*kadambagolakākaraiḥ*), as she discharges streams of nectar from her "mouth" into the mouth of the practitioner.[139] As we have noted, the sixth current of the Kubjikā traditions is said to flow from the nether mouth of the Yoginī, called the *picuvaktra;* and here as well, the reference appears to be botanical: alone, the term *picu* means "cotton," but in compound, *picu-manda* or *picu-marda* refers to the same margosa tree as is identified with the goddess Śītalā throughout northern India.[140]

"Male" white milk and a "female" red flower were also prominent, in an analogous way, in the orthodox Śaiva ritual of *liṅgābhiṣeka,* the "aspersion of the *liṅgam*," in which I participated in the spring of 1999. Here, a group of brahmin priests chanted Vedic mantras whilst a stream of milky water was poured (by myself) over a *bāṇ-liṅgam* (a portable metal *liṅgam* set into a yoni) floating in a pool of the same milk, in a round shallow metal tray. The milky fluid flowing over the tip of the *liṅgam* was channeled via the sculpted groove representing the yoni so as to drip back into the basin, setting up interference patterns in the milky fluid that recalled for me the lines of a mandala or yantra. Floating together with the *bāṇ-liṅgam* at the center of the ensemble was a red flower, representing the Goddess. According to the priests performing the ritual, the purpose of pouring the milky fluid over the *liṅgam* was "to cool Śiva's head, which was heated up by yoga, ganja, and datura"—although another more sexualized interpretation would seem also to apply. And while the priests insisted that the entire configuration was in no way a yantra, the observations of Jan Gonda appear to be apposite here:

> Ancient and widespread ideas in connection with "initiation" and "consecration" (*abhiṣeka*) have here been embedded in the typically Śaiva pattern of Hinduism and are put into practice in the framework of Hindu ritual requiring different *kuṇḍas* (receptacles for fire [but also fluids]) and *maṇḍalas*. . . .[141]

Chapter 5

THE POWER OF THE YOGINĪ:
Tantric Actors in South Asia

It has commonly been assumed that Hindu Tantra has been a marginal, "underground," even subversive tradition. It is nonetheless untrue that esotericism, mysticism, and secrecy—arguably hallmarks of Tantra—need necessarily imply that this body of religious practice has at all times been outside of the South Asian "mainstream." In fact, when one looks at the secular literature and art historical data of the medieval period, as well as at the religious landscape of Nepal, whose public and private religion have remained Tantric down to the present day, one finds that many if not most Tantric actors are not marginal, and that much Tantric practice is public. This is particularly true in cases where Tantra is the "religion of state" and the king the prime Tantric actor in the kingdom. Here, Tantra and Tantric practices become, in the words of Robert Levy, "advertised secrets."

1. Tantric Theories of Kingship: The Heart of the Mandala

Tantric actors in South Asia—who have included Virile Heroes, gurus, monks and nuns, yogins, sorcerers, witches, rulers, royal preceptors, royal chaplains, spirit-mediums, visionary bards, oracle priests, healers, and lay or householder practitioners—may be classified into three main groups: (1) Tantric specialists who have received initiation into a textual, teaching lineage and their generally elite clients; (2) Tantric specialists lacking formal initiation, whose training is effected through oral transmission (or divine possession) alone, and their generally nonelite clients; (3) householder or lay nonspecialists whose personal practice may be qualified as Tantric, but whose goal is liberation rather than supernatural enjoyments. While the third category is numerically the largest, lay or householder Tantric practice is generally "soft core,"[1] and will therefore not enter significantly into this discussion. Of course, there is overlap among these groups, with householder practitioners, for example, calling upon one or another type of specialist for teachings, guidance, and ritual expertise and mediation. The purview of the Tantric actor par excellence, the Tantric sovereign, covers all three of these categories. Himself a householder practitioner, he interacts with both elite and popular, "clerical" and "shamanic"[2] practitioners in his public life as a potentate and in his private life as his own person. Apart from the king of Nepal, there are no Hindu Tantric sovereigns remaining in the world, and it is for this reason, I would maintain, that most modern-day scholarly and popular accounts of Tantra have tended to view it either as little more than popular superstition or "sympathetic magic," on the one hand, or as a sublime theoretical edifice, on the other, without seeking to describe the relationship between these two types of practice and their respective practitioners.

A central element of Tantric theory and practice, the mandala is the mesocosmic template through which the Tantric practitioner transacts with and appropriates the myriad energies that course through every level of the cosmos. The Kāmakalā, Saṃvarta, and Śrīcakra, already mentioned, are but three among a galaxy of Tantric mandalas that are so many graphic representations of the universe as a clan (*kula*) of interrelated beings, as an "embodied cosmos." Here, it is important to note that the mandala was, in its origins, directly related to royal power. Indeed, "mandala" was simply a term for an administrative unit or county in ancient India[3] and has continued to bear that meaning since at least the sixth century C.E. in the expression "Nepāla-Maṇḍala" for the Kathmandu Valley and its surrounding territory.[4]

The concept of the king as *cakravartin*—as both he who turns (*vartayati*) the wheel (*cakra*) of his kingdom or empire from its center and he whose chariot wheel has rolled around its perimeter without obstruction—is one that goes back to the late Vedic period. Central to this construction of kingship is the notion that the king, standing at the center of his kingdom (from which he also rules over the periphery), mirrors the godhead at the center of its realm, its divine or celestial kingdom. However, whereas the godhead's supermundane realm is unchanging and eternal, the terrestrial ruler's kingdom is made so through the "utopia" of the mandala. As such, the idealized "constructed kingdom" of the mandala is the mesocosmic template between real landscapes, both geographical and political, and the heavenly kingdom of the godhead, with the person of the king as god on earth constituting the idealized microcosm. Ruling from his capital at the conceptual center of the universe, the king is strategically located at the pivot of the prime channel of communication between upper and lower worlds—between the human, the divine, and the demonic—which he keeps "open" through the mediation of his religious specialists.[5]

In South Asia the practice of the mandala is tantamount to the millenarian royal conquest of the four directions (*digvijaya*), which, beginning with a fire sacrifice (*homa*), has the king process through the cardinal compass points, around the theoretical perimeter of his realm, before returning to his point of origin, which has now been transformed into his royal capital and center of the universe.[6] This last detail is an important one, because it highlights the king's *dual* role as pivot between heaven and earth. On the one hand, he is the microcosmic godhead incarnate, ruling from the center; yet on the other, he is the mundane representative of Everyman, struggling against a myriad of hostile forces that threaten him from the periphery. This latter role is brought to the fore in the Tantric ceremonial of Nepal, in which the ritual performances that reenact the goddess Durgā's victory over the enemies of the gods mobilize every stratum of society, down to the lowly Poḍe Sweepers.[7]

It is here that, in terms of the practice of the mandala and of Tantric practice in general, the king constitutes the link that binds together elite and nonelite practitioners and traditions. In reality, the king's hold on the mandala of his realm has often been more utopian than real. Conversely, given the intrinsically utopian (belonging to "no-place") nature of the mandala, Tantric practitioners have often flourished, or at least survived, in situations of political anarchy or oppression; that is, in the absence of a religiously sanctioned ruler. In this latter case, religious power, when forced to operate on a clandestine level, controls the invisible forces of the universe from the hidden "center" of the *tāntrika*'s "peripheral" shrine, lodge, or forest. It is not for nothing that in India the abbot of a powerful monastery or leader of a religious order continues to be addressed, down to the present day, as *guru-rāja*, "preceptor-king." In this sense, the Tantric practitioner is a crypto-potentate, transacting like a king with the boundless energy of the godhead that flows from the elevated center of his worship mandala. Here, then, we see that the utopia of the Tantric mandala may serve both to ground legitimate royal authority and power when the king is a Tantric practitioner, as well as to subvert illegitimate power or create a covert nexus of power when the wrong king or no king is on the throne.

2. Kings and Goddesses

The widely advertised secret practices prescribed and described in sacred and secular literature need not necessarily have taken place far from political centers of power or social centers of human activity. So, for example, a nineteenth-century tract from Gujarat, likely the work of a member of the reformist Vaiṣṇava Swāmīnārāyaṇ movement—a tract whose expressed purpose was to unmask the excesses of Tantric practice—asserts that "every city has one-fourth part of its population as Śāktas (i.e., *tāntrikas*)—and the ceremonies are performed very secretly in the middle of the night; if a king be a supporter, they are also observed publicly."[8] As I will show in the final sections of this chapter, Tantric dissimulation may have played a part in public denials of not particularly secret practices that would have been observed by a broad swath of the population.

What happens when, as appears to have been the case in a number of South Asian kingdoms since the medieval period, a king becomes a Kaula practitioner? What impact does his Kaulism have on the nature of both public and secret ritual? What are the sociopolitical conditions that might foster or support a Kaula royal cultus—what one could call a "Kaula polity"? In the opening chapter of this book, I suggested that "classical" *bhakti* in some way corresponded to the religious productions of what Harald Tambs-Lyche has termed "urban society"[9] in South Asia—the brahmin intelligentsia, a certain Indian aristocracy, and the merchant classes. A—Tantric or Kaula—alternative appears to have emerged out of a seventh- to twelfth-century "ruralization of the ruling class," during which the ruling aristocracy of north India severed or reduced its socioeconomic ties with "urban society" in favor of more direct links with farmers and pastoralists.[10] As a means to reinforcing these socioeconomic links with agrarian society—to the land, their allies, and their subjects—these rulers embraced the cults of rural tutelary deities. For the Rajput society of western India that is Tambs-Lyche's focus, this meant an eschewing of the Sanskritized cult of the high Hindu god Śiva in favor of close ties with the *kuladevīs*, the clan goddesses of the land, considered to be the source of all life in an agrarian society.[11] This trend enters into the political theory of the 1131 C.E. *Mānasollāsa*—an encyclopedia attributed to the Cāḷukyan ruler Someśvara III, whose kingdom comprised much of the Deccan plateau—which adds *śakti*, as the eighth element comprising a kingdom, to the standard list of seven found in the *Arthaśāstra* of Kauṭilya. According to this source, a king's *śakti*, which takes the form of his "command" (*ājñā*), controls the seven other elements.[12]

I believe it can be shown that the central Indian kingdoms that were the settings for the documented origins of the Kaula, as well as the post-fifteenth-century Kathmandu Valley kingdoms that revived Kaula practice,[13] display the same ruralization pattern as that found in Tambs-Lyche's Rajput contexts. It is not my intention here to make the reductionist argument that South Asian agrarian political economies that disfavor urban elites have stood at the origin of the various "Kaula polities"; yet I would suggest that there may be an elective affinity between these socioeconomic, political, and religious formations, just as there appears to have been between urban society and classical Hindu devotionalism.

Of greater moment for our concerns is the wealth of empirical historical data pointing to the clear emergence of a public cultus of powerful martial goddesses among the ruling houses of South Asia in the early medieval period. These tutelary goddesses, which were often identified with the great Goddess Durgā or with a group of Mother goddesses—the Seven Mothers, the Nine Durgās,[14] and so on—were at bottom royal *kuladevīs*, goddesses of land and clan that cemented alliances between ruling families (fig. 5.a).[15] This is not to say that the high gods of Hinduism disappeared from the royal cultus in this period: it is in the seventh and eighth centuries precisely that, with the appearance of the first great monumental temples in India, we see the great male gods of Hinduism being sculpturally depicted with the features of the kings who were their devotees.[16] But this identification of king with high god had a limited place in the royal cultus. Viṣṇu (as Kṛṣṇa, Narasiṃha, Jagannātha, and later Rāma) as well as Śiva remained at the sacred center precisely in order to afford the king who identified with these high gods a modicum of transcendence over the alliances and ties to the land that his tutelary goddesses provided.[17] But it was the latter group that ratified and energized the pragmatic religious life of the kingdom as a whole, both as the great family of the king and his people, and as an embodied cosmos of people, ancestors, animals, and land. This pattern has been repeated since Malla times in Nepal, where Viṣṇu and Śiva are the gods of state (*rāṣṭradevatā*) and the goddess Taleju, the personal, tutelary, and lineage goddess (*kuladevatā*) of the rulers of that kingdom.[18] The intimate, even sexual, nature of the king's relationship to his goddess is underscored by their living arrangement: under the Mallas, Taleju, in distinction to the great male gods, resided within the royal palaces, which were at once princely dwellings and goddess temples.[19]

Perhaps the earliest mythic account of a king worshiping a group of "Tantric" goddesses is that found in certain manuscript traditions of the MBh, in which Arjuna calls upon Durgā and a host of other great Goddesses on the eve of a definitive battle in the great Epic war.[20] Slightly earlier, a classical Tamil poem, the circa 100–300 C.E. *Neṭunalvāṭai*, depicts the relationship between warrior king and warrior goddess by describing the royal bedroom situated at the symbolic heart of the Pāṇḍya kingdom.

Figure 5.a. Rajasthani *kuladevīs* and popular goddesses portrayed as emanations of Durgā. Polychrome, ca. 1995.

In this bedroom is a round bed, symbolizing the round Vedic fire altar and the earth, and on this bed is the queen, who lies naked, awaiting the oblation of soma-semen from her husband. Known as "The Clan-founding Goddess" (*kula-mutaltēvi*), she embodies the Mother goddess to whom her maidservant prays for victory, as well as the *aṇaṅku* (a Tamil term whose semantic field corresponds to that of *śakti* in Sanskrit) that pervades the royal capital-fortress. That *aṇaṅku*, transmitted by her to the king each time they have sexual intercourse (*kūṭal*), is carried inside of him as the energy that wins him victory in battle.[21] Nearly all of the elements of the later *kuladevī* cults appear to be present in this early Tamil poem.

In the centuries that follow these two literary sources, royal inscriptions of northern Indian warrior kings first begin to associate the Mothers with war— because war, too, is a cause of death—as well as with Skanda, the war god.[22] This powerful, but also malevolent, aspect of the great Goddess emerges most prominently in a hymn to Vindhyavāsinī, sung by King Yaśovarman, in the ninth-century C.E. *Gaūḍavaho* of Vākpati, in which the description of this goddess mirrors that of Caṇḍikā and her shrine in the seventh-century *Kādambarī* of Bāṇabhaṭṭa as well as that of Cāmuṇḍā in the eighth-century *Mālatī-Mādhava* of Bhavabhūti.[23] Down to the nineteenth century, the kings of Nepal worshiped the Nine Durgās at the end of the autumnal festival of the Nine Nights (*navarātrī*) precisely because this was the beginning of the season of military campaigns, which lasted until the onset of the rainy season (fig. 5.b).[24]

In both Nepal and India, records of royal patronage of goddess cults and temples multiply during the early medieval period, as evidenced in inscriptions and numismatics,[25] with mythologies of the adoption of clan goddesses proliferating. One such goddess is Kubjikā, "She Who Is Hunched Over," whose medieval cult is richly attested in massive manuscript traditions in Kathmandu, where, according to Mark Dyczkowski, the present-day royal cult of the goddess Taleju in fact masks that of Kubjikā. Kubjikā's myth, which links her to the royal power of the Kadambas of Koṅkaṇa (present-day coastal Maharashtra, Goa, and Karnataka), is brief but to the point. A sage named Siddhanātha comes to the Kadamba capital of Candrapura and initiates the king, named Candraprabhā, into the cult of Kubjikā, admonishing him that he have his subjects do the same.[26] Another such goddess is Khoḍīyār, "She Who Limps," a goddess who is worshiped throughout modern-day Gujarat, and who, according to legend, raised Naughan, the founder of the Cūḍāsamā dynasty, to power in 1025 C.E. (fig. 5.c).Three elements of this goddess's myth are worthy of note: First, she is a goddess born in the household of a Charan, a gift of the great Goddess Jagadambā, "Mother of the Universe"; second, she is one of seven sisters who are intimately related to the sixty-four Yoginīs, and who

Figure 5.b. Navadurgā masks, Navadurgā temple, Theco village, Kathmandu Valley. Photograph by David Gordon White.

demand and receive blood (buffalo) sacrifice; and third, she elevates Naughan to power after having been gratified by the sacrificial offering of a human child.[27] Kubjikā and Khoḍīyār are not the sole Tantric goddesses marked by a physical deformity. There are also a number of goddesses whose names denote deformed eyes (Virūpākṣī, Vikaṭākṣī). It is tantalizing to see in these deformed goddesses the continuation of such earlier ambiguous female figures as the Vedic Kunaṃnamā ("Unbowed"), Kuvaṇṇā ("She of Evil Color") of the Sri Lankan *Mahāvamsa*, and the Epic Ambā, who is transformed into a crooked (*kuṭila*) river.[28]

While South Asian mythology knows of a number of kings with physical deformities (the Epic Dhṛtarāṣṭra, Paṇḍu, and Śiśupala being three well-known cases in point), none of their deformities appear to be "congenitally" inherited from goddesses. Yet there is a feature of the ritually constructed person of the king that intimately identifies his body, his very being, with that of the Goddess. In the *Devī Māhātmya*, the great Goddess is generated from the conjoined splendor (*tejas*) of the great male divinities.[29] According to Thomas Coburn, this image directly parallels—if it does not simply appropriate it—the ritual "construction" of a king, from "particles" of the eight divine regents of the directions, as described in the circa first-century B.C.E. *Mānava Dharma Śāstra*.[30] This ontological identification of goddess with king in mythology and royal ideology must have

Figure 5.c. Khoḍīyār, *kuladevī* of the medieval Cūḍāsamā dynasty, now regional goddess of Gujarat. Polychrome, ca. 1990.

been a conscious one, even if, in both of these cases, king and goddess are tributary to male deities.

The South Asian king has played a dual role through history, both generating and revivifying his kingdom from within, and hurling himself outward to the royal periphery to do battle against the demonic forces of his enemies, and, by extension, disease, famine, and pestilence. The king's dual role has mirrored that of the royal Goddess herself, both as symbolic progenetrix of the kingdom at its center and a fearsome female warrior at its periphery. In this latter role, she has long been called Durgā, who was first and foremost a warrior goddess, embodied in the walls of the fortress (*durga*). The very name Durgā, "She Who Is Difficult of Access"— one of the earliest names found in Hindu literature for the Goddess as a powerful, independent, martial deity—is very likely a derivate of terms for "fortress," "stronghold," or distant, outer battlement. Asko Parpola has in fact argued that Tantric diagrams may have their origin in the ground plans of ancient Bactrian and Harappan palace-fortresses.[31] Nowhere do we find such strong evidence for this dual role as in Nepal. The Mallas, the dynasty responsible for the "Tantric revival" in Nepal from the fourteenth century onward, worshiped the Nine Durgās during the season of military campaigns and called upon the Eight Mothers to protect the borders of their city-states from invasion. Durgā, their goddess of war, also identified as their clan goddess Taleju, had a shrine in every fort and garrison, and presided over the defense of the kingdom. When the kingdom was at peace, the sanctum of her royal temple at the kingdom's center housed the royal weapons.[32]

Like Durgā, the Eight Mothers of the three city-states of the Kathmandu Valley have both inner and outer forms, the former anthropomorphic images housed in temples within the city and the latter aniconic stones located at or outside the original city walls.[33] The fierce or wrathful deities located at the periphery of the royal mandala have often been female—circles of wild animal- or bird-headed goddesses—a reminder once again that the activated energy that flows through the Tantric mandala is nearly always feminine. This role is illustrated in the twelfth-century Jain poet Hemacandra's *Dvyāśraya-Kāvya,* which describes an encounter between the Gujarati king Jayasiṃha and a group of Yoginīs. These latter, protecting the kingdom of Malwa at their shrine on the Sipra River, try to kill the invading king with their mantras, but Jayasiṃha wins them over.[34] Kaula and Tantric sources often divide the host of the Yoginīs into two groups, the airborne (*khecarī*) and land-based (*bhūcarī*) divisions. My choice of military terminology is not facetious here: Yoginīs were the semidivine war goddesses of many a medieval South Asian kingdom, as a section of the eleventh-century *Mānasollāsa* also attests. Entitled "The Circle of Yoginīs," it combines a discussion of military strategies with descriptions of astrological diagrams for determining when and where to attack: the last of these diagrams, which places a goddess at each of the eight directions, is called the *yoginī-cakra*.[35]

The Yoginīs' liminal and tutelary status is powerfully evoked, once again, in the *Dvyāśraya-Kāvya*, in its description of the nocturnal exploits of the eleventh-century Cāḷukya monarch Siddharāja (fl. 1094–1143):

> [Even when the night comes] the duties of the king are by no means finished . . . he must rise from his couch to perform the "Veerchuryâ" [*vīra* practice]. He goes forth, sword in hand, alone . . . extend[ing] his rambles beyond [the city] walls to some spot frequented only by the filthy birds of night, the Yogeenee [Yoginīs] and the Dâkin [Ḍākinīs], female sprites, whom he compels to reply to his questions and to inform him of future events.[36]

Walking alone with sword in hand, the king takes the role of Everyman not only because he is the representative and protector of every one of his people, but also because he is himself his own person, subject to many of the same trammels of existence as everyone else in his realm. Like them, he has a home and a family, a body that is prey to disease and death, and deceased relations who come to visit him in his dreams. In this respect, he must transact with the same gods, ghosts, and ancestors as have most Asian individuals from time immemorial—beings that, because they are closer to the human world than are the high gods, are generally viewed as having a more immediate impact on human life.

3. Royal and Tantric Consecration

In South Asia the royal courts of Hindu and Buddhist kings have often constituted the privileged clienteles of Tantric specialists. This symbiotic relationship between Tantric "power brokers" and their power-wielding royal patrons is particularly apparent in Tantric rituals of initiation (*dīkṣā*), and consecration or empowerment (*abhiṣeka*). Tantric consecration has long been the special prerogative of Asian rulers, and royal participation in Tantric ritual colors much of Tantric literature. The intimate relationship between royal and Tantric initiation has recently been clearly delineated by Ron Davidson, with reference to Buddhist Tantric traditions:

> The monk obtains consecration (*abhiṣeka*) from his preceptor (*vajrācārya*) so that he takes pride in himself as a divinity (*devatābhimāna*) and

> will be given dominion over a circle of divinities (*mandala*), of different families (*kulas*). He comes into the company of yogins with spells (*mantrins*) so that he can employ their secret spells (*guhyamantra*). He is protected by Vajrapāṇī, the Lord of Esoteric Literature (*tantrādhipati*). He becomes authorized to engage in ritual behavior (*karma*) which varies from pacific (*śāntika*) to destructive (*abhicāraka*).
>
> The prince obtains coronation (*abhiṣeka*) from his priest (*purohita*) so that he is recognized as composed of fragments of divinity (*devāṃśa*) and will be given dominion over a circle of vassals (*mandala*) of different lineages (*kulas*). He comes into the company of his counselors (*mantrins*) so that he can make use of their confidential counsel (*guhyamantra*). He is protected by the head of the army (*tantrādhipati*). He becomes authorized to engage in royal behavior (*rājakarma*) which varies from pacific (*śāntika*) to ritually destructive (*abhicāraka*).[37]

The implications of this parallelism have been noted and commentated by a number of scholars. Michel Strickmann stresses the attractiveness of Tantric ritual to Asian royalty, both within and beyond the borders of South Asia: ". . . the central ritual of Tantra—consecration—was modeled on the ancient Indian ritual of royal investiture, which not only transformed monks into Tantric kings, but also kings into Tantric masters. . . . [The] Tantric homa-master imagined himself as a cosmocrat, a universal monarch. . . ."[38] This was emphatically the case in Malla-era Nepal, in which a king's Tantric initiation into the use of the goddess Taleju's mantra was what effectively gave him the power to rule over the men as well as many of the divinities of his kingdom.[39]

Similarly, the persons of kings in royal consecrations and icons in ritual worship are consecrated in identical ways, through the ritual act of aspersion, sprinkling with the "water of five oceans."[40] Per Kværne has discussed the sexual connotations of the ritual of *abhiṣeka*, noting the term's derivation from the root *sic*, "to pour out, sprinkle, soak," and, by extension, "impregnate." The hypothesis—that the overtly sexual language employed in textual descriptions of Tantric initiation goes back to South Asian consecration rites, of both kings and divine images, that were so many ritual reenactments of a *hieros gamos*[41]—is supported by both iconography (as in the case of Gaja-Lakṣmī, for example[42]) and ritual description. We have already mentioned the Kaula rite of *yoni-abhiṣecana*, the "sprinkling of the vulva" of the ritual consort. Another example comes from the easternmost extension of Hindu Tantra, medieval Indonesia, where the massive presence of water in Tantric ritual lies at the root of the Balinese term for the Hindu religion that was imported in the medieval period: *āgama tīrtha* is the "religion of holy water."[43] While Bali is the sole Indonesian island to have remained Hindu down to the present day, it must be recalled that Hinduism or Buddhism was the religion of state for much of the archipelago from the seventh century onward, and in some places down to the colonial period.[44] An Old Javanese court poem, the *Smara-Dahana* ("The Burning of Kāma"), translated and commented by C. Hooykaas, ends on the following verses:

> Such is her loveliness, moving and sweet,
> to be compared with mead in a chalice;
> together with her as his principal spouse
> did Smara come down to earth;
> King and Queen as Ardhanareśvarī
> continuously on the jewel lion-throne;
> King Kāmeśvara in [the] lotus' inner part,
> having as śakti the eight goddesses after their arrival.[45]

This poem is in fact a reference to the Indonesian royal consecration, which was Tantric. Hooykaas explicates this verse on the basis of Balinese Śaiva ritual, in which Ardhanareśvarī is praised in the following terms: "Hence a rain of nectar pours down, therefore on all the limbs and junctions, born from the meeting of husband and wife, this is proclaimed to be the 'real life.'"[46] Here, the king and his queen, husband and wife, embody the divine pair Śiva and Umā, who together are called *amṛti-karaṇī,* the "making of nectar, holy water." It is at this moment in the ritual, in which nectar or holy water is said to descend from the sky to earth, that the water in the vessel before the priest becomes transformed into holy water.[47]

This is the central mystery of Balinese Hindu religion. On the one hand, this consecration ritual transforms a man into a king: whereas as a boy, the king may have had an ordinary name like Ayam Vuruk, the Young Cock, following his *abhiṣeka* he is given the official name of Kāmeśvara. On the other hand, it transforms him and his spouse into the central deities of the Tantric mandala, vivifying the world with the nectar of their union: in the moment of their consecration, the newly consecrated King Kāmeśvara and his spouse are identified with Śiva and Umā bestowing the nectar of their supreme bliss upon humanity.[48] The mandala is completed by the array of women that surround the royal couple: the king, together with his spouse, as Ardhanareśvarī, are said to be seated in the *padma-guhya*, the hidden recess of the lotus, where they are surrounded by their eight Śaktis, perhaps the king's lesser queens.[49] However, as we noted in the previous chapter, the lotus and its heart are, in Tantric parlance, none other than the female sexual organ, and certain Kaula groups represented the Śrī Cakra as a yoni surrounded by eight lesser yonis.[50] Behind this Indonesian consecration ritual, then, we see a projection, onto a political space, of a fundamental Tantric configuration: Kuleśvara and Kuleśvarī, surrounded by the Eight Mothers, whose life-giving energy flows downward and outward, through the clan hierarchy, to create the "embodied cosmos" of the kingdom.[51] The same dynamic appears in accounts of the holy city of Madurai, in Tamil Nadu, a city whose mandala is generated, once again, from a "lotus."[52] The center of this lotus is, as we have seen, the royal bed, in the middle of a house called the *karu* ("embryo")—like the inner sanctum, the "womb house" (*garbha-gṛha*) of the Hindu temple—in the heart of the royal palace.[53]

4. Royal Patronage of Tantric Temples

Perched atop a strategic high point on the Narmada River at Bheraghat stands a massive Yoginī temple that was, according to R. K. Sharma, the greatest religious edifice built in the history of the entire Kalacuri dynasty. In a period in which temples were, like the cathedrals of Europe, major repositories of a kingdom's wealth, pivots for the distribution of royal patronage if not motors of economic expansion, and emblems of royal prestige and clan identity, this temple's importance would have been immense. Also known as the Golakī Maṭh ("Circular Lodge"), the renown of this temple as well as of its builder, a Kalacuri royal preceptor, extended southward across the entire Deccan plateau, to the courts of the Cholas of Tamil Nadu and the Kākatīyas of Andhra Pradesh.[54] Built in the first years of the eleventh century by the Kalacuri king Yuvarājā II (circa 975–1025 C.E.), it is unique among extant Yoginī temple ruins in that its circular inner course is comprised of not sixty-four but eighty-one niches, each containing the image of a Yoginī.[55] Eighty-one is in fact the "royal number" for such arrays: a passage from the *Śrīmatottara Tantra* describing the benefits that accrue from the worship of the eighty-one Yoginīs of the *mūla-cakra*—the expansion of one's territory, personal health, and prosperity—suggests their worship by royalty and nobility. A number of extant painted mandalas that show arrays of eighty-one Yoginīs were also originally intended for the use of kings.[56] The sculptures filling these eighty-one niches document, as it were, the practices of the "Circles of Mothers" (*mātṛcakras*)[57] in which their royal builders were likely the main participants. The Yoginī temples were also built for protection against epidemics and public calamities, as evidenced in the fact that many of their ruins are found near the former dynastic capitals. This is supported by a passage from the 1558 C.E. *Mantramahodadhi* of Mahīdhara: "wherever there are fields, secondary fields, mounds or secondary mounds,[58] may the goddesses who are fit to be worshipped by kings (*vīrendra vandyā*), and who are pleased by incense, protect us."[59]

The Bheraghat temple is particularly rich in its depictions of the cremation-ground practices of the Yoginīs.[60] On the inner wall of this temple are figured voluptuous and terrible images of these goddesses, who originally faced inward on a now missing image of a dancing Śiva or Bhairava at the open center of the edifice.[61] Each seminude, multi-armed Yoginī is seated on an animal, bird, or human *preta* vehicle, and their heads are likewise animal, avian, or human. Among all the extant Yoginī temples, Bheraghat is exceptional in the sculptural detail surrounding each of these figures in its niches. Most are cremation-ground scenes, populated by a supporting cast of (generally male) flesh-eating ghouls together with their female counterparts: jackals, birds, and what are clearly two-armed female human figures—the "human" Yoginīs or Yogeśvarīs. There are, however, virtually no representations of sexual practices in the Bheraghat sculptures. The human Yoginīs that are portrayed are often figured with severed human appendages in their hands or mouths (fig. 5.d); a certain number of emaciated but ithyphallic male figures, standing apart from these, are the sole references to sexuality in these images.[62]

Over a dozen ruins of ninth- to twelfth-century Yoginī temples lie scattered across the same central Indian region that saw Kaula or Tantric practice become popular in royal and aristocratic circles in the early medieval period. Moving from west to east, these include the Cāḷukyas of Badami, the Chandellas of Khajuraho, the Kalacuris of Tripurī, and the Somavaṃśis of Orissa. Yoginī temples in various stages of ruin have been found at Khajuraho, Bheraghat, Shahdol, Mitauli, Surada, Naresar, and Satna (all in Madhya Pradesh); Ranipur-Jharial and Hirapur (in Orissa);[63] Rikhiyan, Dudhai, Lukhri, and Tindwali (in Uttar Pradesh);[64] and Coimbatore (Tamil Nadu).[65] Certain of these, in addition to the Bheraghat and Khajuraho temples, can be attributed to specific royal houses: the circa 900 C.E. Hirapur temple was constructed by a ruler of the Bhañja dynasty, while the Mitauli temple was commissioned by the Kachchhapaghāta king Devapāla (1055–1075) at a time when this family was breaking away from the Chandellas, the powerful lords who built Khajuraho.[66] More numerous than such surviving ruins are the monumental constructions that have disappeared over the centuries. Fourteenth-century Jain sources evoke Yoginīpura (Delhi), Ajmer, Ujjain, and Bhṛgukaccha as the four great Yoginī *pīṭhas* of India, although no temple ruins exist at any of these sites,[67] and four Kashmiri kings, queens, or ministers are described in the Kalhaṇa's 1148–49 C.E. *Rājataraṅgiṇī* as having endowed "Circles of Mothers" surrounding a central image of Śiva or Bhairava.[68]

Figure 5.d. Detail from image of Bhāvnā Yoginī, tenth century C.E., Shahdol, Shahdol District, Madhya Pradesh, now housed in Dhubela Museum. *Above,* an animal-headed demon is raising an infant to its mouth; *below,* a human Yoginī nibbles on the fingers of a severed arm. Photograph by David Gordon White.

It is in the fifth century C.E. that we encounter the earliest inscriptional evidence for a permanent structure built for the worship of the Mothers, whose cult is linked to both Ḍākinīs and "Tantra." This is the Gangdhar (Jhalavar District, Rajasthan) stone-tablet inscription,[69] dated to 423 C.E., which records the commissioning by Mayūrākṣaka, a minister to King Viśvavarman, of a temple to Viṣṇu together with a drinking well and a temple to the Mothers.[70] Gangdhar lies in the heart of a region that enshrines many of the earliest Gupta-age sculptures of the Mothers; it also lies within the belt of the ruins of the many medieval Yoginī temples of central India that were constructed in the centuries that followed.[71] In this inscription we find not only evidence for royal worship of multiple goddesses, but also the same sort of combination of the propitiation of both Kaula and Vaiṣṇava deities as found in later Rajput traditions from the same region. This is a pattern that recurs among the early Cāḷukyas of Badami and the Kadambas—both sixth- to seventh-century dynastic lineages of the Deccan—who adopted the Mothers together with Skanda as tutelary deities, even as they were devotees of the great god Viṣṇu;[72] The former claim to have been nourished by the *saptaloka-mātṛ*, the "Mothers of the Seven Worlds," while the latter enjoyed the favor of the god Skanda and the horde of Mothers (*mātṛgaṇa*).[73] So, too, the Cāṅgu Nārāyaṇ temple complex, constructed in the fifth century C.E. by the Licchavis of Kathmandu in honor of their royal god Viṣṇu, also houses shrines to Chinnamastā, the "Severed-Headed Goddess," and a host of other Mothers.[74] Eastern India as well, from Bengal to Assam, has long been a region in which the syncretic worship of Viṣṇu or Kṛṣṇa together with the Tantric Durgā or Kālī has long predominated in the royal cultus.[75]

As inscriptions at Gangdhar and on the "flying pavilions" of the tenth- and eleventh-century Khajuraho temples attest, it was kings and their aristocratic ministers who were the most avid seekers of the *siddhis* afforded through contact with the dangerous yet powerful Mothers or Yoginīs.[76] No South Asian temple built in the medieval period is without erotic sculpture on its walls, and many of the sexual practices so depicted—because they are condemned in the Indian treatises on erotics (*kāmaśāstra*)—are likely depictions of Tantric rituals.[77] In Orissa, where the earliest *maithuna* motifs appear on late-sixth-century Śailodbhāva period temples, explicit depictions of sexual activities multiply significantly near the beginning of the tenth century and are frequently arranged in a sequential manner to imply specific stages of prescribed rites. They appear on Śaiva, Vaiṣṇava, and Śākta structures alike and are no longer confined to relatively hidden temple recesses, but are rather brought to the fore, for example at the Vārāhī temple at Caurasi, mentioned in the last chapter, in which what may have been an eight-stage *kāmakalā* ritual replaces the "entourage deities" standard on earlier temples.[78]

Many of the couples portrayed in the *maithunas* carved into the great royal temples of Bhubanesvar and Konarak in Orissa and Khajuraho in Madhya Pradesh are clearly aristocrats or members of the royal household, even when they are stripped down to their royal headdresses.[79] Now, many of these erotic carvings may be of harem scenes or representative of flights of fancy in which kings took their kingdom to be "Kāmadeva's Pleasure Garden."[80] But when "condemned poses" (including *rajapāna*) and "orgy scenes" depicting ascetics and royal figures are portrayed, the likelihood is great that these were representations of Tantric rituals.[81] So, for example, in orgiastic scenes portrayed on the eleventh-century temples of Modhera and Roda and the twelfth-century Galteśvara temple, ascetics are shown making particular hand gestures, as if reciting mantras.[82] Elsewhere, an erotic scene on the south joining wall of the Viśvanātha temple of Khajuraho depicts orgiastic groups in which attendants, while helping the central aristocratic couple, are themselves part of the erotic action. The presence of a male attendant indicates that the scene does not represent the harem, where only female and eunuch attendants would have been admitted. Moreover, a preceptor is part of the scene, as if chanting mantras and conducting an orgiastic ceremony. The scene seems to represent a religious ritual in which kings and Tantric specialists participated.[83]

The depiction of actual Kaula or Tantric rituals on Indian temples appears to have been a short-lived phenomenon, of no more than two centuries' duration. With the twelfth century, *maithunas* begin to be treated as independent motifs in the overall iconographic program, thereby losing their sequential, and ritual, significance. The introduction in this period of *devadāsīs* as temple prostitutes likely contributed to this new glorification of sexual pleasure as an end in itself, as opposed to a ritual means to an end.[84] The sexualized ritual of the Kaula "gave place to hedonistic practices . . . and most of the kings and feudal chiefs who courted Tantrism were hardly *sādhakas*."[85]

5. Kings and *Tāntrikas* in Medieval Narrative

"Listen O king and I will tell you a story." Many are the medieval Indian fantasy and adventure anthologies that open with these words, or whose multiple embedded stories begin with the same framing device.[86] And what is it that one finds in the content of the various episodes so framed? Stories about kings. There are several obvious reasons for this commonplace of Indian secular literature. The great majority of such anthologies were written under the patronage of, and *a fortiori* for the enjoyment of, royalty. Furthermore, the king, both as a private person and as the most important social and political actor in his kingdom, epitomized the possibilities and aspirations of Everyman. He was the human free agent par excellence with the greatest access, through his pivotal role at the center of his royal mandala, to the higher worlds of the divine as well as to the lower realms of the demonic. One should not conclude from this that the kings of story were nothing more than ideal or virtual beings: many of their adventures and exploits reflect ground-level realities in the relationships between men and their antagonists—the women, gods, goddesses, demons, and demonesses of Tantric tradition. Many of the kings and "good people"[87] of the medieval South Asian aristocracy were Tantric practitioners, and their specifically Tantric practices color the pages of the medieval literary canon.

The most celebrated such anthology is the 21,388-verse *Kathāsaritsāgara* ("The Ocean of Rivers of Story"), composed by Somadeva between 1063 and 1081 C.E., which offers a magnificent *tableau vivant* of the Tantric or Kaula culture of its time. In this sprawling narrative, the heroic king is epitomized by the person of Trivikramasena, the hero of the "Twenty-five Vampire Tales" whose 2,196 verses comprise over one-tenth of the entire work. The frame story of this particular series of tales places the king in a cremation ground, where he is to take part, together with Kṣāntaśila, a perfidious Tantric sorcerer, in a Tantric ritual for supremacy over the semidivine Wizards, the Vidyādharas. This sorcerer has instructed King Trivikramasena to procure a corpse for the Tantric corpse ritual (*śava-sādhanā*) that he has planned; however, the body that the king cuts down from a tree is possessed by a *vetāla*, who proceeds to tell him a series of riddling stories, often about kings like himself involved in practices redolent of Tantra. These "Vampire Tales," a set of narratives within this frame story, epitomize the content of the KSS as a whole, as an embedded collection of tales about the "embodied cosmos" of the Tantric universe.[88]

The kings who are the most frequent protagonists of the broader KSS are at once embodiments of the divine and exemplary humans who undertake heroic quests to realize a divinity that remains virtual for them until it has been won. Indeed, the outermost frame story of the entire cycle is that of Prince Naravāhanadatta, a "fallen" Vidyādhara who recovers his semidivine rule over the atmospheric realm through a series of conquests against human, demonic, and semidivine rivals, as well as through a multitude of amorous conquests of women who nearly always turn out to be Vidyādharīs, his spouses or lovers from former lives.[89] Behind the Vidyādhara Naravāhanadatta and his stable of Vidyādharī paramours, we once again find the Tantric godhead at the heart of the mandala, the Tantric

Virile Hero and his accompanying circle of Yoginīs, as well as the king as aspiring demigod and his semidivine queen. Such aspirations were mirrored in royal self-representations. So, for example, between the seventh and thirteenth centuries, when Vidyādhara stories were at the height of their popularity in Jain literature, the Śilāhāras—Cāḷukya tributaries who ruled a portion of the coastal strip of western India from their capitals in Goa, Kolhapur, and Thana—claimed to be descendants of the Vidyādharas.[90] In the same region, one encounters a significant number of eleventh-century personal and place-names including the term "Siddha": Siddharāja, Siddhanātha, Siddhapura, Siddheśvara.[91]

Narrative becomes the basis for royal precept in the 1131 C.E. *Mānasollāsa*.[92] A chapter of this Indian "mirror of kings" is entitled "Sports of the Virile Hero" (*vīrakrīḍā*). A guide to the attainment of the supernatural enjoyments, the chapter opens by stating that these are to be realized by kings like Vikramāditya and Śālivāhana—that is, men who are Virile Heroes (*vīrapuruṣaiḥ*)—and by none other (*naitaraiḥ*).[93] This prescriptive account finds its mirror in a description, found in the coeval *Dvyāśraya* of Hemacandra, of the Heroic Practice (*vīrācāra*) of King Siddharāja, whose nocturnal forays beyond his city walls bring him face-to-face with the same Yoginīs and Ḍākinīs as are found in the *Mānasollāsa*.[94]

In these various literary sources, the king acts as a Virile Hero, without the mediation of a Tantric specialist. This was the case, to a limited degree, in medieval Nepal, in which Malla kings maintained intimate relationships with their tutelary goddess Taleju and communicated with Tantric deities directly or in dreams. Also in Nepal, the king continues to legitimate his power, down to the present day, through a direct exchange of swords with the Tantric deity Pacalī Bhairava, with minimal priestly mediation (by a Vajrācārya in this case). This is of a piece with enthronement rituals in Maharashtra and Rajasthan, where the throne itself communicates the Goddess's *śakti* to a prince, thereby empowering him to rule.[95] More often, however, in order to become a Virile Hero, a king must first be initiated by a male guru and a female Yoginī or Dūtī. It is only after initiation that a practitioner, royal or otherwise, may become an independent ritual agent, able to act as his own priest and as a priest for other members of his lineage.[96]

Who are the people who initiate the king, and what is the position and role of Tantric specialists in the life of the royal palace? A significant number of literary works from medieval north India attest to the powerful presence of *tāntrikas* in royal courts.[97] Perhaps the earliest of these is the *Karpūramañjarī* of Rājaśekhara, a tenth- to eleventh-century royal poet to the Pratīhāra kings Mahendrapāla and Mahīpāla, and later to the Kalacuri king Yuvarājā II, the builder of the Bheraghat Yoginī temple.[98] The pivotal character of the entire play is a Kaula thaumaturge named Bhairavānanda, who describes his Kula path (*kulamagga*) as one of "mantra and tantra," a path whose practices of "drinking alcohol and enjoying women lead to liberation."[99] The play's fourth act features the installation by Bhairavānanda of an image of Cāmuṇḍā, a ritual accompanied by a series of dances, performed by women clad as goddesses, which the king and queen witness from their palace terrace: "Yet others, bearing in their hands offerings of human flesh and terrible with their groans and shrieks and cries and wearing the masks (*paḍisīsa*) of night-wandering ogresses, are enacting a cemetery scene."[100] It would appear that Bhairavānanda is here orchestrating a Yoginī-type cremation-ground ritual beneath the windows of the royal palace itself. Whether the masks these Hindu maenads are described as wearing were those of animals or birds, or of the type that one finds in the royally patronized dances of the Nine Durgās in the cities of the Kathmandu Valley, cannot, unfortunately, be known on the basis of the text itself. However, it does provide us a glimpse into one of the ways that human women may have played the roles of Yoginīs in medieval ritual performance.

While the orthodox Rājaśekhara[101] was likely ill at ease with the forms of religiosity that his leading Tantric character embodied, he nonetheless was writing for a patron who was eager for the sorts of miracles that religious specialists like Bhairavānanda were able to deliver. Furthermore, as this and other plays demonstrate, the presence of Tantric elements in or near the royal court was a reality in this period, which could not be glossed over.[102] So it is that in Rājaśekhara's play, the king, queen, and their brahmin fool (*viduṣaka*) fall under the thrall of the supernatural powers wielded by their Tantric superman, because he has promised to elevate the king to the status of *cakravartin*, universal conqueror. He makes good on this by magically producing at the court, through his *siddhi* (of *ākārṣaṇa*, "attraction"?), the person of Karpūramañjarī, the play's heroine; and it is through her marriage with him that the king attains the exalted status he is seeking.[103]

While Rājaśekhara portrays Tantric practitioners and their influence on the royal court in an ambiguous light, others are far more negative in their accounts. A remarkable case in point is that of Kṛṣṇamiśra, whose 1070–90 C.E. *Prabodhacandrodaya* (PC) may be read as an allegory of events that transpired in the Chandella royal house of Khajuraho in the first decades of the eleventh century. That is, one may discern behind the play's allegorical presentation—that pits King Discrimination against King Great Delusion, who, supported by Agnosticism, Hypocrisy, Avarice, and Vanity, abducts Religion and attempts to conquer the world through Heresy—a second level of allegory, this time historical. This is the argument of

Hermann Goetz, which I summarize here.[104] The title of this work may itself be a play on words, with both a literal ("The Dawning Moon of Consciousness") and an occulted meaning: "*Prabodha*(śiva) and (Chedi)*candra*'s Rise (*udaya*)," Prabodhaśiva being the name of a Kaula "missionary" sent by the Kalacuri king Yuvarājā II (also known as Chedicandra) as a means to bringing down the Chandella dynasty.[105] This he would have done through Kaula infiltrators, who debauched and thereby weakened the Chandella kings Dhaṅgadeva (ruled 954–999) and Gaṇḍadeva (ruled 999–1003) through the sexual excesses of their practices. An important by-product of this undercover campaign would have been the construction of what is arguably the most glorious example of medieval Indian temple architecture, the Kandariyā Mahādeva temple of Khajuraho, a temple especially rich in sculptural motifs of possible Kaula influence.[106]

The PC is in fact the celebration of the return to power—and to their Vaiṣṇava senses—of the Chandellas in the person of Kīrtivarman (fl. ca. 1060–1100), following a sixty-year period of occultation under the influence of the rival Kalacuri kings of Chedi,[107] coupled by military losses at the hands of Mahmūd of Ghazni. The same Kīrtivarman would also have commissioned the (Vaiṣṇava) Lakṣmaṇa temple, according to Goetz. If one accepts Goetz's well-documented hypothesis that the Kalacuris, although feudatories of the Chandellas in this period, had managed to infiltrate and weaken the court at Khajuraho from within through the use of Kaula "operatives," then the allegorical plot of the PC becomes a transparent dramatization of those historical events.[108] Why the kings Dhaṅgadeva and Gaṇḍadeva, rulers in a time when the Chandellas were at the apparent height of their power, would have been vulnerable to the blandishments of the Kaulas is explained by Goetz on the basis of their age: Dhaṅgadeva was over a hundred years old when he died, and Gaṇḍadeva in his eighties or nineties when he was defeated in a crucial battle against Mahmūd of Ghazni, in 1019.[109] This rendered both vulnerable, on the one hand, to younger, more vigorous courtiers with hidden agendas and, on the other, susceptible to the introduction of young maidens as sexual partners for the magico-medical purpose of gerocomy, bodily rejuvenation (*kāyasādhanā*), if not their deification through Tantric rites (fig. 5.e).[110] This deification of the Chandella kings is also represented, according to Goetz, in the form of three superimposed sculptural tableaus on the northern and southern joining walls of the Lakṣmaṇa, Kandariyā Mahādeva, and Viśvanātha temples.[111] As we will see in chapter 7, more than one aging king fell prey to the seductions of lithe and youthful Yoginīs: in his *Rājataraṅgiṇī*, Kalhaṇa relates how Baka, an elderly Kashmiri king, was tricked into becoming the sacrificial victim of a "Feast of Yoga" (*yogotsava*) orchestrated by a "Mistress of Yoga" (*yogeśvarī*).[112] The same author also chronicles the

Figure 5.e. Orgy scene accompanied by preparation of an elixir, Lakṣmaṇa temple, Khajuraho, ca. 950 C.E. Courtesy of the American Institute of Indian Studies.

last days of King Harṣa (1089–1101), who was offered slave girls as Kaula "goddesses" by his courtiers. He worshiped them, had sexual intercourse with them, and "as he was anxious to live for a very long time, they granted him, in his foolishness, hundreds of years to live."[113]

Now there are certain problems with Goetz's analysis. First, one has to accept dates of 1000 C.E. and 1070 C.E. for the Kandariyā Mahādeva and Lakṣmaṇa temples, respectively, for their construction to have coincided with the rulers under whose reigns he claims they were built. This is at variance with Devangana Desai's accurate dating of the completion of the "former" to 1030 C.E. and the "latter" to 954 C.E.![114] The dedicatory inscription of the Lakṣmaṇa temple, dated 954 C.E., speaks of an image of the Vaikuṇṭha form of Viṣṇu, that was brought from Kīra (Kashmir), perhaps via Kanauj, to Khajuraho. This provenience, together with the iconography of this image, are evidence for a likely tenth-century Pāñcarātra presence at Khajuraho, which may have been revived under the patronage of Kīrtivarman. Curiously, a relief on the Lakṣmaṇa temple's platform depicts a master of a Śaiva order together with a female attendant and four bearded disciples, an indication of a certain religious latitudinarianism.[115] Second, the historical Prabodhaśiva, whom Goetz identifies as a "Kaula missionary," was in fact a leader of the Mattamāyūras ("Drunken Peacocks"), from the far more conventional Śaivasiddhānta order. There is, moreover, rich historical documentation to prove that the Mattamāyūras were patronized and richly supported by the Kalacuri kings. At the same time, it is likely that the Kaulas occupied important places in the Kalacuri kingdom under Yuvarājā II, whose Bheraghat Yoginī temple they controlled in the years following its construction,[116] precisely the same years in which Goetz places Kaula agents, sent by the Kalacuris, in Khajuraho. Even though wrong in certain of its details, Goetz's theory is not entirely without merit with regard to Kaula influence at Khajuraho in the eleventh century, especially when one notes that the PC itself mentions "a Somasiddhāntin in Kāpālika garb,"[117] a reference to the practice of Tantric dissimulation, the adopting of double or triple sectarian identities, to which we will return.

Other medieval authors present the relationship between the royal court and Kaula and Tantric practitioners in a matter-of-fact, even positive light. These include the late twelfth-century Jayaratha, who concludes his commentary on the TĀ with a long account of the relationship between his lineage and the Kashmiri aristocracy that were its patrons (when the two were not one and the same persons).[118] In addition, there are Tantric works which include passages that clearly designate the king and his family as the primary beneficiaries of Tantric ritual. So, for example, the *Netra Tantra* explicitly relates a king's health and prowess and the prosperity of his kingdom to the ritual worship of the Mothers, the powers of the *amṛteśa* mantra, and the performance of Tantric rituals.[119] These include "water-pot" treatments against demonic afflictions: "Because the many defilement [demons] are fond of smiting [all creatures] beginning with the king, protection that is auspicious and that promotes the general welfare ought to be effected. Therefore one should 'worship the water-pot' for the protection of the king while he is asleep." The same chapter, describing how Seizers afflict fortunate children, enjoins: "A child should always be protected, especially the prince."[120] The *Lakṣmī Tantra* enjoins the Tantric practitioner to offer his services to the king in times of national disaster,[121] and many are the sacred and secular texts that portray kings and their Tantric specialists defending the kingdom through the powers afforded them by Tantric mantras and rites.

6. Rivalries among Tantric Elites

We have noted that the Tantric mandala becomes "utopian" when there is no temporal ruler to be identified with the godhead at the center. In such cases, Tantra lies outside of the mainstream, potentially subversive and antinomian, the province of the practitioner as crypto-potentate. When, however, the ruler is himself a Tantric practitioner or client, then the mandala takes on a real-world referent and stands as the mesocosmic template between politico-religious realities and their supermundane prototype, the realm of the divine. In the first instance, the Tantric mandala is covert and occulted; in the latter, it is overt and hegemonic. When the king is a Tantric practitioner, Tantric ritual provides a protective shield around the space of his kingdom, with his Tantric specialists standing as bearers of religious authority. When, however, there is no ruler, or when the "wrong king" is on the throne, the Tantric specialist becomes a covert operative, an occult cosmocrat, controlling a universe of which he is, through his identity with the god at the center of the mandala, the creator, preserver, and destroyer. This latter state of affairs is, of course, threatening to the "wrong king" in question, and Siddha mythology is replete with accounts of the triumph of Tantric masters over wrong-headed temporal rulers. There are, however, other possible scenarios, productive of other strategies on the part of Tantric actors, that need to be explored. These concern relationships among power elites—Tantric specialists and their royal or aristocratic clients, in which the former, whether they consider their royal client to be legitimate or not, seek to find ways by which to assert their authority over the latter. These are the strategies of secrecy and dissimulation.

Until recent times, Tantric ritual constituted a bulwark for the state in the Indianized and Sanskritized monarchies of Asia, from Nepal to Bali.[122] Reciprocally, it has especially been through royal support (protection, land grants, tax-exempt status, etc.) that Tantric orders as well as independent specialists have been empowered both to propagate their sectarian teachings and to consolidate their socioeconomic position in the realm. In this symbiotic relationship, Tantric lineages—of families, teaching traditions, and royal, priestly, and monastic succession—have often been closely intertwined. It is only in Nepal, however—where the royal preceptor (*rāj guru*) has, since the thirteenth century, been the king's chief religious adviser, initiating his royal client into the circles of deities that comprise and energize the *nepāla-maṇḍala*[123]—that the relationship between the *tāntrika* and his king has remained in official force down to the present day.[124] The illustrious Pratāp Malla, who ruled from Kathmandu from 1641 to 1674, surrounded himself with no fewer than five Tantric advisers. Three of these were brahmin specialists in different branches of Tantra, and these are in fact the sole brahmins mentioned in the royal chronicles of Pratāp's reign: Jñānānanda, a brahmin *tāntrika* from the Deccan; Lambakarṇa Bhaṭṭa, a brahmin "magician" from Maharashtra; and Narasiṃha Thākur, a brahmin from northeastern Bihar, who had acquired immense powers by reciting the Narasiṃha mantra for three years. In addition to these, Pratāp was also advised by two Buddhists: Jamanā Gubhāju, a local Newar Vajrayāna priest possessed of prodigious supernatural powers; and a Tibetan lama named Syāmarpā.[125]

In many ways, royal ceremonial has been as essential to royal power in Nepal as it formerly was in premodern Bali and medieval Tamil Nadu, some of whose royal ritual and symbolism we have already outlined in this chapter.[126] In the Kathmandu Valley (which was, it must be recalled, overwhelmingly Buddhist down into the eighteenth century, even as its power elites have generally been Hindu), this ceremonial and the channels to power, both political and supernatural, that undergird it, have been controlled by a number of religious specialists. It is the relationship among these religious power elites that is of signal interest here. Just as in Rajput western India, the lower-caste Charan bard who "made the ruler a true Rajput" was closer to the person of the king than his high-status brahmin chaplain, so, too, the Karmācārya Tantric priests of the kings of Nepal have often enjoyed greater power in the royal cultus than their brahmin homologues, the Rājopādhyāya brahmins.[127] The Karmācāryas belonged to the same *kṣatriya* subcaste, even the same lineages, as the Malla kings, and for this reason, together with the mantras and initiations they controlled, they dominated the politico-religious life of fifteenth- to eighteenth-century Kathmandu. Nonetheless, the Rājopādhyāya brahmins, who have managed to negotiate a dual role—both Vedic and Tantric—for themselves in the religious life of the kingdom, have since become the prime brokers of royal access to the Goddess's power in the Kathmandu Valley.[128]

Control of the cult of the great royal goddess Taleju lies at the heart of the power relationship that has obtained between that goddess's "indigenous" Newar Rājopādhyāya brahmin priesthood and the present royal family of Nepal, itself descended from the eighteenth-century conquerors who invaded from Gorkha, to the west of the valley.[129] After reviewing the cults of the gods of the Newars' public religion, the gods of the "civic space" or "mesocosm," Mark Dyczkowski offers the following scenario:

> But there is an[other] "inner" secret domain which is the Newars' "microcosm." This does not form a part of the sacred geography of the Newar civitas, although, from the initiates' point of view, it is the source and reason of much of it. The deities that populate this "inner space" and their rites are closely guarded secrets and, often, they are the secret identity of the public deities known only to initiates.
>
> The two domains complement each other. The outer is dominantly male. It is the domain of the attendants and protectors of both the civic space and the inner expanse, which is dominantly female. By this I mean that while the deities in the public domain may be both male and female, the male dominates the female, while the secret lineage deities of the higher castes [of the Tantric ritual specialists] are invariably female accompanied by male consorts. . . . [T]he inner domain is layered and graded in hierarchies of deepening and more elevated esotericism that ranges from the individual to the family group, clan, caste, and out through the complex interrelationships that make up Newar society. Thus the interplay between the inner and outer domains is maintained both by the secrecy in which it is grounded and one of the most characteristic features of Newar Tantrism as a whole, namely, its close relationship to the Newar caste system.[130]

The outer domain described by Dyczkowski is that of the outer limits of the royal mandala. Here, the multiple Bhairabs (Bhairavas) who guard the boundaries of villages, fields, and the entire Kathmandu Valley itself are so many hypostases of the great Bhairabs of the royal cultus at the center: Kāl Bhairab, Ākāś Bhairab, et cetera. As we have noted, however, it is only by transacting with the transcendent deity at the heart of the mandala that one may access and maintain supreme power. It is here that secrecy becomes a prime strategy. The Rājopādhyāya brahmins offer Bhairava initiations to the king as the maintainer of the outer, public state cultus; however, it is only among themselves that they offer initiations and empowerments specific to Taleju, their lineage goddess (*kuladevī*)—and it is precisely through these secret initiations and empowerments that they maintain their elevated status vis-à-vis all the other castes of the Kathmandu Valley, including that of their principal client, the king himself. Because the goddess at the center of the mandala is their lineage goddess, and theirs alone, and because her higher initiations are their secret prerogative, the Newar priesthood is able to "control" the king and the *nepāla-maṇḍala* as a whole.[131] Higher levels of initiation into the Kubjikā Tantras, accessible only to these elite *tāntrikas*, afford them hegemony over the religious life of the kingdom, which translates into an occult control of the Nepal royal administration, which in turn enhances their social status and economic situation. Simply by withholding the highest Taleju initiations and their corresponding mantras from the king, they maintain her supernatural power over him.[132]

A comparison with the world of espionage is a useful one here: only those of the privileged *inner circle* (the heart of the Tantric mandala) have the highest *security clearance* (Tantric initiations) and access to the most *secret codes* (Tantric mantras) and *classified documents* (Tantric scriptures). The Newar priesthood of Kathmandu, *tāntrikas* to the king, are the "intelligence community" of the kingdom, and their secret knowledge affords them an invisible power greater than that of the king himself. In this way, the political power that the Newars lost—through the eighteenth-century invasion of the Kathmandu Valley by the founder of the present Śāh dynasty—has been recovered through their monopoly over their *kuladevī*, Taleju, the goddess at the heart of the royal mandala. This has translated into political power, through their control of the administration of the kingdom.

When one looks at the strategy of secrecy employed by the Newar priesthood of Nepal to exert occult control over a kingdom whose political power they lost over two centuries ago, one is not far from the practice of dissimulation, of pretending to be someone other than who one is. Dissimulation is a particular strategy for maintaining secrecy that is most often employed when the "wrong king" is on the throne and practitioners are forced "underground." Here, the oft-quoted aphorism concerning the triple identity of Kaula practitioners is most apposite: "Outwardly Vedic, a Śaiva at home, secretly a Śākta."[133] This strategy is altogether comprehensible in a situation of political or religious oppression: curiously, or not so curiously, it is a strategy employed in times of relative freedom as well. This is the stuff secret societies are made of, the world over. The question of why one would wish to dissemble when fear of oppression is not one's principal motivation may again be approached by borrowing terminology from the world of espionage. Dissimulation allows for covert operatives to possess a double (or triple) identity, and to inhabit more than one world at the same time. It is also a means for "insiders" to recognize one another without being recognized by "outsiders," through the use of secret signs (*chommas*, *mudrās*), language (mantras), codes (forms of mantric encryption), and so on. It is a means for creating an elite, even if its eliteness be known to none but the insider community.

7. Documentation on Kaulas and Kāpālikas in Medieval India

There has been no small controversy in scholarly circles concerning the sociopolitical *signifiés* of the terms "Kāpālika" and "Kaula": Are both more often applied by outsiders than by insider practitioners? Or are these emic terms, used by practitioners themselves? There is evidence to support both arguments, albeit for different reasons.

There appears to have been a certain a self-consciousness on the part of Kaula practitioners of their own clan identities, as witnessed in the significant number of works having the term "Kula" or "Kaula" in their titles (Gopinath Kaviraj lists over fifty extant titles as Kaula works).[134] In addition, numerous epithets of Śiva, Bhairava, and the Goddess bear witness to these divinities' relationship to human Kaula practitioners. These include *kulagocarā* and *kaulāgamā*, the KJñN epithets of the Goddess, already discussed.[135] Elsewhere, the circa tenth-century "Lalitā Sahasranāma" of the *Brahmāṇḍa Purāṇa*[136] describes the Goddess as "She Who Has the Special Taste of the Kula Nectar," the "Protectress of the Kula Secrets," the "Kula Woman," "She Who Is Internal to the Kula," the "Female Member of the Kaula" (*kaulinī*), the "Kula Yoginī" (*kulayoginī*), "She Who Is Clanless" (*akulā*), "Our Lady of the Kula" (*kuleśvarī*), and "She Who Is Worshipped by Persons Devoted to the Kaula Path."[137] In his court epic, the *Haravijaya*, the mid-ninth-century Kashmiri author Ratnākara portrays Kaulas as singing the praises of Cāmuṇḍā in terms that appear to be disclosive of an "insider" knowledge on his part:

> Those who have adopted the Kaula path
> contemplate you [O Goddess] in your Bhairava form . . .
> the form of the sixteen *vīras*
> who are the gurus beginning with Śrīkaṇṭha . . .
>
> Having contemplated you [O goddess] here
> in your two modes, supreme and lower:
> enthroned on the beautiful pericarps
> of the lotuses resting on the tips of
> the trident within the circle;
> in Bhairava's permanent embrace—
> we Kaulas attain the mastery of powers.[138]

This Kaula self-identification could also take the form of a hierarchization of schools or types of practice. So, for example, Kṣemarāja, in his eleventh-century commentary on the *Vijñāna Bhairava,* states that "the Śaiva path transcends those of the Vedas; higher than the Śaiva is the path of the Left and likewise of the Right; the Kaula transcends the Right, and the Trika transcends the Kaula."[139] Likewise, the Kubjikā traditions refer to themselves as the "final transmission" (*paścimāmnāya*) of the Kaula, and to all others as Tāntrika, collectively, with the exception of the "prior transmission" (*pūrvāmnāya*) of the earlier Kaula schools, all of which were received and transmitted by Matsyendranātha.[140] This distinction becomes a subject for rhetorical flourish in works belonging to the later Tantric revivals. So, for example, chapter 2 of the thirteenth- to fourteenth-century *Kulārṇava Tantra* opens with a paean to the greatness of the Kaula and the Clan Practice:

> The Veda is higher than everything [else]; the Vaiṣṇava [teachings] are superior to the Veda. The Śaiva [teachings] are higher than the Vaiṣṇava [teachings]; the teachings of the Right are higher than the Śaiva. The teachings of the Left are higher than those of the Right; those teachings "whose end is realization" (Siddhānta) are higher than those of the Left. The Kaula teachings are higher than those teachings whose end is realization. There is no [teaching] whatsoever that is higher than the Kaula. O Goddess, the Kula [teaching], [which has] gone from ear to ear, which is the manifest state of Śiva-hood, is higher than the highest, the essence of the essence, more secret than the secret. Having churned the ocean of the Vedas and Āgamas with the churning stick of gnosis, the Kula practice was extracted by me who am the knower of the essence, O Goddess![141]

Yet even as the Kaula literature makes ample reference to the Kaula as an empirical as opposed to a virtual or ideal entity, the testimonies of outsiders remain at variance with insider accounts. Of the terms "Kaula" and "Kāpālika," the latter is far more frequently encountered than the former in both secular and "heresiological" literature,[142] as has been richly documented by David Lorenzen. The KSS is particularly harsh in its depictions of Kāpālikas, treating them as lecherous impostors of authentic Tantric practitioners, who use their ill-gotten magical powers to subjugate women and enslave them sexually. So, for example, a brahmin describes a Kāpālika who had kidnapped his wife through the powers of a magic bedstead (*khatvāṅga*) as a "cheat" (*śaṭha*), and his order as a band of "heretics" (*pākhaṇḍin[aḥ]*) and "imposters" (*viḍambin[aḥ]*).[143] Few works have survived that were authored by persons calling themselves Kāpālikas; with the term "Kāpālika" in their title; or with the "Kāpālika doctrine" as their subject matter.[144] Epigraphical evidence for royal or aristocratic patronage of the Kāpālikas is equally lacking. As Lorenzen has noted, apart from four epigraphical records of royal donations to Mahāvrātins (and not Kāpālikas per se) and an inscription on the Kathmandu Paśupatināth temple from circa 630 C.E. mentioning a gift offered in the presence of the "congregation of those wearing a chain of heads," the entire epigraphical record on these Skull-Bearers treats them more as antitypes of more respectable orders—or worse, as mercenaries, dangerous charlatans, or battlefield scavengers—than as a religious order.[145]

So, for example, the Vaiṣṇava *Padma Purāṇa*, which presents a long disquisition by Śiva on the heretical orders, describes these heretics as Kaulikas or Kāpālikas, but attacks the doctrines of the Śaiva, Pāśupata, Nyāya, Sāṃkhya, Materialist, and Buddhist heresies: "Kāpālika doctrine" is nowhere to be found.[146] Numerous Purāṇas blame social disorder on heretics like the Buddhists, Jains, and Kāpālikas, using stock descriptions from a common, and perhaps ancient source, but again, skirting the issue of Kāpālika doctrine.[147] The orthodox Vaiṣṇava founder Rāmānuja, who claims in his *Śrībhāṣya* (2.35–37) to be refuting Pāśupata and Kāpālika doctrines, in fact writes a broadside against *all* of the Śaiva heresies.[148]

Tantric dissimulation may have played a role here: following the mythological example of Śiva-Bhairava after his decapitation of Brahmā's fifth head,[149] Śaiva practitioners may have "disguised" themselves as Kāpālikas at various points in their lives. More than this, Kāpālika dress may have simply been a means for going "undercover." In addition to Goetz's hypothetical reconstruction of the political background to the PC, the KSS and the *Nalavilāsa* of Ramacandrasūri, a twelfth-century Gujarati work, also depict the Kāpālikas as spies working in the service of kings,[150] and, as we have seen, the PC itself mentions "a Somasiddhāntin in Kāpālika garb."[151] This garb, or more properly speaking the "six marks" of the Kāpālika, are listed by Rāmānuja: necklace, *rucaka* neck ornament, earrings, crest jewel, ashes, and sacred thread.[152] Curious by their absence from this list are references to the bedstead, human bone ornaments, begging bowl, and so on, found in nearly every literary description of Kāpālikas. Yet these are present in *Svacchanda Tantra* instructions for the dress of the ascetic officiant of the "unexpurgated" cult of Svacchanda Bhairava, which Alexis Sanderson has identified as partaking of the "cremation ground asceticism of the Kāpālikas."[153]

R. K. Sharma, who notes that there is no written evidence for the existence of the Kāpālikas in the same medieval Kalacuri lands that likely spawned the Śaivasiddhānta sect and in which the Pāśupatas thrived, nonetheless states that the Kāpālika order was somehow linked to the Kaulas.[154] As we have seen, the Tantric wonder-worker who was the central character of the *Karpūramañjarī* is called a Kaula Siddha; a later commentator on this work refers to the same figure as a Kāpālika.[155] Somadeva, a Jain author of the medieval period, identifies the followers of the Trika doctrine as Kaulas who worship Śiva in the company of their Tantric consorts by offering him meat and wine, and condemns these, saying, "If liberation were the result of a loose, undisciplined life, then thugs and butchers would surely sooner attain to it than these Kaulas!"[156] Haribhadra, an eighth-century Jain author, lists the "Kula Yogis" as the lowest of a succession of four sects, calling them "drunken and dull," in contrast to the highest sect, the Jain "Avañcaka (Authentic) Yogis."[157] The Kashmiri author Kṣemendra describes Kāpālika or Kaula practitioners as a generally depraved and worthless lot. In his 1066 C.E. *Daśāvatāracarita*, they and the heterodox practices associated with their "feasts" (*utsavas*), including drinking and consumption of the *kaulagola*, epitomize the late Kali age and hasten the coming of Kalkin (called Karkyavatāra here), the tenth and future incarnation of Viṣṇu.[158] The same author condemns a host of religious actors, including Kaulas and *tāntrikas*, in his *Narmamālā*,[159] a satirical description of the hypocrisy and villainy of the Kāyasthas who controlled the royal administration of the kingdom of Kashmir in his time. The Kāyastha "protagonist" of this work interacts with a number of social lowlifes who pose as Tantric teachers to dupe both himself and other credulous members of his class. These characters include a Śaiva guru who had previously been a Buddhist and a "pseudo-Vaiṣṇava"—who now "together with his wife, and for the sake of protection, had a budding interest in the Kaula teachings"[160]—and who indulges to excess in orgiastic Tantric practices with his many low-caste hirelings.[161]

For all this, there is even less epigraphic evidence for royal patronage of the Kaulas as an institutionalized order or sect than there is for the Kāpālikas. A 973–74 C.E. inscription from the Shekhavati region of eastern Rajasthan states that Allaṭa, a preceptor of the Sāṃsārika-kula order, was the disciple of Viśvarūpa, the preceptor of the Pañcārthika branch of the Pāśupata order.[162] According to Sharma, when the Bheraghat Yoginī fell out of the control of the Kaulas, it was taken over by the Pāśupatas (led by a preceptor named Rudrarāśi of Lāṭa, present-day Gujarat), with the Kaulas migrating a kilometer away to the site of the present-day village of Gopalpur.[163]

Establishing the fact that the terms "Kaula" and "Kāpālika" seem not to correspond to the language used in royal inscriptions and edicts only proves that practitioners who referred to themselves by these names did not have the visibility that identifiable orders with religious establishments, such as the Śaiva Siddhāntins and other contemporary groups, appear to have had.[164] Alternately, it indicates that the Kaulas or Kāpālikas were not institutionalized religious orders at all, but rather secret societies whose memberships were comprised of persons from secular society. Here, as we have already hypothesized, dissimulation would have played an important role in the practice and self-identity of the Kaula practitioner.

8. Tantric Dissimulation in an Eighteenth-Century Account

The French regular Jean-Antoine Dubois, better known as Abbé Dubois, passed some thirty years of his life, toward the beginning of the nineteenth century, among the Indian people whose customs, institutions, and ceremonies he chronicled in a dispassionate if not sympathetic way, in a work that has become a classic: *Moeurs, Institutions et cérémonies des peuples de l'Inde*.[165] An exception to the rule is his wholly unsympathetic depiction of the following ritual, which he ascribes to Vaiṣṇava practitioners:

> People have seen so-called magicians organize nocturnal gatherings at a deserted spot known to me, and indulge in incredible excesses of intemperance and debauchery there. The leader of these orgies was a Vaisnavite Brahmin, and several Sudras were initiated into the mysterious iniquities carried out there. . . . Among the abominable mysteries current in India, there is one that is all too well-known: this is the practice called *sakty-poudja* [*śakti pūjā*]. . . . The ceremony takes place at night, with more or less secrecy. . . . The *Namadharis*, or followers of Vishnu, are the most frequent perpetrators of these disgusting sacrifices.[166] People from all castes, from the Brahmin to the Pariah, are invited to attend. When the company are assembled, all kinds of meat, including beef, are placed before the idol of Viṣṇu. . . . The celebration of these mysteries, invariably foul as concerns their content, can at times vary in their form. In certain cases, the immediate objects of the sacrifice to *Sakty* are a large vessel that has been filled with local alcohol and a girl who has reached the age of puberty. This latter, entirely naked, stands in an altogether indecent pose. They then summon the goddess *Sakty*, whom they presume accepts their invitation by simultaneously establishing herself in the vessel of alcohol and that portion of the girl's anatomy which modesty prohibits me from naming. Next, the people offer these two objects a sacrifice of flowers, incense, sandalwood, akchatta [*akṣata:* unhulled rice], and a lighted lamp; and, as *neiveddia* [*naivedya:* offering of edible foods], a portion of all the meats that have been prepared. Once this has been done, Brahmins, Sudras, Pariahs, men and women all become drunk on the alcohol consecrated to *Sakty*, which they drink from the same vessel, touching it with their lips. . . . The men and women then throw them-

> selves on the food, avidly gobbling it down. The same chunk of food passes from mouth to mouth, and is successively chewed away until it has been entirely consumed. . . . In this case, the people are persuaded that they are in no way sullied by eating and drinking in such a revolting manner. When they have at last become entirely intoxicated, men and women mingle freely and pass the remainder of the night together. . . .[167]

There are a number of elements of this description that do not ring entirely true. The first concerns its source. At first blush, one has the impression that Abbé Dubois had direct knowledge of these mysteries, these secret nocturnal rites; yet what is it that he actually states? (1) *People have seen* (2) *so-called magicians* organize nocturnal gatherings (3) *at a deserted spot known to me*. In fact, Dubois is not claiming to have been an eyewitness to these practices; it is other people who have seen them. But then we have to ask the question: Who but a participant in these rites would have seen them? One can hardly imagine that nonparticipants would have been invited as spectators to these secret rituals. Therefore, Dubois' informants were either participants in these rites, or spies of some sort, or simply liars or gossips. In every one of these three possible scenarios, these informants are making a value judgment about the officiants of these rites: they are *so-called* magicians. Now, magicians have historically been ranked among the bottom feeders of Indian society, together with petty thieves, swindlers, and false ascetics—so what would a *so-called* magician be? And what would a *so-called* magician be if reports of him are coming to Dubois from people who are likely spies, liars, or gossips? The sole eyewitness claim Dubois makes concerning these nocturnal rites is that they take place *at a deserted spot known to me*. Here as well, we find ourselves at an interpretive impasse. If Dubois, a foreign regular, knows where these mysteries take place, how mysterious and secret can they be? Presumably everyone in the district would have been au courant in that case. Finally, as it turns out, the biggest liar in this entire scenario is Dubois himself: Sylvia Murr has demonstrated beyond a doubt that Dubois' celebrated ethnography was plagiarized from the writings of a late-eighteenth-century French regular, Father Coeurdoux.[168]

While we can be certain that Dubois was not an eyewitness to them, it nonetheless remains the case that certain elements of his description of these nocturnal mysteries correspond quite precisely to those found in a number of Tantric ritual texts on the secret rites. Now we have a new set of questions: If these rites are secret, why would they have been written down? And even if these ritual texts were withheld from outsiders—and threats in post-tenth-century texts themselves describing the dire punishments of persons leaking such information are an indication that although committed to writing, they were nonetheless intended to be kept secret—how is it that a foreign cleric could have had such authentic knowledge of the contents of the rites described in them, their participants, and the site of those practices?

Let us return to Dubois' description of the rite, which states that "Brahmins, Sudras, Pariahs, men and women all become drunk on the alcohol consecrated to *Sakty*." Persons from every walk of life and every segment of the social spectrum are participating in a nocturnal rite. What happens on the following day? Everyone dissembles, going about their daily life as if nothing had happened the night before. Yet everyone knows where they were the night before, and in the Gemeinschaft society of traditional India, everyone in the village, town, or neighborhood would also have been privy to the fact that something was going on in the cremation ground or forest grove out on the edge of town on the last new-moon night, or some other temporal conjuncture. So in the end, there is very little secret about these secret nocturnal Kaula rites: it's as if half the town were Freemasons, with the other half knowing the former had a lodge and regular meetings, and pretty much everyone knowing who was who and what was what, but saying they were not telling.

9. The Tantric Turn and the Strategy of Dissimulation

I have used this protracted discussion as a means of indicating that in the Tantric context what has perhaps been essential is not keeping a secret itself, but rather maintaining a cult of secrecy, that is, the notion that there is a secret being kept, and that that secret is so very powerful and so very secret that it is necessary that people dissemble, maintaining a secret identity in a society where keeping secrets is a near impossibility. This is not to say that there did not or do not exist *tāntrikas* who have practiced their religion in totally isolated sites far removed from all human habitation. However, as I have argued, textual, ethnographic, sculptural, and archaeological evidence from the seventh century down to the present day indicate that the great bulk of Kaula or Tantric practice has occurred within or near domesticated or public spaces, and that its secrets have been less important than their cult of secrecy.

Perhaps the most celebrated textual example of the Tantric cult of secrecy is Abhinavagupta's TĀ, whose twenty-ninth book is entitled "An Exposition of the Secret Precepts" (*rahasyavidhiprakāśana*). Once again, we are brought up short by an apparent internal contradiction: Why would this master of masters offer a written exposition of, throw light upon (*āloka*), the secrets of his tradition? Might these not have been transmitted orally, thereby obviating the need for a written description that could have fallen under the eyes of persons from whom he would have wished to conceal them? As we have seen, many of the contents of this twenty-ninth book describe precisely the sort of rites that Abbé Dubois chronicles in his purloined nineteenth-century account. We may therefore conclude that these secret practices were as poorly kept secrets in the eleventh century as they were in the nineteenth. A passage from the twenty-eighth book of the same TĀ indicates that Abhinavagupta was aware of the penetrability of his secret circle:

> . . . when a group of people gather together during the performance of a dance or song, and so on, there will be true enjoyment when they are concentrated and immersed in the spectacle all together and not one by one.
>
> . . . This is the reason why during the rites of adoration of the circle one must remain attentive and not allow anyone to enter whose consciousness is in a dispersed state . . . because he will be a source of contraction [of the collective pleasure of expansive consciousness]. If through some negligence a stranger succeeds in entering, the initiated ritual may proceed together with him provided that he does not enter in a state of contraction. Such a one, if divine grace falls upon him, will become concentrated and absorbed with the various rituals, but if he is struck by a sinister and malevolent power of the Lord [i.e., a demon], he will criticize the group.[169]

If we are to take Abhinavagupta at his word here, it is fear of outside criticism that is the motor to his concern for secrecy, even as he commits all his group's secrets to writing.[170] In fact, as Alexis Sanderson has forcefully argued, it was public opinion that motivated Abhinavagupta and his school to effect a radical reformulation, even a reformation, of Hindu Tantra.

> By the tenth century, the Śaiva scene [in Kashmir] was dominated by the confrontation of two radically opposed schools, on the one hand, a group of nondualistic [Tantric] traditions . . . and on the other, the [orthodox] dualistic Śaiva Siddhānta. . . . The rise of the nondualist theology that opposed the Śaiva Siddhānta . . . sought to accommodate orthodox life. . . . While the dualists adapted Śaivism to the orthodox view of the castebound ritual agent, the nondualists offered the initiate an esoteric self *concealed within his perceived individuality*, a blissful, transindividual consciousness which, being the cause and substance of all phenomena, could be seen as freely assuming the appearance of his limitation by an

> "outside world" and its values, as though it were an actor playing a role. Behind this outer conformity the Śaiva householder initiated into the Trika could experience the power of transcendence through contemplative worship that involved not only consumption of meat and wine but—in the case of the elite of *vīras* ("heroes")—sexual intercourse.[171]

In other words, dissimulation or role-playing by the Tantric practitioners possessed of such a divine, transindividual consciousness was, in this tenth- to eleventh-century context, a means by which householders could maintain an acceptable public persona—even as they continued to observe the old heterodox sectarian rites of the Kaula in secret, while competing with the entrenched Śaivasiddhānta orthodoxy for the hearts and minds of the general Kashmiri populace. Therefore, it is safe to say that the Trika's theological "reformation" was driven in part by its socio-religious agenda; in this case, to gain some sort of control over the principal worship deity of the vale of Kashmir, Svacchanda Bhairava.[172] Regardless of its immediate ends, Abhinavagupta's reformation of earlier Kaula theory and practice quickly became normative within Tantric circles well beyond the geographical limits of Kashmir. And so it is that dissimulation has, since the time of Abhinavagupta, lain at the heart of much of Tantric practice, even of Tantric identity. What began, then, as a particularly ingenious and theologically compelling response to the specific issue of putting a good public face on Kaula practice in Kashmir, later came to be seized upon by high-caste Hindu householders throughout medieval South Asia as a window of opportunity to experiment with a double (or triple) religious identity. Dissimulation was a means to do what one said one was not doing—or better still, to do what one said one was doing, when the saying was done in a secret language so encoded as to obscure from the uninitiated the true nature of the practice it was describing (i.e., partaking of the "sexually transmitted messages" of the silent Dūtī). This, I would argue, lies at the root of Father Coeurdoux's familiarity with a "secret" Tantric rite practiced in the eighteenth century: his informants, probably high-caste householders, were dissembling, describing to him practices in which they were themselves participants, by putting on their public face of orthodox Hindus shocked by the content of such practices. With this, we find further confirmation that the strategy of dissimulation is one that has been employed by actors from a wide spectrum of society, for a variety of reasons—psychological, philosophical, pecuniary, and political.

In this chapter I have sketched out in broad strokes what a hypothetical "Kaula polity" might have looked like, and the place of Tantra in South Asian society. In the two chapters that follow, I will attempt to reconstruct the multiple roles of the Kaula virtuosi, the Siddhas and Yoginīs.

Chapter 6

THE CONSORT OF THE YOGINĪ: *South Asian Siddha Cults and Traditions*

1. Siddha Demigods and Their Human Emulators in Medieval India

In chapter 4 we evoked the metaphysical explanation for the relationship between human Kaula practitioners and the supernatural beings with whom they transacted in their practice: the semidivine Siddhas and Yoginīs inhabit the bodies of selected human Kaula practitioners in order to "spontaneously sport with one another."[1] In the preceding chapter, we described the narrative appropriation of the same principal: Prince Naravāhanadatta is a "fallen" Vidyādhara who rediscovers his inherent demigod status through his karmically determined encounters with Vidyādharī women who have similarly fallen into human rebirths. Once these figures recover the knowledge of their past lives, a carnal knowledge, they return to their semidivine station and become the kings and queens of the firmament that they had been before their fall.[2] Naravāhanadatta is also a prince, whose elevation to a prior or innate semidivine station coincides with his realization of the status of universal conqueror, *cakravartin*. What these sources make clear is that, regardless of the innate power of the Yoginī, the prime Tantric actors in South Asia have always been male, and the historical record of Tantric practice, in literature, architecture, and the arts, has always been told through the eyes of a male protagonist, who sought or claimed for himself the status of Virile Hero or Perfected Being. We now trace the history of these beings in South Asian traditions.

Since at least the time of the Hindu epics, cults of a group of demigods known as the Siddhas have figured in the pantheons of South Asian Hindus, Buddhists, and Jains alike. These beings form the cast of thousands in the pageant of heaven: whenever a hero performs some great deed or travels to the atmospheric regions, a host of Siddhas, Vidyādharas (Wizards), and Cāraṇas (Coursers)[3] sings his praises and showers him with flowers. Who were the semidivine Siddhas? Already in the time of the Epics, they were (and in some cases they remain) the object of popular cults. The *Amarakośa*, a fifth-century lexicon, classes them—together with the Vidyādharas, Yakṣas, Apsarasas, Rākṣasas, Kinnaras, Gandharvas, Piśācas, Guhyakas, and Bhūtas—as *devayonayaḥ*, demigods "born from a divine womb" and therefore not subject to death.[4] Over time the notion arose that the realm or level of the Siddhas was one to which humans, too, could accede, and so it was that in the course of the medieval period, a growing pool of "human" Siddhas and an expanding body of Siddha legend came to be constituted.[5] With the emergence of the Kaula, the semidivine Siddhas became associated with the Yoginīs, their female counterparts of the atmospheric regions. These latter, too, had their human emulators, called Yoginīs or Dūtīs, and the origins of Tantra are intimately entwined with the ritual interactions of these self-made gods and goddesses. Beings called Siddhas—now identified as demigods, now as human virtuosi who become possessed by the same—also play important roles in the popular religion of western India. In this chapter I will trace the religious history of the Siddhas, from their lofty origins at the cope of heaven or the tops of distant mountains, to their identification with human practitioners whose greatest aspiration was, precisely, to fly to the realm of their semidivine role models, and, finally, to their internalization within the yogic body of those same human practitioners.

While the hills of central India are dotted with the ruins of Yoginī temples from the early medieval period, there is not a single edifice on the subcontinent that one could qualify as a "Siddha temple" in the sense of a temple to the Siddhas (although a handful of temples to Śiva Siddheśvara, "Lord of the Siddhas," did exist in the medieval period).[6] Despite this, it is nonetheless the consort of the Yoginī, the male Siddha, who is the heroic "protagonist" of much of the literature of the period, both secular and sacred. The various Kaula and Tantric liturgies are always described from the perspective of the male practitioner, who, in addition to being termed the "Son of the Clan" or the "Virile Hero," is also often referred to as a Perfected Being in a lineage of Perfected Beings going back to the founders of the various Kaula lineages. These lineages, as we have seen, constitute the "flow of gnosis" (*jñāna-pravāha*), whose initiates, "conversant in the secret signs and meeting places of the various lineages . . . range among the *pīṭhas*," to receive initiations and supernatural empowerments from the mouths of Yoginīs.[7]

The fourteenth- to fifteenth-century *Śaṅkaravijaya* of Ānandagiri,[8] which devotes its forty-ninth chapter to a description of the Siddhas, clearly demonstrates the power-based nature of these traditions:

> Then the Siddha practitioners Cirakīrti, Nityānanda, Parārjuna, etc., came together and said to the Swami [Śaṅkarācārya], "Hey Swami!
>
> "Our own doctrine is based on what is manifestly real. It is, to be sure, a highly multifaceted doctrine that flows from the diverse nature of our Siddha practices. Here, by means of the complete perfection of mantras obtained through the Siddha teachings, we have realized our goals and are eternally free. . . .
>
> "Having gained possession of special herbs and mantras at Srisailam and other lofty sites where divine beings make themselves visible, Satyanātha and others became Siddhas, persons who had realized their goal and long life. We are of the same sort [as they, living] according to their [Siddha] precepts. The entire expanding universe is fully known to us.
>
> "Through our special knowledge of [various powers of sorcery], and our special expertise in gaining mastery over [each of the five elements], and by virtue of drinking poisons, drinking mercury, and drinking [specially prepared] oils . . . [and] by means of special forms of yogic practice, [we effect] the removal of accidental or untimely death. By means of special [acts of] sorcery (*kriyā*) . . . through special Śaktis . . . Yakṣiṇīs . . . [and] Mohinīs, by means of the various divisions of *Kakṣ[y]apuṭa* knowledge, iron-making, copper-making, silver-making, gold-making, etc., by means of various types of metallurgical expertise . . . [and] through the special use of black mercuric oxide, roots, and mantras, magic and great magic, we can strike people blind and bind lions, *śarabhas*, and tigers. By means of this panoply of specialized practices, we are, in fact, *omniscient*."

In this precious text, we find not only clear evidence for the scope of the medieval Siddha traditions, but also early references to specific centers for Siddha practice (Srisailam),[9] Siddha literature (*Kakṣ[y]apuṭa*),[10] and Siddha practitioners (Nityānanda, Satyanātha, Cirakīrti, Parārjuna).[11] It also brings into focus what one may call the "Siddha distinction," as such has been defined by the great Tantric practitioner-scholar Gopinath Kaviraj: "Some . . . were accomplished (*siddha*) in the alchemical path (*rasamārga*), some accomplished in *haṭha yoga*, and still others had perfected themselves through Tantric practices or through the use of sexual fluids (*bindu-sādhanā*)."[12] To these we might add sorcery that generally involved the use of mantras to conjure and control powerful female entities—the Śaktis, Yakṣiṇīs, and Mohinīs mentioned in this passage. The guiding principle here seems to have been one of controlling a universe that was understood to be a *body*, the body of the divine consort of Śiva, the body of one's own consort, the feminine in one's own body, and the embodied universe.

2. Siddhas and Yoginīs in the *Kaulajñānanirṇaya*

Some of my discussion of the Siddhas in this chapter revisits matters discussed in *The Alchemical Body*, and the reader is invited to consult that work for further data on the Nāth Siddhas in particular. There was, however, another important sectarian offshoot of the earlier mythological, cosmological, and soteriological Siddha traditions: this was the Siddha Kaula, the Kaula sect of which Matsyendra(nātha) was an adherent if not the legendary founder. With the Siddha Kaula, we perhaps find ourselves in the presence of the earliest group of Indian practitioners seeking to identify themselves with the demigod Siddhas. A ninth- to tenth-century account of them, found in the *Mṛgendrāgama*, juxtaposes them with a number of other groups, whose ontological statuses are equally ambiguous:

> The sages know of eight [other] currents, connected respectively to Śiva, the Mantreśvaras, the Gaṇas, Gods, Ṛṣis, Guhyas, the Yoginī Kaula and the Siddha Kaula. . . . The Yoginīs received a wisdom that immediately causes yoga to shine forth. It was called Yoginī Kaula because it never went beyond the limits of their circle. The same is the case for the other [i.e., the Siddha Kaula current].[13]

In fact, the Yoginīs' wisdom did go beyond the limits of their circle, and it was Matsyendra, precisely, who is held to have been responsible for this development. This is the subject of the KJñN mythology of the theft and recovery of the Kaula scriptures, discussed in chapter 4. As we also have shown, it is for his fusion of the Siddha Kaula with the Yoginī Kaula that Matsyendra is venerated by the great Abhinavagupta in the opening lines of his TĀ. Matsyendra's pivotal role in the history of Hindu Tantra has been described by Alexis Sanderson:

> The distinction between Kula and Kaula traditions . . . is best taken to refer to the clan-structured tradition of the cremation-grounds seen in the *Brahmayāmala-Picumata*, *Jayadratha Yāmala*, *Tantrasadbhāva*, *Siddhayogeśvarīmata Tantra*, etc. (with its Kāpālika *kaulikā vidhayaḥ*) on the one hand and on the other its reformation and domestication through the banning of mortuary and all sect-identifying signs (*vyaktaliṅgatā*), generally associated with Macchanda/Matsyendra.[14]

A reference to the Kaula practitioner's concealment of sectarian marks (*guptaliṅgin*) is found in chapter 22 of the KJñN, which groups the Siddhas together with the deities who are receiving the oral teachings of Bhairava.[15] Chapter 9 of the same work presents the various categories of Kaula practitioners, in which the text's divine revealer Bhairava states:

> I will describe the array of the assemblies of the preceptors, Siddhas and Yoginīs . . . [as well as] the entire group of Airborne (Khecarī) Mothers of all the Siddhas and Yoginīs [and] the entire group of Lords of the Fields[16] [present at] the dwellings of all the Land-based (Bhūcarī) Yoginīs. All of the Mantra-born, Yoga-born, Mound-born, Innately-born, and Clan-born [beings, as well as] all of the Door Guardians and all of the Womb-born Yoginīs and Siddhas[17] are worshiped in different ways in the four ages—in the Kṛta, Dvāpara, Treta and greatly afflicted Kali age.[18]

Then, following a list of eighteen Siddhas and five Yoginīs that are to be worshiped, the chapter goes on to give the following mytho-historical account of the Siddhas:

> One first makes the [utterance] *hrīṃ*, followed by *śrīṃ*. One should place the display of this pair of syllables beyond the boundary [of the mandala].[19] The one [represents] the Siddhas and [the other] the Yoginīs, [who taken together constitute] the perfected beings. . . . There has never been such a Gnosis as this, and there never will be. In [this], the most terrifying, exceedingly fearsome and savage Kali age, the sixteen Siddhas are well known. In the Kṛta, Dvāpara and Treta, they are worshiped as Virile Heroes. [These are the Siddhas called the] Mṛṣṇipādas, Avatārapādas, Sūryapādas, Dyutipādas, Omapādas, Vyāghrapādas, Hariṇipādas, Pañcaśikhapādas, Komalapādas and Lambodarapādas.[20] These are the first great Siddhas, those who brought the Kula and the Kaula down [to earth]. In each of the four ages, these are the ones who animate the independent Clan. Through the power of knowledge of this [Clan], many are the men who have become perfected. This Kaula has an extension of ten *koṭis* beyond the world of existence.[21]

The balance of chapter 9 recounts the transmission of the highest essence of the Mahākaula through a series of exclusively female deities, from "the Yoginī called Icchā(-śakti) by the Siddhas" down through the Airborne Mothers, and the Land-based Yoginīs. The chapter concludes with the promise that the mortal (male) practitioner who receives this gnosis (*jñāna*) shall obtain enjoyment (*bhukti*), liberation (*mukti*), and supernatural power (*siddhi*), and become the beloved of the Yoginīs.[22] The source of this transmission is detailed in the second chapter of the KJñN, entitled "Emission and Retraction," in which the relationship between Śiva and Śakti in her three forms is shown to be a circular or cyclical one: "Śakti is gone into the midst of Śiva; Śiva is situated in the midst of Kriyā [-śakti]; Kriyā[-śakti] is absorbed into the midst of Jñāna[-śakti]; [and] Jñāna[-śakti][23] is absorbed by Icchā[-śakti]. Icchā[-śakti] goes to the state of absorption there where the transcendent Śiva [shines in his] effulgence." The importance of this dynamic is underscored in the final verse of this chapter: "The foundation of the Clan [as regulated] by [the cycle of] emission and retraction has been briefly described."[24]

The classes of Siddhas and Yoginīs mentioned in passing in chapter 9 of the KJñN are described in greater detail in the preceding chapter,[25] which opens with an account of six types of Śaktis, known as "Field-born," "Mound-born," "Yoga-born," "Mantra-born," "Innately-born," and "Clan-born." The Kaula practitioner is instructed to practice, together with the last two of these—along with another type of Śakti, the "Lowest-born" —in an isolated, uninhabited spot, using flowers, incense, fish, meat, and other offerings.[26] Here, the term "Lowest-born" refers to an outcaste woman; a married woman is called "Innately-born," and a prostitute is called "Clan-born."[27] Three of these are stationed within the body, while three are external.[28]

Following this, a sexual ritual involving the Kaula practitioner and a "Lowest-born" woman is described: their conjoined sexual fluids, placed in a set of two vessels (*yugmapātra*), are offered to the sixty-four Yoginīs and the fifty-eight Vīras, "all [of them] clad in blood[-red] garments, and effulgent with armlets and bracelets of gold."[29] Next the text evokes the worship of the great Field-born Yoginīs and Siddhas, together with the great Goddess, at the eight Indian cities or shrines of Karavīra (Karnataka, western Deccan), Mahākāla (Ujjain), Devīkoṭa (Bengal), Varanasi, Prayaga, Caritra-Ekāmraka (Bhubanesvar), Aṭṭahāsa (Bengal?), and Jayantī.[30] A number of Hindu and Buddhist Tantric works present similar lists of centers of Yoginī and Kaula worship, lists that appear to indicate the geographical parameters of Kaula practice in the early medieval period. These would have been the sites at which male Virile Heroes and female Yoginīs would have met on specified nights of the lunar calendar to observe the Kaula *melakas* and other rites.

Associated with these because they were born at and preside over these sites are sixteen "Field-born" male Siddhas. This is the first of six groups of Siddhas, which correspond to six types of Śaktis.[31] Hereafter, the KJñN enumerates four Mounds (*pīṭhas*)—Kāmākhyā, Pūrṇagiri, Uḍḍiyāna, and Arvuda[32]—each of which comprises numerous secondary mounds (*upapīṭhas*), fields, and secondary fields (*upakṣetras*). Then, stating that it will provide instructions for worship of these and their divinities, the text offers a second list, this time of sixteen Mound-born Siddhas who were born at these sites.[33] The Siddhas who became perfected (*siddha*) through the practice of yoga are called "Yoga-born"; those who propitiate [with] mantras are "Mantra-born."[34] Next, referring to a well-known Puranic myth of the Goddess's defeat of the demon Ruru at Blue Mountain (usually identified with Kāmākhyā), the text explains the origins of the "Innately-born" Siddhas.[35] Hereafter, eight goddesses—many of whose names correspond to the classical listing of the Seven Mothers—are listed as the "Pervading Mothers."[36] Also mentioned are the female Door Guardians. All of these, the text states, are to be worshiped, together with their retinues of Siddha preceptors, in every town and city.[37]

Chapter 20 of the KJñN gives another account of these same actors, with certain variations in terminology. It begins by making a distinction between the Clan Śaktis and Virile Heroes and "another Śakti," Icchā-śakti, already identified in chapter 9 as the supreme Goddess. Following this, the Goddess, saying that Jñānā-śakti is already known to her, asks the narrator Bhairava to give an account of Kriyā-śakti.[38] In answer, the text gives a description of the Śakti of the Virile Hero—that is, the human consort of the male practitioner—such as is found in dozens of Tantric descriptions (her Buddhist homologue would be the "Karma-Mudrā"). This is followed by that of her counterpart, the Virile Hero, described in equally idealized terms. Both are clearly human figures, possessed of the requisite physical, emotional, and mental qualities for admission into and participation in Clan ritual.[39] Chapter 11 of the KJñN gives additional data, listing the *kulasamay[in]* ("pledge"), *kulaputra* ("son of the clan"), and *sādhaka* ("master") levels of initiation. These appear to correspond to the standard terminology, found in the Āgamas of the Śaivasiddhānta, for ascetics having undergone the three successive initiations known as *samayin*, *putra*, and *sādhaka*. Other inferior levels of initiation described in various Tantric sources include the *miśraka*, the "mixed" initiate, and the *daiva* ("divine") category of initiate: both refer to the occasional practitioner, the householder who temporarily ventures into the ritual circle of Tantric practice, to return to his household and householder lifestyle at the end of the ritual period.[40]

Most of the data found in these three chapters of the KJñN concern entities named Mothers, Śaktis, Yoginīs, Vīras, and Siddhas. Among these, the females entities are located both within and outside the body, with the latter being identified with—or incarnating in—different types of human women. More often than not, the males appear to be human, born at different locations identifiable as cities, mountains, temples, or shrines situated on the territory of the Indian subcontinent. However, both Siddhas and Vīras are objects of (often internal) worship in this text,[41] an indication that some if not all of these had raised themselves to divine or semidivine status through their practice, through their interactions with females identified as goddesses, in earlier ages. This, precisely, is the major innovation of the medieval Siddha traditions. Whereas the Siddhas were in earlier mythological, cosmological, and soteriological traditions superhuman demigods who had never entered a human womb, the Siddhas of the Kaula clans were humans who, through their practice, acceded to semidivine status and the power of atmospheric flight. At a still later stage, they were also internalized, to become objects of worship within the bodies of male initiates, who also called themselves Siddhas or Vīras. We will discuss the process of their internalization later in this chapter, and the internalization of the Yoginī in chapter 8.

3. Siddhas as Mountain Gods in Indian Religious Literature

Well before the KJñN and other Kaula works, the place of the Siddhas whom human practitioners emulated and venerated had long been established in the mythology, symbol systems, and "systematic geography"[42] of the subcontinent. Generally speaking, Hindu, Jain, and to a lesser extent Buddhist sources offer three primary venues as the abodes of the semidivine Siddhas: atop mountains located near either the center or the periphery of the terrestrial disk (Bhūloka); in atmospheric regions above the sphere of heaven (Svarloka); and at the summit of the cosmic egg, at the level variously known as Brahmaloka, Satyaloka, or Siddhaloka.

The first of these venues appears to be the earliest and the most widely attested. In fact, certain of the high gods of Hinduism were identified, early on, as mountains. In Tamil traditions, Murukaṉ is the "Lord of the Mountains" (*malaikiḻavōṉ*), more closely identified with the "mountain landscape" than with the son of Śiva in the *saṅgam* literature. Similarly, Govardhana, the mountain of Kṛṣṇa mythology, was worshiped as a mountain in its own right before being incorporated, relatively late, into the cult of that god. Moreover, it continues to be worshiped as a mountain today by the tribal inhabitants of Braj, independent of its associations with Kṛṣṇa.[43] Before the many strands of his earlier traditions coalesced into the familiar elephant-headed form in which he has been worshiped for centuries, Gaṇeśa, too, had his origins in mountain cults of the northwestern regions of the Indian subcontinent. Going back to Epic traditions, we find the mountain-dwelling Śiva wedded to Pārvatī ("Mountain Girl"), the daughter of Himavān ("Himalaya"); still earlier, the RV characterizes *all* mountains as supernatural beings, possessed of the power of flight, until Indra, the king of the gods, clips their wings![44]

In western India in particular, one encounters very early traditions of (1) a god named Śrīnāth, Nāthjī, Jālandharnāth, Siddheśvara,[45] and so on; (2) a grouping of semidivine figures, known as the Siddhas, who frequent the upper levels of the atmosphere, below the heaven of the gods, but who also walk the earth in human guise;[46] and (3) a group of deities known as the Nine Nāths (*navanātha*), who originally had nothing to do with the *historical* Nāth Siddhas and their legendary histories of the nine founders of their order. Quite often, these divine Nāths were identified as mountains: the mountain itself was named either "Nāth" or "Siddha." This tradition of identifying mountains as divine Nāths or Siddhas is one that also continues down to the present day in Maharashtra, Nepal, Rajasthan, and Himachal Pradesh.[47] However, even after the advent of the Nāth religious orders, the cults of mountains called "Nāth" or "Siddha" have persisted.

These traditions are particularly strong in western India, as a number of royal chronicles and popular traditions demonstrate. A relatively recent case concerns Mān Singh of Jodhpur, the early nineteenth-century Rathore king of Marwar. Mān Singh's story begins at Jalore fort, in southwestern Rajasthan, where he and his army were besieged by his evil relation Bhīm Singh between the months of July and October 1803. Mān Singh was poised to surrender to Bhīm Singh, when the latter suddenly died, opening the way for the young prince to return to Jodhpur and claim the throne, which he did in early November. This story, which has been told and retold by many historians and hagiographers, has also been told by its protagonist, Mān Singh himself. In his own version of the story, recorded in his *Mahārāja Mān Singh rī Khyāt*, *Jalandhar Carit*, and *Jalandhar Candroday*,[48] it is a Nāth Siddha named Āyas Dev Nāth, the stronghold of Jalore itself (whose ancient names include Jālandhara, Jālandharī, and Jālīndhar), and its local deity, named Jālandharnāth, that are highlighted.[49]

Mān Singh had decided on September 16, 1803, that he would surrender ten days later, on Dīpāvalī, if there was no change in his situation. It is here that the supernatural intervenes in his accounts. Writing in his *Jalandhar Carit*, Mān Singh states that he placed all his faith in the venerable Jālandharnāth,[50] whom he also calls Siddhanāth, Siddheśvara, Jogendra, Jogrāj, and Nāth at other points in the text. So it was that on the eve of Dīpāvalī itself a miracle occurred:

> The Nāth produced a miracle in that difficult time,
> giving his proof one day at morningtide—
> On the tenth of the bright fortnight of Aśvin,
> at an auspicious hour and moment on that holy day,
> His two beautiful footprints shone,

on the pure and fine-grained yellow stone . . .
The king touched his forehead to those feet:
Śrīnāth has come to meet the king![51]

Jālandharnāth left the yellow mark of his footprints on the living rock of the mountain stronghold in which Mān Singh and his army were besieged. The name of this mountain, upon which the fort was built, is Kalashacal ("Water-Pot Mountain"), a peak already identified with Jālandharnāth prior to this epiphany: in fact, Mān Singh had passed much of his youth at Jalore and was steeped in its traditions concerning the god.[52] Below that summit there existed a cave that is still identified with Jālandharnāth, known as Bhanvar Gupha, "Black Bee Cave," whose name is a clear reference to the uppermost *cakra* of the yogic body.[53] It would likely have been at this site that the epiphany of Jālandharnāth's footprints would have taken place.

Mān Singh took the mark of Jālandharnāth's feet to be visible proof that the god had come there, and that the siege would soon be lifted. The *Mahārāja Mān Singh rī Khyāt* further relates that on the following night, Āyas Dev Nāth—the custodian of the site, who had himself gone to worship the god—received the order from Jālandharnāth that if Mān Singh would hold the fort until October 21 (the bright sixth of the lunar month of Karrtik), he would not have to surrender, and that the kingdom of Jodhpur would be his.[54] When he related this to Mān Singh, the prince replied that if such should come to pass, Āyas Dev Nāth would share his kingdom with him.[55] With one day remaining, Mān Singh received the news of Bhīm Singh's death. He then praised Āyas Dev Nāth and acknowledged that the Nāth Siddha was truly Jālandharnāth incarnate: "Your body too is that of a Nāth, in matter and form; you are yourself the world-protector Jālandharnāth!"[56]

It is important to note here that, apart from the mention of the yellow mark of his footprints left on the floor of his shrine, Mān Singh himself never states that Jālandharnāth intervened in his miraculous deliverance from the siege of Jalore. Rather it is his relationship to the undeniably human figure Āyas Dev Nāth, whom the young king rewards following his enthronement in Jodhpur in November 1803, that is emphasized in his writing. Mān Singh's poetic treatment of Jālandharnāth squares with the nature of the latter's cult in Jalore, and in Marwar in general: Jālandharnāth, although he once lived as a yogin on the *tapobhūmi* of Water-Pot Mountain and the Black Bee Cave, is in fact a god who chose to incarnate himself as a yogin at that time.[57] The *Nāth Caritr*, a work commissioned by Mān Singh, is deliberately ambiguous on the subject: "I know not whether

Figure 6.a. Rajput prince kneeling before Nāth Siddha in a mountain setting. Freize from Mahāmandir, Jodhpur, built by Mahārāja Mān Singh in 1804 C.E. to honor Āyas Dev Nāth. Photograph by David Gordon White.

it was a muni, a Siddha, or a man who made his seat at that place. His ancient supreme form has dwelt there for many eons."[58]

Jālandarnāth's role as a local mountain god intersects that of a number of other regional deities from western India. Mallināth, another figure in the history of the Rathore Rajputs, is another Rajasthani case in point. This historical figure, who was a fourteenth-century military champion of the Rathores, has a name that may be construed as "lord of the mountain" (*male* in Kannada; *mallai* in Tamil).[59] Tradition maintains that he was, in addition to being a warrior, a perfected man (*siddh puruṣ*) and a yogin. When he died, in 1399, a tumulus (*samādhi*) and temple were erected at his place in Tilwada village in Barmer District, where a cattle fair is held annually in the month of Caitra. The entire mountainous region of western Marwar, called Malani, is named after him.[60] Near the town of Alwar in eastern Rajasthan, there is a hill named Booti Siddh ("Perfected One of Healing Herbs"), to which Ayurvedic physicians come to collect those herbs (*jaḍī-būṭī*), and which is said to be named after a hermit who lived there.[61] Here, I would argue, it was originally the hill itself that was called "Siddha," and that its identification with a human who dwelt there was made at a later date. Simon Digby reports a similar denomination of a hill, near Monghyr in Bihar. In this case, the holy man identified with the hill, whose site is marked by a shady margosa tree,[62] is a Muslim saint. The hill is therefore called Pīr Pahāṛī, the "Hill of the Saint"; in India the

Islamic "Pīr" is the cognate of the Hindu "Nāth Siddha," as witnessed in the Islamicized name of Matsyendranāth, which is "Morcha Pīr."[63]

A similar situation obtains at Jodhpur, where the imposing royal fort standing atop the towering promontory that dominates the modern city of Jodhpur was built, according to legend, at the site of a hermit's lair. That site, called Cīḍiyānāth kī Dhūnī, the "Fireplace of the Lord of the Birds," is located at the base of a cliff that rises up to form the western face of the fort's promontory. Atop the cliff, perhaps fifty meters above Cīḍiyānāth kī Dhūnī, is the great royal temple of the goddess Cāmuṇḍā; and constantly rising and falling on the winds that blow constantly at that place are dozens of kites, the same dark, massive birds that are emblazoned on the coat of arms of the house of Marwar. Here again, it was most probably the mountain itself that was called "Lord of the Birds," before the site became identified with a solitary human inhabitant. And if the Lord of the Birds was in fact a "Siddha mountain" itself, its Yoginī consorts were already there as well, in the form of the birds that made it their home: we have demonstrated the avian origins of the Yoginīs in chapter 2.

In the light of these data, we may see that the "birthplaces" of the Siddhas and Yoginīs outlined in chapter 8 of the KJñN, as well as the prescribed sites at which human Siddhas and Yoginīs are to gather together for the Kaula rites—that is, on clan mountains (*kula-parvatas*), mounds (*pīṭhas*) generally identified with mountaintops, and fields (*kṣetras*)—correspond precisely to the early mythology and lore of the semidivine Siddhas, who were themselves mountains, and their Yoginī consorts, who were the wild creatures inhabiting those mountains (fig. 6.b).

Apart from the great Himalayan peaks, the prototypical mountain god of India is Srisailam, the "Venerable Peak" located in the heart of the Deccan, in the Kurnool District of Andhra Pradesh.[64] The Maharashtran legend of Siddharāmayya—closely connected, according to Günther Sontheimer, with the story of Siddheśvara (also a name of Jālandharnāth in Mān Singh's writings) of Sholapur—relates man and mountain in ways that we have already seen. Here, a mute Liṅgāyat herder child named Siddharāmayya is taking care of his father's cattle when Mahādeva (Śiva) appears to him in the form of a wandering Jaṅgama (Liṅgāyat) ascetic and asks him for some *hurḍā* (immature kernels of millet or barley). Siddharāmayya gives him these, at which point the ascetic, whose name is Mallayya, asks the child for some rice mixed with yogurt. Siddharāmayya runs to his mother and asks for food for the Jaṅgama. His mother is astonished that he can speak. He runs back to the spot, but the ascetic has disappeared.[65]

Here, the ascetic Mallayya is a human incarnation of the Srisailam

Figure 6.b. Thāṇī Yoginī, Bheraghat Yoginī temple, Jabalpur District, Madhya Pradesh, ca. 1000 C.E. The swirling motifs in the foreground represent either mountain peaks or clouds. Courtesy of the American Institute of Indian Studies.

mountain itself, which was worshiped as a deity in its own right, under the name of Mallana or Mallayya ("Mountain") before becoming identified in later centuries with the Śaiva *jyotirliṅgam* named Mallikārjuna.[66] Among the Liṅgāyats, whose historical base has always been the western Deccan plateau, the Vīra-Baṇañjas, the master merchants of this western region, had a mountain (*guḍḍa-dhvaja*) as the coat of arms on its banner. Khaṇḍobā, a widely worshiped deity in this region—himself said to be the "apotheosis" of a Liṅgāyat merchant—is also known by the name of Mallayya in Karnataka. The most common names for Liṅgāyat and Kuruba men are Mallayya, Mallāppā, Malleś, and Mallināth. As an incarnation of Śiva, the divine Khaṇḍobā-Mallayya has a close connection with mountains: this points to the likelihood that the name Mallayya is derived from the Kannada *male* ("mountain") and *ayya* ("father," "lord").[67]

The same Siddheśvara of Sholapur is the subject of a rich body of mythic tradition in other parts of the interior of Maharashtra, where he is variously named Siddheśvara, Śid, Śidobā, Mhasvaḍ-Śid, Siddhanāth, or simply Nāth.[68] This figure is identified with the deity of the Siddheśvara temple of Mhasvad (Satara District), whose cult was established there, according to an 1138 C.E. inscription, through a land grant made by an ancestor of the Kalacuri king Bijjala of Kalyāṇī, a Cāḷukyan vassal.[69] In one of these local myths, Siddhanāth is a "*sannyāsī*" sent to the underworld by Śaṅkara (Śiva) to confront Jogeśvarī, one of the "Seven Sisters" of Dhangar tradition, whom he wins and makes his wife.[70]

The same Siddheśvara is identified as a human figure who in 1136 C.E. constructed a great water reservoir in Sholapur (Sholapur District), and who, through the performance of religious austerities, attained many *siddhis*. Curiously, or not so curiously, Siddharāja, a Cāḷukya king of Anahilvāḍa between the years of 1094 and 1143 C.E., is said to have carried out an identical construction project, of the Sahasraliṅga tank, in his capital city, in modern-day Gujarat, hundreds of miles to the northwest.[71] Yet Siddheśvara has also been a title applied to powerful holy men in western India. So, for example, Revaṇa, a founder of the Liṅgāyat order, "killed the goddess Māyī [in Kolhapur], who held captive by her valor nine hundred thousand Siddhas or Liṅgāyat saints."[72] Ritual specialists at temples of the deified Revaṇa and others are themselves called "Śids" (Siddhas): these are possessed by the god when they beat their own bodies with swords or sticks. Jostling with these local Śid traditions are those of Vīrs (Vīras). In this context, a Vīr is someone who knows how to gain special yogic abilities. He has the power to subject the fifty-two spirits or deities (also called Vīrs!) to himself, or to master the *siddhis*, by virtue of which he himself becomes a Siddha.[73]

4. Locations of the Siddhas in Indian Cosmologies and Soteriologies

Already in the *Agni Purāṇa,* Srisailam was known as a *siddhakṣetra,* a term that may be read in two ways, on the one hand, as field (*kṣetra*) of the demigod Siddha identified with the mountain itself, and as the field upon which human Siddhas lived and practiced.[74] The KSS calls the Mountain of Sunrise the "field of the Siddhas" (*siddhakṣetra*),[75] and in a battle scene describes thirteen Vidyādhara warrior kings, each in terms of the mountain of which he is the master.[76]

Jain cosmological sources dating as far back as the second century B.C.E. are particularly rich in detail on the mountain haunts of the demigod Siddhas.[77] According to Jain cosmology, the easternmost peak of each of the six parallel east-to-west mountain ranges that divide the central continent of Jambudvīpa into seven unequal parts is crowned by a Siddha sanctuary, and therefore named either Siddhāyatana ("Abode of the Siddhas") or Siddhakūṭa ("Peak of the Siddhas").[78] Also according to Jain cosmology, four elephant-tusk-shaped mountain ranges radiate outward from Meru, the central pillar of the entire world system. The first peak of each of these ranges is named "Siddha."[79] Located closer to the periphery of the terrestrial disk is Nandīśvaradvīpa, the eighth continent of the Jain cosmos, at which this configuration is repeated, with the important difference that this mountain system features a Siddha temple sanctuary on every one of its peaks.[80] As such, Nandīśvaradvīpa is a veritable Siddha preserve, a continent reserved for the festive gatherings of these demigods.[81] Here, it is most particularly four Mountains of Black Antimony (Añjanagiris), located at the four cardinal points of this continent, that are crowned by Siddha shrines. The earliest extant graphic representation of this continent is a bas-relief in stone, dated to A.D. 1199–1200, and housed in a temple on Girnar, itself a Siddha mountain.[82]

Hindu religious literature locates the Siddha demigods in a number of venues. According to certain recensions of the MBh—which adhered to the early "four-continent system" of Hindu cosmography—the paradise "Land of the Northern Kurus" (Uttarakuru), located to the north of Mount Meru, lies on the far shore of the Śailoda ("Rock Water") River, whose touch turns humans to stone. On either shore of this river grow reeds that carry Siddhas to the opposite bank and back. This is a country where the Siddhas live together with divine nymphs in forests whose trees and flowers, composed of precious stones, exude a miraculous resin that is nothing other than the nectar of immortality itself.[83] This Uttarakuru location is found again in the circa fourth-century *Vāyu Purāṇa,* which names the site Candradvīpa, "Moon Island." This appears to be the earliest reference to this important mythic toponym, which I have discussed at length elsewhere, and which has already been evoked in chapter 4:

> To the south of Uttarakuru, there is a moon-shaped island known as Candradvīpa, which is the residence of the Devas. It is one thousand *yojanas* in area and is full of various kinds of fruits and flowers. . . . In its center there is a mountain, in shape and lustre like the moon . . . frequented by the Siddhas and Cāraṇas. . . . Therefore, that mountain and land are named as Moon Island and Moon Mountain after the name of the moon. . . .[84]

The *Varāha Purāṇa* locates Siddhas in mountain valleys immediately to the west of Mount Meru. According to this source, there lies between the Kumuda and Añjana mountains a wide plain called Mātuluṅga. No living creature walks there, save the Siddhas, who come to visit a holy pool. This association of Siddhas with a mountain called Añjana ("Black Antimony") reminds us of the Jain toponym mentioned above;[85] while the "moon-shaped" mountains of Candradvīpa appear to replicate the "elephant-tusk-shaped" mountain ranges of Jain cosmology simply by another name.

The sixth-century C.E. *Bṛhat Saṃhitā* of Varāhamihira and a number of Hindu astronomical works locate Siddhapura, the City of Siddhas, at the outermost edge of the central island-continent of Jambudvīpa, on the northern point of the compass on the terrestrial equator.[86] Several other Hindu sources locate the semidivine Siddhas at an atmospheric, if not heavenly level. The *Bhāgavata Purāṇa* (BhP) situates the Siddhas and Vidyādharas at the highest atmospheric level, immediately below the spheres of the sun and Rāhu, the descending node of the moon; immediately below them are the other *devayoni* beings listed in the *Amarakośa*, the "demonic" Yakṣas, Rākṣasas, Piśācas, and so on.[87] This last detail may appear strange, since the Puranic literature generally locates such beings beneath the terrestrial disk, in the netherworlds. We will return to this apparent anomaly later in this chapter. A number of Indian sources situate the Siddhas at the very summit of the cosmic egg. This uppermost level is termed either Satyaloka ("Real World") or Brahmaloka ("World of Brahmā/Brahman") in the Hindu literature. In Buddhist literature as well, the term Brahmaloka (or Brahmakāyika) is employed.[88] In Jain sources, in which the term Brahmaloka is employed to designate the entire world system, the name for this highest level of the universe is Siddhaloka, the "World of the Perfected Beings."

The Jains, who have historically been far more attentive to cosmology than both the Hindus and the Buddhists—by far the greatest number of

Figure 6.c. Siddhaloka, portrayed as crescent moon in the forehead of Jain Loka Puruṣa ("Universal Man"), ca. 1700 C.E. Photograph by Rusty Smith. Courtesy of the University of Virginia Art Museum, Charlottesville, Virginia.

extant cosmographies are Jain, and cosmography continues to form an important part of Jain religious education—have produced a significant number of descriptions and graphic images of this realm. The Jain Siddhaloka is located at the summit of the "middle world," on the border between the world (*loka*) and the nonworld (*a-loka*). This abode is represented graphically by a crescent moon often described as having the shape of an open umbrella, shown in profile on the forehead of the Loka Puruṣa, the Universal Man (fig. 6.c).[89] According to Jain soteriology, the soul, having regained its purity at the end of its ordeals, will leave its mortal remains behind and leap upward, in a single bound, to the summit of the universe, where it will alight beneath the umbrella-shaped canopy that shelters the assembly of the Siddhas.[90] Here as well, we may perhaps see in the crescent moon–shaped world of the Jain Siddhas the homologue of the Moon Island of the KJñN.

Now, a number of Jain representations of the world system in its anthropomorphized form of the Universal Man, or of Siddhaloka, the World of Perfected Beings, inscribe a man seated in yogic posture at the summit of that world. In these representations, we see, as it were, a yogic homunculus seated in or superimposed upon the cranial vault or forehead of a great man. When we turn to Hindu sources, we find a number of parallel data. An early source is the *Bhagavad Gītā* (8.16), in which Kṛṣṇa evokes the worlds up to the level of brahman (*brahmabhuvana*) from which creatures return (i.e., are reborn) eternally; "but having reached me, their rebirth does not occur." Later (15.16–18) he also speaks of three Puruṣas, which he calls the perishable, the imperishable, and the supreme. The first of these is the stuff of all living creatures; the third, which Kṛṣṇa identifies as himself, is transcendent; and the second, the imperishable, is *kūṭastha*, "seated on the peak." Now, when Kṛṣṇa says "seated on the peak," is he referring to the magnificent isolation of the yogin who practices his austerities on an isolated mountaintop? Or might he not be referring to the subtle peak located within the cranial vault of a meditating yogin (the term *trikūṭi*, "triple-peaked," is used for a region of the cranial vault in a number of sources), since Kṛṣṇa also refers to the human yogin as being "seated on the peak" at another point in the *Gītā* (6.8)? Artistic depictions of the yogic body often represent either the god Śiva or a yogin seated in lotus posture in the cranial region (fig. 6.d).[91]

In many Purāṇas, yogins figure prominently in the highest world, the World of Brahman. The *Viṣṇu*, *Vāyu*, and *Skanda Purāṇas* place the ascetic sons of Brahmā, together with yogins, renouncers, and others who have completed a course of religious austerities, in Satyaloka or Brahmaloka.[92] The *Brahmāṇḍa Purāṇa* locates "Siddha practitioners of yoga who have achieved immortality" in Brahmaloka; and places Gorakṣa—in a likely reference to the historical founder of the Nāth Siddhas and haṭha yoga—there: "There dwell the Siddhas, divine sages, others who practice breath control, and other Yogins the chief of whom is Gorakṣa. They have gaseous bodies. . . . They are eagerly devoted to the practice of yoga."[93] Another Puranic source says of the world of Brahman: "Here, Brahman, the Universal Soul, drinks the nectar of yoga (*yogāmṛta*) together with the yogins."[94] Here, we must pose the same question as we did regarding the term *kūṭastha* in the *Bhagavad Gītā:* Is this lofty station where the nectar of yoga is drunk located at the summit of the cosmic egg, or rather that of the cranial vault, where the yogin drinks the nectar of immortality that he has produced through his practice?

5. Exiting the Subtle Body

While most Western scholars tend to view the Purāṇas as repositories of a particularly baroque genre of Hindu mythology, Hindus themselves are more inclined to see them as encyclopedias of early scientific knowledge. When one looks at the mythology of the Siddhas in these works, one finds very little: they are a generally nameless, faceless aggregate whose mythological role is limited to cheering on more individualized gods or heroes.

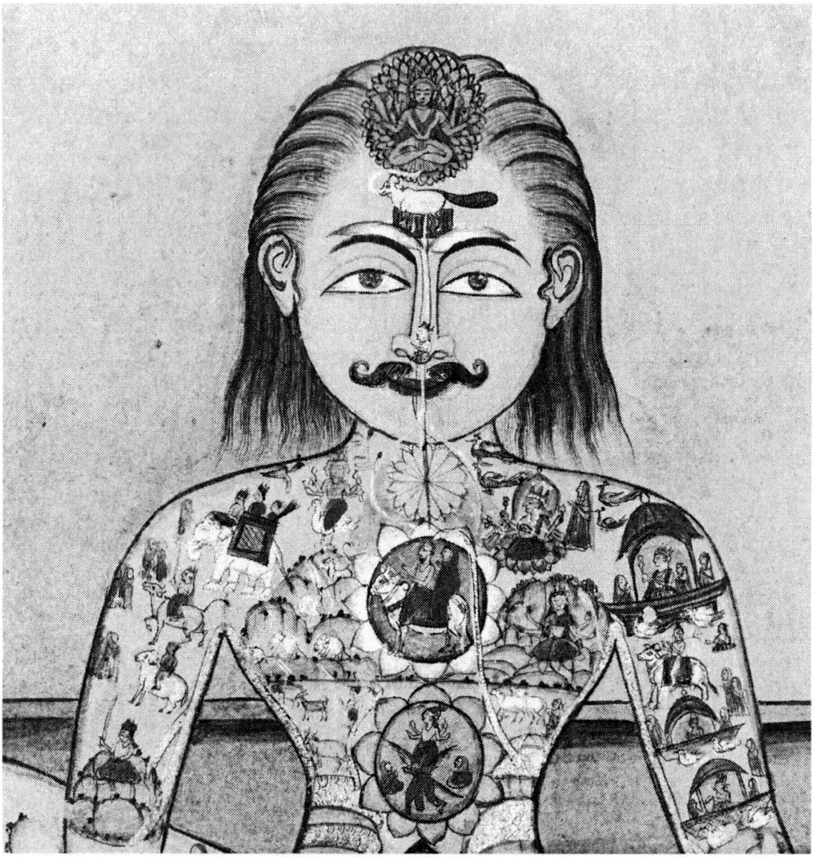

Figure 6.d. Seated yogin, circumscribed in cranial vault of seated yogin, from a drawing by an Indian artist commissioned by a British officer, 1930 C.E. British Library ADD 24099, f118 (detail). By permission of the British Library.

When, however, one turns to religious and scientific inquiry on the nature and location of the Siddhas, the situation changes dramatically: they are the subject of a sustained and highly sophisticated body of speculation that may have had its origins in Greek astronomy, and that "scientifically" described the *process* by means of which the practitioner truly realized the transcendence of his human condition. In a provocative article on the cosmology of the fourth-century C.E. *Viṣṇu Purāṇa*, W. Randolph Kloetzli demonstrates that, according to the Puranic "logic of projection"—based, as he argues, on an image of the heavens as seen through the stereoscopic projection of the "northern" astrolabe, whose theoretical principles would have been introduced to India from the Hellenistic world in this period—it is through the eye of the supreme god Viṣṇu, located at the southern celestial pole (his toe is at the northern celestial pole), that Puranic cosmology is both viewed and projected.[95]

The most sophisticated and fully developed early discussion of yogic body cosmology, or microcosmology, and its underlying soteriology is found in a slightly later Vaiṣṇava work, the circa eighth-century C.E. *Bhāgavata Purāna* (BhP). As I will discuss in chapter 8, it is here that the earliest allusion to the location of the six *cakras* of the subtle body is found: "the sage should, having pressed his heel into the anus, indefatigably raise the breath into the six sites (*ṣaṭsu . . . sthāneṣu*),"[96] culminating in the forehead or fontanel (*mūrdhan*), from which he "will then surge upward into the beyond (*param*)." I will return to this final element of the yogin exiting his own body momentarily. However, it will first be necessary to give an account of the Śrīvaiṣṇava theology and cosmology that undergirds the BhP's microcosmology.[97] According to the Śrīvaiṣṇava doctrine of the four *vyūhas* ("bodily arrays"), it is the supreme deity Vāsudeva who impregnates his own central womb and gestates the fetus that will develop into the cosmic egg (*brahmāṇḍa*) within which we exist.[98] The Vāsudeva *vyūha* is thus at once "the body at whose center we exist, [and] the body at the center of our own consciousness. . . ."[99] As Dennis Hudson explains:

> In the case of humans, the mapping places the gross body on the outside with the subtle body and soul enclosed by it and the *vyūha* Vāsudeva controlling from the center as the Self of all selves. . . . In the case of God, however, the organization of the three bodies is reversed. . . . A difference between God and humans, then, is this: As a microcosm, the human is a conscious soul looking outward through its encompassing subtle body and, by means of that subtle body, through its encompassing gross human body. The Bhagavān, by contrast as the macrocosm, is pure being and consciousness looking "inward" to the subtle body that he encloses and by means of that subtle body, "into" the gross body enclosed within his subtle body. God, one might say, gazes inward at his own center. . . . The ordinary person is not aware that he or she is being watched continuously, literally being seen through at all times by the Pervading Actor (Viṣṇu) within space-time who never winks. . . .[100]

A significant number of medieval works on both cosmology and microcosmology afford just such a "god's-eye view" of the inner cosmos. So, for example, the KJñN, in a very early description of yogic ascent, states that "he [the yogin] sees the threefold universe, with its mobile and immobile beings, inside of his body."[101] Indeed, this is the view ultimately attained by the Nāth Siddhas and other "self-made gods" of the medieval period, who incorporated haṭha yoga into their practice. The means by which the Siddha is able to gain a god's-eye view is central to Siddha soteriology, to the bodily apotheosis that is the point of intersection between theology, cosmology, and "microcosmology."

This notion of apotheosis appears to be addressed in the BhP account of the "six sites"—which portrays the practitioner as exiting his own body to surge upward into "the beyond." Before we go into the details of this process, let us pause for a moment to consider its context. The second chapter of the second book of the BhP is entitled "Description of the Great Man" (*mahāpuruṣa*), by which, of course, the god Viṣṇu is intended, as is made clear by an extended description of the "four-armed Puruṣa" who is to be visualized, "by Lords Among Yogins (*yogīśvaras*), within their hearts."[102] The departure of the yogin from his own body into the beyond is presented in this passage as the first of two alternatives. The second alternative is introduced in the verse that follows: "If [however], the wise one wishes to accede to the realm of the highest [Brahmā], which is none other than the abode of the Sky-Dwellers . . . he may go there with his mind and senses [intact]."[103] While the first alternative may be read as a sort of "out-of-body experience," this second appears to approximate most closely the notion of bodily apotheosis. The ambiguity of this state is addressed directly in the following verse: "It is said that the realm (*gati*) of the Masters of Yoga, whose souls are [contained] within their [yogic] breaths, *is [both] inside and outside of the triple-world.* They do not reach this realm through acts. They partake [of it] through *vidyā* (occult knowledge, the magical arts), *tapas* (heat-producing austerities), yoga, and *samādhi*."[104] This idea is not original to the BhP: the Epic Valakhilyas constituted a class of Siddhas, that "include[d] saints of both worlds," who "ha[d] attained the Siddha realm (*siddhagati*) through asceticism."[105]

The BhP continues, in a passage likely inspired by the fourth- to second-century B.C.E. *Maitri Upaniṣad*,[106] by describing the practitioner as rising, via "the resplendent medial channel that is the path of *brahman*," to a series of higher and higher worlds, identified with the high Hindu gods. Then,

> wheeling over the top of the navel of the universe [which is] venerated by knowers of *brahman*, he ascends alone, with a soul that has been purified and reduced to the size of an atom, [to that world] of Viṣṇu at which the wise enjoy a lifespan of one *kalpa*. Here, beholding the universe [as it is] being consumed by the fire [spat] from the mouth of Ananta, he proceeds to that [world] of the highest [Brahmā], where the Lords of the Siddhas are wont to dwell, [which endures] for a period of a life of Brahmā (*dvaiparārdhyam*).[107]

Four of the verses that follow are of signal interest, because they indicate a simultaneity, if not an identity, between transformations occurring on both microcosmic and macrocosmic levels. Here, the practitioner rises to ever-subtler levels of being, piercing or merging with the seven sheaths of the cosmic egg as he simultaneously implodes their corresponding elements into their higher evolutes within his bodily microcosm. Having now transcended the hierarchy of subtle and gross elements, he effects the dissolution or implosion of these into the ego (here termed *vikārya*), and so on until the final dissolution of the *tattvas* into pure consciousness (here termed *vijñāna-tattva*). It concludes: "In the end, [the yogin who is] composed of bliss . . . attains the [state of the] universal self, peace, and beatitude. He who has reached that divine station is never drawn back here again. These . . . are the two eternal paths whose praises are sung in the Vedas."[108] The *Virāṭa Purāṇa* makes a similar statement: "Having risen above the highest void, the yogin neither dies nor is [re]born, neither goes nor comes. The yogin who has entered into the luminous [firmament] remains [there] from age unto age." So, too, the *Svacchanda Tantra* enjoins the practitioner to travel through his own body simultaneous to his peregrenations through the cosmic egg: when he reaches the top, he will find Daṇḍapāṇi (the "Staff-Bearer"), who with his staff cracks open the egg/his skull for him to ascend beyond it.[109]

A remarkably similar ascent, with a strong Kaula coloring, is found in the KM. This same work also provides a glimpse into an intermediary stage in subtle body mapping, inasmuch as it identifies its set of five *cakras* with the five elements, which it portrays both as encompassing one another like the sheaths of the cosmic egg and aligned vertically above one another along the axis of the spinal column.[110] Other Kubjikā traditions locate the Siddhas inside the yoni of the goddess, which is itself located above the cranial vault at a site knows as "Beyond the Twelve" (*dvādaśānta*) that is both "inside" the yogic body and "outside" the physical body. As the source of mantras, the triangle of the yoni is subdivided into fifty smaller triangles, nested inside of it, each of which contains a Sanskrit phoneme, worshiped as a Bhairava or a Siddha.[111]

Yet another type of yogic apotheosis is described in the eleventh-century C.E. *Rasārṇava*, an alchemical work that offers a great wealth of data on becoming a Siddha, a self-made god. In its discussion of "revivifying water" (*sañjīvanījalam*), this source relates that the alchemist who has drunk three measures of this elixir swoons, and then awakens to find himself transformed and possessed of supernatural powers. After further treatment, "he suddenly disappears from human sight and becomes the lord of the Wizards (Vidyādharas), surrounded by a circle of Siddha-maidens for a period of fourteen *kalpas*."[112] Later it concludes a description of *khecarī jāraṇa* ("calcination of mercury that is possessed of the power of flight") by stating that the alchemist who ingests said mercury is uplifted immediately into the presence of the gods, Siddhas, and Vidyādharas, with whom he flies through the air at will.[113] The entire work concludes on a similar note: "When all the fixed and moving beings in the universe have been annihilated in that terrible flood of universal dissolution, the Siddha is absorbed into the same place as are the gods."[114]

The place in question is, once again, Brahmaloka or Siddhaloka, which Puranic soteriology describes as a holding tank of sorts for gods, demigods, and liberated souls. This soteriology centers on the fate of creatures located in the three uppermost levels of the cosmic egg at the end of a cosmic age (*mahāyuga*). The lowest of these, the fifth of the seven worlds (*lokas*), is called the World of Regeneration (*janarloka*), for it is here that those souls whose karma has condemned them to rebirth are held in suspension while all that lies below within the cosmic egg—bodies and mountains, the entire earth and the subterranean worlds—has been burned up and flooded out in the universal dissolution (*pralaya*). The two worlds above the world of regeneration, the highest worlds within the cosmic egg, are called the World of Ascetic Ardor (*tapoloka*) and the World of Brahman (*brahmaloka*), respectively. Their names are descriptive of the nature of their inhabitants, for it is in these that the souls of practitioners who have realized the absolute (*brahman*) through their heat-producing austerities (*tapas*) reside during the cosmic night.

The division between these upper levels, that is, between the world of generation and the paired Worlds of Ascetic Ardor and Brahmā/Brahman, is brought to the fore in the process of the reordering of the internal contents of the cosmic egg at the beginning of a new cosmic age. After the god Brahmā has restored the earth, netherworlds, heavens, landforms, and bodies of creatures to their respective places, then those souls that are bound by their karma to rebirth in the world—souls that have been held in suspension in the World of Regeneration—are reinjected into the bodies befitting their karmic residue. However, those souls that have, through yogic practice, realized liberation, remain ensconced in *tapoloka* and *brahmaloka*. Suspended high above the general conflagration, they are saved from universal dissolution and, most importantly, from reincarnation into a transmigrating body. According to the same Puranic traditions, these souls remain in the two uppermost levels until the end of the *kalpa*, at which point the entire cosmic egg is dissolved. Yet, as we have seen in the *Rasārṇava* passage just quoted, the self-made Siddha sports in that lofty world for no less than fourteen *kalpas*, that is, through fourteen *mahāpralayas*. How is it possible for Siddhas to remain at the summit of the cosmic egg through fourteen *mahāpralayas* in the course of which the entire universe—the "egg" itself—is itself destroyed and reduced to ashes?

Where are they when they sport with the Siddha maidens and Wizards for fourteen *kalpas*?

An indirect response to this question may be found in the *Harivaṃśa*, the BhP, the TĀ, and the *Svacchanda Tantra*, all of which ambiguously represent the Siddhas and Vidyādharas as inhabitants of both atmospheric and lower regions, as well as mountains. As we have already noted, the BhP (5.24.2–5) situates these perfected beings at the highest atmospheric level, immediately below the spheres of the moon and Rāhu, the descending node of the moon. A series of verses from the TĀ, which is in fact a reworking of an earlier *Svacchanda Tantra* passage,[115] offers a somewhat different account. Having described a number of atmospheric levels located above the terrestrial disk, Abhinavagupta states:

> Five hundred *yojanas* higher . . . at the level of the wind called "Lightning-Streak" are stationed . . . the "lowest-level Wizards (Vidyādharas)." These are beings who, when in the prior form of human wizards (*vidyāpauruṣe*), carried out cremation-ground-related practices. When they died, that *siddhi* rendered them Siddhas, stationed in the midst of the "Lightning-Streak" wind.[116] . . . Five hundred *yojanas* higher . . . there at Raivata itself are the primal Siddhas (*ādisiddhāḥ*) named Yellow Orpiment, Black Antimony, and Mercury-Ash.[117]

The toponym Raivata, mentioned in the midst of these sources' descriptions of atmospheric levels located thousands of miles above the earth's surface, appears to correspond to a terrestrial location. Raivata was in fact a medieval name for the ring of mountains known today as Girnar, in the Junagadh District of Gujarat. Already in the MBh, one finds Subhadrā, the sister of Kṛṣṇa, circumambulating and worshiping Raivātaka mountain; and it is during a festival worship of the mountain itself that she is abducted by Arjuna.[118] A Jain source entitled the "Raivatācala Māhātmya" calls it the fifth of the twenty-one Jain *siddhādris* (Siddha mountains) and states that "here sages who have ceased to eat and who pass their days in devotion . . . worship Nemīnāth [the 22nd *tīrthaṃkara*]. Here divine nymphs and numerous heavenly beings—Gandharvas, Siddhas, and Vidyādharas, etc.—always worship Nemīnāth."[119] A number of Purāṇas, beginning with a circa ninth-century C.E.[120] passage from the *Matsya Purāṇa*, also devote long descriptions to the site, which they term Raivātaka. In these sources we clearly appear to be in the presence of a direct identification of Girnar as both a terrestrial site to which humans come to perfect themselves through Siddha techniques and as an atmospheric or celestial site at which they dwell in their definitively transformed state of semidivine Siddhas. A parallel situation is found in the KSS in which

Mount Ṛṣabha, described as an abode of Siddhas, is the site to which the Vidyādhara Naravāhanadatta goes for his consecration (15.2.43–66), and to which he retires to sojourn for an entire cosmic eon, in the concluding verses of that monumental work (18.5.248).

The pedigree of Raivata-Girnar goes back further still, mentioned as it is in the *Mahābhārata* both by the name of Raivata and that of Gomanta.[121] A detailed description of Gomanta is given in the *Harivaṃśa.*[122] This description is important for a detail it gives concerning its formation and its inhabitants:

> The mountain called Gomanta, a solitary heavenly peak surrounded by a group of lesser peaks, is difficult to scale, even by the Sky-goers . . . its two highest horns have the form of two shining gods.[123] . . . The interior of this mountain is frequented by Siddhas, Cāraṇas, and Rākṣasas, and the surface of the peak is ever thronged with hosts of Vidyādharas.[124]

6. Upside Down, Inside Out

In this passage Siddhas, Cāraṇas, and Rākṣasas are depicted as dwelling *inside* Gomanta while the Vidyādharas are said to dwell *on its surface*. Here, I will offer an empirical explanation for this description, followed by a more esoteric one. Like many sacred mountains, Girnar is riddled with caves, of which at least two (the caves of Dattātreya and Gopīcand) are identified with Nāth Siddhas, and one could conceive that cave-dwelling Siddhas might be portrayed as living inside this mountain, with other beings, human and semidivine, inhabiting its surface.

But this is not the sole possible explanation. Here, let us recall Kṛṣṇa's *Bhagavad Gītā* discussion of both the universal Puruṣa and the human yogin as *kūṭastha*—situated on or in the peak—and the fact that the "triple peak" (*trikūṭi*) is a feature of the yogic body, located within the cranial vault. This corresponds to a feature of Śiva's abode of Mount Kailāsa, as described in the KSS (15.1.61–75): one may pass through this mountain via a cave called "Triśirṣa," a name that may also be read as "triple peak." Let us also recall the BhP description of the apotheosis of the yogin, whose ascent to the realms of the Siddhas in Brahmaloka and his implosion of the lower *tattvas* into their higher essences are shown to be one and the same process.[125] Finally, we should also bear in mind the Puranic doctrine concerning the fate of the souls of this universe at the end of a *kalpa*, with the *mahāpralaya*. Unlike the *pralaya* that marks the transition between two *mahāyugas*, the *mahāpralaya* entails the calcination of the entire cosmic egg, rather than merely its contents. While the ashes that are the end product of this process come to constitute the body of Ananta, Viṣṇu's serpent couch, it is the fate of souls to be reabsorbed into Viṣṇu, the Great Yogin (*mahāyogin*), who holds them in his yogically entranced consciousness. In his state of deep yogic trance, Viṣṇu's consciousness would be concentrated in his cranial vault, and perhaps the subtle triple-peak configuration (*trikūṭi*) located therein.

Might this be an explanation for the Jain imagery of the Siddhaloka, which depicts a yogin seated in the forehead area of the Loka Puruṣa, beneath a crescent moon–shaped umbrella? And might not the locus of the world of the Siddhas—now portrayed as a mountaintop, now as an atmospheric region, and now again as the level located just beneath the inner shell of the top of the cosmic egg—in fact also be a place located just beneath the cranial vault of god, the cosmic yogin? This reading appears to be supported by statements made in Patañjali's *Yoga Sūtras* (YS 3.5) on the attainment of supernatural powers of insight (*jñāna*) through the meditative practice of mental restraint (*saṃyama*).[126] Whereas Patañjali simply states, in YS 3.26, that "through *saṃyama* on the sun, [one gains] insight into the cosmic regions,"[127] the *bhāṣya* to this work, later attributed to Vyāsa, adds a detailed "Puranic" cosmology of the cosmic egg and its inhabitants, stating in its conclusion that the yogin, by concentrating on the "solar door" of the subtle body, obtains a direct vision of the universe in its entirety. A few verses later (YS 3.32), Patañjali concludes his discussion with "In the light of the fontanel is the vision of the Siddhas,"[128] which the *bhāṣya* glosses by stating: "There is an opening within the cranial vault through which there emanates effulgent light. By concentrating on that light, one obtains a vision of the Siddhas who move in the space between heaven and earth."[129]

Where are these Siddhas that one sees through one's yogic practice? Are they inside or outside of the body? And if the latter, are they to be situated inside mountains or on their surface, or indeed under the cope of heaven; that is, are they inside or outside of the structure of the universal macrocosm or of some intermediate space-time? Perhaps it is not a matter of either/or here. As we have seen, the BhP portrays the practitioner's apotheosis as his simultaneous piercing of the seven sheaths surrounding the cosmic egg *and* his internal implosion of their corresponding elements into their higher evolutes within his bodily microcosm. In the medieval Siddha traditions, a mountain cave was the macrocosmic replica of the cranial vault of the meditating yogin as well as of the upper chamber of a mesocosmic alchemical apparatus within which the alchemist transformed himself into the *opus alchymicum*. The Möbius universe of the Siddhas was so constructed as to permit its practitioners to at once identify cosmic mountains with their own subtle bodies, and to enter into those mountains to realize the final end of their practice, the transformation of themselves into the semidivine denizens of those peaks. In other words, the Siddha universe was so constructed as to enable the practitioner to simultaneously experience it as a world in which he lived, and a world that lived within himself. The realized Siddha's experience of the world was identical to that of the supreme godhead.

Let us return here to Kloetzli's discussion of the impact of the "logic of projection" that undergirded the Puranic cosmographies, and that led to the development of the astrolabe in India and the West. Noting that the spatial projections of the Puranic *dvīpas* (concentric island continents) present us with mathematical divisions reminiscent of the divisions of time known as the *yugas* (cosmic ages),[130] Kloetzli demonstrates that Mount Meru, the prototypical sacred mountain, is the key to the entire projection of the Puranic cosmograph.[131] According to the Puranic cosmology, Meru is an "upside-down" mountain, having the form of an inverted cone, whose flat summit and angled sides, Kloetzli argues, are projections of the celestial Tropic of Cancer and the lines of extension from the southern celestial pole, respectively.[132] It is at this pole that the eye of Viṣṇu is located, the toe of whose upraised foot (*uttāna-padam, paramam-padam*) is located at the north celestial pole.[133] Kloetzli concludes:

> If the Hindu cosmograph is not an astrolabe in every detail, it is nevertheless certain that it is a scientific instrument whose design is intended for the measure of time—time considered as the body of the deity for theological purposes by the *Viṣṇu Purāṇa*—and involving a projection of the heavens and their motions onto a planar surface. Mount Meru—represented as an inverted cone—is the definition of that projection as it connects the celestial Tropic of Cancer with the south celestial pole, which is the viewing point from which the projection is made. . . . The fact that 16,000 *yojanas* of the mountain are said to be "underground" may be understood as a statement that this portion of Mount Meru is below the equatorial plane. . . . Since the shape of Mount Meru confronts us again with a logic of projection . . . it means that what is "above" is also here "below." . . . *The gods (devas) and demons (asuras) who reside in the heavens and hells above and below the earth also reside in the mountains of the earth.*[134]

From the perspective of the divine Viṣṇu or of the perfected Siddha, above and below, inside and outside, even time and space converge. It is this that allowed the Siddhas to locate themselves in the world, and the world in themselves—viewed as if through a camera obscura—and armed with this knowledge, to transcend this world and look "down" on it from "below," to situate themselves atop and inside sacred mountains, or within and without the shell of the cosmic egg and their own cranial vaults, at the endpoint of a space and time they now controlled. Additionally, it was in this way that human Siddha practitioners were enabled to view the divine Siddhas located beneath the vault of heaven within their own cranial vaults—in a word, to internalize them—in their own efforts to join their heavenly ranks. It is at this intersection of cutting-edge medieval cosmology and soteriology that the Tantric internalization—of the entire cosmic egg into the subtle body microcosm—was first theorized.

It is tantalizing to note that the prototype for this Hindu body of theory and practice—of both the "logic of projection" and "inner" travel to "higher" worlds—may have been Greek. The notion of the spinal column as a channel for semen and seminal thoughts (*logoi spermatikoi*) was both a medical and a mystical notion dear to the Stoics. Here, however, I wish to concentrate momentarily on a pre-Pythagorean doctrine that was formative to Plato's theory, found in the *Phaedo*, of cyclic rebirth and the recovery of lost knowledge as "recollection," *anamnesis*. This doctrine identified the female soul (*psyche*) with the breath (*pneuma*) that was flung upward through the head via the action of the diaphragm (*prapides*) to travel to higher worlds. The female *psyche* was a divinity that inhabited the human body and a person's spiritual double, whose function it was to link individual destinies to the cosmic order. Whereas in most people the female *psyche* did not leave the body to travel to the higher worlds until their death, the case was a different one for persons initiated into the esoteric practices of the diaphragm and breath. These persons, as part of their "spiritual exercises" of rememoration and purification, would undertake "practice in dying" (*melete thanatou*), by which they would fling their female *psyche* into the higher worlds to rememorate all the wisdom they had lost in the process of rebirth. The *psyche* would be made to rise along the same channel as the seminal thoughts, but would then continue beyond the cranium to the higher worlds where wisdom resided.[135]

Chapter 7

THE FLIGHT OF THE YOGINĪ:
Fueling the Flight of Tantric Witches

1. From Mothers to Yoginīs

As one moves forward in time from the Kushan into the Gupta period, one finds a change in terminology taking place, in which the multiple female divinities formerly called Mothers, female Seizers, or female Dryads come to be known as Yoginīs. In the early stages of this shift, nothing but the general term changes, with the names of the individual goddesses themselves remaining the same. Once again, these goddess's cults have little or nothing to do with the classical Seven Mothers, whose "invention" was, as we have noted, a rear-guard action on the part of Śaiva and Vaiṣṇava sectarians attempting to recuperate the groundswell of goddess cults, both royal and popular, in this period.

A window on this change are the iconographic chapters of the *Agni Purāṇa* (AP), which fall into two groups, dating from the sixth and the ninth to eleventh centuries C.E., respectively. Both the sixth-century C.E. chapter 52 and the ninth- to eleventh-century chapter 146 of this work offer quite nearly identical lists of sixty-four Yoginīs. However, whereas the former, in its descriptions of the circles of Yoginīs, closely connects them to the female Dryads and Mothers, the latter (AP 146.1) calls them "Mothers of Space" (*ākāśamātaraḥ*) and presents them as abstract principles.[1] Certain of the Yoginīs' names in both lists are reminiscent of those of the female Seizers and Mothers of earlier traditions: these include Revatī, Biḍalī ("Kitty"), and Piśācī.[2] In fact, seven of the names of the Yoginīs listed in AP 52 and 164 are identical to those of the female Seizers listed in the 299th chapter of the same work. These are Rākṣasī, Bālakeśī, Lālasā, Tapanī, Dhamanī, Vāyuvegā, and Pūtanā.[3]

The most striking parallels between the Mothers and female Seizers of the Epic period and the later Yoginīs are to be found in their appearance, behavior, and function. The Kushan-era "Revatī Kalpa" of the *Kāśyapa Saṃhitā* (KS) enumerates three types of Revatīs or Jātahāriṇīs: the divine, the human, and the lower animals and plants (of which the avian is the primary subset). Some seven to eight hundred years later, a KJñN description of the Yoginīs also divides them into human, animal, and avian groups. In response to the Goddess's question "How do the Kaula-knowing Yoginīs move about on earth?" Bhairava replies:

> Hear, O Passionate Lady, the movement of [these] deities in this world of mortals. [They move about in the form of] the female pigeon and vulture, the goose . . . the wagtail . . . the babbler and the cuckoo . . . the owl or the *pecakī* owl, the *saralī* (*Pavo bicalcaratus*) as well as the *gulī*. [They also move about in the form of] the she-jackal, the ewe, the she-buffalo, the she-camel, the she-cat and the she-mongoose, the tigress, the cow elephant, the pea-hen and the hen. . . . Having taken the aforementioned forms, the Yoginīs sport about on the earth. When they fall [die] they, O Fortunate One, are [classed] among the [creatures] not to be eaten, O Ruler of the Clan! They are said to have the form [of] the horse, creatures with talons, the creeping snake . . . scorpion . . . mouse [and] frog. . . . Assuming these multiple forms . . . the sixty-four Yoginīs speedily overpower their victim [fig. 7.a.].[4]

These textual accounts square with the Yoginī images found at their medieval temple sites, or taken from the ruins thereof. While many of the images are headless, subject to the ravages of time, vandalism, and pillage, those that do have faces fall into the following groups: one-quarter of the Yoginīs have benign human faces; one-quarter, terrible human faces; one-quarter, animal heads; and one-quarter, bird heads.

2. Food and Sex

The Mothers or female Seizers of the Kushan era were often bird or animal demonesses who preyed upon the bodies of fetuses, infants, and children in particular, but also on those of pregnant women and adult males. When they were birds, they were naturally possessed of the power of flight. When they were the cause of interrupted pregnancies or childhood diseases, they either introduced themselves into the womb of the pregnant woman to provoke an abortion or a monstrous birth, or they poisoned the mother's

Figure 7.a. Cobra-headed Yoginī, Hirapur Yoginī temple, Puri District, Orissa, ninth century C.E. Courtesy of the American Institute of Indian Studies.

breast milk to harm the nursing infant. In the mythology of Kṛṣṇa, for example, Pūtanā directly offers her own poisoned breast to the blue-skinned baby. Later traditions of the smallpox goddess Śītalā and the Seven Sisters or Seven Virgins portray these as possessing their victims and preying upon them from within, causing their skin to erupt in pustules identified with their "eyes" or "vulvas."[5] As a general rule, then, these goddesses or demonesses of disease in some way penetrate the bodily envelope of their prey to inject them with their own fiery or virulent bodily fluids. Yet their penetration results in a pathological condition that consumes or burns up their victims from within. It is as if they at once devour and force-feed their victims. Put another way, they both destroy and re-create their victims, in their dual roles as "goddesses of the breast" and "goddesses of the tooth." In her typology of these two goddess types, Wendy Doniger O'Flaherty has stated that "although food is given to the low-ranking goddesses [or witches, who are sexually free and attack men] to placate them, there is no reciprocity in this transaction; but the high-ranking goddesses, by contrast, are able to give back the food given to them, in the form of the *prasāda* distributed to the worshipers."[6]

In the light of what has been shown in the preceding chapters, this statement does not stand. The blood offerings made to the female Seizers in exchange for their protection and nurture, as described in the Epic, medical, and Tantric literature, do in fact fit the reciprocity model. More than this, the worship of the female Seizers, like that of the female Dryads, is of the same nature and fully as old as that of the Hindu high gods whose *bhakti* cults emerged in the same Kushan era.[7] Of course, the reciprocity between devotees and goddesses of the tooth is often an extremely dangerous undertaking and is reserved in Hindu Tantra for the Virile Hero or Perfected Being. A lapidary account of such transactions is that told by an unnamed character about himself in the KSS:

> Out of despair, I left my home and renouncing all, visited the sacred fords and came to see the Goddess who dwells in the Vindhyas. Upon seeing her, I said to myself, "People satisfy the Goddess by offering her an animal sacrifice: I, stupid animal that I am, it is I whom I will sacrifice on this site!" So resolved, I took up a sword to cut off my head. Immediately, the Goddess herself, pleased with me, spoke: "My son, you are [now] a Siddha (*siddho'si*). Do not take your life. Remain here in my presence!" Having obtained this divine boon, I became a fully realized divinity (*samprāptā divyatā mayā*).[8]

In the Tantric context, the Virile Hero is one who has become empowered, through initiation, ritual practice—or divine grace, as in the story above—to transact in bodily fluids with the devouring Yoginīs, wild goddesses who would otherwise consume the unprepared with their fiery energy, concentrated in their sexual fluids, as well as with their animal claws, teeth, and talons. In this, they carry forward the legacy of the female Seizers and Mothers of the earlier medical tradition. This continuity between the Kushan-age female Seizers and the post-Gupta-age Yoginīs is best illustrated by comparing the stories of the Epic king Jarāsandha and the Kashmiri royal minister Sandhimati.

The conditions of the Epic Jarāsandha's birth are well known. To the sonless King Bṛhadratha of Magadha comes the hermit Caṇḍakauśika, who is welcomed with honor. Bṛhadratha refuses a boon from the sage, but laments that he has no son. A mango drops in the hermit's lap; he enchants it and gives it to the king. The king gives it to his two wives to eat: both become pregnant, and each gives birth to half a child; their midwives expose these half-children at a crossroads. The Protectress Jarā carries them off and joins them together, and they become a complete infant. The child cries out, the king and his wives come outside, and Jarā, assuming a human form, returns the child, who is their son. The king names his son Jarāsandha ("Mended by Jarā") and proclaims a festival in honor of the Protectress.[9]

The critical edition of the MBh states that Jarā, although a Protectress, has the power to change her form (*kāmarūpiṇī*) and appears to King Bṛhadratha as a beautiful shining goddess. More than this, as she announces to the king, she has long been living in his house, where she has been the object of worship! At this point the Calcutta edition of the Epic inserts the following speech by Jarāsandha, which demonstrates that Jarā was in fact a Mother or female Seizer of the same order as Ṣaṣṭhī, Āryā, and Harītī:

> I am a Protectress who stands eternally in every human dwelling. Gṛhadevī ("House-Goddess") is my name, and I was created long ago by Svayambhū. I have been established with a divine form for the destruction of demons. Prosperity reigns in the home of him who draws me and my son [Skanda?], together in a row with [other] young people, on the wall [of his house]. If he fails to do so, scarcity afflicts him. I am installed on the walls of your house. I receive constant worship. I who am drawn [there] surrounded by my many children am well-worshipped with fragrant flowers, incense, and edible foods. I am always mindful of doing good to you in return.[10]

Jarā is a Kushan-era "goddess of the tooth" who nonetheless reciprocates worship with prosperity. Her soliloquy, which highlights her nurturing side, ought not to make us forget, however, who she is and what she is doing in this myth. She is a Protectress who has assembled (*samghaṭṭayām āsa*) the two halves of the future Jarāsandha in order to more easily carry them to the place in which she intends to eat them.[11] Like her female Seizer sisters, Jarā eats babies. Yet it is for her assembly or fusion of the infant child that the future king is given the name Jarāsandha: he has been mended (*samdhā*) by Jarā. Jarā, the erstwhile baby-eater, is also a baby-mender.

The Tantric Hero, in his cremation-ground cult of the Yoginīs, incites these multiple female beings to devour him—both from within through their fiery sexual fluids, and from without, by making him "food for the Yoginīs"—in order precisely that they might transform him into their superhuman lover and master. Behind his Tantric quest lies both the mythology and modus operandi of the Mothers and female Seizers, as well as the Vedic paradigm that every victim is but a surrogate for the sole true sacrifice, which is—following the example of the cosmic man, Puruṣa-Prajāpati—the sacrifice of one's own self. In the case of the Vedic cosmic man, Puruṣa is dismembered through a primary sacrifice, but re-membered, mended, restored to wholeness, through a second sacrifice. In the case of the Tantric Hero, the restoration to wholeness that follows his self-sacrifice to the ravening Yoginīs seems to be effected through a mending process that is quite identical to that carried out by Jarā. We have already seen this in chapter 3, in the KM "bolt practice[s] . . . of the knife," in which the practitioner is instantaneously restored to wholeness by the Yoginīs after seven nights of self-sacrifice. This same process is described in narrative form in the 1148–49 C.E. *Rājataraṅgiṇī* account of the royal minister Sandhimati.[12]

> The king had a minister named Sandhimati, the greatest of sages, who was distinguished by his wonderful life and devotion to Śiva. . . . Wicked men raised the king's hatred against that trusted advisor. . . . At that time there spread by the force of future events a mysterious report from house to house which declared: "To Sandhimati will belong the kingdom." The king thereupon . . . threw him into prison. There he pined . . . until the tenth year was completed, and [with it] the king's term of life. Then by the king's order Sandhimati was at night put to death on the stake by savage executioners. . . . When the news of Sandhimati's end reached his guru, Īśāna by name . . . he proceeded to the place of execution (*śmaśāna*). . . . He found him reduced to a skeleton, from which the wolves tore away [the flesh] with force, but which was held fast by the bones fixed under the foot of the stake. . . . He stayed at that very place . . . and watched the skeleton. Then once in the middle of the night . . . Īśāna smelled a heavenly perfume of incense. Upon hearing the terrific clamor [produced] by the ringing of many bells struck with great clappers and by the violent rattle of two-headed drums,[13] he . . . saw on the burial ground Yoginīs enveloped in a halo of light. . . . Hidden behind a tree, he noticed that the skeleton had been placed by the troops

of witches in the midst of their circle, and that all its limbs were being mended (*samdhīyamāna*).[14] Intoxicated by drink, they had felt the desire for sportive enjoyment of a lover, and not finding a Virile Hero, had carried off that skeleton. One by one, each of them placed [upon the skeleton] one of her own limbs, and then quickly bringing a male organ from somewhere, they made his body complete.[15] Next, the witches, magically drawing back (*yogenākṛṣya*) the spirit of Sandhimati—which was still roaming about without having entered into another body—put it into that [body]. Resembling a person just risen from sleep, he was covered by them with heavenly ointments, and he, the leader of their circle, was carnally enjoyed by them to their fullest desire.[16] As the night grew short, Īśāna was filled with terror that those goddesses would again take back the limbs which they had lent him [Sandhimati]. In order to guard these [limbs], he resolutely approached that place with a shout, and at once the band of witches disappeared. Then their voice was heard: "May you not fear, O Īśāna. We miss no limb, and do not defraud him whom we have chosen as our lover. He who, when chosen by us, was mended (*saṃdhitaḥ*) with a heavenly body, will be known on earth [by the name of] Sandhimān and on account of his noble character as Āryarāja." Then Sandhimān, who wore a magnificent dress and a wreath, and was adorned with heavenly ornaments, recovered the memory of his past and reverently greeted his guru. . . . At the bidding of his guru he who was free from desires reluctantly consented to the prayer of the citizens to rule the country which had no king. Brahmins conducted him . . . and to the sound of music made him take the bath of the consecration ceremony (*abhiṣeka*).

The most salient point of this account for our interests is the etymology of the rebuilt Sandhimān's name: it is based on the same verb, *sam-dhā*, "to mend," as that of the second half of Jarāsandha's name. Like Osiris by Isis in Egyptian mythology, he is given new life by these Yoginīs through their mending of him. Yet who was it who had torn apart and devoured his lifeless body in the first place? The wolves that haunt cremation grounds are but animal forms of the same shape-changing Yoginīs, who are very frequently portrayed as the wolf's female cousins—she-jackals (*śivās*).[17] Having enjoyed him as food and thereby devoured his mortal body, they put him back together again in order to enjoy him a second time, as a source of sexual pleasure.[18]

As we know, a prime locus of Kaula ritual was the cremation ground, where blood offerings to terrible deities were the hallmark of practice. Then, with what Alexis Sanderson has termed the "Kaula reformation," a move away from *thanatos* in favor of *eros* was effected. In this episode we have a window, as it were, upon the nature of this shift. Goddesses who formerly offered their grace by restoring to life those who had sacrificed themselves to them for their gustatory enjoyment now offer the same to those who yield up their vital fluids to them for their sexual pleasure. In both cases, he who offers (himself as) "food for the Yoginīs" is rewarded with sovereignty over the Yoginīs themselves, as the leader of their circle (*cakranāyaka*); or, as in the case of Sandhimān, over the mundane world, as its king.

An extended discussion of the origin and cosmological raison d'être of the Yoginīs, found in the twentieth chapter of the *Netra Tantra*, sheds further light on this belief system. In what might otherwise be dismissed as an exercise in casuistry, this passage is quite profound inasmuch as it underscores a particular etymological reading of their name: they are called "Yoginīs" (which could be construed as "Joiners," from the root *yuj*) because they "join together" (*yojayanti*). The text's rationale (or rationalization) for this reading runs as follows: Śiva created human sacrificial victims (*paśus*) precisely in order that they might be liberated from suffering existence. This the Yoginīs effect by killing them, since all they are killing, in truth, are the bonds that trap said victims in suffering existence. So it is that they join the souls of these *paśus* to their lord (*pati*), Śiva. Therefore, their destruction of life is a form of grace (*anugraha*), a term to which we will return. The Yoginīs' "utilization" (*upa-yuj*) of these victims effects their attainment of a higher station (*ūrdhvagati*). In this way, "the Yoginīs join together by their power: in this instance, they do not kill."[19]

Following this, the *Netra Tantra* launches into a discussion of three types of "yoga" whereby humans are empowered to confront the Yoginīs who would so join them together, that is, kill and eat them, techniques that transform them into Siddhas or Virile Heroes. These techniques bring us back to the most frequently encountered "happy ending" of medieval fantasy literature accounts of male interactions with these powerful beings: the shared power of flight enjoyed by a Yoginī and her beloved Virile Hero. But in the paradigm presented by the *Netra Tantra*, even the brutish uninitiated human becomes "joined together" and elevated to a higher station, simply by becoming food for the Yoginīs. An interesting corollary to this discussion is the question of whether one may eat Yoginīs: in the KJñN passage quoted at the beginning of this chapter, we saw that the eating of the flesh of the horse, creatures with talons, snakes, scorpions, mice, and frogs is prohibited because these creatures tend to be inhabited by Yoginīs. The ambiguity between the animal and the human as well as between eating and sex is highlighted in a slab, from the tenth-century Ranipur-Jharial Yoginī temple, on which a scene of copulation with an animal appears beneath each standing Yoginī image.[20]

3. Early South Asian Aviators

The historical origins of Indian traditions of flying Yoginīs have already been demonstrated: the Yoginīs are medieval heiresses to the earlier female Seizers, female Dryads, or Mothers, who flew because they were birds, birds whose power of flight was generated from the food they ate. We now turn to specifically Tantric principles of the flight of the Yoginī.

There is a passage in an article by Alexis Sanderson that many students of Hindu Tantra have learned and repeated over the years as a kind of catechism:

> The Kāpālika . . . sought the convergence of the Yoginīs and his fusion with them (*yoginīmelaka, -melāpa*) through a process of visionary invocation in which he would attract them out of the sky, gratify them with an offering of blood drawn from his own body, and ascend with them into the sky as the leader of their band. The Kaulas translated this visionary fantasy into the aesthetic terms of mystical experience. The Yoginīs became the deities of his senses (*karaṇeśvarīs*), revelling in his sensations. In intense pleasure this revelling completely clouds his internal awareness: he becomes their plaything or victim (*paśu*). . . . The Yoginīs of the senses relish this offering of "nectar" and gratified thereby they converge and fuse with the *kaula* [practitioner's] inner transcendental identity as the Kuleśvara, the Bhairava in the radiant "sky" of enlightened consciousness (*cidvyomabhairava*).[21]

In a single compact paragraph, Sanderson manages to describe quite comprehensively an important aspect of the transformation from the early traditions of the Kula or Kaula to the exegetical traditions of the later Trika and Śrīvidyā in particular. Yet, there is something troubling in the language of the first sentence of this passage, in which Sanderson states that the Kāpālika's was a *visionary* invocation of the Yoginīs. As I understand it, the term "visionary" means a thing or person seen in a dream or trance, or in the imagination, in which case the translation of "this visionary fantasy into the aesthetic terms of mystical experience" does not appear to me to constitute a significant transformation in practice.[22] In both the "before" and "after," the encounter with the Yoginīs takes place at the level of aesthetic cognition: there are no "real" Yoginīs out there with which the practitioner is interacting. Sanderson appears to put a finer point on matters in another article, in which he states that the initiate "mapped out a world of ecstatic delirium in which the boundaries between actual women and the hordes of their celestial and protean counterparts, between the outer and the inner, was barely perceptible,"[23] but nowhere, as far as I can tell, does he allow the possibility that the Yoginīs with whom the practitioner transacted were more than figments of overactive imaginations.

Here, I intend to dance around this question of the reality of the Yoginīs' flight, and to probe the question of whether theirs was something more than a flight of fancy, and if so what it has meant to those Indians who have claimed to interact with them. In my considerations, I will draw on a typology suggested by Mircea Eliade, which distinguishes between apotheosis ("flying" to heaven at death), mystic ascension (the visionary experience of flight referred to by Sanderson), and magical flight (of the "shamanic" variety). In his *Shamanism*, Eliade states that

> the chief difference between the . . . types of ascent is the intensity of the experience, that is, it is finally psychological. But whatever its intensity, this ecstatic experience becomes communicable through universally current symbolism, and is validated to the extent to which it can enter into the already existing magico-religious system. The power of flight can . . . be obtained in many ways (shamanic trance, mystical ecstasy, magical techniques), but also by a severe psychological discipline, such as the Yoga of Patañjali, by vigorous asceticism, as in Buddhism, or by alchemical practices. . . . This "magical power" is not an isolated element, valid in itself, based entirely on the personal experience of magicians; on the contrary, it is an integral part of a theologico-cosmological complex far more embracing than the various shamanic ideologies.[24]

Mystic ascension of a meditative variety is already present in certain Vedic and Theravada sources. "Among all the things that fly, the mind is the swiftest," says the *Ṛg Veda* (6.9.5); "those who know have wings," says the *Pañcaviṃśa Brāhmaṇa* (14.1.13); and the *Kāliṅgabodhi Jātaka* states that flight depends on "clothing the body with the raiment of contemplation."[25] So, too, are descriptions of apotheosis, as in the Vedic *vājapeya* rite, in which the sacrificer and his wife, having mounted a "pillar," spread their arms like wings and cry, "We have come to heaven, to the gods; we have become immortal";[26] or in the *Pañcaviṃśa Brāhmaṇa* (5.3.5), which states, "The sacrificer, having become a bird, soars to the world of heaven." But what of flight of a more empirical or verifiable sort? The *Buddhacarita* of Aśvaghoṣa, a first-century C.E. Hindu convert to Buddhism, contains the following description of the power of flight in its fifth canto:

> Then longing for spiritual peace, he [Siddhārtha, the future Buddha] set forth outside with the king's permission in order to see the forest. . . . While this pure passionless state of mind grew within his lofty soul, there came up to him a man in mendicant's clothes, unseen of other men.[27] . . .

> The king's son asked him, "Tell me, who are you?" On this he explained to him, "O bull among men, I am a *śramaṇa*, who in fear of birth and death have left the home life for the sake of salvation. . . . I dwell where I happen to be, at the root of a tree or in a deserted temple, on a hill or in the forest, and I wander without ties or expectations in search of the highest good, accepting any alms I may receive." After saying this, he flew up to the sky before the prince's very eyes; for he was a sky-dweller (*divaukas*) who in that form had seen other Buddhas and had encountered him to rouse his attention. When that man was gone like a bird to heaven (*gaganaṃ khagavad-gate*), the best of men was thrilled and amazed.[28]

In this first-century C.E. source, a hermit in ascetic's garb (*bhikṣu-veṣa*), who is invisible to normal humans, shows himself to be a sky-dweller possessed of the power of flight. Yet he is not the first such being in Indian literature. Here, let us recall the famous Rig Vedic hymn of the longhaired (*keśin*) ascetic.

> Long-hair holds fire, holds the drug, holds sky and earth. . . . These ascetics, swathed in wind, put dirty red rags on. When gods enter them, they ride with the rush of the wind. "Crazy with asceticism, we have mounted the wind. Our bodies are all you mere mortals can see. . . . He moves with the motion of heavenly girls and youths, of wild beasts. . . . The wind has churned it up; Kunaṃnamā has prepared it for him. Long-hair drinks from the cup, sharing the drug with Rudra.[29]

Here, a longhaired (*keśin*) ascetic, dressed in the red rags associated with renunciation, partakes of a poisoned brew prepared by a female figure named Kunaṃnamā in the company of Rudra, to fly through the air in the company of celestial nymphs (Apsarasas) and boys (Gandharvas). Transcendence of the human condition, ecstasy, and Tantric flight are all present, in embryonic form, in this very early hymn. In her translation of this hymn, Wendy Doniger O'Flaherty surmises that Kunaṃnamā is a female deity, whose "name may indicate a witch or a hunchback";[30] and one is struck by the similarity between her name and that of a dread *yakkhiṇī* described in the fifth-century C.E. *Mahāvamsa*, the Buddhist chronicle of Ceylon. Here, the powerful *yakkhiṇī* Kuvaṇṇā (whose attendants have the form of she-dogs) kidnaps seven hundred of the soldiers of Prince Vijaya and holds them prisoner in a chasm. Prince Vijaya comes to save them, which he does by throwing a noose over Kuvaṇṇā's neck.

> She frees his men, and Vijaya and Kuvaṇṇā sup together. She then transforms herself into a beautiful sixteen-year-old maiden and, making a bed

at the foot of the tree, invites Vijaya to lie with her. And seeing this, the king's son [Vijaya], looking forward to the time to come, [takes] her to him as his spouse and [lies] with her blissfully on that bed. Vijaya hears singing in the night, and is told by Kuvaṇṇā that these are the *yakkhas* who rule the island, and that their capital city of Sisiravatthu is close at hand. Vijaya slays all the *yakkhas* and himself puts on the garments of the *yakkha* kings.[31]

Modern-day Sri Lankan cults of the demonic Yakās (*yakkas*; *yakṣas*) identify Kuvaṇṇā as the "mother" of two of the most powerful, malevolent Yakās of the island: Kalu ("Black") Yakā is the offspring of Prince Vijaya's union with Kuvaṇṇā, while Riri Yakā is born from her tongue, which was cut out for her betrayal of the other Yakās in favor of Vijaya. The *Mahāvamsa* account, which features theriomorphic female "witches" whose male consorts' places are usurped by a human hero in Sri Lanka, a land that is itself replete with supernatural—serendipitous—connotations, recalls to mind Gail Hinich Sutherland's statement, quoted earlier, that the transfer of the role played by the Hindu, Buddhist, and Jain female Dryads onto the Yoginīs constituted one of the "earliest examples of the enshrinement and employment of demigods as instruments of power" typical of the later Kaula and Tantric traditions.[32] The magical subjugation of these figures is central to the Tantric quest for occult powers, including flight. With these examples we have broached the two principal bodies of techniques for flight, as known to or imagined by medieval India: flight as practiced by male Siddha-type practitioners alone; and flight as practiced by female Yoginī-type practitioners alone or in tandem with their male consorts.

4. Men Flying Solo

While lists of *siddhis* in India are as numerous as varieties of cheese in France, nearly all may be categorized under two general headings, "magical" and "abstract." The latter, better known, are especially found in yogic and high Hindu Tantric sources: atomicity (*aṇimā*), levity (*laghimā*), greatness (*mahimā*), attainment (*prāpti*), irresistible will (*prākāmya*), control (*vaśitva*), mastery (*īśitva*), and resolution (*yatrakāmāvasayitva*). The former, found in both Buddhist and Hindu sources are, in spite of having fallen out of vogue among Tantric authors and commentators, nonetheless more original and authentic: *khaḍga* (magical sword), *añjana* (invisibility ointment), *pādalepa* (foot-paint), *antardhāna* (disappearance), *rasa-rasāyana* (elixir of immortality), *khecara* (flight), *bhūcara* (telekinesis), and *pātāla* (ability to see into the netherworlds). Of all of these, the greatest supernatural power sought after and claimed by Indian practitioners in the medieval period was the *siddhi* of flight.[33] It was the great obsession of the age, and medieval Indian literature, both religious and popular, is full of instructions for and accounts of flying through the air (*khecara*). There were no less than eight techniques for flying, which we now pass in review.

The least extraordinary form this flight took was apotheosis, flying up to heaven or the world of the Siddhas (Siddhaloka) upon death (or dying to the world by flying up to the world of the Siddhas). An eleventh- to twelfth-century Kalacuri inscription from Madhya Pradesh alludes to this goal of Siddha practice. Here, after having described a temple donor named Malayasiṃha as a yogin whose goal was perfection (*siddhārtha-yogī*), the inscription goes on to say that "having performed painful penance, Siddhas go to high heaven."[34] Other medieval sources describe the Siddha's rise in alchemical or yogic terms. The Siddha alchemist, having obtained mercury that is possessed of the power of flight, may, by holding said mercury in his mouth, himself fly through the air.[35] The fourteenth-century *Śārṅgadhara Paddhati* provides a very matter-of-fact description of how the practitioner of haṭha yoga becomes airborne:

> When perfected isolated diaphragmatic retention occurs without inbreath or outbreath, nothing in the three worlds is difficult of access for him. Thereupon, from greater practice, sweating and trembling arise. Then, from still greater practice, hopping like a frog surely occurs. Just as a frog moves over the ground, hopping and hopping, so goes the yogin, who has assumed the lotus posture, over the ground. Thereupon, from greater practice, abandonment of the ground occurs [i.e., he flies].[36]

As we noted in the last chapter, many of the Purāṇas locate yogic practitioners in the uppermost levels of the cosmic egg.[37] A quite detailed description of yogic ascent to these higher worlds is provided by the *Bhāgavata Purāṇa* (BhP). While the question of whether this ascent or flight is embodied or disembodied remains open, there can be no question that the principle of yogic flight is operative here as well:

> The sage should, having pressed his heel into the anus, indefatigably raise the breath into the six sites. Drawing [the breath situated] in the navel upward into the heart, he should then raise it along the path of the up-breath into the breast. Then, the wise one, conjoining [breath] with knowledge, brings it slowly to the root of the palate. From there, he whose seven paths [i.e., the eyes, ears, nostrils and mouth] have been blocked [and] who is without distraction brings it to the place between the eyebrows. Remaining [in this state] for twenty-four minutes, he whose gaze is sharp, having pierced his cranial vault, then surges upward

> into the beyond (*param*). Gone via the sky, [i.e.,] via the resplendent median channel that is the path of *brahman*, he goes to [the world of Agni] Vaiśvānara. Hereupon, he who has shaken off all impurity goes on to the sphere of Hari, [located] on high, [who] has the form of a dolphin [i.e., Śiśumāra].[38]

Hereafter, the yogin ascends to higher and higher levels of being, eventually surpassing even the gods, remaining untouched even as the entire universe is being consumed in the final conflagration. In fact, evocations of the travels of the soul or meditating mind to other worlds are already found in a number of early Upaniṣads, including the *Chāndogya*, *Bṛhadāraṇyaka*, *Kauśītaki*, and *Praśna*,[39] as well as in the MBh. In its Droṇa Parvan, the great Epic presents the following scenario: having made a nocturnal offering to Śiva Tryambaka, Kṛṣṇa enters into a state of yoga, awakens, and then "visits" Arjuna, who is himself lying nearby, asleep (*svapne*) or in a meditative state (*dhyāyantam*). Speaking to Arjuna in this dream state, Kṛṣṇa exhorts him to request the powerful Pāśupata weapon from Śiva. Now seated on the ground, Arjuna concentrates his devoted mind upon Bhava (Śiva). He then sees himself traveling through space, holding Kṛṣṇa by the hand. Passing Mount Himavant and other northern regions, the two come into the presence of Śiva (whom the text names Sādhana, "Practice," here), who is accompanied by Pārvatī and surrounded by dancing *bhūtas*.[40] Whereas the ambiguous language of Arjuna and Kṛṣṇa's nocturnal flight to Mount Kailās may be read as either mystic ascension or magical flight, the rise of the yogin described in the BhP more likely falls under the heading of apotheosis.

5. Men Flying Spacecraft

If we are to believe the KSS, our richest medieval source on every imaginable form of flight, kings also had recourse to "wind-driven flying contraptions" (*vātayantravimānam*)—that is, gliders, built by clever craftsmen, to fly from place to place.[41] And, in at least one case, persons of lesser stature could, with knowledge of the proper mantras, transform cowsheds into airships that traveled across entire countries in the wink of an eye.[42]

Kubera, the lord of the Yakṣas, flies through the heavens on a man: for this reason, he is known from the Epic period onward as *naravāhana*, "he who has a man for his vehicle."[43] The protagonist of the frame story of the KSS is named Naravāhanadatta, "Kubera's gift," an apt designation given the fact that he is constantly flying through the air in the embrace of one of the many Vidyādharī maidens with whom he keeps falling in and out of love. The same source gives several accounts of a stock piece of Tantric sorcery, known as *śava-sādhanā*, "corpse practice," which entails, precisely, the use of a man, albeit a dead man, as one's hot air balloon. The hero of one such episode, a certain Vidūṣaka ("Jester," "Fool"), comes to a cremation ground in the dead of night, where he secretly beholds a wandering religious mendicant seated upon a corpse and uttering mantras:

> Suddenly, the corpse beneath the mendicant began making a "put-put" noise (*phāṭ-kāra*), as flames belched from its mouth and mustard seeds[44] shot out of its navel. Thereupon the mendicant, taking those mustard seeds and standing up, slapped the corpse with the palm of his hand. The corpse, which was inhabited by an enormous *vetāla*, rose up, and the mendicant then climbed up on its shoulder. Thus mounted, [the vampire] began to move quickly away. . . . [Then, having completed some business in a Durgā temple], the mendicant went out, and again striking him with his hand, caused the *vetāla* to rise up with the sound of *phāṭ*. And climbing up on the shoulder of him whose mouth was spewing flames of fire, he flew up, and went across the sky.[45]

Here, the "vampire"-inhabited corpse is clearly a kind of flaming coolie in the sky, powered by the life force that, reactivated by the mendicant's mantras, blasts its way across the heavens, propelled by the jet of flames issuing from its mouth and navel.[46] Clearly, it is the head and mouth of the corpse that are essential to its propulsion through the air, which squares with many of the cranium-based techniques proper to the "Aviator's Science" (*khecarī vidyā*), which I have described elsewhere.[47] Such beliefs and practices continue into the present, as June McDaniel has shown in her research on "folk Tantra" in Bengal:

> Skulls are really not dead but alive, companions and friends of the *sādhus*. They are inhabited by earth-bound entities who seek spiritual knowledge rather than pleasure, but were never educated in this field during their lives. Skulls give their power, and this is the *sādhu*'s offering: he may become guru to the dead. He can teach them the way to the heavens, and initiate them with empowered mantras, the keys to the kingdom. Spirits are said to cluster around meditating *sādhus*, but the *sādhu* will only give mantras to those spirits who bring their skulls to him. They travel through the midnight air, carrying their skulls to offer, and the ones he accepts belong to the spirits who will be initiated.[48]

There is a certain fluidity in the terminology used for the powerful lost souls of the cremation ground that come to inhabit corpses or offer their skulls to high-flying practitioners. The KSS episode uses the term *vetāla*, for which the standard translation of "vampire" is inadequate, the *vetāla* being more like a giant genie that comes out of the "bottle" of its corpse when forced to do so by practitioners using powerful mantras. *Pretas* ("ghosts"; literally "the departed") and *bhūtas* ("beings," "spirits") are terms currently used throughout South Asia in ways more or less synonymous with *vetāla*. When uncontrolled, these lost souls—usually victims of suicide, epidemic, or violent death—can wreak havoc on the living, usually close relatives. This is illustrated by a curious reversal of the skull-riding configuration described above, as observed by Jonathan Parry in his encyclopedic study of postmortem rituals in Benares: "The one who gives fire [the principal mourner, ideally the son of the deceased] becomes the 'vehicle of the *pret*' (*pret kā savārī*). Because he has burnt him, the deceased is always behind him. Because he has cracked open the dead man's skull the latter rides on *his* [the principal mourner's] skull."[49]

The second type of medieval Indian manned spacecraft is the royal airship or chariot in the sky, which, if we are to follow an argument advanced by Michael Rabe, was not restricted to the area of mythology. In a very witty article,[50] this author notes that

> of all the metaphoric formulations of the Hindu temple—mountain, palace, altar, divine embodiment, chariot—for me it is the last that provides the surest key to unlocking the mystique surrounding its [the medieval Hindu temple's] sexual imagery. To expand upon my favorite phrase to the Pali Text Society Dictionary's definition of *vimāna* (undeniably the most common architectural term for the sanctuary structure proper), they are "immeasurably" palatial residences of the meritorious celestials (*devatās*), capable in myth of appearing suddenly or darting off again at their occupants' will, UFO-like. . . . By way of textual authority for this admittedly bold assertion, I cite Krishna Deva's passing mention of an early twelfth-century description of *svargārohaṇa-prāsāda*, literally "temples for flying to heaven."[51]

In support of his theory, Rabe offers two medieval inscriptions from Madhya Pradesh in which temples are described as mountains reaching up to heaven. What is of greater interest to us here is the ostensible reason for kings to desire to fly up to heaven, which is essential to Rabe's explanation for the erotic imagery found on Khajuraho temples. The divinely beautiful women portrayed in every conceivable state of undress and sexual position on the walls of such remarkable edifices as the eleventh-century Kandariyā Mahādeva temple at Khajuraho are none other than the female demigods—the Apsarasas, Vidyādharīs, and Siddha maidens who welcome the royal Virile Hero to their atmospheric haunts.[52]

6. The Flight of the Yoginī

But humans are not the sole passengers to ride *vetālas*, *pretas*, corpses, or skulls. The twelfth-century Pacalī Bhairava image of Kathmandu[53] has a giant *vetāla*, more than five times his size, for his vehicle, a configuration that reflects the textually sanctioned iconography of the medieval cult of Svacchanda Bhairava, who rides on the shoulders of the *preta* Sadāśiva.[54] Far more often, however, it is goddesses who ride *pretas*. These include Kālī,[55] Kubjikā,[56] and Cāmuṇḍā,[57] the three most independent goddesses of the Hindu tradition in the sense that, unlike nearly all the other great goddesses or Mothers of Hinduism, these goddesses always stand alone, without a male consort, their *śakti* entirely their own. A significant number of miniature paintings of Kālī portray her corpse vehicle as a truly "inflated" male, a human dirigible, lying on his stomach.[58] The goddess Kāmākhyā is described as standing on a "white ghost" in the *Kālikā Purāṇa*.[59] Finally, the Yoginīs who are portrayed astride *pretas* are legion in medieval iconography. At least thirty tenth- to eleventh-century Indian sculptures show the great body of a generally mustached figure craning his neck to look upward at the Yoginī seated on his back. This motif becomes even more commonplace in the later medieval period, in both India and Nepal, where all manner of male and female figures are shown riding *pretas* in this way. There is a relationship here between this imagery and the corpse practice (*śava-sādhanā*) depicted in the KSS account related above: it is when the corpse, which is lying facedown, "looks up" at the practitioner that the practice is known to have succeeded (fig. 7.b).[60]

The majority of the Yoginīs depicted in Indian sculpture are multi-armed figures, an indication that they are divine "goddesses" rather than human "witches," by which it would logically follow that their power of flight is not dependent on *preta* propulsion. At the ninth- to tenth-century Yoginī temple at Hirapur (Orissa), however, where many Yoginīs are two-armed (and so perhaps represent human "witches"), a significant number of these figures are depicted standing over a (generally smiling) face or head.[61] Here, the iconographic reference may be to corpse or skull practice, rather than to the *preta* or *vetāla* as vehicle for a Tantric deity. In both cases, we may see a reference to this technique for flight that was so widely evoked in the medieval literature.

Although divine Yoginīs are, together with certain goddesses, portrayed iconographically as riding on vehicles of various sorts, they are most often described in both religious and secular literature as self-propelled, flying through the air under their own power. Indeed, the standard Buddhist etymology for the term *ḍākinī*, a term used synonymously with *yoginī*, is

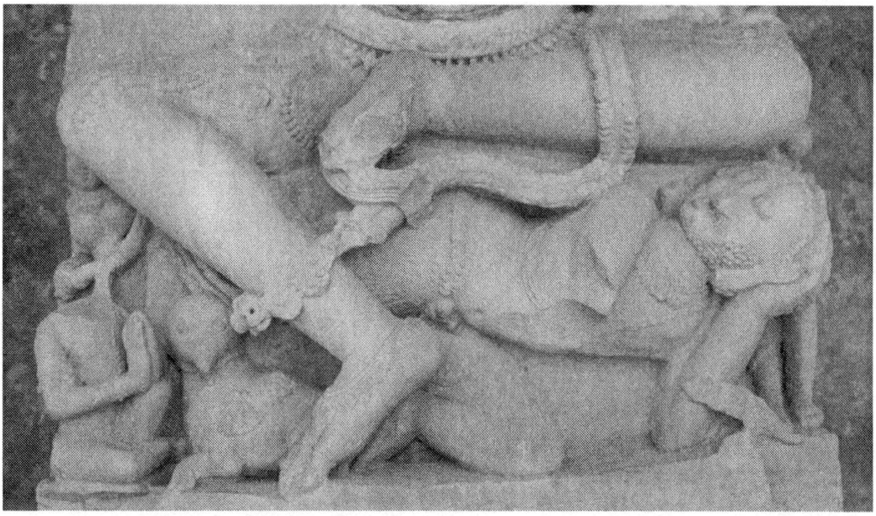

Figure 7.b. Vetāla-possessed corpse looking up at Yoginī for whom it is a vehicle. Bheraghat Yoginī temple, Jabalpur District, Madhya Pradesh, ca. 1000 C.E. Photograph by David Gordon White.

"she who flies," from the Sanskrit root *ḍi*, or *ḍai*, "fly."[62] The flight of the Yoginī—or at least the airborne (*khecara*) division of Yoginīs—is altogether natural once one recalls the origins of their cults. Like a great number of female deities (or demonesses) before them, the Yoginīs were often identified in mythology, sculpture, and ritual as winged figures, or indeed as *birds*. These are in fact the living creatures most frequently encountered at their favorite terrestrial haunt, the cremation ground, where human "witches," jackals (*śivās*), and carrion-eating birds are all identified as Yoginīs, whence their description, in the twelfth-century *Dvyāśraya*, as "the filthy birds of night."[63] It is altogether natural, then, that so many of the medieval Yoginī images portray them as zoocephalic or avicephalic figures, possessed of human bodies and limbs, but the heads of animals or birds. Like their Kushan-era forerunners, the Yoginīs are quite frequently portrayed as bird-headed in temple sculptures from ninth- to tenth-century Madhya Pradesh: these include the Yoginī Piṅgalā at the Bheraghat Yoginī temple, Jabalpur; Jaūti, from Rewa, now housed in the Dhubela Archaeological Museum, Dhubela; and the Yoginī Umā from the Naresar Yoginī temple, now housed in the Gwalior Archaeological Museum (fig. 7.c). To these may be added *kuladevīs* of modern-day north and south India who are also represented as birds,[64] and painted images of bird-headed Indian female Seizers from the "Caves of the Thousand Buddhas" in inner Asia.[65]

Figure 7.c. Animal- or bird-headed Yoginī from the Naresar Yoginī temple (Madhya Pradesh), ca. 1000 C.E. Presently housed in Gwalior Archaeological Museum. Photograph by David Gordon White.

The principle of the Yoginīs' flight is the same as that of the many winged Mother goddesses of earlier Hindu traditions, and, indeed, of birds in general. Thus the *Brahmāṇḍa Purāṇa* states, with reference to the "Mother Protectresses" (*rākṣasamātaraḥ*), that "those beings among them whose energy is drawn upward (*utkṛṣṭa*) are known as 'airborne' (*khecarāḥ*)."[66] In other words, their food fuels their flight. Other Tantric sources indicate that it is the consumption of blood and other bodily constituents that allows demonesses to change their forms, a power, it will be recalled, that was possessed by the demoness Jarā: "A Śākinī is a female Attractor (*ākarṣinī*) of the blood, etc. of her victim, [which she uses] in order to change her form."[67] Attraction and eating somehow go together in the Tantric sources: among the multitude of references to feeding the Yoginīs, one from the KJñN (11.18) states that "by whatever means [possible], one should always devour [the victim one is] attracting (*ākṛṣṭim*). One should honor the horde of Yoginīs with food and [sexual] pleasure." Beyond this, there was a notion in the medieval period that women had, in some way, a natural propensity for flight that was absent in men, as a statement from the twelfth-century alchemical *Kākacaṇḍeśvarīmata* clearly implies: "I will now speak of other female aviators who move through the heavens. Difficult of attainment for all women, how much more must it [i.e., the power of flight] be for a man!"[68]

A watershed for Yoginī traditions in everything but name, the 423 C.E. Gangdhar stone-tablet inscription, mentioned in chapter 5,[69] reads as follows:

> Also for the sake of religious merit, the king's minister caused to be built . . . this most terrible abode, strewn with a multitude of [images of] Ḍākinīs [i.e.,] of the Mothers, that drove of joyous over-the-top gong-bangers who are pumped up to the rain clouds[70] [on] the powerful winds raised by the Tantras [in this context, "ritual practices"].

This early fifth-century passage introduces a number of elements that become staples of later Yoginī traditions. First, the Mothers are associated with loud percussion instruments, as evidenced in two coeval passages from the *Harivaṃśa*, which qualify the Goddess as being "renowned for the great clamor of her bells," and the female Seizers as bird-faced beings "whose harsh cries resemble the booming of kettle-drums."[71] So, too, the later *Rājataraṅgiṇī's* description of a cremation-ground ritual portrays the Yoginīs as violently ringing bells and beating drums.[72] A number of goddesses in later Tantric sources have names that evoke this propensity for clamor: one of these is Caṇḍaghaṇṭā ("She of the Furious Bells").[73] Indeed, it has been argued that the etymological root of the term *ḍākinī* is perhaps *ḍam* ("to sound"), rather than the more widely accepted *ḍī* ("to fly")[74] (fig. 7.d).

Figure 7.d. Yoginī beating a drum, Hirapur Yoginī temple, Puri District, Orissa, ninth to tenth century C.E. Courtesy of the American Institute of Indian Studies.

The second salient feature of the Mothers described in the Gangdhar inscription is that they are "pumped up" into the sky on winds produced by Tantric rites. Here, a connection may be made with an eighth-century C.E. play, the *Mālatī-Mādhava* of Bhavabhūti. In the thrilling opening scene of the play's fifth act, the Yoginī[75] Kapālakuṇḍalā ("She Who Has Skulls for Earrings")—who is the consort of a Kāpālika named Aghoraghaṇṭa ("Hell's Bells")—is flying to a cremation ground. On her way she explains the principle of her flight:

> Beholding by the power of resorption the eternal Supreme Spirit in the form of Śiva—[who], superimposed upon my six members [and] placed in the six circles, manifests himself in the midst of the heart lotus—here I have now come, rending asunder the cloud-laden sky before me, without experiencing any fatigue from my flight by virtue of my extraction of the five nectars (*pañcāmṛta-akarṣaṇād*) of moving creatures (*jagataḥ*), [which I have effected] by the gradual pumping of the breath channels (*nāḍīnām-udaya-krameṇa*).[76]

Commenting on this verse, Jagaddhara states that this female figure's power of flight is acquired by drawing upward (*ākāśagāmitva-utkarṣā-pratipādanāt*) the five constituent elements of the human body (*śarirasya pañcabhūtātmakasya*). Here, Jagaddhara glosses *ā-kṛṣ* ("draw toward," "attract") with the term *ut-kṛṣ*, "draw upward," which we have already encountered in the *Brahmāṇḍa Purāṇa*'s explanation for the flight of the "Mother Protectresses."[77] *Ut-kṛṣ* ("draw upward") is also one of three Sanskrit verbal roots that may be translated as "extraction," the others being *ā-kṛṣ* ("draw toward," "attract"), and *ud-dhṛ* ("bear upward").[78] The root *kṛṣ*, an extremely important one for Tantric "vernacular technologies" in general, denotes the "traction," the simultaneous "cutting" and "drawing" action of the blade of a plow through the soil. Attraction (*ākarṣaṇa*), the technique that lies at the heart of Tantric sorcery, is an omnipresent term in the Tantras. Two episodes in the final book of the KSS depict evil Kāpālikas using mantras of attraction to magically draw a woman and a Yakṣiṇī, against their will, into their lairs. We have also encountered it in the *Rājataraṅgiṇī* account of Sandhimati, in which the Yoginīs yogically "draw back" (*yogena ā-kṛṣ*) his spirit;[79] as well as in the KJñN use of the mantra *hro hraḥ* for the extraction (*ākṛṣṭi*) of the blood of the Yoginīs.[80] In the *Netra Tantra* passage discussed above, the Yoginīs are described as able to "extract (*ākarṣayanti*), in a moment, life from others (literally, 'from foreign cities')."[81] Flight, quite nearly as ubiquitous as attraction, while it is more often termed *khecara*, has "drawing upward" (*utkṛṣṭi*) as its root cause. This feminine power of traction takes on a cosmic dimension in the case of the goddess Kālī, who stands at the heart of the Krama Kaula mandalas: called Kāla-saṃkarṣaṇī, "She Who Contracts Time," she draws back all of time and space into herself at the end of a cosmic eon.

This *Mālatī-Mādhava* passage is immediately preceded by what I identified—in error, I now believe—as the earliest reference to the six *cakras* in all of Indian literature.[82] Here, Kapālakuṇḍalā says:

> Victorious is the lord of Śakti surrounded by the Śaktis, whose self is situated in the midst of the wheel of sixteen channels (*nāḍīcakra*), [and] who, when his form is realized as dwelling in the heart, affords *siddhis* to persons possessed of this arcane knowledge, [and who is] sought after by practitioners whose minds are unwavering.[83]

The power of a female figure's flight through the clouds afforded by the pumping of her wind or breath channels and a cacophony of percussion instruments appear to be the common features of both the Gangdhar inscription and this passage from Bhavabhūti's play. They may also explain the *Kākacaṇḍeśvarīmata*'s statement on women's "natural" propensity for flight. If we juxtapose these concepts with those found in a certain number of yogic and Tantric works, to the effect that, in contradistinction to men, a woman's "flow" through the *nāḍīs* is constant and strong,[84] then we may have found the physiological principles of the flight of the Yoginī. This feminine power of flight may even have its source in the particular aerodynamics of a woman's subtle body as imagined in these medieval sources: Kapālakuṇḍalā's inner "wheel of [sixteen] channels" (*nāḍīcakra*)[85] would have been a "turbine" of sorts, through which the channeling of air propelled her into space. At the same time, it was a yantra in both senses of the term—a "device" for flying and a circular "array" surrounding the god Bhairava, enshrined in her heart. This same principle—of the "pumping up" (*udaya*) of a "wheel of channels" at the heart of which the god Bhairava is enshrined—is found in what Abhinavagupta judged to be the most prestigious of all the Tantras, the circa tenth-century *Jayadrathayāmala*.[86] In the third hexad of this massive work, we find the same terminology as found in *Mālatī-Mādhava* 5.1–2, but with one important difference: even as it refers to the "secret and manifold workings of the hidden Śaktis," the *Jayadrathayāmala* has clearly internalized these within the body of a *male* practitioner, whose combined techniques of meditation and breath control serve to afford him the power of attraction (*ākarṣaṇa*). As I will show in chapter 8, this trend of the "sublimation" and internalization of these powerful feminine entities, and of the "masculinization" of their powers, was one that would gradually reduce the Yoginī to the internal energy, the *śakti* or *kuṇḍalinī* located within the body of the initiated male practitioner.

As *Mālatī-Mādhava* 5.2 and Jagaddhara's commentary make clear, what fueled the Yoginī's flight was her "extraction of the essence" of the five nectars (human semen, blood, urine, excrement, and marrow)[87] or five elements (earth, water, air, fire, ether) of the human body. This is precisely the role played by the *kuṇḍalinī* in the subtle body of hathayogic practice. As she rises upward along the medial channel, she implodes earth into water at the level of the *svādhiṣṭhāna* (navel), water into fire at the *maṇipura* (navel), fire into air at the *anāhata* (heart), and air into the ether through which she rises at the *viśuddhi* (throat). The *cakra*s that she pierces in this process of extraction or refinement are called "cremation grounds" in a number of hathayogic sources, bringing us back to the locus of the Yoginīs' anthropophagy in the outside world.[88] Moreover, the *kuṇḍalinī*, a serpent, was preceded, by millennia, in Indian discussions of the energies of the subtle body by a creature for which flight is an entirely natural mode of being: this is the *haṃsa*, the migratory gander, whose flight upward and downward in the subtle body marks the movement of breath in the body.[89]

The verse that follows, *Mālatī-Mādhava* 5.3, continues to emphasize Kapālakuṇḍalā's percussivity, evoking a bell mounted atop her staff, and more clanging bells of another sort, whose din resonates through hollow skulls. This last detail reminds us, once again, of the skull-riders of other Tantric traditions. Kapālakuṇḍalā is the Yoginī consort of a Kāpālika, and in this scene she is flying to a cremation ground. Thus we are in the presence of another commonplace of medieval Indian literature, which locates Tantric Virile Heroes together with Yoginīs or Ḍākinīs in cremation-grounds settings. In the case of the latter, they are always there to consume human flesh, a role that extends as far back as literature on multiple goddesses takes us. To those Siddhas or Vīras who offer human flesh (their own or someone else's), they offer their form of grace, that is, *siddhi*s, among which the power of flight figures prominently. This connection between the power of flight and the consumption of human flesh is also made clear in a passage from the *Rājataraṅgiṇī*, in which the last days of King Baka are described:

> Hereupon a Mistress of Yoga (*yogeśvarī*) named Bhaṭṭā, having taken the form of a beautiful woman, approached the king as night was falling. His memory of what was proper having been dissipated by her many captivating words, he was delighted to accept her invitation to view the munificence of her "yoga feast" (*yogotsava*). Then when he had come there at dawn, together with hundreds of his sons and grandsons, that

> world-conqueror was transformed by her into an offering to the circle of goddesses (*devīcakropahāratām*). She who had become perfected (*siddhā*) by means of that act left the mark of her rise into the sky (*vyomakramaṇa*). Resembling the imprint of her two knees, it is visible down to this very day. Even today, the memory of the event is perpetuated in the lodges (*maṭhas*) of Kherī, [in the form of] the god named the "Lord of the One Hundred Skulls," the Circle of Mothers [temple], and that rock [bearing the imprint of her knees].[90]

As is the case in so many of these sources, an ambiguity remains concerning the identity of this *yogeśvarī*, this human sorceress who has taken on the role of a Yoginī: Is her power of flight the direct result of her consumption of the flesh of her sacrificial victims, or is it the result of the grace offered *to her* by the semidivine Yoginīs, in exchange for her offering of the same? Here, it would appear that the latter is the case; yet in the *Mālatī-Mādhava* and a number of other sources, "human" Yoginīs appear to become airborne directly through their extraction of the essence of the bodies they consume. Perhaps the question is moot, given the KJñN's depiction of the Yoginīs as "deities moving in this world of mortals" in the form of female humans, birds, and animals.[91] Similarly, Kṣemarāja, in his commentary on *Netra Tantra* 19.71, evokes a group of female beings called the Śābarīs, whose minds are concentrated on mantras, who steal away the five nectars of human beings, and who travel over the earth in a moment, taking on a variety of forms. Whatever the case, the consumption of human flesh as the source of the Yoginīs' power of flight and shape-changing abilities becomes a commonplace in the medieval period. Nearly all of the twentieth chapter of the KSS is devoted to descriptions of the Yoginīs, and it is here that we find a long disquisition on their power of flight, as narrated by Queen Kuvalayāvalī, who has become a member of a witches' coven, a circle of Yoginīs:

> At the conclusion of my worship, I suddenly saw that my friends, having flown upward, were roaming about in the field of the sky, each by means of her own supernatural power. Beholding that [sight], I called in amazement, and made them descend from the sky; and, questioned by me regarding the nature of their supernatural power, they immediately said this: "These supernatural powers of witches' spells arise from the eating of human flesh. . . ."[92] Thus addressed by my friends, [and] most eager for the supernatural power of flight (*khecarīsiddhi*) but anxious about eating human flesh, I hesitated for a moment. But then, out of my ardent desire for that supernatural power [of flight], I said to my friends, "May this, my instruction [in these matters], be conferred by you."[93]

7. Men Who Fly with the Yoginīs

Regardless of the venue—cremation ground, isolated "mound" or "field,"[94] or royal Yoginī temple—there was a certain uniformity to the nature of the transactions that occurred between male and female participants in the Kaula rites. Males fed the Yoginīs the vital bodily constituents they craved, in exchange for which Yoginīs bestowed *siddhis*, including flight.[95] With this, we may return to the quote from Alexis Sanderson with which we opened the third section of this chapter. In Sanderson's words, the male practitioner, having "gratif[ied] the [Yoginīs] with an offering of blood drawn from his own body, [would] ascend with them into the sky as the leader of their band."[96] Here, the male practitioner takes the place of Bhairava-Śiva at the center of the circle of Yoginīs, a configuration found not only in stone-cut Yoginī temples but also in nearly every other representation—on paper, metal, or in textual description—of Yoginī mandalas (fig. 7.e).[97] This is narrativized into the happy ending of many an episode of the KSS, an example being the story of Kandarpa, which, while it glosses over the reasons for the favor he eventually finds with a certain Yoginī, does end on the essential note of their shared flight:

> A brahmin named Kandarpa from Ratnapura comes upon a deserted Mother goddess temple (*mātṛdevagṛha*) in the night. Entering, he sees a brilliant light. He prays to the Mothers to protect him. When the daylight comes, he finds garlands of bones and the skulls of children. He realizes they are from a host of Mothers [i.e., witches]. He later hears the group of Yoginīs speaking among themselves: "Today we must go to the gathering of the circle (*cakramelaka*) that is taking place in Cakrapura." The Yoginīs find him hiding there, and carry him off with them. . . . One of their number, named Sumanā, marries him. Leaving the circular gathering of the Yoginīs (*yoginyaścakramelaka*), she carries him away with her, up into the sky.[98]

A clue to the theoretical means by which a Yoginī could have afforded the power of flight to her male consort may be gleaned from the concluding verses of the twenty-second chapter of the KJñN, already discussed in chapter 4.[99]

> The [work known] by the name of the "Bringing Forth of the [Kaula] Gnosis" was one million five hundred thousand [verses in length]. This [teaching] is the essence, O Lord, extracted upward (*samuddhṛtam*) from the midst of that.[100] This teaching [is found] in every one of the Yoginīs' lodges in Kāmākhyā (the "Place Called Love"). [Bhairava concludes:]

Figure 7.e. *Left*, dancing Śiva shrine at center of Ranipur-Jharial Yoginī temple, Balotra District, Orissa, tenth century C.E. Courtesy of the American Institute of Indian Studies.

> Through their pure knowledge of this [teaching], O Goddess, the [Yoginīs] confer "seizure" and "release" (*nigrahānugraha*), supernatural power, and union (*melāpaka*) with themselves.[101] That which was in the condition of the Fish-Belly—the great [textual] teaching (*mahāśāstra*) that was brought down at Moon Island, O Mistress—is *sung* in Kāmākhyā.[102]

We have already seen that upward extraction is the stated principle of female flight in texts from this period. Here, the juxtaposition of the term *samuddhṛtam* with the Yoginīs' conferred powers of seizure, release, and union (*melāpaka*) with themselves is a clear reference to a broader body of Yoginī-related practice, also found in Kubjikā traditions. *Melāpa[ka]* is of two sorts in these traditions, called "pleasing union" (*priyamelāpa*) and "violent union" (*haṭhamelāpa*), respectively. In the former, the male practitioner's union with the human Yoginī, or his consumption of her female discharge or their mixed fluids, "generates the lineage of Siddhas and the world of sacred places in which they reside." The latter is precisely that process by which the male practitioner is freed from the ignorance barring his path to self-deification: "Like a witch who sucks out the vitality of the unwary male, [the human Yoginī] withdraws the [practitioner's] ignorance . . . 'churning' his energies into a dynamic, active state."[103] Whereas in *priyamelāpa* the male practitioner is nurtured by the Yoginī, who shares her sexual fluids with him, in *haṭhamelāpa* she extracts fluid from him, preying on him sexually like the Goddess who mounts the corpselike Śiva in reverse sexual intercourse. This imagery would appear to be a reversal of Freud's celebrated "wolf-man" case, in which the wolves drawn by his patient represented men he saw in coitus with his mother while still a child. Here, the image is of female predators—jackals (*śivā*), the most commonly represented carrion feeder on Yoginī temple sculptures and in Tantric literature,[104] or predatory birds—preying on their male victims sexually even as they tear them apart with their teeth or beaks (fig. 7.f).

Exchange in both directions may be cast as types of drinking through the oral cavities of the partners, or as types of upward genital extraction—called *vajrolī mudrā* in both men ("urethral suction") and women ("vaginal suction").[105] The relationship between these two readings of the term *melāpa[ka]*, on the one hand, and the pair "seizure" and "release" (*nigrahānugraha*) in KJñN 22.11, on the other, is explained by Dorothea Heilijger-Seelens, on the basis of data found in KM descriptions of the *yoginīcakra*, in what she identifies as "the essential meaning of the Yoginīs."[106] Here, precisely, it is the opposition between the Yoginīs as inauspicious, ill disposed, and prone to destruction (*nigraha*) and their role as auspicious, benevolent, and related to creation (*anugraha*) that is highlighted. In the "upward progress" (*utkrānti*) and other ritual practices, there are two types

Figure 7.f. Yoginī standing above representations of human head and jackals, Hirapur Yoginī temple, Puri District, Orissa, ninth to tenth century C.E. Courtesy of the American Institute of Indian Studies.

of interactions that a male practitioner may have with the Yoginīs. The one in which he offers them his bodily fluids, and in which they torment him, is called the "southern course," which is further identified with upward movement, from the lowest to the highest of the six internal *cakras*; the other, in which these goddesses bestow bliss, is conversely termed the "northern course" and is identified with downward movement, from the highest to the lowest of the six *cakras*. These two directions of exchange are further identified with the terms *kula* (the Goddess, as Clan[ned]) and *kulākula* (the Goddess, complementing her male, Unclanned consort), respectively. Behind this, we can detect a still earlier phase of the Kubjikā traditions, in which motion would have been rotary before being projected upon a vertical axis. As I indicated in chapter 3, the earliest mentions of the "Kubjikā maṇḍala" describe this as a hexagon whose six goddesses are enumerated from the northwestern corner, and whose rituals are constructive when the offerings are made in a clockwise direction and destructive when they are made in a counterclockwise direction (the term *nigraha* in KM 23.146 signifying both the counterclockwise direction and its destructive result). Going back still further, this rotary motion of the Yoginīs, which is also mentioned in Buddhist Tantras, evokes women's circular thigh-slapping dances in Vedic fertility rites.[107] We may illustrate these oppositions with a chart:

female consumption of male fluids	male consumption of female fluids
violent union (*haṭha-melāpa*)	pleasing union (*priya-melāpa*)
seizure (*nigraha*)	release (*anugraha*)
counterclockwise motion	clockwise motion
upward movement	downward movement
utkarṣaṇa, uddhṛti	*nirṇaya*
southern course	northern course
kula	*kulākula*
male power of flight through removal of impediments	"clanning" of male through ingestion of female discharge

This Hindu dynamic is confirmed in a Buddhist Highest Yoga Tantra initiation practice, which combines the language and imagery of *haṭha yoga* (which, like *haṭha-melāpa*, may also be translated as "violent union") with that of the female consumption of male sexual fluids and the power of flight. In the Buddhist context, this is called the "fierce recitation" (again, the equivalent of "violent union"), with seminal fluid being semanticized into a stream of syllables:

> First the male emits from his mouth a stream of sacred syllables. Then he visualizes the goddess before him, the "diamond demoness" (*vajra-yoginī*

> or *vajra-ḍākinī*). He then visualizes himself as the god and visualizes the Mother on his lap. The white *vajra* (penis) of the Father unites with the red *padma* (vulva) of the Mother: *then the deities enter into union in the sky* and enter the male adept through his mouth or between his eyebrows: they descend, pass through his *vajra* and fall and mix into the lotus of the Mother. Then the mantra goes "upward from mouth to mouth" [i.e., from the woman's back into the man's]. This is regarded as the forward recitation of the mantra; *but if the direction is reversed, upward* through the diamond path and *into the mouth of the goddess, this is the fierce recitation* . . . and [one] practices these in turn. *This reverse direction has the seed-mantra travelling up the spine, out of the mouth of the man and into that of the woman*, down into her womb and out into his *vajra*, up through the spine and so forth as the cycle continues and is continually reversed.[108]

Here, one of the principles of the Yoginī's own flight is being applied as the means by which she transfers that same *siddhi* to her male partner: her power to "draw upward" (*ut-karṣaṇa*) not only allows her to lift off the ground herself, but also to draw upward—either through her upper or nether mouth—the impediments to her partner's flight, and to activate his own energies, to the same end.[109] The circular Yoginī temples, open to sky, were landing fields and launching pads for Yoginīs and their consorts, the Virile Heroes and Perfected Beings. Over time these circles of Yoginīs became internalized into the energies of the *cakras* of hathayogic practice, and their cultic practices—in which love and death become intimately intertwined through their extraction of the essence of their male lovers-*cum*-victims—internalized into the raising of the *kuṇḍalinī*.

Chapter 8

THE SUBLIMATION OF THE YOGINĪ: *The Subordination of the Feminine in High Hindu Tantra*

In the opening chapter of this book, I suggested that it was sexual practice and in particular the ritualized consumption of sexual fluids that gave medieval South Asian Tantra its specificity—in other words, that differentiated Tantra from all other forms of religious practice of the period. This, the "hard core" of South Asian Tantra, first appeared as a coherent ritual system—the Kaula—in about the eighth century in central India; and there have since been more recent revivals of the original Kaula impetus, in fourteenth- to sixteenth-century Bengal and Nepal in particular. However, throughout most of South Asia, a marginalization of Kaula practice occurred in elite brahmanic circles, from a very early time onward, which sublimated the "hard core" of Kaula practice into a body of ritual and meditative techniques that did not threaten the purity regulations that have always been the basis for high-caste social constructions of the self.

The sublime edifice of what I have been calling "high" Hindu Tantra in these pages has been, in the main, an internalization, an aestheticization, and a semanticization of Kaula practice. It has been the transformation "from a kind of doing to a kind of knowing," a system of "overcoding" that has permitted householder practitioners to have it both ways and lead conventional lives while experimenting in secret with Tantric identities.[1] This transformation, which was effected over a relatively brief period of time, between the tenth and the twelfth centuries, especially involved the subordination of the feminine—of the multiple Yoginīs, Mothers, and Śaktis (and their human counterparts) of Kaula traditions—to the person of the male practitioner, the male guru in particular. This subordination occurred on a number of levels that involved: (1) the internalization of the Yoginīs and their circles into the *cakras* of hathayogic practice; (2) the semanticization of the Yoginīs into seed mantras; (3) the masculinization of Tantric initiation; and (4) the introduction of ritual substitutes for the referents of the five M-words, including *maithuna*.

1. Prehistory of the *Cakras*

In his masterful book *The Kāpālikas and Kālāmukhas*, David Lorenzen makes the following cogent point concerning the goals of yogic practice:

> In spite of abundant textual references to various *siddhis* [supernatural enjoyments] in classical Yoga texts, many modern Indian scholars, and like-minded western ones as well, have seized on a single *sūtra* of Patañjali (3.37) to prove that magical powers were regarded as subsidiary, and even hindrances, to final liberation and consequently not worthy of concentrated pursuits. This attitude may have been operative in Vedāntic and Buddhist circles and is now popular among practitioners imbued with the spirit of the Hindu reformist movements, but it was not the view of Patañjali and certainly not the view of mediaeval exponents of Haṭha Yoga.[2]

It suffices to cast a glance at the *Yoga Sūtras* to see that the acquisition of *siddhis* was at the forefront of yogic theory and practice in the first centuries of the common era: nearly all of the fifty-five *sūtras* of book 3 of this work are devoted to the *siddhis*, and the "disclaimer" in verse 37 of this book—that "these powers are impediments to *samādhi*, but are acquisitions in a normal fluctuating state of mind"— seems only to apply, in fact, to the *siddhis* enumerated in the two preceding verses. This is a view shared by P. V. Kane.[3]

One finds very little of yogic practice, in the sense of techniques involving fixed postures (*āsanas*) and breath control (*prāṇāyāma*), in the *Yoga Sūtras*. They are, of course, the third and fourth limbs of Patañjali's eight-limbed yoga (2.29); however, in the grand total of seven *sūtras* (2.46–52) he devotes to them, Patañjali gives absolutely no detail on these matters, save perhaps a veiled reference to diaphragmatic retention, which he terms *stambha-vṛtti* (2.50). References to the subtle body, the channels (*nāḍīs*) and energy centers (*cakras*), are entirely absent from this work (although the *bhāṣya* does briefly describe a limited number of *āsanas*). It would appear in fact that the circa sixth-century B.C.E. *Chāndogya Upaniṣad* (8.6.6) had already gone far beyond Patañjali and his commentators when it stated: "There are a hundred and one channels of the heart. One of these passes up to the crown of the head. Going up by it, one goes to immortality. The others are for departing in various directions."

Moreover, Patañjali's "classical" definition of "yoga" notwithstanding,[4] many if not most pre-twelfth-century accounts of the practice of "yoga," going back to the MBh,[5] describe it *not* as a form of meditative or physical practice, but rather as a battery of techniques for the attainment of *siddhis*, including out-of-body experience, entering the bodies of others as a means to escaping death or simply to feed on them, invisibility, the power of flight, transmutation, and so on.[6] Similarly, the term "yogin" (or *yogeśvara*, "master of yoga"), like its feminine form *yoginī* (or *yogeśvarī*), most often means "sorcerer" or "magician" in pre-twelfth-century sources: thus, for example, Kṣāntaśila, the rogue ascetic of the frame story of the KSS, is called a yogin; and Bhaṭṭā, who makes a meal of King Baka in the *Rājataraṅgiṇī*, is called a *yogeśvarī*.[7] The "Tantric yoga" that is being marketed in places like Hollywood has elided several centuries from the history of the origins and development of yoga, and altered its content beyond recognition.

In this section I will trace the development of a number of elements specific to *haṭha yoga* as such emerged in a variety of Hindu and Buddhist sources between the eighth and twelfth centuries C.E. These sources are the eighth-century Buddhist *Hevajra Tantra* and the following Hindu sources: the eighth-century *Bhāgavata Purāṇa* (BhP) and *Tantrasadbhāva Tantra*; the ninth- to tenth-century KJñN; the tenth- to eleventh-century KM and *Jayadrathayāmala*; the eleventh-century TĀ; the eleventh- to twelfth-century *Rudrayāmala Tantra*; and the twelfth-century *Śrīmatottara Tantra*. In this historical analysis, I will discuss (1) the emergence of the subtle body system of the *cakras*; (2) the projection of powerful feminine figures from the external world of Tantric ritual onto the grid of the subtle body; and (3) the role of these now-internalized feminine energies, including that known as the *kuṇḍalinī*, in the male practitioner's attainment of *siddhis*.

One need not go back very far to find the principal source of the seemingly timeless system of the six plus one *cakras*: this is Arthur Avalon's edition and translation of a late work, the *Saṭcakranirūpaṇa*, as the principal element of his seminal study, *The Serpent Power*.[8] Perhaps due to the power of the illustrations of this configuration in Avalon's work, many scholars have taken this to be an immutable, eternal system, as old as yoga itself, and grounded, perhaps, in the yogin's actual experience of the subtle body. A case in point is a recent work by Rahul Peter Das, which, while it offers an encyclopedic account of subtle body systems in Bengal, is constantly plagued by the author's frustration in the face of the inconsistencies and contradictions between those systems.[9] In fact, there is no "standard" system of the *cakras*. Every school, sometimes every teacher within each school, has had their own *cakra* system. These have developed over time, and an "archaeology" of the various configurations is in order.

We have already noted that Hindus have been worshiping groups of Mothers (*mātṛcakras*) since at least the sixth century.[10] These were circular arrays of goddesses "in the world," that is, outside of the body, circles represented in mandalas of every sort, including the circular, hypaethral Yoginī temples. The gradual internalization of these powerful female entities was effected by internalizing their formations into the hierarchized *cakras* of the yogic body. Two early instances of this process may be found in the KJñN and the KM.

We begin with the presentation in the KJñN of six categories of Śaktis—the "Field-born," "Mound-born," and so on—that were outlined in chapter 6.[11] Here, a comparison may be drawn with a slightly later source, Kṣemarāja's eleventh-century commentary to *Netra Tantra* 19.71. Citing the *Tantrasadbhāva*, Kṣemarāja names these same six categories of Śaktis, specifying that unlike the Yoginīs, who dwell in the worlds of Brahmā, Viṣṇu, and Indra, these six types of Śaktis all dwell within the body. He then goes on to identify these with six powerful and terrible classes of female entities: the Yoginīs, Devatās, Rupiṇīs, Śākinīs, Śābarikās, and Śivās. Most of these are described as draining the human body of its "five nectars," its vital fluids, but the language is ambiguous and seems to imply that they do so from without rather than from within. Following its division of the six Śaktis into internal and external groups of three, the KJñN continues with a description of a seventh type, called "Lowest-born"—that is, an outcaste woman—and then shifts to a description of the worship of a *cakra* comprised of the sixty-four Yoginīs and the fifty-eight Virile Heroes, "duly presided over by the Sons of the Clan."[12] Fifteen verses later, two sets of seed mantras—termed the "Clan Group of Eight" and the "Wisdom Group of Eight," comprised of vowels and consonants, respectively—are presented. These are to be written out eight times, with Clan and Wisdom graphemes interspersed. This entire sixty-four-part arrangement is termed the "Yoginī Sequence."[13]

It is at this point that the term *cakra* first comes to be employed in a systematic way in this chapter. One who is devoted to meditation upon and worship of the first *cakra*, named "Mingling with the Yoginīs" (*yoginīmelakam*), obtains the eight supernatural powers (*siddhis*); with the second *cakra*, one obtains the power of attraction; and with the third, entering into the body of another person; and so on to the eighth, which confers the power of realizing one's desires and mastery of the six powers of Tantric sorcery. This Great Cakra (*mahācakra*), raised at its apex (i.e., conical), is ascended through devotion to the Clan. The chapter concludes with the promise that one who knows the sixty-four arrangements becomes perfected, and that the "Sequence of the Sixty-four Yoginīs" is the concealed true essence of these arrangements.[14] This data is repeated with variations in chapter 10, with the practitioner meditating on eight *cakras* of eight petals each, with the total of sixty-four corresponding to eight sets of eight seed mantras.[15]

In these KJñN passages, the term *cakra* is being used in a nontechnical way, to simply denote a circle or grouping of divinities, identified with arrangements of the Sanskrit graphemes. A similar situation obtains in the KM. This work—whose five-"*cakra*" system comprises groups of *devīs*, *dūtīs*, *mātṛs*, *yoginīs*, and *khecarī* deities aligned along the vertical axis of the yogic body—nearly never refers to these groupings as *cakras*.[16] According to Dorothea Heilijger-Seelens, the meaning of the term *cakra* was, in the period in which this work was compiled, generally restricted to the groups of deities located in a mandala, which served as their base or support. The term did not denote a circular array, and even less so one located within the yogic body. Moreover, in those rare cases in which the KM did present the six energy centers by their "standard" names (this is the earliest source in which these are found), it only once referred to one of these—the *anāhata*—as a *cakra*.[17] These conceptual connections would be made later.

While the KM nonetheless insists that these are internal centers or groupings, it betrays a macrocosmic model when it speaks of their dimensions. The lowest group, the Devīcakra, identified with the element earth, is said to be one hundred *koṭis* (of *yojanas*, according to the commentary[18]) in size, with the other, higher groups a thousand, hundred thousand, 10 million, and 1,000 million *koṭis* in diameter, respectively. These are the precise measurements and proportions given in the tenth chapter of the *Svacchanda Tantra*—a text that predates the KM by at least a century—of the cosmic egg (one hundred *koṭis*), and the surrounding spheres of water, fire, air, and ether.[19] This understanding is already present in the KJñN, a text coeval with the *Svacchanda Tantra*, which gives a measure of ten *koṭis* "beyond the visible [world]" for "this Kaula," that is, this embodied universe. Also according to the KJñN, when the practitioner reaches a certain threshold of practice, "he sees the threefold universe, with its mobile and immobile beings, inside of his body. . . . With [an extension of] one thousand *koṭis*, he is Śiva himself, the maker and destroyer [of the universe]."[20] The clear implication here is that the various dimensions of the "outer space" of the universe are being directly projected onto the "inner space" of the human body. In these early references, the circles or spheres of the outer elements, even when they are identified with various groupings of female divinities, are still far removed from the later, "standard" notion of the six *cakras* of the yogic body.[21]

2. The Emergence of the *Cakras* as Components of the Yogic Body

The earliest accounts of the *cakras* as "circles" or "wheels" of subtle energy located within the yogic body are found in the *Caryāgīti* and the *Hevajra Tantra*, two circa eighth-century Buddhist Tantric works that locate four *cakras* within the human body at the levels of the navel, heart, throat, and head.[22] These *cakras* are identified with four geographical sites (*pīṭhas*), which appear to correspond to points of contact between the Indian subcontinent and inner Asia: these are Kāmākhyā (Gauhati, Assam), Uḍḍiyāna (Swat Valley?),[23] Pūrṇagiri (Punjab?), and Jālandhara (upper Punjab). This tradition is repeated in numerous sources, including those of the Nāth Siddhas, whose twelfth-century founder Gorakṣanātha identifies the same set of four *pīṭhas* with sites aligned along the spinal column within the yogic body.[24] The TĀ offers a slightly longer list of *pīṭhas* "in the world," before locating the same within the yogic body, a few verses later.[25] The *Hevajra Tantra*[26] also homologizes these four centers with a rich array of scholastic tetradic categories, including Buddha bodies, seed mantras, goddesses, truths, realities, schools, et cetera.[27] Their locations in the yogic body appear to correspond as well to the mystic locations of the mind in its four states as described in a number of late Upanishadic traditions, which declare that while one is in a waking state, the mind dwells in the navel; during dreamless sleep, it dwells in the heart; during dream sleep, it resides in the throat; and when in the "fourth state" only attainable by the yogin, it resides in the head.[28] Later sources locate ten and, still later, fifty-one *pīṭhas* (identified with the Sanskrit phonemes) within the subtle body.[29]

The vertical configuration of the six plus one *cakras* that many identify with Hindu subtle body mapping emerges slowly, in the course of the latter half of the first millennium C.E. Perhaps the earliest Hindu source on this system is the BhP, discussed in previous chapters.[30] Here, the "six sites" (*ṣaṭsu . . . sthāneṣu*) named are the (1) navel (*nābhī*); (2) heart (*hṛd*); (3) breast (*uras*); (4) root of the palate (*svatālumūlam*); (5) place between the eyebrows (*bhruvorantaram*); and (6) cranial vault (*mūrdhan*), from which he "will then surge upward into the beyond (*param*)." What is the source of this enumeration in the BhP? A glance at the early medical literature indicates that these sites correspond quite exactly to anatomical notions of the vital points of the body (*mahā-marmāṇi*) or the supports of the vital breaths (*prāṇāyatana*). These are listed in the circa 100 C.E.

Caraka Saṃhitā as follows: head (*mūrdhan*), throat (*kaṇṭha*), heart (*hṛdaya*), navel (*nābhī*), bladder (*basti*), and rectum (*guda*).[31] Certain later sources add the frenum,[32] the membrane that attaches the tongue to the lower jaw, to this list: this would correspond to the root of the palate listed in the BhP.

Śaivasiddhānta sources give a slightly different account of the centers. These most commonly list five centers, which they call either sites (*sthānas*), knots (*granthis*), supports (*ādhāras*), or lotuses—but almost never *cakras*. These are the heart (*hṛt*); throat (*kaṇṭha*); palate (*tālu*); the place between the eyebrows (*bhrūmadhya*); and the fontanel (*brahmarandhra*). Quite often, the End of the Twelve (*dvādaśānta*)—because it is located at twelve finger-breadths above the fontanel—will also be mentioned in these sources, but not as a member of this set of five. So, too, Śaivasiddhānta works will sometimes evoke the root support (*mūlādhāra*) in its bipolar relationship to the *brahmarandhra*, but without mention of the intervening centers.[33]

The first Hindu source to list the locations found in the BhP, and perhaps the first to apply the term *cakra* to them as well, is the KJñN:

> The various spokes [of the wheels] of divine maidens (*divyakanyāra*) are worshiped by the immortal host in (1) the secret place (genitals), (2) navel, (3) heart, (4) throat, (5) mouth, (6) forehead, and (7) crown of the head. [These maidens] are arrayed along the spine (*pṛṣṭamadhye*) [up] to the trident (*tridaṇḍakam*) [located at the level of] the fontanel (*muṇḍasandhi*). These *cakras* are of eleven sorts and comprised of thousands [of maidens?], O Goddess! [They are] five-spoked (*pañcāram*) and eight-leaved (*aṣṭa-pattram*), [as well as] ten- and twelve-leaved, sixteen- and one hundred–leaved, as well as one hundred thousand–leaved.[34]

This passage continues with a discussion of these divine maidens, through whom various *siddhis* are attained, each of whom is identified by the color of her garb (red, yellow, smoky, white, etc.). So it is that we find in this source a juxtaposition of (1) the locations of the *cakras*; (2) the use of the term *cakra*; (3) a description of the *cakras* as being composed of spokes *and* leaves (but not petals); and (4) a portrayal of color-coded divine maidens as dwelling in or on the spokes of these *cakras*. The problematic remark in this passage, that the *cakras* are in some way elevenfold, or of eleven sorts, appears to be explicated in the seventeenth chapter of the same source, which names eleven sites, of which six correspond to the six sites or *cakras*:

> The (1) rectum, (2) secret place (genitals), along with the (3) navel [and] (4) the downturned lotus (*padma*) in the heart, (5) the cakra of breath and utterances (*samīrastobhakam*) [i.e., the throat], (6) the

cooling knot (*granthi*) of the uvula, (7) the root (or tip) of the nose, and the (8) End of the Twelve;[35] the (9) [site] located between the eyebrows; (10) the forehead; and the brilliant (11) cleft of brahman, located at the crown of the head: it is the stated doctrine that [this] elevenfold [system] is located in the midst of the body.[36]

In addition to using the term *cakra*, this passage also refers to the downturned *lotus* (and not wheel) in the heart, as well as to a knot (*granthi*) located at the level of the uvula.[37] It would appear that Matsyendra's yogic body system contributed to the synthesis presented in the writings of Abhinavagupta. In TĀ 29.37 he names the End of the Twelve, the "upward *kuṇḍalinī*" (*ūrdhvagakuṇḍalinī*), the place between the eyebrows (*baindava*), heart, umbilicus, and the "bulb" (*kandam*) as the six "secret places" (*chommas*) through which the *kula* is transmitted from teacher to disciple.[38] Abhinavagupta's system also features a trident (*triśula*), located at the level of the fontanel, and a thousand-spoked End of the Twelve. However, we must note that whereas the KJñN discusses these centers as wheels possessed of spokes or leaves, or as lotuses, the *cakras* of the subtle body in Trika Kaulas sources are whirling spoked wheels that, in the body of the nonpractitioner, become inextricable tangles of coils called knots (*granthis*) because they knot together spirit and matter.[39]

Another likely source of Abhinavagupta's synthesis is the *Netra Tantra*, of which his disciple Kṣemarāja wrote an extensive commentary. The seventh chapter of this work, entitled the "Subtle Meditation on the 'Death-Conquering' [Mantra]," comprises a discussion of two subtle body systems, which Kṣemarāja qualifies as belonging to the "Kaula" and "Tantric" liturgies, respectively.[40] Taken together, the two systems presented in the text and commentary appear to be more direct forerunners of the later haṭha yoga system of Gorakṣanātha than do the KJñN and other works attributed to Matsyendranātha, who was Gorakṣanātha's guru, according to Nāth Siddha tradition. The *Netra Tantra*'s presentation of yogic practice combines breath control, meditation, "the piercing" of knots and the central channel, the raising of the "Śakti who is filled with one's semen" the length of that channel,[41] and the internal production of the nectar of immortality.[42] At the same time, the *Netra Tantra* agrees with the KJñN on a number of subtle body locations; for example, the "Fire of Time" (*kālāgni*), which it locates at the tips of the toes; and "Fish-Belly," which it locates at the level of the genitals.[43] Such is not the case, however, for the *Netra Tantra*'s presentation of the six *cakras*, which is idiosyncratic with regard to every other yogic body system: "The *nāḍīcakra* is [located] in the 'place of generation'; the [*cakra*] called *māyā* is in the navel; the *yogicakra* is placed in the heart; while the [*cakra*] known as *bhedana* is placed in the uvula. The *dipticakra* is placed in the 'drop' (*bindu*) and the [*cakra*] called *śānta* is in the 'reverberation' (*nāda*)."[44] The sole source to mention any one of these *cakras* is the eighth-century *Mālatī-Mādhava*, in which it is the *nāḍī-cakra* that powers Kapālakuṇḍalā's flight.[45] A mention in the *Jayadrathayāmala* of "*māyā* [as] the mother of the phonemes . . . the *kuṇḍalinī*" may be a reference to the second of the *Netra Tantra cakras*.[46]

Returning to the KJñN, yet another discussion of subtle body mapping occurs in this source under the heading of sites (*sthānas*). Here, it describes eleven of these in terms of their spokes, leaves, and petals (*dalas*): in order, they are the four-leaved, eight-spoked, twelve-spoked, five-spoked, sixteen-spoked, sixty-four-petaled, one hundred–leaved, one thousand–petaled, 10 million–leaved, 5 million–leaved, and 30 million–leaved.[47] It then goes on to discuss a number of other subtle sites (*vyāpaka*, *vyāpinī*, *unmana*, etc.), located in the upper cranial vault, that one finds in other Kaula sources, including the *Svacchanda Tantra* and *Netra Tantra*.[48]

A final KJñN evocation of the workings of the subtle body will serve to orient us, once again, toward the KM.[49] This is the work's fourteenth and longest chapter, much of which comprises a rambling account of supernatural powers realized by "working the mind" through a sequence (*krama*) of yogic body locations, variously called *cakras* and "*kaulas*" ("clans of internal Siddhas"?).[50] Toward the end of this meditative ascent, the KJñN (14.92) evokes "this seal, which is called 'Unnamed'" (*anāmā nama mudreyam*), and states that "sealed with the five seals . . . one should pierce that door whose bolts are well-fitted." One finds similar language in the KM, for which "Unnamed" is one of the names of the goddess Kubjikā.[51] Here, the statement "applications of the bolts on the openings of the body,"[52] occurs at the beginning of this work's discussion of "upward progress" (*utkrānti*),[53] which appears to be a type of hathayogic practice. The KM passage continues: "The rectum, penis, and navel, mouth, nose, ears and eyes: having fitted bolts in these places (i.e., the nine 'doors' or bodily orifices), one should impel the 'crooked one' (*kuñcikā*) upward."[54] Then follows a discussion of a number of yogic techniques—including the Cock Posture (*kukuṭṭāsana*)—which effect the piercing of the knot[s], confer numerous *siddhis*, and afford firmness of the self.[55]

Bhairava, the divine revealer of the KM, next states that he will provide a description of what he calls the "bolt-practices" of the knife (*kṣurikādyargalābhyāsa*), and so on, which effect upward progress (*utkrānti-kāraṇam*) in him who is empowered to use it, and great affliction in the unempowered. Having already discussed this ritual in earlier chapters, I will not go into a description of its details at this point.[56] Here, the salient point of this passage concerns the names of the goddesses invoked and the bodily constituents offered to them. In order, their names are Kusumamālinī ("She Who

Is Garlanded with Flowers"),[57] Yakṣiṇī, Śaṅkhinī, Kākinī, Lākinī, Rākiṇī, and Ḍākinī. These Yoginīs are named in nearly identical order in the eighteenth chapter of the *Śrīmatottara Tantra*, a later text of the same Kubjikā tradition. Here, the names listed are Ḍākinī, Rākiṇī, Lākinī, Kākinī, Śākinī, Hākinī, Yākinī, and Kusumā.[58] They are listed in the same order in *Agni Purāṇa* 144.28b–29a. In this last case, their names are enumerated in instructions for the construction of the six-cornered Kubjikā mandala, with the ordering proceeding from the northwest corner.[59] This mandala is identical to the Yoginīcakra, the fourth of the five *cakras* of the Kubjikā system, located at the level of the throat, as described in the fifteenth chapter of the KM itself.[60] A shorter, variant list of these Yoginīs is found in two places in the KJñN, and chapter 4 of the KJñN, which is devoted to Tantric sorcery, appears to be a source for the data found in a number of later Kubjikā traditions.[61]

What the Yoginīs are offered is of signal interest here: the first of these, Kusumamālinī, is urged to take or swallow (*gṛhṇa*) the practitioner's "prime bodily constituent," that is, semen; the second, Yakṣiṇī, to crush his bones; the third, Śaṅkhinī, to take his marrow; the fourth, Kākinī, to take his fat; the fifth, Lākinī, to eat his flesh; the sixth, Rākiṇī, to take his blood; and the seventh, Ḍākinī, to take his skin.[62] Clearly, the bodily constituents these goddesses are urged to consume constitute a hierarchy. These are, in fact, the standard series of the seven *dhātus*, the "bodily constituents" of Hindu medical tradition (with the sole exception being that skin has here replaced chyle [*rasa*]), which are serially burned in the fires of digestion, until semen, the "prime bodily constituent," is produced.[63] With each goddess invoked in this passage, the practitioner is offering the products of a series of refining processes.

To all appearances, this is a rudimentary form of the hathayogic raising of the *kuṇḍalinī*. What is missing here is an identification between the goddesses to whom one's hierarchized bodily constituents are offered and subtle body locations inside the practitioner. This connection is made, however, in another KM passage, which locates six Yoginīs, called the "regents of the six fortresses," as follows: Ḍāmarī is located in the *ādhāra*, Rāmaṇī in the *svādhiṣṭhāna*, Lambakarṇī in the *maṇipura*, Kākī in the *anāhata*, Sākinī in the *viśuddhi*, and Yakṣiṇī in the *ājñā*.[64] In another chapter the KM lists two sequences of six goddesses as *kulākula* and *kula*, respectively. The first denotes the "northern course" of the six *cakras*, from the *ājñā* down to the *ādhāra*, and the latter the "southern course," in reverse order. The former group is creative, and the latter—comprised of Ḍākinī, Rākiṇī, Lākinī, Kākinī, Śākinī, and Hākinī—is destructive.[65]

A number of later sources,[66] beginning with the *Rudrayāmala Tantra*, identify these goddesses, which they call Yoginīs, with the *cakras* as well as with the *dhātus*, the bodily constituents. The *Rudrayāmala Tantra*'s ordering identifies these Yoginīs with the following subtle body locations: Ḍākinī is in the *mūlādhāra;* Rākiṇī in the *svādhiṣṭhāna;* Lākinī in the *maṇipura;* Kākinī in the *anāhata;* Śākinī in the *viśuddhi;* and Hākinī in the *ājñā.*[67] Kusumamālā, who is missing from this listing, is located in the feet in the *Śrīmatottara Tantra;*[68] other works place a figure named Yākinī at the level of the *sahasrāra.*[69] These *Rudrayāmala Tantra* locations correspond, of course, to the "standard" names of the six *cakras* of later hathayogic tradition. They are, in fact, first called by these names in the KM, which correlates the six standard yogic body locations with its Yoginīs of the "northern course."

Mark Dyczkowski has argued that it was within the Kubjikā traditions that the six-*cakra* configuration was first developed into a fixed coherent system.[70] The KM, the root Tantra of the Kubjikā tradition, locates the *cakras* and assigns each of them a number of "divisions" (*bhedas*) or "portions" (*kalās*), which approximates the number of "petals" assigned to each of these "lotuses" in later sources.[71] We also encounter in the KM the notion of a process of yogic refinement or extraction of fluid bodily constituents, which is superimposed upon the vertical grid of the subtle body, along the spinal column, leading from the rectum to the cranial vault. Nonetheless, it would be incorrect to state that there is a hathayogic dynamic to the KM's system of the *cakras*. What is lacking are the explicit application of the term *cakra* to these centers, the explicit identification of these centers with the elements,[72] and the deification or hypostasization of the principle or dynamic of this refinement process: here I am referring to that commonplace of hathayogic theory, the female *kuṇḍalinī* or serpent power—who has perhaps been evoked, albeit not by name, in the statement made in this source that one should, through *utkrānti*, "impel the crooked one upward" (KM 23.114a).

3. The *Kuṇḍalinī* and the Channeling of Feminine Energies

The KM makes a number of other statements that appear to betray its familiarity with a notion of this serpentine feminine nexus of yogic energy.[73] In KM 5.84 we read that "[*śakti*] having the form of a sleeping serpent [is located] at the End of the Twelve. . . . Nevertheless, she is also to be found dwelling in the navel. . . ."[74] This serpentine (*bhuja[ṅ]ga-ākārā*) *śakti* is connected in this passage to mantras and subtle levels of speech, through which she is reunited with Śiva. A later passage (KM 12.60–67) describes the sexual "churning" (*ma[n]thanam*) of an inner phallus (*liṅgam*) and vulva (yoni) that occurs in the *maṇipura cakra,*[75] that is, at the level of the navel. Here, however, the language is not phonematic, but rather fluid: this churning of Śiva and Śakti produces a flood of nectar.

This is not, however, the earliest mention of this indwelling female serpent to be found in Hindu literature. This distinction likely falls to the circa eighth-century C.E. *Tantrasadbhāva Tantra*,[76] which similarly evokes her in a discussion of the phonematic energy that also uses the image of churning:

> This energy is called supreme, subtle, transcending all norm or practice. . . . Enclosing within herself the fluid drop (*bindu*) of the heart, her aspect is that of a snake lying in deep sleep . . . she is awakened by the supreme sound whose nature is knowledge, being churned by the *bindu* resting in her womb. . . . Awakened by this [luminous throbbing], the subtle force (*kalā*), Kuṇḍalī is aroused. The sovereign *bindu* [Śiva], who is in the womb of Śakti, is possessed of a fourfold force (*kalā*). By the union of the Churner and of She that is Being Churned, this [Kuṇḍalī] becomes straight. This [Śakti], when she abides between the two *bindus*, is called Jyeṣṭhā. . . . In the heart, she is said to be of one atom. In the throat, she is of two atoms. She is known as being of three atoms when permanently abiding on the tip of the tongue. . . .[77]

In this passage we may be in the presence of the earliest mention of a coiled "serpent energy"; however, the term that is used here is *kuṇḍalī*, which simply means "she who is ring-shaped." This is also the term that one encounters in the KJñN, which evokes the following goddesses in succession as the Mothers (*mātṛkās*) who are identified with the "mass of sound" (*śabdarāśi*) located in "all of the knots" (*sarvagrantheṣu*) of the subtle body: Vāmā, Kuṇḍalī, Jyeṣṭhā, Manonmanī, Rudra-śakti, and Kāmākhyā.[78] Also mentioned in this passage are the "female" phonemes called the Mātṛkās ("Little Mothers") and the "male" phonemes called the Śabdarāśi ("Mass of Sounds"). Here we already detect the process of the semanticization of the Goddess and her energies, a process that becomes predominant in later Tantric traditions.[79] In another passage the KJñN describes Vāmā as having an annular or serpentine form (*kuṇḍalākṛti*) and extending from the feet to the crown of the head: the raising of this goddess from the rectum culminates with her absorption at the End of the Twelve.[80] Once again the *kuṇḍalinī* serpent appears to be present here in everything but precise name.

Let us dwell for a moment on the names of the Mother goddesses evoked in the KJñN. In Śaivasiddhānta metaphysics, the goddess Jyeṣṭhā(devī), mentioned in the KJñN and *Tantrasadbhāva* passages, is described as assuming eight forms, by which she represents eight *tattvas*: these are Vāmā (earth), Jyeṣṭhā herself (water), Raudrī (fire), Kālī (air), Kalavikaraṇī (ether), Balavikaraṇī (moon), Balapramathinī (sun), and Manonmanī (Śiva-hood). This group of eight are said to be the *śaktis* of the eight male Vidyeśvaras of the Śaivasiddhānta system, the deifications of the eight categories of being that separate the "pure" worlds from the "impure."[81] With this enumeration, we may surmise that Matsyendranātha was drawing on the same source as the Saiddhāntika metaphysicians.[82] In addition, we once more see a hierarchization of internalized goddesses, identified here with the five elements (and a number of their subtler evolutes), as well as with the ordering of phonemes within the yogic body. That these are projected upon the grid of the yogic body is made clear by the fact that they are said to be located "in all the knots." Finally, this list of deities from the Saiddhāntika system is complemented by the Mother named Kuṇḍalī whom the KJñN locates between Vāmā (earth) and Jyeṣṭhā (water).[83] It is a commonplace of later subtle body mapping to identify the five lower *cakras* with the five elements: Kuṇḍalī would thus be located, according to this schema, between the rectal *mūlādhāra* (earth) and the genital *svādhiṣṭhāna* (water).

Jyeṣṭhā ("Eldest") is a goddess whose cult goes back to the time of the fifth- to second-century B.C.E. *Baudhāyana Gṛhya Sūtra*.[84] As was indicated in chapter 2, she is a dread goddess who is mentioned together or identified with such terrible Mothers as Harītī, Pūtanā, and Jarā,[85] and inauspicious (*alakṣmī*) astrological configurations: in the Indian calendar, the month of Jyaiṣṭḥa, falling as it does in the deadly heat of the premonsoon season, is the cruelest month. Jyeṣṭhā's names and epithets are all dire—"Ass-Rider," "Crow-Bannered," and "Bad Woman" (Alakṣmī)—and she is depicted in her iconography with a sweeping broom, the symbolic homologue of the winnowing fan carried by the smallpox goddess Śītalā.[86] Jyeṣṭhā belongs to an early triad of goddesses—the other two being Vāmā and Raudrī—who would later become identified with the three Śaktis (Icchā-, Jñānā- and Kriyā-), the three phonemes A, Ā, and Ī, as well as the goddesses Parā, Aparā, and Parāparā of the Trika pantheon. References to Parā, Aparā, and Parāparā in the *Mālinīvijayottara Tantra* (3.30–33) indicate that this triad was an appropriation of an earlier threefold division of classes of Mothers: those that liberate souls (*aghorāḥ*), those that impede souls (*ghorāḥ*), and those that drag souls downward (*ghorātarāḥ*).[87]

Both the KJñN account of the raising of the ring-shaped goddess Vāmā from the level of the rectum to the End of the Twelve and the statement in KM 5.84 that Śakti dwells in the form of a sleeping serpent in both the cranial vault and the navel are precursors of the dynamic role of the *kuṇḍalinī* in later hathayogic sources. In the KJñN passage, the goddess's ring shape evokes the circles of Yoginīs that rise into the air at the conclusion of their cremation-ground rites—and it should be recalled here that the *cakras* themselves are referred to as cremation grounds in the later hathayogic literature.[88] In the KM passage, it is the upward motion of feminine energy that is stressed.

Perhaps the earliest occurrence of the term *kuṇḍalinī* (as opposed to *kuṇḍalī*) is found in the third hexad (*ṣaṭka*) of the tenth- to eleventh-century *Jayadrathayāmala*,[89] which, in a discussion of the origin of mantras from the supreme god Bhairava, relates the *kuṇḍalinī* to phonemes as well as to the *kalās*, to which we will return:

> Māyā is the mother of the phonemes and is known as the fire-stick of the mantras. She is the *kuṇḍalinī* Śakti, and is to be known as the supreme *kalā*. From that spring forth the mantras as well as the separate clans, and likewise the Tantras. . . .[90]

Abhinavagupta, who likely took his inspiration from all of the sources we have been reviewing, develops this principle in his discussion of the upper and lower *kuṇḍalinīs*, which are two phases of the same energy, in expansion and contraction, that effects the descent of transcendent consciousness into the human microcosm, and the return of human consciousness toward its transcendent source. Often he portrays these as spoked wheels that, aligned along a central axis or axle, rise and descend to whirl in harmony with one another. In spite of the highly evocative sexual language he employs, Abhinavagupta's model is nonetheless one of phonematic, rather than fluid, expansion and contraction.[91]

It not until the *Rudrayāmala Tantra* and the later hathayogic classics attributed to Gorakṣanātha that the *kuṇḍalinī* becomes the vehicle for fluid, rather than phonematic transactions and transfers. This role of the *kuṇḍalinī* in the dynamics of yogic body fluid transfer is brought to the fore in a portion of the Tantric practice of the five M-words, which Agehananda Bharati describes:

> When the practitioner is poised to drink the liquor, he says "I sacrifice"; and as he does so, he mentally draws the coiled energy of the Clan (*kula-kuṇḍalinī*) from her seat in the base cakra. This time, however, he does not draw her up into the thousand-petaled *sahasrāra* in the cranial vault, but instead he brings her to the tip of his tongue and seats her there. At this moment he drinks the beverage from its bowl, and as he drinks she impresses the thought on his mind that it is not he himself who is drinking, but the *kula-kuṇḍalinī* now seated on the tip of his tongue, to whom he is offering the liquid as a libation. In the same manner he now empties all the other bowls as he visualizes that he feeds their contents as oblations to the Goddess—for the *kula-kuṇḍalinī* is the microcosmic aspect of the universal Śakti.[92]

Here, the coiled energy at the tip of the practitioner's tongue is not spitting phonemes, as in the *Tantrasadbhāva Tantra* passage quoted above, but rather drinking ritual fluids, which are so many substitutes for, or actual instantiations of, vital bodily fluids. One may speculate as to why it is that the feminine principle of yogic energy comes to be represented as a serpent, now coiled, and now straightened. Of course, there seems to be some sort of elective affinity between the *kuṇḍalinī*'s function and form—however, the avian gander (*haṃsa*), which doubles for the *kuṇḍalinī* in a number of sources, appears to fulfill the same function of raising energy from the lower to the upper body.[93] The KJñN's discussion of the "goddess named Vāmā" is framed, tellingly, by a disquisition on the *haṃsa:*

> From below to above the gander sports, until it is absorbed at the End of the Twelve. Seated in the heart it remains motionless, like water inside a pot. Having the appearance of a lotus fiber, it partakes neither of being nor of nonbeing. Neither supporting nor supported, it is omniscient, rising in every direction. Spontaneously, it moves upward, and spontaneously it returns downward. . . . Knowing its essence, one [is freed] from the bonds of existence. . . . In the ear [orally] and in the heart, the description of the gander is to be made known. [Its] call becomes manifest in the throat, [audible] near and far. From the base of the feet to the highest height, the [goddess] named Vāmā has the form of a ring (*kuṇḍalākṛtim*). It is she who, seated in the anus, rises upward until she is absorbed at the End of the Twelve. Thus indeed the gander sports in the midst of a body that is both auspicious and inauspicious.[94]

Lilian Silburn suggests that it is the serpent's coiling and straightening that explain its projection upon the subtle body: a venomous serpent, when coiled, is dangerous; straightened, it is no longer threatening. This would be of a piece with the characterization of the *kuṇḍalinī* as "poison" when she lies coiled in the lower body and "nectar" when she is extended upward into the cranial vault. Or, Silburn suggests, the image of the *kuṇḍalinī* is one that borrows from the Vedic creatures Ahir Budhnya and Aja Ekapāda, or the Puranic Śeṣa and Ananta. In fact, the KJñN describes the Goddess's body as being "enveloped in fire and having the form of Ekapāda (i.e., of a serpent)."[95] I am more inclined to see the *kuṇḍalinī*'s origins in the role of the serpent in Indian iconography. Temples and other buildings are symbolically supported by a serpent that coils around their foundations, an image represented graphically by a certain number of Hindu temples in Indonesia. Similarly, images of the Buddha and later of Viṣṇu are figured with a serpent support and canopy. Finally, the phallic emblem of Śiva, the *liṅgam*, is often sculpted with a coiled serpent around its base, whose spread hood serves as its canopy. This is a particularly evocative image when one recalls that the *kuṇḍalinī* is figured in the classical hathayogic sources as sleeping coiled three and a half times around an internal *liṅgam*, with her hood or mouth covering its tip. When the yogin awakens her through his practice of postures and breath control, she pierces the lower door to the medial *suṣumṇā* channel and "flies" upward to the place of Śiva in the cranial vault.

4. Transformations in the Art of Love

The theoreticians of post-tenth-century C.E. high Hindu Tantra were especially innovative in their integration of aesthetic and linguistic theory into their reinterpretation of earlier theory and practice. As such, the acoustic and photic registers lie at the forefront of their metaphysical systems, according to which the absolute godhead, which is effulgent pure consciousness, communicates itself to the world and especially to the human microcosm as a stream or wave of phosphorescent light, and as a "garland" of the vibrating phonemes of the Sanskrit language. And because the universe is brought into being by a divine outpouring of light and sound, the Tantric practitioner may return to and identify himself with this pure consciousness by meditatively recondensing those same photemes of light and phonemes of sound into their higher principles.

This is, in the main, a gnoseological process, in which knowing takes priority over doing. In fact, as Alexis Sanderson has argued, one may see in the high Hindu Tantra of the later Trika and Śrīvidyā the end of ritual: "since [the] Impurity [that is the sole impediment to liberation] has been dematerialized, ritual must work on ignorance itself; and to do this it must be a kind of knowing."[96] Of course, a similar transformation had already occurred over two millennia earlier in India, in what Jan Heesterman has termed the transformation of sacrifice into ritual:

> The "science of ritual" . . . should be rated as a paradigm of what Max Weber called "formal rationality." Its rational bent becomes apparent when we notice that it is not just to be done but is required to be "known." What has to be known are the equivalences, the keystone of ritualistic thought, to which the ubiquitous phrase "he who knows thus" refers.[97]

In a sense, high Hindu Tantra ritualizes—that is, "gnoseologizes"—Kaula sacrifice in the same way that the Brāhmaṇas did the sacrificial system of the Vedic Saṃhitās; and it is worth recalling here that the term "Tantra" originally applied to the auxiliary acts of the ritual complex of a given sacrifice. It is the general and largely unchangeable part of the complex and the same for all sacrifices of the same type.[98]

With this, we return to the practice of the *kāmakalā*, introduced in chapter 4.[99] In the high Hindu Tantric context, the ritual component of the *kāmakalā*—that is, *rajapāna*, the drinking of female discharge—becomes abstracted into a program of meditation whose goal is a nondiscursive realization of the enlightened nondual consciousness that had theretofore been one's object of knowledge. Through the meditative practice of mantras (phonematic, acoustic manifestations of the absolute) and of mandalas or yantras (photemes, i.e., luminous, graphic, visual representations of the same), the consciousness of the practitioner is uplifted and transformed to gradually become god-consciousness. But what is the nature of the "practice" involved here? It is reduced to knowing, as the most significant Śrīvidyā work on the *kāmakalā*, aptly entitled *Kāmakalāvilāsa* ("The Love-Play of the Particle of Desire"),[100] makes clear (verse 8): "Now this is the *vidyā* of Kāma-kalā, which deals with the sequence of the cakras [the nine triangles of the Śrīcakra] of the Devī. He by whom this is known becomes liberated and [the supreme Goddess] Mahātripurāsundarī Herself."

Yet even as the acoustic and the photic, phosphorescing drops of sound lay at the forefront of high Hindu Tantric practice, there was a substratum that persisted from other traditions, a substratum that was neither acoustic nor photic but, rather, fluid, with the fluid in question being sexual fluid. As we have seen in these earlier or parallel traditions, it was via a sexually transmitted stream or flow of sexual fluids that the practitioner tapped into the source of that stream, usually the male Śiva, who has been represented iconographically, since at least the second century B.C.E., as a phallic image, a *liṅgam*. Śiva does not, however, stand alone in this flow of sexual fluids. In most Tantric contexts, his self-manifestation is effected through his female hypostasis, the Goddess, whose own sexual fluid carries his divine germ plasm through the lineages or transmissions of the Tantric clans, clans in which the Yoginīs play a crucial role. In the earlier Kaula practice, it was via this flow of the clan fluid through the wombs of Yoginīs that the male practitioner was empowered to return to and identify himself with the godhead. It was this that lay at the root of the original practice of the *kāmakalā*, the Art of Love.

5. Śrīvidyā Practice of the *Kāmakalā*

Here I present a detailed account of the multileveled symbolism of the *kāmakalā*, as it is found in the primary Śrīvidyā sources, in order to demonstrate how the description itself of the *kāmakalā* diagram represents a semanticization or overcoding of the Kaula ritual upon which it is based. A word on the meanings and usages of this term is in order, composed as it is of two extremely common nouns, both of which are possessed of a wide semantic field. The simplest translation of the term might well be "The Art (*kalā*) of Love (*kāma*)." Two other important senses of the term *kalā* yield the additional meanings of "Love's Lunar Digit" or "Love's Sixteenth Portion." Earlier, we also saw the use of the term *kalā* in early yogic body descriptions as a subtle force, synonymous with the *kuṇḍalinī*, and the mother of phonemes.[101] Commenting on Abhinavagupta's *Tantrāloka* (TĀ), Jayaratha (fl. ca. 1225–1275) refers to the *kāmakalā* or *kāmatattva* as the "Particle (or Essence) of Love," a gloss to which I will return.[102]

Nowhere in the history of these medieval traditions is the *kāmakalā* accorded greater importance than in Śrīvidyā, which, likely born in Kashmir in the eleventh century, came to know its greatest success in south India, where it has remained the mainstream form of Śākta Tantra in Tamil Nadu, down to the present day.[103] The *kāmakalā* is of central importance to Śrīvidyā because it is this diagram that grounds and animates the Śrīcakra or Śrīyantra, the primary diagrammatic representation of the godhead in that tradition. Thus verse 8 of the thirteenth-century *Kāmakalāvilāsa* [KKV] of Puṇyānandanātha states that "the *Vidyā* of the Kāmakalā . . . deals with the sequence of the Cakra [of the Śrīcakra] of the Devī. . . ."[104]

The Śrīcakra is portrayed as a "drop" (*bindu*) located at the center of an elaborate diagram of nine nesting and interlocking triangles (called *cakras*), surrounded by two circles of lotus petals, with the whole encased within the standard gated frame, called the "earth citadel" (*bhūpura*). The principal ritual practice of Śrīvidyā is meditation on this cosmogram, which stands as an abstract depiction of the interactions of the male and female forces that generate, animate, and ultimately cause to reimplode the phenomenal universe-as-consciousness. The practitioner's meditative absorption into the heart of this diagram effects a gnoseological implosion of the manifest universe back into its nonmanifest divine source, and of mundane human consciousness back into supermundane god-consciousness, the vanishing point at the heart of the diagram. In the Śrīvidyā system, these male and female principles are named Kāmeśvara and Kāmeśvarī, "Lord of Love" and "Our Lady of Love," a pair we have already encountered in an Indonesian ritual of royal consecration.[105]

To maintain the image of the drop, as the Śrīvidyā sources do, it is appropriate to conceive the entire diagram, with its many "stress lines" of intersecting flows of energy and consciousness, as a diffraction pattern of the wave action initiated when the energy of a single drop, falling into a square recipient of calm water, sends out a set of ripples that interfere constructively and destructively with one another. This, too, appears to be the image the Śrīvidyā theoreticians had in mind when they described the relationship of the nonmanifest male and manifest female aspects of the godhead in terms of water and waves. In his commentary on *Yoginīhṛdaya* (YH) 1.55, the thirteenth- to fourteenth-century Amṛtānanda (whose teacher, Puṇyānandanātha, was the author of the KKV) [106] states:

> The waves are the amassing, the multitude of the constituent parts of Kāmeśvara and Kāmeśvarī. It [the heart of the Śrīcakra] is surrounded by these waves and ripples as they heave [together]. . . . Here, the word "wave" (*ūrmi*) means that Parameśvara [here, a synonym of Kāmeśvara], who is light, is the ocean; and Kāmeśvarī, who is conscious awareness, is its flowing waters, with the waves being the multitude of energies into which they [Parameśvara and Kāmeśvarī] amass themselves. Just as waves arise on the [surface of the] ocean and are reabsorbed into it, so too the [Śrī]cakra, composed of the thirty-six *tattvas* . . . arises from and goes [back to Parameśvara].[107]

It is, then, a phosphorescing (*sphurad*) drop of sound (*bindu*) that animates this cosmogram and the universe, and into which the mind of the person who meditates upon it is resorbed. This drop is the point located at the center of the Śrīcakra, and the *kāmakalā* is a "close-up," as it were, of this drop. When one zooms in on it meditatively, one sees that it is composed of three or four elements whose interplay constitutes the first moment of the transition, within the godhead, from pure interiority to external manifestation, from the pure light of effulgent consciousness (*prakāśa*) to conscious awareness (*vimarśa*). I now give an account of these constituent elements of the *kāmakalā* and the means and ends of meditation upon them, as described in the Śrīvidyā and the broader Tantric literature.[108]

Dirk Jan Hoens has translated *kāmakalā* as the "Divine Principle (*kalā*) [manifesting itself as] Desire (*kāma*)." In this context,

> the triad of Śiva-Śakti-Nāda [are given] the name Kāmakalā. . . . Śiva and Śakti are called Kāmeśvara and Kāmeśvarī . The kāmakalā symbolizes the creative union of the primeval parental pair; a pulsating, cosmic atom with two nuclei graphically represented by a white and red dot which automatically produce a third point of gravity. This situation is often represented in graphical form as a triangle. This can be done in two ways: with the point upwards or downwards. . . . A final step is taken when this triad is enriched with a fourth element so as to constitute the graphic representation of the most potent parts of Devī's mystical body

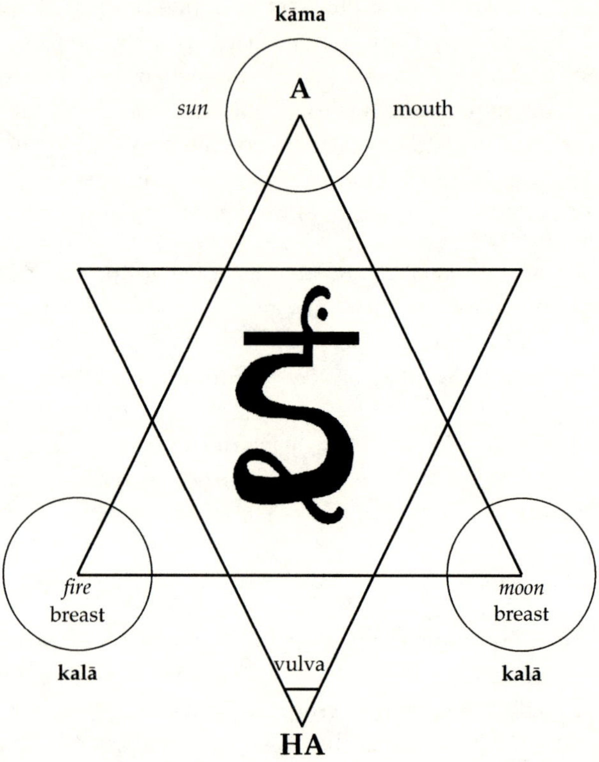

Figure 8.a. *Kāmakalā* yantra according to the *Yoginīhṛdaya Tantra*. Adobe Photoshop image.

> (also in this context she is called Kāmakalā or Tripurāsundarī): her face, two breasts (the white and red *bindus*) and womb [yoni]. They are represented by the letter Ī written in an older form akin to the Newari [or Brahmi] sign, or by the *ha* (the "womb" is often called *hārdhakalā*, "the particle consisting of half the *ha*," i.e., its lower part). . . .[109]

In this yantra (fig. 8.a),[110] the upturned triangle represents Śiva, and the downturned triangle, his consort Śakti.[111] At the apex of the upturned Śiva triangle, we find the Sanskrit grapheme A, which is also the sun and the mouth of the maiden who is the support for this meditation. This is also termed the "medial *bindu*." The two *bindus* or points that form the *visarga* (the surd Sanskrit phoneme represented by two *bindus*) are the two base angles of this triangle: they are identified with fire and the moon. They are also the breasts of the maiden. Located between these two and pointing downward is the apex of the downturned Śakti triangle, which is the yoni of the maiden and the locus of the grapheme HA. Natānandanātha, the commentator of the KKV, explains that these elements, taken together, constitute a phonematic rendering of the *kāmakalā*, since Kāma is Paramaśiva (whose desire to create gives rise to the universe), pure effulgence, and the first phoneme, which is A; and Kalā signifies reflective consciousness and the last phoneme, which is HA.[112]

Located in the heart of the hexagon formed by the two intersecting triangles is the *kuṇḍalinī*, the coiled serpent who here takes the form of the Sanskrit grapheme Ī (which, together with the *bindu*—the graphic dot over a Sanskrit character that represents the nasalization of a sound—becomes Īṃ) However, Īṃ is also the special grapheme of the supreme Śrīvidyā goddess, Tripurāsundarī. Termed the *trikhaṇḍā* ("having three parts"), it is meditatively viewed as the body of the goddess, composed of head, breasts, and yoni.[113] As such, it constitutes a redoubling of the symbolism of the intersecting Śiva and Śakti triangles. It is in the form of the Īṃ grapheme then, that energy, in the coiled form of the *kuṇḍalinī* serpent, dwells between the *bindu* and the *visarga*, that is, between the first and last phonemes and graphemes of the Sanskrit "garland of letters." Lastly, the *kuṇḍalinī* is represented in the form of the serpentine grapheme Īṃ because it is a commonplace of the Hindu yogic tradition that the female Śakti, which dwells in a tightly coiled form in the lower abdomen of humans, can be awakened through yogic practice to uncoil and rise upward, along the spinal column, to the cranial vault. Here then, the grapheme Īṃ also represents a yogic process that extends from the base to the apex of the yogic body. Later commentators would find additional correlates to this configuration, identifying the four components of face, breasts, and yoni with four goddesses, four stages of speech, and four *cakras* within the subtle body.[114]

There are no less than six levels of overcoding in the Tantric interpretation of this diagram, which reflect so many bipolar oppositions mediated by a third dynamic or transformative element. These oppositions are (1) Śiva and Śakti, the male and female principles of the universe in essence and manifestation; (2) the phonemes A and HA, the primal and final utterances of the phonematic continuum that is the Sanskrit alphabet; (3) the effulgent graphemes or photemes representing the phonemes A and HA, here the *bindu* (a single point or drop) and the *visarga* (a double point or drop);[115] (4) two subtle or yogic "drops," the one red and female and the other white and male, which combine to form a third "great drop";[116] (5) male and female sexual emissions; and (6) the corporeal mouth and vulva of the maiden upon whom this diagram is projected in Kaula-based practice.

These bipolarities are mediated by the serpentine nexus of female energy, the *kuṇḍalinī*, who in her yogic rise from the base to the apex of the system is described as telescoping the lower phonemes and graphemes of the Sanskrit garland of letters back into their higher evolutes, until all are absorbed in the *bindu*, the dimensionless point at which all manifest sound and image dissolve into silence and emptiness, in the cranial vault. Also bearing a yogic valence in this diagram and its interpretation are the elements sun, moon, and fire. Identified here with the upper *bindu* and lower *visarga*, respectively, these also represent the three primary channels of yogic energy, the right, left, and central channels, respectively.

Finally, we also detect a sexual substrate to this diagram. First of all, the first member of the compound is, after all, "*kāma*," erotic love, and the name of the Indian Eros or Love, whose arts are described in works like the *Kāma Sūtra*. Second, the ritual support of this meditation is a maiden's naked body. Of course, in high Hindu Tantra, the flesh-and-blood maiden substrate is done away with, with the abstract schematic visualization sufficing for the refined practitioner. Yet she remains present, just beneath the surface of her geometric and semantic abstraction, as such was effected in these later cosmeticized traditions. In a discussion of the *kāmakalā*, the *Yoginīhṛdaya* describes the two *bindus* that make up the corners of the base of the Śiva triangle and the breasts of the maiden as red and white in color. Here, the white and red drops are "Śiva and Śakti absorbed in their movement of expansion and contraction."[117] Clearly, the *bindus* so described are not abstract points but rather subtle drops of sexual fluids, that is, male semen and female uterine blood.[118] Thus, the *bindu* as photic grapheme (dimensionless point of light) and the *bindu* as acoustic phoneme (dimensionless vibration, particle of speech) are overcodings of the abstract red and white *bindus* of the subtle body physiology of yogic practice, which are in turn overcodings of concrete drops of male and female sexual fluids (particles of love). These unite, in the upper *bindu* at the apex of the triangle, in the mouth (*mukham*) of the maiden, into a *mahābindu*, a "great drop." We are reminded, however, that her mouth, the apex of the upturned Śiva triangle, is "reflected" in her vulva, the apex of the downturned Śakti triangle.[119] Furthermore, as we have noted, a woman's oral cavity is reflected, redoubled in her vulva, her "nether mouth."

The fact that these divine principles were transacting in something more concrete than graphemes and phonemes is made abundantly clear even in these scholasticist, semanticizing sources. On the basis of terminology alone, we can see that the conceptual matrix is sexual. The absolute flashes forth, in phosphorescent effulgence (*sphurattā; ullāsa*). It expands as a phosphorescent wave, a welling, a swelling (*sphurad-ūrmi*)[120] . . . thereby manifesting the cosmos made up of the thirty-six metaphysical categories (*tattvas*), from Śiva down to the element earth. . . . The Goddess is luminously conscious (*prakāśāmarśana*). . . . She is "throbbing incarnate" (*spandarūpinī*), being immersed in bliss (*ānanda*). . . . The cosmos is her manifest form, but, though shining as the "essence of divine loveplay" (*divyakrīḍāra-sollāsa*), the Absolute is pure undivided light and bliss.[121]

The subliminal sexual referents of this abstract image of the "Art of Love" were not entirely lost on the Śrīvidyā theoreticians. That they were aware of such is made clear from a debate that raged within the school concerning the relative legitimacy of conventional (*samaya*) meditation on the *kāmakalā* as opposed to the Kaula form of the same. It was in this latter (and earlier) case that a maiden's naked body was used as the meditational substrate.[122] A number of Śrīvidyā commentators, led by the venerable seventeenth-century master Bhāskararāya, insisted on the literal use of this meditation support, together with the referents of the five M-words, all of which smacked of the Kaula practices.[123] Finally, the names of "Our Lord and Lady of Love," in addition to their associations evoked above, are also identified, in the pre-fourteenth-century *Kālikā Purāṇa*, with the *pīṭha* of Kāmākhyā, whose sexual associations are legion in Tantric traditions.[124]

Elsewhere the worship of the sixteen Nityā goddesses who constitute the Goddess's retinue, and which Śrīvidyā tradition identifies with the sixteen lunar *tithis*,[125] includes offerings of meat and alcohol. It is especially the names of these sixteen Nityā goddesses that constitute the most obvious bridge between this and the earlier Kaula version of the same, given that these sixteen names are identical to those of the sixteen *kalā-śaktis* of the *Śilpa Prakāśa*.[126] In Śrīvidyā sources these sixteen form the immediate entourage (*āvaraṇa*) of the Goddess, to whom sacrifices are to be offered, either in the central triangle or between the sixteen-petaled lotus and the square of the Śrīcakra. In other words, they occupy the same place in these sources as the sculpted images of the "eightfold practice of the kāmakalā" occupied on the early Tantric temples of Orissa.[127] The sole variation between the two lists lies in the name of the first Śakti: she is Kāmeśvarī in Śrīvidyā sources and Kāmeśī in the Kaula diagram.[128]

6. Mantric Decoding and *Kāmatattva* in the Later Trika

It was the Kashmiri theoreticians, specifically Abhinavagupta and his disciple Kṣemarāja, who were most responsible for the semanticization of Kaula ritual into a form acceptable to the Hindu "mainstream," to married householders, seekers of liberation, for whom the antinomian practices of the former were untenable. Here, in the socioreligious context of eleventh-century Kashmir, these reformers of the Trika sought to win the hearts and minds of a conformist populace by presenting a cleansed version of Kaula theory and practice, while continuing to observe the original Kaula rites in secret, among the initiated virtuosi. This trend of the progressive refinement of antinomian practice into a gnoseological system grounded in the aesthetics of vision and audition culminates in the Śrīvidyā tradition. Quite significantly, it is the image of a drop (*bindu*) that recurs, across the entire gamut of Tantric theory and practice, as the form that encapsulates the being, energy, and pure consciousness of the divine; and so it is that we encounter a multiplicity of references to drops of fluid, drops of light, drops of sound, and drops of gnosis. The language of phonemes and photemes, of mantras and yantras, make it possible for practitioners of high Ḥindu Tantra to discuss, in abstract, asexual terms, what was and remains, at bottom, a sexual body of practice. Through it, particles of love become transformed into particles of speech.

This is the explicit teaching of the (twelfth-century?) *Vātūlanātha Sūtra* (VNS) and its commentary by the sixteenth-century Anantaśaktipāda,[129] according to which the mystic is effortlessly initiated, without the aid of external gurus or masters, by his own divinized powers of cognition, called "Yoginīs."[130] In the sixth verse to his commentarial introduction, Anantaśaktipāda evokes the "*sūtras* emitted from the mouth of the Yoginī," and, in fact, each of the aphoristic teachings of this text is, according to him, presented by an internal Yoginī. It is in this way that that the overtly sexual language of the fifth *sūtra*, "From the sexual union of the Siddha and the Yoginī the great mingling (*mahāmelāpa*) arises,"[131] is entirely sublimated and semanticized by Anantaśaktipāda:

> The expression "Siddha-Yoginī" designates those who are Yoginīs and Siddhas, that is, the divinities of the senses and the objects of the senses. Their close contact is the "sexual union" of the two: the coming together of object [what is grasped] and subject [grasper]; or, again, their mutual and perfect embrace. By virtue of this embrace, an uninterrupted "great mystic union" (*mahāmelāpa*) occurs; that is, a sudden awakening or fluid equilibrium (*mahāsāmarasya*) which takes place constantly and everywhere in the ether of transcendent consciousness, when the duality of subjectivity and objectivity has melted away.

Here, the ritualized and sexualized Kaula "minglings" (*melāpas*) of flesh-and-blood Yoginīs and Siddhas that once took place on isolated hilltops on new moon nights now occur at all times within the "heart" of the enlightened Tantric practitioner, where they form the entourage of Bhairava-as-pure-consciousness and are characterized by their "extremely subtle vibrational activity."[132] In the context of these semanticized renderings, it is mantras that render one's practice effective, containing in their very sound structure a mystic gnosis that, in a gnoseological system, is liberating. In every Tantric tradition, mantras are phonematic embodiments of deities and their energies, such that to know the mantra, and to be able to pronounce and wield it correctly, becomes the sine qua non of Tantric practice.[133] These mantras, nondiscursive agglomerations of syllables, are entirely meaningless to an outsider; yet knowledge of their arcane meaning and, perhaps more importantly, the very divine energies embedded in their phonematic configuration render them incalculably powerful in transforming the practitioner into a "second Śiva" and affording him unlimited power in the world.

It is for this reason that mantras are themselves a matter of great secrecy and thereby subject to a wide array of security measures in their use and transmission.[134] First of all, a mantra will generally be pronounced silently or inwardly, so as to not fall upon the wrong ears. When it is transmitted orally, as in the case of the initiation of a disciple by his teacher, this process is called "ear-to-ear" transmission (*karṇāt karṇopadeśena*). There exists, however, a massive textual corpus (called *mantraśāstra*) devoted to the discussion of secret mantras, which, in order to maintain the secrecy of these powerful, sect-specific utterances, are only given in code.[135] In these sources, mantric encoding and decoding can take a number of forms, including the embedding and "extraction" (*uddhṛti*) of a mantra[136] from its concealment in the midst of a mass of mundane phonemes, through one or another sort of cryptogram,[137] or through more simple strategies of writing the mantra in reverse order, interchanging the syllables of a line, substituting an occult term for a phoneme, et cetera. However, we find in the texts of *mantraśāstra*, as well as in commentaries on texts in which mantras are given in code, "skeleton keys" that explain how to construct the mantric cryptograms, sets of equivalents for decoding occult terms, and so on. Here again, we find that a strategy of secrecy—implied in the encrypting of mantras—is undermined, in this case, by written instructions for their decryption.

It is nonetheless essential to note here that in high Hindu Tantra the knowledge and manipulation of extremely complex mantras are, by simple virtue of the fact that they are utterances in the Sanskrit tongue, the privileged prerogative of the Indian literati, who are, nearly by definition, comprised of the brahmin caste.[138] For this reason, the likelihood of their being decrypted and used by non-brahmins is minimal—and high Hindu Tantra has been, from the outset, a mainly brahmanic prerogative. Now, Paul Muller-Ortega has argued, quite cogently, that the concealment of mantras through encoding/encryption, followed by their "revelation" through decoding/decryption, is of a piece with the theology of high Hindu Tantra, which maintains that these are the two modes of being that characterize the godhead in its expansion and contraction, into and out of manifest creation.[139] That is, the decrypting of the mantra is, in and of itself, a mystic experience, a powerful communication of the Tantric gnosis to the initiate.

In high Hindu Tantra, the acoustic practice of the mantra flows directly into, or is simultaneous with, the visual practice of the mandala. This we have already seen in the context of the *kāmakalā* diagram: the *bindus* are simultaneously mantric utterances and photic graphemes. The Goddess is said to have a "body composed of letters" (*lipitanu*), which renders the act of reading them an audiovisual voyage of sorts through her body. Another grapheme will aid us in moving from this discussion of mantric encoding and encryption to an earlier time in the history of Hindu Tantra, when secrecy seemed not to have been such a vital and vexing issue. This is the phoneme E, whose grapheme, in the Sanskrit alphabet, more or less has the form of a downturned triangle. Because of its form, E is considered to be the privileged grapheme of the Goddess, the site of creation and joy, because it is identified as the "mouth of the Yoginī." As before, the term "mouth" here refers to the Goddess's or Yoginī's vulva, which is called a site of creation and joy and "beautiful with the fragrance of emission"[140] because, in early Hindu and Buddhist Tantra, one was reborn, re-created through initiation, and was assured the joy of liberation through the nether mouth of the Yoginī.[141]

Now, it is true that the Goddess, as the source of all mantras, is described in the high Hindu Tantric sources as *bhinnayoni*,[142] "she whose vulva is spread"—but the question then arises as to how a woman embodying the Goddess would have been able to transmit mantras, sound formulas, through her vulva. This depiction of the Goddess is in fact found in a discussion, by Abhinavagupta, of Mālinī, the goddess identified with the energy of intermediate speech (*madhyamā vāc*) in the form of the "Garland of Phonemes": "And this [Little Mother], by banging together with the Mass of Sounds, becomes the Garland of Phonemes, whose vulva is spread."[143]

The fluid dynamic of this complex is made explicit in Kubjikā traditions, which locate the Goddess's yoni at the level of the End of the Twelve of the subtle body, impaled there upon a subtle Śiva *liṅga* that rises out of the cranial vault.[144] This yoni is simultaneously a "womb of mantras" and the nexus of the energy of transmission of gnosis, in the form of the Goddess's "command" (*ājñā*). As the source of mantras, the triangle is subdivided into fifty smaller triangles, nested inside of it, each of which contains a Sanskrit phoneme. "Each letter is worshiped as a Bhairava or a Siddha. Each one of them lives in his own compartment, which is itself "a yoni said to be 'wet' with the divine Command (*ājñā*) of the energy of the transmission that takes place through the union they enjoy with their female counterparts."[145]

The acoustic *kāmakalā* (or *kāmatattva*), whose practice Abhinavagupta also describes is, once again, the *visarga*, comprised of two *bindus*, as found in the Śrīvidyā *kāmakalā*.[146] "Therefore, the venerable *Kulagahvara* ['Cave of the Clan'] states that 'this *visarga*, which consists of the unvoiced [*avyakta*] *ha* particle [*kalā*],[147] is known as the Essence of Desire [*kāmatattva*].'" Still quoting from this lost source, he continues: "[It is] the unvoiced syllable which, lodged in the throat of a beautiful woman, [arises] in the form of an unintentional sound, without forethought or concentration [on her part]: entirely directing his mind there [to that sound, the practitioner] brings the entire world under his control."[148] Here, Abhinavagupta's bridge, between external ritual (if not sexual) practice and internalized speech acts, is the sound a woman makes while enjoying sexual intercourse—a barely articulated "ha, ha, ha."[149] It is this particle of speech (*kalā*) that is the essence of desire or love: in other words, the "ha" sound of the *visarga* is the semanticization of sex in Abhinavagupta's system. However, as in the case of Śrīvidyā, the "practice" of the *kāmakalā* is reduced to meditative concentration, this time upon a syllable. Ritual doing has been reduced, once again, to a nondiscursive form of knowing. However, the presence of a sexual signifier again orients us back in the direction of a Kaula substratum that involved ritual practices of a sexual order.

7. The Masculinization of Tantric Initiation

In chapters 3 and 4, I presented a wealth of data to argue that the "insanguination" of the male initiate by a Yoginī lay at the heart, if not the source, of Kaula initiation and ritual. At the same time, many of these rituals also brought a male actor into play in the person of the teacher or master (guru or *ācārya*),[150] with the combined sexual emissions of the pair transforming the initiand from an undetermined biologically given *paśu* into a *kulaputra*, a son of the clan. As one moves forward in time, and out of the Kaula context and into more conventional forms of Tantra, the role of the Yoginī becomes increasingly eclipsed by that of the male master. In fact, this shift toward "guru-ism" is one of the most fundamental dynamics in the development of later Tantra. The male guru gives birth to a new member of the Tantric order by inseminating his novice with male sexual fluid, which is nothing other than the seed of the male Śiva himself.

This transmission is termed initiation by penetration (*vedha[mayī] dīkṣā*) in a number of contexts,[151] with the next move—the total sublimation of the sexual drop (*bindu*) or seed (*bīja*) into a seed mantra (*bīja-mantra*)—occurring in nearly every high Hindu Tantric tradition. Śiva, the divine revealer of the *Liṅga Purāṇa*, states that "initially my eternal command (*ājñā*) arose out of my mouth."[152] Mark Dyczkowski links this statement to a description found in an early Kaula work, the *Kularatnoddyota*, in his discussion of the term *ājñā*, which is reproduced in chapter 3. In this latter text, the guru initiates the disciple by literally transmitting the "command" to him through the recitation of mantras, at the level of the *ājñā cakra*, the "Circle of Command."[153] In his account of *vedhadīkṣā*, Abhinavagupta states that the disciple should press himself against the master, who, in order to effect a perfect fusion (*samarasībhavet*), should be mouth to mouth and body to body with him.[154]

In fact, rituals of male-to-male transmission or initiation predate Śaivism and Kaula traditions by at least two millennia. They constitute the Vedic norm, as it were, as evidenced in the *Atharva Veda* (AV) statement that "the teacher, when he initiates his pupil, places him, like a fetus, inside of his body. And during the three nights [of the initiation], he carries him in his belly. . . ."[155] The *Bṛhadāraṇyaka Upaniṣad* (1.5.17) describes the transmission (*sampratti*) of breath from a dying father to his son in similar terms: "When he dies to this world, he penetrates his son with his breaths. Through his son, he maintains a support in this world, and the divine and immortal breaths penetrate him." Finally the *Kauśītaki Upaniṣad* (2.15) anticipates Abhinavagupta's instructions for *vedhadīkṣā* by at least twelve hundred years: "When the father is at the point of dying, he calls his son [to him]. . . . [The] father lies down, dressed in new clothing. Once he has arrived [there], the son lies down upon him, touching [his father's] sense organs with his [own] sense organs."[156]

As Paul Mus argued over sixty years ago, the guiding principle of these ancient sources was "not that one inherits *from* one's [father]; rather, *one inherits one's father*."[157] This was not, however, the implicit or explicit model of initiation in the later Tantric traditions. Rather than being the extension of a preexisting brahmanic mode of male self-reproduction, this was rather a reversal and masculinization of the Kaula model of heterosexual reproduction. That is, the Tantric *vedha[mayī] dīkṣā* and other initiations and consecrations self-consciously removed the feminine from the reproductive process, usually by internalizing and semanticizing her as the guru's *śakti*, the "mother of the phonemes" and "fire stick of the mantras" passively transmitted from the guru's mouth into that of his disciple.[158] So, for example, in his general introduction to Tantric initiation in the TĀ, Abhinavagupta quotes the *Ratnamālā Tantra* in stating that when the master places the *mālinī* (mantra) on the disciple's head, it's effect is so powerful that it makes him fall to the ground.[159] Here as well, the Yoginī—however instrumentalized she may have been in the Kaula rites in which the silent discharge from her nether mouth transformed an initiate into a member of the clan—has now been semanticized out of existence. As I argued in chapter 3, advances in Indian medical knowledge were such that a woman's contribution, in the form of her "female discharge," to the conception of a fetus, was well known by the time of the emergence of the Kaula rites. This understanding of the biology of reproduction, so important to the development of the Yoginī Kaula, was therefore consciously censored and sublimated in the initiation rites of later high Hindu Tantra. This paradigm nonetheless persists in the Bengali traditions of the *dīkṣā guru* (master of initiation) and the *śīkṣā guru* (teaching master). In both Sahajiyā Vaiṣṇava and Bāul traditions, the former, who is a male transmitter of mantras, plays a secondary role to the latter, who is female and whose "teaching" is received through her sexual emissions.[160]

In these rituals and their mythological representation, the guru inseminates his disciple by spitting into his mouth,[161] a masculinized alloform of transmitting a chew of betel between mouths.[162] Curiously, this type of transmission also becomes transposed into Indian Sufi hagiographical literature from the time of the Delhi Sultanate:

> Now there was one man who had that very day become a disciple of the Shaykh; he was called Jamāl-al-dīn Rāvat. The Shaykh told him to go forth and give an answer to the [unnamed] Jogī's display of powers. When Jamāl-al-dīn hesitated to do so, the Shaykh called him up close to him and took some *pān* out of his own mouth and placed it with his own hand in Jamāl-al-dīn's mouth. As Jamāl-al-dīn ate the *pān* he was overcome by a strange exaltation and he bravely set out for the battle. He went to the Jogī. . . . When the Jogī had exhausted all his tricks he then said, "Take me to the Shaykh! I will become a believer." . . . At the same time all the disciples of the Jogī became Muslims and made a bonfire of their religious books.[163]

Another tradition that blends Sufi and Tantric imagery, if not practice, is that of the Nizarpanthis of western India, whose "way of the basin" ritual was described in chapter 3.[164] Here, it will be recalled that the term *pāyal* is used by Nizarpanthis for the mixture of sperm and *chūrma* that all participants consume at the end of this ritual. This terminology appears to have been inspired by Sufi traditions, in which "taking the cup" (*piyālā lenā*), that is, sharing a drink of milk with the master, is a transformative moment in initiation rites. However, here as well, the "milk" in the cup may have originally been the semen of the initiating *pīr*, diluted in water.[165]

8. Prescriptive Dreams and Visions

Gananath Obeyesekere and, more recently, Isabelle Nabokov[166] have provided compelling analyses of the relationship between individual dreams and visions, on the one hand, and the cultural norms for the interpretation of the same, on the other. Most often dreams and visions involve possession by a demonic being, which can only be expelled by a narrativized interpretation (within the cultural idiom, in these cases, Tamil or Singalese) followed by a dramatic ritual exorcism either improvised by the dreamer or choreographed by an independent ritual specialist, a *cāmi*. These *cāmis*, generally low-caste individuals, do not choose to practice their charismatic calling. Rather, they have been "recruited" by a deity, usually a goddess; that is, they too have been the objects of repeated possessions, invasions of their person, by a foreign being. It is their prior and ongoing possession experience that empowers them to diagnose and cure other similarly possessed persons.[167] In this role, *cāmis* are similar—if not identical—to *tāntrikas*. As Michel Strickmann has observed, the Tantric mantra master[168] is a person who is enveloped by his dreams and visions, with the goal of Tantric ritual being to generate a sustained state of (wakeful) dreaming, such that a Tantric ritual, when properly performed, constitutes a "perfect dream."[169] Here, we may speak of what Sigmund Freud termed the "dream work,"[170] the *tāntrika*'s ritual processing of the terrible nightmare demonesses that possess his own mind and body that permits him to see in them the one nurturing Mother goddess (or her male consort) that grounds *their* being as well as his own. This dream work, which is part and parcel of Kaula and Tantric initiation, continues throughout the practitioner's career.

But dreams—or rather what one makes of dreams once one has "awakened," as dictated by one's cultural idioms—vary widely in their content and psychological impact. Here, a comparison between the prescriptive and transformative dreams and visions of two Tantric traditions—one Kaula and the other Śaivasiddhānta—will offer us a window onto the ways in which high Hindu Tantra sublimated the transformative sexuality of Kaula rites that were, as Obeyesekere's and Nabokov's research and analysis show, commensurate with real-life experiences of many South Asians. Here, our proof texts will be the circa ninth- to tenth-century *Brahmayāmala* (BY)[171] and the 1095 C.E. *Somaśambhupaddhati* (SŚP).[172]

The BY passage describes a series of ritually induced dreams or visions that noncelibate practitioners are to undertake to succeed in their practice and attain a number of supernatural enjoyments, including the power of flight. Three rituals are presented, whose increasing complexity is accompanied by assurances of enhanced results; here I will only present the third and most elaborate of the series.[173] As in the two envisioning rituals that precede this one, the practitioner seeks to know his past lives—in order to discern whether acts committed in those lives may be creating impediments to the success of his Kaula practice in his present life—by meditating on the vulvas of a circle of ritual consorts. These rites therefore involve the "viewing of his own yoni," in which the yoni in question is at once the vulva that is his meditation support and the womb of the prior existence he is seeking to know.

"Concerning the 'viewing of his own yoni,' listen now to the following [practice on the part] of the practitioner. . . . It is the bestower of fruits: pure and impure nectar, [and] the [eight supernatural powers] beginning with atomicity." Here, the practitioner is instructed to take a group of eight women, "the Śaktis, etc., those [women] who are devoted to the [one] Śakti, who have authority over the pure stream, and who are likewise without shame and without aversion." Next, he is to prepare an underground chamber, equipped with a water circulation system, and a store of worship items, food (including 100,000 sweetmeats), drinking water, and a couch—but no fire: only an oil lamp is to be used to see in the dark.[174] He then arranges the eight women around himself, at each of the cardinal and secondary directions. Then, he sexually arouses his Śaktis in succession,[175] "effecting as many 'rebirths' [i.e., serial acts of sexual intercourse?] as his energy allows." This day sets the pattern for the "sequential method" that the practitioner will observe for up to six months. Having aroused the eight Śaktis by day, the practitioner eats together with them by night. In this way, he "sees the vision of his own yoni, going back over eight births."

At this point the text evokes a practice of the "Five Women of the Seal," in the context of which the most vivid visions occur. The male practitioner, who is "sealed in" here by a circle of four or five women, now experiences the arising of

> the great obstructors (*mahāvighnāni*), all of them very terrifying. . . . He should not be frightened either by these creatures . . . or when he sees a fearsome serpent that seems to be devouring [him]. He sees a she-cat with sharp teeth and a deformed body. Even seeing her, he ought not to be frightened, nor should he halt the ritual. He sees a very terrifying she-rat, with the body of an obstructor. Drawing toward (*ākarṣya*) herself the person who abandons his worship [out of fear], that Śakti . . . kills [him]. [A demoness] will say the words: "Stand up! I devour [you]!" . . . He is not to be frightened. . . . Voices will come from outside [the underground chamber]. [He will hear] the words "Kill! kill! Throw out food! Draw in [this] sinner!" . . . [and] "Get up, get up, you witless one! You are taken by the order of the king!" Seeing [these demonesses], he is not to fear, and his mind should not depart from its meditation. The practitioner [will see] dreadful gape-mouthed forms. [There will be] buck-toothed Śaktis licking [him] with their tongues. Seeing them, he should not fear. . . . Without a doubt, they lick the essence [that is] inside the practitioner

> for the sake of knowledge. While this is taking place, supernatural experiences [will] arise, one at a time. . . . His supernatural power, pervading the triple-world, will manifest itself. When the full six months [have passed], there is the visible manifestation of the [great] Goddess. . . . [Even when she appears] with her gape-mouthed form, she should not be feared by the possessor of mantras. . . . [The] completion [of the practice] is to be carried out by the practitioner in [the midst of the circle of] the eight [women]. In the [circle of] seven, nothing more than the viewing of the yoni occurs. In the group of eight, there is, without a doubt, the daily arising of [supermundane] wisdom. Having attracted the bodies of every one of these beings, he thereby obtains that [wisdom]. He becomes a Virile Hero, surrounded by yonis.

At the conclusion of this heroic practice, the Tantric practitioner of this rite becomes a Virile Hero, standing alone, like the supreme male godhead itself, at the center of a mandala of feminine entities he now controls. This he has succeeded in doing through his "dream work," through his ability to maintain his sangfroid when assaulted by hordes of demonesses, howling beasts with sharp teeth and long tongues seeking to drain him of his vital essence both from without and within. This is the modus operandi of the modern-day *tāntrika*, a visionary who *induces* possession by—or the vision of—a divinity, through a series of "spiritual exercises" by means of which lower beings, usually demonesses, are driven out or brought under control by the higher god, with whom he identifies. In fact, the configuration of the male practitioner at the center of a circle of eight females exactly reproduces a Kaula representation of the "clan transmission" (*kulāmnāya*) as described in the *Netra Tantra* and other sources, in which the male deity Bhairava is enthroned in the heart of a lotus, on the eight petals of which are seated eight Mother goddesses.[176] As with the popular demonological traditions of South Asia, it is the family that is at the center of one's dream- or trance-induced experience; what has changed here is that the family or clan is now comprised of superhuman families of goddesses whose powers sustain and energize the entire universe.

The specificity of this Kaula tradition further lies in its privileging of the power (and the male conquest) of female sexuality, represented by eight Śaktis in the *Brahmayāmala* passage. Eight is of course the "clan number": through the *kulayāga* and other initiation rituals, Kaula practitioners were reborn into families of the eight Mothers, which proliferated into the broader clans of the sixty-four Yoginīs. In both the early Buddhist and Hindu Tantras, one finds ritual instructions for entering into the cosmic body of the divine clan via the powers of one of the eight Mothers, in initiation rites that involved possession (*āveśa*). In the controlled environment of the ritual, the danger of possession by these demonic female entities was both reduced and voluntarily induced by the heroic male practitioner: rather than being their passive victim, he actively transformed them into his instrument for the attainment of supernatural enjoyments.[177] Through these rites, the eight Mothers became internalized, making the (male) body a temple in which to worship these powerful female entities. Now linked to the eight parts of the practitioner's subtle body, the Mothers were seen as grounded in and projections of this new center, from which they were emitted and into which they were reabsorbed.[178] The notion of "family" is at once retained and expanded here: the threatening female nightmare horde, now identified with the vivifying powers of a cosmic family (*kula*), is sublimated into the mind-body complex of the male practitioner. Yet the initiatory role of the Yoginī never fully disappears in the Clan traditions, as in the case of the "Great Feast" (*mahotsava*) of the Siddhas and Yoginīs, at which "only men and women initiated by a Yoginī . . . in a dream are invited. . . ."[179]

At the opposite end of the spectrum from the Kaula are those high Hindu Tantric traditions in which the popular goddess-based demonological traditions have been fully occulted by a direct male (god)–to–male (practitioner) initiation process and transmission of the Tantric gnosis. A case in point is the metaphysician Vāsugupta (circa 825–875 C.E.), to whom the supreme male deity Śiva revealed himself, in a dream, in the form of a text that became known as the *Śivasūtra*, the "Aphorisms of Śiva."[180] This sublimation of the feminine becomes the rule in elite brahmanic forms of Hindu sectarian practice, in which a technique of "divine envisioning" (*divyadṛṣṭi*) is employed to identify directly with the supreme male godhead.[181]

The *Somaśambhupaddhati*'s description of the highest Śaivasiddhānta initiation, called *nirvāṇa-dīkṣā*,[182] epitomizes this censoring of the female from high Hindu Tantric practice. The passage opens with an instruction to the Tantric guru to "install . . . his disciples [for the night] . . . the renouncers lying on a bed of pure ashes, their heads to the south, their topknots knotted with the *śikha* [mantra], [and] protected by the *astra* [mantra]. After having prayed to the God of Dreams, he leaves them." Here, a preliminary mantric protection is effected to ensure that no demonic power, no spirit of the dead, and especially no female entity invade the space of the initiation or the consciousness of the initiands. This is made clear in a number of Āgamas, which, in their discussions of this initiation rite, place great emphasis on the means of protection (*rakṣitān*) of the sleeping initiands, comparing the protective mantras to a citadel with ramparts. Two such sources mention blood offerings (*bali*) and blood offerings to the "beings" (*bhūtabali*),[183] clear references to the demonological underpinnings of this ritual.

The SŚP continues its exposition by stating that the aim of this initiation rite is to stimulate dreams in the initiands through the teaching of the mantra of the "Little Dream Man" (*svapnamāṇavaka*), the Indian equivalent of the Sandman, who is here identified with Śiva.[184] This mantra, given in the verses that follow, concludes with this prayer to Śiva: "O God of Gods! I beg of you to reveal to me, here in my sleep, all the acts [hidden] in my heart!"[185] As Hélène Brunner notes, this prayer is made to the God of Dreams to know whether there remain any karmic traces that may bar their initiation on the following day. The god's reply will come in the form of the intervening night's dreams, which must of course be interpreted. The *Siddhāntaśekhara* states the matter aphoristically: "The guru invokes the dream mantra in order that they [the disciples] have visions in their sleep." This is the essence of the ritual: the disciples *must* dream![186]

The extremely tame list of dreams that follows in the SŚP, dreams whose karmic content the guru is called upon to interpret and to remedy through ritual expiations (*prāyaścittas*), indicates that we are, in this Śaivasiddhānta initiation, worlds away from the nightmare scenarios of the Kaula envisionings of "one's own yoni." Not one of the dreams has either a sexual or a horrific content—they range from eating clotted milk to falling down an empty well.[187]—precisely because the sleeping initiands have been protected from demonic invasions of their bodies and minds by a "citadel of mantras." And such is precisely the situation in these elite traditions: no fearsome female entity troubles the sleep and dreams of the male practitioners, whose ritual practice is quite entirely directed toward the supreme male deity Śiva and his male entourage. The "dream work" has been elided here, with the total sublimation, or exclusion, of the terrifying feminine, in favor of an unthreatening male "Sandman." Yet these troublesome beings retain an occult presence in these elite rituals, the elaborate protective measures being taken against them constituting ample evidence of their invasive power.

Despite their differences in emphasis, we can see that these two Tantric traditions share three common approaches to dreams and visions. First, both require that practitioners undergo a dream experience as part of their spiritual itinerary: for a number of reasons, they *must* dream. Second, both traditions work from the same worldview that places multitudes of dead and demonic beings at the periphery of a hierarchized mandala governed by a supreme deity, either male or female. Third, both give full value to the possession experience: for in high Hindu Tantra traditions, the ultimate end of the vision practice is *samāveśa*, the "co-penetration" or "mutual possession" of two beings—the human practitioner and the divine—until they are realized to be one. However, whereas in the earlier Kaula traditions, success is only attained through transactions with terrifying female beings, the later Śaivasiddhānta source examined here literally walls these out from the practitioner's consciousness while denying the importance of the subconscious to his mind-body composite. The Yoginīs have no place in this all-male universe.

9. Sublimation of the Five M-words

We have shown that high Hindu Tantra defeminized Kaula practice, either internalizing the feminine or simply removing women from its sublimated ritual program. If indeed, *maithuna*, the fifth *makāra*, has been excised from these sources, what of the referents of the other four M-words, the proscribed (for the purity-conscious upper castes) substances that also gave Kaula practice its specificity? As will be shown, these substances too, and the pollution and power they represent, are dispensed with through ritual substitutes and casuistic argumentation. In the end, there is nothing left of the Kaula legacy in high Hindu Tantra, which becomes indistinguishable from other forms of orthodox householder religious practice.

We begin by looking at the transgressive language of the Kaula sources themselves. When the KJñN enjoins the Kaula practitioner to eat "the flesh, clarified butter, blood, milk, and yogurt of a cow," in what appears to be a conflation of an orthodox abomination (bovicide) with an orthodox requirement (three of the *pañcagavya*, the five pure products of the cow), we find ourselves in the presence of a deliberate subversion of orthodox canons and categories of purity. A few verses later, the same source recommends the ritual consumption of the flesh of the jackal, dog, and other impure animals.[188] The *Vīrāvalī Tantra*, quoted by Jayaratha in his commentary to TĀ 4.243, undermines orthodox categories through a historical argument, stating that "the ancient *ṛṣis* ate both beef and human flesh";[189] and Jayaratha quotes an unnamed source in his commentary on TĀ 29.10 by declaring, "Tantric adepts who are Virile Heroes should eat that which the common man detests and, being revolting, is censorable and prohibited by the scriptures." The *Bṛhat Saṃnyāsa Upaniṣad*, not a Tantric text, simply reverses the poles of licit and illicit when it maintains that for the renouncer, "clarified butter is like dog's urine, and honey is equal to liquor. Oil is pig's urine and broth is equal to garlic. Bean cake and the like are cow's meat, and milk is equal to urine. With every effort, therefore, an ascetic should avoid clarified butter and the like. . . ."[190]

Of course, the Kaula traditions were less concerned with shocking the conventional sensibilities of the wider South Asian society than they were with the transformative effects, for the uninitiated, of eating the final member of the series, the clan fluid. We should also recall here that five M-words do not belong to the original Kaula traditions. One instead finds other sets of five—the Five Essences (*pañcatattva*),[191] Five Nectars, Five Lamps (in Kālacakra Buddhism),[192] or Five Jewels (urine, semen, menstrual blood, feces, and phlegm). A set comprised of these five, combined with seven other prohibited foods, is termed the "Set of Twelve Fluids" (*dravyadvādaśaka*).[193] Alternately, it is an earlier set of three M-words, comprised of liquor, meat, and sexual fluids, that one finds in the TĀ and other Trika sources.[194] When, however, one examines treatments of the five M-words in works belonging to the later Tantric revivals, they are most often presented in order to be equated with ritual substitutes.

Even when the language is subversive in these later sources, the intention is casuistic. A prime example is a rhetorical sally found in the fifteenth-century *Haṭhayogapradīpikā* of Svātmarāman: "[The practitioner] should always eat the flesh of a cow (*gomāṃsa*) and drink strong liquor (*amara-vāruṇī*). Him I consider to be well-born, whereas those who do otherwise are the ruin of their families." Svātmarāman, however, provides his own gloss on this verse: "By the word *go* (cow), the tongue is intended. Its entry into [a cavity in] the palate is *gomāṃsa-bhakṣaṇa* ('eating the flesh of a cow'). This indeed destroys the [five] great sins."[195] In the later Tantric works, one finds for each of the five M-words a ritual substitute (*pratinidhi*). The *Āgamasāra*[196] declares that *madya*, liquor, refers to the nectar internally drunk in the cranial vault at the culmination of yogic practice; that *māṃsa*, flesh, refers to the practitioner's tongue in the yogic technique of *khecarī mudrā;* that *matsya*, fish, refers to the absorption into the medial channel of the breaths moving in the right and left channels of the subtle body (these breaths, styled as two fish swimming in the Ganges and Yamuna Rivers, are to be swallowed into the central *suṣumṇā* channel, the Sarasvati River); that *mudrā* refers to the dawning of inner knowledge in the *sahasrāra cakra*, located in the cranial vault; and that *maithuna*, sexual union, refers to the supreme essence (*paramatattva*), from which *siddhis* and the knowledge of the absolute arise.[197] A similar yogic interpretation is found in the *Kulārṇava Tantra*,[198] which, in spite of the rhetorical glorification of the Kaula in its opening chapter,[199] shows itself to be an altogether conventionalist work in its fourth chapter when it provides long lists of such equivalents and condemns the consumption of the referents of the original five M-words.

Casuistry gives rise to countercasuistry, as in the case of the *Jñānārṇava*,[200] a pre-sixteenth-century work that quite nearly reverses all of the *Āgamasāra*'s "soft" readings of the five M-words, no doubt to make a point concerning the doctrine of radical nonduality (*advaya*)—that is, that there is no difference between the absolute and the lowest forms of manifest being—as held by many of the Kaula schools:[201]

> From the perspective of one who has a consummate knowledge of *dharma* and *adharma*, there is purity even in the things of this world. . . . The eating of cow dung and urine . . . is prescribed as an expiation for such sins as the murder of a brahmin, so what stain can there be in [human] excrement and urine . . . ? It is by means of menstrual blood that a body is in fact generated. How then can that by means of which liberation is realized be polluting (*duṣaṇa*)? . . . Semen, as the root cause of the body, is assuredly pure. How is it that [men] revile it?[202]

But countercasuistry can, in turn, give rise to counter-countercasuistry. The KĀN repeats the verse quoted above from the *Jñānārṇava* on the subject of menstrual blood and semen.[203] Yet, after having effected a reductio ad absurdum of every sort of brahmanic purity regulation, this same source then goes on to catalog the numerous ritual substitutes that orthodox brahmin practitioners were permitted to resort to in their practice.[204]

This spirit of scrupulousness and attention to purity regulations, inspired no doubt by the real fear that contact with dangerous fluids would destroy one's very being, flies in the face of the fundamental Kaula and Tantric ideologies. More than this, they epitomize the "contracted consciousness" that is the antitype of the expanded god-consciousness of the Tantric practitioner, and they bar the path to the powers and supernatural enjoyments that give Tantra its specificity. The inhibitions, or sorts of dread or fear (*śaṅkā*) by which the consciousness of the orthodox brahmin becomes contracted, have been enumerated by Jayaratha, in his TĀ commentary on the *kulayāga*. They are dread of loss of identity, dread of participation in non-Vedic rites, dread of impure Tantric incantations, dread of fluids (*dravyaśaṅkā*), dread of contamination by untouchables in caste-promiscuous sexual rites, dread of entering the cremation grounds and the other impure sites in which the Tantric rites are observed, dread of assault or possession by the demonic beings that inhabit these sites (*bhūtaśaṅkā*) and dread of the human body (*śarīraśaṅkā*), and, finally, dread of [nonbrahmanic] categories (*tattvaśaṅkā*).[205] Finally, in a total reversal of standard notions of demonic possession, Abhinavagupta, citing the *Kulagahvara Tantra* and the *Niśisaṃcāra Tantra*, dismisses such orthodox obsessions with conventionalist categories as so many Seizers (Grahas), "because they conceal the true self (autonomous, unitary consciousness) beneath a phantasmagoric pseudo-identity, contaminating and impoverishing it with categories unrelated to its essence." These "Eight Seizers," which combine to create the limited persona of the orthodox householder practitioner, are conformist obsessions with birth, traditional knowledge, family (*kula*), discipline, the body, one's country, conventional virtues, and wealth.[206]

In this exegetical synthesis, the ultimate referent of purity regulations, like that of sexual practice, becomes an exalted state of consciousness. Once again, doing becomes subsumed under knowing. Thus, while there remains a place in the secret initiations of the Abhinavan corpus for the consumption of prohibited foods and sexual fluids, the goal of such practice has now become a breakthrough of consciousness rather than the transformative effects of these substances themselves. Kaula practice and its effects are now explained in terms of the value of transcending the "psychosis" of conformity to the exoteric religion,[207] as epitomized in the use of the Five Jewels, mentioned above.

> The hesitation which prevents the majority from accepting the validity of the Kaula and Tantric revelation becomes identical in this perspective with the contraction which consciousness takes on when it projects itself as bound individuals and their world. . . . Such is the power attributed to this contact with impurity that it is believed that it may take the place of the conventional process of initiation (*dīkṣā*) into the Kaula cult. Instead of that ritual the Kaula officiant may simply present the candidate with a skull-cup containing wine and the [Five] Jewels or other such substances. If he swallows the contents without hesitation (*śaṅkā*) he is considered to have attained direct realization of consciousness in its essential nature uncontaminated by conceptual or ethical dualities (*vikalpaḥ*). Termed the "consumption of the oblation" (*caruprāśanam*) this act is listed accordingly among the contexts in which enlightenment may occur without recourse to meditation, ritual or any other means of liberation.[208]

Even as, however, Abhinavagupta allows for the ingestion of the *dravyams* of the original Kaula rituals in his high Hindu Tantric synthesis, the referent of the practice has been entirely displaced, from the power inherent in the clan fluids themselves—to transform a biologically given "inert being" (*paśu*) into a Virile Hero or Perfected Being—to the transformative psychological effect of overcoming conventional notions of propriety through the consumption of polluting substances. This emphasis on aesthetic experience and gnoseological transformation, coupled with a system of equivalencies between Vedic and Tantric ritual, could not help but have a leveling effect on all later forms of Tantra, whether of the more Kaula or Śākta "left" or the more Śaiva "right."[209] In the end and regardless of Tantric theory, the impetus behind the Tantric rituals became one of achieving parity with the Vedic rituals, with the "need to match these orthodox rituals . . . strong enough to compromise the very beliefs which justified the separate existence of the Tantric system."[210] This is precisely what has happened over the centuries. Heterodox Kaula or Tantric ritual has so shaded into orthodox Vedic or Śaivasiddhānta ritual as to become indistinguishable from it, as in the case of South Indian Smārta communities. The various waves of "Tantric revival" have only further clouded the picture. Everything becomes Tantra, because nothing is Tantra. In the late twentieth century, New Age Tantra has rushed in to fill the vacuum.

But this is not where the story ends, nor is it where it began.

Chapter 9

TANTRA FOR THE NEW MILLENNIUM

With the gradual extinction of the lineages that constituted its fluid connection back to its divine source, the practices of the Kaula became increasingly abstracted from the eleventh century onward into Tantra. With its gradual loss of royal patronage, Tantric practice became increasingly removed from its real-world referents, with its external rites being internalized, semanticized, and brahminized. From the ruins of its past, modern-day entrepreneurs have cobbled together the pathetic hybrid of New Age "Tantric sex." The Kaula's flame, which burned brightest in the centuries around the turn of the first millennium, and which was subsequently rekindled in Nepal and Bengal some five hundred years later, has forever been extinguished. What of Tantra? In the opening chapter of this book, I argued that "mainstream" religion in South Asia was more aptly termed "Tantra" than *bhakti*. Here, what I mean by "Tantra" has little or nothing to do with the sexualized ritual that gave the Kaula rites their specificity. Rather, it is a perennial and pervasive form of religiosity that has persisted on the Indian subcontinent since well before the emergence of the Kaula sects, down to the present day.

1. The Periphery of the Mandala

As noted in chapter 5, some of the most basic structures of Tantric or Kaula polity have been predicated on a strategic concern with the sealing off of one's boundaries. This is a concern that has permeated every level of Tantric practice. In the last chapter, we saw this in the "citadel of mantras" constructed to protect sleeping initiands from demonic invasion, a practice that is of a piece with a standard preliminary ritual called the "binding of the directions" (*digbandhana*), by which hostile demonic forces are fenced outside the worship mandala. In fact, the *tāntrika*'s ritual techniques for driving away, immobilizing, confusing, and annihilating demonic enemies are legion; and once again we see the importance of the Tantric specialist's role as a defender of inhabited human space. It is here that the fierce and heavily armed deities pictured at the borders and gates of the Tantric mandalas have their place: they are the protectors of the realm.[1]

Here, it may be helpful to reintroduce into our discussion the typology of the "transcendental" and "pragmatic" aspects of religion. This typology, first proposed in the 1960s by the anthropologist David Mandelbaum[2] on the subject of village-level religious practice in India, will serve as our theoretical bridge between what appear today to be two distinct types of Tantric specialists and their clients, and two distinct and generally disconnected types of Tantric practice in South Asia. When practitioners pay homage to the great gods of their tradition in the controlled atmosphere of a religious festival or periodical ritual observance, such is an example of "transcendental" religion. When, however, an uncontrolled epidemic breaks out in their village or territory, and the local or regional deity of the disease in question is worshiped to protect and save them from their affliction, such is an example of "pragmatic" religion. Tantric elites—kings and their priestly specialists, householder practitioners, and so on—will generally take a "transcendental" approach to their religion, transacting with high gods through the controlled template of the mandala. But far from the center and the exalted concerns of these generally urban elites, Tantric specialists from lower levels of society—healers, exorcists, spirit-mediums, shamans, et cetera—will generally be called upon by their clients for their "pragmatic" abilities to transact with a malevolent spirit world that has *already* erupted into their lives, far away from the mandala's quiet center.

Most of pragmatic religious life in South Asia revolves around family gods, that is, those deceased family members, distant or recent, who have died untimely or unusual deaths. Such a death has barred their path to the protected world of the ancestors, the happy dead; and so these unhappy and unsettled spirits find themselves condemned to a marginal and dangerous existence. Because these beings inhabit the limen between the living and the dead, they are most readily encountered in the places at which they departed from this world: graveyards and charnel and cremation grounds. As such, these sites become the privileged venues of certain types of Tantric practice (exorcism, subjugation, killing, etc.), as described

Figure 9.a. Bound male victim being led away by two female figures, Chinnamastā shrine, Patan, Kathmandu Valley, twentieth century. Photograph by David Gordon White.

in gruesome detail in sacred and secular medieval literature, and graphically illustrated on the lower portions or borders of Buddhist mandala art in particular.

In their unhappy situation, the dead will often seek to avenge themselves against their family, clan, or village, and so become malevolent ghosts, the *bhūt-prets* of South Asia. The protean horde of these lesser entities form or hem in the outermost fringes of the great mandala that the king, as incarnation or representative of the godhead, rules from the center. Yet, it is one and the same mandala, the same mesocosm of interpenetrating energies: all that changes is the perspective from which it is viewed. At the pragmatic outer fringes of the mandala, possession, exorcism, divination, and healing have historically been the most pervasive forms of Tantric practice, and it has been in their roles as ritual healers, "psychoanalysts," clairvoyants, and ground-level problem solvers that popular Tantric specialists first established and have continued to maintain their closest ties with every level of South Asian society. The dark counterpart to these protective practices is ritual sorcery or black magic, the manipulation of the same low-level deities or demons to strike down one's enemies with the same afflictions as those they are called upon to placate or eliminate (fig. 9.a).

As Michel Strickmann has argued, data from throughout medieval Asia indicate that Tantra was the province of the highest strata of Asian society—of kings and pretenders to kingship—and that it therefore spread downward and outward from the elevated center to lower echelons of society located at the periphery.[3] If his reading is correct, this means that the "sanskritization" of medieval South Asian religious society occurred in a Tantric—in addition to, or rather instead of—a *bhakti* mode. In other words, the low-caste, rural margins of medieval South Asian society would have adopted the Tantric practices of their rulers as a means to social uplift in much the same way that low-caste peasant communities of the nineteenth- and twentieth-century Hindu heartland of India have more recently embraced the *bhakti* cults of Rāma and Kṛṣṇa to assert their Hinduness and claim higher-caste identities and privileges. This is quite the opposite of the widely received notion that Tantra was a grassroots "shamanic" tradition that welled up from a non-Aryan periphery of South Asian religious society. It also raises the question of the sources of the popular Tantric practices of present-day village India: are they the rustic vestiges of elite practices introduced "from above" a millennium ago, or are they the continuation of a perennial body of practice that has remained unchanged for millennia, and that was one of the sources, "from below," of the elite Tantric traditions that emerged in the early medieval period? To be sure, there has always been a give and take between elite and popular traditions in South Asia, and as I argued in chapter 2, the very notions of "elite'" and "popular" break down when, since the time of the *Atharva Veda*, every level of society was practicing the same "pragmatic" religion with regard to certain constants in life—the dangers of childbirth, the threats of illness and insanity, and so on. An examination of Whitney's English captions to his translations of the hymns of the *Atharva Veda* shows that over half of these are devoted to protection against disease, demonic beings, and sorcery for oneself and one's family, or *for* sorcery against one's enemies.[4] One finds the same preoccupations in much of the earliest Kaula literature; in addition, present-day mainstream Indian understandings of "*tantra-mantra*" also identify it with exorcism, sorcery, and demonology.

What differentiates elite Tantric specialists from their nonelite counterparts is not the basic transactions they effect with their deities, but rather the name and attributes of the deities with whom they transact. Elite practitioners—by virtue of their higher Tantric empowerments, textual lineages, and formal instruction—are able to transact with the supreme transcendent-yet-immanent deity of the Tantric universe at the center to control *all* of the beings of the mandala—divine, semidivine, and demonic—for the protection of the king, his court, and the state as a whole.

The principal deity with whom the nonelite specialist or practitioner will transact—some low- or intermediate-level *bhūtanātha* ("Lord of Spirits")—will not be absent from the elite mandala; rather, he or she will be relegated to a zone nearer to its periphery, as a fierce tutelary deity guarding the mandala of the king's (and the supreme deity's) realm from incursions by malevolent spirits from the outside, that is, enemies.

As I argued in chapter 5, the Tantric ruler is the Tantric actor par excellence, with galactic polity operating on the level of mandalas of deities as well as that of agglomerations of peoples, clans, and territorial units. Furthermore, the office and person of the king have perennially constituted the vital link between elite and nonelite forms of Tantric practice. Without him, the center is missing, and the phenomenon that is Tantra becomes cloven into two bodies of practice—the one transcendent and quietistic and the other pragmatic and "shamanistic"—that appear to have little or no relationship to one another. Yet, with the possible exceptions of the kingdom of Bhutan, Nepal (now a constitutional monarchy), and Tibet (a theocracy in exile), there are no Tantric systems of galactic polity remaining on the planet.

What effect has this loss of the center had on Tantra? It has apparently split Tantra into two styles of practice whose connections are barely recognizable to either practitioners or scholars. On the one hand, the powerful Tantric rites of subjugation, immobilization, annihilation, and so on—the "Six Practices" (*ṣaṭkarmāṇi*)—have become the sole province of individuals practicing for their own prestige and profit, or on behalf of other individuals on a for-cash basis. In the absence of state patronage, deployment of these ritual technologies often amounts to little more than black magic. When no longer employed in the service of the state, what had previously been a coherent body of practice for its protection can appear to be little other than a massive "protection racket" against supernatural thugs. It is in this context that many Hindus in India today deny the relevance of Tantra to their tradition, past or present, identifying what they call "*tantra-mantra*" as so much mumbo-jumbo.

The second body of practice that has emerged from this loss of a political center generally involves Tantric elites. When it becomes the case that there no longer is a royal client to support them, many of those elite specialists who had been royal chaplains or preceptors have tended to turn their energies toward "perfecting" the rituals and liturgies for which a performance arena no longer exists. Closeted in monasteries or secret "*pūjā* rooms," these specialists have tended to elaborate Tantric theory and internalize, sublimate, or semanticize external Tantric practice. Taken to its extreme, this scholasticizing tendency has removed Tantra from its this-worldly concerns and transformed it into an idealized and intellectualized inner exercise generally reserved for an elite group of insiders.

There have been two major upshots to these developments in South Asia. On the one hand, much of high Hindu Tantra has become highly philosophical, and it is the case that many of the most brilliant Tantric *summa* have been the work of "pure theoreticians." Even when the language of such forms of Tantra remains antinomian, this is a purely ritual or philosophical antinomianism cut off from the outside world. On the other hand, as we have already noted, Tantric specialists often have, in the absence of politically powerful patrons, adopted the strategy of dissimulation, of hiding their "true" Tantric identity behind a facade of conventional behavior in the public sphere. In this context, elite "Tantra has moved towards the doctrinally orthodox and politically unobjectionable. . . . The magical and shamanic powers have lost their importance, the 'disreputable' sexual practices are avoided, and Tantric ritual has become little more than a supplement to the ordinary Brahmanic cult. . . ."[5] These two strategies, of appropriating Tantric ritual technologies as means to self-promotion and of dissimulation combined with scholasticist theorization, only *appear* to be the legacy of two different traditions. In fact, they are two sides of the same coin; however, the coin is one that no longer bears a royal head or device on its face.

2. Interview with a *Tāntrika*

Every village, town, and city in South Asia has its complement of *tāntrikas*, Tantric entrepreneurs whose services include an often eclectic combination of astrology, yoga, exorcism, sorcery, and other problem-solving techniques. Some are the sons or disciples of other *tāntrikas*, others self-trained specialists, others persons with particular psychological dispositions that open them to communing with the spirit world,[6] others individuals with a gift for healing, and others cynical charlatans.

The most sustained relationship I had with a *tāntrika* grew out of a chance meeting during the spring of 1999. My friend in the western Indian city where I was staying worked in the employ of the local *mahārāja*, whom he counted as a friend, and who was in fact a quite close relative. Like many of his aristocratic brethren, he enjoyed his food and drink, and as a result was suffering from pains in the lower legs that I took to be gout. Like most of the men of his class, he was religious in a ceremonial sort of way, publicly displaying his fealty to the god of his lineage when custom dictated that he should do so, but leaving matters of daily worship to the women living under the roof of his family compound. Yet it was he who told me that he had been seeing a *tāntrika* for several months with regard to his leg condition. This *tāntrika*, my friend told me, had not yet determined whether or not his condition was the result of demonic possession, and if so, whether such had been provoked by human sorcery. This was, however, his working hypothesis, and he had told my friend that he would be able to pronounce on the matter at their next meeting.

As I came to learn, this *tāntrika*, whom I will call Madanlal, had a citywide reputation as an exorcist. He called himself a *tāntrika*, a practitioner of Tantra, because the mantras he used to manipulate and bend demons to his will were taken from the Tantric canon, as it had been taught to him by his guru. Two nights a week, he offered his services pro bono to a large and generally well-heeled clientele. He would begin shortly after he had eaten his dinner, and it would often be well past midnight before the last of the troubled souls he treated left his "clinic." This was a very small, bare, low-ceilinged underground cell located at the bottom of a stairway that led down from the public courtyard in front of his house. On the nights when he received clients, a brilliant reddish glow would flood up into the courtyard; at all other times, the stairway and the cell were closed by a padlocked trap door. Sitting at a crazy angle to the house not far from the trap door was an old Ambassador car, covered with a tattered piece of canvas. Madanlal would later tell me (it was the only time I ever saw him show pride) that he was the sole *tāntrika* in the entire city to drive an Ambassador: it had been the gift of a grateful client for whom he had depossessed the car of a demon that insisted on tapping him on the shoulder while he was driving.

Apart from one evening when he invited me to an excellent vegetarian dinner in his attractive home, a meal shared with himself and his two sons—both graduate students at the local university—all of my meetings with Madanlal took place in his shop, which faced on the same courtyard as his home. This was a small rectangular cube, all of whose walls (including the front window display) were lined with shelves crammed with cast aluminum sculptures, depicting both religious and secular subjects. At the back of the shop were a small counter and three stools; a door behind the counter opened onto the small workshop in which Madanlal smelted, molded, and finished his wares. This was his trade and source of income, a gift from God, he said, in thanks for which he offered his services as a Tantric healer to the haunted and possessed people of his community. Madanlal called his shop Madhusudana Handicrafts: this was also what it said on his visiting card, three-fourths of which was taken up by a polychrome image of the Goddess astride her tiger. On the card, next to the word "proprietor," was Madanlal's legal name, with the name Madanlal in parentheses.

My original interest in meeting Madanlal stemmed from a remark my aristocrat friend had made concerning Madanlal's own guru, a *tāntrika* who had considered himself so powerful that he had installed an image of the head of the god Bhairava beneath his porch stairs: shortly thereafter he had died a sudden and painful death. What sort of person could have the courage to step on the head of Bhairava with (what he had thought would be) impunity? I wanted to know more about this guru, but it was Madanlal's own story and many of the other stories he told me that kept me coming back to the Madhusudana Handicrafts shop. There was, for example, the story of Madanlal's guru's guru, a *tāntrika* who was so powerful that the then *mahārāja* (this was back in the 1940s) forbade him from so much as lighting an oil lamp in his house for fear that he would use the fire to practice some sort of sorcery. Then one day the *mahārāja* fell deathly ill, and no one in the country was able to heal him. At death's door, the *mahārāja* had the *tāntrika* brought to him, and Madanlal's guru's guru—using mantras he had perfected through years of cremation-ground vigils—exorcised the demons that were the cause of the great man's illness. Wanting to show his gratitude, the *mahārāja* offered to grant the *tāntrika* anything he wished. The *tāntrika* asked for two things, both prized possessions of the *mahārāja:* his favorite mare and his hunting rifle. It was on this ambiguous note that Madanlal's story ended: he wouldn't tell me what his guru's guru did with the gun and the horse. Did he simply ride off into the sunset, or shoot the one with the other? The true message of the story, as I understand it, was precisely to emphasize the ambiguity of the power of the Tantric practitioner, to give life or to destroy it, according to the whim of the true man of power.

But it was Madanlal's accounts of his own practice that were the most fascinating to me. As he put it, the powers he had over *bhūt-prets*—the spirits of the unhappy dead that haunted most of his clients—had been gained by spending the better part of his nights, for a period of twenty years, reciting the mantras his guru had taught him on the local cremation ground. By his reckoning, he had recited those mantras as many as 125,000 times on a given night, and the accumulated power of those recitations had given him dominion over a constellation of powerful male and female deities—led by Bhairava and several goddesses whose names he would not divulge—that now battled and drove away demons at Madanlal's bidding. As he understood it, he was not only combating malevolent beings from the spirit world, he was also fighting the human sorcerers and witches who, through *their* practice, had unleashed these demons against the human victims who were Madanlal's clients. This was the power of Tantric mantras: they controlled the gods who controlled the spirits and demons that possessed Madanlal's clients.

The gods and goddesses Madanlal controlled were not different from those controlled by the Bhopas, the low-caste or tribal "shamanic healers" of this part of India, but there was an important difference between Madanlal's and their practice. For whereas the Bhopas would "embody" these divinities by becoming possessed by them, Madanlal controlled them from without, through the power of his mantras. For him, this made "his" Bhairava more powerful than that of the Bhopas because simply by being inside of their bodies, Bhairava was weaker than when he was unhindered by a human vehicle. Another distinction, but one that Madanlal did not himself speak to, was the difference in socioreligious ranking between himself and the Bhopas. They were generally illiterate *ādivāsīs* ("aboriginals," "tribals"), whereas he, a high-caste Hindu, manipulated complex Sanskrit mantras.

On the evening that I had dinner with him, Madanlal showed me documentation of the spirit world he was fighting. Pages torn from copybooks with strange shadowy characters from no known script traced across their surface: this was "ghost writing" that would appear on paper inside the private homes of his clients. Photographs of every sort. A bed scattered with all manner of clothing, slashed as if with razors. Women with their hair chopped away at crazy angles—again, the work of *bhūt-prets* who had broken into people's homes, people's wardrobes and beds, to wreak their havoc. The roof of a factory covered with stones that had rained down on it, the work of demons. Of course, many of Madanlal's clients were beset by demons whose effects on their lives could not be photographed: my friend's gouty knee, for example, but far more often, mental afflictions—insomnia, voices inside their heads, insanity. Madanlal's clients were haunted by demons, whom he fought with Tantric mantras.

Yet, who was Madanlal? What was he? A rather frail, mild-mannered man with a quiet voice. A vegetarian. A father of two sons attending university. A successful businessman who named his shop after Viṣṇu but whose business card bore the image of the Goddess. A man who had spent most of the nights of his adult life on cremation grounds, reciting mantras. A man with intimate knowledge of the pantheon of divine and demonic beings whom he recognized by the quality of the heat and light they radiated. A man who healed his clients, including members of the local aristocracy, in an underground cell. A man whose guru had died after walking on the head of Bhairava. A man whose disciple, an athletic young man in his twenties, spoke BBC English. A man who had perhaps undergone Tantric initiations that he was not telling me about.

Is Madanlal not a twenty-first-century paragon of the perennial Tantric practitioner who has multiple social identities and who lives simultaneously in several parallel worlds—the human, the divine, and the demonic? And if Madanlal is a twenty-first-century avatar of the *tāntrikas* of medieval India, is he the most recent link in an unbroken line of teachers and disciples? And where would that line have begun? In the eighth to tenth century, in this part of India that would have been precisely the "original" homeland of Kaula practice? Or perhaps at a much earlier time, before the phenomenon recognizable as Tantra first emerged?

3. Yoginīs of the New Millennium

Female counterparts to male *tāntrikas* like Madanlal: what has been the fate of Yoginīs in South Asia? Much of the modern-day South Asian discourse concerning Yoginīs differs but little from their medieval legacy. Now as then, "Yoginī "(or "Jognī," Joginī, or "Yakṣī") is a term applied to female supernatural beings, usually of the wild forest, who demand blood sacrifice from the humans who venture into the wilderness lands they inhabit. So, for example, the "jungle" of the Vindhya mountain region of southern Uttar Pradesh and Madhya Pradesh is the province of the Jognī who troubles the lives of those who do not show her proper respect.[7] Similarly, in the Kulu region of Himachal Pradesh, Jognīs are dread goddesses of the uninhabited "jungle" to whom elaborate blood offerings must be made whenever one of their trees is cut down. According to local traditions, every February, all of the Jognīs of the entire region, from as far away as Chamba and Tibet, come to the village of Lahaul, each straddling a roof beam as she flies through the air, carrying a sacrificial animal (a yak, ibex, dzo, or sheep) to consume at the feast. Villagers take every possible precaution to protect themselves from these Jognīs, and to keep them away from their inhabited space.[8] In southern Rajasthan the Līlāḍ (from the Sanskrit *līlā*, "[Where the Gods] Play") temple on the outskirts of the village of Ghatiyali remains a living Yoginī shrine, with these goddesses (and the Bhairavas with whom they are associated) being represented by naturally occurring stones, covered with vermilion paint and metal foil, the former representing the blood offerings that sustain their bodies (fig. 9.b). In all of these contexts, failure to show respect to these powerful, petulant female beings brings down their wrath in the form of possession, disease, miscarriage, and death.

The relationship between these supernatural or preternatural Yoginīs and human "witches," in many ways the female counterparts of the male *tāntrikas*, remains as ambiguous today as it was in the medieval period. In the Kulu Valley once again, local traditions maintain that the leader of the

Figure 9.b. Painted stones representing Yoginīs outside Līlāḍ temple, Ghatiyali, Rajasthan. The temple is said to enshrine the sixty-four Yoginīs and the fifty-two Bhairavas. The stones coated with vermilion paint and foil in the foreground represent Yoginīs. Photograph by David Gordon White.

Jognīs who haunt the village of Gosal is the spirit of the circa 1500 C.E. queen of a local Rajput ruler named Jhinna Rana, who, upon learning of the death of her husband, burned his fort (Madankoṭ) to the ground, with her and her ladies inside. She became a Jognī and his family built a shrine to her in the ruins of the fort.[9] Far more common is the identification of living women with Yoginīs, that is, as witches. In Bengal *ḍains* (a vernacularization of the term *ḍākinī*) are human witches who serve as accomplices to the malevolent supernatural Yoginīs.[10] An identical pattern is found in many other parts of village India, where aged, widowed, and socially marginalized women are accused of witchcraft, of consorting with the Yoginīs, and of "eating the livers"[11] of their human victims when an untimely death or some other calamity befalls a village. Like many of the unfortunate women of post-Reformation Europe and North America, accused witches are still occasionally put to death in South Asia. G. M. Carstairs's *Death of a Witch*, a study based on thirty years of participant anthropology in the Udaipur District of rural southern Rajasthan, is a classic account of this fatal dynamic.

This having been said, not all "human" Yoginīs are mere scapegoats or victims in traditional South Asian society. In certain cases they have a well-defined social role that affords them a certain modicum of empowerment, even if they remain socially and economically excluded. A "reminiscence" of one such Yoginī was reported recently in the daily English-language newspaper of Kathmandu, the *Rising Nepal.* Under the title "Reminiscence: Juddha Shumsher and the Sorceress," the unsigned story begins:

> Nobody knew her name. She was just [a] Yogini (nun) who had come to Kathmandu from India on Shivaratri. During the Rana [r]egime. . . . Indians were not allowed to come to Nepal without [a] passport and visa. Only on such occasion[s as these religious festivals] they could come to Kathmandu for a day and visit the Pashupatinath temple. . . . The hermits and yogis could remain for three days and leave. . . . The Yogini who had come during the reign of Juddha Shumsher . . . did not go back to India [with]in [the] stipulated time. She roamed about the Pashupati area for many days and surprised people with her accurate prediction[s]. She was a middle-aged lady of dark complexion and wore a cotton sari, blouse and a shawl. She smiled while speaking but anyone could guess [that] she never cleaned her teeth. She accepted the invitation of some devotees if she was pleased, and went to their residence as well. But she never entered the house and preferred to stay out: on a bench or under a tree in the garden.
>
> The relatives and neighbours of the host used to come to see the lady. Many of them brought some fruits and even clothes as offerings. . . . But she did not accept anything and told the host to distribute it among friends present in the garden. Sometimes she would point towards a person and say to the host that the man was a criminal—he had taken a bribe just a day before. Sometimes she would not allow a lady to touch her feet saying the lady was a concubine of some rich person. Almost all of the devotees charged by her did not stay there [*sic*] and quietly returned bowing to the assembled crowd. But they spread rumours that the so-called Yogini was a sorceress and she was in command of an evil spirit called Karnapinchash [*karṇapiśāca*]. The then prime minister Juddha Shumsher also heard . . . the rumour. He ordered the police chief Chandra Bahadur Thapa to expel the sorceress from Nepal within a week. She used to stay in [the] Pashupati area and was always surrounded by devotees who regarded her [as] a divine Yogini, not a sorceress.
>
> The police chief also was one of her devotees and he did not dare to arrest her immediately. He was trying to [find] the opportunity [to beg] the P[rime] M[inister] to let the divine lady remain in Nepal. . . . On the fourth day, a strange thing happened. The Prime Minister had gone to [the gardens around the] Balaju [temple] for a stroll in the evening

> [w]here he saw the sorceress on a platform under a tree. . . . At that very moment the sorceress saw the Prime Minister approaching in [a] rage. . . . Juddha Shumsher stood before her and signalled Major Thapa to come forward. The Major ran to him with folded hands but before he could speak, the Yogini stopped him, raising a hand. She then asked the Prime Minister to lend her his ears so that she could tell him some matters of importance privately. . . . She whispered in his ear for three minutes and he nodded several times. In the end, he saluted her and requested her to remain in this country forever. . . . No one knows [w]hat the divine lady told Juddha. Some guessed that she must have told him his past and future, otherwise he would not have cancelled his own order [to deport her]. After some months the sorceress from India disappeared. . . . When Juddha abdicated in favour of Padma Shumsher and went to Ridi in the guise of a hermit, people started spreading rumours that she had predicted Juddha's future to him in Balaju garden. No one knows whether this is true or not, but people, including myself, still remember the lady who had created [a] sensation in Kathmandu more than five decades ago.[12]

Less prosaic, perhaps because more realistic, is the case of the Jōgammas ("Yoga-Mothers") of Karnataka, who as the female servants of Yellammā, the south Indian goddess of sterility, are the heiresses of the former south Indian *devadāsī* traditions as well as of Yakṣī mythology. Here, generally low-caste families continue the custom of offering one of their children, usually a daughter, to Yellammā, to serve as her servant and co-wife to the great god Śiva.[13] Revered on worship days, festival times, at marriages, and following childbirth as representatives of this goddess, they are considered auspicious.[14] More than this, Jōgammas are, like Yellammā, sterile fertility goddesses, who offer their fertility and sexuality without reproduction: Jōgammas never become mothers. This is of a piece with their role in Karnataka society, where they are prostitutes. Thus, outside of festival times and life-cycle rites, far from being considered embodiments of the Goddess, the divine *śakti*—as the *devadāsīs* perhaps once were—Jōgammas are treated as simple whores, "public property," by their generally well-heeled male clients.[15] One may nonetheless glimpse, even today, some vestige of the relative autonomy that the Yoginīs of past ages might have enjoyed. So, for example, during village festivals of Kāma in Karnataka, the Jōgammas mimic a combat against the young men of the village with obscene gestures, salacious insults, and suggestive dances. Their pantomime of battle sometimes becomes real, with the help of alcohol, as they attempt to fend off the spray of colored liquids sent their way by battalions of boys.[16] It is also during these festival periods, punctuated by ritual reversals of the established order, that Jōgammas will tend assert their individual dignity and worth over and against the male society that dominates them at all other times of the year. In an incident witnessed by Jackie Assayag in the village of Saundatti in the southeastern corner of the Belgaum District during the 1987 Holi festival, a group of Mātaṅgīs (women closely related to the Jōgammas in status and function) began berating a man of the merchant caste, circling him, insulting him, and spitting on him, with some mimicking the sexual act. As was later learned, the reason for the uproar was insufficient payment by the man for sexual services, to which he was visibly accustomed.[17] Like the Jōgammas and unlike the mysterious Yoginī who briefly rubbed shoulders with the high society of 1950s Kathmandu, the vast majority of the "living" Yoginīs of South Asia are poor marginalized women whose sexuality is idealized and glorified in words even as it is exploited in practice.

Yet South Asia is beginning to witness a revalorization of the Yoginī, even if such subverts the Kaula system that first enshrined her as a living goddess. So it is that the spiritual head of one of a "chain" of *āśrams* established by Tamil devotees of the gods Rāma and Murukaṉ is a woman known by the name of Mataji Om Prakash Yogini. According to the website of the Sri Ramji Ashram, one can learn the practices of *Rām nām* and *guru bhakti* there.[18] Nothing in the description of this south Indian neo-*bhakti* shrine justifies the name or title of "Yoginī" borne by its Mātā-jī caretaker; and one may safely say that such would have been an abomination to Śaṅkarācārya—arguably the founder of both the orthodox Hindu devotional style and the Advaita Vedānta philosophy that undergirds it—who penned a ringing condemnation of the Yoginī cults in the eighth century.[19]

Once again, in the absence of a centralized Tantric "church," "canon," and "pope," people are free to plunder and reinvent the Yoginī traditions in whatever way they please, in this case to effect the bricolage that has been the hallmark of the stories humans have told about themselves from time immemorial, here in a revisionist religious mode. But none of the developments taking place in modern-day India can rival the commodification of the Yoginī going on in California and other Western "Meccas" of New Age spirituality. So, for example, a story from the business section of the *New York Times*, with a Beaverton, Oregon, dateline, begins: "She called herself the Yogini . . . ":

> She could twist her body in all kinds of ways. . . . Her body quivered like a plucked guitar string. She was teaching at a yoga studio in Los Angeles when she was discovered by Nike, which plastered her face across magazines and beamed her body over television.

> "We love the Yogini," said . . . a spokeswoman for Nike, as she paused a tape of the commercial in Nike's headquarters here [in Beaverton]. . . . From opening women's stores in the Los Angeles area to starting a Web site called nikegoddess.com to creating sneakers that have a snakeskin look, Nike is trying to dominate a market where having a trendy image scores more points than macho advertising.[20]

One might view this globalization of the Yoginī as her final victory, a last howling laugh against the male forces that have tried for over a millennium to domesticate her. But such would be to forget that every day, ersatz entrepreneurs of ecstasy, male and female, are still in the business of selling Yoginī kisses.

Notes

Preface

1. The nom de plume of Sir John Woodroffe, which he used on title pages of works that he had edited rather than written or translated himself.

2. It seems fitting that the Dhubela Museum (Chattarpur District, Madhya Pradesh), which houses the largest collection of Yoginī images of any in India, also includes a room of funhouse mirrors, for which the prince whose collection this originally was also had a passion.

3. Thus, for example, the treatment of Kāpālikas in the *Kathāsaritsāgara:* see below, chap. 5, n. 143.

4. Although, as will be shown in chapter 4 in particular, the production of sexual fluids remains central to the *kula prakiyā*, the secret ritual of Abhinavagupta's synthesis, treated in book 29 of his *Tantrāloka*.

5. "Bliss language" is used in a *Kaulajñānanirṇaya* description of the consecration rite; however, the "state of intoxicated bliss" enjoyed by the practitioner and his consort is produced through their consumption of sexual fluids: see below, chap. 4, n. 81.

6. On this element of Abhinavagupta's exegesis of the Tantric rites, see Sanderson, "Meaning in Tantric Ritual" (1995), pp. 78–87.

7. Urban, "Cult of Ecstasy" (2000), 268–304; and id., *Tantra* (2003).

8. Kakar, *Shamans, Mystics, and Doctors* (1982), p. 151.

9. LeGoff, *L'Imaginaire médiéval* (1985), pp. 17–39, 64; and id., *Pour un autre Moyen Age* (1977), p. 298. See also White, *Myths of the Dog-Man* (1991), p. 10.

10. For a general discussion of the European experience of India, see Halbfass, *India and Europe* (1988).

11. On the other hand, some are sick-minded manipulators of psychologically fragile persons in search of a father or mother figure. The guru-disciple relationship combined with the sexual content of "Tantric sex" often make for a dangerous cocktail. On this, see Kramer and Alstad, *Guru Papers* (1993), esp. pp. 91–99.

12. Here, I am referring to freelance purveyors of mainly "Hindu Tantric sex," as opposed to the Tibetan Buddhist missions to the West, which have a direct lineage going back to Indian teachers and a rigorous standard concerning the Sanskrit-language origins of its root texts. In any case, overt "Tantric sex" is not part of the Tibetan Buddhist agenda.

Chapter 1

1. Strickmann, *Mantras et mandarins* (1996).

2. Mandelbaum, "Transcendental and Pragmatic Aspects of Religion" (1966).

3. Here, I am mainly referring to the progressive "Hindu Renaissance" movement of the early twentieth century, but also to the neo-orthodox "Eternal Religion" (*sanātana dharma*) movement of the same period: for a short, concise overview, see Lutgendorf, *Life of a Text* (1991), pp. 360–71.

4. Tambs-Lyche, *Power, Profit, and Poetry* (1997), pp. 18–19.

5. A particularly astute study of this sort is Pollack, "Deep Orientalism?" (1993), pp. 96–117, in which Pollock generates an archaeology of the elite categories through which the British viewed Indian religion and culture.

6. Lévi, "Le Catalogue des Yakṣa" (1915), esp. pp. 32–37, 55. The earliest version of the *Mahāmāyuri*, a Buddhist "protection" against demons (*rakkhās*) in which the comprehensive list of tutelary "yakṣas" is found, dates from the fifth century C.E. (pp. 20–26).

7. Vaudeville, *Myths, Saints and Legends* (1999), pp. 158–72, 182; and Narain, "Gaṇeśa" (1991), pp. 25, 34.

8. See Couture and Schmid, "*Harivaṃśa*" (2001); and Eschmann et al., "Formation of the Jagannātha Triad" (1978), pp. 180–81. See below, chap. 2, n. 97.

9. *Rāmāyaṇa of Vālmīki, Vol. 1: Bālakāṇḍa*, ed. and trans. Goldman (1984), p. 46 n. 90. A "revisionist history" of *bhakti* is in preparation.

10. Ramanujan, *Hymns for the Drowning* (1981), pp. 128–29.

11. Pinch, *Peasants and Monks* (1996), pp. 82–92.

12. Lutgendorf, *Life of a Text*, p. 363.

13. Pinch, *Peasants and Monks*, pp. 33–34.

14. Ibid., p. 37.

15. Toffin, *Le Palais et le temple* (1993), p. 211 n. 8.

16. Clothey, "Tamil Religions" (1986), p. 267.

17. Obeyesekere, *Medusa's Hair* (1981); Caldwell, *Oh Terrifying Mother* (1999); Assayag, *La Colère de la déesse décapitée* (1992).

18. This process began in the Tamil country in the fourteenth century, with the incorporation of female tutelary cult figures, previously enjoying the devotion and patronage of local communities, into Chola state religion through their marriage to the great *bhakti* gods, notably Śiva: Nabokov, *Religion Against the Self* (2000), p. 27.

19. Brooks, "Encountering the Hindu 'Other'" (1992).

20. Dyczkowski, "Kubjikā, Kālī, Tripurā and Trika" (2000), p. 1 n. 2.

21. Gupta and Gombrich, "Kings, Power and the Goddess" (1986), p. 123.

22. Avalon, *Principles of Tantra* (1960), p. 1.

23. Clémentin-Ojha, *Le Trident sur le palais* (1999), p. 99.

24. Ibid., pp. 66–67.

25. Ibid., pp. 237, 240. In his commentary on *Manu Smṛti* 2.1, Kullūka Bhaṭṭa states that revelation (*śruti*) is twofold: Vedic and Tantric.

26. Hudson, "The Śrīmad Bhāgavata Purāṇa in Stone" (1995), pp. 147, 155, with reference to *śūdra* kings of Kancipuram. The *Jayākhya Saṃhitā*, a foundational Pāñcarātra source on this initiation, dates from the seventh to tenth century: Flood, "Purification of the Body" (2000), p. 509. The Narasiṃha *mantra* and *nyāsa* are central to the secret royal *navakalevara* ritual of the Jagannātha temple of Puri: Eschmann et al., "Formation of the Jagannātha Triad," p. 171.

27. Willis, "Religious and Royal Patronage," p. 55; and Pinch, *Peasants and Monks*, p. 97. See also below, chap. 5, nn. 165–67, for an eighteenth-century account of Vaiṣṇava "Tantric" practices.

28. For example, the same members of the high-ranking "Sanskritized" Tamil castes who publicly stigmatized possession rituals at goddess temples as "superstitious" and "inferior" were active participants in those very rituals: Nabokov, *Religion Against the Self*, p. 4.

29. Lévi, *La Doctrine du sacrifice*, 2nd ed. (1898; 1966), p. 107.

30. Shulman, *Hungry God* (1993), pp. 16, 35, 144.

31. Sanderson, "Meaning in Tantric Ritual" (1995), p. 79; id., "Purity and Power" (1985), pp. 203, 214 n. 108; and id., "Śaivism and the Tantric Tradition" (1988), pp. 664–66.

32. Sanderson, "Meaning in Tantric Ritual," p. 83 n. 244; citing *Jayadrathayāmala*, fourth hexad, fols. 206r7–209r (vīratāṇḍavaḥ); and *Kālīkulakramārcana* of Vimalaprabodha, fols. 18r5–19v2 (see bibliography); and id., "Purity and Power" (1985), p. 214 n. 110; citing *Tantrāloka* 13.301, 320–21b; and *Mahānāyaprakāśa* 1.30.

33. Sanderson, "Śaivism and the Tantric Tradition" (1988), pp. 669–79.

34. Full- and new-moon nights, as well as the lunar eighth and fourteenth, according to most sources, including *Kaulajñānanirṇaya* (KJñN) 21.8b (in *Kaulajñānanirṇaya and Some Minor Texts*, ed. Bagchi [1934]); and *Hevajra Tantra* 1.7.20.

35. The term *pīṭha* also refers to the base or chasing of a Śiva *liṅga*, as well as to the vulva. The term *pīṭha-nāyikā*, "heroine of the *pīṭha*," applied to a premenstrual girl of fourteen who impersonates Durgā during that goddess's festival, seems to presuppose all three senses of the term: Monier-Williams, *Sanskrit-English Dictionary* (1899; 1984), s.v. "pīṭha," p. 629.

36. My reading of the term *dravyam* as "fluid" may appear to be idiosyncratic, given that the standard reading of the term is simply "substance." However, as a derivate of the root *dru*, "flow, run," *dravyam* may in fact be read as a gerundive, as "that which is to, which ought to flow," which is entirely appropriate in the contexts in which it is used in Tantric sources.

37. For example, in *Tantrāloka* 29.24 (for editions, see bibliography), which states that in the natural body of the Female Messenger (Dūtī) there is obtained an excess of the "real thing" (*adhika-sadbhāva*).

38. See bibliography for editions and translations of the KSS. The eleventh-century *Rasārṇava*, which calls itself a "Tantra," describes this type of ascent in its concluding verses: 18.221–27. See bibliography for editions.

39. *Rudrayāmala Tantra* 17.151b–52b. For edition, see below, n. 102.

40. Referred to by Geoffrey Samuel with reference to Tibetan Buddhist society as "shamanic" and "clerical" specialists: *Civilized Shamans* (1993), pp. 7–10.

41. In Śākta-Śaiva traditions only: in such purely Śākta traditions as the Krama, the source of the Yoginī clans is the Goddess.

42. Sharma, *Temple of Chaunsaṭha-yoginī* (1978), p. 5.

43. *Mānasollāsa* 2.17–20, vv. 1031–145: *Mānasollāsa*, ed. Srigondekar (1925, 1939, 1961), vol. 1, pp. 122–32. See below, chap. 5, n. 35.

44. There are two principal emic perspectives on Tantra in present-day south India: those of the householder practitioner whose goal is liberation, and those of the popular Tantric specialist whose goal is pragmatic control over supernatural entities. These perspectives and related practices are discussed in chap. 5, parts 8 and 9; and in chap. 9, parts 1 and 2.

45. This applies to Buddhist as well as Hindu Tantra. On the latter, Kværne ("On the Concept of Sahaja" [1975], p. 133) states: "In fact, the uniqueness of Buddhist tantricism is not . . . to be found in the mystic experience to which the yogin aspires, but in the *ritual* which—as a 'means-of-approach' (*upāya*), i.e., as a preliminary procedure—plays a fundamental part in the whole Tantric scheme of salvation."

46. Sanderson, "Purity and Power," p. 201. See below, chap. 8, n. 177.

47. Sanderson, "Meaning in Tantric Ritual," pp. 22, 25; and id., "Śaivism and the Tantric Traditions," pp. 670–89. See below, chap. 5, n. 171.

48. The classic sources on Tamil Śrīvidyā are Brooks, *Auspicious Wisdom* (1992); and id., *Secret of the Three Cities* (1990). On the redundancy of much of high Tantric ritual vis-à-vis Smārta ritual, see Sanderson, "Meaning in Tantric Ritual," pp. 27–53.

49. Houellebecq, *Les Particules élémentaires* (2000), p. 108.

50. Padoux, "Tantrism" (1986), p. 273.

51. *Tantrāloka*, ed. Shastri et al. (1918–38); reprint, ed. Dwivedi and Rastogi, 8 vols. (1987). See bibliography for translations.

52. Dyczkowski, "Kubjikā, Kālī, Tripurā and Trika," p. 45 n. 129.

53. Sanderson, "Meaning in Tantric Ritual," p. 46.

54. As Hélène Brunner has argued convincingly, this text of the *Netra Tantra* itself was originally a work on demonology, onto which was grafted, for the most part clumsily, a treatise on the god Amṛteśa and the *netra* mantra: Brunner, "Tantra du Nord" (1974), p. 127.

55. Sanderson, "Doctrines of the Mālinīvijayottaratantra" (1992), pp. 293, 306, 308.

56. My categorization here may give rise to some confusion, given the fact that the term "Tantraśāstra" is one that is also applied for the *entire* Tantric corpus, including both root or core ritual texts and theoretical exegesis. I intend it in the same limited sense as is found in the compound *mantraśāstra*, "treatises on mantras."

57. See especially Urban, "The Extreme Orient" (1999).

58. Smith, *Reflections* (1989), p. 126; citing the *Āśvalayana Śrauta Sūtra* 1.1.3.

59. This is not to say that Tantras are wholly bereft of internal exegesis: Tantras like the *Kubjikāmata* are rich in metaphysical speculation; and even the KJñN contains speculative passages.

60. Brunner states that the earliest Āgamas may date from as early as the sixth or seventh centuries C.E.: Brunner, Oberhammer, and Padoux, *Tāntrikābhidhānakośa I* (2000), p. 26. However, in the absence of any solid historical evidence to support such dating, there is no reason to date them any earlier than foundational works of the Hindu Śākta corpus—the Yāmalas and early Tantras—i.e., the eighth century C.E. On the dating of the Pāñcarātra Saṃhitās, see above, n. 26.

61. It is the Sanskrit cognate of the Latin *vir* that has the same semantic field.

62. Sanderson's ("Meaning in Tantric Ritual," esp. pp. 23, 79–83) subtle and detailed account of the Kaula and Tantric perspectives of the principal Śaiva cults of medieval India employs different criteria than I do in this study, concentrating as it does on married seekers of liberation, as opposed to nonmarried seekers of supernatural powers.

63. KJñN 11.5b, 7b (employing the vernacularized term *kaulave*).

64. See, for example, TĀ 29.4 and 35.31–34, discussed in Skora, "Consciousness" (2001), pp. 377–78, 391–92.

65. Muller-Ortega, *Triadic Heart* (1989), pp. 58–63.

66. On the origins of this triad of goddesses, see below, chap. 8, n. 87.

67. For a brief history, see Sanderson, "Śaivism: Trika Śaivism" and "Śaivism: Śaivism in Kashmir" (1986). Cf. Dyczkowski, "Kubjikā, Kālī, Tripurā and Trika," pp. 27–28.

68. *Kulārṇava Tantra* 3.7b (ed. Vidyaratna [1965; 1975]).

69. For a discussion, see Dyczkowski, *Canon* (1988), pp. 123–25. See below, chap. 4, nn. 38–41.

70. Thus the *Kulārṇava Tantra* 3.7a states: "The five transmissions arose from my

five mouths." The KJñN 16.10a speaks of "five streams" (*pañcasrotas*), a term first encountered in the Āgamas of the Śaivāsiddhānta, for its lines of transmission.

71. Dyczkowski, *Canon*, pp. 64, 168–69 nn. 54–57; citing the TĀ, *Saṭsāhasrasaṃhitā*, *Brahmayāmala*, *Jayadrathayāmala*, and other sources. Cf. *Kubjikāmata* 3.7–10 (ed. Goudriaan and Schoterman [1988]).

72. Lidke, "Goddess" (2001), p. 2 and passim. Cf. Dyczkowski, "Kubjikā, Kālī, Tripurā and Trika," pp. 42–44.

73. TĀ 29.127b–29a. For discussion, see also White, *Alchemical Body* (1996), pp. 79, 137; Dyczkowski, *Canon*, pp. 60, 62, 82; and Skora, "Consciousness," pp. 289–90.

74. Monier-Williams, *Sanskrit-English Dictionary*, s.v. "kula," p. 294.

75. *Parātriśika Vivaraṇa* of Abhinavagupta, ed. and trans. Singh (1989), p. 594; cited in Dyczkowski, "Kubjikā, Kālī, Tripurā and Trika," p. 1 n. 2. Cf. HT 1.4.10. See also *Tantrāloka, Abhinavagupta, Luce dei tantra*, trans. Gnoli (1999), p. 549 n. 1.

76. For a recent historical and theoretical overview, see Tambs-Lyche, *Power, Profit, and Poetry*, pp. 64–92.

77. Weinberger-Thomas, *Cendres* (1996), pp. 155–57.

78. Dyczkowski, "Kubjikā, Kālī, Tripurā and Trika," p. 1 n. 2; and White, "Tantra in Practice" (2000), p. 14.

79. The hierarchy of units in the Jaina *saṅgha* uses a terminology that is reminiscent of the lineage structure of the earlier tribes—*gaṇa*, *kula*, *śākhā*, *anvaya*, and *gaccha:* Thapar, *Ancient Indian Social History* (1978), p. 87.

80. These are summarized in Bagchi's introduction to the *Kaulajñānanirṇaya* (pp. 36–39) and numerous other sources.

81. In the introduction to her translation of the *Vātūlanātha Sūtra*, Lilian Silburn (*Vātūlanātha Sūtra*, rev. 2nd ed., trans. Silburn [1995], p. 8) proposes a more metaphysical reading of the term, as it is found in this and other exegetical Tantric works: ". . . the Light of Consciousness always reveals itself to itself, without limitation or differentiation. Whether the world does not appear in it (*akula*) or manifests itself in it (*kula*). . . . Consciousness remains one in its essence, and is unaffected by this alternation."

82. KJñN 1.1, 14.89a, 18.7a.

83. KJñN 16.14b. For a discussion, see below, chap. 3, n. 72.

84. *Netra Tantra* 19.80b–81a (in *Netratantram*, ed. Dwivedi [1985], p. 171). The *Netra Tantra* places this statement in the context of a discussion of Skanda and other Seizers of infants: on these, see below, chap. 2, part 5.

85. *Netra Tantra* 19.71, with the commentary of Kṣemarāja, whose discussion of Yoginī "types" intersects that of several other Tantric texts, including the KJñN. Such a rite, to "the servant of the fever demon who kills fevers," consisting of a blood offering on a Śiva *liṅga*, is described in detail in KSS 12.4.215–19.

86. Apfel-Marglin, *Wives of the God-King* (1985), pp. 51, 57.

87. Ibid., p. 58.

88. *Manu Smṛti* 9.32–51; *Mānava Dharma Śāstra* 9.9–10; *Aitareya Brāhmaṇa* 7.13.7–8 (see bibliography for editions). Cf. Daniel, *Fluid Signs* (1984), p. 163.

89. The model was, in fact, one based on the observation of animals, and bovines in particular, throughout the ancient world: Jöchle, "Traces of Embryo Transfer" (1984).

90. See below, chap. 3, part 7.

91. Indeed, one often has the impression that the role and preponderance of feminine sexual fluids gradually "drowns" those of males in later systems, contributing to the later development of the South Asian "cultural disease" of male sexual disorders, *guptā rog:* see White, *Alchemical Body*, pp. 339–42.

92. See above, n. 77; and Tambs-Lyche, *Power, Profit, and Poetry*, p. 73 and nn. 18, 188, 271.

93. Ibid., pp. 61, 271; see also pp. 74, 82–83, 91–92, 107, 111.

94. A compelling description and analysis of this ritual is found in Nabokov, *Religion Against the Self*, pp. 125–50, esp. pp. 144–45.

95. Dyczkowski, "Kubjikā, Kālī, Tripurā and Trika," p. 30 n. 82. The Puranic traditions of Śiva as Ardhanarīśvara, the androgynous "God Who Is Half-Female," never refer to him as emitting both male and female seed, or both semen and menstrual blood.

96. Sanderson, "Śaivism and the Tantric Traditions," p. 679.

97. Dyczkowski, "Kubjikā, Kālī, Tripurā and Trika," p. 17 n. 36.

98. Bagchi's dating is based on paleographical comparisons with earlier Nepalese manuscripts held in the Cambridge University Library and analyzed by Bendell in his *Catalogue of the Cambridge Mss.*, published in 1883.

99. Heilijgers-Seelen, *System of the Five Cakras* (1994), pp. 9, 33; and Dyczkowski, "Kubjikā, Kālī, Tripurā and Trika," p. 28.

100. TĀ 1.7.

101. For a summary of this early literature and its dating, see Brunner, Oberhammer, and Padoux, *Tāntrikābhidhānakośa*, pp. 26–30; and Sanderson, "Remarks" (2002), 1–2.

102. This is the *Rudrayāmala Tantra* that was edited by the Yogatantra Department of the Sampurnanand Sanskrit University in Benares (see bibliography), as opposed to a lost earlier work that is cited by Abhinavagupta and the *Jayadrathayāmala*. See below, chap. 7, n. 86, for the relative dates of these works.

103. *Yoni Tantra*, ed. Schoterman (1980). Dated on the basis of its enumeration of the ten Mahāvidyā goddesses (at 3.15–16), a late configuration.

104. *Kaulāvalī-Nirṇayaḥ*, ed. Avalon (1929). Dated on the basis of the numerous Tantras that it cites in its opening verses (KĀN 1.2–13). See Goudriaan and Gupta, *Hindu Tantric and Śākta Literature* (1981), p. 141.

105. The Mallas ruled in the Kathmandu Valley from the thirteenth to the eighteenth century, with the greatest flowering of Tantric culture occurring between the fifteenth and eighteenth centuries: Toffin, *Le Palais et le temple*, pp. 30, 127, 193. It was in the eleventh century, however, that Tantra was first introduced into the valley, since it was then that the earliest Kubjikā manuscripts were either brought to, or composed or copied, and archived there: Dyczkowski, "Kubjikā, Kālī, Tripurā and Trika," pp. 22–23.

106. KJñN 16.11a–14b.

107. Sadāśiva and Śrīkaṇṭha are names of Śiva in the Śaivasiddhānta.

108. Here I have emended *trāyate* to *trāyame*.

109. KJñN 16.15a–20a.

110. Here, I have emended *kāmarūpī* to *kāmarūpe*.

111. KJñN 16.20b–22a.

112. KJñN 16.38ab.

113. This difficult passage (KJñN 16.38b) is nearly identical to verse 22b of the same chapter. The former reads "avyaktagocaraṃ tena kulairjātam mahākṛpe," whereas the latter reads "avyaktaṃ gocaraṃ tena kulajātaṃ mama priye." Clearly, the compiler or copyist of this text was doing some cutting and pasting to make these narrative transitions.

114. KJñN 16.39a–40b, 44b–46a.

115. Jayā and Vijayā are identified with the goddess Durgā (and Kālī) as early as the so-called "Durgā Stotra" of the MBh (appen. I, no. 1, line 11: for editions, see bibliography): see below, chap. 2, n. 88.

116. Nepali legend holds that this goddess was brought from Ujjain to the Kathmandu Valley by a king named Vikramāditya in 426 B.C.E.: Toffin, *Le Palais et le temple*, pp. 176–78.

117. KJñN 16.40b, 46a. A similar line of transmission is detailed in KJñN 22.1b–3a: Harasiddhi, Vināyaka, Skanda, Mahākāla, the Yoginī Kālikā, Nandi, Bhaṭṭakā, Droṇakā, Vijayā, and the "highly illustrious Mothers, the six Yoginīs." This appears to be a reference to the six Mothers or Yoginīs of later Kubjikā traditions. On these, see below, chap. 7, n. 107; and chap. 8, nn. 64, 65.

118. KJñN 16.41a–43b.

119. It may be the case that standing skeletal males figured on the pedestals of certain Yoginīs at Bheraghat, who, in a heightened state of sexual excitement, are intended to be seen as an indication of the ritual of *maithuna:* Dehejia, *Yoginī Cult and Temples* (1986), p. 64. On the other hand, these may simply be early Hindu versions of the common Buddhist Tantric sprites, known as *citipatis*, figured together with Yoginī-type females on Buddhist edifices in present-day Nepal and Bhutan. An excellent eighteenth-century Tibetan Buddhist *thangka* depicting such a couple is found in Béguin, *Art ésotérique de l'Himâlaya* (1990), plate 54 and p. 106.

120. KJñN 16.46b–48b. "Fish-Belly" refers to the means by which the Kaula scripture was recovered by Bhairava in the form of a fisherman. This myth is discussed below, in chap. 4, part 3.

121. Silburn, *Kuṇḍalinī* (1983), p. 76. I have argued elsewhere that in addition to these meanings, "Fish-Belly" is also a reference to hathayogic diaphragmatic retention, a practice better known as *kumbhaka:* White, *Alchemical Body*, pp. 222–29. See below, chap. 4, nn. 53, 58, 65.

122. KJñN 21.5a–7b.

Chapter 2

1. A growing number of scholars are arguing that these cults were originally controlled by women. These include Miranda Shaw (*Passionate Enlightenment*, 1994, passim) for early Buddhist Tantra; Caldwell (*Oh Terrifying Mother*, pp. 195–251) for cults of Bhadrakālī in Kerala; and Assayag (*La Colère de la déesse décapitée*, pp. 189–200, 265–88) for the Jōgammas in Karnataka.

2. Here, I am referring to haṭha yoga, the combination of postures and breath control that was innovated, for the most part, by Gorakhnāth (Gorakṣanātha) in the twelfth to thirteenth century C.E.: on this date, see White, *Alchemical Body*, pp. 90–101.

3. Mallmann, *Enseignements* (1963), p. 3. Her dating is based on comparisons with passages from *Viṣṇudharmottara Purāṇa* 3, *Bṛhat Saṃhitā* 58, and the *Hayaśīrṣa Pañcarātra*. A passage found in several manuscript versions of the *Harivaṃśa*, but omitted from the critical edition, mentions "a Yoginī": appen. 1, no. 35, line 27, in *Harivaṃśa*, (1969–71), ed. Vaidya, 2 vols., vol. 2, p. 487. See below, n. 87; and chap. 7, n. 1. The same verse also contains the two seed mantras, *hrīṃ* and *śrīṃ*, an indication that this is a relatively late interpolation. See below, chap. 6, n. 19

4. *Caryāgīti* 4.1–2, in *Caryāgīti* (1986), ed. Kværne, pp. 86–91. See below, n. 9.

5. Inden ("Hierarchies of Kings" [1982], p. 99) defines "early medieval" as the period between the collapse of the Cāḷukya kingdom around 750 C.E. and the establishment of the Delhi sultanate early in the thirteenth century. The Gupta age ran from the fourth to sixth century C.E.; however, its "classical pattern" evolved in north India through the end of the seventh century: Thapar, *A History of India* (1968), vol. 1, p. 136.

6. Sergent, *Genèse* (1997), pp. 121–23.

7. Ibid., pp. 123–24.

8. Ibid., p. 124.

9. Tiwari, *Goddess Cults* (1988), p. 183. The Sanskrit word for "kiss" (*cumba*) is phonetically close to the term used for the secret signs (*chumma, chomma*) employed by Tantric sectarians to recognize one another.

10. Sergent, *Genèse*, p. 140.

11. Parpola, *Deciphering* (1997), p. 261 and fig. 14.35; and id., *Sky-Garment* (1985), pp. 121, 151. This seal (DK 6847) is held in the National Museum of Pakistan.

12. Parpola, *Sky-Garment*, p. 84; citing Kirfel, *Der Kosmographie* (1920), pp. 139, 281.

13. Erndl, *Victory to the Mother* (1993), pp. 4, 39. The shrine of Nainā Devī also enshrines three portable *piṇḍīs*, but one of these represents the male Gaṇeśa (p. 54). Other goddesses in this ensemble are worshiped as individual *piṇḍīs* (pp. 50–52).

14. Although the term "Dryad" is a quite literal translation of the Sanskrit Vṛkṣakā, another class of beings identified with trees, I use it to translate Yakṣa, following an old scholarly convention, and because the Yakṣas as well, even if their (contested) etymology does not support it, are also closely identified with trees, and more important to the Hindu pantheon than the Vṛkṣakās. For a discussion, see Tiwari, *Goddess Cults*, pp. 22–24; and below, nn. 133, 195.

15. Hymns to these three are found in AV 7.46–48: for editions, see bibliography. The *Āpastamba Śrauta Sūtra* (3.9.4–5) prescribes offerings to Rākā if the sacrificer desires a son, Sinīvālī for abundant cattle, or Kuhū for general prosperity: Smith, "Indra's Curse" (1992), pp. 27–29. Smith hypothesizes that these offerings were derived from an independent prototype that women originally performed for themselves. Another Vedic goddess associated with childbirth, abundance, and (sometimes) Indra was Puraṃdhi: RV 2.38.10; 4.26.7; 4.27.2. See bibliography for editions.

16. Smith, "Indra's Curse," pp. 37–38.

17. Jamison, *Sacrificed Wife* (1996), pp. 63–64; citing the *Mānava Śrauta Sūtra* 6.1.2.4–12 and *Maitrāyaṇī Saṃhitā* 2.7.6.

18. Described in detail in Jamison, *Sacrificed Wife*, pp. 240–45. The Sākamedha and Aśvamedha are *śrauta* rites; the Gavāmayanam is a *sattra* rite. According to Shulman (*Tamil Temple Myths* [1980], p. 227), "having three mothers" is the "natural" meaning of *tryambaka*.

19. According to Tiwari (*Goddess Cults*, p. 85), Ambikā as Rudra's "sister" (in *Vājasaneyi Saṃhitā* 3.57a and *Taittirīya Saṃhitā* 1.8.6) is the earliest forerunner of that god's later relationship, in the form of Śiva, with the Goddess as consort. The *Śatapatha Brāhmaṇa* (2.6.2.13–14) calls Ambikā a "dispenser of happiness" and enjoins maidens to call upon her brother Tryambaka, who is "the fragrant bestower of husbands": Coburn, *Devī-Māhātmya* (1984), p. 102. Ambikā is portrayed in the *Taittirīya Brāhmaṇa* (ibid., p. 214) as a cruel goddess and killer. It is only later that she is presented as Rudra's spouse.

20. The molehill (*akhara:* animal's lair) and mole (*akhu:* Rudra's emblem) both have probable sexual connotations, representing the female sexual organ: Jamison, *Sacrificed Wife*, p. 245.

21. *Āpastamba Śrauta Sūtra* 20.17.12, translated in Jamison, *Sacrificed Wife*, p. 243. Mantras against disease-causing demons are addressed to Tryambaka and Garuḍa in the *Yogataraṅginī:* Filliozat, *Kumāratantra* (1937), p. 64.

22. MBh 5.187.18–40, 5.193.4.

23. Jamison, *Sacrificed Wife*, p. 244. See below, chap. 7. n. 107.

24. RV 8.91.1–7, in ibid., p. 240.

25. RV 1.133.2–3, 10.155.4.

26. Hiltebeitel, *Ritual of Battle* (1976), p. 180. A list of goddesses in the circa fourth-century A.D. Jaina *Aṅgavijja* includes the name of Apālā, together with Aṇāditā, Airāṇī, and Sālimāliṇī. According to V. S. Agrawal and Moti Candra, these may be the Greek and Persian goddesses Pallas Athena, Anāhitā, Irene, and Selene: introduction to *Aṅgavijja*, pp. 53–54, 78, 83; cited in Tiwari, *Goddess Cults*, p. 12.

27. Feldhaus, *Water and Womanhood* (1995), pp. 41, 48. They are also referred to as *paryā*, a word that is etymologically related to the English word "fairy."

28. Ibid., pp. 54–55. At one of their shrines, located in the courtyard of the Mahālakṣmī temple in Kolhapur, they are named. At least four of them have the name of (female) animals: Matsyī, Kurmī, Karkarī, and Makarī (p. 63 n. 31).

29. The identification of a major river with a goddess by this name extends well beyond India's borders: the Mekong River of Southeast Asia is a cognate of the Indian "Mother Ganges," Mā Gaṅgā.

30. Kurtz, *All the Mothers Are One* (1992). I am unable (because unqualified) to follow Kurtz, however, in his analysis of the psychological effect that the multiple female caretakers of Indian child rearing have on children's image of the mother.

31. Tiwari, *Goddess Cults*, p. 23. For a modern continuation of this tradition, see Sontheimer, *Pastoral Deities*, (1989), p. 34. See below, part 6.

32. Generated from the prefix *ku-* plus a nominalized form of the intensificative of the root *nam*, "to bow, bend, subject, submit oneself."

33. RV 10.136.1–7. This is presented as a hymn *to* the Keśins (Agni, Sūrya, and Vāyu), from the seven sons of a seer named Vātaraśana ("Wind-Girt"), who mention themselves in verse 2: *Rig Veda*, ed. Nooten and Holland (1994), p. 557.

34. Monier-Williams glosses their name as *ap* + *sṛ*, "going in the waters or between the waters of the clouds": *Sanskrit-English Dictionary*, s.v. "apsaras," p. 59.

35. *Śatapatha Brāhmaṇa* 11.5.1.1–13.

36. RV 7.104.17a, 20a, 22ab, translated in *The Rig Veda*, trans. O'Flaherty (1981), p. 294.

37. See above, n. 17. Cf. RV 10.16.6, 10.165.2; and AV 7.64.1–2, discussed in Filliozat, *Kumāratantra*, p. 80; and *Śatapatha Brāhmaṇa* 13.5.2.4. In the most sexually charged ritual of the entire Vedic corpus, the senior queen's ritual copulation with the sacrificial horse, the priestly dialogues consistently refer to sexual organs of both the parties involved as "little birds" (*śakuntaka, śakuntika*): *Vājasaneyi Saṃhitā* 23.22–23, discussed in Jamison, *Sacrificed Wife*, p. 70.

38. *Atharva Veda* 2.2.1–5, cited in Tiwari, *Goddess Cults*, p. 163. As Tiwari indicates in his detailed analysis (p. 161), this is one of three Atharvavedic hymns referred to by the *Kauśika Sūtra*, the others being AV 6.111 and 8.6. The *Atharvaveda Pariśiṣṭa* entitled *gaṇa-mālā*, the "garland of the host," refers to these as well as AV 4.20 and gives an alternative name of the group as *mātṛgaṇa*, the "host of mothers."

39. *Atharva-veda-saṃhitā*, trans. Whitney, (1905; reprint, 1984), vol. 1, p. 39; and Tiwari, *Goddess Cults*, p. 167.

40. AV 4.38.1–4. Some of the discussion that follows is taken from White, "Dogs Die" (1989).

41. Pāṇini (3.3.70), discussed in Lüders, "Das Würfelspiel im alten Indien" (1907), pp. 26–28.

42. White, "Dogs Die," p. 294.

43. *Āpastamba Gṛhya Sūtra* 7.18.1–2; *Hiraṇyakeśin Gṛhya Sūtra* 2.2.7.1–5; *Pāraskara Gṛhya Sūtra* 1.16.24–25; and *Mantrapāṭha* 2.16.1–11 (see bibliography for editions). I choose to see the use of the term *kumāra* in the ritual texts as a reference to the boy;

others see it as a proper name and a reference to the god Skanda-Kumāra, who emerges in the MBh as the leader of the demons known as Seizers (*grahas*). See White, "Dogs Die," pp. 294–96; and Agrawala, *Skanda-Kārttikeya* (1967), p. 15.

44. RV 10.161.1 and AV 2.9.1 and 16.5.1 refer to disease-causing demons (*grāhis*) and demonesses (*grahīs*). Cf. RV 10.162 and AV 2.25.

45. *Śrīlaghukālacakratantrarāja* 2.152 (with the Vimalprabhā commentary), discussed in Wallace, "Buddhist Tantric Medicine in the Kālacakratantra," (1995), p. 162. Similar data are found in the Tibetan translation of the circa seventh-century C.E. *Aṣṭāṅgahṛdaya* of Vāgbhaṭṭa (6.3.40–59); nearly identical is the Tibetan version of the *Amṛtāhṛdayāṣṭāṅga-guhyopadeśatantra* (3.73.1–36): Filliozat, *Kumāratantra*, pp. 133–42.

46. MBh 1.114.49–54.

47. Hiltebeitel, *Ritual of Battle*, p. 145.

48. MBh 12.99.45. Cf. *Kaṭha Upaniṣad* 1.25. This is an idea that has persisted down to the modern period among the Rajputs. In the words of Forbes, "Like the virgins of Valhalla, the choosers of the slain, the Upsurâs [Apsarasas] continually hover above the field of battle, ready to convey to Swerga [*svarga:* heaven] the warriors who pass to heaven through its carnage": *Râs-Mâlâ* (1924), p. 425.

49. Rabe, "Sexual Imagery" (1996), nn. 106, 107.

50. MBh 3.207.2–3.219.43. Skanda appears on the coinage of the Kushan Huviṣka: Rana, *Study* (1995), p. 21. One of the earliest standing images of the Kṛttikās, dating from the year 11 C.E. and held at the Mathura Archaeological Museum (no. F. 38), shows them accompanied by Skanda, who is holding a spear: Schastok, *Śāmalājī Sculptures* (1985), p. 64.

51. MBh 6.10.33–35.

52. RV 6.50.7. For additional Rigvedic references to Agni's multiple mothers, see Shulman, *Tamil Temple Myths*, pp. 227, 254, and notes.

53. Harper, *Iconography* (1989), p. 55.

54. Joshi, *Mātṛkās* (1986), pp. 80–83. For further discussion of the origins and early history of the Seven Mothers, see Tiwari, *Goddess Cults*, pp. 103, 106–7, 110–11, 126–27, 131. For changes in iconographic conventions at sixth-century Rajasthani sites, see Schastok, *Śāmalājī Sculptures*, p. 79.

55. Meister, "Regional Variations" (1986), pp. 244–45. See also Coburn, *Devī-Māhātmya*, pp. 313–30; and Harper, *Iconography*, pp. 75, 84, 148.

56. MBh 3.214.7–17.

57. MBh 3.215.16. Shulman (*Tamil Temple Myths*, p. 245) takes these to be the Kṛttikās. A similar compound is found in the late-sixth-century C.E. inscription at Deogarh Fort (Jhansi Dist., U.P.): see below, n. 113. This inscription is engraved directly above a niche containing a panel of the "standard" Seven Mothers, flanked by Vīrabhadra and Gaṇapati: Tiwari, *Goddess Cults*, pp. 101–2. In the earliest Tamil version of the Skanda birth myth, six of the seven sages' wives cook and eat the infant: Shulman, *Tamil Temple Myths*, pp. 248–49.

58. MBh 3.215.18.

59. For example, a sexually frenzied Kālī is calmed by the sight of the two infant gods, Gaṇeśa and Nandikeśan, and milk begins to flow in her breasts. In some variants Śiva himself becomes the baby, making his breastfeeding the equivalent of his sexual penetration; both calm the goddess: Caldwell, *Oh Terrifying Mother*, pp. 169–70.

60. See below, chap. 3, part 7.

61. MBh 3.215.22–23. She is explicitly named Lohitāyanī in MBh 3.219.39.

62. Naigameya appears to be an alloform of both the Vedic Nejameṣa and the

Naigameṣa of the medical tradition. As for the Vedic figure, Nejameṣa, he is not goat-headed and is moreover portrayed as flying through the air! Whereas Nejameṣa—like the Jaina Naigameṣa and the Buddhist Nemeso—is a granter of male offspring, the Naigameṣa of *Suśruta Saṃhitā* (SS) 6.37.6 is a male Seizer who harms male children, albeit created to protect the infant Skanda. On this, see Winternitz, "Nejamesha, Naigamesha, Nemeso" (1895), pp. 149–55; Filliozat, *Kumāratantra*, p. 81; Agrawala, *Skanda-Kārttikeya*, p. 80; Joshi, *Mātṛkās*, p. 41; and Coomaraswamy, *Yakṣas* (1928–31; reprint, 1971), pp. 12 n. 2, 25.

63. Parpola, *Deciphering*, pp. 237–39, who also provides several citations from fifth- to third-century B.C.E. *gṛhya sūtra* literature and reproduces a stunning first-century C.E. Buddhist frieze of the goat-headed "Lord Nemeṣo."

64. Joshi, *Mātṛkās*, pp. 20, 69–70. Agarwala ("Mātṛkā Reliefs" [1971], pp. 81–82) identifies the head on the jar's top as that of a ram (*meṣa*), and that of the goddess as a goat's head, and opines that she is either Harītī (see below, nn. 241–51) or a female counterpart to the male Naigameṣa. The panel is reproduced as fig. 8 in Agrawal: the goddess looks more like a great bird than a goat- or lion-headed figure to me.

65. Harper, *Iconography*, pp. 68–69.

66. Schastok, *Śāmalājī Sculptures*, p. 87 and fig. 132.

67. Agarwala, "Kṛttikā Cult" (1969), pp. 56–57, plate 23, fig. 3. Cf. Gaston, *Śiva* (1982), pp. 124–30.

68. "Rare Bust of a Yakṣiṇī Found" (1990), p. 8; and Agrawala, *Skanda-Kārttikeya*, p. 51 and plate 12. A set of two bells was part of Skanda's early iconography: MBh 3.220.18–19. A male goat-headed figure, also from Mathura, bears the inscription "Bhagavā Nemeso": see above, n. 62, and below, n. 244.

69. On the connections between Skanda and Khaṇḍobā, see Sontheimer, *Pastoral Deities*, p. 155. On Malla's representation as a goat's head, see Stanley, "Capitulation of Maṇi" (1989), pp. 275–77 and plate 21.

70. *Kātyāyana Śrauta Sūtra* 9.2.6 with the commentary of Sarala. For this and other sources on the soma-*grahas*, see Dharmadhikari, ed., *Yajñāyudhānī* (1989), pp. 49–54.

71. MBh 1.60.22–23 names Śākha, Viśākha, and Naigameṣa as *sons* of Skanda.

72. MBh 3.217.1–2a.

73. Literally, they "resolved upon Viśākha's paternity": "viśākhaṃ taṃ pitṛtve saṃkalpayan."

74. MBh 3.217.2b–4a, 6ab. As Coburn (*Devī-Māhātmya*, p. 320) notes, the text is ambiguous about the origins of the Daughters, saying first that they were "born from the impact of Indra's thunderbolt (MBh 3.217.2a), and later that they were born of the Fire called Tapas" (6a).

75. Literally, they "resolved upon Skanda's sonship": "saṃkalpya putratve skandaṃ."

76. MBh 3.217.9.

77. There are thus three goat-headed figures in this account: Agni-Naigameya, Viśākha, and Skanda himself.

78. MBh 3.215.10–12, 3.217.10–15, 3.211.2. For discussion, see Harper, *Iconography*, p. 96; and Coburn, *Devī-Māhātmya*, p. 152.

79. Monier-Williams, *Sanskrit-English Dictionary*, s.v. "palāla," p. 609; and "halīmaka," p. 1293. Cf. *Kāśyapa Saṃhitā*, Cikitsā Sthāna 4.1–8, in *Kāśyapa Saṃhitā* (1996), ed. Tewari, pp. 179–80. Hereafter, KS.

80. This is the feminine form of Dhṛtarāṣṭra, which is the name of the father of the Kauravas in the MBh. However, the Epic also assigns the name Dhṛtarāṣṭra to a serpent and a Gandharva.

81. MBh 1.60.54–59. Kākī is the name given to the demoness later identified as

Pūtanā (a female Seizer: see below, part D) slain by the infant Kṛṣṇa whom she had attempted to kill by offering him her poisoned breast: Gadon, "Hindu Goddess" (1997), p. 296.

82. MBh 3.219.40ab.

83. *Angavijja*, chaps. 51, 58; cited in Joshi, *Mātṛkās*, p. 61. Cf. Tiwari, *Goddess Cults*, p. 6 n. 28.

84. *Mānava Gṛhya Sūtra* 2.13–15, cited in Rana, *Study*, p. 18.

85. This is Tiwari's (*Goddess Cults*, p. 22) reading of *āryavṛddhā* in *Bāṇa's Kādambarī*, ed. Kale, 4th ed. (1968), p. 120.

86. Tiwari, *Goddess Cults*, p. 102.

87. *Harivaṃśa*, appen. 1, no. 8, lines 1, 2, 4, 35, 39; and appen. 1, no. 35, line 27. These are considered to be late interpolations; however, the former continues, without repetition, a praise of the goddess included in the critical edition (which ends at 47.54) and is found in every recension and manuscript version of the critical edition, except the Malayalam: *Harivaṃśa*, ed. Vaidya, vol. 1, pp. xxiv, xxx, xxxi. See also Couture and Schmid, "*Harivaṃśa*," p. 177; and above, n. 3. On the dating of the *Harivaṃśa*, see id., p. 185.

88. MBh 6.23.4–11, in appen. 1, no. 1, lines 4, 7–9, 11, 15, 22. This hymn immediately precedes the *Bhagavad Gītā*. It is found in the K_2, K_4, B, D_a, D_n, and D_2 manuscripts of the MBh.

89. MBh 3.218.23–30.

90. MBh 3.218.43–49.

91. On the relationship between the Vedic Kuhū, the Epic Ekānaṃśā ("One and Indivisible") and the black Kālī, see Couture and Schmid, "*Harivaṃśa*," pp. 179, 186 n. 16; see also above, n. 15.

92. See, for example, Coburn, *Devī-Māhātmya*, p. 330.

93. See Filliozat, *Kumāratantra*, pp. 123–58, on Tibetan, Chinese, Cambodian, and Arabic traditions.

94. Ibid., p. 122; quoting Hippocrates, *Sacred Disease*, para. 2.

95. *Bāṇa's Kādambarī*, ed. Kale, pp. 119–20. Cf. Tiwari, *Goddess Cults*, pp. 7–8. Also in the birth chamber are an old he-goat (*jarachāgam*), tied near the door, and a piece of cloth upon which figures of the Mothers (*mātṛpaṭa*) were painted (p. 120). Ṣaṣṭhī continues to be represented in this way in village Bengal, with an image of dung and cowrie shells plastered on the wall of the lying-in chamber: Gadon, "Hindu Goddess," p. 300. In the MBh, Jarā plays a similar role: Banerjea, "Some Folk Goddesses" (1938), pp. 101–2 (see below, chap. 7, n. 10). Cf. Joshi, *Mātṛkās*, p. 44; and Tiwari, *Goddess Cults*, p. 125 n. 182.

96. KS, Cikitsā Sthāna 4.9, in *Kāśyapa Saṃhitā*, ed. Tewari, p. 170. However, an image of a goat-headed Mother goddess, held in the Mathura Museum, has been identified as Ṣaṣṭhī: Harper, *Iconography*, p. 59.

97. Rana, *Study*, pp. 92–93; Agrawala, *Skanda-Kārttikeya*, pp. 38–43. Cf. Agrawala, *Ancient* (1970), pp. 92–93, 95; Tiwari, *Goddess Cults*, p. 8; and Couture and Schmid, "*Harivaṃśa*," p. 87. See above, chap. 1, n. 8.

98. Joshi, *Mātṛkās*, p. 11. Joshi (p. 68) also suggests that Ṣaṣṭhī's six heads represent the female Skanda-Seizers of MBh 3.219.26–21.

99. *Mānava Gṛhya Sūtra* 2.13–15, cited in Agrawala, *Skanda-Kārttikeya*, p. 35.

100. *Mānava Gṛhya Sūtra* 2.13–15, cited in Rana, *Study*, p. 18; and Agrawala, *Ancient*, p. 92. Cf. Joshi, *Mātṛkās*, p. 66.

101. In addition to Skanda, Ṣaṣṭhī has four other brothers: Mahāsena, Kumāra, Viśākha, and Nandikeśvara (a form of Śiva) or Naigameṣa: Agrawala, *Ancient*, pp. 91, 93.

102. The importance of the date is explained in this MBh (3.218.49b) passage: "His

goal (union with the goddess) was consummated on the sixth: therefore the sixth ('Ṣaṣṭhī') is a great lunar day."

103. All of these aspects of Ṣaṣṭhī's "six-ness" are mentioned in KS, Cikitsā Sthāna 4.11–13, in *Kāśyapa Saṃhitā*, ed. Tewari, pp. 170–71. This source identifies Ṣaṣṭhī as a form of Revatī (see below, part C): elsewhere, she is identified with Jyeṣṭhā (see below, nn. 142, 157, 188), or the modern Vimātā (Agrawala, *Ancient*, p. 93).

104. Gadon, "Hindu Goddess," pp. 293–308.

105. White, *Alchemical Body*, pp. 210–17. On the Seizers in the *Suśruta Saṃhitā*, see especially the excellent article, with illustrations, by Wujastyk, "Miscarriages of Justice" (1999), pp. 1–20. Cf. Zysk, "*Mantra* in *Āyurveda*" (1989), appendix, pp. 135–38.

106. Stewart, "Goddess Ṣaṣṭhī" (1995), pp. 352–66; and Gadon, "Hindu Goddess," pp. 296–98, 305. As Gadon notes, however, Ṣaṣṭhī is most commonly worshiped in aniconic form in Bengal, as a great rough stone smeared with red paint and placed at the foot of the jack tree, or as a great cylindrical grinding stone (pp. 297, 302–3). She was worshiped in the same form in Puranic times: Joshi, *Mātṛkās*, p. 67.

107. MBh 3.219.1–11.

108. MBh 1.14.12b, 22a.

109. See above, n. 57.

110. The verbal form is *pra-kalpitāḥ*: the same verb root *klṛp* is employed here as in the expressions noted above, in which the Youths "resolved upon Viśākha's paternity" and the host of Mothers upon that of Skanda (*sam-klṛp* in both constructions): see above, nn. 73, 75.

111. MBh 3.219.14, 16–17.

112. Coburn, *Devī-Māhātmya*, p. 318; quoting MBh 3.219.6a and 15a.

113. Sahni, "Deogarh Rock Inscription" (1925–26), p. 127. The inscription reads: "mātṝṇāṃ lokamātṝṇāṃ maṇḍalaṃ bhūtayestu vaḥ//." See above, n. 57.

114. See above, nn. 57, 75.

115. MBh 3.219.18–20. Cf. *Suśruta Saṃhitā* 6.37.11–12.

116. *Mahābhārata; Book 2, The Book of the Assembly Hall; Book 3, The Book of the Forest*, trans. van Buitenen (1975), p. 834. This opinion is shared by Filliozat (*Kumāratantra*, p. 75). Other scholars (Shulman, *Tamil Temple Myths*, p. 245; Tiwari, *Goddess Cults*, pp. 114–15; and Kinsley, *Hindu Goddesses* [1986], p. 152) see the Kṛttikās in this role: they are the last group to be mentioned in the text prior to this dialogue.

117. Sutherland, *Disguises of the Demon* (1991), p. 145.

118. KS, Kalpa Sthāna, "Revatī Kalpa" 68, in *Kāśyapa Saṃhitā*, ed. Tewari, pp. 363–65. The "Revatī Kalpa" constitutes the sixth chapter of the Kalpa Sthāna. Wujastyk ("Miscarriages of Justice," pp. 10–13), who offers four pages of brilliant summary, notes that the archaic language of the "Revatī Kalpa" may date it to as far back as the first millennium B.C.E.

119. Weber, "Zwei vedische Texte" (1859), pp. 349–53; cited in Tiwari, *Goddess Cults*, pp. 155–57.

120. Sutherland, *Disguises of the Demon*, p. 145. This is also the explicit case of the Cambodian homologues of the female Seizers: Filliozat, *Kumāratantra*, p. 155. See below, chap. 3, n. 38.

121. Tambs-Lyche, *Power, Profit, and Poetry*, p. 28 n. 24; Caldwell, *Oh Terrifying Mother*, p. 182.

122. Shulman, *Tamil Temple Myths*, p. 250.

123. Skandāpasmāra, whose description evokes the "deformed face" of a child suffering from an epileptic seizure, is identified with Viśākha in *Suśruta Saṃhitā* 6.29.9.

124. *Pongamia glabra*, according to Filliozat, *Kumāratantra*, p. 76.

125. She is also described in MBh 3.215.22–23. See above, n. 61.

126. *Nauclea cadamba*, a tree with orange-colored fragrant blossoms: Monier-Williams, *Sanskrit-English Dictionary*, s.v. "kadamba," p. 247.

127. MBh 3.219.23–44. The Calcutta edition of the MBh (3.14501ff.) continues with a description of a "seizure" by one of these Graspers: Filliozat, *Kumāratantra*, p. 26 n. 5. This insertion is not found, however, in either the critical text or the appendix to the critical edition of the third book.

128. *Netra Tantra* 19.15–33, 20.4–10.

129. The Protectors are identified, more than any other group, with the Seizers, in both religious and medical literature: Filliozat, *Kumāratantra*, pp. 30–31, 40, 42.

130. MBh 3.219.45–58. In his eleventh-century commentary on *Netra Tantra* (19.69, 70, 80), Kṣemarāja, citing the *Kriyākālaguṇottara*, gives detailed descriptions of the symptomology of possession by these various Seizers.

131. Agrawala, *Skanda-Kārttikeya*, pp. 10–11.

132. *Taittirīya Saṃhitā* 2.5.1.

133. MBh 3.220.9–16. The Kumbhakoanam edition gives the alternate reading of Vṛkṣakā or Vṛkṣikā, "Tree Woman": Tiwari, *Goddess Cults*, p. 22. See below, n. 195.

134. *Mārkaṇḍeya Purāṇa* 3.221.52–66.

135. See lists from the *Bhāgavata Purāṇa* 2.10.37–39, 10.63.9–11; and *Amarakośa* 1.1.11. See bibliography for editions.

136. She is so named in MBh 6.60.66a.

137. For example, *Aṣṭāṅgahṛdaya* 6.3.1–32, edited and translated in Filliozat, *Kumāratantra*, pp. 48–59. This source, which closely follows SS 6.27.1–20, lists twelve Seizers, of which five are male and seven female. Cf. SS 3.10.51; *Śārṅgadhara Saṃhitā* 1.7.189b–190b; and *Viṣṇudharmottara Purāṇa* 1.227 (in Tiwari, *Goddess Cults*, p. 126).

138. SS 6.27.16–20. White mustard is a "destroyer of Protectors," according to AH 6.3.43.

139. See above, n. 42.

140. Agrawala, *Skanda-Kārttikeya*, pp. 92–95. Thirteen Seizers are shown on this column.

141. I owe this felicitous translation of her name to Wujastyk, "Miscarriages of Justice," pp. 10–15.

142. AV 6.110.2–3 and *Kauśika Sūtra* 46.25, discussed in Tiwari, *Goddess Cults*, pp. 6–7, 154. Cf. Banerjea, "Some Folk Goddesses," pp. 104–7; and Rao, *Elements of Hindu Iconography* (1914–16), vol. 1, part 2, pp. 390–400.

143. MBh 1.211.7; *Viṣṇu Purāṇa* 4.1.65–66, 5.25.19. On the identification of Raivata or Raivātaka with Girnar, see White, *Alchemical Body*, pp. 329–32.

144. MBh 3.232.6 (of the Bombay edition, cited in Hopkins, *Epic Mythology*, p. 227) and critical ed., vol. 4, p. 1076, appen. 1, no. 22, 1.13.

145. See above, n. 87.

146. SS 6.31.11. Her *Viṣṇu Purāṇa* myth mentions this: Balarāma cuts her down to size with the end of his ploughshare.

147. Bahuputrikā seems to have had a cult of her own: Tiwari, *Goddess Cults*, p. 121.

148. KS, Cikitsā Sthāna 4.4–6, in *Kāśyapa Saṃhitā*, ed. Tewari, p. 169.

149. Elsewhere in the KS (Indriya Sthāna 11.2–21.2), in *Kāśyapa Saṃhitā*, ed. Tewari, pp. 152–54), ten *grahas* are mentioned, most of which are identical to those found in the MBh and SS lists.

150. KS, Kalpa Sthāna, "Revatī Kalpa" 3–7, in ibid., pp. 351–53. For the Brahmanic mythology of Dīrghajihvī, see O'Flaherty, *Tales of Sex and Violence* (1985), pp. 101–3. On Saramā, see below, nn. 179–84.

151. KS, Kalpa Sthāna, "Revatī Kalpa" 69, in *Kāśyapa Saṃhitā*, ed. Tewari, pp. 366–67.

152. KS, Kalpa Sthāna, "Revatī Kalpa" 62–69, in ibid., pp. 362–69. She is also the subject of a Tibetan Tantric work, the *Guhyāgnicakra:* Filliozat, *Kumāratantra*, pp. 145–46.

153. Joshi, *Mātṛkās*, pp. 11–12; and Mallmann, *Enseignements*, p. 176.

154. Filliozat, *Kumāratantra*, p. 61.

155. On her modern cult in Bengal, see Stewart, "Encountering the Smallpox Goddess" (1995), pp. 389–98. Her Tamil counterpart is the very popular Māriyammān, whose name means "smallpox/death" (*māri*) "mother" (*ammā*). See below, nn. 198, 199. The term *mahāmārī* is often used to designate cholera: Filliozat, *Kumāratantra*, pp. 109–10, 112 n. 1. A number of dread Tantric goddesses have names ending in the suffix *-mārī*.

156. Filliozat, *Kumāratantra*, p. 114.

157. *Bhāvaprakāśa*, Masūrikādhikāra 7.1–38: see bibliography for edition. Both the *Bhāvaprakāśa* and *Skanda Purāṇa* passages are cited without reference in Filliozat, *Kumāratantra*, pp. 117–19.

158. Joshi, *Mātṛkās*, pp. 45–46; Filliozat, *Kumāratantra*, p. 171.

159. SS 6.32. This source (6.27.4–5, 6.37.6–7) lists nine Seizers, which differ only slightly from those of the MBh. They are Skanda the Seizer, Skandāpasmāra, Śakunī, Revatī, Pūtanā, Andhapūtanā, Śītapūtanā, Mukhamaṇḍikā, and Naigameṣa. See above, text to nn. 123, 124.

160. That goddess shrines were often abandoned broken-down buildings may be adduced from the *Kādambarī* (*Bāṇa's Kādambarī*, ed. Kale, p. 341), according to which a priest of the Caṇḍikā temple had been attacked by a bear in an abandoned *mātṛgṛha*. Already in Vedic times, sorcerers and sorceresses (*yātumatīs*) were said to inhabit the ruins of old cities: Burrow, "Significance of the Term *arma, armaka*" (1963), pp. 159–66.

161. In his harangue against Kṛṣṇa, Śiśupala mocks his "killing Pūtanā and other previous acts": MBh 2.38.4.

162. BhP 10.6.1-20-44. For other early versions of this myth, see *Harivaṃśa* 50.20–29; *Padma Purāṇa* 6.245; and *Viṣṇu Purāṇa* 5.5.

163. A concise analytical discussion of this branch of Ayurveda is found in chapter 2 of Braverman, "Totally Soaked" (2002). The Ayurvedic sources juxtapose a "scientific" explanation for mental disorders to the demonic, without attempting to reconcile the two: Filliozat, *Kumāratantra*, pp. 27–28.

164. These and other demonic habitats were precisely the sites at which Kaula practitioners actively *sought* possession by these dread demonic beings: see above, chap. 1, n. 46. The entire nineteenth chapter of the *Netra Tantra* is a primer in demonology. See also Wujastyk, "Miscarriages of Justice," passim.

165. Patricia Jefferey, Roger Jefferey, and Andrew Lyon, *Labour Pains and Labour Power: Women and Childbearing in India* (London: Zed, 1989), quoting an informant from the early 1980s; quoted without page reference in Wujastyk, "Miscarriages of Justice," epigram to p. 1.

166. Joshi (*Mātṛkās*, pp. 21, 71): one of these is housed in the Mathura Museum (GMM. 75. 20). Pūtanā is also represented as a bird in an eighteenth-century Pahari miniature painting: Fisher and Goswamy, *Pahari Masters* (1992), plate 60.

167. *Harivaṃśa* 50.20. She is called a bird in AH 6.3.2a.

168. Humes, "Vindhyavāsinī" (1996), p. 57. Humes notes that the head of the Vindhyavāsinī image is that of a bird, and that the name Kauśikī given to the image may

be derived from *kauśika*, a word that means "owl," as well as the more generally accepted "sheath."

169. *Harivaṃśa* 65.48–57.

170. *Harivaṃśa*, appen. 1, no. 24, lines 87–91, 95–97, p. 191. See also the "Hymn to Āryā," (appen. 1, no. 8, lines 1–58), which also names no fewer than twenty-seven early goddesses: this number is difficult to establish, given the abstract or epithetical nature of many of the names. I have translated *krauñca* here (line 97) as (Sarus) crane, following Leslie, "A Bird Bereaved" (1998), pp. 455–87.

171. *Harivaṃśa*, appen. 1, no. 24, lines 107–8, 112. The same passage (lines 113–57) continues with a discussion of a number of winged (*garutmantaḥ*) male disease demons, including Skandagraha.

172. AP 52.8, 299.19, 49. She is also listed as a Yoginī in the *Mayadīpikā*, whose list of the sixty-four Yoginīs is nearly identical to that found in the AP. The Yoginī lists in question are reproduced in Mallmann, *Enseignements*, pp. 292–306; the same author discusses their content and chronology in ibid., pp. 169–82.

173. *Śrīmatottara Tantra* 20.211b.

174. MBh 9.45.3–30. For multiple "lists of goddesses" in the MBh, *Harivaṃśa*, various *Purāṇas*, a Jain source, and Ayurvedic works, see Joshi, *Mātṛkās*, pp. 50–63. See also below, nn. 172–78.

175. *Saddharmapuṇḍarika Sūtra* chap. 21, line 30: see bibliography.

176. *Mānasollāsa* 5.18.966–67, in *Mānasollāsa*, ed. Srigondekar, vol. 3, p. 268. A single goddess named Śuṣkarevatī appears in the *Matsya Purāṇa* (179.65), in which she leads a host of Mothers created by Viṣṇu to drink the blood of Andhaka's demon army: Tiwari, *Goddess Cults*, p. 111. Śākinī is discussed at length in Kṣemarāja's commentary on *Netra Tantra* 19.55, in which he cites the *Tantrasadbhāva*.

177. *Śrīmatottara Tantra* 27.79b–81a (Pandey's edition of the *Gorakṣa Saṃhitā*).

178. *Hārītā Saṃhitā* 3.54; *Brahmāṇḍa Purāṇa* 2.3.7.158. See also Filliozat, *Kumāratantra*, pp. 65–66.

179. RV 10.108.1–11.

180. MBh 1.3.1–9.

181. Hopkins, *Epic Mythology*, p. 42.

182. *Jaiminīya Brāhmaṇa* 2.440–42; translated in O'Flaherty, *Tales of Sex and Violence*, pp. 99–100.

183. Filliozat, *Kumāratantra*, pp. 53–54 (translation of AH 6.3.9–17), 61.

184. AV 4.37.11; AH 6.3.16.40–61.

185. MBh 1.165.1–44. The same story is told in MBh 9.39.11–29. For a discussion, see White, *Myths of the Dog-Man*, p. 79.

186. Shulman, *Tamil Temple Myths*, p. 266. For further discussion of the theme of the murderous, feral cow, see ibid., pp. 231–33, 258.

187. RV 6.74.2; AV 7.42.1; in Filliozat, *Kumāratantra*, pp. 30 n. 2, 168, 177.

188. Shulman, *Tamil Temple Myths*, p. 258; and Rao, *Elements of Hindu Iconography*, vol. 1, part 2, pp. 390, 394, and plate CXXII.

189. Heesterman, *Broken World* (1993), pp. 25, 38, and nn. 141, 142; and Jamison, *Sacrificed Wife*, pp. 106–7.

190. MBh 1.14.5–1.31.18. The names of Kadrū's principal serpent sons are given in MBh 1.31.5–16. Vinatā has only two sons, Garuḍa and Aruṇa. Recall as well that Svāhā takes the form of a female kite (*garuḍī*) to deposit Agni's seed: see above, n. 56. On this myth's dating, see Winternitz, *A History of Vedic Literature* (1981), vol. 1, p. 292.

191. TS 6.1.6. A still earlier version may be adduced from *Śatapatha Brāhmaṇa* 3.6.2.2–7, in which the rivals are named Kadrū and Suparṇī ("Fair-feathered").

192. Knipe, "The Heroic Theft" (1967), pp. 337–45.

193. O'Flaherty, *Women* (1980), pp. 168, 182, 200, 202.

194. Malamoud, *Cooking the World* (1996), pp. 288–89 n. 66.

195. MBh 3.220.16. The alternate reading is found in the Kumbhakoanam manuscripts of the MBh: Tiwari (*Goddess Cult*, pp. 21–22) sees these as references to Āryā; another possibility is Jyeṣṭhā, ("Eldest"), who is identified with a tree in northern Indian and Nepali traditions. See above, nn. 142, 157.

196. *Jātakas* 50 and 307, summarized in Coomaraswamy, *Yakṣas*, part 2, p. 9.

197. See below, chap. 4, nn. 137–39.

198. Henry, *Chant the Names of God* (1988), pp. 84–90.

199. Adams, *The Western Rajputana States* (1899), pp. 230–35; and Balfour, *Cyclopaedia*, s.v. "Azadirachta indica," vol. 1, p. 212.

200. Boulnois, *La Caducée* (1989), pp. 134–39. See above, n. 155.

201. Fuller, *The Camphor Flame* (1992), pp. 112–14; Weinberger-Thomas, *Cendres*, p. 109.

202. Desirens, "Les *Yoginī*" (1991), pp. 62, 63, 70; and Willis, "Religious and Royal Patronage," p. 57.

203. Coomaraswamy, *Yakṣas*, part 1, p. 33 n. 1.

204. KSS 2.5.101–18.

205. KSS 7.3.7–31.

206. A bas-relief held in the Bharat Kalā Bhavan (acc. no. 22318), Varanasi, depicts two Mothers, of which one has a human face and the other the face of a parrot: Agrawala, "Early Brahmanical Sculptures" (1971), p. 180 and fig. 347. The Mathura (AMM 00.U.92; AMM 00.G.57; AMM 33.2331) and Lucknow (SML 60.168) Museum collections include a significant number of Kushan-age bird-headed Mother goddesses images, including a series of five Mothers, all of whom have the faces of birds (AMM. 33.2331): Joshi, *Catalogue* (1972), pp. 55–56.

207. Zysk, "*Mantra* in *Āyurveda*," p. 124. On plagues of parrots, see Ron Inden, "Cultural and Symbolic Constitutions in India" (Princeton: Princeton University, 1978, typescript), pp. 303–31; cited in Sax, "Ramnagar Ramlia" (1990), p. 144.

208. *Brahmāṇḍa Purāṇa* 2.3.7.154a: "utkṛṣṭabalasattvā ye teṣāṃ vai khecarāḥ smṛtāḥ." The context is found in 2.3.7.156–58. See below, chap. 7, n. 66.

209. A fascinating discussion of the relationship between this phenomenon and the human domestication of fire can be found in Heesterman, *Broken World*, pp. 20–21.

210. Stewart, "Encountering the Smallpox Goddess," pp. 389–97. Skanda's connection to them devolves from his sonship to Agni, fire. "As the son of Agni Skanda was identified with all burnings (fevers) and other afflictions": Hopkins, *Epic Mythology*, p. 229.

211. Dehejia, *Yoginī Cult and Temples*, pp. 55, 57, 83.

212. Contrariwise, they may be in some way related to such popular disease-causing goddesses as the Seven Sisters of south India (Filliozat, *Kumāratantra*, pp. 119–20), the Seven Sisters of northwest India, the Sātī Āsarā of Maharashtra, etc.

213. MBh 3.219.24–35 names nine Seizers and then speaks of a total of eighteen (which includes their consorts); nine are listed in SS 6.27.4–5. See above, n. 125.

214. The AV (19.9.7) mentions the *grahas* moving in the sky: however, there is no basis for determining that it is planets rather than birds that are intended here. The MBh (13.14.156, 14.43.6) names Sūrya as the "greatest of the *grahas*" in a sense that clearly means "heavenly body," but does not mention the nine *grahas*; furthermore, no single Epic passage gives the positions of the planets in relationship to the days of the

week or the signs of the zodiac: Kane, *History of Dharmaśāstra*, 2nd ed. (1974), vol. 5, part 1, p. 532.

215. Kaye, *Hindu Astronomy* (1924), vol. 18, p. 36; cited in Markel, *Origin* (1995), p. 79.

216. Markel, *Origin*, p. 16.

217. Ibid., p. 164.

218. Ibid., pp. 9–13; citing Trivedi, "Mother and Child Sculpture" (1974), pp. 141–45; Pal, *Indian Sculpture* (1986–88), vol. 2 (A.D. 700–1800), p. 194, plate 93.

219. *Kathāsaritsāgara, Ocean* ed. Penzer (1924–28), vol. 4, p. 69 n. Penzer gives their number as 16 or 14. In its chapter on architecture, the *Bṛhat Saṃhitā* (53.83) names Carakī, Vidārī (Biḍālī), Pūtanā, and Rākṣasī as "those who dwell outside the corners of the house." See also Tiwari, *Goddess Cults*, pp. 6–7, on Revatī as a *nakṣatra* and Jyeṣṭhā as the goddess identified with a dire month in the Indian calendar.

220. Slusser, *Nepal Mandala* (1982), vol. 1, pp. 344–45.

221. *Bṛhat Saṃhitā* 48.26 and *Viṣṇudharmottara Purāṇa* 1.227 (Mothers), 228 (Kṛttikās), 231–32 (*navagrahas*), both discussed in Tiwari, *Goddess Cults*, pp. 154–55.

222. Meister, "Regional Variations," pp. 240 n. 27, 243 n. 35. Cf. Markel, *Origin*, pp. 9–10.

223. Brunner, "Tantra du Nord," p. 132.

224. Desai, *Religious Imagery of Khajuraho* (1996), p. 165. This "reversal" is likely due to the Kaula orientation of the founder or the royal builder of the Kandariyā temple, as opposed to the Vaisnavism of the Dhaṅgadeva, the royal patron of the Lakṣmaṇa temple. On Dhaṅgadeva, see below, chap. 5, nn. 106, 109.

225. See above, n. 42. Cf. Agrawala, *Skanda-Kārttikeya*, p. 65.

226. Filliozat, *Kumāratantra*, pp. 19–20. This is a system of twelve Skanda-Seizers, whose names are Nandanā, Sunandā, Pūtanā, Mukhamaṇḍikā, Kaṭapūtanā, Śakunikā, Śuṣkarevatī, Aryakā, Bhūsūtikā, Nirṛtā, Pilipicchika, and Kāmukā.

227. Described in detail (as the 299th chapter) by Mani, *Purāṇic Encyclopedia* (1964; English trans. 1975, 1993), s.v. "Grahapīḍā," pp. 297–99. Nine of the names of the Grahīs described in AP 299 correspond to those inscribed beneath the images of the Yoginīs of the Bheraghat temple: Mallmann, *Enseignements*, p. 306. Chapters 72–103 of the AP are copied from the 1073 or 1096 C.E. *Somaśambhupaddhati* (SŚP, ed. Brunner-Lachaux, part 4 [1998], pp. lix–lx: see bibliography), and one may assume that this chapter as well, which has close connections to the tenth- to eleventh-century KM, is also post-eleventh century.

228. This is the second text in a codex of five short works, entitled the *Ḍākinīkalpa*. Texts 1 and 3, likely later works than text 2, the *Tithiḍākinīkalpa*, present similar systems, based on the seven-day week and the twenty-seven lunar mansions (*nakṣatras*): these, however, rarely if ever present the *ḍākinīs* by name. This is one of only two Hindu Tantras having the word *ḍākinī* in their title; in contrast, the term is very common in Buddhist Tantric works, in which the term *yoginī* is far less frequent. All of the information presented here is drawn from Herrmann-Pfandt, "The So-Called *Ḍākinīkalpa*" (1997), esp. pp. 53–57, which also contain a critical edition and translation of text 1 (pp. 68–75). Texts 2 and 3 are forthcoming in the same journal; texts 4 and 5 of this codex are on other topics.

229. Klein, "Nondualism and the Great Bliss Queen," p. 79. On *ḍākinīs*, see below, chap. 7. nn. 62, 70, 74, 108.

230. Filliozat, *Kumāratantra*, po. 69–70.

231. KS, Kalpa Sthāna, "Revatī Kalpa" 47, in *Kāśyapa Saṃhitā*, ed. Tewari, pp. 359–60; AP 52, discussed in Mallmann, *Enseignements*, pp. 6–7, 176. Mallmann (pp. 173–74) notes that this is the sole passage in which the number sixty-four is given

in connection with an arrangement that runs from east to northeast, i.e., in *pradakṣiṇa* order.

232. He is named Mārtaṇḍa Bhairava, the solar form of Bhairava, in AP 301.12b: however, this is a post-eleventh-century addition to the "core" text: Mallmann, *Enseignements*, p. 105. Bhairava stands or stood at the center of the Yoginī temple ruins of Hirapur and Ranipur-Jharial in Orissa; he likely stood at the center of the Khajuraho and Bheraghat Yoginī temples: Desai, *Religious Imagery of Khajuraho*, pp. 86, 88; Sharma, *Temple of Chaunsaṭha-yoginī*, pp. 35, 40; and Mallmann, *Enseignements*, pp. 7, 97–98, 170. Some temples would have had an image of Śiva or a *liṅgam* at the center. For textual references to this configuration, see below, chap. 7, n. 97.

233. Harper, *Iconography*, p. 163, referring to the circle of Mātṛkās surrounding the dancing (*tāṇḍava*) Śiva at the Rāmeśvara Cave at Ellora. Evidence for a circle of Mothers surrounding a *goddess* (the Mātṛkā Sārvāṇī) is found in a late-fifth-century inscription from the Kathmandu Valley: Lidke, "Goddess," p. 141.

234. Bhairava is described in this role in dozens of medieval sources: Mallmann, *Enseignements*, p. 173; Dehejia, *Yoginī Cult and Temples*, pp. 35, 40. On the king as *cakravartin*, see below, chap. 5, nn. 5, 103; on the Kaula practitioner in the same role, see below, chap. 8, n. 176.

235. Curiously, a passage from the KJñN (7.15a) instructs a practitioner to betake himself to a "place of the Yoginīs" (*yoginīsthānam*) that is "dark and black in color," which is at variance with the unenclosed structures of the surviving Yoginī temples. See below, chap. 8, n. 174.

236. Mallmann, *Enseignements*, pp. 102–5, 115–16, 176.

237. Desai, *Religious Imagery of Khajuraho*, p. 77.

238. One of these is the online "Vedic Astrology Magazine": www.vedicastro.com/yogini1.htm.

239. M. R. Kale's notes to his edition of the *Daśakumāracarita* (1966), chap. 6, p. 170; cited in Dehejia, *Yoginī Cult and Temples*, p. 17.

240. Personal communication from Purusottama Locan Srestha, Bhaktapur, Nepal, June 4, 1999.

241. Her Buddhist legend is retold in Coomaraswamy, *Yakṣas*, p. 9. Cf. Filliozat, *Kumāratantra*, pp. 149–50; and Joshi, *Mātṛkās*, pp. 74–75.

242. A goddess of the Harītī type plays a primary role in the birth myth of Jarāsandha: see below, chap. 7, n. 10.

243. Banerjea, "Some Folk Goddesses," p. 108. Kokā means "cuckoo" in Sanskrit, and Durgā is called *kokamukhā* in the "Durgā Stotra" of the MBh (Bhīṣmaparvan, appen. 1, no. 1, line 16). See above, n. 88.

244. Tiwari, *Goddess Cults*, p. 52. On Naigameṣa, see above, n. 68.

245. Strickmann, *Mantras et mandarins*, p. 248.

246. *Mārkaṇḍeya Purāṇa* 48.103–4, 107–9 (p. 266 of Pargiter's edition; cited in Tiwari, *Goddess Cults*, pp. 4–5). Cf. Agrawala, *Ancient*, p. 82.

247. *Harṣacarita* (ucchvāsa 4, lines 6–7): "The old nurses danced encircled by a great throng of boys like the incarnate Jāta-mātṛ-devatā surrounded by a troop of dwarfs and deaf people, with laughing upturned faces" (*The Harshacarita of Bāṇabhaṭṭa*, 2nd ed., ed. Kane [1965], ucchvāsa 4, p. 7; and notes to ucchvāsa 4, p. 26). In their iconographic and literary representations, all of these goddesses (if they are not one and the same figure) are surrounded by infants: Tiwari, *Goddess Cults*, pp. 7–8; and Agrawala, *Ancient*, p. 94. Another Kushan-age goddess, named Carcikā, had the form of a cat: Tiwari, *Goddess Cults*, p. 52. Kubjikā is identified with Carcikā in the "Kumārikākhaṇḍa" of the *Manthānabhairava Tantra* 3.78: Dyczkowski, "Kubjikā, Kālī, Tripurā and Trika," p. 29 n. 78.

248. Agrawala, *Catalogue* (1951), p. 88 (describing holding no. F 30, an image of Harītī). Cf. Agrawala, *Skanda-Kārttikeya*, plate 18.b. A Kushan-age sculpture of Harītī with Pāñcika-Kubera from Sahri-Bahlol is shown in Coomaraswamy, *Yakṣas*, plate 15, fig. 1. Other such sculptures, from Mathura, are listed in Joshi, *Mātṛkās*, p. 77. See also Harper, *Iconography*, pp. 62–64; and Schastok, *Śāmalājī Sculptures*, figs. 90, 115. For discussion, see Sutherland, *Disguises of the Demon*, pp. 143–45; Joshi, *Mātṛkās*, pp. 75–77; and Agrawala, *Catalogue*, p. 80. In Tamil tradition the six Kṛttikās are termed *iyakkamātar*, i.e., "Yakṣa Mothers": Shulman, *Tamil Temple Myths*, p. 251.

249. Dhawan, *Mother Goddesses* (1997), p. 189 n. 149.

250. Discussed in Coomaraswamy, *Yakṣas*, p. 9; and Filliozat, *Kumāratantra*, pp. 149–51.

251. *Samyuktavastu*, recounted in Dhawan, *Mother Goddesses*, p. 189 n. 146.

252. *Rāmāyaṇa* 1.24.5–13, 1.25.4–14, in *The Rāmāyaṇa of Vālmīki*, trans. and ed. Goldman (1984), vol. 1, Bālakāṇḍa, pp. 172–75.

253. *Rāmāyaṇa* 7.4.9-13; quoted in Sutherland, *Disguises of the Demon*, p. 55; and discussed in Coomaraswamy, *Yakṣas*, p. 5 n. 1; and Hopkins, *Epic Mythology*, p. 41.

254. *Jātaka* 50; *Matsya Purāṇa* 180.9–10.

255. *Mahāvamsa* 7.9–37, trans. Geiger (1912), pp. 54–57. For a Tamil variant, see Shulman, *Tamil Temple Myths*, pp. 204–5.

256. For discussion, see Coomaraswamy, *Yakṣas*, vol. 1, pp. 13–14; Hiltebeitel, *Ritual of Battle*, pp. 183–85; and Sutherland, *Disguises of the Demon*, pp. 139–40.

257. Coomaraswamy, *Yakṣas*, vol. 1, p. 16.

258. Kapferer, *Celebration of Demons*, 2nd ed. (1991).

259. *Valāhassa Jātaka* (no. 196), discussed in Sutherland, *Disguises of the Demon*, p. 139.

260. *Telapatta Jātaka* (no. 96), translated in Sutherland, *Disguises of the Demon*, pp. 138–39.

261. KSS 5.2.139–52; the Keralan description is discussed below, chap. 3, nn. 35–36.

262. Caldwell, *Oh Terrifying Mother*, p. 182.

263. *Jayadissa Jātaka* (no. 513); discussed in Sutherland, *Disguises of the Demon*, p. 142.

264. Coomaraswamy, *Yakṣas*, vol. 1, pp. 17–20, 24 n. 2; Desai, *Religious Imagery of Khajuraho*, pp. 83–85; and Mallmann, *Enseignements*, p. 176.

265. Rana, *Study*, p. 84.

266. Coomaraswamy, *Yakṣas*, vol. 1, pp. 8–9; Hopkins, *Epic Mythology*, p. 142. See also MBh 2.10.3.

267. Schastok, *Śāmalājī Sculptures*, pp. 59, 68, 70. See also Harper, *Iconography*, p. 64.

268. Caldwell, *Oh Terrifying Mother*, p. 141.

269. Schastok, *Śāmalājī Sculptures*, p. 60; Meister, "Regional Variations," p. 240 n. 27, 243 n. 35; and Markel, *Origin*, pp. 9–10.

270. Caldwell, *Oh Terrifying Mother*, pp. 141–42.

271. *Bhūtaḍāmara Tantra* (Hindu version: see bibliography) 3.21, 4.24, 5.17. For a discussion, see Bühnemann, "Buddhist Deities and Mantras" (2000), p. 41.

272. Sutherland, *Disguises of the Demon*, p. 146.

273. Dehejia, *Yoginī Cult and Temples*, p. 36. See, for example, KSS 8.6.162b–187b; 18.2.3–33; 18.5.3–23. See also below, chap. 7, n. 79.

274. Goetz, "Historical Background" (1974), p. 108.

275. O'Flaherty, *Women*, pp. 279–80.

Chapter 3

1. For a discussion, see Weinberger-Thomas, *Ashes of Immortality*, pp. 210–14; Caldwell, *Oh Terrible Mother*, esp. pp. 114–22, 131–42; and Bhattacharyya, *Indian Puberty Rites*, 2nd rev. ed. (1980), pp. 11–19.

2. Khan, "Deux rites tantriques" (1994).

3. KSS 3.6.104–12, in Dehejia, *Yoginī Cult and Temples*, pp. 55–57; Carstairs, *Death of a Witch* (1983), p. 56.

4. See below, part 7.

5. Sanderson, "Purity and Power," pp. 198–99, 205–6, 211–12 n. 69.

6. *Taittirīya Saṃhitā* 2.5.1; discussed in Smith, "Indra's Curse," p. 23.

7. White, *Alchemical Body*, pp. 25–26, 339–42.

8. RV 10.85.28–30, 34–35; discussed in Menski, "Marital Expectations" (1992), pp. 57–58.

9. *Atharva Veda* 14.1–2, discussed ibid., pp. 59–62.

10. Allen, "Kumari or 'Virgin' Worship" (1976), p. 297.

11. Menski, "Marital Expectations," p. 65.

12. Bhattacharyya, *Indian Puberty Rites*, pp. 33–34.

13. Caldwell, *Oh Terrible Mother*, pp. 218–19. The *tāli* itself is a gold pendant having the form of the *aśvatthā* ("sacred fig") leaf, whose form and ribbing is compared with that of the vulva in Sanskritic traditions.

14. Allen, "Kumari or 'Virgin' Worship," p. 314.

15. In addition to India and Nepal, puberty rites found in Sri Lanka, among both Hindu and Muslim populations, appear to reflect similar concerns and betray similar patterns of belief and practice: McGilvray, "Sexual Power and Fertility" (1982), pp. 25–73.

16. Allen, "Kumari or 'Virgin' Worship," p. 314.

17. Kapadia, *Śivā* (1995).

18. Ibid., pp. 68–69, 75.

19. Ibid., p. 77.

20. Caldwell, *Oh Terrible Mother*, p. 116.

21. *Bṛhadāraṇyaka Upaniṣad* 6.4.13, 20–22. Cf. *Manu Smṛti* 5.135 and *Vyāsa Saṃhitā* 2.37–40, quoted in Bhattacharyya, *Indian Puberty Rites*, pp. 13–14.

22. *Arthaśāstra* 3.153, cited in Bhattacharyya, *Indian Puberty Rites*, p. 15.

23. MBh 1.113.25–26.

24. Caldwell, *Oh Terrible Mother*, p. 115.

25. Kapadia, *Śivā*, p. 16; White, *Alchemical Body*, p. 195; Apfel-Marglin, *Wives of the God-King*, p. 240; Caldwell, *Oh Terrible Mother*, p. 115.

26. Caldwell, *Oh Terrible Mother*, p. 128.

27. Ibid., p. 146.

28. KM 23.126–40.

29. KM 23.141–46. As Heilijger-Seelens makes clear (*System of the Five Cakras*, pp. 140–46), there are two sets of six (or seven) goddesses in these *cakras*, the ones malevolent and the others benevolent. For further discussion, see below, chap. 7, nn. 107, 108; and chap. 8, nn. 56–65.

30. Heilijger-Seelens, *System of the Five Cakras*, pp. 131, 134–35.

31. *Śrīmatottara Tantra* 27.79b–81a (partially edited by Janardana Pandeya as the *Gorakṣa Saṃhitā*: see bibliography).

32. Strickmann, *Mantras et mandarins*, p. 320.

33. *Rasārṇava* 18.103, 105cd–6cd.

34. *Telapatta Jātaka* (no. 96), translated in Sutherland, *Disguises of the Demon*, pp. 138–39.

35. Caldwell, *Oh Terrifying Mother*, pp. 116–18, 164–66; and Gough, "Female Initiation Rites" (1955), pp. 45–80 (cited in Allen, "Kumārī or 'Virgin' Worship," p. 297).

36. Caldwell, *Oh Terrifying Mother*, p. 163. Obeyesekere (*Medusa's Hair*, pp. 86, 138) reports the case of a Tamil woman of Sri Lanka whose possession by the incubus named Kalu Kumar (Black Prince) in her dreams culminated in the emission of *dhatu* (semen, essence) from her vagina. This is the same figure as Kalu Yakṣa (the Black Dryad): see below, chap. 7, n. 32. Cf. RV 10.162.4–6.

37. Daniel, *Fluid Signs*, pp. 165–69.

38. Harper, *Iconography*, p. 35. The name Churelin is a likely variant on the term *cuṛel*, which is applied to the wrathful ghosts of women who died untimely deaths, and who are identifiable by the fact that their feet are turned backward. See above, chap. 2, n. 120.

39. Kakar, *Shamans, Mystics, and Doctors* (1982), pp. 27–28.

40. An intended play on words: *adharamadhu* means simply "the moisture of the lips" (Monier-Williams, *Sanskrit-English Dictionary*, s.v. "adhara," p. 19), but the clear meaning here is that the lower lips (*adharas*) in question belong to the vulva, and that their exudation, their "honey" (*madhu*), is female sexual discharge.

41. *Hevajra Tantra* 2.11.10b–12b; 11.10b–12b, 14b–15b. Cf. 2.3.48, 63. My translation differs from that of Shaw (*Passionate Enlightenment*, p. 157), who bases her translation on the Tibetan version of this work. Cf. HT 2.5.60.

42. For the dating of this text, see above, chap. 1, n. 104.

43. KĀN 5.36–40. Cf. 5.81–82.

44. Zvelebil, *Siddha Quest* (1996), pp. vii–viii. For a fifteenth-century cognate Japanese evocation, see Faure, *Red Thread* (1998), p. 113.

45. Zvelebil, *Siddha Quest*, pp. 100 n. 2, 109.

46. Tellingly, the Buddhist *Tārā Tantra* declares Vasiṣṭha and Buddha to be two Kula Bhairavas: Bhattacharyya, *Religious Culture of North-Eastern India* (1995), p. 124.

47. I have emended *varāṅganām* to *varāṅganāḥ*: otherwise, there is only one woman. Note, however, that most references to Kāpālikas portray them as solitary wandering ascetics, occasionally joined by *a single female disciple*: Lorenzen, *Kāpālikas and Kālāmukhas* (1972), p. 14.

48. *Rudrayāmala* 17.130b–31b.

49. KĀN 5.81a–82a.

50. KJñN 3.17b–18b.

51. KJñN 18.22a. I have emended *samayahīne* to *samayine*.

52. KJñN, unnumbered mixed prose following 4.15b.

53. KJñN 6.14b.

54. KJñN 11.11ab. It should be noted that this set of five is *not* termed *pañcamakāra*, the "Five M-words." See below, nn. 102, 103, 108, 109.

55. KJñN 11.18a–19a.

56. KJñN 11.32a–33b.

57. KJñN 18.1.

58. KJñN 18.2–6.

59. KJñN 18.7a–14b.

60. Mark Dyczkowski, e-mail message, April 5, 2001. This is also a reference to the fact that in yogic body physiology, the *kuṇḍalinī* is coiled three and a half times around an internal *liṅgam*.

61. McDaniel, *Madness of the Saints* (1990), pp. 180–82.

62. Khan, *Conversions and Shifting Identities* (1997), p. 131. See below, chap. 8, n. 165.

63. KĀN 5.33ab.

64. KĀN 5.48a–73b.

65. See also Jayaratha's commentary to TĀ 29.14, 29.21, and 29.128 (*Tantrāloka*, ed. Dwivedi and Rastogi, vol. 8, pp. 3304, 3308–9, 3382–83); and *Tantrāloka, Abhinavagupta, Luce dei Tantra*, trans. Gnoli, pp. 551 n. 1, 552 n. 2.

66. Cited in Bhattacharyya, *Indian Puberty Rites*, p. 17.

67. *Mātṛkabheda Tantra* 5.17–33.

68. *Kulacūḍāmaṇi Tantra*, trans. Finn (1986), p. 87 n. 71.

69. *Muṇḍamālā Tantra* 2, quoted in Bhattacharyya, *Indian Puberty Rites*, p. 16.

70. Snellgrove, *Indo-Tibetan Buddhism* (1987) vol. 1, p. 276. Male blood may bear the same symbolic valence. In the *Basava Purāṇa* of Somanātha, a thirteenth-century Vīraśaiva work, a male devotee grinds his own arm down to pulp in order to offer it to Śiva in place of sandalwood paste: Narayana Rao, trans. and ed., *Śiva's Warriors* (1990), pp. 23 (for Somanātha's dates), 162 ("The Story of Eṇumārti Nārayanāru").

71. RA 15.131–32.

72. KJñN 16.14b. Cf. Monier-Williams, *Sanskrit-English Dictionary*, s.v. "āgama," p. 129.

73. Dyczkowski, "Kubjikā, Kālī, Tripurā and Trika," p. 42.

74. Dyczkowski, "Kubjikā the Erotic Goddess" (1995–96), p. 127.

75. *Manthānabhairava Tantra*, Kumārikākhaṇḍa 2.10b, translated in Dyczkowski, "Kubjikā, Kālī, Tripurā and Trika," p. 42.

76. *Ciñcināsāramatasamucchaya* 1.5b–6b, translated in ibid., p. 42.

77. Ibid., pp. 46–47. For a similar literal tracing of a lineage's bloodline, this time masculine, see the Japanese Zen Buddhist case described in Bodiford, "Emptiness and Dust" (2000), p. 301.

78. KĀN 17.136b–40b. This passage is a variant on Jayaratha's commentary on TĀ 29.109b–10a (*Tantrāloka*, ed. Dwivedi and Rastogi, vol. 7, pp. 3368–69).

79. KCM 1.20, 33. The term *dravyam* is employed in the RA to signify the sexual fluids (2.121b) offered in Tantric worship (*siddhadravyam*), as well as all the "secret" fluids (124b–25a), including mercury, used in alchemy.

80. Brunner, Oberhammer, and Padoux, *Tāntrikābhidhānakośa I*, s.v. "āṇavamala," pp. 181–82.

81. *Somaśambhupaddhati*, ed. Brunner-Lachaux, part 4 (1977), p. vii.

82. Lorenzen, *Kāpālikas and Kālāmukhas*, p. 91.

83. TĀ 1.23–28, with the commentary of Jayaratha, in *Tantrāloka, Abhinavagupta. La Lumière sur les Tantra*, trans. Silburn and Padoux (1998), pp. 82–83.

84. Sanderson, "Meaning in Tantric Ritual," p. 20.

85. *Amanaskayoga* 2.33: "kecit kāṣṭāṃ praviṣṭā yuvatibhagagataṃ bindum ūrdhvaṃ nayati/ . . . naiteṣāṃ dehasiddhir vigatanijamano*rājayogād* ṛte syāt//." Translated by James Mallinson, personal communication by e-mail, July 1995.

86. "rajaso retaso yogād rājayoga iti smṛtāḥ." For a discussion, see Kaviraj, "Siddhoṃ kī Cakra-Sādhanā," in *Bhāratīya Sādhanā kī Dhārā* (1984), p. 117. Cf. the *Āgama Prakāśa*, in Stewart and Rinehart, "Anonymous *Āgama Prakāśa*" (2000), p. 276, which states that "the Kaula is called Rāj[y]ayoga."

87. Bharati, *Tantric Tradition* (1965), p. 242. The term *mudrā* can, however, denote a substance to be eaten, rather than the vulva as "seal." So, for example, a verse in chapter 45 of the *Brahmayāmala* reads: "tvaśaktyāsādhako nityaṃ yathāvibhavasa[mbh]av[āt] mudrāṃ caiva yathānyāyaṃ madhyañcaiva pradāpayet" ("But the practitioner who is without a consort [should] constantly [offer] according to what is possible for him. One should also offer *mudrā*, according to the rule, as well as liquor").

88. If, indeed, it was at all possible. In a recent article, Darmon ("Vajrolī Mudrā" [2002]) argues, on the basis of field research carried out in Lonavla, Maharashtra, that

vajrolī mudrā is anatomically impossible. However, the subjects of his research were male yogins who attempted to reabsorb fluids from an external container, via a catheter, through the urethra. They did not attempt to do so (in Darmon's presence, at least) in the way described in the Nāth Siddha sources, i.e., in tandem with a female partner following sexual emission. I discuss the terms *vajrolī, mudrā,* and *sampuṭa* in *Alchemical Body*, pp. 199–201, 256–57.

89. See above, nn. 60–61.

90. Salomon, "Bāul Songs" (1995), pp. 195–96. In certain Bāul traditions, woman herself is the *sahaj manuṣ* (here, "Natural Person"), while her male partner is the *siddhamanuṣ* ("Cultivated Person"): Openshaw, "'Killing" the Guru" (1988), p. 14.

91. On this identification, see KM 6.100b–1a; and Brunner, Oberhammer, and Padoux, *Tāntrikābhidhānakośa*, s.v. "anāmā," p. 117.

92. KJñN 14.93–94: "devyā bhūtvā ca yoginyā mātṛcakrāvaśānugā/ līyante khecarīcakre kṣobhayet paramāmṛtam//amṛtaṃ vinā devi amaratvaṃ kathaṃ priye/ amṛtaṃ kaulasadbhāvaṃ śṛṇu kāmakalātmakam//." See also below chap. 8, n. 49.

93. KJñN 14.37b–41a.

94. *Śilpa Prakāśa* , trans. Boner and Sarma (1966), pp. 136–37. The *Kaulacūḍāmaṇi* mentioned here is not the same text as the *Kaulacūḍāmaṇi Tantra:* see below, chap. 4, n. 22; and bibliography.

95. Lorenzen, *Kāpālikas and Kālāmukhas*, pp. 2–3; quoting Rāmānuja, *Śrī-bhāṣya* 2.2.35–37. Cf. Sharma, ed., *Kalacuri Rājvaṃś aur Unkā Yug*, (1998), vol. 2, p. 297.

96. Described in Kværne, "On the Concept of Sahaja," passim, who provides other, Buddhist, synonyms for the Tantric consort on p. 95: *vidyā, prajñā, devī.*

97. *Hevajra Tantra* 1.1 and *Guhyasamāja Tantra* 1.1, in Snellgrove, *Indo-Tibetan Buddhism*, vol. 1, p. 121.

98. *Sekoddeśaṭīkā*, p. 22; quoted in Kværne, "On the Concept of Sahaja," pp. 99, 101 (and n. 61), 106, 117–20. It is useful to note, in this context, that a number of early (seventh- to tenth-century C.E.) Buddhist Tantric classificatory systems considered these works to belong to the class of "Ḍākinī-," "Bhaginī-," or "Yoginī-Tantras": Orofino, "Notes on the Early Phases" (2001), pp. 545–46.

99. TĀ 29.150b–54a; discussed in Skora, "Consciousness," pp. 305–6.

100. Jayaratha's commentary on TĀ 3.95–96, discussed in Silburn, *Kuṇḍalinī*, pp. 232–35; and Skora, "Consciousness," p. 309.

101. *Toḍala Tantra* 2.68, translated by Gupta, "The Worship of Kālī" (2000), p. 487. Gupta dates the *Toḍala* to the eleventh century on the basis of its treatment of the Tārā worship, which is in keeping with the *Nīlasarasvatī Tantra* and the *Mahācīnācāra Tantra:* personal communication by e-mail, March 18, 2001.

102. For example, TĀ 29.98, with the commentary of Jayaratha, who cites *Manu Smṛti* 5.56.

103. KĀN 4.15–44.

104. Monier-Williams, *Sanskrit-English Dictionary*, s.v. "mithuna," p. 816.

105. KĀN 5.110b, 17.140b.

106. KĀN 4.44a: "asaṃskṛtaṃ pibed dravyaṃ balātkāreṇa maithunam//."

107. Stewart and Rinehart, "Anonymous *Āgama Prakāśa*," p. 281.

108. TĀ 29.97a–98b, with the commentary of Jayaratha.

109. TĀ 29.99ab: "tadvarjitā ye paśava ānandaparivarjitāḥ/ ānandakṛttrimāhārāstadvarjaṃ cakrayājakāḥ//." Jayaratha's commentary on *trimāhārāstadvarjaṃ* reads: "trīn mānāharanti makāratrayamupabhuñjate."

110. Bharati, *Ochre Robe* (1970), p. 99.

111. Apfel-Marglin, *Wives of the God-King*, pp. 223–28. Apfel-Marglin further notes that in a dance of the *devadāsīs* of Puri, called the Kālī or Śakti Ucchiṣṭa, the

divine *ucchiṣṭa* ("leavings of eaten food") in question were identified with drops of feminine sexual fluid secreted from the vagina of the devadāsī, the *kulāmṛta:* ibid., p. 240.

112. Sanjukta Gupta, personal communication by e-mail, March 18, 2001, referring to the discourse of Kashmiri Kaulas in Allahabad and Tantrics in Benares.

113. The most complete account of the practice remains the remarkable appendix 2 to volume 8 of *Kathāsaritsāgara, Ocean*, "Romance of Betel-Chewing," ed. Penzer, pp. 237–319.

114. An early Western traveler to give such an interpretation is Niccolao Manucci, a Venetian who visited Surat in 1653: *Kathāsaritsāgara, Ocean*, ed. Penzer, vol. 8, p. 268.

115. An abundance of historical sources indicate that the practice of *pān* chewing was as widespread among women as men in India: Ibid., vol. 8, pp. 244, 261, 263, 269, etc.

116. These are detailed in Stevenson, *Rites of the Twice-Born* (1920), passim, as summarized in *Kathāsaritsāgara, Ocean*, ed. Penzer, vol. 8, p. 277 n. 1.

117. *Kathāsaritsāgara, Ocean*, ed. Penzer, vol. 8, pp. 282–83.

118. Ibid. vol. 8, p. 258, quoting 'Abdu-r Razzāq, a fifteenth-century ambassador to the court of Vijaynagar, who stated: "It is impossible to express how strengthening it is, and how much it excites to pleasure. It is probable that the properties of this plant may account for the numerous harem of women that the king of the country maintains."

119. Dimock, *Place of the Hidden Moon* (1966; 1989), pp. 133–34, 203–4.

120. *Bhāgavata Purāṇa* 2.32.5a.

121. See above, chap. 2, n. 4.

122. See above, chap. 2, nn. 24–26; and below, chap. 4, n. 116.

123. The words of this priest, who will remain nameless, were communicated to me by Anand Krishna, Benares, January 1999.

124. *Prabodhacandrodaya*, ed. and trans. Nambiar (1971), pp. 84–89. See below, chap. 4, nn. 119, 123.

125. Snellgrove, *Indo-Tibetan Buddhism*, vol. 1, p. 179; citing Kværne, *Anthology*, pp. 181–88.

126. KJñN 8.12: "eṣā śaktirmahātmāna antyajā vyomamālinī/ tāmbūlapūritaṃ vaktraṃ viliptaṃ muktakeśañ ca//." I have emended *muktamena ca* in the text to *muktakeśañ ca*, which is a formula frequently found in Tantric sources.

127. Mylius, "Kokkokas *Ratirahasya*" (1997), p. 152.

128. Finn (*Kulacūḍāmaṇi Tantra*, p. 21) argues that this work may date from as early as the ninth century; however, its mention of the *Kubjikāmata* (ibid., p. 20) militates against this.

129. KCT 2.31b–32b, 3.5ab, 3.7b, 3.32b–33b, 3.47ab, 5.73a–74a.

130. Vaudeville, *Myths, Saints and Legends*, esp. pp. 181–85.

131. The text of the *Dhanyaśloka*, based on a single extant manuscript from Benares, has been edited in Pandey, *Abhinavagupta*, p. 738, and translated in Masson and Patwardhan, *Śāntarasa* (1969), p. 39.

132. Quoted in Pandey, *Abhinavagupta*, p. 617.

133. KJñN 17.174b, 191a–98b.

134. KJñN 17.199a–203a.

135. I am grateful to Mark Dyczkowski for providing me the Sanskrit of this unedited text. His reading is based on several manuscript sources of the MBhT: see bibliography.

136. *Mātṛkabheda Tantra* 2.5–6.

137. *Manthānabhairava Tantra*, Yoga Khaṇḍa 4.138b–40b, 142ab. I am grateful to

Mark Dyczkowski, who is preparing an annotated translation and study of this massive work, for providing me with the Sanskrit of this passage.

138. *Catuṣpīṭha*, the "fourfold mound," is a reference to the pubic triangle with the vulva at its center, which is conceived in Kaula traditions as the triangle of the *pīṭhas* of Uḍḍiyāna, Pūrṇagiri, and Jālandhara surrounding Kāmākhyā in the center.

139. RA 2.17b, 25b.

140. *Manthānabhairava Tantra*, Yoga Khaṇḍa 4.141ab.

141. *Nāthaṣoḍaśāmnāyakrama*, MSL MSS no. 1668/3059, fol. 2b, lines 4–8.

142. Bharati, *Tantric Tradition*, p. 260; RA 7.63a.

143. For an extended discussion of the lunar number sixteen, see White, *Alchemical Body*, pp. 36–44.

144. KĀN 5.111b–14b. On the *kāmakalā*, see below, chap. 4, part 1; and chap. 8, part 4.

145. Desai, *Erotic Sculpture of India* (1975), p. 77.

146. See below, chap. 7, n. 6.

147. Da Vinci's anatomical study is found in *Leonardo da Vinci, Anatomical Drawings* (Fribourg-Geneva: Productions Liber and Editions Minerva, 1978), p. 175. I owe this entire discussion to the veterinary historian Wolfgang Jöchle, who provided it to me in a letter dated December 23, 1998, in which he cites two of his own papers: "Traces of Embryo Transfer and Artificial Insemination in Antiquity and the Medieval Age" (1984); and "Treasured Breasts, A Historical View of Human Lactation" (1997).

148. Aristotle, *Generation of Animals*, book 1, 727a2–29a33; book 2, 738a9–39a33; book 4, 765b18–66b5. Hippocrates shares this view: *On the Nature of the Infant* 21.4. See bibliography for edition.

149. Apfel-Marglin, *Wives of the God-King*, pp. 57–58. Cf. Heilijger-Seelens, *System of the Five Cakras*, pp. 61–64, esp. p. 63 n. 65, for an overview of the relationship between female sexual and menstrual emissions, conception, and nurture of the human embryo. For similar modern-day Sri Lankan data, see McGilvray, "Sexual Power and Fertility," pp. 31, 54–56, 61.

150. Whence the multiplicity of terms used by scholars for *rajas*, "female discharge": it is either endocrinal fluid (Miranda Shaw's terminology), cataminal fluid (in Donaldson's terminology ["Erotic Rituals," p. 156]), or postpartum lochial discharge (facsimile communication from Wolfgang Jöchle, Denville, New Jersey, August 17, 1997).

151. Dyczkowski, "Kubjikā, Kālī, Tripurā and Trika," p. 30 n. 82. Cf. HT 2.8.8b.

152. KĀN 5.34a–35a.

153. Dyczkowski, "Kubjikā, Kālī, Tripurā and Trika," pp. 30, 33–34; "Kubjikā the Erotic Goddess," p. 128; and personal communication from the author, Todi, Italy, July 2001.

154. *Caraka Saṃhitā* 4.2.11–12. For further discussion, see White, *Alchemical Body*, p. 340. See also Daniel, *Fluid Signs*, pp. 163–64, on *intiriam*, the Tamil term popularly employed for the combination of male and female sexual fluids that gives rise to an embryo; and McGilvray, "Sexual Power and Fertility," pp. 52–54, on Sri Lankan understandings of the same.

Chapter 4

1. *Śilpa Prakāśa*, trans. Boner and Sarma, p. vii. There is an "oral tradition" among historians of South Asian art that Boner and Sarma's source was in fact a "pastiche" of medieval manuscripts, and that there was no single manuscript entitled *Śilpa Prakāśa*. Nonetheless, such specialists of Orissan and Tantric art as Thomas Donaldson

and Devangana Desai continue to accept the authenticity of this source in their writings.

2. *Śilpa Prakāśa*, trans. Boner and Sarma, introduction, p. viii. A new translation of ŚP 1.90–106 and 2.498–539 is Rabe, "Secret Yantras" (2000).

3. *Śilpa Prakāśa*, trans. Boner and Sarma, introduction, pp. xi–xii.

4. Ibid., p. xv.

5. ŚP 1.99.

6. ŚP 2.508–29.

7. ŚP 2.526b–28.

8. *Śilpa Prakāśa*, trans. Boner and Sarma, pp. liv–lv. On the Vārāhī temple, see below, n. 20.

9. *Mālatī-Mādhava*, act 5, verse 1, ed. and trans. Kale (1983), p. 95. See below, chap. 7, n. 83.

10. Shaw, *Passionate Enlightenment*, p. 160. The *vajrapadma* configuration of the *yoginīcakra* of KM 15.40, 49, in which six goddesses encircle Kuleśvara (and sometimes Kubjikā), may also draw on this image of female anatomy. Cf. TĀ 29.150b–53a.

11. *Kāma-kalā-vilāsa*, verses 15–17, trans. Avalon, p. 33. See below, chap. 8, nn. 104, 106, 112, and bibliography.

12. ŚP 2.163–79, 408–705.

13. The *jāṅgha* is a "pilaster-like projecting wall-element between two chamfers, reaching from the *pañcakarma* to the upper *bandhanā*": *Śilpa Prakāśa*, trans. Boner and Sarma, p. 147.

14. ŚP 2.432.

15. ŚP 2.498–505, following Boner and Sarma's translation.

16. ŚP 2.526. Cf. KJñN 14.94, which employs the term *kāmakalātmaka* as a synonym for the clan nectar that the same goddesses carry in their wombs. See above, chap. 3, n. 92; and below, n. 29.

17. ŚP 2.534–35, 538–39, following Boner and Sarma's translation.

18. Michael Rabe has suggested the same for the erotic imagery of the southern joining wall of the Lakṣmaṇa temple at Khajuraho. Figure 4.b is composed of Rabe's photo reproduction of this image of the same, with the ŚP *kāmakalā* superimposed upon it.

19. *Śilpa Prakāśa*, trans. Boner and Sarma, introduction, p. xix.

20. These eight images are clustered around a central diamond-shaped window on the *mukhaśāla* of the Caurasi temple: for a discussion and photographs of two of the images, see Dehejia, *Early Stone Temples* (1979), pp. 127–28. See also Donaldson, "Erotic Rituals" (1986), p. 156; and id., "Propitious-Apotropaic Eroticism" (1975), p. 95. See below, chap. 8, n. 127.

21. Hudson, "Śrımad Bhāgavata" (1995), p. 167, who finds further parallels in the "courtesan bowl" motif of medieval literature.

22. Banerjea, "Vārāhī Temple" (1965), pp. 349–54. Banerjea states that the manuscript of the *Kaulacūḍāmaṇi* was held by Sadashiva Ratha Sarma, the manuscript collector of the Orissa government, who gave him the extract quoted below (p. 354 n. 4). Sarma had procured the manuscript from Ganjam and showed it to Banerjea. The Sanskrit of the *Kaulacūḍāmaṇi* passage (in Banerjea, "Vārāhī Temple," p. 352) reads: "śṛṇu tvaṃ kāmapūjāṅgaṃ prayogakramameva ca/ hetuvādaśca matraśca tahā kāmakalādayaḥ// sukumārī tu samprāpte varayettu vidhānataḥ/ kaulajñānaṃ tu samvakṣya tvayā jñānārtha kevalam// vaśīkaraṇamādyañca sammohaṃ pakṣameva ca/ vede ākarṣaṇañcaivamuccāṭādi tathā caret// yuge yonyābhiṣekaśca vidhipūrvaṃ sācaret/ puraścaraṇa vāṇe ca indrīye rajapānakam/ prastāvamsindhu tadantaḥ nivṛtiraṣṭame tathā//."

23. Two of the eight *kāmakalā* bas-reliefs from the Vārāhī temple are reproduced in

Donaldson, "Propitious-Apotropaic Eroticism" (1975), p. 82, figs. 12, 13. Cf. id., "Erotic Rituals," p. 157.

24. On the distinction between Tantric art and "art as influenced by Tantrism without being functionally related to Tantric *sādhanā*," see below, chap. 5, n. 85.

25. Donaldson, *Kāmadeva's Pleasure Garden* (1987), figs. 45, 47, 186, 194, and discussion, pp. 280–82, 325–26; id., *Hindu Temple Art* (1987), vol. 3, figs. 4044–47, 4053–63; and id., "Erotic Rituals," figs. 37, 38, 40, 41, 44–46. It was also portrayed in temple sculpture from both south and north India, between the seventh and eighteenth centuries C.E. For two examples, see Mookerjee, *Kali* (1988), pp. 30, 42. Scenes of cunnilingis (*aupariṣṭaka*) may also have been portrayals of *rajapāna*: Donaldson, *Kāmadeva's Pleasure Garden*, p. 334.

26. Donaldson, "Erotic Rituals," p. 158 and fig. 37.

27. Donaldson, *Kāmadeva's Pleasure Garden*, pp. 326–27. Cf. Desai, *Religious Imagery of Khajuraho*, p. 201.

28. The "Goddess of the Kāmakalā" is invoked in KJñN 7.32ab. See KJñN 14.93–94, discussed in chap. 3, n. 92.

29. For example, in *Kubjikāmata* 23.133–44. For a discussion, see Heilijgers-Seelen, *System of the Five Cakras*, pp. 35–38. Cf. Munidatta's commentary on the *Caryāgīti* (see above, chap. 2, n. 4), which is, in the words of Kværne ("On the Concept of Sahaja," p. 120), "nothing but a sustained paean to the divine Yoginī in the yogin's body."

30. The *khecarī mudrā* is, however, described, without being named and in asexual terms, in KJñN 6.18–19.

31. Additionally, several Buddhist sources refer to the Buddha as dwelling in the vulvas of Adamantine women: see above, chap. 3, n. 97. The Buddhist *Caṇḍamahāroṣaṇa Tantra* calls the clitoris a "red Buddha": see below, n. 135.

32. Another part of female anatomy also consistent with this imagery is the cervix, located behind the vulva, which is the inner orifice from which menstrual blood flows. This would be a possible explanation for the numerous medieval sculpted images of female sexual display, in which the interior of the yoni is made visible. A photographic image of a female cervix issuing menstrual blood, viewed with the aid of a speculum, may be found at www.heck.com/annie/gallery/cervixmain.html.

33. It is explicitly so depicted in the Keralan myth of the birth of the goddess Bhadrakālī, who is born from Śiva's third eye: Caldwell, *Oh Terrible Mother*, p. 176. On the female yoni as the "eye of love," see Jayakar, *Earth Mother*, pp. 100, 124.

34. See above, chap. 3, nn. 73–75.

35. KJñN 16.10a: "pañcasrotātmakaṃ caiva gopitaṃ siddhigocaram//."

36. Goudriaan and Gupta, *Hindu Tantric and Śākta Literature*, pp. 10, 16.

37. Sadyojāta, Vāmadeva, Aghora, Tatpuruṣa, and Īśāna. For a discussion, see Brunner, Oberhammer, and Padoux, *Tāntrikābhidhānakośa*, pp. 24–25; and Dyczkowski, *Canon*, pp. 123–25.

38. Dyczkowski, *Canon*, pp. 64, 168–69 nn. 54–57. Cf. KM 3.7–10. See also above, chap. 1, n. 71.

39. Dyczkowski, *Canon*, p. 64 n. 56.

40. On the construction of the *liṅgam-yoni* ensemble, see Brunner-Lachaux's introduction to the fourth volume of her translation of the SŚP (1998), pp. xviii–xix. In addition, *liṅgas* had removable casings (*kośas*), sometimes in precious metals. Two eighth-century Cambodian inscriptions record six-faced *kośas*: Bagchi, *Studies in the Tantras* (1975), pp. 20–21. On the portable *liṅgas* that were used for mantra deities in Tantric practice, see Sanderson, "Meaning in Tantric Ritual," p. 20.

41. *Kālikā Purāṇa* 72.78–84, 89.

42. *Nalavilāsanāṭakam, Rāmacandrasūri*, ed. Misra (1996), pp. 60–62.

43. KJñN 16.3a, 5ab, 7a–8a.

44. KJñN 16.21a, 22b. The *Yoginī Tantra* (2.3.6, 2.4.6; cited in *Yoni Tantra*, ed. Schoterman, p. 5) location of a "Moon Peak" (*candrakūṭa*) within Kāmarūpa may be a reference to the same site. However, this text, which shows a strong Vaiṣṇava influence typical of eastern India in later centuries, refers to the male deity as Mādhava, and his consort as Mādhavī.

45. Here, I emend Bagchi's reading of *prājñā* to *prajñā*.

46. KJñN 16.23ab.

47. KJñN 16.26b. Here, I emend Bagchi's reading of *sarvaśāstrāvatārakaḥ* to *sarvaśāstrāvatārakau*.

48. KJñN 16.27.

49. KJñN 16.27b–30b.

50. KJñN 16.31a–36a.

51. See also TĀ 29.32 and Jayaratha's commentary to TĀ 1.18.

52. KJñN 16.38a–48b.

53. KJñN 16.49a–51c. Cf. the effects of the *kauladīkṣā* in TĀ 29.202a, which makes the disciple fall to the ground; and HT 1.10.12 and 2.4.68. See below, chap. 8, n. 159.

54. Sanderson, "Śaivism and the Tantric Tradition," p. 672.

55. KJñN 22.7ab.

56. KJñN 22.8b.

57. KJñN 22.9b–12b.

58. For example, the *Kriyākālaguṇottara* fol. 1, lines 2–3 (see bibliography); and the *Mālinīvijayottara Tantra* (1.4), both eighth- to ninth-century texts.

59. For example, the *Siddhayogeśvarimata Tantra*, of which the *Mālinīvijayottara Tantra* was considered to be a portion (*Mālinīvijayottara Tantra* 1.8ff.; cited in Gonda, *Medieval Religious Literature* [1977], p. 203), was transmitted from Śiva's Aghora mouth to Parameśa to the Goddess, to Kumāra (Kārttikeya), and thereafter to Nārada and the sages.

60. Sanderson, "Śaivism and the Tantric Tradition," pp. 696–99.

61. KJñN 16.40b. See above, chap. 1, n. 117.

62. White, *Alchemical Body*, pp. 229–40.

63. Personal communication from Mark Dyczkowski, Todi, Italy, July 2001.

64. TĀ 5.54–61, with the commentary of Jayaratha, in Silburn, *Kuṇḍalinī*, pp. 76, 78.

65. See below, chap. 7, part 6, and n. 66.

66. *Kāma Sūtra* 2.1.17, 22: "The followers of Babhravya say: 'A young woman reaches a climax continually, from the very beginning of lovemaking; a man, by contrast, only at the end. . . . Men's sensual pleasure comes at the end of sex, but women's is continual. And the wish to stop occurs only when fluids are used up" (in Doniger and Kakar, *Kāmasūtra of Vatsyāyana* [2002], pp. 33–34).

67. *Haṭhayogapradīpikā* 3.100, 102; *Śiva Saṃhitā* 4.1–5; and Silburn, *Kuṇḍalinī*, pp. 204–6.

68. TĀ 29.122a, with the commentary of Jayaratha (*Tantrāloka*, ed. Dwivedi and Rastogi, vol. 7, p. 3377).

69. *Akulavīratantram* (A), verse 78a (= verse 61a of *Akulavīratantram* [B]). Both manuscript versions, A and B, are found in *Kaulajñānanirṇaya* of Matsyendranātha, ed. Bagchi (see bibliography). Bagchi identifies Mīnasahajānanda with Matsyendra. An alternate reading of *sugocaram* is *svagocaram*, "naturally accessible." The Bāul tradition (Openshaw, "'Killing' the Guru," p. 13) attributes this innate perfection to a woman's

absence of male seed, or to the fact that her seed, even when it is emitted, produces no progeny. This last alternative seems to square with Indian notions of the clan as well: see above, chap. 1, nn. 86–87.

70. It may be significant in this context to note that a temple to Śiva, Lord of the Siddhas (Siddheśvara), was consecrated in 1030 C.E. in Candrapura ("Moon City"), the purported historical seat of the cult of Kubjikā, arguably a Yoginī Kaula–type cult, into which the king of that place was initiated by a figure named Siddhanātha, within a few decades of the consecration of that temple: White, *Alchemical Body*, p. 94; and Dyczkowski, "Kubjikā, Kālī, Tripurā and Trika," pp. 20–21.

71. KJñN 21.1b–4a. The nine titles are the *Pañcapañcaśikha*, *Kulapañcaśikhāmūlam*, *Kulasāgara*, *Kulogha*, *Hṛdaya*, *Bhairavodyānaka*, *Candrakaula*, *Jñānanirṇaya*, and *Saṃvara*. None of these titles are attested in other works, with the possible exceptions of the *Pañcapañcaśikha* and the *Hṛdaya:* works with similar names are mentioned in the TĀ. An exhaustive list of Abhinavagupta's cited sources is found in *Tantrāloka, Abhinavagupta, Luce dei tantra*, trans. Gnoli, pp. 699–706, "Texte ed autori citati nel <Tantrāloka>."

72. "karṇāt karṇopadeśa samprāptam," in *Yoginīhṛdaya Tantra* 1.3 (see bibliography for edition). In his commentary Amṛtānanda stipulates that this transmission passes serially from the divine to the semidivine to the human: "divaysiddhamānavakrameṇa" (in *Yoginīhṛdaya Tantra*, trans. Padoux [1994], pp. 99, 101).

73. KJñN 18.22b; TĀ 29.125b ("vaktrādvaktrastham"). For other references, see White, *Alchemical Body*, pp. 255–56.

74. See *Yoni Tantra*, ed. Schoterman, pp. 18–21 and passim.

75. TĀ 29.96–166. For discussion, see Flood, *Body and Cosmology* (1993), pp. 283–301; and Brunner, Oberhammer, and Padoux, *Tāntrikābhidhānakośa*, s.v. "ādiyāga," p. 189.

76. TĀ 29.6b–7b. Jayaratha glosses the term *yāmala* as *ādiyāga* in Abhinavagupta's list of the six types of *kulayāga* (*Tantrāloka*, ed. Dwivedi and Rastogi, vol. 7, p. 3295). Each of these six types are detailed in TĀ 29: for versification, see *Tantrāloka, Abhinavagupta, Luce dei Tantra*, trans. Gnoli, p. 550 n. 3.

77. Donaldson, "Erotic Rituals," p. 150 and passim. *Kumārī-pūjā* occurred during the maiden's menses: Nandi, *Religious Institutions and Cults* (1973), p. 125.

78. Donaldson, "Erotic Rituals," p. 156 n. 7.

79. Although *vāmāmṛtam* is read as "alcohol" in TĀ 29.10 and its commentary, I translate it as "woman's nectar" (i.e., female discharge) here, since the term *surā*, "alcohol," occurs in the same hemistich in the instrumental.

80. Here, I have emended Bagchi's *bhaktiyukto* to *śaktiyukto*. On the *buka* flower, see below, n. 128.

81. Here, I have emended Bagchi's *parijalpayet* to *parikalpayet*.

82. KJñN 18.7a–14b.

83. Here, I have emended Bagchi's *makṣabhojyayutam* to *bhakṣyabhojyayutam*.

84. Here, I have emended Bagchi's *yena* to *tena*.

85. Here, I have emended Bagchi's *samayahīna* to *samayine*.

86. KJñN 18.15a, 17a–19b, 21a–23a.

87. George, *Caṇḍamahāroṣaṇa Tantra* (1974), p. 51.

88. Discussed in Kværne, "On the Concept of Sahaja," pp. 97–101; and Snellgrove, *Indo-Tibetan Buddhism*, vol. 1, pp. 256–64.

89. www.tantra.com/boston2.html. This is a highly informative 1998 article by Alicia Potter, posted on the tantra.com website, which originally appeared in the *Boston Phoenix* under the title "Truly, Slowly, Deeply: Men Don't Ejaculate, Women Do, and You Have to Learn to Find Your Chakras. Tantric Sex Is Not Your Average Roll in

the Hay" (1998). In it, Potter interviews and quotes a number of Western Tantric sex gurus and practitioners. Another website, meditationfrance.com, quotes Rajneesh (Osho) as saying, in a work entitled "Vighyan Bharav Tantra" (vol. 1, chap. 34): "The Tantric sex act is fundamentally different. . . . You remain in the act without ejaculation. . . ."

90. HT 1.8.26–29; 1.10.5–6; 2.3.13–14; and Kværne, "On the Concept of Sahaja," pp. 112–22.

91. According to the *Kālī Sahasranāma Stotra*, one is to recite the names of Kālī, many of which emphasize her sexual organ and sexual appetites, while meditating on a menstruating yoni: personal communication from Mark Dyczkowski, Todi, Italy, July 2001.

92. The first two chapters of the *Yoni Tantra* are devoted to this ritual, which concludes with the drinking of the *yonitattva*: YT 2.22–24. Drinking of the *yonitattva* is also prescribed in this text at 6.33a; and in the *Mātṛkabheda Tantra* 5.40.

93. The mouth of the Yoginī is identified as the *picuvaktra* by Jayaratha in his commentary: *Tantrāloka*, ed. Dwivedi and Rastogi, vol. 7, p. 3371. See above, n. 39. For an eighteenth-century south Indian representation of a woman emitting torrents of discharge, see Mookerjee, *Kali*, p. 42.

94. "Arisen form" (*abhyuditaṃ rūpam*) in the text, glossed by Jayaratha as *kuṇḍagolaka* (*Tantrāloka*, ed. Dwivedi and Rastogi, vol. 7, p. 3381).

95. TĀ 29.122a–26a, 127b–28b.

96. Here, I am referring to much of the first part of the entire twenty-ninth *āhnika* of the TĀ, from its presentation of the six types of *kulayāga* (29.6b–7b) to the end of the description of *adiyāga* (29.166b), in *Tantrāloka*, ed. Dwivedi and Rastogi, vol. 7, pp. 3215–404.

97. Here, the "Śakti" may be the same woman as the "Yoginī," given that, as Flood has noted (*Body and Cosmology*, p. 287), "the yogi or siddha, also called the 'hero' (*vīra*), becomes the possessor of Śakti, while the yoginī or 'messenger' (*dūtī*) becomes Śakti." Cf. Masson and Patwardan, *Śāntarasa*, pp. 40–41.

98. Jayaratha's commentary on TĀ 29.127b–29a (*Tantrāloka*, ed. Dwivedi and Rastogi, vol. 7, p. 3382). See also Flood, *Body and Cosmology*, pp. 298, 387. Parallel practices from the Buddhist "Highest Yoga Tantra" tradition of the *Hevajra Tantra* and other sources are described in detail in Beyer, *Buddhist Experience* (1974), pp. 140–53; Snellgrove, *Indo-Tibetan Buddhism*, vol. 1, pp. 256–64; and Kværne, "On the Concept of Sahaja," pp. 88–135.

99. TĀ 29.29a. Presented in diagrammatic form in Dyczkowski, *Canon*, p. 81: as Dyczkowski himself notes ("Kubjikā, Kālī, Tripurā and Trika," p. 47 n. 135), this diagram was published upside down. Remarkably, Jain Tantric traditions also knew of a Siddha Cakra as a meditation support: the *Yoga Śāstra* of Hemacandra states that "the Circle of the Siddhas should always be learned from the guru and meditated upon for the destruction of karma": *Yoga Shastra of Hemachandracharya* ed. Bothara and trans. Gopani (1989), p. 223.

100. TĀ 29.26b–54b, with the commentary of Jayaratha (*Tantrāloka*, ed. Dwivedi and Rastogi, vol. 7, pp. 3313–29).

101. TĀ 29.32b. Kṣemarāja presents the same configuration in his commentary to the term *kulāmnāyadarśana* in *Netra Tanta* 12.1 (in *Netratantram*, ed. Dwivedi, p. 91).

102. TĀ 29.32b–36b. For discussion, see *Tantrāloka, Abhinavagupta, Luce dei Tantra*, trans. Gnoli, p. 553 n. 1; and Sanderson, "Śaivism and the Tantric Tradition," p. 681.

103. Jayaratha's commentary to TĀ 29.36b (*Tantrāloka*, ed. Dwivedi and Rastogi, vol. 7, p. 3318).

104. TĀ 29.40.

105. TĀ 29.43.

106. *Caraka Saṃhitā* 6.9.20–21. See above, chap. 2, n. 164. See also below, chap. 6, n. 1; and chap. 7, nn. 18, 19, on the vicissitudes of becoming food for the Yoginīs.

107. TĀ 29.37–39, 59–72.

108. On the centrality of the sexual commerce with the Dūtī, and the consumption and offering of her sexual or menstrual fluids in Kaula practice, see Sanderson, "Meaning in Tantric Ritual," pp. 83–86.

109. Jayaratha, introduction to TĀ 29.96 (*Tantrāloka*, ed. Dwivedi and Rastogi, vol. 7, p. 3353): *dautam vidhim*. See above, chap. 3, n. 107, for a similar use of the term *dūtīyāga*.

110. Masson and Patwardhan, *Śāntarasa*, pp. 40–41.

111. Shaw (*Passionate Enlightenment*, pp. 140–78, esp. 154–58, 176, and notes) provides detailed discussion of parallel practices, involving Yoginīs/Dūtīs in Buddhist Tantra. Shaw, however, imputes greater agency and intentionality to these female figures than I find in the Hindu material.

112. A manuscript entitled *Madyapānavidhi* ("Rules for Drinking Alcohol"), MSL MSS no. 1786A/3079, fol. 5a, line 9, retains the "mouth-to-mouth" sense of such transmissions while reversing the polarity I have been stressing: "The doctrine of Vāsudeva, which was issued (*āgatam*) from Śambhu's mouth, went into the mouth of the Mountain-born (Pārvatī). Therefore it is called 'issue' (*āgamam*)." See above, chap. 3, n. 72, for the term *āgamā*.

113. See, for example, KSS 9.5.183–224. Cf. *Harivaṃśa* 65.48–57, cited above, chap. 2, n. 169. The Goddess is already referred to as Vindhyavāsinī in the "Durgā Stotra" of the MBh: see above, chap. 2, n. 88.

114. Compare KJñN 16.42, which describes the same vegetative model, but in a masculine mode.

115. KĀN 5.121a–23b.

116. See above, chap. 2, nn. 24–26, and chap. 3, n. 122.

117. Alampur, Archaeological Museum, no. 52; reproduced in *In the Image of Man* (1982), p. 110, plate 55.

118. Silburn, *Kuṇḍalinī*, p. 224.

119. Monier-Williams, *Sanskrit-English Dictionary*, s.v. "bakula," p. 719.

120. *Prabodhacandrodaya*, ed. and trans. Nambiar, pp. 84–89. See above, chap. 3, n. 124. Curiously, the female character who allegorizes a more exalted "Faith—Daughter of *Sattva*" in this work, is a "Yoginī" named "Viṣṇubhakti": Woodward, "Lakṣmaṇa Temple" (1989), pp. 30–31.

121. "śaktijihvāviloḍitam": KĀN 5.57b–59b.

122. Caldwell, *Oh Terrible Mother*, pp. 20, 178–79.

123. In fact, the compound *kṛṣṇāsava* may be a reference to the palmyra and the toddy produced from it: in Sanskrit lexicography, the compound *āsavadru* refers to the palmyra tree *Borassus flabelliformis*, whose juice, on fermenting, affords a spirituous liquor: Monier-Williams, *Sanskrit-English Dictionary*, s.v. "āsava," p. 160.

124. Caldwell, *Oh Terrible Mother*, p. 110. Also in Kerala, outcaste Mātaṅgī women, who have served as village shamanesses and "special representatives of the Goddess" since the tenth century, will periodically become possessed by the Goddess, drinking toddy and dancing in a wild frenzy as they run about spitting toddy on the assembled crowd, uttering strange wild cries and hurling obscene verbal abuse at all present: ibid., pp. 23–24; citing R. L. Brubaker, *The Ambivalent Mistress*, University of Chicago dissertation (1978), p. 269. Ucciṣṭa-matāṅginī, a form of the Mahāvidyā named Mātaṅgī, accepts "leftover" offerings of menses stained clothing: Kinsley, *Tantric Visions* (1997), p. 216. See below, chap. 9, n. 17.

125. Kripal, *Kālī's Child* (1995), pp. 243–306, esp. pp. 249–50.
126. Apfel-Marglin, *Wives of the God-King*, p. 215.
127. See above, n. 79.
128. See above, n. 80.
129. Monier-Williams, *Sanskrit-English Dictionary*, s.v. "āsava," p. 160.
130. KĀN 5.85a–89a.
131. KĀN 5.96b–98a.
132. Kinsley, *Tantric Visions*, p. 245.
133. Personal communication with David Knipe, Madison, Wisconsin, October 1992.
134. Shaw, *Passionate Enlightenment*, pp. 155–57.
135. Ibid., quoting George, *Caṇḍamahāroṣaṇa Tantra*, pp. 112–13. The flower of the *bandhūka* (*Pentapetes phoenicia*, sometimes called scarlet marrow) is of a brilliant orange-red color, with six petals and a prominent whitish stamen. Verse 22 of the *Saṭcakranirūpaṇa* (see below, chap. 8, n. 8) identifies the six-petaled *anāhata cakra* with this flower; it is also identified with the red six-cornered Kālī yantra.
136. "Bṛhadpīṭhādikāravarṇana," which constitutes fols. 394–427 of the "Yoga-khaṇḍa" of the *Manthānabhairava Tantra*; cited in Dyczkowski, "Kubjikā the Erotic Goddess," p. 136 n. 18.
137. See above, chap. 2, n. 126.
138. Dyczkowski, "Kubjikā, Kālī, Tripurā and Trika," p. 56; citing *Manthāna-bhairava Tantra*, Kumārikākhaṇḍa 3.125b–26a, 11.22b–23b, 17.30ab; and personal communication from the author, Todi, Italy, July 2001.
139. *Siddhayogeśvarīmata Tantra* 12.4–11, quoted in Sanderson, "Visualisation" (1990), pp. 36–37. Cf. *Jayadrathayāmala*, second hexad, fol. 112a4–8 (quoted in ibid., pp. 43–44), in which the goddess Vidyāvidyeśvarī plays the same transmissive role.
140. Böhtlingk and Roth, *Sanskrit Wörterbuch* (1855–75, reprint 1990) vol. 4, p. 705, s.v. "picu-marda." See above, chap. 2, nn. 198–200.
141. The ritual was held in late March 1999 in the home of Radhakrishna Srimalli, an eminent Jodhpur-based astrologer and Śaiva scholar. On yantras and ritual implements, see Gonda, "Dīkṣā," in *Change and Continuity* (1965), p. 430. Gonda cites Rao, *Elements of Hindu Iconography*, vol. 2, part 1, pp. 10–11. However, the quotation is found neither here nor anywhere else in Rao's four-volume work.

Chapter 5

1. See above, chap. 1, n. 48.
2. See Samuel's classic discussion of these terms in his *Civilized Shamans*, pp. 7–10.
3. Gupta and Gombrich, "Kings, Power and the Goddess," p. 130 and n. 17, referring to the sixth book of Kauṭilya's *Arthaśāstra*, whose title is "Maṇḍalayoni" ("Source of the Realm").
4. Slusser, *Nepal Mandala*, epigraph to vol. 1, p. vii.
5. Gupta and Gombrich, "Kings, Power and the Goddess," pp. 130–31; Toffin, *Le Palais et le temple*, pp. 126–27, 168, 224.
6. Sax, "Ramnagar Ramlila," pp. 143, 145.
7. Toffin, *Le Palais et le temple*, pp. 95, 107–10.
8. Stewart and Rinehart, "Anonymous *Āgama Prakāśa*," p. 280. On the possible Swāminārāyaṇ stamp of this work, see ibid., pp. 268–69.
9. See above, chap. 1, n. 4.
10. Tambs-Lyche, *Power, Profit, and Poetry*, p. 41.
11. Ibid., pp. 25, 122–27, 260, 267–71, and passim. For a south Indian example, see below, chap. 7, n. 64.

12. *Mānasollāsa* 2.8.696, cited in Gupta and Gombrich, "Kings, Power and the Goddess," p. 131. See above, chap. 3, part 4, for an extended discussion of the term *ājñā*.

13. Although the three kingdoms of the Kathmandu Valley have been dominated by their royal capitals, ancient urban centers, these began as, and have remained, overwhelmingly rural in their demography and agricultural in their economies: for a discussion, see Toffin, *Le Palais et le temple*, pp. 123–25.

14. Lidke, "Goddess," pp. 100–21; and Toffin, *Le Palais et le temple*, p. 43.

15. Tambs-Lyche, *Power, Profit, and Poetry*, pp. 60–61.

16. Inden, "Ritual, Authority, and Cyclic Time" (1978).

17. As Tambs-Lyche notes, the public cultus of the Rajput kings, at first Saivite, eventually came to favor the god Rāma, to "sanctify kingship over kinship," and mainly as a means to maintain a link with the divine that transcended the family alliances sacralized by their cults of the *kuldevīs*: ibid., pp. 85–86, 92. See below, nn. 72–75.

18. Taleju Bhavānī played an identical role among the Marāthas of Maharashtra: Toffin, *Le Palais et le temple*, p. 43 n. 22. Cf. Dyczkowski, "Kubjikā, Kālī, Tripurā and Trika," p. 10; and Weinberger-Thomas, *Ashes*, p. 87, for a Rajasthani parallel.

19. Toffin, *Le Palais et le temple*, pp. 31, 43, 46. Taleju's temples date from the fourteenth century in Bhaktapur, 1501 in Kathmandu, and 1620 in Pathan. See also Bledsoe, "An Advertised Secret" (2000).

20. See above, chap. 2, n. 88.

21. Hudson, "Madurai" (1993), p. 134. See also id., "Śrīmad Bhāgavata," p. 167, on the power of *rajas*, menstrual blood obtained in Tantric rites, to empower the king, in other Tamil traditions.

22. Harper, *Iconography*, p. 158.

23. *Gaūḍavaho*, vv. 285–338, and introduction, pp. xxi–xxiii; cited in Tiwari, *Goddess Cults*, p. 67.

24. Toffin, *Le Palais et le temple*, p. 104.

25. Tiwari, *Goddess Cults*, pp. 41–47; and Toffin, *Le Palais et le temple*, p. 219.

26. Dyczkowski, "Kubjikā, Kālī, Tripurā and Trika," pp. 20–21; citing his unpublished critical edition of chapter 43 of the *Saṭsāhasrasaṃhitā*.

27. Tambs-Lyche, *Power, Profit, and Poetry*, pp. 23–25, 32–33.

28. See above, chap. 2, nn. 22, 32; and below, chap. 7, nn. 29–31.

29. *Devī Māhātmya* 2.11.

30. *Mānava Dharma Śāstra* 7.1, 3–8, 10–11; discussed in Coburn, *Devī-Māhātmya*, pp. 229–30.

31. Parpola, *Deciphering*, pp. 255–56 and figs. 14.30, 14.31, which link the floor plan of the ruins of the circa 1900–1700 B.C.E. Bactrian Dashly-3 palace, in northern Afghanistan, with the *bhūpura* ("earth citadel") configuration of Tantric mandalas.

32. Toffin, *Le Palais et le temple*, pp. 43, 69–70, 114. Cf. Gupta and Gombrich, "Kings, Power and the Goddess," p. 133, for a survival of the same practice in Mysore.

33. Toffin, *Le Palais et le temple*, p. 194.

34. Desai, *Religious Imagery of Khajuraho*, p. 83.

35. *Mānasollāsa* 2.17–20 is devoted to royal polity. Chapter 20 of part 2, devoted to "enforcement" (*daṇḍa*), is divided into four parts, of which the first, entitled "Yoginī-Cakra," is comprised of vv. 1031–145. See especially vv. 1031–82, 1141–45.

36. Retold in Forbes, *Râs-Mâlâ*, vol. 1, p. 238.

37. Davidson, "Political Dimension" (1999), p. 15. Davidson has thoroughly revised and expanded this material in a forthcoming book: *Indian Esoteric Buddhism: A Social History of the Tantric Movement* (New York: Columbia University Press).

38. Strickmann, *Mantras et mandarins*, pp. 40, 348.

39. Toffin, *Le Palais et le temple*, p. 45.
40. Ibid., p. 195.
41. Strickmann, *Mantras et mandarins*, p. 37.
42. Ibid., p. 197.
43. Ibid., p. 420. Much of Balinese Tantric ritual can be traced back to Indian sources. For example, the *Somaśambhupaddhati* description of the *homa* ceremony at the conclusion of the *nirvāṇa-dīkṣā* ritual is identical to that found in Balinese Śaivism: ibid., p. 360. A portion of this ritual is described below, chap. 8, nn. 182–87.
44. Schwartzberg, ed., *Historical Atlas* (1992), pp. 36, 43, 193, 201–2.
45. Hooykaas, *Āgama Tīrtha* (1964), p. 138.
46. Ibid., p. 139. The text is found in Lévi, *Sanskrit Texts* (1933), p. 14, no. 52. The Sanskrit reads: "amṛtaṃ varṣate tasmāt sarvāṅga-sandhiṣu yataḥ / dampatayoḥ saṅgato jātam jīvitaṃ parikīrtitam //."
47. This language of vessel and fluid, identified with this divine pair, is also found in *Yoginīhṛdaya* 1.54 (with the commentary of Amṛtānanda, in *Yoginīhṛdaya Tantra, Coeur*, trans. Padoux, p. 150), in which "the container is Kāmeśvara. That which he receives is the supreme effulgence named Kāmeśvarī."
48. Hooykaas, *Āgama Tīrtha*, p. 139.
49. Ibid., p. 140. According to Hooykaas, this *karṇikā* configuration corresponds to that prescribed in chapter 26 of the *Rauravāgama*, a Śaivasiddhānta work widely used in Indonesia in this period. See below, chap. 8, n. 176.
50. *Karpūra-Mañjarī by Kavirāja Rājaśekhara*, ed. Suru (1960), pp. 137–38 (note to line 22); and referring to the same play, Sharma, ed., *Kalacuri*, vol. 2, p. 279.
51. See Brunner, "Tantra du Nord," pp. 151–52, for similar configurations in the *Netra Tantra*, Śaivasiddhānta, and other systems.
52. Hudson, "Madurai," p. 129.
53. Ibid., pp. 133–34.
54. Sharma, ed., *Kalacuri*, vol. 2, pp. 291–93, 295–96. On the medieval phenomenon of royal patronage of monumental temples in India, see Willis, "Religious and Royal Patronage" (1993), esp. pp. 56–59, 62.
55. Sharma, *Temple of Chaunsaṭha-yoginī*, p. 5.
56. Desai, *Religious Imagery of Khajuraho*, p. 83; Dehejia, *Yoginī Cult and Temples*, pp. 56, 125. The sole temple ground plans about which Varāhamihira gives any detail in his *Bṛhat Saṃhitā* (53.42–56, 56.10) are the sixty-four- and eighty-one-square plans. The ideal Nepali city plan was based on an eighty-one-square template: Toffin, *Le Palais et le temple*, p. 84.
57. Documented as early as the sixth-century C.E. *Bṛhat Saṃhitā* (60.19).
58. On these terms, see above, chap. 1, n. 35; and below, chap. 6, n. 33.
59. Quoted in Desai, *Erotic Sculpture of India*, p. 81. Yoginī temples or shrines also protected the borders of kingdoms: see above, nn. 34–36.
60. A similarity of sculptural style and epigraphy, found among the temples of Bheraghat, Shahdol, and Mitauli, indicates a common workshop and school of sculpture for these temples.
61. On the pivotal Śiva or Bhairava image, see above, chap. 2, nn. 232, 233. In 1155 C.E. the Bheraghat Yoginī temple was "converted" into a "Gaurī-Śaṅkar" temple, an edifice that fills the southern part of the open central area, and which involved the displacement of central Bhairava or dancing Śiva images: Sharma, *Temple of Chaunsaṭha-yoginī*, p. 33.
62. Dehejia, *Yoginī Cult and Temples*, pp. 63, 137.
63. Ibid., p. 84 and passim; Mallmann, *Enseignements*, pp. 175–79.
64. Documented in *Khel, the Play*, video by Roy and Dewan (1994).

65. Mallmann, *Enseignements*, pp. 174–75.

66. Desai, *Religious Imagery of Khajuraho*, p. 83. A significant number of the Yoginī sculptures from the Mitauli temple are housed in the nearby Gwalior Archaeological Museum.

67. Ibid., p. 83. Delhi's reputation as a "City of Yoginīs" continued, among Jains at least, well into the thirteenth century: Dundas, "Jain Monk Jinapati Sūri" (2000) .

68. *Rājataraṅgiṇī* 1.122, 1.350, 3.99, 5.55; cited in Mallmann, *Enseignements*, p. 173. See below, n. 113.

69. Gangdhar is a village located in the western Malwa region of Madhya Pradesh, some fifty-two miles southwest of Jhalrapatan, Kotah District, Rajasthan: Meister, "Regional Variations," p. 240 n. 26.

70. The inscription is found in Fleet, "Gangdhar Stone Inscription" (1888), vol. 3, no. 17, pp. 76–78, lines 35–37. See below, chap. 7, n. 69.

71. See maps in Dehejia, *Yoginī Cult and Temples*, p. 84; and Atherton, *Sculpture* (1997), p. xiv. For discussion, see Joshi, *Mātṛkās*, pp. 84–88; and Schastok, *Śāmalājī Sculptures*, passim.

72. Tiwari, *Goddess Cults*, pp. 102–3. On the dates and territories of these two dynasties, who conquered one another over a period of several centuries, see Schwartzberg, *Historical Atlas*, pp. 26 (plate III.d.2), 180–82.

73. Sircar, "Śakti Cult in Western India," in *Śakti Cult and Tārā* (1967), p. 89.

74. Lidke, *Viśvarūpa Mandir* (1996), pp. 134–38; citing Mukunda Raj Aryal, who posits a Licchavi date for the Chinnamastā image. The earliest mention of the temple dates from 464 C.E.: Toffin, *Le Palais et le temple*, p. 34.

75. See, among many others, Dimock, *Place of the Hidden Moon*; Hayes, "*Necklace of Immortality*" (2000); Eschmann, Kulke, and Tripathi, "Formation of the Jagannātha Triad," pp. 178–81; and Bhattacharyya, *Religious Culture*, pp. 50–58 and passim.

76. On Gangdhar, see below, chap. 7, n. 69; on Khajuraho, see Rabe, "Sexual Imagery."

77. Donaldson, *Hindu Temple Art of Orissa*, vol. 3, p. 1160; id., "Propitious-Apotropaic Eroticism" (1975), pp. 76, 95; id., *Kāmadeva's Pleasure Garden*, p. 280; and Desai, *Erotic Sculpture of India*, pp. 75, 83, 145.

78. Donaldson, "Erotic Rituals," p. 180; and id., "Propitious-Apotropaic Eroticism," p. 94. See also above, chap. 4, nn. 22–26.

79. Desai, *Erotic Sculpture of India*, p. 79.

80. Naravāhanadatta, the protagonist prince of the KSS, is a partial incarnation of Kāma: 9.4.45. Recall as well that the king of Indonesian initiation rituals was identified with Kāmeśvara: see above, n. 45.

81. Desai, *Erotic Sculpture of India*, p. 86.

82. In a *liṅgam*-worship scene portrayed on the Modhera temple, ascetics are shown making exactly the same gesture: Ibid., p. 78 and plates 138, 146, 147.

83. Desai, *Religious Imagery of Khajuraho*, pp. 190–91 and plate 198.

84. Donaldson, "Erotic Rituals," pp. 162, 167, 180; and id., *Kāmadeva's Pleasure Garden*, pp. 326, 332.

85. Donaldson, *Kāmadeva's Pleasure Garden*, p. 200.

86. On the specificity and symbolism of Indian narrative frames, see O'Flaherty, *Dreams* (1984), esp. pp. 197–205.

87. Somadeva—the eleventh-century author who actually composed the *Kathāsaritsāgara*, the greatest of such anthologies, for a queen (Sūryamatī)— offers it, in the final lines of his work, to "good people" (*sanskṛtāḥ*), i.e., the Kashmirian aristocracy.

88. The KSS is not the sole, or even the earliest, South Asian source of the "Vampire Tales": see the introduction to *Vetālapañcaviṃśati, Contes du Vampire*, trans. Renou (1963) pp. 10–18.

89. Naravāhanadatta has married nineteen semidivine or human women (KSS 15.2.114–18) by the end of the epic (KSS, books 14, 15), in which he also realizes his destiny as a Vidyādhara king and a universal conqueror (*cakravartin*).

90. Pathak, "Navasāhasāṅkacarita" (1965), p. 429. The same author indicates that from the early medieval period onward, Jains adapted Puranic and Epic mythology, transforming demons and animals (e.g., the monkey king Sugrīva) into Vidyādharas (p. 428).

91. Goetz, "Historical Background," p. 119. See below, chap. 6, n. 71.

92. On the chronology and the geographical spread of the later Cāḷukyas of Kalyāṇī, see Schwartzberg, *Historical Atlas*, p. 147, plate XIV.3.e.

93. *Mānasollāsa* 5.18.914–18.

94. See above, n. 35.

95. Toffin, *Le Palais et le temple*, pp. 48, 72, 250; and Gupta and Gombrich, "Kings, Power and the Goddess," p. 132.

96. Dyczkowski, "Kubjikā, Kālī, Tripurā and Trika," p. 7.

97. In another medieval play, the *Āgamaḍambara*, a *tāntrika* disturbs the peace of a royal court: personal communication from Richard Gombrich, London, February 2001. I have been unable to consult this play of which an edition exists: *Āgamaḍambara*, ed. Raghavan and Thakur (1964). A new critical edition and translation is presently being prepared by Csaba Dezso, a graduate student at Oxford University.

98. In addition to Suru's edition of the *Karpūra-Mañjarī* (see above, n. 50), I have also used *Rāja-Çekara's Karpūra-mañjarī*, ed. Konow, trans. Lanman (1901). My analysis is based in part on Chattopadhyaya, *Making* (1994), pp. 223–32.

99. *Karpūramañjarī* 1.22, in *Karpūra-Mañjarī*, ed. Suru, pp. 137–38; and discussed in Chattopadhyaya, *Making*, pp. 226–27.

100. *Karpūramañjarī* 4.15.

101. He was a Yāyāvara brahmin: Chattopadhyaya, *Making*, p. 223.

102. Ibid., p. 228.

103. Ibid., pp. 227–28.

104. Goetz, "Historical Background," pp. 108–21. A similar argument is also developed in Desai, *Religious Imagery of Khajuraho*, pp. 181–89, who nonetheless comes to different conclusions.

105. Desai, *Religious Imagery of Khajuraho*, p. 121.

106. See above, chap. 4, n. 18 and fig. 4.b.

107. Desai, *Religious Imagery of Khajuraho*, pp. 109–10.

108. Ibid., pp. 115–16.

109. Ibid., p. 113.

110. Ibid., pp. 117–18; Desai, *Erotic Sculpture of India*, p. 77 and plate 141, which depicts the preparation of aphrodisiac drugs amidst a scene of sexual orgy, from the Lakṣmaṇa temple, Khajuraho; and Donaldson, *Kāmadeva's Pleasure Garden*, p. 332.

111. Goetz, "Historical Background," p. 119.

112. See below, chap. 7, n. 90.

113. *Rājataraṅgiṇī* 7.1129–32, quoted in Goetz, "Historical Background," p. 118 and n. 32. In his chronicle of King Kalaśa (fl. 1063–1089), Kalhaṇa depicts that depraved ruler as falling in with evil Tantric gurus from both high- and low-caste society: *Rājataraṅgiṇī* 7.273–83, in *Rājataraṅgiṇī*, ed. Pandey (1985).

114. Desai, *Religious Imagery of Khajuraho*, p. 1, in which she indicates, on the basis of inscriptional evidence, that the Lakṣmaṇa temple was consecrated by Dhaṅgadeva, and the Kandariyā Mahādeva temple by Vidyādhara, the son of Gaṇḍadeva. Desai furthermore identifies sculptures on the joining walls of the Lakṣmaṇa temple as architectural references to the PC: ibid., pp. 181–89. This raises new chronological problems, however, since the PC (1070–1090 C.E.) is dated over a century later than the 954 C.E.

Lakṣmaṇa temple. Hiram Woodward ("Lakṣmaṇa Temple," p. 31) hypothesizes a "lost prototype" of the PC.

115. Ibid., p. 27; and Willis, "Religious and Royal Patronage," p. 61 and fig. 21.

116. Sharma, ed., *Kalacuri*, vol. 2, pp. 282–302, 305; Davis, "Inscriptions of the Drunken Peacocks" (2000). See above, nn. 54–62.

117. Quoted in Sharma, ed., *Kalacuri*, vol. 2, p. 281: "tataḥ praviśati kāpālikarūpadhārī somasiddhāntinaḥ//."

118. Jayaratha's commentary following the end of book 37 of the TĀ, in *Tantrāloka*, ed. Dwivedi and Rastogi, vol. 8, pp. 3718–25.

119. *Netra Tantra* 12.6–8, 17.5–7, 19.88–100, 20.54–57.

120. *Netra Tantra* 19.93b–94b, 211a.

121. *Lakṣmī Tantra*, trans. Gupta (1972), pp. 312–13, 315–16, 318–20, 323–24.

122. Strickmann, *Mantras et mandarins*, p. 348.

123. Toffin, "La Voie des <héros>" (1989), pp. 24–25.

124. A similar situation obtains in Buddhist Bhutan. The palace massacre of August 2001 may change the relationship between the royal family and the Tantric priesthood in Nepal.

125. Toffin, *Le Palais et le temple*, pp. 215, 216, 223.

126. Ibid., pp. 24–25.

127. Tambs-Lyche, *Power, Profit, and Poetry*, pp. 220–22; and Toffin, *Le Palais et le temple*, pp. 46, 112–13.

128. Toffin, "La Voie des <héros>," pp. 19–39. See also id., *Le Palais et le temple*, pp. 46–47, 110–13, who also notes that while these brahmins are nearly entirely excluded from the cult of Taleju in Kathmandu, they remain linked to those of Bhaktapur and Patan (p. 49).

129. See Toffin (*Le Palais et le temple*, p. 44) on the myth of Taleju's curse on the Gorkha conqueror Pṛthivinārāyaṇ Śāh as the reason for the exclusion of the Gorkha-Śāh kings from her inner sanctum.

130. Dyczkowski, "Kubjikā, Kālī, Tripurā and Trika," p. 2.

131. This is because, unlike the Malla kings before them—whose link to Taleju was direct, since she was their lineage goddess as well—the Śāh kings did not completely "inherit" Taleju from the kings they ousted from power in the Kathmandu Valley, and therefore can only access the tutelary goddess of their kingdom through the Taleju Rājopādhyāya and his assistants.

132. Toffin (*Le Palais et le temple*, p. 45), who also notes that the rivalry—religious, political, and economic—between brahmin Rājopādhyāya and *kṣatriya* Karmācārya priests continues to rage in the valley (p. 112).

133. TĀ 4.24b–25, 4.251a, with Jayaratha's commentary, in Rastogi and Dwivedi, *Tantāloka*, vol. 3, pp. 643, 893–94. Cf. *Yonitantra* 4.20 and other sources cited in *Yoni Tantra*, ed. Schoterman, p. 16; and KĀN 10.94b. The KT 11.83 alters the aphorism to read: "Secretly Kaula, outwardly Śaiva, and Vaiṣṇava among men."

134. These include the *Kulārṇava Tantra*, *Kulacūḍāmaṇi*, *Rudrayāmala*, *Bhāvacūḍāmaṇi*, *Kulakamala*, *Kulagahvara*, *Kulatattvasāra*, *Kulapañcāmṛta*, *Kuladīpinī*, *Kulapañcāśikā* (and thirty other works with "Kula-" in their titles), as well as the *Meru Tantra*, *Kaula Tantra*, *Kaulikārcanadīpikā*, *Āgamasāra*, *Vāmakeśvaratantra*, *Tantrarāja*, *Śāmbhavītantra*, *Gandharva Tantra*, *Paramānanda Tantra*, *Dakṣiṇamūrti Saṃhitā*, *Śrītattvacintāmaṇi*, and the *Rahasyārṇava:* Kaviraj, *Tāntrik Sāhitya* (1972), p. 49.

135. See above, chap. 1, nn. 82, 83; and chap. 3, n. 72.

136. Rocher (*Purāṇas*, [1986], p. 157) dates the *Brahmāṇḍa Purāṇa* to 400–1000 C.E. The "Lālitā Sahasranāma," which comprises *Brahmāṇḍa Purāṇa* 3.4.5–44, would necessarily date to the lower end of this period.

137. *Lalitā-Sahasranāma*, trans. Sastry (1899; 6th reprint of 3rd ed., 1988), titles 90–96 (pp. 86–90), and title 441 (p. 216).

138. *Haravijaya* 47.96, 98, in Smith, *Ratnākara's* Haravijaya, (1985), pp. 263–64.

139. Kṣemarāja, commentary on *Vijñāna Bhairava*, p. 4; quoted in Kaviraj, *Tāntrik Sāhitya*, p. 48. Kṣemarāja makes a similar defense of the Kaula in his commentary on *Netra Tantra* 12: Brunner, "Tantra du Nord," pp. 154–55 n. 6.

140. Dyczkowski, "Kubjikā, Kālī, Tripurā and Trika," pp. 27–28.

141. KT 2.7–10. The praises of the Clan Practice and the Clan Gnosis continue for another thirty verses.

142. Lorenzen, *Kāpālikas and Kālāmukhas*, pp. 13–95. For Puranic myths that identify Kāpālikas as heretics, see O'Flaherty, *Origins of Evil* (1976), pp. 272–320; stock condemnations of heretical sects are found in numerous Puranic sources, surveyed in Hazra, *Studies in the Purāṇic Records* (1936), pp. 207, 223–25.

143. KSS 18.5.3–23, especially verses 15b–16b. See also KSS 18.2.3–33.

144. A lost Ayurvedic work is entitled *Svargavaidya-kāpālika;* the "rapid Kāpālika method" for perfecting mercury is discussed in the eleventh-century *Rasārṇava:* White, *Alchemical Body*, pp. 148, 166, 173, 417. Two late south Indian manuscripts, entitled *Kāpālika Tantra*, are alchemical works: MSS no. 772, University of Mysore; MSS no. 7475, University of Travancore.

145. Lorenzen, *Kāpālikas and Kālāmukhas*, pp. 24–31; id., "New Light on the Kāpālikas" (1989), pp. 231–38. The four grants to "Kāpālikas" are all from western India. One dates from the sixth century C.E., one from the seventh century, and two from the eleventh century.

146. *Padma Purāṇa* 1.60.37–43, 6.235–36: see bibliography. See also O'Flaherty's discussion of *Padma Purāṇa* 6.263 in *Origins of Evil*, p. 286.

147. *Kurma Purāṇa* 1.29.13; *Matsya Purāṇa* 144.40; and *Vāyu Purāṇa* 58.64; discussed in Hazra, *Studies in the Purāṇic Records*, p. 207.

148. Lorenzen, *Kāpālikas and Kālāmukhas*, p. 2. Cf. Sharma, ed., *Kalacuri*, vol. 2, p. 297.

149. The image of Śiva as a wandering Kāpālika begging ascetic (Bhikṣātaṇamūrti) who also seduces the *ṛṣis*' wives in the Pine Forest predominates in Orissan temple sculpture during the ninth century (Donaldson, "Erotic Rituals," pp. 141–47 and figs. 6,10–13), before being superseded by images of "Tantric sex" in the tenth (p. 148).

150. KSS 3.5.74–85. The *Nalavilāsa* passage is cited without reference in Lorenzen, *Kāpālikas and Kālāmukhas*, p. 52.

151. See above, n. 117. Compounds containing the term "yoga" seem to have had the same signification: the *Arthaśāstra* (1.21.29, 5.2.32) as well, perhaps, as the *Harivaṃśa* (96.13–15) use the terms *yogapuruṣa* and *yogakanyā* or *yogastrī* to designate male and female "secret agents": Couture and Schmid, "*Harivaṃśa*," p. 179 n. 14.

152. Rāmānuja, *Śrībhāṣya* 2.35–37; quoted in Lorenzen, *Kāpālikas and Kālāmukhas*, p. 2.

153. Sanderson, "Meaning in Tantric Ritual," pp. 79–80; citing *Svacchanda Tantra* 3.2a–4b, with the commentary of Kṣemarāja.

154. Sharma, ed., *Kalacuri*, vol. 2, p. 279.

155. Dehejia, *Yoginī Cult and Temples*, p. 86.

156. Dyczkowski, *Canon*, p. 6; citing *The Yaśastilaka and Indian Culture*, by K. K. Handiqui (Sholapur, 1949), p. 204. This is not the same Somadeva as the author of the KSS.

157. *Yogadṛṣṭisamucchaya*, vv. 222; quoted and discussed in Chapple, "Haribhadra's Analysis" (1998), pp. 22, 24.

158. *Daśāvatāracarita* 10.26, 27, 29, in *Daśâvatâracharita of Kshemendra*, ed. Durga-

prasad and Parab (1891), p. 162. *Kaulagola* is a likely variation on *kuṇḍagolaka*, discussed above, chap. 3, nn. 63–66.

159. *Minor Works of Kṣemendra*, ed. Sharma et al. (1961), introduction, p. 1.

160. *Narmamālā* 2.101, in ibid., p. 331.

161. *Narmamālā* 3.1–20, in ibid., pp. 335–37. The same author portrays a king being bamboozled by a female *tāntrika* in his *Samayamātṛkā* (2.95–96), cited in Gupta and Gombrich, "Kings, Power and the Goddess," p. 132.

162. Lines 28–30 of the "Harṣaparvata" inscription of the Chāhamāna king Vigrahapāla, discussed in Pathak, *Śaiva Cults* (1960), pp. 27–28.

163. Sharma, ed., *Kalacuri*, vol. 2, p. 305.

164. For a discussion of this group's important religious establishments, patronized in late-tenth-century Madhya Pradesh by the Kalacuri kings, see Davis, "Inscriptions of the Drunken Peacocks," pp. 131–45. On the same religious order at Khajuraho, see Desai, *Religious Imagery of Khajuraho*, pp. 57–60.

165. Dubois, *Moeurs* (1985).

166. On the Tantric practice of colonial-period Vaiṣṇava sectarians, see above, chap. 1, n. 23.

167. Dubois, *Moeurs*, pp. 243–45. Translation my own.

168. Murr, *L'Inde philosophique* (1987).

169. TĀ 28.373–80, translated by Muller-Ortega in "Power of the Secret Ritual" (1990), pp. 53–54.

170. An alternative explanation for keeping such secrets would be rivalries between different Tantric teachers: see for example Brunner, "Tantra du Nord," p. 161, discussing *Netra Tantra* 15.29b–30a.

171. Sanderson, "Śaivism: Śaivism in Kashmir" (1986), vol. 13, p. 16.

172. Sanderson, "Purity and Power," pp. 204–5; and id., "Meaning in Tantric Ritual," p. 78.

Chapter 6

1. See above, chap. 4, n. 105.

2. See above, chap. 5, n. 89.

3. The Charans, the traditional bards of the Rajputs discussed in chapter 1 (n. 77), claim the semidivine Cāraṇas as their mythic ancestors. This follows an Epic tradition that maintains that the semidivine Cāraṇas are earthly wandering minstrels who were raised to a heavenly station: Hopkins, *Epic Mythology*, p. 186.

4. *Amarakośa* 1.1.11.

5. A Buddhist parallel, following the same chronology, is found in traditions of the atmospheric *devamānuṣas* ("God-Men") and *vidyarājas* ("Wisdom Kings"), whose status as well was attainable by humans through esoteric practice: Przyluski, "Hommes-Dieux" (1938), pp. 123–28.

6. The long surrounding wall of the Mallikārjuna temple at Srisailam, probably sculpted in the thirteenth or fourteenth century C.E., is an edifice that glorifies the Siddhas: Shaw, "Srisailam" (1997), pp. 161–78. On Siddheśvara temples in western India, see White, *Alchemical Body*, pp. 60, 95–96; on the same in Orissa, see Smith, "Images of Divine Kings" (1991), pp. 94, 103. See also above, chap. 5, n. 91; and below, nn. 68–69.

7. See above, chap. 4, nn. 103, 104.

8. *Śaṅkaravijaya*, ed. Veezhinathan (1971).

9. Srisailam, a sacred mountain located in the Kurnool district of Andhra Pradesh in the central Deccan, is the site of one of Śiva's fourteen *jyotirliṅgas* ("liṅgas of light"), over which stands the Mallikārjuna temple. It has, since at least the time of the

Mahābhārata (3.83.16–21), been a site associated with Siddhas and the attainment of *siddhis*. On this site, see White, *Alchemical Body*, 110–12.

10. This is an apparent reference to the *Kakṣapuṭa Tantra*, a twelfth- to thirteenth-century work by Siddha Nāgārjuna (in *Indrajālavidyāsaṃgrahaḥ*, ed. Bhattacharya [1925], pp. 264–390). Much of this work is little more than a plagiarization of the Mantra Khaṇḍa of the *Rasratnākara* of Nityanātha Siddha. This latter is a Hindu alchemical classical, whose fifth portion, the (unedited) Mantra Khaṇḍa, is instead devoted to Tantric sorcery.

11. The Nāth Siddhas claim a certain Satyanāth to be a founder of one of their suborders; Nityānanda, named earlier in this text, may be identical with Nityanātha, who was also very likely a Nāth Siddha. On these figures, see White, *Alchemical Body*, chap. 4, parts 3, 5b; chap. 5, parts 1, 4h.

12. Kaviraj, *Tāntrik Sādhanā* (1979), p. 392. *Bindu-sādhanā* refers to practices involving "drops" (*bindu*) of sexual fluids.

13. *Mṛgendrāgama*, Caryāpāda 1.36b–37, 40b–41a, trans. Brunner-Lachaux (1985), pp. 364, 366. The later Western Transmission claimed to belong both to the sequence of the Yoginīs (*yoginīkrama*) and the secret of their oral transmission, as well as to the Siddha lineages: as such, its teachings were not to be revealed to anyone not belonging to the Siddha Kaula: Dyczkowski, *Canon*, p. 65.

14. Sanderson, "Purity and Power," p. 214 n. 110; citing TĀ 13.301, 320–21b; and *Mahānāyaprakāśa* 1.30.

15. KJñN 22.6a.

16. Throughout, the KJñN gives the reading of *kṣatra*, which I emend to *kṣetra*.

17. The KJñN often gives the reading of *siddhi* where *siddha* is expected, as in this verse.

18. KJñN 9.1a–4a. Much of this chapter is directly paralleled in the twenty-seventh chapter of the twelfth- to thirteenth-century Kubjikā text, the circa twelfth-century *Śrīmatottara Tantra*.

19. I have emended *anyanteṣu* in the text to *atyanteṣu*. On a parallel case of placing syllables identified with Siddhas outside of a mandala, see below, n. 111. The same seed mantras are identified with a Yoginī in certain recensions of the *Harivaṃśa:* see above, chap. 2, n. 3.

20. On names ending in -pāda in these traditions, see Dyczkowski, *Canon*, p. 62.

21. KJñN 9.6a–10a. The measurement appears to be to that of the cosmic egg, which is a hundred *koṭis* of *yojanas*, according to the *Svacchanda Tantra;* the Kaula is thus ten measures greater than the *brahmāṇḍa*—perhaps after the fashion of the Puruṣa of RV 10.90.1? Compare this measure with those found in the *Kubjikāmata:* below, chap. 8, nn. 18–20.

22. KJñN 9.11–15.

23. I have emended Bagchi's reading of *kriyā*, which makes no sense here, to *jñāna*.

24. KJñN 2.6a–7b, 10a.

25. This chapter appears to be the source of ten verses of the 1131 C.E. *Mānasollāsa* (5.18.956–65): see above, chap. 5, n. 93.

26. KJñN 8.2ab, 4–5. Cf. *Mānasollāsa* 5.18.963b–64a; and Kṣemarāja's commentary to *Netra Tantra* 19.71.

27. KJñN 8.6–7.

28. KJñN 8.9a–10a. Kṣemarāja gives a similar summary of the types of Yoginīs in his commentary on *Netra Tantra* 19.71.

29. KJñN 8.10b–15a. If it is images that are being described here, one is reminded of the forms taken by the sixty-four Yoginīs and the fifty-two Bhairavas (often identified with the fifty-two Bīrs—Vīras) at the Līlāḍ temple located on the outskirts of Ghati-

yali, Ajmer District, Rajasthan. These are stones, smeared with vermilion and covered with silver paper. See fig. 9.b.

30. KJñN 8.16b–17b. Cf. HT 1.7.13–16; TĀ 29.39; *Mānasollāsa* 5.18.958b–60b; *Śrīmatottara Tantra* 27.121–22; *Pīṭharvarṇanam*, MSL MSS no. 1722, fol. 9b, lines 2–8. In its chapter colophons, this last text claims the same pedigree as a number of Kubjikā works held in the Mān Singh Library at Jodhpur: see White, *Alchemical Body*, p. 156. I have relied on Schwartzberg, ed., *Historical Atlas* (p. 22, pl. III.C.3; and p. 27, pl. III.D.3) for my identifications of the probable locations of these sites.

31. KJñN 8.16–18. Each of the sixteen has a name ending in -pāda, and each name is preceded by the seed mantras *hrīṃ śrī hrīṃ śrī*.

32. Kāmākhyā is the name of an ancient and important goddess shrine in the Gauhati District of Assam; Pūrṇagiri is possibly in the Punjab; many have seen in Oḍiyāna a reference to the kingdom of Uḍḍiyāna in the trans-Himalayan Swat Valley (the early-seventeenth-century Tibetan author Tāranātha identifies Oḍiyāna with Ghazni and states that "a great number of *kṣetra-yoginīs* dwell there": *Tāranātha's Life of Buddhaguptanātha*, 539L4, draft translation by David Templeman, p. 7); Arvuda is Mount Abu, in the Sirohi District of western Rajasthan. This is at variance with most Tantric works, which replace Arvuda with Jālandhara, which is usually located in the upper Punjab. The *Mānasollāsa* (5.18.958a) substitutes Ujjayinī (Ujjain) for Arvuda.

33. KJñN 8.19–22a.

34. KJñN 8.24.

35. KJñN 8.25–26.

36. KJñN 8.27a–28a. They are Brāhmī, Māheśvarī, Kaumārī, Vaiṣṇavī, Vārāhī, Vajrahastā, Yogeśvarī, and Aghoreśī.

37. KJñN 8.28b–29b.

38. On the origins of these three Śaktis, see below, chap. 8, n. 87.

39. KJñN 20.13a–22a. Cf. KJñN 14.5a–16b.

40. Brunner-Lachaux, *Somaśambhupaddhati*, part 1 (1963), p. xxiii. On the *sādhaka* in particular, see id., "Le Sādhaka, personnage oublié" (1975), pp. 411–43; and id., "Place of Yoga," pp. 452–54.

41. KJñN 24.3b.

42. O'Flaherty, *Dreams*, p. 203.

43. Sontheimer, *Pastoral Deities*, p. 91; Vaudeville, *Myths, Saints and Legends*, pp. 72–92, 187–96. The names and cults of Khaṇḍobā and Murukaṉ closely relate them to Skanda. Cf. Ramanujan, *Interior Landscape* (1967), pp. 92, 105.

44. Narain, "Gaṇeśa," pp. 25, 34; RV 2.12.2.

45. *Riporṭ Mardumaśumārī*, ed. Singh (1895), p. 241. On the cult of Siddheśvara in Maharashtra, see Sontheimer, *Pastoral Deities*, pp. 23, 94–95.

46. This tradition has a strong textual grounding in the Purāṇas; however, it is also richly represented in late medieval, colonial, and modern Jain iconography from western India: for a discussion see White, "Le Monde dans le corps du Siddha" (2002).

47. Sontheimer, *Pastoral Deities*, pp. 91–92, 187–90; Lecomte-Tilouine, "Des Dieux aux sommets (Népal)" (1993), pp. 159–62; and *Chamba State with Maps, 1904* (1910), pp. 183–84.

48. In my analysis of Mān Singh's Marwari-language accounts, I have relied heavily upon the meticulous work of the Jodhpur-based historian Bhagavatilal Sharma: *Śrī Jalandharanāth* (1995). Sharma's Hindi rendering of Mān Singh's Rajasthani-language account of the events that transpired at Jalore are ibid., pp. 147–62 and notes.

49. Ibid., p. 55.

50. "gaḍh madhy nāth mandir anūp/ nit pūjan jāvat sahit bhūp//tan kī sudhi nāhiṃ

na lok pher/ dil rākhyau nāth pratāp gher//." Ibid., p. 154, quoting *Jalandhar Carit*, pp. 6–7.

51. "nāth nai agam paricay dikhān/ ik divas prāt velā pramān// āsoj dasam sit pakṣ ker/ subh gharī muharat sudh ver// pāṣān pīt sukumār param/ dedīpyamān jug caran ramy// [. . .] nṛp lae caran mastak caḍhāy/ mān kūṃ mile śrī nāth āy//": *Jalandhar Carit*, p. 7; quoted in ibid., p. 155. Cf. *Jalandhar Carit Granth*, Gu. Sam. 2 Ka., p. 35, quoted in ibid., p. 155.

52. Ibid., pp. 122, 148.

53. Sharma, *Śrī Jalandharanāth*, pp. 71–72. In addition to the Black Bee Cave, a well that is known as Candrakūpa, a pool called Sūrya Kuṇḍ, and a Śiva shrine named Ratneśvara Mahādev were already in situ on Kalashacal.

54. The language of the *Mahārāja Mān Singh rī Khyāt* (ed. Bhati [1979], p. 4) is vague here: "āyas devnāthjī jāḷandharnāthjī rī sevā kartā jiṇāṃ nai śrī jāḷandharnāthjī rī rāt rā ājñā huī" ("Jālandharnāth gave his order in the night to Āyas Dev Nāth, who was performing his worship service.") It is not said whether the order was given face-to-face or in a dream.

55. Sharma, *Śrī Jalandharanāth*, pp. 155–56.

56. "deh bhi nāthmaya nāthrupa/apu hi jalandharnāth bhupa" (ibid., pp. 159–61; quoting *Jalandhar Carit*, p. 9).

57. Ibid., pp. 71, 76–77. The 1891 Census Report of Marwar quotes H. H. Wilson when it states that "the Naths are a respectable order within the Kanphata-Jogis, and are also known by the names of Jogeshur, Sarup, or Aisji. They are the disciples of Jallundur Nath. . . .": Singh, *Castes of Marwar* (1894; reprint, 1993), p. 106.

58. *Nāth Caritr*, verse 7: "nahi jānat muni śiddh nar kab taiṃ āsan kīn/bahut jugani taiṃ vās wahāṃ param rūp prācīn//."

59. Sontheimer, *Pastoral Deities*, p. 91.

60. Sukla, *Rājasthān ke Pramukh Sant evaṃ Lok Devatā* (1996), pp. 6–7.

61. Ram, *Rajasthan District Gazetteer, Alwar* (1968), p. 625.

62. On the margosa tree and its importance in goddess worship in north India, see above, chap. 2, nn. 198–200.

63. Digby, "To Ride a Tiger or a Wall?" (1994), pp. 128–29.

64. I have discussed this peak and its Siddha mythology at length in *Alchemical Body*, esp. pp. 110–12.

65. Sontheimer, *Pastoral Deities*, p. 94.

66. Shaw, "Srisailam," p. 161.

67. Sontheimer, *Pastoral Deities*, pp. 91–92. The Kuruba are a dominant caste of northern Karnataka, specializing in agriculture and pastoralism: ibid., p. 9.

68. Ibid., p. 23.

69. Ibid., pp. 22–23.

70. Ibid., pp. 27–29, 40.

71. Ibid., p. 95; and Forbes, *Râs-Mâlâ*, vol. 1, p. 109.

72. Sontheimer, *Pastoral Deities*, p. 107.

73. Ibid., pp. 116, 146, 202.

74. Shaw, "Srisailam," pp. 161–62.

75. KSS 3.4.348a.

76. KSS 8.5.42–64.

77. The earliest of these, the *Jivājivābhigama Sūtra*, dates, according to Dixit (*Jaina Ontology* [1971], pp. 62–63) to roughly between the second century B.C.E. and the first century C.E. He is clear that the cosmographical portion was originally an independent text that was grafted onto an earlier source. Other sources include the second- to

fourth-century *Tattvārtha Sūtra* of Umasvati; the sixth-century *Digambar Tiloyapannatti* of Yativṛṣabha; eleventh-century *Trilokasāra* of the Digambara Nemicandra; and the twelfth-century *Bṛhatsaṅgrahaṇi*, of the Śvetambara Candrasuri. E-mail message from John Cort, Dennison University, August 15, 1996.

78. Kirfel, *Kosmographie*, p. 215, and table, p. 218.

79. Ibid., p. 233. This configuration is repeated on a reduced scale, with each of the four quarters, which are subdivided, once again by four elephant-tusk-shaped ranges: the first peak of each range is named Siddhāyatanakūṭa. So, for example, Pūrvavideha, the eastern zone (the other three zones are Paścimavideha, Uttarakuru, and Devakuru), is itself divided into four subregions by four elephant-tusked ranges. The eastern quadrant of Pūrvavideha is Kaccha, on the eastern rim of which is the Citrakūṭa mountain range, which runs from south to north: this has four peaks, the southernmost of which is called Siddhāyatanakūṭa (ibid., pp. 237–39).

80. Ibid., p. 253.

81. Harley and Woodward, eds., *Cartography* (1992), p. 296.

82. Caillat and Kumar, *Jain Cosmology* (1981), plates on pp. 111, 114. See below, nn. 118–24.

83. *Encyclopedia of Religion and Ethics*, ed. Hastings (1908), s.v. "Abode of the Blest (Hindu)," by Hermann Jacobi, pp. 698–700. The Śailoda has been identified as the Khotan River, referred to as Silas by Ctesias and Side by Megasthenes: White, *Myths of the Dog-Man*, pp. 122–23. The slightly later Dharmaśāstra literature locates the Siddhas in more or less the same region, on the slopes of Mount Nīla, the northern mountain pillar flanking Meru to the north: Kirfel, *Kosmographie*, p. 60.

84. *Vāyu Purāṇa* 33.51–54, 58; quoted in Ali, *Geography of the Puranas* (1966), p. 77. See chap. 4, nn. 45–50.

85. Kirfel, *Kosmographie*, p. 101.

86. Ibid., p. 174; and Harley and Woodward, *Cartography*, p. 356.

87. BhP 5.24.4–5. These two nodes are those points at which the orbit of the moon intersects that of the sun and where, as a result, eclipses occur: Kloetzli, "Maps of Time" (1985), p. 121.

88. Kirfel, *Kosmographie*, p. 191.

89. Caillat and Kumar, *Jain Cosmology*, p. 21, illustrated, p. 52.

90. Ibid., p. 35.

91. There is a possible connection here with the triple-peaked Mount Śṛṅgavān, the range that separates Uttarakuru from the rest of Jambudvīpa, whose three peaks correspond to the vernal and autumnal equinoxes and summer solstice along the arc of the ecliptic: Kloetzli, "Maps of Time," pp. 133–34. See below, n. 125.

92. *Vishnu Purána*, trans. Wilson (1840; reprint, 1961), pp. 175–76 n. 3.

93. *Brahmāṇḍa Purāṇa* 3.4.2.74–75, 78; 3.4.33.68.

94. Cited without source reference in Kirfel, *Kosmographie*, p. 142.

95. Kloetzli, "Maps of Time," pp. 121–26, 144–45, on the astrolabe and the "logic of projection" by which that instrument was used to measure the movements of the stars, sun, and moon. On the eye of Viṣṇu, see below, n. 133.

96. BhP 2.2.19b–21b. See below, chap. 7, n. 38.

97. This discussion is based on Hudson, "Vāsudeva Kṛṣṇa" (1993), pp. 139–70.

98. Ibid., p. 146.

99. Ibid., p. 149.

100. Ibid., pp. 162–64.

101. KJñN 14.65a.

102. BhP 2.2.8–13.

103. BhP 2.2.21b–22b.

104. BhP 2.2.23ab.

105. *Rāmāyaṇa* 3.1.23, 2.70.30; and MBh 3.145.9, 3.146.93, 3.158.84; cited in Hopkins, *Epic Mythology*, p. 186.

106. *Maitri Upaniṣad* 6.30: "... Unending are the rays of him who like a lamp dwells in the heart. They're white and black and brown and blue; they're tawny and of pale red hue. Aloft arises one of these, which piercing through the sun's round disk, on to the Brahma-world extends. Thereby men go the highest course." Cf. the circa sixth-century B.C.E. *Chāndogya Upaniṣad* (8.6.6): "There are a hundred and one channels of the heart. One of these passes up to the crown of the head. Going up by it, one goes to immortality. The others are for departing in various directions."

107. BhP 2.2.24–26.

108. BhP 2.2.28–31.

109. The *Virāṭa Purāṇa* passage is quoted without verse reference in Kaviraj, *Bhāratīya Sādhanā kī Dhārā*, p. 115. The *Svacchanda Tantra* reference is paraphrased in TĀ 8.159b–60, as discussed in Dyczkowski, "Sacred Geography" (1999), p. 23.

110. KM 16.95–104, discussed in Heilijgers-Seelen, *System of the Five Cakras*, pp. 179–80; and Dyczkowski, "Sacred Geography," pp. 23–25.

111. Dyczkowski, "Kubjikā the Erotic Goddess," p. 133; and id., "Sacred Geography," pp. 6–7. The fiftieth phoneme, *kṣa*, is in fact located outside of the triangle, opposite its downturned point, identified with the Kāmarūpa *pīṭha* (ibid., p. 6 and fig. 1). Here, we are reminded of the two seed mantras, representing the Siddhas and the Yoginīs located "outside of the mandala," according to KJñN: see above, n. 19.

112. RA 12.252–58, esp. 12.254, 257.

113. RA 11.104b–6. Cf. 12.337.

114. RA 18.228. Cf. RA 11.107: "There where the gods are absorbed [at the end of a cosmic eon], there too the Siddha is absorbed." In fact, three half-verses follow RA 18.228.

115. TĀ 8.119–38. In his commentary, Jayaratha indicates selected passages borrowed from the *Svacchanda Tantra* (10.424–51). The original source of these traditions appears to be the *Rāmāyaṇa*: Hopkins, *Epic Mythology*, p. 60.

116. *Vajrāṅka* in TĀ 8.128, but *vajrāṅga* ("Lightning-Limbed") in SvT 10.446, which adds that the "lowest-level Vidyādharas are travelers on the winds of the mind (*manaḥpavanagaminaḥ*)."

117. TĀ 8.133. The names of these Siddhas are *[go]rocanā*, *añjana*, and *bhasma*. *Gorocana* is an organic dye having the same intense yellow color as orpiment (auripigmentum).

118. MBh 1.211–12, esp. 1.212.6–7.

119. The "Raivatācala Māhātmya" constitutes chapters 10 through 13 of the Jain *Śatruñjaya Māhātmya* (translated in Burgess, *Report on the Antiquities of Kāthiāwāḍ and Kacch* [1884–85; reprint, 1971], p. 157n.).

120. The bulk of the MP is older than this; the praise of the Narmada River region in which Raivātaka is mentioned is a late addition, made by a Śaiva resident of Maharashtra: Bhardwaj, *Hindu Places of Pilgrimage* (1973), pp. 66–67; Hazra, *Studies in the Purānic Records*, p. 46; Kantawala, *Cultural History* (1964), appen. 3.

121. On the identification of Raivata and Gomanta, see Mani, *Purāṇic Encyclopedia*, s.v. "Gomanta I," p. 294.

122. The passage concerning Gomanta is found only in the Bombay and Calcutta recensions of the *Harivaṃśa* (2.40, entitled "The Climbing of Gomanta" or "The Journey to Gomanta"); in the critical edition, it forms a portion of appendix 17 and all of appendix 18, found in vol. 2, pp. 92–98 (lines 380–507). Cf. Mani, *Purāṇic Encyclopedia*, s.v. "Gomanta I," p. 294.

123. *Harivaṃśa*, appen. 17, lines 381–82, 386. Girnar is a cluster of peaks, of which twin crags, today identified by Hindus as Gorakh and Dattātreya, are by far the highest. Lines 390–91 state that Kṛṣṇa and Balarāma would later defeat Jarāsandha at that site; the battle is drawn in line 487.

124. *Harivaṃśa*, appen. 18, lines 448–49.

125. Here as well (BhP 2.2.34b), the yogin seemingly finds himself identified with the supreme god, who is, once again, *kūṭastha*. For the *Bhagavad Gītā* discussion of Kṛṣṇa as *kūṭastha*, see above, n. 91.

126. *Saṃyama* is defined in Vyāsa's commentary on YS 3.16 as the combination of *dhāraṇa*, *dhyāna*, and *samādhi*, the three culminating limbs or stages of Patañjali's "yoga": *Yoga Sūtras* of Patañjali, *Yoga Philosophy*, ed. and trans. Aranya (1981), p. 254. Larson (*Classical Sāṃkhya*, 2nd rev. ed. [1979], p. 150) follows J. W. Hauer in dating this portion of the YS to the second century B.C.E.

127. "bhuvanajñānaṃ sūrye saṃyamāt/."

128. "mūrddhajyotiṣi siddhadarśanam/."

129. *Yoga Sūtras* of Patañjali, *Yoga Philosophy*, ed. and trans. Aranya, p. 308. This is echoed in the circa fifteenth-century *Śiva Saṃhitā* (4.46; 5.202, 204).

130. Kloetzli, "Maps of Time," p. 132.

131. Ibid., p. 135.

132. Ibid., p. 137.

133. Ibid., p. 142. This posture is similar to that of the Zodiacal Man, who looks up at the constellations inside his body, which culminate in the Pole Star ensconced in his big toe.

134. Ibid., pp. 144–45, 137–38; my emphasis. A Buddhist parallel may be adduced here as well: the *Divyāvadāna* locates the *devamānuṣa* and *asuras* in the atmosphere, between heaven and earth: Przyluski, "Hommes-Dieux," p. 124; citing p. 614 of a version of the *Divyāvadāna* for which he does not provide a bibliographical reference.

135. Vernant, *Mythe et pensée* (1981) vol. 1, pp. 95–114.

Chapter 7

1. Mallmann, *Enseignements*, pp. 2–3, 6–7, 169–82. The *Agni Purāṇa*'s account of the Mothers, in chapter 50, concerns the "standard" Seven Mothers; the same chapter (verses 30–37) describes the "Maternal Group of Eight" (*ambāṣṭaka*), who are hypostases of Cāmuṇḍā, the last and most important of the Seven Mothers: ibid., pp. 150–57.

2. AP 52.8b. This list and description are virtually identical to those found in the *Mayadīpikā*, cited by Hemādri under the title of *Catuḥṣaṣṭiyoginīrūpāṇī*: Mallmann, *Enseignements*, p. 170. Synoptic lists from the three sources are found ibid., pp. 304–5.

3. Mallmann, *Enseignements*, p. 306.

4. KJñN 23.1a–7b, 10ab. The *Kulacūḍāmaṇi Tantra* (7.47b) makes essentially the same statement: "The animal Śakti, the human Śakti, and also the bird Śakti are thereby worshiped."

5. See above, chap. 2, n. 210.

6. O'Flaherty, *Women*, pp. 90–91. See above, chap. 2, n. 275.

7. MBh 3.219.43–44; SS 1.1.3, 6.27.16–20. Coomaraswamy (*Yakṣas*, pp. 27–28, 36) argues forcefully that "we may safely recognize in the worship of the [dryads] (together with Nāgas and goddesses) the natural source of the Bhakti elements common to the whole sectarian development which was taking place before the beginning of the Kuṣāna period."

8. KSS 1.6.78–82.

9. MBh 2.16.10–50, 2.17.1–6; summarized in *Mahābhārata*, trans. van Buitenen, vol. 2, pp. 54–55.

10. MBh (Calcutta ed.) 2.18.2–6, reproduced and translated in Banerjea, "Some Folk Goddesses," pp. 101–2. I have modified Banerjea's translation. See also MBh 2.16.36–42 (critical edition). See above, chap. 2, nn. 82–106, 241–51. The goddess Ekānaṃśā employs the same shape-changing powers to deceive Kaṃsa in *Harivaṃśa* 47.50: Couture and Schmid, "*Harivaṃśa*," p. 176.

11. MBh 2.16.38–39. Jarā's name may be related to those of Jaritā and Harītī: Agrawala, *Skanda-Kārttikeya*, p. 33. The latter has been discussed in chapter 2; the former is a *bird*, who takes her husband to task for improper care of their fledglings (and herself): MBh 1.220.17, 1.224.17–26.

12. *Rājataraṅgiṇī* 2.65b–117b, trans. Stein, *Kalhaṇa's Rājataraṅgiṇī* (1900; reprint, 1979), vol. 1, pp. 61–65. See bibliography for Sanskrit edition. I have slightly modified Stein's translation. See above, chap. 3, n. 29.

13. *Rājataraṅgiṇī* 2.99ab: "uccaṇḍalāḍanādaṇḍodghṛṣṭaghaṇṭaughaṭāṅkṛtaiḥ/ caṇḍaḍāmaru nirghoṣairghargharaṃ śrutavāndhvanim//."

14. *Rājataraṅgiṇī* 2.102ab: "sandhīyamānasarvāṅgaṃ kaṅkālaṃ yoginīgaṇaiḥ//."

15. *Rājataraṅgiṇī* 2.104ab: "ekamekaṃ svamaṅgaṃ ca vinidhāya kṣaṇādatha/ kuto 'pyānīya puṃlakṣma pūrṇāṅgaṃ taṃ pracakrire//."

16. *Rājataraṅgiṇī* 2.106b: "samabhujyata tābhiḥ sa yathecchaṃ cakranāyakaḥ//."

17. In the *Devī Māhātmya* (88.22–23, 26–27), the goddess produces a *śakti* named Śivadūtī, "Jackal-shaped Female Messenger," from her own body, the description of which includes evocations of jackals.

18. There is a relationship here between the iconography of Śiva as the corpse (*śava*) lying inert beneath the activated body of the terrible devouring goddess Kālī: as Wendy Doniger O'Flaherty (*Women*, p. 116) has pointed out, such Tantric goddesses restore corpses to life through sexual intercourse.

19. *Netra Tantra* 20.4b–10b; see below, nn. 81, 106, 107.

20. Donaldson, "Propitious-Apotropaic Eroticism," p. 88 n. 54. See above, n. 4.

21. Sanderson, "Śaivism and the Tantric Tradition," p. 680.

22. I am grateful to Steven Collins for bringing this "nondistinction" to my attention, in his questions and comments following a paper I presented at the University of Chicago, on March 6, 1997, entitled "Fluid Typologies in Early Tantra."

23. Sanderson, "Purity and Power," p. 201.

24. Eliade, *Shamanism* (1972), pp. 411–12.

25. Cited in Eliade, *Myths, Dreams, and Mysteries* (1967), p. 108.

26. *Taittirīya Saṃhitā* 1.7.9, cited in Eliade, *Shamanism*, p. 404.

27. *Buddhacarita*, ed. and trans. Johnston, 2nd ed. (1936; 1972), vol. 1, p. 47; vol. 2, p. 64: "puruṣair aparair adṛśyamānaḥ puruṣaś ca upasasarpa bhikṣu-veṣaḥ" (*Buddhacarita* 5.16b).

28. *Buddhacarita* 5.17ab, 19a–21a.

29. RV 10.136.1a, 2a–3b, 6a, 7ab, in *Rig Veda*, trans. O'Flaherty, pp. 137–38.

30. Ibid., p. 138 n. 8. A similar combination of themes is found in *Atharva Veda* 11.5.6: "[The muni] repairs to both oceans, the eastern and the western . . . wandering in the track of the Apsarasas and the Gandharvas . . . and the wild beasts."

31. *Mahāvamsa* 6.47, 7.9–7; in *Mahāvamsa*, trans. Geiger, pp. 54–57.

32. Sutherland, *Disguises of the Demon*, p. 146; Kapferer, *Celebration*, pp. 167, 169. See above, chap. 3, n. 36.

33. *Yoga Sūtra* 3.45, with the commentary of Vyāsa (in *Yoga Sūtras* of Patañjali, *Yoga Philosophy*, ed. and trans. Aranya, pp. 325–26; *Sādhanamālā*, ed. by Bhattacarya (1925,

1928), vol. 2, p. 350; and KM 25.53–64, discussed in Dyczkowski, "Sacred Geography," p. 24.

34. Sharma, *Temple of Chaunsaṭha-yoginī*, p. 19, describing the Reva stone inscription of Vijayasiṁha of Kalacuri Era 944 (in *Corpus Inscriptionum Indicarum*, vol. 4, pt. 1, inscription no. 7, verse 4; and inscription no. 67, verses 27, 42). The temple Malayasiṁha has dedicated is to the god Rāma; yet the inscription also invokes the Buddhist bodhisattva Mañjughoṣa!

35. *Rasārṇava* 11.104b–6. Cf. 12.337.

36. *Śārṅgadhara Paddhati* 4385a–88a. This hopping technique has been adopted by the transcendental meditation movement, whose practitioners claim it leads to levitation.

37. See above, chap. 6, parts 5 and 6.

38. BhP 2.2.19–21, 24–26. See also above, chap. 6, n. 107.

39. *Chāndogya Upaniṣad* 5.10.1–7; *Bṛhadāraṇyaka Upaniṣad* 6.2.15–16; *Kauśītaki Upaniṣad* 1.2–3; *Praśnā Upaniṣad* 1.9–10.

40. MBh 7.56–59 [= 7.79–81 of the critical edition], summarized in Scherer, *Śiva dans le Mahābhārata* (1982), pp. 255–60.

41. KSS 7.9.38a, 135a.

42. KSS 3.6.115–85.

43. Hopkins, *Epic Mythology*, p. 142. According to Dhawan (*Mother Goddesses*, p. 188), the term *nara* in *nara-vāhana* did not originally mean "man," but rather a mythical figure, a type of winged horse.

44. Mustard seeds are a standard fixture of Tantric sorcery, due in no small part to the brilliant flame and loud crackling sounds they emit when thrown into fire.

45. KSS 3.4.152a–57a, 164–65.

46. McDaniel ("Sitting on the Corpse's Chest" [1999], p. 25) refers to the corpse used in such practices as a battery that stores energy; while Michael Walter, evoking Buddhist sources, states that it is the Tantric practitioner's own superheated breath energy (*prāṇa*) that, transferred into the corpse through the mantra, affords it the power of flight: personal communication, Nagarkot, Nepal, May 1999.

47. White, *Alchemical Body*, pp. 240–58 and passim.

48. McDaniel, "Interviews with a Tantric Kālī Priest" (2000), p. 72.

49. Parry, *Death in Banaras* (1994), p. 183.

50. Rabe, "Sexual Imagery." See above, chap. 2, n. 49.

51. Deva, *Temples of Khajuraho* (1990), vol. 1, p. 33; quoted in Rabe, "Sexual Imagery," n. 104.

52. Rabe, "Sexual Imagery," nn. 107–9.

53. The 1993 C.E. inscription (presumably a reiteration of earlier inscriptions) at Pacalī Bhairab identifies Pañcaliṅgeśvara (Pacalī) with Svacchanda Bhairava, dating the original establishment of the deity at that site to 724 C.E., and the inauguration of his festival *jātra* to 1140 C.E.

54. *Svacchanda Tantra* 2.281a. See also Sanderson, "Maṇḍala and Āgamic Identity" (1986), p. 182; and Toffin, *Le Palais et le temple*, pp. 55, 56, 61, 70.

55. TĀ 5.322a.

56. *Manthānabhairava Tantra*, "Kumārikā Khaṇḍa" 29.34–end; cited in Dyczkowski, "Kubjikā the Erotic Goddess," p. 130 n. 14.

57. A circa 750–850 C.E. rendering of the Seven Mothers, found in the "Hall of Sacrifice" within the Kailāsanātha temple of the Ellora Caves, depicts Cāmuṇḍā seated on a large corpse whose face is tilted upward: Zimmer, *Art of Indian Asia* (1955), vol. 1, p. 410; vol. 2, plate 221; from the same period, a sculpture of Cāmuṇḍā standing on a

corpse has survived in the so-called "Kālī" temple at the Candrabhāgā site in the Sirohi District of southwestern Rajasthan: Atherton, *Sculpture*, p. 103.

58. For seventeenth-century miniature paintings of the Goddess, usually identified as Kālī, astride a great corpse or *preta*, see Fisher and Goswamy, *Pahari Masters*, plates 7, 8, 12.

59. *Kālikā Purāṇa* 72.63.

60. Avalon (Sir John Woodroffe), *Serpent Power*, 4th ed. (1950), p. 204 n. 1: "At the conclusion of a successful rite, it is said, that the head of the corpse turns round, and, facing the Sadhaka, speaks, bidding him name his boon, which may be spiritual or worldly advancement as he wishes. This is part of the Nila Sadhana done by the 'Hero' (Vira), for it and Savasana are attended by many terrors."

61. Donaldson (*Kāmadeva's Pleasure Garden*, p. 348) identifies these figures, of which there are nine at Hirapur, as Kātyāyanīs; Dehejia identifies them as either Yoginīs or Durgās (*Yoginī Cult and Temples*, p. 101).

62. The circa ninth-century *Yogaratnamāla* of Kaṅha, one of the few extant Sanskrit commentaries on the *Hevajra Tantra* (2.3.3), states that "*ḍākinī* derives from the root *ḍai*, which means to fly in the sky and which corresponds to the power (*siddhi*) of moving anywhere in the sky." For another possible etymology, see below, n. 74.

63. Quoted in Forbes, *Râs-Mâlâ*, vol. 1, p. 238.

64. In Rajasthan the Goddess is represented as a kite (*cīl*) on the arms of Jodhpur; and as another bird (*palam*) on the arms of Jaisalmer. In Tamil Nadu, a mural at Tirugorkarnam, in the state temple of the former kingdom of Pudukkottai, depicts Śiva together with the goddess Brihadambal ("Great Mother"), the royal *kuldevī*, who has the head of parrot and is called "the Parrot that Prattles Always": Waghorne, *Raja's Magic Clothes* (1994), p. 208, plate 73.

65. Drawings of bird- and animal-headed female Seizers are found in a ninth-century manuscript from central Asia: Farrer and Whitfield, *Caves of the Thousand Buddhas* (1990), no. 69, pp. 88, 90, 91.

66. *Brahmāṇḍa Purāṇa* 2.3.7.154a. The reference to the Mother Protectresses is at 2.3.7.156b: note that in Epic mythology, it is Pūtanā who is specifically singled out as a Protectress. See above, chap. 2, n. 208, for Sanskrit.

67. Kṣemarāja's commentary on *Netra Tantra* 19.71. Cf. a commentary on KM 2.13–14, quoted by Heilijger-Seelens, *System of the Five Cakras*, p. 126.

68. "athānyaṃ sampravakṣyāmi khecarākāśagāminī/ durlabhaṃ sarvanārīnāṃ kiṃ punar mānuṣāya ca//": *Kākacaṇḍeśvarīmata*, Wellcome Institute MSS Indic g473, fol. 12, lines 14–15; Nepal-German Manuscript Preservation Project Reel no. E1796/8, fol. 6b, lines 3–4.

69. The inscription (in Fleet, "Gangdhar Stone Inscription": see above, chap. 5, n. 70) reads: "mātṝṇāñca [pramu]dita-ghanātyarttha nihrādinīnām, tantrodbhūta-prabala-pavanodvarttitāmbhonidhīnām, [. . .] gatam idaṃ ḍākinī-samprakīrṇṇam, veśmātyugraṃ nṛpati sacivo [']kārayat puṇyahetoḥ." My translation, while differing in substantial ways from it, is particularly inspired by that of Basham in his "Notes on the Origins of Śāktism and Tantrism" (1984), pp. 148–50. See also Tiwari, *Goddess Cults*, pp. 100, 126–27; and Dehejia, *Yoginī Cult and Temples*, p. 67.

70. Basham reads the compound *ambhonidhi* as the waters of the ocean. In the light of the *Mālatī-Mādhava* passage cited below (n. 76), and the ambiguity of both the term "ambhas" and "apsaras" ("going in the waters or between the waters of the clouds," according to Monier-Williams: see above, chap. 2, n. 34), I prefer to read the term as "rain clouds."

71. *Harivaṃśa*, appen. 1, no. 8, line 12 ("ghaṇṭāninādabahulā viśrutā"); and

appen. 1, no. 24, line 99b ("kharabherisamasvanāḥ"). Although neither of these passages is contained in the critical edition, both are found in every recension and in nearly every manuscript used in its establishment, and must therefore be nearly as old as the third- to fourth-century C.E. dating of this *khila* to the MBh. See Vaidya, *The Harivaṃśa*, vol. 1, pp. xxiv, xxx, xxxi.

72. *Rājataraṅgiṇī* 2.99ab.

73. *Rasārṇava* 3.13.

74. Heilijger-Seelens (*System of the Five Cakras*, p. 126 n. 21), who also points out that in KM 15.52a an alternate reading for *ḍākinī* is the adjective *ḍamarī*. Cf. Böhtlingk and Roth, *Sanskrit Wörterbuch*, vol. 3, p. 185, s.v. "ḍāṃkṛta," "ḍāṃkṛti." See also above, n. 62.

75. Although she is not called a Yoginī in the text, this is her role, as the consort of a Kāpālika. Another figure in the play, Saudāminī, is referred to as a Mistress of Yoga (*yogeśvarī*), when she displays the supernatural power of flight (*akṣepiṇī siddhi*) arising from her knowledge of ". . . austerities, mantra, Tantra, yoga . . . ": *Mālatī-Mādhava*, act 9, verses 52–53; in *Bhavabhūti's Mālatī-Mādhava*, ed. Kale, pp. 202–3.

76. *Mālatī-Mādhava*, act 5, verse 1; in ibid., p. 95.

77. Jagaddhara's commentary to *Mālatī-Mādhava*, act 5, verse 1; in ibid., pp. 95–96.

78. See below, n. 100; and chap. 8, n. 136.

79. KSS 18.2.3–33, 18.5.3–23. See above, n. 15; and chap. 5, n. 143. Cf. HT 2.2.19, 2.19.21.

80. KJñN, unnumbered mixed prose following 4.15b.

81. *Netra Tantra* 20.2. The Kashmirian commentator Harihara, who lived between 950 and 1216 C.E., interprets the "extraction of the essence" of *Mālatī-Mālava* 5.2 as echoing the Krama doctrine of the "goddesses of the five flows" (*pañcavāhadevīs*): Sanderson, "Śaivism," p. 680. See above, n. 19; and below, nn. 106, 107.

82. White, *Alchemical Body*, p. 73.

83. *Mālatī-Mādhava*, act 5, verse 2; in *Bhavabhūti's Mālatī-Mādhava*, ed. Kale, with Jagaddhara's commentary, pp. 96–97. See above, chap. 4, n. 9.

84. See above, chap. 4, nn. 66–69.

85. In the *Netra Tantra*, which was perhaps coeval with the *Mālatī-Mādhava*, the name of the lowest of the six *cakras* of the yogic body is *nāḍīcakra*: see below, chap. 8, n. 45.

86. The *Jayadrathayāmala* is the root Tantra of the Kashmiri Kālīkrama cult of Kālasaṃkarṣaṇī, and of the cult of Siddhilakṣmī, later identified with the Newar goddess Taleju: Dyczkowski, "Kubjikā, Kālī, Tripurā and Trika," p. 19 n. 42, 24, 39 n. 113. Whereas Abhinavagupta refers to the *Jayadrathayāmala* as the "Venerable King of the Tantras" in his early-eleventh-century TĀ, the third hexad of this work includes in its list of over fifty of its sources (in fols. 170ab) the *Kubjikā[mata]*, which it calls a "root Tantra," the *Siddhayogeśvarīmata*, the *Picu[mata]* (i.e., the *Brahmayāmala*), and the *Rudrayāmala*. The *Siddhayogeśvarīmata* and *Tantrasadbhāva* are sources of the KM, which predates the third hexad of the *Jayadrathayāma*, with the *Rudrayāmala* named here not being the same as the circa thirteenth-century work that was edited by the Yogatantra Department of the Sampurnanand Sanskrit University in Benares: see bibliography, and Sanderson, "Remarks," pp. 1–2.

87. KJñN 11.11. Certain Buddhist Tantras list brains and flesh in place of urine and feces.

88. TĀ 29.71b–72a, with the commentary of Jayaratha (*Tantrāloka*, ed. Dwivedi and Rastogi, vol. 7, pp. 3340–41). Cf. HYP 3.4. Nepali images of the "Eight Śmaśānas" (at which a Yoginī, a Bhairava, and a Siddha are located) situate these in the heart *cakra*: Pott, *Yoga and Yantra* (1966), p. 84. On the intimate links between the eight

Mothers, the eight Bhairavas, and the eight cremation grounds in Nepali religious cosmography, see Toffin, *Le Palais et le temple*, p. 54. Cf. the "eight cremation grounds" as an element of the iconography of the cult of Svacchanda Bhairava: Sanderson, "Meaning in Tantric Ritual," p. 20.

89. See below, chap. 8, n. 94.

90. *Rājataraṅgiṇī* 1.331–35.

91. See above, n. 4.

92. "imā nṛmāṃsāśanajā ḍākinīmantrasiddhayaḥ/."

93. KSS 3.5.102a–4a, 105a–6b.

94. On these terms, see above, chap. 1, n. 35; and chap. 6, nn. 32, 33.

95. This they would do, according to certain Kaula traditions, by feeding the male Siddhas the ritual oblation (*cāru*): personal communication from Mark Dyczkowski, Todi, Italy, July 2001. See KJñN 8.25, 18.22.

96. See above, n. 21.

97. Bhairava is so portrayed in *Agni Purāṇa* 52, 146; KJñN 16.1; KSS 20, 47, 56; and the *Mayadīpikā*: see Mallmann, *Enseignements*, pp. 7, 170–73. Iconographic examples of this configuration are listed above, chap. 2, nn. 232–34.

98. KSS 18.4.204–22.

99. See above, chap. 4, n. 57.

100. See above, n. 78; and below, chap. 8, n. 136.

101. KJñN 22.11a: "nigrahānugrahañcaiva siddhi[ṃ] melāpakaṃ tathā//." The powers of *nigraha* and *anugraha*, which I have translated literally here, are more often translated as "auspicious" and "inauspicious" or "creative" and "destructive" in the context of Tantric practice. On the power or gift of *melāpakam*, which in this spelling may be read either as "union" or "drinking of mixed [fluids]" with the Yoginīs, see above, chap. 3, n. 58; chap. 4, n. 43; and below, chap. 8, nn. 14, 131, 132.

102. KJñN 22.9b–12b.

103. Dyczkowski, "Kubjikā, Kālī, Tripurā and Trika," p. 30. A similar division appears to obtain in the Krama school, which distinguishes two levels of practice, one for "*melāpa* Siddhas devoted to union," and the other for Siddhas who have reached the perfect equality of spirit. In the former, a practitioner undergoes a *kulayāga*-type initiation followed by sexual union with the Dūtī, which, if he remains dispassionate, transforms him into a Virile Hero: Skora, "Consciousness," p. 306.

104. They are so described in the eighty-seventh chapter of the Ājñā Khaṇḍa of the *Manthānabhairava Tantra* (see *Caturviṃśatisāhasra Tantra* in bibliography), Mān Singh Library MSS no. 1488, fol. 164b, line 3; fol. 167b, line 4; fol. 170a, line 11. See also Atherton, *Sculpture of Early Medieval Rajasthan*, p. 102; Michaels, "Paśupati's Holy Field" (1989), p. 52; Donaldson, *Kāmadeva's Pleasure Garden*, p. 349; Sharma, *Temple of Chaunsaṭha-yoginī*, p. 100; *Mālatī-Mādhava* 5.5, in *Bhavabhūti's Mālatī-Mādhava*, ed. Kale, pp. 100–1; and Coburn, *Devī-Māhātmya*, pp. 136–38, 142.

105. *Haṭhayogapradīpikā* 3.83–91, 99–103.

106. Heilijger-Seelens, *System of the Five Cakras*, p. 139.

107. Ibid., pp. 139–46, and esp. p. 145, quoting KM 15.81ab. On Buddhist Tantric classifications according to the rotation of the Yoginīs, see Orofino, "Notes," p. 546 n. 20. See also above, chap. 2, n. 23; chap. 3, n. 29; and below, chap. 8, nn. 59, 64–65.

108. O'Flaherty, *Women*, p. 269; my emphasis. Cf. Sanderson, "Visualisation of the Deities" (1990), p. 36, in which he quotes the *Prapañcasāratantra* (attributed to Śaṅkara) 9.42: "He must then visualize the goddess of the syllable . . . then imagine the alphabet pouring forth from her mouth again and again [rising up from his heart] and emerging from his mouth in an unbroken stream."

109. See above, n. 77.

Chapter 8

1. I borrow all of this terminology from the writings of Alexis Sanderson. See, for example, Sanderson, "Meaning in Tantric Ritual," pp. 47, 87. See also Masson and Patwardhan, *Śāntarasa*, pp. 40–41.

2. Lorenzen, *Kāpālikas and Kālāmukhas*, pp. 93–94.

3. Ibid., p. 94, citing Arthur Koestler, *The Lotus and the Robot* (London: Hutchinson, 1960), pp. 110–11. A similar situation may be found in early Buddhism, in which admonitions in the *Vinaya Piṭaka* against magical powers may be contrasted with statements to the effect that "a magical feat quickly converts an ordinary person": Strong, *Legend of King Aśoka* (1983), p. 75.

4. *Yoga Sūtra* 1.2. "yogaścittavṛttinirodhaḥ": "yoga is the suppression of the states of consciousness."

5. MBh 12.289.26.

6. *Netra Tantra* 20.28–40; TĀ 28.292–302, citing the *Svacchanda Tantra* (10.787b) and the *Mālinīvijaya;* KSS 8.2.55–62, 78–82; and Renou and Filliozat, "L'Inde classique" (1947, 1953), vol. 1, p. 614. The power of the yogin to enter the body of another is the necessary condition for his ability to initiate disciples, most especially through "initiation by penetration": see Gupta and Gombrich, "Kings, Power and the Goddess," p. 129; and below, nn. 53, 151.

7. *Vetālapañcaviṃśati*, *Contes du Vampire*, trans. Renou, pp. 13, 39 n. 1. See above, chap. 2, nn. 3, 87; chap. 5, n. 151; and chap. 7, n. 10.

8. Avalon, *Serpent Power*, pp. 317–508. The Sanskrit text of the *Saṭcakranirūpaṇa* is appended to this work, with a separate title page and Devanagari numbering (see bibliography).

9. Das, "Problematic Aspects" (1992), pp. 396–402.

10. See above, chap. 2, nn. 113, 233.

11. See above, chap. 6, nn. 18, 26–28.

12. KJñN 8.10b–15b. Verse 15 reads: "yoginīvīracakrantu yathāśaktyā [pra]pūjayet/ itthambhūtaṃ kulācāryaḥ kulaputrairadhiṣṭitam//."

13. KJñN 8.30b–32a. KJñN 8.16–29 was discussed above, chap. 6, nn. 31–37.

14. KJñN 8.32b–43b.

15. KJñN 10.6a–32b.

16. Heilijger-Seelens, *System of the Five Cakras*, p. 34.

17. Ibid., pp. 34–35, 38, and n. 60, citing KM 11.109a.

18. A *koṭi* is 10 million; a *yojana* approximately nine miles.

19. *Svacchanda Tantra* (1.618–20). Similar data is provided in a number of Purāṇas, including the *Vāyu* (1.50.82–84) and the *Liṅga* (1.70.54–56), in Heilijger-Seelens, *System of the Five Cakras*, pp. 23–24 and n. 17.

20. KJñN 9.10a, 14.65a, 66a. See above, chap. 6, n. 21, and chap. 6, parts 5 and 6.

21. However, see above, chap. 6, nn. 130–34, for an explanation of how such projections might have been effected in the Purāṇas.

22. *Hevajra Tantra* 2.4.51–55, in *The Hevajra Tantra, a Critical Study*, ed. Snellgrove (1959), vol. 2, p. 68.

23. Buddhist traditions specifically identify Uḍḍiyāna with the Yoginī cults: David Templeman, personal communication, New York, April 7, 1997.

24. *Siddha Siddhānta Paddhati* 2.1c, 2b, 8b, 9c; in *Siddha Siddhānta Paddhati and Other Works of the Natha Yogis*, ed. Mallik (1954). See above, chap. 6, n. 32, for the four *pīṭhas* as they are listed in the KJñN.

25. TĀ 29.39, 59–63.

26. *Hevajra Tantra* 1.7.12. A similar list is found in the coeval Buddhist *Sādhana-*

mālā (pp. 453, 455) and Hindu *Kālikā Purāṇa* (64.43–45): on these sources see Sircar, *Śākta Pīṭhas*, 2nd rev. ed. (1972), pp. 11–14.

27. *Hevajra Tantra* 1.1.22–30, discussed in Snellgrove, *Indo-Tibetan Buddhism*, vol. 1, p. 248. The KM (11.50, 60, etc.) locates these four *pīṭhas* in the *viśuddhi cakra*.

28. *Brahma Upaniṣad* 2 (82–83), in Olivelle, *Saṃnyāsa Upaniṣads* (1992), p. 149. Early references to the four states of consciousness are found in the circa first-century C.E. *Māṇḍukya Upaniṣad*, without reference to subtle body locations. The *Mālinīvijayottara Tantra* (11.35) describes four centers—*mūlādhāra*, *kanda* (above the genitals), palate, and *dvādaśānta*—with their respective effects on the practitioner: Padoux, "Transe" (1999), p. 139.

29. For a discussion, see Sircar, *Śākta Pīṭhas*, pp. 17–18; and Pal, *Hindu Religion and Iconology* (1981), pp. 24–29.

30. *Bhāgavata Purāṇa* 2.2.19b–21b. This work has been dated to the eighth century by Hudson, "Śrīmad Bhāgavata Purāṇa in Stone," pp. 137–38, 177. See, however, MBh 12.289.39–40. See above, chap. 6, n. 96; and chap. 7, n. 38.

31. *Caraka Saṃhitā* 4.7.9, cited in Roşu, "*Marman*" (1981), p. 418. Over time the number of vital points or organs rises to 107: ibid., pp. 419–26.

32. *Rasanabandha*, listed in the *Aṣṭāṅgahṛdaya* and *Aṣṭāṅgasaṃgraha* of Vāgbhaṭṭa; the *Viṣṇudharma;* and other sources: Roşu, "*Marman*," p. 418.

33. Brunner, "Place of Yoga" (1994), pp. 436–38. These sources are difficult to date. It would appear that the earliest Śaivasiddhānta monastic orders to receive royal patronage were those that flourished under the central Indian Kalacuris from the ninth century onward (Sharma, ed., *Kalacuri*, vol. 2, pp. 282–95).

34. KJñN 5.25–27.

35. This mention of the *dvādaśānta* appears to be out of place, unless some other subtle center, within the contours of the body, is intended.

36. KJñN 17.2b–4b.

37. In this, it mirrors Śaivasiddhānta terminology to a certain extent: only the heart is termed a lotus, with the other centers generally termed *granthis*: Brunner, "Place of Yoga," p. 438.

38. TĀ 29.37, with the commentary of Jayaratha (*Tantrāloka*, ed. Dwivedi and Rastogi, vol. 7, pp. 3317–18). As Gnoli notes (*Abhinavagupta, Luce dei Tantra*, pp. 553–54 n. 4), the term *chomma* more often designates a "secret sign" or "secret name" in these traditions. For Buddhist parallels, see HT 1.6.1–8; 2.3.55–67.

39. Discussed in Silburn, *Kuṇḍalinī*, pp. 25–35.

40. Kṣemarāja's introductory commentary to *Netra Tantra* 7.16, in *Netratantram*, ed. Dwivedi, p. 55. For a detailed discussion of this system, see Brunner, "Tantra du Nord," pp. 141–45.

41. *Netra Tantra* 7.18–19.

42. Ibid., 7.47–49.

43. Ibid., 7.17a (with the commentary of Kṣemarāja) and KJñN 2.2, for *kālāgni-[rudra]; Netra Tantra* 7.32a and KJñN 22.12b, for *matsyodara*.

44. *Netra Tantra* 7.28b–29b. Kṣemarāja glosses *bindu* as "between the eyebrows" and *nāda* as "forehead."

45. See above, chap. 7, nn. 83, 86.

46. See below, n. 90.

47. KJñN 3.6a–8a.

48. KJñN 3.9–12. See Padoux's discussion of *Svacchanda Tantra* 4 and *Netra Tantra* 22 in *L'Énergie de la parole* (1994), pp. 225–30.

49. I have discussed the connections between the Kaula traditions (*kaulamata*) and

the Western Transmission of the Kubjikā Tantras through the person of Matsyendra-(nātha) at length in *Alchemical Body*, pp. 88–89, 133–37. See especially p. 135, in which I argue for the primacy of the KJñN over the KM. Heilijger-Seelens notes (*System of the Five Cakras*, p. 9) that the sole source in which the KM system of the five *cakras* is found, if only by name, outside of Western Transmission sources, is KJñN 14.93. Other passages in this text that refer to these *cakras* are KJñN 7.2a, 7.32a, 14.20a, 19.1a, and 24.5a. The mention of the *devī cakra* together with the fourfold *ādhāra* and the *brahmagranthi*—in KJñN 14.20, 24—is a further indication that the KJñN was familiar with the five *cakra* system, as later elaborated in the KM: cf. Heilijger-Seelens, *System of the Five Cakras*, pp. 55–61.

50. The term *cakra* is found at KJñN 14.15a (*mūlacakra*), 20b (*devyāścakrorddhaṃ*), 58b (*imaṃ cakram*), and 103b (*aṣṭāṣṭavidhinā cakram*). The term *kaula* forms the second half of a number of surprising compounds, which seem also to relate to bodily locations: the "Kaula rooted in the hair follicles [above the genitals]" (14.28b, 32b); the "Kaula of the testicles" (14.32a); the "Kaula of upraised feet" (14.48a); and the "highest and very secret" Yoginī Kaula (14.59a).

51. KJñN 14.92: "anāmā nāma mudreyaṃ . . . mudritam pañcamudrābhi[ḥ] . . . bhedayettatkapāṭañca argalāyāsusañcitā//." See above, chap. 3, nn. 92, 93, for further discussion.

52. KM 23.112b: "dvāreṣu argalasaṃyogam kuryāc codghāṭanaṃ." An excellent discussion of many elements of the subtle body system of the KM, together with a fine translation of chapters 14 through 16 of the text is Heilijgers-Seelen, *System of the Five Cakras*. On the term *argala*, see Brunner, Oberhammer, and Padoux, *Tāntrikābhidhānakośa*, s.v. "argala," p. 140.

53. Goudriaan ("Some Beliefs and Rituals" [1983], pp. 96–98) defines *utkrānti* as follows: "the method by which a *yogin* may chose to take leave of mundane existence." Here, we are reminded of the upward progress of the yogin as described in the BhP, above, nn. 6, 31; and above, chap. 6, n. 96; and chap. 7, nn. 38, 107. The earliest Indian reference to *utkrānti* as a *siddhi* is *Yoga Sūtra* 2.39, in which the term refers to the power to exit the body.

54. KM 23.113b–14a.

55. KM 23.115–25.

56. See above, chap. 3, nn. 28–30; and chap. 7, n. 107.

57. Heilijger-Seelens (*System of the Five Cakras*, p. 124 n. 14) opines that her name "seems to express the idea of the *ātman* being represented by a flower," citing the use of flowers in Balinese ritual. See also Sanderson, "Śaivism and the Tantric Tradition," p. 672; and Tripathi, "Daily Puja Ceremony" (1978), pp. 297, 301, on Tantric uses of the same.

58. *Śrīmatottara Tantra* 18.8–57, discussed in Heilijger-Seelens, *System of the Five Cakras*, p. 147. Further discussion of alternative listings of these goddesses' names are found in ibid., pp. 121–25.

59. This passage belongs to that portion of the *Agni Purāṇa* comprised of material inserted from Kubjikā sources after the ninth century C.E.: Mallmann, *Enseignements*, pp. 3, 6–7, 205–6 (including fig. 2, p. 206).

60. The KM locates the Yoginīcakra in the *ghaṭasthāna*, the "Place of the Jar" in the throat region. The Yoginīs are born from the water of said jar: Heilijger-Seelens, *System of the Five Cakras*, pp. 119, 131. Heilijger-Seelens notes the presence of the same series of goddesses in the *Saṭsāhasratantra* 24.1–59, *Yoginīhṛdaya* (3.3), *Saṭcakranirūpaṇa*, and *Kaulāvalinirṇaya* , chapter 21 (pp. 119–20). Contrasting this multiplicity of references to the "empty" categories of the twenty Devīs, the eighty-one Dūtīs, and the sixty-four Mātṛs of the lower three *cakras* of the KM system, this author sees in them evidence for

actual cults of these six goddesses (p. 119), which perhaps originated from six different border regions of the Indian subcontinent (pp. 126–28).

61. In the mantra following 4.15, the KJñN names Kusumamālinī, Ḍākinī, Rākṣasī, Lākinī, and Yoginī; the mantra following KJñN 9.5 lists Lākinī, Ḍākinī, Śākinī, Kākinī, and Yākinī.

62. KM 23.140.1–7. Another passage from the KM (15.63b–77a) identifies these goddess's favorite foods with nearly the same bodily constituents: Heilijger-Seelens, *System of the Five Cakras*, p. 137. The language with which these goddesses are invoked is quite similar to that addressed to disease-causing Mothers in *Agni Purāṇa* 299.50 (quoted in Filliozat, *Kumāratantra*, p. 70).

63. These six (or seven) goddesses are also identified in Kubjikā sources with the sixfold *adhvan*, the *ṣaṭcakra*, the six *aṅgas*, and the six *tattvas*: Heilijger-Seelens, *System of the Five Cakras*, pp. 135–36.

64. KM 15.49b–54a; cited in Heilijger-Seelens, *System of the Five Cakras*, pp. 137–38.

65. KM 14.3–4; discussed in ibid., p. 146.

66. These include the *Vidyārṇava Tantra*, *Saundaryalaharī*, *Śrīmatottara Tantra*, and "Lalitā Sahasranāma" of the *Brahmāṇḍa Purāṇa*: Dehejia, *Yoginī Cult and Temples*, pp. 48–49.

67. *Rudrayāmala Tantra* 27.54b–56b. The identification is made by juxtaposition; in addition, six forms of Śiva are also listed.

68. *Śrīmatottara Tantra*, chaps. 19, 27; cited in Dehejia, *Yoginī Cult and Temples*, pp. 48–49.

69. Some of these works further identify these Yoginīs with the *dhātus* they are offered in the KM; however, these same works alter their hierarchical arrangement along the vertical axis of the subtle body. The *Vidyārṇava Tantra*, *Saundaryalaharī*, and *Lalitā Sahasranāma* place Śākinī (bone) in the *mūlādhāra*; Kākinī (fat) in the *svādhiṣṭhāna*; Lākinī (flesh) in the *maṇipura*; Rākiṇī (blood) in the *anāhata*; Ḍākinī (skin) in the *viśuddhi*; Hākinī (marrow) in the *ājñā*; and Yākinī (semen) in the *sahasrāra*: Dehejia, *Yoginī Cult and Temples*, pp. 48–49.

70. Dyczkowski, "Kubjikā the Erotic Goddess," p. 139.

71. KM 11.34b–37b. This source calls the *mūlādhāra* "gudam." It assigns four "portions" to it, six portions to the *svādhiṣṭhāna*; twelve to the *maṇipura*; ten to the *anāhata*; sixteen to the *viśuddhi*; and two to the *ājñā*. The *viśuddhi* is discussed in KM 11.44–99a; the *anāhata* in 11.99b–12.29; the *maṇipura* in 12.30–69; the *svādhiṣṭhāna* in 12.70–13.36; the *ādhāra* in 13.37–52; and the *ājñā* in 13.53–86.

72. Heilijger-Seelens, *System of the Five Cakras*, p. 38.

73. This source actually uses the term *kuṇḍalinī*, but in no case does it have the hathayogic sense of female serpent energy. It is rather employed to signify a *japa-mālā* thread (5.118); as a synonym for Śakti (6.4); and as a synonym for the yoni (6.108). It is used in a mantra (following 18.43); at end of a description of the highest path of practice, the *śāmbhava-adhvan* (in 18.111); and in a discussion of visions leading to the power of prognostication (19.76).

74. "[śakti] prasupta-bhujaga-ākārā dvādaśānte varānane/ nābhiṣṭhā tu tathāpy evaṃ draṣṭavyā parameśvari//."

75. Even so, her energy dwells in the *svādhiṣṭhāna*, the second *cakra*, in these same Kubjikā traditions. This is the place where the erect penis makes contact with the cervix at the base of the womb during sexual intercourse. Thus this wheel is the center of the first point of contact in the union of Śiva and Śakti from which the emission (*visarga*) that generates the universe originates: Dyczkowski, "Kubjikā, Kālī, Tripurā and Trika," p. 32 n. 90.

76. Dated by Sanderson, "Śaivism: Trika Śaivism," p. 14. The KM calls itself a portion of the *Tantrasadbhāva*, of which it reproduces substantial portions. This passage is quoted by both Kṣemarāja in his *Śiva Sūtra Vimarṣinī* (2.3) and Jayaratha in his commentary on TĀ 3.67 (in *Tantrāloka*, ed. Dwivedi and Rastogi, vol. 2, p. 429).

77. Translated in Padoux, *Vāc*, trans. Gontier (1989), pp. 128–30. See bibliography for the relationship of this translated text to the revised French edition, cited in the next footnote.

78. KJñN 20.11ab. Also mentioned here is the goddess Icchā-śakti, who arose from Śiva, and who is also called the "Ethereal Garland of Letters" (*vyomamālinī*) and "Airborne" (*khecarī*), and who is herself "the foremost among all [goddesses], neither written and read"—a reference to the Sanskrit grapheme A: KJñN 20.10ab, 12a. In later traditions Icchā-śakti is identified with the phoneme I: on this, see Padoux, *L'Énergie de la parole*, pp. 134.

79. KJñN 20.12b. See Padoux, *L'Énergie de la parole*, pp. 161–70; and below, parts 5 and 6.

80. KJñN 17.23: "āpādatalamūrddhāntā vāmākhy[a]ṃ kuṇḍalākṛtim/ gudasthamudayantasyā dvādaśānte layam punaḥ." Here Kuṇḍalī is not a distinct goddess, but simply a quality of Vāmā.

81. This group of eight is found in the Purāṇas (Michaël, *La Légende immémoriale* [1991], p. 157 n. 3; Mallmann, *Enseignements*, pp. 55, 57; citing *Agni Purāṇa* 74, 308, and *Garuḍa Purāṇa* 23); as well as Śaivasiddhānta works (*Īśānaśivagurudevapaddhati* 3.5.12–14; and *Tantrasamuccaya* 7.46; Rao, *Elements*, vol. 1, part 2, pp. 398–400; citing the *Siddhāntasārāvali* of Trilocana Śivācārya).

82. The same sequence figures in Śaivasiddhānta soteriology. "A wife ascends [the hierarchy of the ancestors] in step with her husband. She is a Rudrāṇī ('wife of Rudra') until incorporation (*sapiṇḍikaraṇam*). Then she becomes first a Balavikaraṇī, then a Balapramathanī, and finally a Bhūtadamanī. These three are the highest of the eight goddesses that surround the goddess Manonmanī on the thirty-second cosmic level (*śuddhavidyātattvam*), the first of those which make up the pure (i.e., liberated) segment of the universe (*śuddhādhvā*)": Sanderson, "Meaning in Tantric Ritual," p. 35; citing *Īśānaśivagurudevapaddhati [Siddhāntasāra]*, Kriyapada 17.217c–19b; *Svacchandatantra* 10.1142c–46b. Cf. Brunner, "Place of Yoga," p. 453, on the subtle body as *puryaṣṭaka*. See below, n. 178.

83. Brunner, "Place of Yoga," p. 438. Kuṇḍali is also the name of a Buddhist Tantric deity.

84. Rao, *Elements*, vol. 1, part 2, p. 390.

85. See above, chap. 2, nn. 87, 142, 157, 162, 188, 243.

86. Rao, *Elements*, vol. 1, part. 2, p. 395. A late Chola image of Jyeṣṭhā, housed in the Bhārat Kalā Bhavan Museum on the campus of Benares Hindu University, portrays her with a broom.

87. *Mālinīvijayottara Tantra* 3.30–33, discussed in Sanderson, "Visualization of the Deities" (1990), pp. 55–56.

88. See above, chap. 7, n. 88.

89. On the dating of this work, see above, chap. 7, n. 86.

90. *Jayadrathayāmala*, third hexad, fol. 169b.

91. Silburn, *Kuṇḍalinī*, pp. 15–83, passim.

92. Bharati, *Tantric Tradition*, p. 260.

93. An excellent overview of *haṃsa* imagery in Indian traditions is found in Padoux, *L'Énergie de la parole*, pp. 72–73.

94. KJñN 17.18b–20a, 21a–24a.

95. KJñN 10.1b.
96. Sanderson, "Meaning in Tantric Ritual," p. 46.
97. Heesterman, *Broken World*, p. 4. Cf. p. 84.
98. Ibid., p. 61.
99. See above, chapter 4, part 1.
100. *Kāma-kalā-vilāsa*, 3rd ed., trans. Avalon (1961), p. 20; French translation by Padoux, *Yoginīhṛdaya Tantra, Coeur*, p. 111.
101. See above, nn. 46, 90.
102. TĀ 3.146a–48a, with the commentary of Jayaratha.
103. Sanderson, "Śaivism and the Tantric Tradition," pp. 688–90.
104. KKV, p. 20. Cf. Natānandanātha's commentary on verse 50 (*KKV*, trans. Avalon, p. 89): "Having in manner described [and] explained the stages of the unfolding of the [Śrī-] Cakra (*cakra-krama*), which is but a manifestation of Kāmakalā (*Kāmakalā-vilāsana-rūpa*). . . ." Simultaneously, the *kāmakalā* syllable (*akṣara*) generates the Śrīcakra on an acoustic register (*Yoginīhṛdaya* 1.24, with the commentary of Amṛtānanda, in *Yoginīhṛdaya Tantra, Coeur*, trans. Padoux, pp. 121–22).
105. See above, chap. 5, nn. 45–51.
106. Brooks, *Auspicious Wisdom*, p. 50.
107. Commentary of Amṛtānanda on YH 1.55. My translations from this text rely in no small part on the French translation of Padoux (*Yoginīhṛdaya Tantra, Coeur*). This passage is found ibid., p. 153.
108. KKV 6–7; YH 1.24, 3.164, with the commentary of Amṛtānanda; *Gandharva Tantra* 30.48–64; *Śaktisaṅgama Tantra* 1.3.77–79, 87–95; *Jñānārṇava Tantra* 10.8; *Paraśurāma Kalpa Sūtra* 5.16, with the commentary of Rāmeśvara; *Vāmakeśvara Tantra* 166; *Śāktakrama* 5.
109. Gupta, Hoens, and Goudriaan, *Hindu Tantrism* (1979), pp. 95–96. Hoens's translation of the term *kāmakalā* is with specific reference to the pre-sixteenth-century *Jñānārṇava Tantra*. Cf. *Yoginīhṛdaya Tantra, Coeur*, trans. Padoux, p. 387 n. 404, who identifies the Ī at the heart of the *kāmakalā* as a Brahmi grapheme.
110. Generated by the author using Adobe Photoshop. This diagram is based on Padoux's rendition in *Yoginīhṛdaya Tantra, Coeur*, p. 202 n. 99.
111. The historical source of the downturned triangle in Tantra, which represents a yoni, is the *catuṣpīṭha* triangle of the Kubjikā Kaula: personal communication from Mark Dyczkowski, Todi, Italy, July 2001.
112. KKV, verse 25a, with the commentary of Natānandanātha, in *KKV*, trans. Avalon, p. 50: "In this way the united Kāma and Kalā (*kāmakalātmakā*) are the (three) letters whose own form is the three Bindus." Commentary: "By Kāma is meant Paramaśiva who is pure Illumination and is the first letter which is A, and Kalā signifies Vimarśa the last of letters (Ha)." Cf. Ramachandra Rao, *Śrī Cakra* (1989), p. 65.
113. Gupta, Hoens, and Goudriaan, *Hindu Tantrism*, p. 144. The *trikhaṇḍā* is also represented by the *mudrā*, the symbolic hand posture adopted while meditating on Tripurā: this "consists of denoting the number three by joining palms and keeping three of the five pairs of fingers in an upright position whilst bending the other two pairs" (*Nityotsava*, p. 72; cited in Gupta, Hoens, and Goudriaan, *Hindu Tantrism*, p. 144).
114. Ibid., p. 96, citing Rāghavabhaṭṭa's commentary on *Śāradātilaka* 1.110. The four goddesses Ambikā, Vāmā, Jyeṣṭhā, and Raudrī correspond to the *mūlādhāra*, *svādhiṣṭāna*, *hṛdaya*, and *kaṇṭha* (or *mukha*) *cakras*, respectively. Cf. *Yoginīhṛdaya Tantra, Coeur*, trans. Padoux, p. 123 n. 127.
115. This movement, from the one to the two, also reflects Hindu medical notions concerning lactation in pregnant women: when a woman has conceived, her uterine

blood (which has only one channel of egress from the body) is transformed into breast milk (which has two points of egress): *Caraka Saṃhitā* 6.15.17; *Mātṛkabheda Tantra* 2.5–6. See above, chap. 3, part 7.

116. On this, see White, *Alchemical Body*, pp. 188, 202.

117. *Yoginīhṛdaya* 1.10–11, with the commentary of Amṛtānanda (in *Yoginīhṛdaya Tantra, Coeur*, trans. Padoux, pp. 109–11). For further discussion of the practice of *bindu* in the context of the *kāmakalā*, see Ramachandra Rao, *Śrī Cakra*, pp. 65–67.

118. In spite of Sir John Woodroffe's protestations to the contrary, in his introduction to the *Kāma-kalā-vilāsa*, p. xi.

119. *Yoginīhṛdaya Tantra, Coeur*, trans. Padoux, p. 202 n. 99. For a parallel discussion, also from the Śrīvidyā tradition, see Brooks, *Secret* (1990), pp. 176–77 (in which the author reproduces verse 11 of the *Tripurā Upaniṣad* with the commentary of Bhāskararāya).

120. Both members of this Sanskrit compound have their English cognates: *sphurad* is the cognate of pho-*sphoresc*-ing; and *ūrmi* of welling or swell. The term *sphuradūrmi* is found in YH 1.55.

121. Padoux, introduction to *Yoginīhṛdaya*, p. 15. I have altered Padoux's prose to render a more literalist reading of certain Sanskrit terms.

122. Ramachandra Rao, *Śrī Chakra*, pp. 68–69.

123. Brooks, *Secret*, p. 82, referring to *Tripurā Upaniṣad* 11–12, with the commentary of Bhāskararāya.

124. Bharati, *Tantric Tradition*, p. 89. See above, chap. 5, nn. 45–48, for the royal associations of these names.

125. YH 3.165–68, with the commentary of Amṛtānanda, in *Yoginīhṛdaya Tantra, Coeur*, trans. Padoux, pp. 372–74; KKV 17, with the commentary of Natānandanātha, in Woodroffe, *KKV*, pp. 33–34; Brooks, *Auspicious*, p. 127; and Ramachandra Rao, *Śrī Chakra*, p. 69.

126. KKV, verses 15–17, in Avalon, *KKV*, p. 33. See above, chap. 4, n. 11.

127. Donaldson, "Erotic Rituals," p. 156. In the KKV of Śrıvidyā tradition, the *āvaraṇa-devatās* are identified as the limbs of the Goddess: "When the Śakti, this all-excelling great Queen, changes into the form of the [Śrī]cakra, then the limbs of her body change into her *āvaraṇa devatās*": KKV, verse 36, in Avalon, *KKV*, p. 70. See above, chap. 4, n. 21.

128. YH 3.165–68, with the commentary of Amṛtānanda, in *Yoginīhṛdaya Tantra, Coeur*, trans. Padoux, pp. 373–74. Cf. ŚP 2.517. Cf. YH 3.156–58, on the four Yoginīs of the Sarvasiddhimaya *cakra* (in ibid., p. 367); YH 3.190, 196, 199 on *makāra* offerings to the Goddess and Śiva and their transformation into nectar (in ibid., pp. 392, 396, 398); and YH 3.203 on the knower of this practice becoming dear to the Yoginīs (ibid., p. 401).

129. The "school" to which this author belonged is contested: Rastogi (*Krama Tantricism* [1979], p. 100) calls him a Krama author and dates him, abusively, to 675–725 C.E.; Silburn offers no date and states that this work and its commentary remain isolated in the Saivite literature of Kashmir, and outside (*Vātūlanātha Sūtra*, trans. Silburn, p. 5).

130. Here, this work follows TĀ 13.141–42; cited in *Vātūlanātha Sūtra*, trans. Silburn, p. 14.

131. "siddhayoginīsaṃghaṭṭanmahāmelāpodayaḥ//" (p. 7 of the Sanskrit text of the VNS, reproduced in *Vātūlanātha Sūtra*, trans. Silburn, p. 89).

132. Abhinavagupta, *Parātrīśikalaghuvṛtti*, p. 19, line 10; discussed by Silburn, trans., *Vātūlanātha Sūtra*, p. 48.

133. It is on this basis that pandits from Benares Hindu University rejected

Madonna's 1998 hit "Shanti Ashtangi," in which she sang mantras from the *Yoga Tarāvalī*, as useless rubbish because her pronunciation of the Sanskrit was faulty. However, the same pandits were gratified when, three months later, they were able to observe, via a live telecast of a Los Angeles concert, that Madonna's pronunciation had greatly improved! For the story, see URL www.tribuneindia.com/1998/98sep17/nation.htm.

134. Douglas Brooks has also devoted some attention to matters of secrecy in Hindu Śākta Tantra: see, for example, his *Auspicious Wisdom*, pp. 11–12, 111–13.

135. For, example, the thirtieth chapter of the TĀ. Much of the discussion that follows borrows from Muller-Ortega, "Ciphering" (2003).

136. Padoux, "L'Oral et l'écrit" (1996), pp. 133–43, esp. pp. 136–37. See above, chap. 7, nn. 78, 100.

137. The most common of these are called *prastāra* or *gahvara*. An extended discussion of these cryptograms is provided, with numerous examples, in appendix 1 to Schoterman, trans.,*The Saṭsāhasra Saṃhitā, Chapters 1–5* (1982), pp. 181–209.

138. Padoux, "L'Oral et l'écrit," p. 142.

139. Muller-Ortega, "Ciphering."

140. Dyczkowski, "Kubjikā, Kālī, Tripurā and Trika," p. 43 n. 125; citing Jayaratha's commentary on TĀ 3.95a.

141. Padoux, "L'Oral et l'écrit," pp. 140, 143 n. 10. Buddhist Tantra had the same tradition concerning the phoneme E: HT 2.2.38, 2.3.4.

142. With specific reference to the goddess Mālinī, whose womb contains both vowels and consonants: Padoux, *L'Énergie de la parole*, pp. 165–71. See above, n. 79.

143. TĀ 3.199ab, translated in Skora, "Consciousness," p. 151. I have slightly altered Skora's translation. See above, chap. 7, n. 108.

144. This "body *liṅgam*" (*dehaliṅgam*) or "*liṅgam* of the mind" (*manoliṅgam*), this "*liṅgam* worshiped by the Siddhas," a feature of the yogic physiology of the KJñN (3.21a–31a), is "superenthroned" by the yoni of the Goddess in Kubjikā subtle physiology: personal communication from Mark Dyczkowski, Todi, Italy, July 2001.

145. Dyczkowski, "Kubjikā the Erotic Goddess," p. 133 and id., "Sacred Geography," pp. 6–7. See above, chap. 6, n. 111.

146. TĀ 3.146a–48a.

147. Glossed by Jayaratha (in *Tantrāloka*, ed. Dwivedi and Rastogi, vol. 2, pp. 499–500) as the "quarter portion of the phoneme *ha*."

148. "ata eva visargo 'yamavyaktahakalātmakaḥ/ kāmatattvamitiśrimatkulagahvara ucyate//tattadakṣaramavyaktakāntākaṇṭhe vyavasthitam/ dhvanirūpamanicchaṃ tu dhyānadhāraṇavarjitam// tatra cittaṃ samādhāya vaśayedyugapajjagat//."

149. See Jayaratha's commentary, in *Tantrāloka*, ed. Dwivedi and Rastogi, vol. 2, p. 503.

150. There is an important distinction between the two terms. Whereas a guru can initiate a disciple into various Kaula and Tantric practices, only an *ācārya* can consecrate a disciple, that is, empower him to initiate or consecrate disciples of his own.

151. White, *Alchemical Body*, pp. 257–58, 311–14. See above, n. 6.

152. Quoted without chapter and verse citation in Dyczkowski, "Kubjikā the Erotic Goddess," p. 125 n. 5.

153. *Kularatnoddyota* 5.148ab, quoted in Dyczkowski, "Kubjikā the Erotic Goddess," p. 125 n. 5. See above, chap. 3, nn. 73–76.

154. TA 29.273–74, discussed in Padoux, "Transe," p. 141.

155. *Atharva Veda* 11.5.3; *Śatapatha Brāhmaṇa* 11.5.4.12.

156. Discussed in Silburn, "Techniques" (1966–67), p. 170.

157. Mus, *Barabudur* (1935), vol. 1, p. 12; my emphasis.

158. See above, nn. 46, 90, 101.

159. TĀ 29.202a, with the commentary of Jayaratha (in *Tantrāloka*, ed. Dwivedi and Rastogi, vol. 7, p. 3422). See above, chap. 4, n. 53.

160. Hayes, "*Necklace of Immortality*," p. 312, concerning the circa 1700 C.E. teacher Ākiñcana-dāsa; and Openshaw, "'Killing' the Guru," pp. 10–13. The same author, referring to a third type of Bāul initiation into a Vaiṣṇava religious order (*bhek* initiation), notes that here, "the tongue of the [male] guru is likened to a penis, and the ear of the disciple to a vagina" (ibid., p. 6). See also above, chap. 3, part 7.

161. For discussion, see White, *Alchemical Body*, pp. 310–14.

162. See above, chap. 3, part 6.

163. The *Laṭā'if-i ashrafī*, quoted in Digby, "Encounters with Jogīs" (1970), p. 16.

164. See above, chap. 3, n. 62.

165. Khan, *Conversions*, pp. 71–72, 136.

166. Obeyesekere, *Medusa's Hair* (1981); Nabokov, *Religion Against the Self* (2000).

167. Nabokov, *Religion Against the Self*, pp. 23–24.

168. The Buddhist Tantric *mantrin* (see above, chap. 5, n. 37) would be the equivalent of the *sādhaka*, the mantra masterers of the Kaula (Sanderson, "Meaning in Tantric Ritual," p. 79 n. 208).

169. Strickmann, *Mantras et mandarins*, p. 322.

170. Freud also used the terms "secondary elaboration" and "rationalization" for this dynamic: Laplanche and Pontalis, *Vocabulaire de la psychanalyse* (1967), s.v. "Élaboration secondaire," "Rationalisation," and "Travail de rêve," pp. 132, 387–88, 505–6.

171. The passages I will quote from are taken from chapter 45 of the *Brahmayāmala*, Nepal National Archives MSS no. 3.370 (Śaiva Tantra 129), fols. 260b–65b.

172. See Brunner, *Somaśambhupaddhati*, introduction to vol. 4 (1998), pp. lix–lx on the chronology of the SŚP and the sources it claims to quote: in fact, the *Uttarakāmikāgama*, which the SŚP "quotes," is a creation of the author Somaśambhu himself, and not an earlier tradition!

173. The pragmatic thrust of Tantra is apparent in the ways in which this and texts like it present their ritual instructions, which are quite identical to those found in the equally pragmatic medical traditions. After a primary ritual instruction, a series of alternatives, variations on a theme, are offered. In the medical works, these variations take the form of variant cures for a given malady: instead of such-and-such an herb, prepared as a decoction, one may use a mineral substance, triturated and distilled. The Tantric sources present rituals in the same way, unambiguously (or totally ambiguously), without explanation for why the "original" ritual should be in need of any variant. Yet there is very often a sort of progression, of the same order as that found in ritual texts of the Vedic tradition, from simple to complex, with an ascending order of results.

174. See above, chap. 2, n. 235, for a description of a "dark, black" place of the Yoginīs.

175. This he does on the second day of practice, following an initial day of preliminary rituals, which nonetheless include arousing the first Śakti (seated to his east) and the sharing, together with all of the Śaktis, of her fluid emission (*taddravyam*).

176. *Netra Tantra* 12.1–4, with the commentary of Kṣemarāja, who refers to the configuration of the Siddha Cakra: see above, chap. 4, nn. 99–104.

177. See above, chap. 1, n. 46.

178. The eight parts, the *puryaṣṭaka*, are sound, sensation, visual form, taste, smell, will, judgment, and ego. See above, n. 82. See also Sanderson, "Śaivism and the Tantric Tradition," pp. 679–80.

179. Described in the *Mahārthamañjari* of Māheśvarānanda, translated by Skora, "Consciousness," p. 304.

180. Skora, "Consciousness," p. 13.

181. The term is employed by the Vaiṣṇava Rāmānandis to denote the divine visions cultivated by initiands to experience transcendent reality through a heightened state of consciousness. The technique and modern-day uses are described in Burghart, "Regional Circumambulation" (1985), pp. 125, 140.

182. *Somaśambhupaddhati, Troisième partie*, ed. Brunner (1977), pp. 216–27.

183. *Kriyādipikā*, pp. 186–87, and *Iśānaśivagurudevapaddhati*, vol. 3, p. 174; quoted in *Somaśambhupaddhati, Troisième partie*, ed. Brunner, pp. 219, 221.

184. *Somaśambhpaddhati, Troisième partie*, ed. Brunner, pp. 216–17 nn. 131, 132, and p. 219. The *svapnamāṇava[ka]* is attested in other medieval sources, the KSS (1.6.137 and 12.5.103) in particular, in which it is also identified with a "dream-producing charm."

185. *Somaśambhpaddhati, Troisième partie*, ed. Brunner, pp. 218–19 (SŚP 3.3.55).

186. Ibid., pp. 220–21 n. 134 (to SŚP 3.3.54).

187. Ibid., pp. 224–27 (SŚP 3.3.58–61).

188. KJñN 11.12, 15–16.

189. In *Tantrāloka*, ed. Dwivedi and Rastogi, vol. 3, pp. 884–85.

190. *Bṛhat Saṃnyāsa Upaniṣad* (pp. 267–68 of Schrader's edition), quoted in Olivelle, *Saṃnyāsa Upaniṣads*, p. 253.

191. See above, chap. 3, n. 103.

192. *Kālacakra Tantra* 2.119, with the "Vimalaprabhā" commentary of Vimalamitra, in Fenner, "Rasayan Siddhi" (1979), pp. 138–39. This source enjoins the practitioner to consume both the Five Nectars and the Five Lamps, comprised of canine, elephantine, equine, and human flesh, taken with honey. On the use of "Five Lamps" in the Trika and Krama, see Sanderson, "Meaning in Tantric Ritual," pp. 82–83.

193. Jayaratha's commentary to TĀ 29.17 and TĀ 29.200 (in *Tantrāloka*, ed. Dwivedi and Rastogi, vol. 7, pp. 3306, 3420). Sanderson ("Meaning," p. 82) refers to this same set of twelve as the *vīradravyam* ("Fluid of the Virile Heroes").

194. See above, chap. 3, nn. 102, 108, 109.

195. *Haṭhayogapradīpikā* 3.47–48.

196. Listed in Kaviraj, *Tāntrik Sāhitya*, p. 35.

197. *Āgamasāra*, cited without reference in Bharati, *Siddh-Sāhity*, 2nd ed. (1968), p. 129. This identification of *maithuna* with a substance further substantiates the hypothesis presented above (chap. 3, part 5) that this term for the fifth *makāra* originally referred to sexual fluids rather than sexual intercourse.

198. KT 5.105–13, which calls the five M-words the "Five Seals."

199. See above, chap. 5, n. 141.

200. Goudriaan and Gupta, *Hindu Tantric and Śākta Literature*, p. 67.

201. Cf. KJñN 11.28–29, which equates brahmanicide with the performance of a horse sacrifice and touching a barbarian with aspersion with the waters of all the *tīrthas*.

202. *Jñānārṇava*, quoted without verse reference in Ghildayal, *Pañcamakāra* (1974), pp. 45–46.

203. KĀN 17.158–59.

204. KĀN 17.147–72. This copies the *Jñānārṇava* passage, quoted in the previous footnote, on the subject of the purity of menstrual blood and semen.

205. Jayaratha's commentary to TĀ 13.196a–96b and 13.197a–97b (in *Tantrāloka*, ed. Dwivedi and Rastogi, vol. 5, pp. 2326–27), quoted in Sanderson, "Purity and Power," p. 212 n. 69. According to the *Garuḍa Purāṇa*, contact with menstrual blood

dooms a person to eternal wandering as a *preta:* Tarabout, "Ancêtres et Revenants" (2001), p. 172.

206. TĀ 15.595–97, cited in Sanderson, "Purity and Power," pp. 211–12 (p. 199 n. 69).

207. Sanderson, "Meaning in Tantric Ritual," p. 87.

208. Ibid., pp. 86–87; citing TĀ 29.198–200 and commentary; *Mahānāyaprakāśa* 2.5.

209. "Left" (*vāma*) and "right" (*dakṣiṇa*) are both elite categories that fall within the purview of Tantric exegesis: Sanderson, "Meaning in Tantric Ritual," pp. 18–19. That is, neither belongs to the original Kaula traditions, nor are they applicable to the nonelite Tantric "mainstream." The "antinomian" left remains as much within the controlled, gnoseological system of high Hindu Tantra as does the "orthodox" right.

210. Ibid., p. 27.

Chapter 9

1. Strickmann, *Mantras et mandarins*, p. 41.

2. Mandelbaum, "Transcendental and Pragmatic," pp. 1175–91.

3. Strickmann, *Mantras et mandarins*, p. 43.

4. *Atharvaveda Saṃhitā*, trans. Whitney (1905), vol. 8, pp. 1024–32. My calculation is based on Whitney's captions to the 486 hymns of books 1–7.

5. Samuel, *Civilized Shamans*, p. 432.

6. Nabokov, *Religion Against the Self*, pp. 19–29.

7. *Khel*, video by Roy and Dewan.

8. Desirens, "Les *Yoginī*" (1991), p. 67 and passim.

9. Ibid., p. 62.

10. Carrin, *Enfants de la Déesse* (1997), pp. 94–96, 113. This relationship appears to reproduce a relationship evoked in a *dhyāna* of the medieval *Tantrasāra*, which, referring to a mantra, states that any woman who takes this mantra "not only becomes a ḍākinī along with other ḍākinīs, but, losing her husband and son, she becomes a perfected Yoginī who can move about at will": Donaldson, *Kāmadeva's Pleasure Garden*, p. 349 n. 11.

11. Carstairs, *Death of a Witch* (1983), p. 56; Jayakar, *Earth Mother* (1990), p. 129.

12. News story dated April 3, 2001, reproduced on the Internet at www.nepalnews.com/contents/englishdaily/trn/2001/apr/apr03/features.htm.

13. Assayag, *Colère*, pp. 160–65, 308. Male servants of Yellammā, called Jōgappas, "Yoga-Fathers," are transvestites: ibid., pp. 25, 229–36. Both Jōgammas and Jōgappas belong to the class of beings called Jōgatis, which is a vernacularization of the Sanskrit *yoginī:* ibid., p. 302.

14. Ibid., pp. 189–95.

15. Ibid., pp. 100, 302–12.

16. Ibid., p. 193.

17. Ibid., pp. 95–96. See above, chap. 4, n. 124.

18. www.xlweb.com/heritage/skanda/ramji_ashram.htm.

19. Nagaswamy, "The Sixty-Four Yoginīs" (1966).

20. *New York Times*, Business Section, June 19, 2001, reproduced on the Internet at college1.nytimes.com/guests/articles/2001/06/19/852652.xml.

Bibliography

Adams, Archibald. *The Western Rajputana States: A Medico-Topographical Account of Marwar, Sirohi and Jaisalmer*. London: 1899.

Āgamaḍambara of Jayanta Bhaṭṭa. *Āgamaḍambara, Otherwise Called Saṇmatanāṭaka of Jayanta Bhaṭṭa*. Edited by V. Raghavan and Anantalal Thakur. Darbhanga: 1964.

Agarwala, R. C. "Early Brahmanical Sculptures from Bharat Kalā Bhavan." In *Cchavi, Golden Jubilee Volume*, edited by Anand Krishna, pp. 173–91. Varanasi: Bharat Kalā Bhavan, 1971.

———. "Kṛttikā Cult in Early Indian Sculpture." *Lalit Kalā* 14 (1969): pp. 56–57.

———. "Mātṛkā Reliefs in Early Indian Art." *East and West*, n.s., 21 (1971): pp. 81–82.

Agrawala, Prthvi Kumar. *Skanda-Kārttikeya [A Study in the Origin and Development]*. Varanasi: Banaras Hindu University, 1967.

Agrawala, Vasudeva S. *Ancient Indian Folk Cults*. Benares: Prthivi Prakashan, 1970.

———. A Catalogue of the Brahmanical Images in Mathura Art. Lucknow: 1951.

Akulavīratantra. In *Kaulajñānanirṇaya and Some Minor Texts of the School of Matsyendranātha*. Edited with an introduction by Prabodh Chandra Bagchi. Sanskrit Series, no. 3. Calcutta: Metropolitan, 1934.

Ali, S. M. *Geography of the Puranas*. New Delhi: People's Publishing House, 1966.

Allen, Michael R. "Kumari or 'Virgin' Worship in Kathmandu Valley." *Contributions to Indian Sociology*, n.s., 10, no. 2 (1976): pp. 293–316.

Amanaskayoga of Gorakṣanātha. Edited by Ramlal Srivastav. Gorakhpur: Gorakhnath Mandir, 1980.

Amarakośa. *Śrīmad Amarasiṃhaviracitaṃ nāmaliṅgānuśāsanam Amarakośa*. 2nd ed. Edited with Hindi and Sanskrit commentaries by Brahmananda Tripathi. Chaukhamba Surbharati Granthamala, no. 52. Benares: Chaukhamba Surbharati Prakashan, 1982.

Āpastamba Śrauta Sūtra. With the commentary of Rudradatta. 3 vols. Edited by Richard Garbe. Calcutta: Baptist Mission Press, 1885–1903.

Apfel-Marglin, Frédérique. *Wives of the God-King*. New York: Oxford University Press, 1985.

Aristotle. *Generation of Animals*. With an English translation by A. L. Peck. Loeb Classical Library, no. 366. Cambridge: Harvard University Press, 1943.

Assayag, Jackie. *La Colère de la déesse décapitée: Traditions, cultes et pouvoir dans le sud de l'Inde*. Paris: CNRS Editions, 1992.

Aṣṭāṅga Hṛdaya of Vāgbhaṭṭa. *Aṣṭāṅgahṛdaya* with the commentary of Hemadri. Bombay: Nirnaysagar Press, 1925.

Atharva Veda. Atharvaveda Saṃhitā. 2 vols. Translated with a critical commentary by William D. Whitney. Revised and edited by Charles R. Lanman. Harvard Oriental Series, vols. 7–8. Cambridge: Harvard University Press, 1905.

Atharvaveda Parīśiṣṭas. The Ancillary Literature of the Atharva-Veda. By B. R. Modak. New Delhi: Rashtriya Veda Vidya Pratishthan, 1993.

Atherton, Cynthia Packert. *The Sculpture of Early Medieval Rajasthan.* Leiden: Brill, 1997.

Avalon, Arthur (Sir John Woodroffe), ed. *Principles of Tantra. The Tantratattva of Śrīyukta Śiva Candra Vidyārṇava Bhattacārya Mahodaya.* 3rd ed. With introductions by Arthur Avalon and B. K. Majumdar. Madras: Ganesha, 1960.

———. *The Serpent Power, Being the Shat-chakra-nirūpana and Pāduka-panchakā.* 4th ed. Madras: Ganesh and Co., 1950.

Bagchi, Prabodh Chandra. *Studies in the Tantras, Part 1.* Calcutta: University of Calcutta, 1975.

Balfour, Edward. *The Cyclopaedia of India and of Eastern and Southern Asia, Commercial, Industrial, and Scientific.* 3 vols. London: 1885; reprint Graz: Akademische Druck-u. Verlagsantstalt, 1967.

Banerjea, J. N. "Some Folk Goddesses of Ancient and Mediaeval India." *Indian Historical Quarterly* 14 (1938): pp. 101–10.

———. "The Vārāhī Temple at Chaurāshi." In *Felicitation Volume (A Collection of Forty-two Indological Essays) Presented to Mahamahopadhyaya Dr. V. V. Mirashi,* edited by G. T. Deshpande, Ajay Mitra Shastri, and V. W. Karambelkar, pp. 349–54. Nagpur: Vidarbha Samshodhan Mandal, 1965.

Basham, A. L. "Notes on the Origins of Śāktism and Tantrism." In *Sudhakar Chattopadhyaya Commemoration Volume,* pp. 148–50. Calcutta: Roy and Chowdhury, 1984.

Béguin, Gilles. *Art ésotérique de l'Himâlaya: Catalogue de la donation Lionel Fournier.* Paris: Editions de la Réunion des Musées Nationaux, 1990.

Beyer, Stephan. *The Buddhist Experience: Sources and Interpretations.* Encino, Calif.: Dickenson Publishing, 1974.

Bhāgavata Purāṇa. Śrimadbhāgavata Purāṇa. 2 vols. Edited and translated by C. L. Goswami and M. A. Sastri. Gorakhpur: Gita Press, 1971.

Bharati, Agehananda. *The Ochre Robe, An Autobiography.* Garden City, N.Y.: Doubleday, 1970.

———. *The Tantric Tradition.* London: Ryder & Co., 1965; reprint, New York: Grove Press, 1975.

Bharati, Dharmavir. *Siddh-Sāhity.* 2nd ed. Allahabad: Kitab Mahal, 1968.

Bhardwaj, Surinder Mohan. *Hindu Places of Pilgrimage in India.* Berkeley: University of California Press, 1973.

Bhattacharyya, Narendra Nath. *Indian Puberty Rites.* 2nd rev. ed. Delhi: Munshiram Manoharlal, 1980.

———. *Religious Culture of North-Eastern India.* New Delhi: Manohar, 1995.

Bhāvaprakāśa of Bhāvamiśra. *Bhāvaprakāśanighaṇṭu.* 2 vols. Edited with an English translation by K. R. Srikantha Murthy. Krishnadas Āyurveda Series, 5. Benares: Krishnadas Academy, 1998–2000.

Bhūtaḍāmara Tantra. Bhūtaḍāmara tantram: mūla evaṃ Hindi anuvāda sahita. Edited and translated by Krsna Kumara Raya. Benares: Pracya Prakasana, 1993.

Bledsoe, Bronwen. "An Advertised Secret: The Goddess Taleju and the King of Kathmandu." In *Tantra in Practice,* ed. White, pp. 195–205.

Bodiford, William. "Emptiness and Dust: Zen Dharma Transmission Rituals." In *Tantra in Practice*, ed. White, pp. 299–307.

Böhtlingk, Otto, and Rudolf Roth. *Sanskrit Wörterbuch hrsg. von der Kaiserlichen Akademie der Wissenschaften*. 7 vols. Saint Petersburg: Kaiserlichen Akademie, 1855–75; reprint, Delhi: Motilal Banarsidass, 1990.

Boulnois, Jean. *La Caducée et la symbolique dravidienne indo-méditeranéenne de l'arbre, de la pierre, du serpent et de la déesse-mère*. With a preface by G. Jouveau-Dubreuil. Paris: Librairie d'Amérique et d'Orient, 1989.

Brahmāṇḍa Purāṇa. *Brahmāṇḍa Purāṇa of Sage Kṛṣṇa Dvaipāyana Vyāsa*. Edited by J. L. Shastri. Delhi: Motilal Banarsidass, 1973.

Brahmayāmala. Nepal National Archives. MSS no. 1-743. Nepal-German Manuscript Preservation Project Reel no. A 166/1. 439 fols.

Braverman, Marcy Alison. "Totally Soaked: Immersion (*samāveśa*) and Intoxication of Devotion (*bhaktyunmāda*) in the Nondual Śaiva Yoga Traditions of Kashmir." Ph.D. diss., University of California, Santa Barbara, 2002.

Bṛhadāraṇyaka Upaniṣad. Edited and translated into French by Emile Sénart. Paris: Les Belles Lettres, 1934.

Bṛhat Saṃhitā of Varāhamihira. *Varāhamihira's Bṛhat Saṃhitā*. 2 vols. Edited and translated by M. Ramakrishna Bhat. Delhi: Motilal Banarsidass, 1981–82.

Brooks, Douglas Renfrew. *Auspicious Wisdom: The Texts and Traditions of Śrīvidyā Śākta Tantrism in South India*. Albany: SUNY Press, 1992.

———. "Encountering the Hindu 'Other': Tantrism and the Brahmans of South India." *Journal of the American Academy of Religion* 60, no. 3 (fall 1992): pp. 405–36.

———. *The Secret of the Three Cities: An Introduction to Hindu Śākta Tantrism*. Chicago: University of Chicago Press, 1990.

Brown, Robert L. ed. *Ganesh, Studies of an Asian God*. Albany: SUNY Press, 1991.

Brunner, Hélène. "The Place of Yoga in the Śaivāgamas." In *Pandit N. R. Bhatt Felicitation Volume*, edited by Pierre-Sylvain Filliozat, S. P. Narang, and C. P. Bhatta, pp. 425–61. Delhi: Motilal Banarsidass, 1994.

———. "Un Tantra du Nord: Le 'Netra-Tantra.'" *Bulletin of the School of Oriental and African Studies* 37 (1974): pp. 125–97.

Brunner, Hélène, Gerard Oberhammer, and André Padoux. *Tāntrikābhidhānakośa I, Dictionnaire des termes techniques de la littérature hindoue tantrique*. Vienna: Verlag der Österreichischen Akademie der Wissenschaften, 2000.

Buddhacarita. *The Buddhacarita or, Acts of the Buddha*. 2 vols. 2nd ed. Edited and translated by E. H. Johnston. Lahore: University of the Punjab, 1936; reprint, New Delhi: Oriental Books Reprint Corporation, 1972.

Bühnemann, Gudrun. "Buddhist Deities and Mantras in the Hindu Tantras: II, the *Śrīvidyārṇavatantra* and the *Tantrasāra*," *Indo-Iranian Journal* 43, no. 1 (spring 2000): pp. 27–48.

Burgess, James. *Report on the Antiquities of Kâthiâwâḍ and Kacch, Being the Result of the Second Season's Operations of the Archæological Survey of Western India, 1874–1875*. London: India Museum, 1876; reprint, Delhi: Indological Book House, 1971.

Burghart, Richard. "The Regional Circumambulation of Janakpurdham." In *L'Espace du temple*, vol. 1, *Espaces, itineraires, et méditations*, edited by Jean-Claude Galey, pp. 121–47. *Puruṣārtha* 8. Paris: Editions de l'EHESS, 1985.

Burrow, T. "On the Significance of the Term *arma, armaka* in Early Sanskrit Literature." *Journal of Indian History* 41, no. 1 (April 1963): pp. 159–66.

Caillat, Colette, and Ravi Kumar. *The Jain Cosmology*. English translation by R. Norman. Basel: Ravi Kumar, 1981.

Caldwell, Sarah. *Oh Terrifying Mother: Sexuality, Violence and Worship of the Goddess Kāḷi*. New York: Oxford University Press, 1999.

Caraka Saṃhitā, with the commentary of Cakrapāṇidatta. Edited with Hindi translation by Jadavji Trikamji Acarya, Chaukhamba Ayurvijnan Granthamala, 34. Bombay: 1941; reprint, Benares: Chaukhamba Surabharati Prakashan, 1992.

Carstairs, G. M. *Death of a Witch: A Village in North India, 1950–1981*. London: Hutchinson, 1983.

Carstairs, G. Morris. *The Twice Born*. London: Hogarth Press, 1958.

Caryāgīti. *An Anthology of Buddhist Tantric Songs: A Study of the Caryāgīti*. Edited and translated by Per Kværne. Oslo: Universitatetsforlaget, 1977; reprint, Bangkok: White Orchid, 1986.

Caturviṃśatisāhasra Tantra. Mān Singh Library MSS no. 1488, 319 fols, 19th century. This work is very likely identical to the Ādi Khaṇḍa of the *Manthānabhairava Tantra*.

Chamba State with Maps, 1904. Punjab States Gazetteer, vol. 22A. Lahore: Civil and Military Gazette Press, 1910.

Chāndogya Upaniṣad. Edited and translated into French by Emile Sénart. Paris: Adrien Maisonneuve, 1930.

Chapple, Christopher Key. "Haribhadra's Analysis of Pātañjala and Kula Yoga in the *Yogadṛṣṭisamucchaya*." In *Open Boundaries, Jain Communities and Cultures in Indian History*, edited by John E. Cort, pp. 15–30. Albany: SUNY Press, 1998.

Chattopadhyaya, Brajadvlal. *The Making of Early Medieval India*. Delhi: Oxford University Press, 1994.

Clémentin-Ojha, Catherine. *Le Trident sur le palais: Une Cabale anti-vishnouite dans un royaume hindou à l'époque coloniale*. Paris: Presses de l'Ecole Française d'Extrême Orient, 1999.

Clothey, Fred. "Tamil Religions." In *The Encyclopedia of Religions*, ed. Eliade, vol. 14, pp. 260–68.

Coburn, Thomas B. *Devī-Māhātmya, The Crystallization of the Goddess Tradition*. With a foreword by Daniel H. H. Ingalls. Delhi: Motilal Banarsidass, 1984.

Coomaraswamy, Ananda K. *Yakṣas*. Washington, D.C.: Smithsonian Institution–Freer Gallery, 1928–31; reprint, New Delhi: Munshiram Manoharlal, 1971.

Corpus Inscriptionum Indicarum. Vol. 3 (*Inscriptions of the Early Gupta Kings and Their Successors*). Calcutta: Government of India, 1888.

Couture, André, and Charlotte Schmid. "The *Harivaṃśa*, the Goddess Ekānaṃśā, and the Iconography of the Vṛṣṇi Triads." *Journal of the American Oriental Society* 121:2 (April–June 2001): 173–92.

Daniel, E. Valentine. *Fluid Signs: Being a Person in the Tamil Way*. Berkeley: University of California Press, 1984.

Darmon, Richard A. "Vajrolī Mudrā: La Rétention séminale chez les yogī vāmācāri." In *Images du corps dans le monde hindou*, edited by Véronique Bouillier and Gilles Tarabout. Paris: Editions du C.N.R.S., 2002.

Das, Rahul Peter. "Problematic Aspects of the Sexual Rituals of the Bauls of Bengal." *Journal of the American Oriental Society* 112, no. 3 (1992): pp. 388–422.

Daśakumāracarita. Edited by Moresvara Ramacandra Kale. Delhi: Motilal Banarsidass, 1966.

Daśāvatāracarita of Kṣemendra. *The Daśâvatâracharita of Kshemendra*. Edited by Pandit Durgaprasad and Kashinath Pandurang Parab. Bombay: Nirnaya-Sagara Press, 1891.

Davidson, Ronald. "The Political Dimension of Indian Esoteric Buddhism." Paper presented at the American Academy of Religion Annual Conference, San Francisco, November 21, 1999.

Davis, Richard. "Inscriptions of the Drunken Peacocks." In *Tantra in Practice*, ed. White, pp. 131–45.

Dehejia, Vidya. *Early Stone Temples of Orissa*. New Delhi: Vikas, 1979.

———. *Yoginī Cult and Temples*. New Delhi: National Museum, 1986.

Desai, Devangana. *Erotic Sculpture of India: A Socio-Cultural Study*. New Delhi: Tata McGraw-Hill, 1975.

———. *The Religious Imagery of Khajuraho*. Mumbai: Franco-Indian Research Pvt. Ltd., 1996.

Desirens, Hélène. "Les *Yoginī* de la haute vallée de Kulu (Himachal Pradesh)." *Bulletin d'Etudes Indiennes* 9 (1991): pp. 61–73.

Deśopadeśa of Kṣemendra. In *Minor Works of Kṣemendra*, edited by Aryendra Sharma et al., pp. 273–306. Hyderabad: Lokavijaya Press, 1961.

Deva, Krishna. *Temples of Khajuraho*. 2 vols. New Delhi: Archaeological Survey of India, 1990.

Dharmadhikari, T. N., ed. *Yajñāyudhānī (An Album of Sacrificial Utensils)*. Poona: Vaidika Samsodhana Mandala, 1989.

Dhawan, Savitri. *Mother Goddesses in Early Indian Religion*. Jaipur: National Publishing House, 1997.

Digby, Simon. "Encounters with Jogīs in Indian Sūfī Hagiography." Typescript of paper read at the School of Oriental and African Studies, London, January 27, 1970.

———. "To Ride a Tiger or a Wall? Strategies of Prestige in Indian Sufi Legend." In *According to Tradition: Hagiographical Writing in India*, edited by Winand Callwaert and Rupert Snell, pp. 99–129. Wiesbaden: Harrassowitz, 1994.

Dimock, Edwin C., Jr. *The Place of the Hidden Moon: Erotic Mysticism in the Vaiṣṇava-sahajiyā Cult of Bengal*. Chicago: University of Chicago Press, 1966; reprint, Chicago: Phoenix Press, 1989.

Dixit, K. K. *Jaina Ontology*. Ahmedabad: L. D. Institute of Indology, 1971.

Donaldson, Thomas E. "Erotic Rituals on Orissan Temples." *East and West* (Rome) 36, nos. 1–3 (September 1986): pp. 137–82.

———. *Hindu Temple Art of Orissa*. 3 vols. Leiden: Brill, 1987.

———. *Kāmadeva's Pleasure Garden: Orissa*. Delhi: B. R. Publishing, 1987.

———. "Propitious-Apotropaic Eroticism in the Art of Orissa," *Artibus Asiae* 37:1 (1975): pp. 75–100.

Dubois, Jean Antoine. *Moeurs, Institutions et cérémonies des peuples de l'Inde*. With a postface by Alain Danielou. Paris: Imprimerie Royale, 1825; reprint, Paris: Métailié, 1985.

Dundas, Paul. "The Jain Monk Jinapati Sūri Gets the Better of a Nāth Yogī." In *Tantra in Practice*, ed. White, pp. 231–38.

Dyczkowski, Mark S. G. *The Canon of the Śaivāgama and the Kubjikā Tantras of the Western Kaula Tradition*. Albany: SUNY Press, 1988.

———. "Kubjikā, Kālī, Tripurā and Trika." *Nepal Research Center Publications*, no. 22, pp. 1–65. Stuttgart: Fritz Steiner Verlag, 2000.

———. "Kubjikā the Erotic Goddess. Sexual Potency, Transformation and Reversal in the Heterodox Theophanies of the Kubjikā Tantras." *Indologica Taurinensia* 21–22 (1995–96): pp. 123–40.

———. "The Sacred Geography of the Kubjikā Tantras with Reference to the Bhairava and Kaula Tantras." Unpublished manuscript. 1999.

Eliade, Mircea. *Myths, Dreams, and Mysteries*. Translated from the French by Philip Mairet. New York: Harper Torchbooks, 1967.

———. *Shamanism, Archaic Techniques of Ecstasy*. Translated from the French by Williard R. Trask. Princeton: Princeton University Press, 1972.

Encyclopedia of Religion and Ethics. 12 vols. Edited by James Hastings. New York: Scribner's, 1908.

Encyclopedia of Religions. 16 vols. Edited by Mircea Eliade. New York: Macmillan, 1986.

Erndl, Kathleen M. *Victory to the Mother: The Hindu Goddess of Northwest India in Myth, Ritual, and Symbol*. New York: Oxford University Press, 1993.

Eschmann, Anncharlott, Hermann Kulke, and Gaya Charan Tripathi et al. "The Formation of the Jagannātha Triad," *The Cult of Jagannath and the Regional Tradition of Orissa*. New Delhi: Manohar, 1978.

Farrer, Anne, and Roderick Whitfield. *Caves of the Thousand Buddhas: Chinese Art from the Silk Route*. London: British Museum, 1990.

Faure, Bernard. *The Red Thread, Buddhist Approaches to Sexuality*. Princeton: Princeton University Press, 1998.

Feldhaus, Anne. *Water and Womanhood: Religious Meanings of Rivers in Maharashtra*. New York: Oxford University Press, 1995.

Fenner, Edward Todd. "Rasāyan Siddhi: Medicine and Alchemy in the Buddhist Tantras." Ph.D. diss., University of Wisconsin, 1979. Ann Arbor: University Microfilms International, 1982.

Filliozat, Jean. *Etude de démonologie indienne: Le Kumāratantra de Rāvaṇa et les textes parallèles indiens, tibétains, chinois, cambodgien et arabe*. Cahiers de la Société Asiatique, 1è série, vol. 4. Paris: Imprimerie Nationale, 1937.

Fisher, Eberhard, and B. N. Goswamy. *Pahari Masters*. Zurich: Museum Rietberg, 1992.

Fleet, John Faithfull. "Gangdhar Stone Inscription of Visvavarman, the Year 480." In *Corpus Inscriptionum Indicarum*, vol. 3.

Flood, Gavin. *Body and Cosmology in Kashmir Śaivism*. San Francisco: Mellen Research University Press, 1993.

———. "The Purification of the Body." In *Tantra in Practice*, ed. White, pp. 509–20.

Forbes, Alexander Kinloch. *Râs-mâlâ: Hindu Annals of Western India, with Particular Reference to Gujarat*. With historical notes by H. G. Rawlinson. London: Richardson, 1878; reprint, New Delhi: Heritage Publishers, 1973.

Fuller, Chris. *The Camphor Flame*. Princeton: Princeton University Press, 1992.

Gadon, Elinor W. "The Hindu Goddess Shasthi: Protector of Women and Children." In *From the Realm of the Ancestors: An Anthology in Honor of Marija Gimbutas*, edited by Joan Marfer. San Diego: Paradigm Publishing, 1997.

Gaston, Anne-Marie. *Śiva in Dance, Myth and Iconography*. Delhi: Oxford University Press, 1982.

Gaūḍavaho of Vākpati. *The Gauḍavaho: A Historical Poem in Prākrit*. Edited by Shankar Pandurang Pandit. Bombay: Government Central Book Depot, 1887.

Ghildayal, Deviprasada. *Pañcamakāra tathā bhāvatraya*. Allahabad: Pandit Devidatta Sukla Smaraka Kalyana Mandira Prakasana, 1974.

George, Christopher S. *Caṇḍamahāroṣaṇa Tantra, Chapters 1–8: A Critical Edition and English Translation*. American Oriental Series, no. 56. New Haven: American Oriental Society, 1974.

Goetz, Hermann. "The Historical Background of the Great Temples of Khajuraho." In *Studies in the History, Religion, and Art of Classical and Medieval India*, edited by Hermann Kulke, pp. 108–21. Wiesbaden: Steiner, 1974.

Gonda, Jan. *Change and Continuity in Indian Tradition*. The Hague: Mouton, 1965.

———. *Medieval Religious Literature in Sanskrit*. History of Indian Literature, II, 1. Wiesbaden: Harassowitz, 1977.

Goudriaan, Teun. "Some Beliefs and Rituals concerning Time and Death in the Kubjikāmata." In *Selected Studies on Ritual in the Indian Religions: Essays to D. J. Hoens*, edited by Ria Kloppenborg. Leiden: Brill, 1983, pp. 92–117.

Goudriaan, Teun, and Sanjukta Gupta. *Hindu Tantric and Śākta Literature*. History of Indian Literature, II, 2. Wiesbaden: Harrassowitz, 1981.

Gough, K. "Female Initiation Rites on the Malabar Coast." *Journal of the Royal Anthropological Institute* 85 (1955): pp. 45–80.

Guhyasamāja Tantra. *Guhyasamāja*. Edited by Benoytosh Bhattacharyya. Gaekwad's Oriental Series, no. 53. Baroda: Oriental Institute, 1931.

Gupta, Sanjukta. "The Worship of Kālī According to the *Toḍala Tantra*." In *Tantra in Practice*, ed. White, pp. 463–88.

Gupta, Sanjukta, and Richard Gombrich. "Kings, Power and the Goddess." *South Asia Research* 6, no. 2 (November 1986): pp. 123–38.

Gupta, Sanjukta, Dirk Jan Hoens, and Teun Goudriaan. *Hindu Tantrism*. Handbuch der Orientalistik, 2.4.2. Leiden: Brill, 1979.

Halbfass, Wilhelm. *India and Europe: An Essay in Understanding*. Albany: SUNY Press, 1988.

Haravijaya of Ratnākara. *Ratnākara's* Haravijaya, *An Introduction to the Sanskrit Court Epic*. Translated by David Smith. Delhi: Oxford University Press, 1985.

Hārītasaṃhitā. *La Hārītasaṃhitā: Texte médical sanskrit*. Edited and translated by Alix Raison. Pondicherry: Institut Français d'Indologie, 1974.

Harivaṃśa. *The Harivaṃśa Being the Khila or Supplement to the Mahābhārata*. 2 vols. Edited by Parasuram Lakshman Vaidya. Poona: Bhandarkar Oriental Research Institute, 1969, 1971.

Harley, J. B., and David Woodward, eds. *Cartography in the Traditional Islamic and South Asian Societies*. The History of Cartography, vol. 2, book 1. Chicago: University of Chicago Press, 1992.

Harper, Katherine Anne. *The Iconography of the Saptamatrikas: Seven Hindu Goddesses of Spiritual Transformation*. Lewiston, N.Y.: Edwin Mellen Press, 1989.

Harṣacarita of Bāṇabhaṭṭa. *The Harṣacarita of Bāṇabhaṭṭa with Exhaustive Notes [Ucchvāsas I–VIII]*. Edited by Pandurang Vamana Kane. Bombay: 1918; reprint, New Delhi: Motilal Banarsidass, 1973.

Haṭhayoga Pradīpikā of Svātmarāman. *Haṭhayogapradīpikā of Svātmarāman*. With the commentary of Brahmānanda. Edited and translated by Srinivasa Iyengar. Madras: Adyar, 1972.

Hawley, John Stratton, and Donna M. Wulff. *Devi: Goddesses of India*. Berkeley: University of California Press, 1996.

Hayes, Glen. "*The Necklace of Immortality*: A Seventeenth-Century Vaiṣṇava Sahajiyā Text." In *Tantra in Practice*, ed. White, pp. 308–25.

Hazra, R. C. *Studies in the Purāṇic Records on Hindu Rites and Customs*. 2nd ed. Delhi: Motilal Banarsidass, 1975.

Heesterman, Jan. *The Broken World of Sacrifice*. Chicago: University of Chicago Press, 1993.

———. *The Inner Conflict of Tradition*. Chicago: University of Chicago Press, 1985.

Heilijger-Seelens, Dorothea. *The System of the Five Cakras in Kubjikāmatatantra 14–16*. Groningen: Egbert Forsten, 1994.

Henry, Edward O. *Chant the Names of God: Musical Culture in Bhojpuri-speaking India*. San Diego: San Diego State University Press, 1988.

Herrmann-Pfandt, Adelheid. "The Good Woman's Shadow: Some Aspects of the Dark Nature of Ḍākinīs and Śākinīs in Hinduism." In *Wild Goddesses in India and Nepal, Proceedings of an International Symposium, Berne and Zurich, November 1994*, edited by Axel Michaels, Cornelia Vogelsanger, and Annette Wilke, pp. 39–70. Bern: Peter Lang, 1996.

———. "The So-Called *Ḍākinīkalpa:* Religious and Astrological Medicine According to a North-West Indian Collective Manuscript (I)." *Journal of the European Āyurvedic Society* 5 (1997): pp. 53–75.

Hevajra Tantra. The Concealed Essence of the Hevajra Tantra. With the "Yogaratnamālā" commentary of Kaṅha. Edited and translated by G. W. Farrow and I. Menon. Delhi: Motilal Banarsidass, 1992.

———. *The Hevajra Tantra, a Critical Study.* 2 vols. Edited and translated by David L. Snellgrove. London: Oxford University Press, 1959.

Hiltebeitel, Alf. *The Ritual of Battle: Krishna in the Mahābhārata.* Ithaca: Cornell University Press, 1976.

———, ed. *Criminal Gods and Demon Devotees: Essays on the Guardians of Popular Hinduism.* Albany: SUNY Press, 1989.

Hippocrates. *On the Nature of the Infant.* In *Hippocrate.* Edited and translated into French by Robery Joly, vol. 11, p. 68. Paris: Les Belles Lettres, 1970.

———. *Sacred Disease.* In *Works.* Translated by Francis Adams, vol. 2, pp. 139–83. New York: Loeb Classical Library, 1981.

Hooykaas, C., trans. *Āgama Tīrtha, Five Studies in Hindu-Balinese Religion.* Amsterdam: N.V. Noord-Hollandsche Uitgevers Maatschappij, 1964.

Hopkins, George Washburn. *Epic Mythology.* Strassburg: Trübner, 1915; reprint, Delhi: Motilal Banarsidass, 1974.

Houellebecq, Michel. *Les Particules élémentaires.* Paris: Editions J'ai Lu, 2000.

Hudson, Dennis. "Madurai: The City as Goddess." In *Urban Form and Meaning in South Asia: The Shaping of Cities from Prehistoric to Precolonial Times*, edited by Howard Spodek and Doris Meth Srinivasan, pp. 125–42. Washington, D.C.: National Gallery of Art, 1993.

———. "The Śrīmad Bhāgavata Purāṇa in Stone: The Text as an Eighth-Century Temple and Its Implications." *Journal of Vaiṣṇava Studies* 3, no. 3 (summer 1995): pp. 137–82.

———. "Vāsudeva Kṛṣṇa in Theology and Architecture: A Background to Śrīvaiṣṇavism." *Journal of Vaiṣṇava Studies* 2, no. 1 (winter 1993): pp. 139–70.

Humes, Cynthia Ann. "Vindhyavāsinī: Local Goddess Yet Great Goddess." In *Devi: Goddesses of India*, edited by John Stratton Hawley and Donna M. Wulff, pp. 49–77. Berkeley: University of California Press, 1996.

In the Image of Man: The Indian Perception of the Universe through 2000 Years of Painting and Sculpture. Hayward Gallery, London, March 25–June 13, 1982. Arts Council of Great Britain. London: Weidenfield and Nicolson, 1982.

Inden, Ronald. "Hierarchies of Kings in Early Medieval India." In *Way of Life: King, Householder, Renouncer: Essays in Honor of Louis Dumont*, edited by T. N. Madan. New Delhi: Vikas, 1982.

———. "Ritual, Authority, and Cyclic Time in Hindu Kingship." In *Kingship and Authority in South Asia*, edited by J. F. Richards, pp. 28–73. Madison: University of Wisconsin Press, 1978.

Īśānaśivagurudevapaddhati. Īśānaśivagurudevapaddhati [Siddhāntaśāstra]. 4 vols. Edited by T. Ganapati Sastri. Trivandrum Sanskrit series 69, 72, 77, 83. Trivandrum: Superintendant, Government Press, 1920–25; reprint, Delhi: Bharatiya Vidya Prakashan, 1988.

Jacobi, Hermann. "Abode of the Blest (Hindu)." In *Encyclopedia of Religion and Ethics*, vol. 1, pp. 698–700.

Jamison, Stephanie. *Sacrificed Wife/Sacrificer's Wife: Women, Ritual, and Hospitality in Ancient India*. New York: Oxford University Press, 1996.

Jātaka. Translated by E. B. Cowell. 6 vols. Cambridge: Cambridge University Press, 1895–1907; reprint, London: Routledge & Kegan Paul, 1973.

Jayadrathayāmala, second hexad. Nepal National Archives. MSS no. 5-4650.

———, third hexad. Nepal National Archives. MSS no. 5-1975. Śaiva Tantra 429. Nepal-German Manuscript Preservation Project Reel no. A 152/9.

———, fourth hexad. Nepal National Archives. MSS no. 1-1468. Nepal-German Manuscript Preservation Project Reel no. B 122/4.

Jöchle, Wolfgang. "Traces of Embryo Transfer and Artificial Insemination in Antiquity and the Medieval Age." *Theriogenology* 21, no. 1 (January 1984): pp. 80–83.

———. "Treasured Breasts: A Historical View of Human Lactation." Paper read at the Australian College of Midwives, Tenth Bienniel National Conference. The Truth, Virtue, and Beauty of Midwifery. Melbourne, April 16–18, 1997.

Joshi, N. P. *Catalogue of the Brahmanical Sculptures in the State Museum, Lucknow (part I)*. Lucknow: State Museum, 1972.

———. *Mātṛkās: Mothers in Kuṣāṇa Art*. New Delhi: Kanak, 1986.

Kādambarī of Bāṇabhaṭṭa. *Bāṇa's Kādambarī (Pūrvabhāga Complete)*. Edited by Moresvara Ramacandra Kale. 4th rev. ed. Delhi: Motilal Banarsidass, 1968.

Kākacaṇḍeśvarīmata. Wellcome Institute Indic MSS g473, 20th century, 74 fols.

———. Nepal-German Manuscript Preservation Project Reel no. E1796/8.

Kakar, Sudhir. *The Inner World: A Psychoanalytic Study of Childhood and Society in India*. New York: Oxford University Press, 1978.

———. *Shamans, Mystics and Doctors: A Psychological Inquiry into India and Its Healing Traditions*. New York: Alfred A. Knopf, 1982; New Delhi: Oxford India Paperbacks, 1982.

Kakṣapuṭa Tantra. In *Indrajālavidyāsaṃgrahaḥ*. Edited by Jivananda Bhattacharya, pp. 264–390. Calcutta: V. V. Mukherji, 1925.

Kālikā Purāṇa. 2 vols. Edited with English translation and introduction by B. N. Shastri. Delhi: Chowkhambha Sanskrit Series, 1972; reprint, Delhi: Nag Publishers, 1992.

Kālīkulakramārcana of Vimalaprabodha. Nepal National Archives MSS no. 5-5188.

Kāmakalāvilāsa. *Kāma-kalā-vilāsa by Puṇyānanda-nātha with the Commentary of Natanānanda-nātha*. 3rd ed. Translated with commentary by Arthur Avalon. Madras: Ganesh and Co., 1961.

Kāmasūtra of Vatsyāyana. *Kamasutra Mallanaga Vatsyayana*. Trans. Wendy Doniger and Sudhir Kakar. New York: Oxford University Press, 2002.

Kane, Pandurang Vaman. *History of Dharmaśāstra*. 5 vols. 2nd ed. Poona: Bhandarkar Oriental Research Institute, 1968–75.

Kantawala, S. G. *Cultural History from the Matsya Purāṇa*. Baroda: M. S. University, 1964.

Kapadia, Karin. *Śivā and Her Sisters: Gender, Caste, and Class in Rural South India*. Boulder: Westview, 1995.

Kāpālika Tantra. University of Mysore. MSS no. 772.

———. University of Travancore. MSS no. 7475.

Kapferer, Bruce. *A Celebration of Demons: Exorcism and the Aesthetics of Healing in Sri Lanka*. 2nd ed. Providence, R.I.: Berg and Smithsonian Institution Press, 1991.

Karpūramañjarī of Rājaśekhara. *Karpūra-Mañjarī by Kavirāja Rājaśekhara*. Edited by N. G. Suru. Bombay: 1960.

———. *Rāja-Çekara's Karpūra-mañjarī, a Drama by the Indian·Poet Rājaçekhara (about 900 A.D.)*. Critically edited with an introduction by Sten Konow and translation into English with notes by Charles Rockwell Lanman. Harvard Oriental Series, vol. 4. Cambridge: Harvard University Press, 1901.

Kāśyapa Saṃhitā. *Kāśyapa Saṃhitā or Vṛddhajīvakīya Tantra (Text with English Commentary)*. Edited by P. V. Tewari. Haridas Ayurveda series, 2. Varanasi: Chaukhambha Visvabharati, 1996.

Kaṭha Upaniṣad. *The Kathaka Upanishad with Shri Shankara's Commentary*. Edited with notes by Swami Satchidanandendra Saraswati. Holenarsipur: Adhyatma Prakasha Karyalaya, 1962.

Kathāsaritsāgara of Somadeva. *Kathāsaritsāgaraḥ kaśmīrapradeśavāsinā Śrīrāmabhaṭṭanūdbhavena mahākavi Śrī Somadevabhaṭṭena viracitaḥ*. Edited by Jagadish Lal Sastri. Delhi: Motilal Banarsidass, 1970.

———. *The Kathâsaritsâgara of Somadevabhatta*. 2nd ed. Edited by Pandit Durgaprasad and Kasinath Pandurang Parab. Bombay: Nirnaya Sagara, 1903.

———. *The Ocean of Story Being C. H. Tawney's Translation of Somadeva's Kathā Sarit Sāgara (or Ocean of Streams of Story)*. 10 vols. Edited by N. M. Penzer. London: Chas. J. Sawyer, Ltd., 1924–28.

———. *Somadeva, Océan des rivières de contes*. Pubished under the direction of Nalini Balbir. Bibliothèque de la Pléiade. Paris: Gallimard, 1997.

———. *Somadeva, Tales From the Kathāsaritsāgara*. By Arshia Sattar. With a foreword by Wendy Doniger. New Delhi: Penguin Books India, 1994.

Kaulajñānanirṇaya of Matsyendranātha. *Kaulajñānanirṇaya and Some Minor Texts of the School of Matsyendranātha*. Edited with an introduction by Prabodh Chandra Bagchi. Sanskrit Series, no. 3. Calcutta: Metropolitan, 1934.

Kaulāvalinirṇaya of Jñānānanda Paramahaṃsa. *Kaulavalī-Nirṇayaḥ*. Edited by Arthur Avalon. Tantrik Texts, vol. 14. Calcutta: Sanskrit Press Depository, 1929.

Kauśītaki Upaniṣad. Edited and translated into French by Louis Renou. Paris: Adrien Maisonneuve, 1948.

Kaviraj, Gopinath. *Bhāratīya Sādhanā kī Dhārā*. Bihar: Rashtrabhasa Parisad, 1984.

———. *Tāntrik Sādhanā aur Siddhānt*. Patna: Bihar Rashtrabhasa Parisad, 1979.

———. *Tāntrik Sāhity (Vivaraṇātmak Granthsūcī)*. Benares: Bhargava Bhushan Press, 1972.

Kaye, George R. *Hindu Astronomy: Memoirs of the Archaeological Survey of India*. Vol. 18. Calcutta: Government of India, Central Publication Branch, 1924.

Khan, Dominique-Sila. *Conversions and Shifting Identities: Ramdev Pir and the Ismailis in Rajasthan*. New Delhi: Manohar, 1997.

———. "Deux rites tantriques dans une communauté d'intouchables au Rajasthan." *Revue de l'Histoire des Religions* 211, no. 4 (1994): pp. 443–62.

———. "L'Origine ismaélienne du culte hindou de Rāmdeo Pīr." *Revue de l'Histoire des Religions* 210 (1993): pp. 27–47.

———. "Rāmdeo Pīr and the Kāmaḍiyā Panth." In *Folk, Faith, and Feudalism*, edited by N. K. Singhi and Rajendra Joshi, pp. 295–327. Jaipur: Rawat Publications, 1995.

Khel, the Play. Video by Rahul Roy and Saba Dewan. New Delhi: Aakaar Productions/ Mass Comunication Research Center, 1994.

Kinsley, David. *Hindu Goddesses: Visions of the Divine Feminine in the Hindu Religious Tradition*. Berkeley: University of California Press, 1986.

———. *Tantric Visions of the Feminine: The Ten Mahāvidyās*. Berkeley: University of California Press, 1997.

Kirfel, Willibald. *Der Kosmographie der Inder nach Quellen dargestellt*. Bonn: 1920; reprint, Hildesheim: Georg Olms, 1967.

Klein, Anne C. "Nondualism and the Great Bliss Queen: A Study in Tibetan Buddhist Ontology and Symbolism." *Journal of Feminist Studies in Religion* 1:1 (1985): 73–98.

Kloetzli, W. Randolph. "Maps of Time—Mythologies of Descent: Scientific Instruments and the Purāṇic Cosmograph." *History of Religions* 25 (1985): pp. 120–45.

Knipe, David M. "The Heroic Theft: Myths from Rgveda IV and the Ancient Near East." *History of Religions* 6 (1967): pp. 328–60.

Kramer, Joel, and Diana Alstad. *The Guru Papers: Masks of Authoritarian Power*. Berkeley: Frog, Ltd., 1993.

Kripal, Jeffrey. *Kālī's Child: The Mystical and the Erotic in the Life and Teachings of Ramakrishna*. Chicago: University of Chicago Press, 1995.

Kriyākālaguṇottara. Kaiser Library [Kathmandu] MSS no. 297. Nepal-German Manuscript Preservation Project Reel no. C 30/16. 88 fols.

Kubjikāmata. *Kubjikāmata Tantra, Kulālikāmnāya Version*. Edited by Teun Goudriaan and Jan A. Schoterman. Orientalia Rheno-Traiectina, 30. Leiden: Brill, 1988.

Kulacūḍāmaṇi Tantra. *The Kulacūḍāmaṇi Tantra and the Vāmakeśvara Tantra with the Jayaratha Commentary*. Introduced, translated, and annotated by Louise M. Finn. Wiesbaden: Harrassowitz, 1986.

———. *Kulachûdâmani Tantra*. Edited by Girisha Chandra Vedantatirtha. In *Tantrik Texts*, ed. Arthur Avalon, vol. 4. London: Luzac & Co., 1915.

Kulārṇava Tantra. Edited by Taranatha Vidyaratna with an introduction by Arthur Avalon (Sir John Woodroffe). Madras: Ganesh and Company, 1965; reprint, Delhi: Motilal Banarsidass, 1975.

Kurtz, Stanley. *All the Mothers Are One: Hindu India and the Reshaping of Psychoanalysis*. New York: Columbia University Press, 1992.

Kværne, Per. "On the Concept of Sahaja in Indian Buddhist Tantric Literature." *Temenos* 11 (1975): pp. 88–135.

Lakṣmī Tantra. *Lakṣmī Tantra: A Pāñcarātra Text*. Translated with notes by Sanjukta Gupta. Leiden: Brill, 1972.

Lalitā Sahasranāma of the *Brahmāṇḍa Purāṇa*. *Lalitā-Sahasranāma with Bhāskararāya's Commentary*. Translated by R. Anantakrishna Sastry. Madras: Thompson Press, 1899; 6th reprint of 3rd ed., Madras: Adyar Library, 1988.

Laplanche, J., and J.-B. Pontalis. *Vocabulaire de la psychanalyse*. Paris: Presses Universitaires de France, 1967.

Larson, Gerald. *Classical Sāṃkhya*. 2nd rev. ed. Delhi: Motilal Banarsidass, 1979.

Lecomte-Tilouine, Marie. "Des dieux aux sommets (Népal)." In *Classer les Dieux? Des Panthéons en Asie du Sud* [*Puruṣārtha* 15], edited by Véronique Bouillier and Gérard Toffin. Paris: EHESS, 1993.

Le Goff, Jacques. *L'Imaginaire médiéval*. Paris: Gallimard, 1985.

———. *Pour un autre Moyen Age: Temps, travail et culture en Occident*. Paris: Gallimard, 1977.

Leonardo da Vinci. *Anatomical Drawings*. Text by Jean Mathe, trans. David Macrae. Geneva: Minerva, 1978.

Leslie, Julia. "A Bird Bereaved: The Identity and Significance of Vālmīki's *Krauñca*." *Journal of Indian Philosophy* 26 (1998): pp. 455–87.

———, ed. *Roles and Rituals for Indian Women*. Rutherford, N.J.: Fairleigh Dickenson University Press, 1992.

Lévi, Sylvain. "Le Catalogue des Yakṣa dans la Mahâmâyurî." *Journal Asiatique*, 11è série, tome 5, vol. 1 (January–February 1915): pp. 19–138.

———. *La Doctrine du sacrifice dans les Brâhmaṇas*. 2nd ed. Saigon, 1898; reprint, Paris: Presses Universitaires de France, 1966.

———. *Sanskrit Texts from Bali*. Gaekwad's Oriental Series, 67. Baroda: Oriental Institute, 1933.

Lidke, Jeffrey S. "The Goddess Within and Beyond the Three Cities: Śākta Tantra and the Paradox of Power in Nepāla-Maṇḍala." Ph.D. diss., University of California, Santa Barbara, 2001.

———. *Viśvarūpa Mandir: A Study of Chaṅgu Nārāyaṇ, Nepal's Most Ancient Temple*. New Delhi: Nirala Publications, 1996.

Lopez, Donald S., Jr., ed. *Religions of India in Practice*. Princeton: Princeton University Press, 1995.

Lorenzen, David. *The Kāpālikas and Kālāmukhas: Two Lost Śaivite Sects*. New Delhi: Thomson Press, 1972.

———. "New Light on the Kāpālikas." In *Criminal Gods*, ed. Hiltebeitel, pp. 231–38.

Lüders, Heinrich. "Das Würfelspiel im alten Indien." *Abhandlungen der Königlich Gesellschaft der Wissenschaftlichen zu Göttingen*. Philologische-historischen Klasse, n.s., 9, no. 2 (Berlin, 1907).

Lutgendorf, Philipp. *The Life of a Text: Performing the* Rāmcaritmānas *of Tulsidas*. Berkeley: University of California Press, 1991.

Madyapānavidhi, Man Singh Library MSS no. 1786A/3079.

Mahābhārata. *Mahābhārata*. 21 vols. Edited by Visnu S. Sukthankar et al. Poona: Bhandarkar Oriental Research Institute, 1933–60.

———. *The Mahābhārata; Book 2, The Book of the Assembly Hall; Book 3, The Book of the Forest*. Translated by J. A. B. van Buitenen. Chicago: University of Chicago Press, 1975.

Mahārāja Mān Singh rī Khyāt. Edited by Narayansinh Bhati. Jodhpur: Rajasthan Oriental Research Institute, 1979.

Mahāvamsa. *The Mahāvamsa; or, The Great Chronicle of Ceylon*. Translated by Wilhelm Geiger. Pali Text Society. London: Henry Frowde, Oxford University Press, 1912.

Maitri Upaniṣad. Edited and translated into French by Marie-Louise Esnoul. Paris: Adrien Maisonneuve, 1952.

Malamoud, Charles. *Cooking the World*. Translated by David Gordon White. New Delhi: Oxford India, 1996.

Mālatī-Mādhava of Bhavabhūti. *Bhavabhūti's Mālati-Mādhava, with the Commentary of Jagaddhara*. 3rd ed. Edited by Moresvara Ramacandra Kale. Delhi: Motilal Banarsidass, 1967.

Mālinīvijayatantra. Translation into the Italian of chapters 1–6, 8–9, and 11 in *Abhinavagupta, Luce dei Tantra*, trans. Gnoli, pp. 645–89.

Mallmann, Marie-Thérèse de. *Les Enseignements iconographiques de l'Agni-Purana*. Paris: Presses Universitaires de France, 1963.

Mānasollāsa of Bhūlokamalla Someśvara. *Mānasollāsa of King Bhūlokamalla Someśvara*. 2nd ed. 3 vols. Edited by G. K. Srigondekar. Gaekwad's Oriental Series, nos. 28, 84, 138. Baroda: Oriental Institute, 1925, 1939, 1961.

Mandelbaum, David. "Transcendental and Pragmatic Aspects of Religion." *American Anthropologist* 68 (1966): pp. 1175–91.

Mani, Vettam. *Purāṇic Encyclopedia: A Comprehensive Work with Special Reference to the Epic and Purāṇic Literature*. English translation by a committee of scholars. Kottayam: 1964; reprint, Delhi: Motilal Banarsidass, 1975, 1993.

Manthānabhairava Tantra. Nepal National Archives. MSS no. 5-4654. This work is divided into four divisions (*khaṇḍas*), the Ājñā (sometimes referred to as Ādi), Kumārikā, Yoga, and Siddha Khaṇḍas. A manuscript of the Ādi Khaṇḍa held in the Mān Singh Library in Jodhpur bears the title of *Caturviṃśatisāhasra Tantra*.

Manu Smṛti. With the commentary of Kullūka Bhaṭṭa. Edited by Gopala Sastri Nene. Kashi Sanskrit Series, no. 114. Benares: Chowkhamba Sanskrit Series Office, 1970.

Markel, Stephen. *Origin of the Indian Planetary Deities*. Lewiston, N.Y.: Edwin Mellen Press, 1995.

Masson, J. L., and M. V. Patwardhan. *Śāntarasa and Abhinavagupta's Philosophy of Aesthetics*. Poona: Bhandarkar Oriental Research Institute, 1969.

Mātṛkabheda Tantra. Edited by Chintamani Bhattacharya. Calcutta Sanskrit Series, no. 7. Calcutta: Metropolitan, 1933, 1958.

Matsya Purāṇa. Edited by Hari Narayana Apte. Anandasrama Sanskrit Series. Poona: Anandasrama, 1907.

McDaniel, June. "Interviews with a Tantric Kālī Priest: Feeding Skulls in the Town of Sacrifice." In *Tantra in Practice*, ed. White, pp. 72–80.

———. *Madness of the Saints*. Chicago: University of Chicago Press, 1990.

———. "Sitting on the Corpse's Chest: The Tantric Ritual of *Śava-sādhana*." Unpublished manuscript, 1999.

McGilvray, D. B. "Sexual Power and Fertility in Sri Lanka: Batticaloa Tamils and Moors." In *Ethnography of Fertility and Birth*, edited by Carol P. MacCormack, pp. 25–73. London: Academic Press, 1982.

Meister, Michael W. "Regional Variations in Mātṛkā Conventions." *Artibus Asiae* 47, nos. 3–4 (1986): pp. 240–45.

Menski, Werner F. "Marital Expectations as Dramatized in Hindu Marriage Rituals." In *Roles and Rituals for Hindu Women*, edited by Leslie, pp. 47–67.

Michaels, Axel. "Paśupati's Holy Field." In *Prêtrise et Pouvoirs en Himalaya*, edited by Véronique Bouillier and Gérard Toffin, pp. 41–59. Paris: Editions de l'EHESS, 1989.

Monier-Williams, Monier [Sir]. *A Sanskrit-English Dictionary Etymologically and Philologically Arranged with Special Reference to Cognate Indo-European Languages*. London: Oxford University Press, 1899; reprint, Delhi: Motilal Banarsidass, 1984.

Mookerjee, Ajit. *Kālī: The Feminine Force*. New York: Destiny Books, 1988.

Mṛgendrāgama. *Mṛgendrāgama, Section des Rites et Section du Comportement avec la Vṛtti de Bhaṭṭanārāyaṇakaṇṭha*. Translated by Hélène Brunner-Lachaux. Publications de l'Institut Française d'Indologie, no. 69. Pondicherry: Institut Français d'Indologie, 1962.

Muller-Ortega, Paul Eduardo. "Ciphering the Supreme: Mantric Encoding in Abhinavagupta's *Tantrāloka*." Forthcoming, *International Journal of Hindu Studies* 6 (2003).

———. "The Power of the Secret Ritual: Theoretical Formulations from the Tantra." *Journal of Ritual Studies* 4, no. 2 (summer 1990): pp. 41–59.

———. *The Triadic Heart of Śiva: Kaula Tantricism of Abhinavagupta in the Non-dual Shaivism of Kashmir*. Albany: SUNY Press, 1989.

Murr, Sylvia. *L'Inde philosophique entre Bossuet et Voltaire*. 2 vols. Paris: Ecole Française d'Extrême Orient, 1987.

Mus, Paul. *Barabudur*. 2 vols. Hanoi: Imprimerie d'Extrême Orient, 1935.

Mylius, Klaus. "Kokkokas *Ratirahasya* übersetzt und erlaütert (III)." *Journal of the Euro-*

pean Āyurvedic Society 5 (1997): pp. 136–179. Parts I and II of Mylius's translation are found in JEĀS 3 (1993): pp. 145–73 and 4 (1995): pp. 163–93.

Nabokov, Isabelle. *Religion Against the Self: An Ethnography of Tamil Rituals*. New York: Oxford University Press, 2000.

Nagaswamy, R. "The Sixty-four Yoginīs and Bhūta Worship as Mentioned by Śaṅkara in His Commentary on the Bhagavadgītā." *Berliner Indologische Studien* 9–10 (1966): 237–46.

Nalavilāsanāṭaka of Rāmacandrasūri. *Rāmacandrasūri, Nalavilāsanāṭakam*. Edited by Dhirendra Misra. With a Hindi commentary by Suresacandra Pandey. Varanasi: Parsvanath Vidyapith, 1996.

Nandi, Ramendra Nath. *Religious Institutions and Cults in the Deccan (c.* A.D. *600–*A.D. *1000)*. Delhi: Motilal Banarsidass, 1973.

Narain, R. K. "Gaṇeśa: A Protohistory of the Idea and the Icon." In *Ganesh, Studies of an Asian God*, edited by Robert L. Brown, pp. 19–48. Albany: SUNY Press, 1991.

Narayana Rao, Velchuru, trans. and ed. *Śiva's Warriors: The* Basava Purāṇa *of Pālkuriki Somanātha*. Princeton: Princeton University Press, 1990.

Narmamālā of Kṣemendra. In *Minor Works of Kṣemendra*. Edited by Aryendra Sharma et al., pp. 307–46. Hyderabad: Lokavijaya Press, 1961.

Nāthaṣoḍaśāmnāyakrama, Mān Singh Library MSS no. 1668/3059.

Netra Tantra. Netratantram [Mṛtyuñjaya Bhaṭṭāraka] with the Commentary Udyota of Kṣemarājācārya. Edited by Vajravallabh Dwivedi. Delhi: Parimal Publications, 1985.

Obeyesekere, Gananath. *Medusa's Hair: An Essay on Personal Symbols and Religious Experience*. Chicago: University of Chicago Press, 1981.

O'Flaherty, Wendy Doniger. *Dreams, Illusion and Other Realities*. Chicago: University of Chicago Press, 1984.

———. *The Origins of Evil in Hindu Mythology*. Berkeley: University of California Press, 1976.

———. *Tales of Sex and Violence: Folklore, Danger, and Sacrifice in the Jaiminīya Brāhmaṇa*. Chicago: University of Chicago Press, 1985.

———. *Women, Androgynes and Other Mythical Beasts*. Chicago: University of Chicago Press, 1980.

Olivelle, Patrick. *The Sannyāsa Upanisads: Hindu Scriptures on Asceticism and Renunciation*. New York: Oxford University Press, 1992.

Openshaw, Jeanne. "'Killing' the Guru: Anti-hierarchical Tendencies of 'Bāuls' of Bengal." *Contributions to Indian Sociology* n.s. 32:1 (1988): 1–19.

Orofino, Giacomella. "Notes on the Early Phases of Indo-Tibetan Buddhism." In *Le Parole e i marmi: Studi in onore di Raniero Gnoli nel suo 70° compleano*, pp. 541–64. Edited by Raffaele Torella. Rome: Istituto Italiano per l'Africa e l'Oriente, 2001.

Padma Purāṇa. Padmapurāṇam. 4 vols. Edited by Narayana Visvanatha Mandalika. Bombay: Anandasrama-mundranalaya, 1893–94.

Padoux, André. *L'Énergie de la parole, cosmogonies de la parole tantrique*. With a postface by Lokenath Bhattacharya. Paris: Fata Morgana, 1994. This is a revised edition of the author's thesis, *Recherches sur la symbolique et l'énergie de la parole dans certains textes tantriques*, translated into English by Jacques Gontier under the title *Vāc: The Concept of the Word in Selected Hindu Tantras*. Albany: SUNY Press, 1989. I have only referred to this English translation in the few cases in which data found therein was not included in the revised 1994 French edition.

———. "L'Oral et l'écrit: Mantra et *mantraśāstra*." In *Traditions Orales dans le Monde*

Indien (*Puruṣārtha* 18), edited by Catherine Champion, pp. 133–43. Paris: Editions de l'EHESS, 1996.

———. "Tantrism." In *Encyclopedia of Religions*, ed. Eliade, vol. 14, pp. 272–76.

———. "Transe, Possession ou Absorption Mystique?" In *La Possession en Asie du Sud (Puruṣārtha 21)*, edited by Jackie Assayag and Gilles Tarabout, pp. 133–47. Paris: Editions EHESS, 1999.

———, ed. *L'Image divine: Culte et méditation dans l'hindouisme*. Paris: Editions du CNRS, 1990.

———, ed. *Mantras et diagrammes rituels dans l'hindouisme*. Table Ronde, Paris, 21–22 juin 1984. Paris: Editions du CNRS, 1986.

Pal, Pratapaditya. *Hindu Religion and Iconology According to the Tantrasāra*. Los Angeles: Vichitra Press, 1981.

———. *Indian Sculpture: A Catalogue of the Los Angeles County Museum of Art Collection*. 2 vols. Los Angeles: LACMA, 1986–88.

Pandey, Kanti Chandra. *Abhinavagupta: An Historical and Philosophical Study*. Varanasi: Chowkhamba Sanskrit Series Office, 1963.

Parātriśika Vivaraṇa of Abhinavagupta. Edited and translated with notes by Jayadeva Singh. Albany: SUNY Press, 1989.

Parpola, Asko. *Deciphering the Indus Script*. Cambridge: Cambridge University Press, 1997.

———. *The Sky-Garment: A Study of the Harappan Religion and Its Relation to the Mesopotamian and Later Indian Religions*. Helsinki: Finnish Oriental Society, 1985.

Parry, Jonathan. *Death in Banaras*. Cambridge: Cambridge University Press, 1994.

Pathak, V. S. "The Navasāhasāṅkacarita (Itihāsa under the Shadow of a Symbolist)." In *Felicitation Volume (A Collection of Forty-two Indological Essays) Presented to Mahamahopadhyaya Dr. V. V. Mirashi*, edited by G. T. Deshpande, Ajay Mitra Shastri, and V. W. Karambelkar, pp. 424–32. Nagpur: Vidarbha Samshodhan Mandal, 1965.

———. *Śaiva Cults in Northern India from Inscriptions (700 A.D. to 1200 A.D.)*. Varanasi: Ram Naresh Varma, 1960.

Pinch, William. *Peasants and Monks in British India*. Delhi: Oxford University Press, 1996.

Pīṭharvarṇanam. Mān Singh Library MSS no. 1722.

Pollack, Sheldon. "Deep Orientalism? Notes on Sanskrit and Power Beyond the Raj." In *Orientalism and the Postcolonial Predicament*, edited by Carol Breckenridge and Peter van der Veer, pp. 76–133. Philadelphia: University of Pennsylvania Press, 1993.

Pott, P. H. *Yoga and Yantra: Their Interrelation and Their Significance for Indian Archaeology*. The Hague: Nijhoff, 1966.

Potter, Alicia. "Truly, Slowly, Deeply: Men Don't Ejaculate, Women Do, and You Have to Learn to Find your Chakras. Tantric Sex Is Not Your Average Roll in the Hay." www.tantra.com/boston2.html. This article originally appeared in the *Boston Phoenix* in 1998.

Prabodhacandrodaya of Kṛṣṇamiśra. *Prabodhacandrodaya of Kṛṣṇa Miśra (Sanskrit Text with English Translation, a Critical Introduction and Index)*. Edited and translated by Sita Krsna Nambiar. Delhi: Motilal Banarsidass, 1971.

Praśna Upaniṣad. Edited and translated into French by J. Bousquet. Paris: Adrien Maisonneuve, 1948.

Przyluski, Jean. "Les Hommes-Dieux dans la mythologie bouddhique." *Journal Asiatique* 229 (January–March 1938): pp. 123–28.

———. "Les Vidyārāja." Bulletin de l'Ecole Française d'Extrême Orient 23 (1923): pp. 301–18.

Rabe, Michael. "Secret Yantras and Erotic Display for Hindu Temples." In White, ed., *Tantra in Practice*, pp. 434–46.

———. "Sexual Imagery on the Phantasmagorical Castles at Khajuraho." *International Journal of Tantric Studies* 2, no. 2 (November 1996). www.shore. net/~india/ ijts.

Rājataraṅgiṇī of Kalhaṇa. *Kalhaṇa's Rājataramginī, Chronicle of the Kings of Kashmir.* 2 vols. Edited by M. A. Stein. London: Constable, 1900; reprint, Delhi: Motilal Banarsidass, 1979.

———. *Rājataraṅgiṇī*. Edited with a Hindi commentary by Ramtej Shastri Pandey. Delhi: Chaukhamba Sanskrit Pratishthan, 1985.

———. *Rājataraṅgiṇī of Kalhaṇa*. 2 vols. Edited by Vishva Bandhu. Hoshiarpur: Vishveshvaranand Vedic Research Institute, 1963.

Ram, Maya. *Rajasthan District Gazetteer, Alwar*. Jaipur: Bharat Printers, 1968.

Ramachandra Rao, S. K. *Śrī Cakra*. Sri Garib Dass Oriental Series, no. 87. Delhi: Sri Satguru Publications, 1989.

Ramanujan, A. K. *Hymns for the Drowning*. Princeton: Princeton University Press, 1981.

———. *The Interior Landscape: Sangam Poems of Classical Tamil Literature*. Bloomington: Indiana University Press, 1967.

Rāmāyaṇa. *The Rāmāyaṇa of Vālmīki, Vol. 1: Bālakāṇḍa*. Edited and translated by Robert P. Goldman. Princeton: Princeton University Press, 1984.

Rāmāyaṇa of Vālmīki. 7 vols. Edited by G. H. Bhatt et al. Baroda: Oriental Institute, 1960–75.

Rana, S. S. *A Study of Skanda Cult*. Delhi: Nag Publishers, 1995.

Rao, T. A. Gopinath. *Elements of Hindu Iconography*. 2 vols. in 4 tomes. Madras: Law Road Printing House, 1914–16.

"Rare Bust of a Yaksini Found." *Motilal Banarsidass Newsletter* (September 1990): p. 8.

Rasārṇava. *Rasārṇavam nama Rasatantram*. Edited with Hindi translation by Indradeo Tripathi and notes by Taradatta Panta. Haridas Sanskrit Series, no. 88. Banares: Chowkhamba, 1978.

Rasendramaṅgala of Nāgārjuna. 39 fols. Paris, Bibliothèque Nationale. Fonds Palmyr Cordier. MSS no. 1222 [Sanscrit].

Rastogi, Navjivan. *The Krama Tantrism of Kashmir*. Vol. 1. Delhi: Motilal Banarsidass, 1979.

Renou, Louis, and Jean Filliozat. *L'Inde classique, manuel des études indiennes*. 2 vols. Paris: Payot, 1947, 1953.

Ṛg Veda. *Ṛg Veda Saṃhitā, Together with the Commentary of Sāyaṇāchārya*. 2nd ed. 4 vols. Edited by F. Max Müller. London: Henry Frowde, 1890–92. First Indian ed. Chowkhamba Sanskrit Series, no. 99. Varanasi: Chowkhamba Sanskrit Series Office, 1966.

———. *Rig Veda, A Metrically Restored Text with an Introduction and Notes*. By Barend A. van Nooten and Gary B. Holland. Cambridge: Harvard University Press, 1994.

———. *The Rig Veda*. Translated by Wendy Doniger O'Flaherty. Harmondsworth: Penguin, 1981.

Riporṭ Mardumaśumārī Rāja Mārvāḍ Bābat san[vat] 1891 Isvī, Tīsrā Hissā. 2 vols. Edited by Raya Bahadur Munshi Haradayal Singh. Jodhpur: Vidyasal, 1895.

Rocher, Ludo. *The Purāṇas*. A History of Indian Literature, vol. II, 3. Wiesbaden: Otto Harrassowitz, 1986.

Roşu, Arion. "Les *Marman* et les arts martiaux indiens." *Journal Asiatique* 269 (1981): pp. 417–51.

Rudrayāmala Tantra. Rudrayāmalam. Edited by the Yogatantra Department. Yogatantra Granthamala, no. 7. Benares: Sampurnanand Sanskrit Vishvavidyalaya Press, 1980.

Saddharmapuṇḍarika Sūtra. Buddhist Sanskrit Texts, no. 6. Darbhanga: Mithila Institute, 1960.

Sādhanamālā. 2 vols. Edited by Benoytosh Bhattacarya. Baroda: Oriental Institute, 1925, 1928.

Sahni, Daya Ram. "Deogarh Rock Inscription of Svamibhata." *Epigraphica Indica* 18 (1925–26): pp. 125–27.

Salomon, Carol. "Bāul Songs." In Lopez, ed., *Religions of India in Practice*, pp. 187–208.

Samuel, Geoffrey. *Civilized Shamans, Buddhism in Tibetan Societies*. Washington, D.C.: Smithsonian Institution Press, 1993.

Sanderson, Alexis. "The Doctrines of the Mālinīvijayottaratantra." In *Ritual and Speculation in Early Tantrism, Studies in Honor of André Padoux*, edited by Teun Goudriaan, pp. 281–312. Albany: SUNY Press, 1992.

———. "Maṇḍala and Āgamic Identity in the Trika of Kashmir." In *Mantras et diagrammes rituels dans l'Hindouisme*, ed. Padoux, pp. 169–207.

———. "Meaning in Tantric Ritual." In *Essais sur le Rituel, III* (Colloque du Centenaire de la Section des Sciences Religieuses de l'Ecole Pratique des Hautes Etudes), edited by Anne-Marie Blondeau and Kristofer Schipper, pp. 15–95. Louvain-Paris: Peeters, 1995.

———. "Purity and Power among the Brahmins of Kashmir." In *The Category of the Person: Anthropology, Philosophy, History*, edited by Michael Carrithers, Steven Collins, and Steven Lukes, pp. 191–216. Cambridge: Cambridge University Press, 1985.

———. "Remarks on the Text of the Kubjikāmatatantra." *Indo-Iranian Journal* 45 (spring 2002): pp. 1–24.

———. "Śaivism: Krama Śaivism," "Śaivism: Śaivism in Kashmir," and "Śaivism, Trika Śaivism." In *Encyclopedia of Religion*, vol. 13, pp. 14–17.

———. "Śaivism and the Tantric Tradition." In *The World's Religions*, edited by S. Sutherland et al., pp. 660–704. London: Routledge and Kegan Paul, 1988.

———. "Visualization of the Deities of the Trika." In *L'Image divine*, ed. Padoux, pp.31–89.

Śaṅkaravijaya of Ānandagiri. *Śrīśaṅkaravijaya of Anantānandagiri*. Edited by N. Veezhinathan, with an introduction by T. M. P. Mahadevan. Madras: University of Madras, 1971.

Śārṅgadhara Paddhati. The Paddhati of Śarṅgadhara, A Sanskrit Anthology. Edited by Peter Peterson. Bombay Sanskrit Series, no. 37. Bombay: Government Book Depot, 1888.

Śārṅgadhara Saṃhitā. Edited and translated by K. R. Srikanta Murthy. Benares: Chaukhamba, 1984.

Śatapatha Brāhmaṇa. The Śatapatha Brāhmaṇa in the Mādhyāndina-Śākhā, with Extracts from the Commentaries of Sāyaṇa, Harisvāmin, and Dvivedagaṅga. 2nd ed. Edited by Albrecht Weber. London, 1855; reprint, Chowkhamba Sanskrit Series, no. 96. Benares: Chowkhamba Sanskrit Series Office, 1964.

———. *The Śatapatha Brāhmaṇa According to the Mādhyandina School*. Translated by Julius Eggeling. Sacred Books of the East, vols. 12, 26, 41, 43, 44. Oxford: Clarendon Press, 1882–1900; reprint, Delhi: Motilal Banarsidass, 1968.

Saṭcakranirūpaṇa. Shatchakranirūpana and Pādukapanchaka. Revised with Variant Read-

ings. Edited by Taranatha Vidyaratna. Tantrik Texts, vol. 2. Madras: Ganesh and Co., 1950. This edited Sanskrit text appears with a separate title page in a Devanagari-numbered appendix to Arthur Avalon, *The Serpent Power*, pp. 5–94.

Saṭsāhasrasaṃhitā. *The Saṭsāhasrasaṃhitā, Chapters 1–5*. Translated by J. A. Schoterman. Leiden: Brill, 1982.

Sax, William S. "The Ramnagar Ramlila: Text, Performance, Pilgrimage." *History of Religions* 31 (1990): pp. 129–53.

Schastok, Sara L. *The Śāmalājī Sculptures and 6th Century Art in Western India*. Leiden: Brill, 1985.

Scherer, Jacques. *Śiva dans le Mahābhārata*. Paris: Presses Universitaires de France, 1982.

Schwartzberg, Joseph E., ed. *A Historical Atlas of South Asia*. Chicago: University of Chicago Press, 1978; 2nd impression, with additional material, New York: Oxford University Press, 1992.

Sergent, Bernard. *Genèse de l'Inde*. Paris: Payot, 1997.

Sharma, Aryendra, ed. *Minor Works of Kṣemendra*. Hyderabad: Lokavijaya Press, 1961.

Sharma, Bhagavatilal. *Śrī Jalandharanāth—Pīṭh Sire Mandir, Jalor*. Jalore: Sri Bherunathji ka Akhada, 1995.

Sharma, Raj Kumar. *The Temple of Chaunsaṭha-yoginī at Bheraghat*. Bhopal: Agam Kala Prakashan, 1978.

———, ed. *Kalacuri Rājvaṃś aur Unkā Yug*. 2 vols. New Delhi: Aryan Books International, 1998.

Shaw, Miranda. *Passionate Enlightenment: Women in Tantric Buddhism*. Princeton: Princeton University Press, 1994.

Shaw, Richard. "Srisailam: Centre of the Siddhas." *South Asian Studies* 13 (1997): pp. 161–78.

Shulman, David. *The Hungry God: Hindu Tales of Filicide and Devotion*. Chicago: University of Chicago Press, 1993.

———. *Tamil Temple Myths: Sacrifice and Divine Marriage in the South Indian Śaiva Tradition*. Princeton: Princeton University Press, 1980.

Siddha Siddhānta Paddhati of Gorakṣanātha. *Siddha Siddhānta Paddhati and Other Works of the Natha Yogis*. Edited with an introduction by Kalyani Mallik. Poona: Oriental Book House, 1954.

Silburn, Lilian. *La Kuṇḍalinī, ou L'Énergie des profondeurs*. Paris: Les Deux Océans, 1983. English translation, *Kuṇḍalinī: Energy of the Depths*. Translated by Jacques Gontier. Albany: SUNY Press, 1988.

———. "Techniques de la transmission mystique dans le shivaïsme du Cachemire." *Hermes* 4 (1966–67): pp. 158–75.

Śilpa Prakāśa. *Śilpa Prakāśa. Medieval Orissan Sanskrit Text on Temple Architecture by Rāmacandra Kulācāra*. Translated and annotated by Alice Boner and Sadasiva Rath Sarma. Leiden: Brill, 1966.

Singh, Munshi Hardyal. *The Castes of Marwar Being (Census Report of 1891)*. With an introduction [to the reprint edition] by Komal Kothari. Jodhpur: Marwar Darbar, 1894; reprint, Jodhpur: Books Treasure, 1993.

Sircar, D. C. *The Śākta Pīṭhas*. 2nd rev. ed. Delhi: Motilal Banarsidass, 1972.

Śiva Purāṇa. *La Légende immémoriale du dieu Shiva, Le Shiva-purâna*. Partial translation by Tara Michaël. Paris: Gallimard, 1991.

Śiva Saṃhitā. 2nd ed. Edited and translated by Sisa Chandra Vasu. Allahabad: Panini Office, 1914; reprint, New Delhi: Munshiram Manoharlal, 1975.

Skanda Purāṇa. 3 vols. Edited by Nag Sharan Singh. Delhi: Nag Publishers, 1984.

Skora, Kerry Martin. "The Consciousness of Consciousness, Reflexive Awareness in the Trika Śaivism of Abhinavagupta." Ph.D. diss., University of Virginia, 2001.

Slusser, Mary Sheperd. *Nepal Mandala: A Cultural Study of the Kathmandu Valley*. 2 vols. Princeton: Princeton University Press, 1982.

Smith, Brian K. *Reflections on Resemblance, Ritual, and Religion*. New York: Oxford University Press, 1989.

Smith, Frederick M. "Indra's Curse, Varuṇa's Noose, and the Suppression of the Woman in the Vedic *Śrauta* Ritual." In *Roles and Rituals for Hindu Women*, ed Leslie, pp. 17–45.

Smith, Walter. "Images of Divine Kings from the Mukteśvara Temple, Bhubaneswar." *Artibus Asiae* 51:1–2 (1991): pp. 90–106.

Snellgrove, David. *Indo-Tibetan Buddhism. Indian Buddhists and Their Tibetan Successors*. 2 vols. Boston: Shambhala, 1987, 1995.

Somaśambhupaddhati. Edited by Hélène Brunner-Lachaux. Publications de l'Institut français d'indologie no. 25, pts. 1–4. Pondicherry: 1963, 1968, 1977, 1998.

Sontheimer, Günther-Dietz. *Pastoral Deities in Western India*. Translated by Anne Feldhaus. New York: Oxford University Press, 1989.

Sprinkle, Annie. "A Public Cervix Announcement." www.heck.com/annie/gallery/cervixmain.html.

Śrīmatottara Tantra. Incomplete edition published as *Gorakṣa Saṃhitā (Part One)*. Edited by Janardana Pandeya. Sarasvatibhavana Granthamala, vol. 110. Benares: Sampurnananda Sanskrit Visvavidyalaya, 1976.

Stanley, John M. "The Capitulation of Maṇi: A Conversion Myth in the Cult of Khaṇḍobā." In *Criminal Gods*, ed. Hiltebeitel, pp. 279–98.

Stevenson, Margaret. *Rites of the Twice-Born*. London: Oxford University Press, 1920.

Stewart, Tony K. "Encountering the Smallpox Goddess: The Auspicious Song of Śītalā." In *Religions of India in Practice*, ed. Lopez, pp. 389–98.

———. "The Goddess Ṣaṣṭhī Protects Children." In *Religions of India in Practice*, ed. Lopez, pp. 352–66.

Stewart, Tony K., and Robin Rinehart, "The Anonymous *Āgama Prakāśa:* Preface to a Nineteenth-Century Gujarati Polemic." In *Tantra in Practice*, ed. White, pp. 266–84.

Strickmann, Michel. *Mantras et mandarins: Le Bouddhisme tantrique en Chine*. Paris: Gallimard, 1996.

Strong, John S. *The Legend of King Aśoka: A Study and Translation of the* Aśokavadāna. Princeton: Princeton University Press, 1983.

Sukla, Dinesh Candra. *Rājasthān ke Pramukh Sant evaṃ Lok Devatā*. Jodhpur: Rajasthan Sahitya Samsthan, 1996.

Suśruta Saṃhitā with the commentary of Atrideva. 5th ed. Edited by Bhaskara Govinda Ghanekar. Delhi: Motilal Banarsidass, 1980.

Sutherland, Gail Hinich. *The Disguises of the Demon: The Development of the Yakṣa in Hinduism and Buddhism*. Albany: SUNY Press, 1991.

Svacchanda Tantra. Svacchandatantram. With the commentary of Kṣemarājā. 2 vols. Edited by Vrajavallabha Dvivedi. Delhi: Parimal Publications, 1985.

Taittirīya Brāhmaṇa. With the commentary of Sāyaṇa. Edited by Rajendrala Misra. Calcutta: Bibliotheca Indica, 1859.

Taittirīya Saṃhitā. With the commentary of Mādhava. Edited by Rajendralal Misra. Calcutta: Bibliotheca Indica, 1860.

Tambs-Lyche, Harald. *Power, Profit, and Poetry: Traditional Society in Kathiawar, Western India*. Delhi: Manohar, 1997.

Tantrāloka of Abhinavagupta. *The Tantrāloka of Abhinavagupta with Commentary by Rājānaka Jayaratha*. 12 vols. Edited with notes by Mukund Ram Shastri et al. Allahabad: Indian Press, 1918–38; reprinted with introduction and notes by R. C. Dwivedi and Navjivan Rastogi. 8 vols. Delhi: Motilal Banarsidass, 1987.

———. *Abhinavagupta. La Lumière sur les Tantra, chapitres 1 à 5 du Tantrāloka*. Translated by Lilian Silburn and André Padoux. Paris: De Boccard, 1998.

———. *Abhinavagupta, Luce dei tantra. Tantrāloka*. Translated by Raneiro Gnoli. Milan: Adelphi Edizioni, 1999.

Tantrasaṃgraha. 4 vols. Edited by Gopinath Kaviraj (vols. 1–3) and Ramaprasada Tripathi (vol. 4). Benares: Sampurnanand Sanskrit Visvavidyalaya, 1973–81.

Tantratattva. See Avalon, Arthur.

Tarabout, Gilles. "Ancêtres et revenants. La construction sociale de la malemort en Inde." In *De la malemort en quelques pays d'Asie*, ed. Brigitte Baptandier, pp. 165–99. Paris: Editions Karthala, 2001.

Tāranātha's Life of Buddhagupta. Unpublished translation by David Templeman, n.d.

Thapar, Romila. *Ancient Indian Social History: Some Interpretations*. New Delhi: Orient Longman, 1978.

———. *A History of India*. Vol. 1. Harmondsworth: Penguin, 1968.

Tiwari, Jagdish Narain. *Goddess Cults in Ancient India [with special reference to the first seven centuries A.D.]*. With a preface by A. L. Basham. Delhi: Sundeep Prakashan, 1985.

Toḍala Tantra. Edited by Bhadrashil Sharma. Allahabad: Kalyan Mandir, 1961.

Toffin, Gérard. *Le Palais et le temple: La Fonction royale dans la vallée du Népal*. Paris: CNRS Editions, 1993.

———. "La Voie des <héros>: Tantrisme et héritage védique chez les brâhmanes rājopādhyāya du Népal." In *Prêtrise, Pouvoirs et Autorité en Himalaya (Puruṣārtha 12)*, edited by Véronique Bouillier and Gérard Toffin, pp. 19–40. Paris: Editions de l'EHESS, 1989.

Tripathi, Gaya Charan. "The Daily Puja Ceremony." In *The Cult of Jagannāth and the Regional Tradition of Orissa*, edited by Anncharlott Eschmann et al., pp. 285–307. New Delhi: Manohar, 1978.

Trivedi, Rakesh Datta. "Mother and Child Sculpture in the National Museum." *East and West*, n.s., 24, nos. 1–2 (1974): pp. 141–45.

Urban, Hugh. "The Cult of Ecstasy: Tantrism, the New Age, and the Spiritual Logic of Late Capitalism." *History of Religions* 40, no. 2 (November 2000): pp. 268–304.

———. "The Extreme Orient: The Construction of 'Tantrism' as a Category in the Orientalist Imagination." *Religion* 29 (1999): pp. 123–46.

———. *Tantra: Sex, Secrecy, Politics and Power*. Berkeley: University of California Press, 2003.

Vājasaneyi Saṃhitā. *Yajurveda Saṃhitā*. Edited by Damodara Satavalekara. Aundharajadhanyam: Svadhyayamandalam, 1946.

Vātūlanātha Sūtra. *Vātūlanātha Sūtra avec le commentaire d'Anantaśaktipāda*. Rev. 2nd ed. Translated by Lilian Silburn. Publications de l'Institut de Civilisation Indienne, fascicule 8. Paris: DeBoccard, 1995.

Vaudeville, Charlotte. *Myths, Saints and Legends in Medieval India*. Delhi: Oxford India, 1999.

Vāyu Purāṇa. *Muniśrīmadvyāsapraṇitaṃ Vāyupurāṇam*. Anandasrama Sanskrit Series, 49. Poona: Anadasrama, 1983.

Vedic Astrology Magazine. www.vedicastro.com/yogini1.htm.

Vernant, Jean-Pierre. *Mythe et pensée chez les Grecs*. 2 vols. Paris: Maspero, 1981.

Vetālapañcaviṃśati. *Contes du Vampire*. Translated from the Sanskrit and annotated by Louis Renou. Paris: Gallimard, 1963. See also bibliographic refererences to *Kathāsaritsāgara*.

Viṣṇu Purāṇa. *The Vishnu Purána: A System of Hindu Mythology and Tradition Translated from the Original Sanskrit and Illustrated by Notes Derived Chiefly from Other Purāṇas*. Translated by H. H. Wilson. With an introduction [to the reprint edition] by R. C. Hazra. London, 1840; reprint, Calcutta: Punthi Pustak, 1961.

———. *Viṣṇupurāṇam*. Edited by Annangara Acarya and Sampatkumara Acarya. Kanci: Liberty, 1972.

Viṣṇudharmottara Purāṇa. Edited by Indian pandits. Bombay: Srivenkatesvara Steam Press, 1912.

Waghorne, Joanne Punzo. *The Raja's Magic Clothes: Re-Visioning Kingship and Divinity in England's India*. University Park: Pennsylvania State University Press, 1994.

Wallace, Vesna A. "Buddhist Tantric Medicine in the Kālacakratantra." *Pacific World*, n.s., 11 (1995): pp. 155–74.

Weber, Albrecht. "Zwei vedische Texte über Omina und Portenta." *Transactions of the Royal Academy of Berlin* (1859): pp. 349–53.

Weinberger-Thomas, Catherine. *Cendres d'immortalité: La Crémation des veuves en Inde*. Paris: Seuil, 1996. English translation by Jeffrey Mehlmann and David Gordon White, *Ashes of Immortality: Widow-Burning in India*. Chicago: University of Chicago Press, 1999.

White, David Gordon. *The Alchemical Body: Siddha Traditions in Medieval India*. Chicago: University of Chicago Press, 1996.

———. "Dogs Die." *History of Religions* 28, no. 4 (May 1989): pp. 283–303.

———. "Le Monde dans le corps du Siddha: Microcosmologie dans les traditions médiévales indiennes." In *Images du corps dans le monde hindou*, edited by Véronique Bouillier and Gilles Tarabout. Paris: Editions du C.N.R.S., 2002.

———. *Myths of the Dog-Man*. Chicago: University of Chicago Press, 1991.

———. "Tantra in Practice: Mapping a Tradition." In *Tantra in Practice*, ed. White, pp. 3–38.

———. "Transformations in the Art of Love: Kāmakalā Practices in Hindu Tantric and Kaula Traditions." In *History of Religions* 38, no. 2 (November 1998): pp. 172–98.

———, ed. *Tantra in Practice*. Princeton: Princeton University Press, 2000.

Willis, Michael D. "Religious and Royal Patronage in North India." In *Gods, Guardians, and Lovers: Temple Sculptures from North India A.D. 700–1200*, ed. by Vishakha N. Desai and Darielle Mason, pp. 49–65. Ahmedabad: Mapin Publishing, 1993.

Winternitz, Moritz. *A History of Vedic Literature*. 3 vols. Translated by V. Srinivasa Sarma. Delhi: Motilal Banarsidass, 1981.

———. "Nejamesha, Naigamesha, Nemeso." *Journal of the Royal Asiatic Society of Great Britain and Ireland* (1895): pp. 149–55.

Woodward, Hiram. "The Lakṣmaṇa Temple, Khajuraho, and Its Meanings." *Ars Orientalia* 19 (1989): pp. 27–48.

Wujastyk, Dominik. "Miscarriages of Justice: Demonic Vengeance in Classical Indian Medicine." In *Religion, Health and Suffering*, edited by Roy Porter and John Hinnells, pp. 1–20. London: Kegan Paul International, 1999.

Yoga Śāstra of Hemacandra. *Yoga Shastra of Hemachandracharya: A Twelfth Century Guide to Jain Yoga*. Edited by Surendra Bothara. Translated by A. S. Gopani. Jaipur: Prakrit Bharti Academy, 1989.

Yoga Sūtras of Patañjali. *Yoga Philosophy of Patañjali* with the commentary of Vyāsa. Edited and translated by Swami Hariharananda Aranya. Calcutta: University of Calcutta, 1981.

Yoginīhṛdaya Tantra. *Le Coeur de la Yoginī,* Yoginīhṛdaya *avec le commentaire* Dīpikā *d'Amṛtānanda*. Translated by André Padoux. Publications de l'Institut de Civilisation Indienne, fasc. 63. Paris: DeBoccard, 1994.

———. *Yoginīhṛdayam with Commentaries Dīpikā of Amṛtānanda and Setubandha of Bhāskararāya*. Edited by Gopinath Kaviraja. Varanasi: Sampurnanand Sanskrit Vishvavidyalaya, 1979.

Yoni Tantra . Edited with an introduction by J. A. Schoterman. Delhi: Manohar, 1980.

Zimmer, Heinrich. *The Art of Indian Asia*. 2 vols. Princeton: Bollingen Press, 1955.

Zvelebil, Kamil V. *The Siddha Quest for Immortality*. Oxford: Mandrake of Oxford, 1996.

Zysk, Kenneth. "*Mantra* in *Āyurveda:* A Study of the Use of Magico-Religious Speech in Ancient Indian Medicine." In *Mantra,* edited by Harvey Alper, pp. 123–43. Albany: SUNY Press, 1989.

Index

Abhidhāncintāmaṇi, 65
Abhinavagupta, xii, xiii, 15, 16, 19, 22, 25, 78, 89, 103, 110, 113, 114, 157, 158, 159, 163, 183, 210, 226, 232, 236, 241, 244, 245, 246, 255, 256
Abhirati. *See* Harītī
abhiṣeka. *See* initiation and consecration
ācārya, 108, 245, 331
Action Seal, 166
Aditi, 30, 46, 48, 49
Ādityas, 48, 49
ādiyāga, 106, 110, 113, 114, 302
Afghanistan, 306
Āgama Prakāśa, 84
āgama tīrtha, 134
Āgamaḍambara, 309
Āgamas, 17, 24, 79, 102, 152, 166, 251, 276. *See also Mṛgendrāgama*
Āgamasāra, 254
Aghoreśvarī, 8
Agni, 29, 30, 36, 40, 43, 47, 49, 201, 288, 289
agnicayana, 30
Ahir Budhnya, 233
Airborne beings, 58, 72, 164, 205. *See also* flight
Aja Ekapāda, 233
Ajmer, 137
ājñā, 11, 79, 80, 101, 121, 126, 244, 245, 306
ājñā cakra, 97, 100, 101, 228, 229, 246, 327
ākarṣaṇa. *See* attraction
akula-kula-kulākula, 19, 24, 151, 217, 228
Akulavīratantra, 105
alchemy, 67, 72, 80, 90, 91, 162, 181, 185, 197, 200. *See also Kākacaṇḍeśvarīmata; Rasārṇava*
alcohol, 71, 76, 77, 78, 83, 84, 85, 108, 116, 117, 118, 143, 155, 157, 232, 241, 253, 270
Allahabad, 51, 165
Āḻvārs, 4
Amanaskayoga, 81
Amarakośa, 161, 175
Ambā, 31, 32, 130. *See also* Jagadambā; Kuṅkuṇāmbā
Ambikā, 30, 31, 329
āmnāyas, 18, 110, 250, 276
amṛta, 84, 85; *amṛti-karaṇa*, 135; *yogāmṛta*, 177. *See also kulāmṛta*
anāhata cakra, 223, 228, 229, 305, 327
aṇaṅku, 129
Ananta, 180, 185, 233
ancestor cults, 21, 45, 84, 89, 203, 259
Andhra Pradesh, 115, 136, 171, 312. *See also* mountains: Srisailam
animal sacrifice, 8, 13, 34, 35, 52, 53, 55, 64, 65, 67, 70, 71, 117, 130, 191, 194, 252, 267
animals, Yoginīs as, 8, 27, 50, 58, 132, 137, 143, 189, 192, 194, 195, 205, 212. *See also* birds; cats; jackals; mice and rats; wolves
anugraha, 47, 195, 217, 323. *See also nigraha*
anuṣṭhāna, 6. *See also* sorcery
Apabharaṇī, 29
Apālā, 31, 87, 115
aparā. *See* flowers and flowering trees
Aparā, 18, 231
Apasmāra, Apasmāras, 37, 52, 53. *See also* epilepsy; Skandāpasmāra
Apfel-Marglin, Frédérique, 20, 85, 92
apotheosis, 180–84, 197, 201
Apsarasas. *See* Nymphs
Āraṇyakas, 55
Ardhanareśvarī, Ardhanarīśvara, 93, 135, 278
Aristotle, 92, 298
Arjuna, 40, 183, 201
arousal, sexual, 72, 82, 83, 100, 106, 249
Arthaśāstra, 70
Arvuda, 165, 314
Āryā, 39, 40, 46, 48, 49, 50, 192, 289
ass, 51, 231
Assam, 139, 314. *See also* Kāmākhyā; Kāmarūpa

Assayag, Jackie, 5, 271
Aṣṭāṅgahṛdaya, 54
Aṣṭāṅgasaṃgraha, 59
astrolabe, 178, 186, 316
astronomy and astrology, 34, 49, 60, 63, 133, 175, 178, 231, 263, 316. *See also* lunar mansions; menstrual horoscopes; moon; planets and planetary deities; stars
Asurī, 83
aśvamedha. *See* Vedic ritual
Atharva Veda, 3, 33, 34, 35, 39, 68, 246, 261
attraction, 99, 117, 143, 194, 207, 209, 210, 222, 249. *See also* extraction
Avadhūteśvarī, 89
Avalon, Arthur, xi, xii, 221. *See also* Woodroffe, Sir John
āvaraṇa-devatās. *See* entourage deities
avyaktam, 24
Āyas Dev Nāth, 168, 169
Āyurveda, 39, 52, 224, 228. *See also* *Bhāvaprakāśa*; *Caraka Saṃhitā*; *Hārītā Saṃhitā*; Kaumarabhṛtya; *Kauśika Sūtra*; *Kumāratantra*; *Suśrūta Saṃhitā*

Bactria, 132
Bagchi, Prabodh Chandra, 22
bāhyāvaraṇa. *See* entourage deities
bakula. *See* flowers and flowering trees
Balapramathinī, 231
Balarāma, 41, 50, 286, 318
Bālatantra, 51
Balavikaraṇī, 231
Bali. *See* Indonesia
bandhūka. *See* flowers and flowering trees
Banerjea, J. N., 98
barha khya, 69
Bāuls, 77, 82, 105, 247, 296, 301, 332
Beings, 32, 53, 56, 57, 71, 201, 203, 252, 255, 260, 262, 265, 266
bells, 193, 207, 210
Benares, 120, 165, 203, 328
Bengal, 41, 45, 77, 165, 219, 247, 258, 268, 284, 285, 287. *See also* Devīkoṭa
betel, 85–90, 116–18, 247. *See also* *tāmbūla*
Bhadrakālī, 40, 117, 300
Bhagamālinī, 96, 99
Bhagavad Gītā, 2, 176, 177, 184
Bhagavatī, 69, 70, 73
Bhairava, 8, 12, 20, 21, 23, 24, 25, 56, 62, 63, 77, 81, 102, 103, 105, 106, 113, 137, 151, 153, 164, 166, 181, 196, 210, 213, 227, 232, 242, 244, 250, 265, 266, 307; Ākāś Bhairab, 149; Bhairavas (class of divinities), 149, 267, 323; Ekapāda Bhairava, 89; fifty-two Bhairavas, 313; Mārtaṇḍa Bhairava, 291; Pacalī Bhairava, 142, 204, 320; Svacchanda Bhairava, 153, 159, 204, 227, 320, 323
Bhairavānanda, 143
bhakti, 2–6, 52, 126, 127, 191, 258, 261, 271, 318
Bhañja kingdom, 137
Bharati, Agehananda, 85, 91, 232
Bharhut, 57, 63
Bhāskararāya, 24
Bhāvaprakāśa, 51
Bheraghat Yoginī temple, 9, 12, 110, 136–37, 142, 146, 205, 279, 290, 291, 307
Bhimbhetka, 41, 42
bhinnayoni, 109, 244
bhoga. *See* supernatural enjoyments
Bhṛgukaccha, 137
Bhubanesvar, 94, 97, 140, 165. *See also* Vaitāl Deul temple
bhūcarī, 72, 132, 164, 199
bhukti. *See* supernatural enjoyments
Bhūtaḍāmara Tantra, 66
Bhutan, 262, 279, 310
bhūtas. *See* Beings
bhūtavidyā. *See* demonology
bhūtnīs. *See* Beings
bhūt-prets. *See* Beings
Biardeau, Madeleine, 15
Biḍalī, Viḍalī, 53, 188, 290
Bihar, 5, 40, 148, 170. *See also* Mithila; Patna; Rājagṛha
bījam. *See* blood-seed
bindu, 121, 230, 236–45, 325, 329
bindupuṣpā, 21, 93
bindusādhanā. *See* *sādhanā*
Bird Seizers, 46
birds, Yoginīs and goddesses as, 8, 27, 33, 39–52, 55, 58, 62, 65, 132, 137, 143, 171, 189, 196, 205, 207, 212, 215, 281, 289. *See also* Cīḍiyānāth; crows; Kauśikī; kites; *mkha' 'gro ma*; owls; Women with Uncut Wings
Bīrs (class of divinites), 313
blood offerings. *See* animal sacrifice
blood-seed, 70, 73, 117
Bollywood, 85
bolt-practices, 70, 193, 227, 228
Boner, Alice, 97
Booti Siddha, 170
Brahmā, 153, 175, 177, 182, 222
brahmacārin, 84, 85
brahmahatyā, 47, 68, 255
Brahmaloka, 167, 175, 177, 182, 184, 317
brahman, 84, 175, 177, 180, 182
Brāhmaṇas, 8, 50, 234; *Jaiminīya*, 54; *Pañcaviṃśa*, 197; *Śatapatha*, 33, 36; *Tāṇḍya*, 50
brahmarandhra. *See* fontanel
Brahmayāmala, 17, 23, 101, 163, 248, 250, 295, 322
brahmins and brahmanic traditions, 3, 7, 12, 15, 68, 69, 108, 126, 143, 148–49, 152, 155, 157, 194, 219, 251, 255, 263, 309; Smārta Brahmins, 5, 15, 257, 276. *See also* royal chaplain; royal preceptor; seven: Ṛṣis
Bṛhadāraṇyaka Upaniṣad. *See* Upaniṣads
Bṛhat Saṃhitā, 61, 175, 307
Brooks, Douglas, 1, 5

broom, 231
Brunner, Helène, 61, 252
Buchanan, Francis, 5
Buddha and Buddhas, 63, 73, 76, 83, 96, 120, 197, 205, 224, 233, 300
Buddhacarita, 197
Buddhism and Buddhist traditions, 4, 27, 29, 43, 53, 55, 57, 62–64, 66, 72, 96, 109, 116, 154, 161, 166, 175, 197, 199, 204, 220, 221, 260, 312, 318, 320, 324. *See also Buddhacarita*; Buddhist Tantra; Jātakas; Prajñā; *Saddharmapuṇḍarika Sūtra*; Zen Buddhism
Buddhist Tantra, 79, 83, 84, 87, 109, 115, 120, 133, 148, 165, 217, 224, 244, 250, 275, 279, 296, 323, 332. *See also* Action Seal; Buddha and Buddhas; *Cakrasaṃvara Tantra; Caṇḍamahāroṣaṇa Tantra;* Great Seal; *Hevajra Tantra;* Highest Yoga Tantra; lotus: Lotus Maiden; *Sekoddeśaṭīkā;* Vajrapāṇī; Vajrayoginī; Wisdom Maiden
Buffalo Demon, 28, 32, 48
buka flower. *See* flowers and flowering trees
butter, 35, 49, 108, 120, 253

Caitanya, 86
caityas, 65
cakras, 82, 112, 124, 169, 211, 218, 220, 221, 293; eleven *cakras*, 225–26; five *cakras*, 100, 181; four *cakras*, 224, 239; *mahācakra*, 223; nine *cakras*, 236; six *cakras*, 179–80; triangles of Śrī Cakra called, 236. *See also ājñā cakra; anāhata cakra;* Devīcakra; Dūtī Cakra; *dvādaśānta;* fontanel; *khecarī:* Khecarī Cakra; *maṇipura cakra;* Mātṛ Cakra; *mūlādhāra cakra; nāḍīs: nāḍīcakra; sahasrāra;* Śrī Cakra; *svādhiṣṭhāna cakra; viśuddhi cakra;* yogic body; Yoginī: Cakra
Cakrasaṃvara Maṇḍala. *See* mandalas
Cakrasaṃvara Tantra, 120
cakravartin, 62, 124, 143, 160, 309
Caldwell, Sarah, 1, 5, 73, 117
Cāḷukya dynasty, 53, 126, 133, 137, 139, 173, 279, 309. *See also* Someśvara III
Cambodia, 285, 300
cāmis, 248
camphor, 73, 80, 87, 88
Cāmuṇḍā, 60, 88, 204, 318, 320
Caṇḍaghaṇṭā, 207
cāṇḍālī. *See* plants and herbs
Caṇḍamahāroṣaṇa Tantra, 83, 109, 120
Caṇḍeśvarī, 56
Caṇḍī(kā), 8, 9, 74, 129, 287
Candra Mountain. *See* moon
Cāṅgu Nārāyaṇ temple, 139
cannabis, 108, 122
Caraka Saṃhitā, 93, 113, 225
Cāraṇas, 48, 129, 143, 151, 171, 312
Carcikā. *See* cats
Carstairs, G. M., 268
Caryāgīti, 27, 32, 87, 224
cats, 43, 53, 63, 189, 249, 291. *See also* Biḍalī
catuṣpīṭha. *See pīṭhas*
Caurasi. *See* Vārāhī temple
Ceylon. *See* Sri Lanka
Chandella dynasty, 12, 137, 143, 144
Charans, 19, 20, 21, 129, 148, 312
chāyāchidrāṇi, 52
childbirth, 30, 35, 37, 38, 40, 41, 42, 45, 63, 66, 91, 115, 261, 270. *See also* conception and gestation; miscarriage
childhood diseases, 35, 41, 48, 49, 51, 52, 189
China: Chinese translations of Indian Buddhist texts, 63; *cīnācāra*, 76; *mahācīna*, 75
Chinnamastā, 139, 308
Chola dynasty, 136
chommas, 151, 226, 280, 325
Cīḍiyānāth, 171
cīnācara. *See* China
ciñca (tamarind). *See* flowers and flowering trees
Circe, 64
circles: *cakras* as, 194, 195, 212, 213, 220, 223, 231, 249, 250; of Mothers, 44, 136, 137, 212, 222, 291 (*see also* Mātṛ Cakra; Yoginī: temples); of the Nine Seizers, 62; of Tantric practitioners, 27, 30, 31, 62, 72, 82, 100, 151, 158, 166
citadel of mantras. *See* mantras
citipatis, 279
clan fluid. *See kuladravyam*
Clan Island, 77
clan mountains. *See kula-parvatas*
clan nectar. *See kulāmṛta*
Clan of the Yoginīs. *See* Yoginī: Kaula
Clan-born Siddhas and Yoginīs, 72, 164, 165
clans: kinship term, 11, 18–21, 127, 136, 149; Tantric lineages, 6, 7, 18, 19, 20, 21, 23, 24, 76, 79, 80, 90, 93, 100, 101, 102, 103, 109, 113, 114, 124, 151, 165, 166, 223, 227, 232, 235, 250, 251, 277
clitoris, 97, 100, 300
Clothey, Fred, 5
Coburn, Thomas, 130
Coeurdoux, Father Pierre, 156, 159
conception and gestation, 20, 57, 67, 90–92, 189. *See also* childbirth
consecration. *See* initiation and consecration
cosmic egg, 167, 175, 177, 179, 181, 182, 185, 187, 200, 313; dimensions of, 164, 223, 324. *See also* cosmology and cosmography; seven: sheaths of the cosmic egg
cosmogony. *See sṛṣṭi*
cosmology and cosmography, 164–87, 315–16. *See also* Brahmaloka; Jambudvīpa; mountains: Meru; Satyaloka; Siddhaloka; Tapoloka
cows, 46, 50, 54, 58, 253, 254, 255. *See also kāmadhenu;* Mūḷi; Surabhī
cranial vault, 100, 104, 105, 176, 177, 184, 185, 187, 200, 202, 224, 227, 231, 232, 234, 240, 244, 254
cremation grounds, 8, 10, 14, 52, 137, 143, 153,

cremation grounds (*continued*) 157, 163, 193, 194, 202, 207, 209, 211, 213, 231, 232, 255, 265, 266. *See also* eight: Cremation Grounds
crows, 39, 53, 80, 231, 283
Cūḍāsamā dynasty, 129
cuḍels, 45; Cuḍelin Mātā 73, 294

daiva, 166
Ḍākinīs, 29, 52, 53, 62, 71, 133, 139, 142, 204, 207, 211, 228, 229, 268, 290, 296, 321, 322, 334. *See also mkha' 'gro ma*
Ḍāmarī, 228
dancing, 34, 64, 137, 143, 158, 201
Daṇḍapāṇi, 181
Dārika, 70, 117
Das, Rahul Peter, 221
Daśāvatāracarita, 154
datura, 122
Davidson, Ronald, 133
Deccan plateau, 53, 126, 139, 148, 171, 173, 312
Dehejia, Vidya, 1
Delhi, 137, 308
demonology, 35, 52, 59, 113, 252, 261, 266, 276. *See also chāyāchidrāṇi*
Deogarh, 44, 52
Desai, Devangana, 1, 97, 146
devadāsīs, 98, 99, 140, 270, 296–97. *See also* prostitutes
Devasenā, 40, 44
devayoni beings, 161, 175. *See also* Dryads; Gandharvas; Kinnaras; Nymphs; Protectors; Siddha demigods
Devī Māhātmya, 48, 59, 130
Devībali Pākhaṇḍ, 7
Devīcakra, 82, 223; *devī cakra*, 326
Devīkoṭa, 165
dhaman, 86
Dhanyaśloka, 89
dhātus, 228
Dhṛtarāṣṭra, 130, 283
Dhubela Archaeological Museum, 205, 273
dice play, 34, 35, 49, 61
dig-bandhana, 259
Digby, Simon, 170
digvijaya, 125
Dikkāravāsinī, 89
dīkṣā. *See* initiation and consecration
Dīrghajihvī, 50, 286
dissimulation, 126, 146, 150, 155, 157, 159, 263. *See also* secrecy
dissolution, 182
Diti, 46
Divine Daughters, 38, 53
Divine Seizers, 47, 49
divyadṛṣṭi, 251
dogs, 46, 53–54, 58, 64, 198, 253. *See also* Saramā; *śva-graha*
Donaldson, Thomas, 1, 99
Doniger, Wendy, 66, 191, 198
door guardians, 164, 166
dravyam, 7, 11, 14, 67, 74, 76, 80, 81, 84, 85, 93, 112, 118, 255, 256, 275, 295. *See also kuladravyam; sadbhāva; yonitattva*
dreams, 72, 196, 201, 224, 247–52, 333
drums, 193, 207, 210
Dryads, 4, 50–53, 63, 64, 64, 71, 161, 175, 199, 201; Dryad Seizers, 47. *See also* Female Dryads; Kalu Kumar; Sthūṇākarṇa
Dubois, Abbé Jean-Antoine, 155–58
Durgā, 7, 40, 41, 48, 125, 127, 128, 132, 139, 202, 275, 278, 291; name derived from *durga*, "fortress," 132
Durgā Stotra, 40
Dūtī Cakra, 82
Dūtīs, 89, 91, 107, 110, 112–14, 142, 159, 161, 223, 275, 303, 304, 323. *See also* Śakti: Tantric consort
dūtīyāga, 84
dvādaśānta, 104, 181, 225, 226, 229, 230, 231, 233, 244, 325
dvārapālas. *See* door guardians
Dvyāśraya, 132, 133, 142, 205
Dyczkowski, Mark, 1, 79, 229, 305

Egyptian Mysteries, xiii, 194
eight: Bhairavas, 323; *cakras*, 223; "Clan Group of Eight" mantras, 222; Cremation Grounds, 322, 323; elements of yogic body, 251; female slaves dance in Vedic ritual, 30; forms of Jyeṣṭhā, 230; goddesses, 11, 66, 88, 135, 166; Heroes, 39; "Maternal Group of Eight," 318; Mothers, 22, 113, 132, 136, 250, 251, 322; Śaktis in Tantric rite, 231, 249–51; Seizers, 255; sets of seed mantras, 223; supernatural powers, 222; *tattvas*, 230; types of *kāmakalā* practice, 96, 98, 241; types of Protectresses, 58; Vidyeśvaras, 231; Wisdom Group of, 222; Yoginīs, 63
eighteen: children of Harītī, 63; Divine Daughters, 53; Seizers, 46, 48, 49; Siddhas, 164
Ekānaṃśā, 4, 40, 41, 284, 319
eleven: *cakras*, 225–26; sites, 227
Eliade, Mircea, 197
Ellora Cave Temples, 37, 62, 291, 320
emission. *See sṛṣṭi*
End of the Twelve. *See dvādaśānta*
entourage deities, 96, 97, 140, 241, 330
epilepsy, 34, 37, 49, 54
excrements, 71, 77, 254
exorcism, 248, 259, 260, 261, 263, 264
extraction, 58, 72, 76, 104, 105, 152, 207, 209, 211, 212, 213, 215, 217, 218, 227, 229, 322; of mantras, 243. *See also* attraction

Father Seizers, 47
Fathers, 45
Female Dryads, 8, 29, 33, 37, 43, 45, 59, 63–66, 72, 82, 121, 162, 188, 191, 196, 198, 199,

201, 209, 228, 267, 270, 292. *See also* Harītī; Tāḍakā
Female Ghouls, 188
Female Seizers, 8, 29, 35, 41, 43, 50, 53, 59, 62–66, 121, 188, 189, 191, 192, 193, 196, 205, 321
female semen. *See strī-vīrya*
Females with Uncut Wings, 30
fertility and fertility rites, 20, 21, 40, 66, 67, 92, 217, 270. *See also ṛtu doṣa*
Field Guardians, 53, 71, 164
Field-born Siddhas and Yoginīs, 72, 165, 166, 222
fields and secondary fields, 10, 136, 165, 174, 213
Finn, Louise, 78
Fish-Belly, 25, 102, 104, 215, 226, 279, 325
five: *cakras*, 100, 181, 223, 225, 228, 326; elements, 211, 231; Essences, 254; gemstones, 108; Jewels, 254, 256; Lamps, 254, 333; mouths of Śiva, 18, 101, 277; *mudrās*, 82, 227; M-words, 82–84, 120, 330, 333; Nectars, 35, 209, 211, 212, 222, 333; pure products of the cow, 253; purifiers, 76; Seals, 333; streams, 101, 277; Women of the Seal, 249; Yoginīs, 164
Flaith, 32, 64
flesh. *See* meat
flight, power of, 7, 10, 27, 58, 65, 96, 105, 161, 167, 181, 182, 188–218, 221, 227, 248
flower, term for menstrual discharge, 78–79, 90
flowers and flowering trees, 21, 22, 24, 55, 80, 89, 103, 108, 115, 120, 155, 165, 174, 175, 192, 326; *aparā*, 115; *bakula*, 116, 117; *bandhūka*, 121, 305; *buka*, 76, 77, 108, 118, 302; *ciñca* (tamarind), 121; *hayāri*, 115; *kadamba*, 46, 121; *khadīra*, 87; *kiṃśuka*, 121; *kṛṣṇa*, 77, 108; *palāśa*, 118; palmyra, 304; saffron, 118; toddy palm, 117. *See also* plants and herbs; trees
fontanel, 179, 185, 225, 226
four: *cakras*, 224, 239, 325; Kula Siddhas, 103, 113; Mounds, 137, 165; states of the mind, 224, 325; *vyūhas*, 179
Freud, Sigmund, 215, 248, 332

Gaja-Lakṣmī, 134
Gaṇas, 48, 65, 163, 282
Gandhapūtanā. *See* Pūtanā
Gandharvas, 30, 33–35, 46, 48, 49, 161, 183, 198, 319; Gandharva Seizers, 47, 49; Gandharvīs, 82
Gaṇeśa, 4, 24, 36, 49, 61, 65, 167, 280; Ucchiṣṭa Gaṇeśa, 63
Gaṇeśvara temple, Khiching, 99
Gaṅgā (Ganges). *See* rivers
Gangdhar stone-tablet inscription, 139, 207, 209–10, 308, 321
garbhagṛha. *See* temple architecture
Garuḍa, 44, 280
garuḍī (female kite), 37, 288
Gaūḍavaho, 129
Gauḍiya Vaiṣṇavas, 86, 87. *See also* Vaiṣṇavas and Vaisnavism
gavāmayana. *See* Vedic ritual
Ghosts, 64, 80, 203, 204, 333
Ghoul Seizers, 47, 49
Ghouls, 32, 48, 52, 161, 175, 269
Girnar, 50, 174, 183–84, 286, 317, 318. *See also* mountains
Gnoli, Raniero, 1, 325
goats, 37, 38, 39, 63, 283, 294. *See also* Naigameṣa, Naigameya
gocaram, 24
Goetz, Hermann, 66, 144, 146, 153
Golakī Maṭh. *See* Bheraghat Yoginī temple
Gomanta. *See* Girnar
Gombrich, Richard, 6
Gonda, Jan, 122
gopīs, 86, 88
Gorakh(nāth), Gorkaṣa(nātha), 81, 177, 224, 226, 232
Gorkha kingdom, 149, 310
Goudriaan, Teun, 1
Govardhana. *See* mountains
grahas. *See* Seizers
grahīs, *grahaṇīs*. *See* Female Seizers
graphemes, 222, 223, 238, 239, 240, 244. *See also bindu*; *visarga*
Great Seal, Buddhist Tantric consort, 73, 83
Greece, possible scientific exchanges with India, 41, 60, 92, 187
Gṛhadevī, 192. *See also* Jarā
Gṛhya Sūtras: *Baudhāyana*, 231; *Mānava*, 39, 41
Guha, 65
Guhya(ka)s, 48, 65, 161
Gujarat, 59, 126, 129, 132, 153, 154, 173, 183. *See also* Bhṛgukaccha; Girnar
guṇas, 77
Gupta, Sanjukta, 1, 296, 297
guru, 6, 19, 22, 80, 88, 105, 108, 112, 123, 142, 194, 202, 220, 245, 246, 247, 251, 252, 264, 265, 266, 271, 331; *guru-rāja*, 125
Gwalior Archaeological Museum, 205, 308

Hākinī, 228, 229
haṃsa, 43, 211, 233, 328
Harappa. *See* Indus Valley civilization
Harasiddhi, 24
Haravijaya, 151
Hārītā Saṃhitā, 53
Harītī, 43, 63–64, 192, 231, 283, 291, 292, 319
Harivaṃśa, 40, 50, 52, 115, 183, 184, 207
Harper, Katherine Anne, 36
Harṣacarita, 63
haṭha yoga, 82, 200, 211, 217, 220, 221, 226–31, 234
Haṭhayogapradīpikā, 81, 254
hayāri. *See* flowers and flowering trees
Heesterman, Jan, 234

Heilijger-Seelens, Dorothea, 215, 223
Hevajra Tantra, 73, 83, 109, 221, 224, 303, 321
Highest Yoga Tantra, 79, 109, 217, 303
Hiltebeitel, Alf, 31
Himachal Pradesh, 57, 168, 267–68
Hiṅglāj Mātā, 77
Hippocrates, 41, 298
Hirapur Yoginī temple, 137, 190, 204, 208, 291, 321
hlādinī. *See* Śakti: hypostasis of the Goddess
Hoens, Dirk Jan, 237
Hollywood, 221
homa, 125
Hooykaas, C., 135
Host of Mothers, 39, 44, 47, 139, 281
householder-practitioners, 123, 124, 159, 166, 219, 253, 255, 259, 275
Hudson, Dennis, 179
human flesh, 211, 212, 253
husband-finding rite. *See* marriage rituals

Icchā-śakti, 164, 231, 328
ihi ceremony. *See* marriage rituals
Indo-European traditions, 28, 29, 32, 53, 55
Indonesia, 134, 135, 148, 236, 307, 308, 326
Indra, 31, 37, 38, 40, 68, 87, 115, 167, 222
Indus Valley civilization, 28, 29, 37, 132
initiation and consecration, 11, 21, 27, 28, 77, 79–81, 83, 85, 106, 108–9, 113, 114, 122, 133–36, 142, 148, 149, 150, 166, 184, 191, 194, 217, 220, 236, 243, 244, 245–47, 250–52, 256, 266, 274, 301. *See also kulasamayin*; *miśraka*; Narasiṃha: *narasiṃha-dīkṣā*; *nirvāṇa-dīkṣā*; *sādhaka*
Innately-born Siddhas and Yoginīs, 164, 165, 166
internalization, 161, 167, 187, 210, 218, 219, 251, 258, 262
Islam and Tantric traditions, 77, 170, 171, 247. *See also* Nizarpanthis
iṣṭa-devatā, 6

jackals, 58, 137, 189, 194, 205, 215, 216, 253, 319
Jagadambā, 129
Jagannātha temple, 85, 89, 98
Jainism and Jain traditions, 4, 29, 38, 39, 65, 66, 116, 117, 137, 142, 153, 154, 161, 167, 174–77, 183, 185, 277, 303, 309, 315–16
Jaipur, 6
Jālandhara (*pīṭha*), 224, 314
Jālandharnāth, 168–71, 315
Jalore, 168, 169, 314
Jambudvīpa, 174, 175
Jammu, 62
Janamejaya, 53
jāṅgha. *See* temple architecture: joining wall
japa, 89. *See also* mantras
Jarā, 63, 192, 194, 207, 231; Jarāsandha, 192, 194, 291
Jātahāriṇī, 63; Jātahāriṇīs (class of female divinities), 45, 50, 51, 189
Jātakas, 55, 64; *Jayaddisa*, 65; *Kāliṅgabodhi*, 197; *Mahāmāyuri*, 274; *Telapatta*, 64, 72; *Valāhassa*, 64
Jayā, 24, 278
Jayadrathayāmala, 17, 23, 163, 210, 221, 227, 232, 278, 322
Jayaratha, 84, 89, 105, 110, 112, 113, 114, 146, 236, 253, 255
jīvanmukti, 10, 15
jñāna, 25; *jñāna-pravāha*, 113, 161; Jñānā-śakti, 165, 166, 231; *kaula-jñāna*, 10, 103
Jñānārṇava, 254
Jöchle, Wolfgang, 298
Jodhpur, 168, 169, 170–71, 305, 314, 321. *See also* Cīḍiyānāth; Mān Singh
Jōgammas, 270, 271, 334
Jogeśvarī, 173
Joginīs, Jognīs, 45, 268; Jala-jogini, 73
Jyeṣṭhā, 40, 49, 51, 52, 54, 63, 230, 231, 285, 289, 290, 328, 329

Kachchhapaghāta kingdom, 137
Kachvaha dynasty, 6
kadamba. *See* flowers and flowering trees
Kadamba kingdom, 129, 139
Kādambarī, 40, 41, 129
Kadrū, 46, 48, 55, 288
Kailās. *See* mountains
Kākacaṇḍeśvarīmata, 17, 80, 207, 210
Kakar, Sudhir, 1, 73
Kākatīya kingdom, 136
Kākī. *See* crows
Kākinī, 228, 229
Kālacakra Tantra, 35, 83, 254
Kalacuri dynasty, 12, 136, 137, 142, 144, 146, 153, 173, 200, 309, 312, 325. *See also* Yuvarājā II
kālāgni, 226
kalās, 91, 229, 230, 232, 236, 237, 241, 245, 329; *kalā-śaktis*, 95, 96, 241. *See also kāmakalā*
Kāla-saṃkarṣaṇī, 210, 322
Kalashacal. *See* mountains
Kālavikaraṇī, 230
Kālī, Kālikā, 18, 24, 37, 40, 53, 93, 119, 204, 210, 230, 278, 282, 284, 296, 303, 319, 321; Kālī Yantra, 305; Twelve Kālīs, 104
Kali Yuga, 23, 103, 113, 164
Kālī-Krama. *See* Krama
kalpa, 180, 181, 182, 183, 184
Kalu Kumar, 294
kāma, 97, 237–40, 270, 308
Kāma Sūtra, 105
kāmaśāstra, xii. *See also Kāma Sūtra*
kāma-bandha. *See* temple architecture
kāma-bindu, 95, 100
kāmadhenu, 54
kāmakalā, 82, 91, 94–100, 140, 234–45, 329;

eight types of practice, 96; *kāmakalā* yantra, 94–97, 98, 238
Kāmakalāvilāsa, 237–38
Kāmakaleśvara, 97, 100; Kāmakaleśvarī, 100; Mahākāmakaleśvarī, 96–97
Kāmākhyā, 89, 105–6, 204, 213, 215, 224, 230, 241, 314; *Kāmākhyā Tantra*, 80. *See also* Kāmarūpa
Kāmapānacāstiram, 74
Kāmarūpa, 24, 102, 104, 106, 301, 317. *See also* Kāmākhyā
kāmatattva, 241–45
Kāmeśvara, 236, 237, 307, 308; Kāmeśvarī, 99, 236, 237, 241, 307
Kaṃsa, 52
Kancipuram, 98
Kandariyā Mahādeva temple. *See* Khajuraho
Kane, P. V., 220
Kapadia, Karin, 69
Kapālakuṇḍalā, 209, 210, 211, 227
Kāpālikas, 80, 81, 87, 96, 102, 117, 146, 151–54, 163, 196, 209, 211, 294, 311, 322; Kāpālinī (female Kāpālika), 116; "six sectarian marks" of, 83, 153, 163–64. *See also* Kapālakuṇḍalā
karañja. *See* trees
karimpana. *See* trees
Karmācārya (Tantric priest). *See* royal chaplain
Karma-Mudrā, 166
Karnataka, 165, 173, 279, 315
Karpūramañjari, 142, 154
Kārttikeya. *See* Skanda
Kashmir, 137, 144, 146, 151, 154, 158, 159, 192, 236, 241, 308, 330
Kaṭapūtanās. *See* Pūtanā
Kathāsaritsāgara, 11, 57, 60, 64, 115, 141, 152, 153, 174, 183, 184, 191, 201, 202, 204, 209, 212, 221, 308. *See also* "Vampire Tales"
Kathmandu Valley, 5, 18, 23, 57, 63, 69, 124, 127, 129, 139, 143, 148–50, 153, 204, 269, 270, 278, 279, 291, 306. *See also* Cāṅgu Nārāyaṇ temple; Nepal; Paśupatināth temple
Kātyāyanī, 40; Kātyāyanīs (class of divinities), 321
Kaulacūḍāmaṇi, 83, 98
kaulāgamā, 151
kaulagola, 154
kaula-jñāna. *See jñāna*
Kaulajñānanirṇaya, 17, 19, 22–26, 50, 76, 79, 82, 89, 100, 101, 102, 105, 108–10, 118, 151, 163–67, 171, 176, 179, 189, 195, 207, 209, 213, 215, 221, 222, 223, 225, 227, 228, 230, 231, 233, 253
kaulasadbhāva, 82, 100. *See also sadbhāva*
Kaulāvalinirṇaya, 17, 23, 74, 76, 78, 80, 84, 89, 91, 93, 115, 117, 118, 255
kaulavit, 17
Kaumarabhṛtya, 52
Kauśika Sūtra, 34, 50, 58, 59, 62, 63
Kauśikī, 40, 287
Kaviraj, Gopinath, 151, 162
kāyasādhanā, 144
Kerala, 45, 62, 64, 65, 69, 70, 72, 73, 117, 304
khadīra. *See* flowers and flowering trees
Khajuraho, 35, 61, 63, 97, 139, 140, 143, 146, 203, 291; Kandariyā Mahādeva temple, 61, 146, 203, 290, 309; Lakṣmaṇa temple, 61, 98, 144, 145, 146, 290, 299, 309, 310; Viśvanātha temple, 140, 144
Khan, Dominique-Sila, 77
Khaṇḍobā, 38, 173, 283
khatvāṅga, 152
khecara. *See* flight
khecarī, 58, 72, 132, 164, 223; Khecarī Cakra, 82; *khecarī mudrā*, 83, 100, 254, 300; *khecarī vidyā*, 202
khejaṛa. *See* trees
Khiching. *See* Gaṇeśvara temple; Kiñcakeśvarī temple
Khoḍīyār, 129, 130, 131
kiṃśuka. *See* flowers and flowering trees
Kiñcakeśvarī temple, Khiching, 62, 99
kings, as patrons, practitioners of Tantra, 2, 12, 19, 21, 31, 56, 102, 123–47, 198, 201, 258, 259, 261. *See also* Pratāp Malla; Siddhanāth; Someśvara III; Trivikramasena
Kinnaras, 48, 82, 161
Kīrtivarman, 144–46
kiss, 28, 31, 57, 73, 80, 87, 115, 272
kites, 171, 288, 321. *See also garuḍī*
Kloetzli, W. Randolph, 178, 186
Knipe, David, 120
Konarak, 140
Koṅkaṇa, 113, 129, 142
Krama, 11, 18, 24, 210, 275, 322, 323, 330
Kriyākālaguṇottara, 17, 59, 286
Kriyā-śakti, 165, 166, 231
Kṛṣṇa, 4, 6, 35, 40, 41, 51, 52, 85, 86, 88, 127, 139, 167, 176, 177, 183, 184, 191, 201, 261, 284, 287, 318
kṛṣṇa flower. *See* flowers and flowering trees
Kṛttikās, 28, 36, 40, 44, 49, 282, 292
kṣatriyas, 148
Kṣemarāja, 16, 59, 89, 152, 212, 222, 226, 241
Kṣetrapālakas. *See* Field Guardians
kṣetras and *upakṣetras*. *See* fields and secondary fields
kṣetra-yoginīs, 314
Kubera, 63, 65, 201, 292
Kubjā. *See* Kubjikā
Kubjikā, 18, 55, 82, 89, 93, 129, 130, 204, 215, 217, 227, 291, 302. *See also* mandalas
Kubjikā Tantras, 22, 79, 93, 100, 101, 104, 121, 152, 181, 228, 229, 244, 278, 326. *See also paścimāmnāya*
Kubjikāmata, 17, 23, 70, 193, 215, 221, 222, 223, 227, 229, 231, 290, 322
Kuhū, 30, 40
kula. *See* clans: Tantric lineages
kula prakriyā, 16, 110, 226, 273
Kula Siddhas, 103, 113

Kula Tantras, 18
kulācāra, 8
Kulacūḍāmaṇi Tantra, 23, 78, 88, 296, 318
kuladevatās, 127
kuladevīs, 20, 21, 126–29, 131, 149, 150, 306, 321
kuladharma, 8
kuladravyam, 11, 22, 80, 105. *See also dravyam*
Kulagahvara Tantra, 245, 255
kulāgamā, 19, 79
kulagocarā, 19, 151
kulamadyam, 117
kulāmṛta, 11, 76, 85, 91, 297
kula-mutaltevi, 129
kula-parvatas, 10, 171
kulaputras, 17, 21, 166, 222, 245
Kularatnoddyota, 93, 246
Kulārṇava Tantra, 18, 23, 105, 152, 254
kulārtham, 110
kulasamayin, 166
kulayāga, 106, 116, 250, 255, 302, 323
kulayoginī, 151
kuldevīs. *See kuladevīs*
Kuleśvara, 136, 196, 299; Kuleśvarī, 113, 136, 151
Kullūka Bhaṭṭa, 6
Kumāra. *See* Skanda
Kumāratantra, 62
Kumārī, 40, 98–99. *See also* Maidens
Kunaṃnamā, 33, 130, 198
kuṇḍā panth, 77
kuṇḍagolaka, 77–79, 108, 112, 115, 303. *See also kaulagola*
Kuṇḍalī, 230, 231, 233, 328
kuṇḍalinī, 43, 77, 82, 211, 218, 221, 226, 227, 228, 229–34, 239
kuṇḍas, 122
Kuṅkuṇāmbā, 113
Kurtz, Stanley, 32
Kushan age, 35–37, 39–41, 48–50, 52, 58–60, 188, 191, 192, 205, 282, 292, 318
Kusumā, Kusumamālinī, 227–29
kūṭastha, 177, 184, 318
Kuvaṇṇā, 64, 130, 198, 199
Kværne, Per, 134

lactation, 90, 91, 92
Lākinī, 228, 229
Lakṣmaṇa temple. *See* Khajuraho
Lakṣmī, 40, 41; *Lakṣmī Tantra*, 147. *See also* Gaja-Lakṣmī; Mahālakṣmī
Lalitā Sahasranāma, 151, 310
Lambakarṇī, 228
land-based beings. *See bhūcarī*
Leonardo da Vinci, 92
Lévi, Sylvain, 8
Levy, Robert, 123
Licchavi dynasty, 139
liṅgam, 78, 87, 101, 119, 244, 229, 233–35, 275, 291, 300, 308; *bāṇ-liṅgam*, 121; *dehaliṅgam*, 331; *ekamukha liṅgam*, 101; *jyotirliṅgam*, 173, 312; *liṅgābhiṣeka*, 121; *liṅga-pīṭham*, 95, 100; *mahāliṅgam*, 97; *manoliṅgam*, 331; *pañca-mukha-liṅga*, 18, 101; portable *liṅgams*, 300
Liṅgāyatas, 171, 173, 295
liquor. *See* alcohol
Lohitāyanī, 37, 46, 48, 49, 121, 282
Loka Puruṣa. *See* Puruṣa
Lorenzen, David, 83, 152, 153, 220
lotus: *cakra* or mandala as, 135, 136, 151, 218, 226, 229, 236, 250; Lotus Maiden, 115; term for woman's nether mouth, 28, 71, 80, 115, 116, 120, 121
Lowest-born Yoginī, 165, 222
lunar mansions, 290

M-words, 83–85, 120, 220, 232, 241, 253–57. *See also* alcohol; *maithuna*; meat; *mudrās*
Macchanda. *See* Matsyendra(nātha)
Madhya Pradesh, 41, 60, 137, 140, 200, 203, 267, 308, 312. *See also* Bharhut; Bheraghat Yoginī temple; Bhimbhetka; Dhubela Archaeological Museum; Gwaloir; Khajuraho; Malwa; Mitauli Yoginī temple; Naresar Yoginī temple; Shahdol Yoginī temple; Ujjain
Madonna, 331
Madurai, 136
Madyapānavidhi, 304
Mahābhārata, 31, 35–63, 65, 70, 91, 121, 127, 174, 183, 184, 192, 201, 221
Mahācaṇḍeśvarī, 89
mahācīna, 75
Mahādeva, 47, 48, 171
Mahākāla, 24, 137, 165; Mahākālī, 29
Mahākaula, 25, 164
Mahālakṣmī, 29
mahāpīṭha. *See pīṭhas*
Maharashtra, 32, 38, 142, 148, 168, 171, 173, 306, 314. *See also* Ellora Cave Temples; Koṅkaṇa
Mahāsarasvatī, 29
mahātman, 24
Mahāvamsa, 64, 130, 198–99
Mahāvidyās, 278, 304
Mahāvrātins, 153
Mahiṣamardinī Stotra, 83
Mahmūd of Ghazni, 144
Maidens, 36, 46, 48, 53, 225
maithuna, 81, 83–85, 139–40, 220, 253, 254, 279, 333
Maitrāvaruṇa, 38
makāras. *See* M-words
malam, as impediment to liberation, 80
Mālatī-Mādhava, 96, 129, 209–12, 227
Mālinī, 244, 331; *mālinī* mantra, 246; *vyoma-mālinī*, 328
Mālinīvijayottara Tantra, 23, 231, 325
Malla dynasty, 23, 127, 132, 134, 142, 148, 278, 310. *See also* Pratāp Malla
Mallayya. *See* mountains

Mallināth, 170, 173
Mallmann, Marie-Thérèse de, 1
Malwa, 132
Mān Singh, king of Marwar, 168–71, 314
Manasā, 41
Mānasollāsa, 53, 126, 133, 142
Mānava Dharma Śāstra, 130
mandalas, 11, 24, 35, 59, 103, 113, 120, 122, 132, 134, 135, 136, 147, 150, 164, 213, 222, 223, 235, 244, 250, 252, 258, 262, 306, 313, 317; as administrative units, royal lands, 123–25, 141, 149; Cakrasaṃvara Maṇḍala, 96; Kubjikā maṇḍala, 217, 228; *saṃvarta* mandala, 55. *See also* lotus: *cakra* or mandala as
Mandelbaum, David, 259
maṇipura cakra, 228, 229, 327
Manonmanī, 230, 231
Manthānabhairava Tantra, 79, 90–91, 121, 291, 305, 323
Mantra-born Siddhas and Yoginīs, 164, 165, 166
Mantramahodadhi, 105, 120, 136
mantras, 6, 13, 30, 31, 34, 47, 51, 52, 66, 71, 72, 74, 76, 85, 88, 109, 117, 121, 132, 134, 140, 143, 147, 148, 150, 151, 162, 164, 166, 201, 202, 209, 212, 220, 222, 223, 226, 229, 232, 235, 242–44, 246, 247, 250–52, 259, 265, 266, 274, 322, 327, 334; citadel of mantras, 251–52, 259; *mālinī* mantra, 246; *mantraśāstra*, 243; *netra* mantra, 276; seed mantras (*see* seeds). *See also* extraction; Narasiṃha: Narasiṃha *mantra;* phonemes
Manu Smṛti, 79
margosa. *See* trees
Māriyammān, 56, 287
marriage rituals, 20, 21, 41, 68, 69, 86, 116, 270; husband-finding rite, 30–31, 115; *ihi* ceremony, 69; *tāli*, tying of the, 69, 293
Marwar, 168–71. *See also* Mān Singh
masks, 143
Masson, Jeffrey, 114
Master. *See ācārya*
Mataji Om Prakash Yogini, 271
Mathura, 37, 41, 50, 52, 63; Mathura Archaeological Museum, 282, 284, 287, 289
Mātṛ Cakra, 82
mātṛcakras. *See* circles: of Mothers
mātṛgaṇa. *See* Host of Mothers
Mātṛkābheda Tantra, 78, 90
mātṛ-nāmāni. *See* Names of the Mothers
Mātṛs. *See* Mothers
Mātṛsadbhāva, 81
Matsyendra(nātha), 22, 23, 25, 100, 103, 105, 113, 152, 163, 171, 226, 231, 326
matsyodara. *See* Fish-Belly
Mattamāyūras, 146
Maurya age, 43
McDaniel, June, 77, 202
McLuhan, Marshall, 114
meat, 46, 76, 78, 83–85, 108, 109, 118, 143, 154, 155, 159, 165, 211, 241, 253, 254. *See also* human flesh
medical literature. *See* Āyurveda
melaka, melāpa(ka), 10, 47, 77, 102, 165, 196, 213, 215, 222, 242, 323; pleasing union, 215, 217; violent union, 215, 217
menstrual horoscopes, 69
mercury, 67, 72, 80, 90, 174, 175, 186, 200
Meru. *See* mountains
Mhasobā, 32
mice and rats, 189, 195, 249
milk, 35, 37, 52, 54, 56, 70, 115, 191, 247, 252, 253, 330; Milk of the Yoginī, 90–93. *See also pāyal*
miscarriage, 48, 59, 63, 64, 267. *See also* childbirth
miśraka (level of Tantric initiation), 166
Mitauli Yoginī temple, 307, 308
Mithila, 7, 78
Mitrā, 39
mkha' 'gro ma, 62
Mohinī, 98; Mohinīs (class of female divinities), 162
moles, 280
monks and monasticism, 72, 123, 125, 133, 134, 148
moon, 30, 60, 63, 68, 77, 81, 89, 90, 91, 238, 240, 316; Moon Island, 24, 102, 104, 105, 106, 174, 175, 176, 215; Moon Mountain, 175
Mother Earth, 70
Mothers, 4, 8, 14, 19, 22, 29, 34, 35, 38, 40, 41, 48, 50, 52, 53, 60, 61, 65, 66, 91, 95, 108, 115, 139, 146, 164, 166, 188, 189, 192, 193, 196, 204, 207, 209, 213, 219, 223, 230, 231, 284, 285; Mother of Cows, 48; Mother of Dogs, 48; Mother of Plants, 46, 48; Mother Protectresses, 58, 207, 209; Mothers of all the World, 39; Mothers of Infants, 39; Mothers of the Seven Worlds, 139; Mothers of Space, 188; Mothers of the Universe, 36; Mothers of the World, 36, 37, 44, 45. *See also* eight: Mothers; Host of Mothers; Names of the Mothers; seven: Mothers
Mound-born Siddhas and Yoginīs, 72, 164, 165, 222
Mounds and Secondary Mounds, 10, 113, 136, 137, 161, 165, 171, 213, 275, 314, 317, 324, 325. *See also pīṭhas*
mountains, 4, 50, 65, 167–73, 203; Añjana, 175; Govardhana, 167; Himavān, 167; Kailās, 184, 201; Kalashacal, 69; Mallayya, 173; Meru, 81, 174, 175, 186, 316; Raivata(ka), 50, 51, 183–84, 317; Srisailam, 62, 102, 173, 312; Vindhya, 267 (*see also* Vindhyavāsinī); White, 37. *See also* Girnar; *kulaparvatas*
mouth, as female sexual organ, 7, 18, 27, 28, 72, 87, 88, 89, 94–122, 161, 215, 218, 240, 242, 323. *See also* lotus: term for women's nether

mouth (*continued*)
mouth; *picuvaktra; pīṭhas*: *catuṣpīṭha; pīṭhas*: *mahāpīṭha*
Mṛgendrāgama, 163
mudrās, 13, 81, 82, 84, 89, 151, 227, 295, 329; *pañcamudrā*, 82; *vajrolī mudrā*, 11, 82, 114, 215, 296
Mukhamaṇḍikā, 46, 48, 50, 58
Mukhamaṇḍitās (class of female divinities), 53
mūlādhāra cakra, 225, 228, 229, 231, 325, 327
Mūḷi, 54
Muller-Ortega, Paul, 1, 18, 243
Muṇḍamālā Tantra, 78
Murr, Sylvia, 156
Murukaṉ, 5, 167, 271
Mus, Paul, 246
mustard seeds. *See* seeds

Nabokov, Isabelle, 1, 247–48
nāda, 227, 325
nāḍīs, 82, 210, 220; *nāḍīcakra*, 96, 322. *See also* path of brahman
nagna-kabandhā, 115
Naigameṣa, Naigameya, 37, 38, 63, 282, 283
nakṣatras, 290
Nalavilāsa, 102, 153
Nāmadhārīs, 155
Names of the Mothers, 34–35
Nandin, Nandikeśvara, 24, 284
Nandinī, 54
Narasiṃha, 89, 127, 148; Narasiṃha *mantra*, 274; *narasiṃha-dīkṣā*, 6
Naravāhanadatta, 141, 160, 184, 201, 308, 309
Nārāyaṇa, 6
Naresar Yoginī temple, 205, 206
Nāth Jogis, 77
Nāth Siddhas, 82, 163, 168–71, 177, 179, 184, 224, 226, 296, 313. *See also* Āyas Dev Nāth; Gorakh(nāth); Jālandharnāth; Matsyendra(nātha); Nāth Jogis; Satyanātha; Siddhanāth
Nāthaṣoḍaśāmnāyakrama, 91
navadurgā. *See* nine: Durgās
navagraha. *See* nine: Seizers; planets and planetary deities
navanātha, 168
navarātrī, 129
Nāyaṉmārs, 4
Nepal, 123, 124, 125, 127, 129, 132, 134, 142, 148, 149, 150, 168, 204, 219, 258, 262, 269. *See also* Gorkha kingdom; Kathmandu Valley; Licchavi dynasty; Malla dynasty; Newar society; Śāh dynasty
nether mouth. *See* mouth
netherworlds, 175, 186
netra mantra. *See* mantras
Netra Tantra, 16, 19, 23, 47, 59, 61, 72, 115, 146, 204, 219, 258, 262, 269
Neṭunalvāṭai, 127
Newar society, 69, 148–50
Nidrā, 53
nigraha, 47, 71, 215, 217, 323. *See also anugraha*
nīm. *See* trees: margosa
Nimbārkīs, 6
nine: *cakras* of Śrī Cakra, 236; Durgās, 61, 127, 129, 130, 132, 143, 321; Kātyāyanīs, 321; Nāthas, 168; Nights, 129; Planets, 61, 63; Seizers, 35, 38, 43, 46, 48, 60, 62, 289; Skanda-Seizers, 49
Nirṛti, 54
nirvāṇa, 83, 88
nirvāṇa-dīkṣā, 307
Niśisaṃcāra Tantra, 255
Nityā (class of goddesses), 96, 241
Nityaklinnā, 80, 96, 99
Nityānanda, 162, 313
Nizarpanthis, 77, 247
nocturnal emissions, 72–73
north: northern course of internal Yoginīs, 217, 228, 229 (*see also* southern course of internal Yoginīs); orientation of shrines, 61, 65, 66
Nymphs, 29, 30, 32–35, 39, 46, 48, 161, 174, 183, 198, 203, 319. *See also* seven: Nymphs

Obeyesekere, Gananath, 1, 5, 247, 248
Obstructors, 249
Ocean of Milk, 91
O'Flaherty, Wendy Doniger. *See* Doniger, Wendy
Orissa, 62, 85, 92, 94–99, 118, 137, 139, 140, 204, 241, 291, 311. *See also* Bhubanesvar; Gaṇeśvara temple; Hirapur Yoginī temple; Jagannātha temple; Kiñcakeśvarī temple; Konarak; Ranipur-Jharial; Vaitāl Deul temple; Vārāhī temple
outcastes, 125, 155, 157, 165, 222, 255
ovallis, 113
owls, 189, 288. *See also* Kauśikī

padma. *See* lotus
Padoux, André, 1, 15, 16
palāśa. *See* flowers and flowering trees
pān. *See* betel
pañcamudrā. *See mudrās*
Pāñcarātras, 6, 17, 146, 274, 276
pañcasrotas. *See* five: streams
pañcatattva. *See* M-words
Paṇḍu, 130
Pāṇḍya kingdom, 127
Pāṇini, 4
Parā, 18, 121, 231
Parāparā, 18, 231
Parātriśika Vivarṇa, 18
pariahs. *See* outcastes
Parpola, Asko, 28, 29, 37, 132
Parry, Jonathan, 203
Pārvatī, 167, 201
paścimāmnāya, 18, 152, 313. *See also* Kubjikā Tantras
paśu, 14, 24, 76, 84, 195, 196, 245

Pāśupatas, 153, 154
Paśupati, 28
Paśupatināth temple, 153, 269
Patañjali, 185, 197, 220, 221
path of brahman, 81, 201, 254
Patna, 5, 40, 43
Patwardhan, M. V., 114
pāyal, 78
penis, 71, 79, 82, 89, 93, 117. *See also liṅgam*
Penzer, N. M., 60
Perfected Beings. *See* Siddhas
Perfection of Wisdom (*prajñā-paramitā*) teachings, 79
phonemes, 181, 227, 230–46. *See also nāda*
picuvaktra, 101, 121
Pinch, William, 4
piṇḍīs, 29
piśācas. *See* Ghouls
piśācīs. *See* Female Ghouls
pīṭhas, 10, 63, 65, 113, 161, 221, 224, 241, 247, 314; *liṅga-pīṭham*, 95, 100; *pīṭhas*: *catuṣpīṭha*, 90, 104, 298; *pīṭhas*: *mahāpīṭha*, 81; *ravi-pīṭha*, 63. *See also* Arvuda; four: Mounds; Jālandhara; Kāmākhyā; Mounds and Secondary Mounds; Pūrṇagiri; Uḍḍiyāna
pitṛs, 45
Place Called Love. *See* Kāmākhyā
planets and planetary deities, 34, 60–63, 69, 289
plants and herbs, 8, 49, 50, 189; *cāṇḍālī*, 79; *rākṣasī*, 79. *See also* betel; flowers and flowering trees; trees
pleasing union. *See melaka*
Pleiades. *See* Kṛttikās
Poḍe "sweepers." *See* outcastes
poison, 33, 76
Pole Star, 318
pollen, 115, 120
possession, 13, 14, 22, 45, 51, 52, 56, 70, 88, 103, 106, 113, 124, 191, 248, 250, 251, 252, 255, 260, 264, 267, 275. *See also* exorcism; *samāveśa*
Prabodhacandrodaya, 87, 116, 143, 146, 153, 309
prajñā, 79
Prajñā (Buddhist goddess), 109
Prakṛti, 77, 80
pralaya, 182
Prapañcasāra Tantra, 323
prasāda, 101, 109, 116, 191
Pratāp Malla, king of Nepal, 148
Pratīhāra dynasty, 57, 142
pretas. *See* Ghosts
prostitutes, in ritual, 31, 108, 116, 117, 140, 165, 270. *See also devadāsīs*
Protector Seizers, 47, 49
Protectors, 52, 53, 64, 71, 161, 175, 184, 286
Protectresses, 30, 46, 48, 54, 64, 189, 192, 321; Mother Protectresses, 58; Protectress Seizers, 53
Pṛthivinārāyaṇ Śāh, 310
puberty rites, 41, 68, 69, 117. *See also barha khya*
Punjab, 224, 314. *See also* Jālandhara (*pīṭha*)
Purāṇas: *Agni*, 27, 53, 62, 65, 174, 188, 228, 290, 326; *Basava*, 295; *Bhāgavata*, 51, 86, 175, 179–85, 200, 201, 221, 224, 225; *Brahmāṇḍa*, 53, 58, 151, 177, 207, 209; *Garuḍa*, 333; *Kālikā*, 204, 241; *Liṅga*, 245; *Mārkaṇḍeya*, 48, 63; *Matsya*, 60, 64, 183; *Padma*, 153; *Skanda*, 51, 177; *Varāha*, 175; *Vāyu*, 174, 177; *Virāṭa*, 181; *Viṣṇu*, 177, 178, 186; *Viṣṇudharmottara*, 61
puraścaraṇa, 99
purity codes, 68, 116, 219, 253, 255–57
Pūrṇagiri, 165, 224, 314
purohita. *See* royal chaplain
Purūravas, 33
Puruṣa, 80, 180, 193, 313; Loka Puruṣa, 176, 185; three Puruṣas, 177
puryaṣṭaka, 332
Pūtanā, 40, 46, 48, 49, 50, 51, 52, 55, 58, 62, 189, 191, 231, 284, 287, 290, 321; Gandhapūtanā, 53; Kaṭapūtanās (class of female divinities), 53, 72; Pūtanās (class of female divinities), 53, 58, 71
pūvāṭaikkāri, 21

Rabe, Michael, 203
Rādhā, 86
Raivata, son of Revatī, 46, 48, 49–50. *See also* mountains
rāj guru. *See* royal preceptor
Rājagṛha, 64
rajapāna, 11, 76, 83, 97, 99, 106, 140, 235
rājaputras, Kaula "princes," 113
Rajasthan, 7, 37, 56, 57, 89, 139, 142, 154, 168, 170, 267, 268, 313. *See also* Ajmer; Arvuda; Gangdhar stone-tablet inscription; Jalore; Jodhpur; Marwar
rājasūya. *See* initiation and consecration
Rājataraṅgiṇī, 137, 144, 193, 207, 209, 221
rājayoga, 81–82
Rajneesh, xiii
Rājopādhyāya brahmins. *See* royal chaplain
Rajput society and polity, 19–21, 126–27, 148, 168, 170, 268, 306, 312
Rākā, 30
Rākiṇī, 228, 229
Rākṣasas. *See* Protectors
rākṣasī. *See* plants and herbs
Rākṣasīs. *See* Protectresses
raktacandana, term for female discharge, 79. *See also* trees
Rām Carit Mānas, 5
Rāma, 4, 5, 6, 64, 127, 261, 271, 306
Rāmānandīs, 6, 7, 333
Rāmaṇī, 228
Rāmānuja, 153
Rāmās (class of female divinities), 53, 71
Rāmāyaṇa, 53, 64, 317
Ranipur-Jharial Yoginī temple, 137, 195, 291

Rasārṇava, 72, 73, 79, 91, 181, 182, 295
rāṣṭradevatās. *See* tutelary deities
Ratirahasya, 88
Ratnamālā Tantra, 246
Raudrī, 230, 231, 329
Rāvaṇa, 51, 54
retraction, 165
Revatī, 40, 46, 48–53, 58, 188, 285, 290; Revatīs (class of female divinities), 53, 189
"Revatī Kalpa," 45, 50, 189
Ṛg Veda, 29, 31, 33, 36, 53, 68, 167, 198
rivers, 31, 32, 130; Gaṅgā, 32, 254; Narmada, 317; Śailoda, 174; Sarasvati, 32, 254; Yamuna, 254. *See also* seven: Nymphs
royal chaplain, 123, 134, 148–49, 262, 310
royal preceptor, 123, 148, 262
ṛtu doṣa, 70
Rudra, 23, 33, 36, 39, 40, 46, 47, 48, 54, 61, 96, 198; Rudrā, 39; Rudra Tryambaka, 30, 31, 280; Rudra-śakti, 230. *See also* Śiva
Rudrayāmala Tantra, 11, 23, 75, 221, 229, 232, 278, 322

Śābarīs (class of female divinities), 212
sacrificer's wife. *See* Vedic ritual
Sadāśiva, 18, 23, 115, 204, 278
sadbhāva, 11, 26, 112, 275. *See also kaulasadbhāva; kulamadyam; kulārtham*; Mātṛsadbhāva; *yonitattva*
Saddharmapuṇḍarika Sūtra, 53
sādhaka, 123, 140, 166, 314
sādhanā, xiv, 6, 97, 105; *bindusādhanā*, 162; *śava-sādhanā*, 202, 204; *yoginīsādhanā*, 66
Sādhanamālā, 324
saffron. *See* flowers and flowering trees
Śāh dynasty, 150. *See also* Pṛthivinārāyaṇ Śāh
sahaj mānuṣ, 82
Sahajiyās, 86, 247
sahasrāra, 229, 232, 254, 327
Śailoda. *See* rivers
Śailodbhava kingdom, 139
Śaivāgamas. *See* Śaivasiddhānta
Śaivas and Saivism, 5, 6, 139, 146, 150, 152, 158, 159, 188, 246, 306, 307. *See also* brahmins: Smārta Brahmins; Kāpālikas; Mattamāyūras; Nāyaṉmārs; Pāśupatas; Śaivasiddhānta; Somasiddhāntins
Śaivasiddhānta, 15, 17, 18, 24, 80, 81, 101, 146, 152–54, 158, 166, 225, 230, 231, 248, 251, 252, 253, 278, 307, 325, 328
Śākinī, 207, 228, 229; Śākinīs (class of female divinities), 53, 76, 118, 222
Śāktas and Saktism, 5, 6, 40, 59, 60, 93, 126, 139, 150, 199
Śākta-Śaiva metaphysics, 19, 23, 36
Śakti: as eighth element of a kingdom, 126; feminine energy, 22, 73, 81, 82, 86, 103, 129, 142, 226, 229, 232 (*see also aṇaṅku; kuṇḍalinī*); hypostasis of the Goddess, 86, 95, 96, 109, 118, 135, 162, 166, 210, 219, 241, 319 (*see also* Icchā-śakti; *jñāna*, Jñānā-śakti; *kalās*: *kalā-śaktis*; Kriyā-śakti; Nityā); name of the great Goddess, 5, 6, 8, 78, 80, 96, 97, 115, 165, 210, 230, 237, 239, 249, 303, 330 (*see also* Prajñā); sole mention in MBh, 39; Tantric consort, 78, 81, 84, 88, 98–99, 105, 112, 117, 118, 120, 157, 165, 166, 210, 249, 332 (*see also* Action Seal; Dūtīs; Great Seal; Kumārī; lotus: Lotus Maiden; Wisdom Maiden); type of yogic practice, 82
Śakti Cakra, 88
Śakti Ucchiṣṭa, 296
Śaktibhedakaula, 25
sakty poudja (śakti pūjā), 155
Śakuna, 33
śakuni. *See* birds
Śakunī, 33, 40, 50, 53
śakuni-graha, 46
samādhi, 170, 180
samāveśa, 14
Samayacāra Tantra, 78
saṃhāra, 165
sampradāya, 112
saṃyama, 185, 318
sanātana dharma, 5
Sanderson, Alexis, 1, 8, 21, 153, 158, 163, 194, 196, 213, 234
Sandhimān, Sandhimati, 192–94, 209
Śaṅkara, 63, 97, 162, 173, 271
Śaṅkaradigvijaya, 81
Śaṅkaravijaya, 162
Saṅkaṭā, 63
Śaṅkhinī, 228
Śānti Kalpa, 34, 35
saptamātṛka. *See* seven: Mothers
Śāradātilaka, 23
Saramā, 46, 50, 53
Sarasvati. *See* rivers
Śārṅgadhara Paddhati, 200
Ṣaṣṭhī, 40, 41, 58, 192, 284, 285
Śatapatha Brāhmaṇa. *See* Brāhmaṇas
Ṣaṭcakranirūpaṇa, 221, 324
Sātī Āsarā. *See* seven: Nymphs
Satyaloka, 167, 175, 177
Satyanātha, 162, 313
Sāyaṇa, 34
secrecy, 113, 126, 155–59, 161, 243–44. *See also* dissimulation
seeds: mustard, 49, 202, 286, 320; seed mantras, 223, 279, 313, 314, 317; sesame, 51
Seizers, 34, 35, 52, 60, 61, 62, 72, 147, 255. *See also* Bird Seizers; Divine Seizers; Dryads: Dryad Seizers; Father Seizers; Female Seizers; Gandharvas: Gandharva Seizers; Ghoul Seizers; nine: Seizers; Protector Seizers, Siddha Seizers; Skanda-Seizers

Sekoddeśaṭīkā, 83
self-sacrifice, 191, 193, 196, 211, 213, 228. *See also* bolt-practices
Sergent, Bernard, 28
serpents, 25, 41, 43, 46, 48, 50, 55, 185, 189, 195, 211, 230, 231, 233, 249, 288. *See also* Ahir Budhnya; Ananta
Śeṣa. *See* serpents
sesame seeds. *See* seeds, sesame
seven: *cakras*, 221; *dhātus*, 228; Mothers, 32, 40, 45, 49, 59, 60, 61, 65, 127, 166, 188, 314, 318, 320; Nymphs, 32, 289; Ṛṣis, 36, 40, 43, 163; sheaths of the cosmic egg, 181, 185; Sisters, 29, 129, 173, 191, 289; worlds, 182
Shahdol Yoginī temple, 137, 307
Sharma, R. K., 136, 153, 154
Shaw, Miranda, 120
Shulman, David, 8, 54
siddh puruṣ, 170
Siddha Cakra, 113, 303, 332
Siddha demigods, 160–87, 227; Kula Siddhas 103, 113; Siddha Nāthas, 91. *See also* Siddhas: as mountain gods
Siddha Kaula, 25, 105, 163, 313
Siddha maidens, 183, 203
Siddha Seizers, 47
siddhagati, 180
siddhakṣetra, 174
Siddhakūṭa, 174
Siddhaloka, 167, 175, 176, 182, 185, 200
Siddhāmṛta Kaula, 25
Siddhanāth, 168, 173, 302
Siddhāntaśekhara, 252
Siddhapura, 175
Siddharāja, 133, 142, 173
Siddhas: Booti Siddha, 170; human, 10, 18, 22, 48, 74–76, 83, 105, 106, 108, 110, 113, 142, 154, 160–87, 195, 199, 211, 215, 242, 244, 251; as mountain gods, 167–74, 183–84; with names ending in -pāda, 164, 242, 313, 314. *See also* Clan-born; Field-born; Innately-born; Mantra-born; Mound-born; Siddha demigods; Sittars; six: groups of Siddhas; Womb-Born
Siddhayogeśvarīmata, 17, 23, 121, 163, 322
Siddheśvara, 142, 161, 168, 171, 173, 302, 312, 314; Siddheśvara Kaula, 25
Siddhilakṣmī, 322
siddhis. *See* supernatural powers
Śilāhāra kingdom, 142
Silburn, Lilian, 1, 16, 25, 116, 233
Śilpa Prakāśa, 94–97, 100, 241
śilpa śāstra. *See* temple architecture
Sinīvālī, 30, 40
Śiśupala, 130
Sītā, 54
Śītalā, 51, 55, 56, 63, 66, 121, 191
Śītapūtanā, 46, 48, 49, 51, 58
Śītavātā ("Cooling Breeze"), 53
Sittars, 75
Śiva, 4, 8, 12, 19, 21, 23, 28, 36, 37, 41, 47, 48, 49, 51, 61, 62, 65, 66, 78, 80, 81, 87, 95, 96, 97, 101, 104, 105, 109, 112, 118, 119, 122, 126, 127, 135, 137, 151, 153, 154, 161, 163, 165, 167, 171, 177, 184, 193, 195, 201, 209, 213, 214, 215, 223, 229, 230, 233, 234, 237, 239, 240, 245, 251, 252, 270, 307, 311, 315, 319, 321, 330; *śivāmbu* (Śiva-Water), 76, 118; *Śivasūtra*, 251
Śivā, 89; Śivās (class of female divinities), 222
Śivadūtī, 319
Śivanārāyaṇ, 5
six: *āmnāyas*, 18; *cakras*, 179–80, 217, 221, 226, 228–29, 322; circles, 209; goddesses, 217, 327; groups of Śaktis, 222; groups of Siddhas, 165; heads of Skanda and Ṣaṣṭhī, 41; *kula* and *kulākula* goddesses, 228; Mothers, 279; mouths of Śiva, 101; practices of Tantric sorcery, 222, 262; secret places, 226; sites, 200, 224; types of Śaktis, 165; Yoginīs, 228, 279
sixteen: channels, 210; *kalās*, 91, 236, 241, 298; *kalā-śaktis*, 241; Nityā goddesses, 96; Siddhas, 164, 165, 166; Virile Heroes, 151
sixty-four: sequence of, 108, 222–23, 307; Yoginīs: 11, 104, 129, 165, 188, 189, 222, 223, 250, 313
Skanda, 4, 24, 35, 37, 38, 40, 41, 43, 45–50, 61, 63, 65, 91, 129, 139, 192, 283, 289; Guha, 65; Kārttikeya, 50, 102, 104, 106; Kumāra, 39, 46, 49, 54, 65, 282. *See also* Khaṇḍobā
Skandamātā, 40
Skandāpasmāra, 46, 48, 54, 58, 285
Skanda-Seizers, 45, 48, 49, 54, 58, 60, 62
skulls, 202–4, 212, 213, 256
slab altars, 50, 65
Slusser, Mary, 1, 61
smallpox, 51, 56, 59, 63, 66, 231. *See also* Māriyammān; Śītalā
Smara-Dahana, 135
Smārta Brahmins. *See* brahmins and brahmanic traditions
Smith, Frederick, 29
soma, 87, 115
Somaśambhupaddhati, 248–52, 332
Somasiddhāntins, 146, 153
Somavaṃśi kingdom, 12, 137
Someśvara III, Cāḷukya king, 53
Sontheimer, Gunther, 171
sorcery, 13, 19, 33, 59, 141, 162, 202, 209, 221, 222, 228, 260, 262–65, 269, 320. *See also* attraction; *uccāṭana; vaśīkaraṇa;* witches and witchcraft
soteriology, 80, 174–79
southern course of internal Yoginīs, 217, 228. *See also* north: northern course of internal Yoginīs
spies and espionage, 146, 150, 153
śrāddha rites. *See* ancestor cults

Śrauta Sūtras, 16, 38; *Āpastamba*, 280; *Āśvalayana*, 16; *Mānava*, 33
Śrī, 24, 32, 40, 41, 64
Sri Lanka, 57, 64, 198, 199, 248, 293, 294, 298
Śrībhāṣya, 153
Śrīcakra, 124, 135, 235–37, 241
Śrīkaṇṭha, 23, 151, 278
Śrīmatottara Tantra, 53, 71, 136, 221, 228, 229, 313
Śrīnāth, 24, 89, 168, 169
Srisailam. *See* mountains
Śrīvaiṣṇavas, 179
Śrīvidyā, 15, 95, 96, 99, 196, 234, 235, 236, 237, 239, 241, 242, 245
sṛṣṭi, 23, 165
Staal, Frits, 28
stars, 29, 34, 36, 44, 62, 63, 69, 316. *See also* Apabharaṇī; Kṛttikās; Pole Star
sterility, 270
Sthūṇākarṇa, 31
Strickmann, Michel, 1, 134, 248, 261
strī-vīrya, 77, 92. *See also śukradevī*
subtle body. *See* yogic body
Sudras, 155, 157
śukradevī, 21, 93. *See also strī-vīrya*
sulfur, 67, 80, 90, 91
sun, 62, 63, 69, 238, 240, 316
supernatural enjoyments, 10, 14, 15, 74, 124, 161, 164, 248, 251, 255
supernatural powers, 6, 8, 10, 12, 15, 22, 71, 73, 77, 80, 90, 108, 120, 124, 139, 143, 164, 173, 181, 183, 185, 199, 200, 210, 211, 212, 213, 215, 218, 220, 221, 225, 227, 250, 254. *See also* flight
Surabhī, 46, 54
Sūrya. *See* sun
Sūryā, daughter of the Sun, 68
Suśruta Saṃhitā, 39, 43, 49, 50, 51, 52, 59, 60, 79
suṣumṇā. *See* path of brahman
Sutherland, Gail Hinich, 45, 66, 199
Svacchanda Tantra, 23, 153, 181, 183, 223, 313
svādhiṣṭhāna cakra, 228, 229, 231, 327
śva-graha, 34, 54
Svāhā, 36, 40, 43, 47
Swāmīnārāyaṇ sect, 126, 305
Śyāmarahasya, 78

Tāḍakā, 64
Taittirīya Saṃhitā, 34, 55, 84
Taleju, 127, 129, 132, 134, 142, 149, 150, 306, 310, 322
tāli, tying of the. *See* marriage rituals
Tambs-Lyche, Harald, 3, 20, 21, 126, 127
tāmbūla, 87–88. *See also* betel
Tamil Nadu, 4, 14, 15, 21, 45, 54, 69, 73, 74, 75, 98, 127, 129, 137, 167, 236, 248, 271, 274, 275, 282, 292, 306, 321. *See also* Kancipuram; Madurai; Pāṇḍya kingdom; Vaikuṇṭha Perumal temple
tantra prakriyā, 16, 226
Tantrāloka, 15, 16, 78, 83, 84, 89, 103, 105, 110, 113, 116, 146, 157, 158, 163, 183, 221, 224, 226, 236, 246, 253, 254, 255
tantra-mantra, 5, 261, 262
Tantrasadbhāva, 17, 23, 163, 221, 222, 230, 233
Tantraśāstra, 15, 16, 276
"Tantric sex," xi–xiv, 14, 73, 100, 109, 258, 303
"Tantrism," 16
tapas, 180
Tapoloka, 182
Tārā, 76, 89, 128, 296
Tāranātha, 314
tattvas, 237, 240
temple architecture, 94–98, 136, 203, 23; *garbha gṛha*, 94, 136; joining wall, 96–97, 299, 309; *kāma-bandha*, 96–97; *vimāna*, 94, 96, 203; *vīra-mandira*, 97
Templeman, David, 314, 324
Tibet, 262, 267
Tithiḍākinīkalpa, 62, 290
Tiwari, J. N., 34
Toḍala Tantra, 83, 296
toddy palm. *See* flowers and flowering trees
tongue, 57, 74, 75, 78, 109, 117, 118, 199, 232, 233, 254, 332
tree divinities, 55–58, 70, 72. *See also* Dryads; Female Dryads; Vaṭayakṣiṇidevī; Vṛddhikās; Vṛkṣakās
trees, 27, 33, 47, 57, 58, 65, 104, 117, 121, 174, 193, 198, 199, 267, 270; *aśvatthā*, 293; jack, 285; *karañja*, 46; *karimpana*, 65; *khejaṛa*, 56; margosa, 56, 121, 170, 315; *raktacandana*, 57. *See also* flowers and flowering trees
Trika, 16, 18, 59, 81, 99, 152, 154, 159, 196, 226, 231, 234, 241, 254. *See also* Abhinavagupta; Aparā; Mātṛsadbhāva; Parā; Parāparā
trikūṭi, 177, 184, 185
Tripurāsundarī, 18, 93, 235, 238, 239, 329
Trivikramasena, 141
tutelary deities, 21, 126, 127, 139, 262. *See also kuladevatās; kuladevīs*

uccāṭana, 99
Uḍḍiyāna, 165, 224, 314, 324
Ujjain, 137, 165, 279, 314
Umā, 8, 24, 47, 135
Universal Man. *See* Puruṣa: Loka Puruṣa
Unnamed. *See* Kubjikā
untouchables. *See* outcastes
Upaniṣads: *Bṛhadāraṇyaka*, 69, 201, 246; *Bṛhat Saṃnyāsa*, 253; *Chāndogya*, 201, 220, 317; *Kauśītaki*, 201, 246; *Maitri*, 180, 317; *Māṇḍukya*, 325; *Praśna*, 201; *Yogaśikha*, 81
upāsanā, 6
Urban, Hugh, xiii
"urban society," 3, 126
urine, 71, 77, 253, 254, 255

Urvaśī, 33
utkrānti, 215, 227, 326
utkṛṣṭa. *See* extraction
utopias, 125, 147
utsavas, 154, 211, 251
Uttar Pradesh, 44, 49, 137, 267. *See also* Allahabad; Benares; Mathura
Uttarakurus, 174, 175, 316

Vaikuṇṭha Perumal temple, 98
Vaiṣṇavas and Vaisnavism, 2, 5, 6, 7, 36, 97, 139, 144, 152, 153, 155, 188, 274, 290, 301, 312; sectarian marks of, 6. *See also* Āḻvārs; Nāmadhārīs; Nimbārkīs; Rāmānandīs; Sahajiyās; Śrīvaiṣṇavas; Vallabhīs
Vaiṣṇo Devī, 29
Vaitāl Deul temple, 97
vajra. *See* penis
vajrācārya, 133, 142
vajrapadma, 71
Vajrapāṇī, 134
vajrapuṣpa, 78
Vajrayoginī, 120, 217
Vajreśvarī, 89
vajrolī mudrā. *See mudrās*
Vallabhīs, 6
Vāmā, 230, 231, 233, 328, 329
"Vampire Tales," 141, 308
Vampires, Vampiresses, 48, 53, 71–73, 117, 141, 202, 203, 204, 205
van Buitenen, J. A., 45
Vārāhī temple, Caurasi, 96–99, 139, 299
Varanasi. *See* Benares
Varuṇa, 28, 117
vaśīkaraṇa, 99
Vasiṣṭha, 54, 75, 76
Vāsudeva, 179
Vāsugupta, 251
Vaṭayakṣiṇidevī, 57
Vātūlanātha Sūtra, 242
Vaudeville, Charlotte, 89
Vedānta, 220, 271
Vedic literature and traditions, 6, 28–32, 40, 49, 54, 68, 87, 115, 121, 130, 150, 152, 193, 234, 246. *See also Atharva Veda; Ṛg Veda*
Vedic ritual, 217, 256, 257; *aśvamedha*, 30, 31; *gavāmayana*, 30; sacrificer's wife in, 30–31, 197; *vājapeya*, 197
vetālas. *See* Vampires
Vibhīṣana, 53
Viḍālī. *See* Biḍalī
vidyā, 180, 235
Vidyādharas, 48, 141, 160, 161, 174, 175, 181–84, 309
Vidyādharīs, 57, 83, 141, 160, 201, 203, 317
Vijayā, 24, 278
Vijñāna Bhairava Tantra, 152
Vikaṭākṣī, 130
Vinatā, 44, 45, 46, 48, 50, 55, 58
Vināyaka, 65, 103; Vināyakas (class of divinities), 48, 52
Vindhyavāsinī, 53, 115, 129, 191, 287, 304
violent union. *See melaka*
Vīrabhadra, 49, 61, 282
vīrācāra, 142
vīrakrīḍā, 142
vīras. *See* Virile Heroes
Vīraśaivas. *See* Liṅgāyatas
Vīrāvalī Tantra, 253
Virile Heroes, 7, 10, 11, 12, 17, 18, 22–24, 47, 73–75, 98, 99, 123, 133, 142, 160, 162, 165–66, 191, 193, 194, 195, 203, 211, 218, 250, 253, 256, 323; as demigods, 164, 173; fifty-eight, 165, 222. *See also* Bīrs
Vīrs. *See* Virile Heroes: as demigods
Virūpākṣī, 130
vīrya, 10, 17, 71, 87, 92
Viśākha, 38, 41, 283, 285
visarga, 238, 239, 240, 245
Viṣṇu, 4, 7, 28, 41, 52, 89, 127, 139, 146, 154, 155, 178, 179, 180, 185, 186, 201, 288; as *mahāyogin*, 185, 222, 266
viśuddhi cakra, 228, 229, 325, 327
Viśvāmitra, 54
Viśvanātha temple. *See* Khajuraho
Vṛddhikās, 48, 55
Vṛkṣakās, 55, 280, 286
Vṛṣṇi triads, 4, 41
Vṛtra, 68
vulva, 18, 28, 29, 71, 74, 78–83, 87, 89, 93, 95, 97, 101, 104, 106, 115–17, 120, 121, 134, 135, 181, 191, 218, 229, 238–39, 244, 249, 250, 294, 300, 327. *See also* lotus; mouth; *pīṭhas*: *catuṣpīṭha; pīṭhas*: *mahāpīṭha; vajrapadma*
vyūhas, 179

warrior goddesses, 127, 129, 132. *See also* Durgā
Weber, Albrecht, 45
Weber, Max, 234
Weinberger-Thomas, Catherine, 20
Whitney, William Dwight, 34, 261
wind, 198, 201, 207, 209, 210
wine, 73, 89, 154, 159
Wisdom Maiden, 79
witches and witchcraft, 10, 25, 27, 30, 31, 55, 67, 68, 123, 191, 193, 194, 198, 199, 204, 205, 212, 213, 215, 265, 267, 268, 269
wolves, 58, 193, 194
Womb-born Siddhas and Yoginīs, 164
Women with Uncut Wings, 33
Woodroffe, Sir John, xii, 1, 6, 16

Yājñavalkya Smṛti, 91, 318
Yakas, Yakkas. *See* Dryads
Yākinī, 228, 229
Yakkhinīs. *See* Female Dryads
Yakṣa Mothers. *See* Female Dryads
Yakṣas. *See* Dryads

Yakṣīs, Yakṣiṇīs. *See* Female Dryads
yantras, 106, 122, 210, 235, 238, 242. *See also* Kālī: Kālī Yantra; *kāmakalā: kāmakalā* yantra; Yoginī: Yantra
Yātudhānas, 48
Yellammā, 270, 334
yoga, early definitions and forms of, 27, 80, 81, 168, 173, 180, 194, 195, 201, 221, 311, 318, 322
Yoga Sūtras, 220. *See also* Patañjali
yogeśvarīs, 137, 144, 211, 212, 221, 322
yogic body, 161, 169, 179, 184, 211, 219–34, 254, 326. *See also ājñā cakra; anāhata cakra; cakras*; cranial vault; *dvādaśānta;* fontanel; *haṃsa; kuṇḍalinī; maṇipura cakra; mūlādhāra cakra; nāḍīs*; path of brahman; *sahasrāra; svādhiṣṭhāna cakra; trikūṭi; viśuddhi cakra*
yogic practice, early forms of, 82, 83, 100, 162, 176, 182, 185, 200, 218, 220, 227, 239. *See also* bolt-practices; *haṭha yoga; saṃyama; utkrānti*
yogin, early definitions of, 77, 97, 108, 123, 134, 170, 177, 178, 181, 184, 185, 200, 201, 221, 234, 324, 326; Avañcaka Yogis, 154; Kula Yogis, 154; *yogīśvaras*, 180
Yoginī: Cakra, 82, 133, 215, 228, 299, 306, 326; etymology of in *Netra Tantra*, 195; Kaula, 22, 103, 105, 163, 247, 326; Sequence, 222, 313; temples, 12, 25, 51, 62, 136–42, 146, 161, 204, 213, 215, 218, 222 (*see also* Bheraghat Yoginī temple; Hirapur Yoginī temple; Khajuraho; Mitauli Yoginī temple; Naresar Yoginī temple; Ranipur-Jharial; Shahdol Yoginī temple); temples with eighty-one niches, 136, 307; Yantra, 94, 95
yoginī-bindu, 95
yoginīdaśa. *See* astronomy and astrology
Yoginīhṛdaya, 237, 240
Yoginīpura. *See* Delhi
yogurt, 171
yoni. *See* vulva
Yoni Tantra, 23
yoni-abhiṣecana, 99, 134
yonipūjā, 106, 109, 110
yonisalila, 102
yonitattva, 11, 303
Youths, 38, 46, 48
Yuvarājā II, Kalacuri king, 136, 142, 144, 146

Zen Buddhism, 294, 295
Zvelebil, Kamil, 74, 75